A SHORT HISTORY
OF CIVILIZATION

A SHORT HISTORY OF CIVILIZATION

BY

LYNN THORNDIKE, Ph.D.

Professor of History in Columbia University

Author of
"The History of Medieval Europe,"
"A History of Magic and Experimental Science,"
etc.

"The book, at least the history, that wants to be abridged, does not deserve to be read."

—Bolingbroke

". . . pour out all . . . as plain
As downright Shippen, or as old Montaigne."

—Pope

No single age can show the true end of man and meaning of civilization. History must reap the harvest of all the ages.

F. S. CROFTS & CO.

NEW YORK - - - - 1926

MANUFACTURED IN THE UNITED STATES OF AMERICA
BY THE VAIL-BALLOU PRESS, INC., BINGHAMTON, N. Y.

PREFACE

When the world war broke out in 1914, I determined to do what little I could to keep civilization alive. This volume is a contribution in that direction. I have written the book because I think it is needed. Historical students, investigators, writers, and readers have long since begun to turn away from the old tale of destruction to survey the past constructively, and to interest themselves in past culture as well as in purely political history. Yet so far there has been no adequate presentation of the main thread of the story of civilization between the covers of a single volume, or, for that matter, in any one work, at least in English. For college students who are preparing to enter, let us say, the medical profession, or to specialize in the natural or mathematical sciences, and any others who hardly have the time to pursue more than one course in history, a course in the history of civilization would seem the most fitting. Indeed, such a survey would seem the ideal introduction to all the other studies of the curriculum, since it would indicate at once their background and their interrelation. Yet many institutions of learning have hesitated to institute such an introductory course, partly from the lack of persons qualified to teach it, partly from the lack of any satisfactory text-book. Such a book would also meet the need of the serious-minded reader whose academic education is over but who wishes to review and unify his impressions of the past, and to keep up with the present current of thought and progress of knowledge. It should also prove serviceable to the many Americans who are now for the first time visiting foreign countries and coming into contact with past civilizations.

This book is based on fairly wide reading, on a good deal of intensive travel and study in historic Europe, and on a varied teaching experience. It may not, for example, be generally known that—leaving medieval history aside—I taught college classes in Greek and Roman History for seventeen consecutive years, and a class in English History for fifteen years. These varied labors as general work-horse and utility-man for history

v

departments I have tried to make work together for good in the present volume. It is more directly the outcome of a course in the history of civilization given during the last two years of my teaching at Western Reserve University.

Some may censure me for having gone too far in the way of new organization of materials, new perspective, and independent historical judgments, but these seem hardly avoidable in a work of such scope. Moreover, specialized historical research has for some time been pointing toward the rejection of many of the old generalizations. Especially have I endeavored to show the actual, not the fancied or the sentimental, antecedents of modern civilization. While we think of modern civilization as primarily European and American, the great cultures of the Far East cannot be omitted from any survey of civilization as a whole, and are here treated both *per se* and in their relations to the west.

On any particular topic it will obviously be desirable for one who has the time to read more than can be said in the present brief survey and general review. For this purpose bibliographies have been added at the close of every chapter, listing particularly the more recent works in English—in which reference may usually be found to the earlier literature of the subject —but often including two or three titles in foreign languages, especially for topics which have not been treated in English, in order to give the reader a taste, or glimpse at least, of foreign scholarship. To avoid repeated citation of different portions of the same book at the close of our various chapters, works which cover long periods or deal with the entire history of some special department of civilization have been grouped in one general bibliography at the close of the volume. As a rule, any place that is mentioned in the text will be found in some one of the maps comprised in the volume. The illustrations are for the most part taken from a collection of some five thousand views selected by the author during various trips abroad for their accuracy and historical interest.

The book as now presented to the reader has profited by the helpful criticism of Professor J. Montgomery Gambrill of Teachers College, who read it in manuscript. Other colleagues have very kindly read certain chapters in proof and offered corrections or suggestions. Professor William Linn Westermann read Chapters VIII to XVI; Professor William R.

Shepherd, Chapters **XXX** to **XXXII**; Dr. Frederick Barry, Chapter **XXXIV**; Professor Parker T. Moon, Chapter **XL**; Mr. Irving W. Raymond, a number of chapters; while Professor Harry J. Carman and Mr. J. B. Brebner have added their good offices. Chapters **XXXVIII** and **XXXIX** have been read in proof by Professor Bernadotte E. Schmitt of the University of Chicago; Chapter **III**, by Dr. Paul Radin. I have further been assisted in proof-reading by one of my graduate students, Miss Anna Campbell, who read certain portions, and by my sister, Miss Mildred L. Thorndike, who read the entire galley proof. I am also indebted to my brother, Professor Edward L. Thorndike, for reading the manuscript and taking up the question of its publication while I was absent in Europe. In the treatment of the history of science I have profited by having been able to read in manuscript two works which I hope will soon appear in print, *The Growth of Biology*, by the late Professor William A. Locy of Northwestern University, my friend and former colleague there, and the portion of Dr. George Sarton's *Introduction to the History of Science* that deals with the fourteenth and fifteenth centuries. In the final revision and verification of the text I have made numerous demands upon the time and patience of the reference librarians of Columbia University and have met with cheerful and unfailing cooperation.

CONTENTS

ix

LIST OF MAPS AND ILLUSTRATIONS

ILLUSTRATIONS

ILLUSTRATIONS

A SHORT HISTORY
OF CIVILIZATION

CHAPTER I

INTRODUCTION

Many civilizations other than ours have achieved things of genuine and unique worth.—Goldenweiser.

IN newspaper headlines attention is called to train collisions and wrecks or to great railroad strikes, but consultation of a time-table would be more useful to a traveler wishing to reach New York or Chicago than would the reading of such news. A person who intended to make railroading his vocation would study railroad construction and transportation, not collisions and strikes. Let us, then, turn away from human wars and disasters to a consideration of man's constructive achievement, to those positive accomplishments in political and social institutions, in art and industry, in science and thought, which we denote by the collective word, civilization. It is the product of our higher faculties as exercised first by original and superior individuals and then accepted or followed by a sufficient number of human beings to make it a social fact.

Civilization has been a gradual, complicated, and often irregular growth. That is to say, a given people or a given period may be highly developed in one respect and very backward in another. The Eskimo, for example, has marked mechanical ingenuity but a crude political and social life. The ancient Mayas of Central America constructed most impressive works of architecture, but in metallurgy were inferior to the present negroes of Africa. They did not employ domestic animals; yet they had developed the art of writing and had an elaborate calendar. Even our present civilization may have, intermingled with it, survivals of animalism, savagery, and barbarism, or while advancing far beyond past cultures in many respects, it may have lost some of their good features. It is therefore highly desirable to study the history of civilization, not only in order to understand how the present state of civilization came about, but also in order to rectify it intelligently. In a national or international crisis, or in an epoch-making hour

(margin note: Collisions or Progress?)

(margin note: Importance of Studying Civilization Historically)

3

for future civilization, the average mind is apt to explode aim-
lessly under the stress of excitement, emotion, altruism, prejudice, self-interest, or, most likely, misapprehension.   The result
is a big flash, a breaking of all the intellectual windows in the
vicinity, and maybe even more serious damage where it was least
intended.   But the historically-trained mind, using the long
gun-barrel of past experience and the sights of dispassionate,
critical, historical method, is far more likely to hit the desired
distant mark.

Relation of
Civilization
to Natural
Change

Before beginning to trace the story of human civilization,
it may be well to call to mind briefly the scene upon which it
has been enacted and the almost interminable drama of natural
change in which it comes as a late and brief episode or climax.
Who can tell which it is?   In those vast vistas of other worlds
which the telescope has revealed to our gaze and which light
alone traverses, our earth, the scene of human civilization, is
but a tiny speck which would be quite invisible to an astronomer in one of the more distant stars, and the drama of human
civilization in which we are engaged shrinks to the insignifi-
cance of a child's toy theater or a puppet-show in a band-
box.   Only after long æons required for the formation of solar
systems from nebulæ, and long ages of rock formation and development of organic life on our planet, does the hour of human
life strike, and, as against the slow evolution of early man, the
period of the development of civilization is but a moment.
Nevertheless, it is the progress of civilization that has invented
the telescope and other scientific instruments, has revealed to us
those other worlds, those long periods of natural change, and
that slow evolution of early man.   It may yet reveal to us signs
of organic life, or even other dramas of civilization, in other
planets or sidereal systems, or otherwise enlarge and improve
our knowledge of space and time, of life and change.

Geological
Strata and
Periods

In studying the crust of our earth, the geologist discerns the
world over successive layers of rocks and soils laid down in the
different periods of rock formation.   The lowest, and therefore
earliest formed, strata contain no relics or evidence of the existence of organic life, but include rocks which were apparently
formed before there was any sea, when the earth was still so hot
that its surface was covered with steam and vapors, and other
rocks that were formed later from the sediment which washed
down into the first seas.   Finally the strata begin to contain

fossilized forms of organic life. These again occur in successive layers, and in different parts of the world the same types of fossils are found in the corresponding geological strata. This indicates a regular evolution of organic life conforming to surrounding conditions and guided by natural selection.

The first forms of life of which we have any knowledge existed in the water and somewhat resembled those forms which can be seen through a microscope today, although they were then sometimes of great size. There were as yet no vertebrates. At a later stage in the long process of rock formation, we find evidences of the spread of plant life from sea to land and of the existence of amphibious animals. Then, leaving primary or palæozoic for secondary or mesozoic times, we enter the age of reptiles. It is from this distant period that are preserved the remains of huge monsters now extinct, like the dinosaur and ichthyosaur. Remains of creatures somewhat approaching the form of birds begin to appear in this mesozoic period but are relatively rare, and if mammals existed at all, they were very small. But in the tertiary or cainozoic period we reach the age of mammals, or vertebrates which suckle their young. At the beginning of that period the ancestor of our horse was about the size of a fox terrier. In place of a hoof he had toes and something like a thumb, and he still bore a close family resemblance to animals from which our tapirs and rhinoceroses are descended. The tertiary period is commonly subdivided into four ages: eocene, oligocene, miocene, and pliocene. The tremendous duration of even these subdivisions may be deduced from the fact that while in the early eocene age the ancestor of the horse was the type of animal described above, by the middle of that age he had already advanced to the stature of a whippet, had lost his thumb splint, and centred his weight on his middle toe. To suppress the lateral toes completely, however, "required two or three million years more." Thus the available evidence indicates a very slow gradual progression or evolution of organic forms. Some species become extinct, new species gradually emerge from their predecessors, though at first the changes are minute and inconspicuous. This transformation of species has been actually traced in the case of ammonites in the successive strata of Jurassic rocks. Why there is such variation is a problem not yet solved, but the fact must be accepted.

Appearance of Life and Origin of Species

PRE-HUMAN AND PRE-HISTORIC PERIODS

PRIMARY OR PALÆOZOIC
SECONDARY OR MESOZOIC (*Age of Reptiles*)
TERTIARY OR CAINOZOIC (*Age of Mammals*)

Eocene
Oligocene
Miocene
Pliocene (Eoliths)

POST-TERTIARY OR PLEISTOCENE (*Man appears*)

Pre-Chellean
Chellean (between the last two glacial periods)
Acheulean
Mousterian (during the last glacial period)
Aurignacian
Solutrean
Magdalenian
Azilian-Tardenoisean
Neolithic (since the last glacial period)

Human Evolution

This fact must be taken into account in studying the history of civilization, since the human species has evolved like other mammals and vertebrates. "Not only in the structure of all his physical parts, bone for bone, muscle for muscle, and nerve for nerve, is man fundamentally like the other mammals, but his specific organic functions are identical. We have the same diseases; we are similarly affected by the same drugs." Some of the organs of the human body can be traced far back into the past, "others are but of yesterday." Man, indeed, "is one of the few surviving animals that have not ceased to progress." This may be partly because he has evolved but recently, geologically speaking. The earliest known human remains can hardly be placed as early as the pliocene period, the latest of the geological eras mentioned in our previous paragraph, but seem to belong to the post-tertiary or pleistocene period, which was subdivided by climatic change and glacial action into several ice ages and intervening warmer periods. The history of developed civilization lies entirely within the comparatively brief interval since the last ice age, which was especially severe.

The close anatomical resemblance between man and certain

apes makes it difficult to determine in some instances whether the bones which have been found are those of early men or of the ancestors of apes, but remains of apes and monkeys are found in the oligocene and miocene periods before we have any traces of man. This fact suggests that the human species evolved from these seemingly earlier primates. Man seems to have at least four distinctive characteristics: (1) the erect attitude: (2) the hand or more strictly the opposable thumb; (3) the enlarged brain, in which respect the mammals surpass all other animals, while man is far ahead of other mammals especially in frontal development; (4) the power of articulate speech. Let us see how far these characteristics appear in some of the earliest remains which seem to be human or semi-human.

Two molar teeth, the top of a skull, and a left thigh-bone, found in Java in 1891 in what is either an uppermost pliocene or earliest pleistocene stratum, indicate, if they really belong together, a being of erect stature, long-headed unlike the anthropoid apes, but with very low brain capacity and undeveloped forehead. This creature has been called *Pithecanthropus erectus*, or the Java ape-man. The Heidelberg jaw, discovered in 1907 at a depth of seventy-nine feet, dates from the second interglacial period of the pleistocene age. It is the most massive and powerful jaw known, but "the bone closes in to such an extent as to interfere seriously with the free use of the tongue in articulate speech," and there is no chin. On the other hand, all the teeth are essentially human and they form a perfect arch, unlike those of apes, the grinders of which are parallel. The Piltdown skull was found in Sussex, England, during 1911–1913 together with pliocene fossils and very early flints, but "cannot safely be described as earlier than the first half of the pleistocene period." The brain capacity is greater than that of Java ape-man and the brow-ridge projects less, but the bone of the skull is very thick and its conformation is more like that of an anthropoid ape than that of a modern man. There is an enormous canine tooth; jaw and teeth in general are ape-like and perhaps unadapted to speech. Reviewing the three remains which we have just described, Marett says, "It is remarkable to note how, though differing widely from each other, all alike converge on the ape." Other prehistoric human remains were unearthed at Foxhall in 1919, in Rhodesia in 1921, in California in 1923, and even more recently in Mongolia and by the shores of Lake Galilee and in Moravia. It seems likely that we shall keep discovering new evidence which will shed light upon the problem of human evolution.

Instinct and Civilization   Many activities characteristic of civilization are found in a more or less rudimentary or developed state among animals other than man, so that the roots of civilized life perhaps go back of the early life of primitive uncivilized man to animal instincts. Instinctive behaviour, we are told, is not determined by individual experience and does not have to be learned. "Instinct precedes intelligence . . . . and it has furnished all the structural foundations employed by intelligence." The high mark attainable by instinctive behaviour is seen in insect life. Bees are "ideal socialists and colonizers"; ants and social wasps carry on a complicated communal life of concerted labor which puts our industrial disputes to shame. The beaver built his dams; the birds constructed their nests and made their regular migrations; the spider spun webs and spread nets long before man thought of these things. The natives of New Guinea still set up frames of bent bamboo on which obliging spiders weave nets for them that are six feet in diameter and will hold fish weighing a pound. In the insect world there were miners, carpenters, and masons long before there were any human craft gilds. The chimpanzee and gorilla lived an affectionate family life before the institution of human marriage. Even the redoubtable institution of private property is not unknown to the dumb beasts, most of which feel an instinctive claim to their nests or lairs or mates and will fight for their rights. Furthermore, "in any discussion of the origins of art animals cannot be ignored. In excited movements and cries and melodious notes, in brilliant colors and pride of port, in a love of what is showy and glittering, in elaborate constructions, they act and produce in a fashion that at any rate reminds us of the artistic activities of man." But æsthetic sense is developed in man alone. He is superior to the other animals in his ability to profit from his observation and experience, to imitate and adapt and improve upon all the varied instinctive activities which are divided among them, and to combine these into one richer life and civilization.

Geographical Change   Through the ages great masses of land are elevated or sink; not only islands but mainlands rise from or subside beneath the waves. Our mountain ranges differ greatly in age. The Himalayas are a comparatively recent uplift, geologically speaking, whereas there are no high mountain ranges in the peninsula of India although it is one of the oldest land areas of the world. This is presumably because there has been time to wear off the mountain tops by erosion. In early pleistocene times, "Sumatra and Java formed an extension of the Malay peninsula reaching more than a thousand miles into the Indian Ocean." At Gibraltar and the Dardanelles there were land bridges instead of the present straits, while the Mediterranean Sea was divided into two smaller lakes by another land bridge from Sicily to Africa. England was once connected with the continent of Europe and inhabited by animals now extinct or found in the tropics. During the successive ice ages of the pleistocene period glacial action wrought great changes in the earth's surface. Even the time since the last ice age has seen both Scandinavia an island and the Baltic a land-locked lake. Geological change of course still goes on unceasingly, altering historic coast lines by river deposits or encroachment of the sea, and recently raising the bed of the ocean between St. Helena and the Cape of Good Hope over a mile nearer the surface than it was when the previous soundings were taken.

Climate has undoubtedly exercised a great influence upon civilization. Regions without rivers or rainfall naturally have very scant flora and fauna, and, unless man has advanced to the mastery of artificial irrigation, can support only a sparse and nomadic population which develops no settled civilized life. In the arid interior of Australia the natives must keep on the move in small bands in order to obtain food, and there are neither wild beasts nor animals to domesticate. There is evidence which suggests that these desert regions have not always been the same, that the distribution of rainfall and moisture has varied, that there once were flourishing settlements and cultures where now we see only dry and dreary wastes. The amount of water in an inland sea like the Caspian has varied greatly at different periods within recorded history. Alexander the Great was able to lead a large army east through areas where a score of men would find it difficult today to travel together. Soon after Alexander's time there were peaks in Crete from which the snow never disappeared, although now it remains only "in the deeper clefts throughout the summer"; but the inhabitants

Climate and Civilization

then testified that the winters were more severe, and that more snow fell than formerly, when the hills used to be planted with grain and fruit, and the island had a large population.   Unfortunately, we do not have sufficient testimony of this sort concerning climatic conditions in times past, when thermometers and weather bureaus were unknown, to work out the correlation between civilization and climate at all satisfactorily. But it has been contended that all the financial crises in the United States during the nineteenth century may be connected with deficiency of rainfall.

Chief Centers of Civilization

As we come to them in our narrative, we shall describe the geography and climate of particular countries and civilizations.   We may briefly list in anticipation those regions which have proved most favorable to the development of civilization in the past, where it has first appeared and endured longest. First comes Egypt, or the lower valley of the Nile, on which the river has bestowed for millenniums an uninterrupted fertility.   The Tigris-Euphrates valley, on the contrary, while an almost equally ancient seat of civilization, has yielded to the encroachments of the sands of Arabia on the one hand and the nomads of central Asia on the other.   China, long protected by natural barriers and favored by wind and climate, and the rich river valleys of the Ganges and Indus have conserved culture uninterruptedly for many centuries.   Egyptian civilization seems to have spread into the interior of Africa but to have there undergone degeneration; in the Mediterranean countries, however, it was carried further and improved upon.   From them civilization spread in later times to northern Europe, and again from western Europe to the American continents.   Apparently man did not evolve in the American continents but entered from the far eastern section of the Old World after the old stone age.   The American natives had probably at one time learned much from Asiatic civilization, just as Japan learned from China in its early history.

The Backbone of the World

The expression, "the backbone of the world," has been applied to the succession of mountainous or highland regions enclosing the Mediterranean Sea on both north and south, slanting across Asia from Syria and Asia Minor to Japan, and running down the American continents along the Rocky Mountains and the Andes.   This territory contains most of the deserts of the world, such as the Sahara, Arabian desert, and wastes of central Asia and Arizona; but it has also included most of the great civilizations of the past. North of it is the tundra zone; south of it, at least in Asia and Africa, the jungle and equatorial tropics,—which both afford better hunting than the *mesa* region of which we have been speaking. On the farthest margins, or in out-of-the-way places like Australia, South Africa, and Patagonia, are found both the oldest surviving species of mammals and the most primitive human cultures.

Too much is often made of the distinction between east and west and the difference between orientals and Europeans. If, however, one had to draw a line between east and west, the best meridian to select would perhaps be that thirty degrees east of Greenwich. West of this line lie the entire Baltic basin, the valley of the Danube, the Ægean Sea and its surrounding shores which were the cradle of ancient Greek civilization. East of the line lie practically all of Russia, whose past history has been connected with oriental rather than European civilization, and all Asia except the west coastal region of Asia Minor which, as part of the Ægean area, has been connected rather with European history. Of Mediterranean islands Cyprus would be oriental; Rhodes and Crete western. In Africa, Egypt lies just east of the line, as do the India Ocean and even its westernmost shore. Cities that in the past have been great meeting-places of east and west, like Alexandria, Constantinople, Kiev, Leningrad, and Novgorod, happen to be situated almost on this meridian.

A Dividing Line Between East and West

BIBLIOGRAPHY [1]

I. CIVILIZATION

Four noted books that in their respective times made perhaps the closest approach to being histories of civilization are:

Pliny the Elder (died 79 A. D.). *Natural History,* translated by Bostock and Riley, London, 1855, 6 vols. See especially its first and seventh books.

Giovanni Villani (died 1348 A.D.) *Selections from the first nine books of the Chroniche Fiorentine of,* ed. by P. H. Wicksteed and translated by Rose E. Selfe, 1906.

Voltaire (1694–1778). *Le siècle de Louis XIV* (The Age of Louis XIV).

Buckle, H. T. *History of Civilization in England,* 1857–61, 2 vols.

[1] A bibliography of general histories of civilization, works covering long periods, and histories of special types and departments of civilization will be found at the end of the book.

A work by a leading exponent of the theory of the diffusion of culture is G. Elliot Smith, *The Migrations of Early Culture.*

The following contain discussions of civilization from varied standpoints:

Crozier, J. B. *Civilization and Progress*, 1898.

Dickinson, G. L. *Essay on the Civilizations of India, China, Japan*, 1915.

Kidd, Benjamin. *Principles of Western Civilization.* 1902.

Poincaré, H. *The Value of Science*, authorized translation, 1907.

Samuelson, James, *Civilization of Our Day*, 1896.

Steinmetz, C. P. "Electricity and Civilization," *Harper's Magazine*, Jan., 1922.

Stoddard, Lothrop. *The Revolt against Civilization*, 1923.

II. HISTORY

An enlightened treatment by an ancient author is "The Way to Write History," in Lucian's *Essays*, translated by H. W. and F. G. Fowler. Besides the well known essays of Bolingbroke, Carlyle, and Macaulay in the eighteenth and nineteenth centuries, we may note a few recent discussions:

Barnes, Harry. *The New History and the Social Studies*, 1925

Davies, W. W. *How to Read History*, 1925.

George, H. B. *Historical Evidence*, 1909.

Johnson, Allen. *The Historian and Historical Evidence*, 1926.

Osler, Sir Wm. *The Growth of Truth*, 1906.

Robinson, J. H. *The New History*, 1912.

Shotwell, J. T. "History," in *Encyclopedia Britannica*, 11th ed.

Teggart, F. J. *Prolegomena to History*, 1916; *Processes of History*, 1918; see pp. 106–23 on "idea systems" of different civilizations; *Theory of History*, 1926.

Vincent, J. M. *Historical Research*, 1911.

III. EVOLUTION AND GEOGRAPHY

Berry, E. W. "The Geologic Evidence of Evolution," *Scientific Monthly*, Aug., 1922.

Brooks, C. E. P. *The Evolution of Climate*, 1922.

Conklin, E. G. *The Direction of Human Evolution*, 1923.

Febvre, L. *A Geographical Introduction to History*, 1925.

Fleure. *Human Geography in Western Europe.* 1918.

George, H. B. *Relation of History and Geography*, 1907.

Huntington, E. *Civilization and Climate*, 1915; and other works.

Jeans, J. H. *The Nebular Hypothesis and Modern Cosmogony*, 1922.

Osborn. H. F. *Orgin and Evolution of Life.* 1917.

Perrier, Edm. *The Earth Before History*, 1925.

Read, C. *Origin of Man*, 1920.

Scharff, R. F. *The History of European Fauna*, 1899.

Scott, D. H. *Studies in Fossil Botany.*

Semple, E. C. *Influences of Geographical Environment*, 1911.

BOOK I. PREHISTORIC AND PRIMITIVE CIVILIZATION

CHAPTER II

THE STONE AGE

To make a connected story out of the still scanty material from palæolithic times is a somewhat thankless task.—History

As it is difficult to distinguish the oldest extant human bones from those of apes, so it is hard to discriminate between the first objects showing evidence of purposive human handiwork and those which may have been shaped, marked, or worn by forces of nature. Flint implements were perhaps not the earliest to be used by our distant forebears, but, partly on account of their durability, they are the oldest and chief product of early human life which has been preserved for our inspection. Therefore the period of early man is spoken of as the stone age. Eoliths are stones dating from the tertiary period which look as if they had been given edges or points by human agency but were probably produced by the action of streams and strata. Recently, however, evidence of human activity at the close of the pliocene period seems to have been found at Foxhall in the form of a number of small flakes of flint which appear to have been shaped into small tools for boring and other purposes. Flint Implements and Eoliths

The most common implement used by primitive man in the early stone age seems to have been the fist-hatchet, a flint of a size and shape to be conveniently grasped in the hand and given an edge by striking it against another stone and chipping off flakes. These flakes were sometimes used as awls and scrapers. Several different types of fist-hatchets have been found; they seem to have been employed throughout Europe, Asia, and Africa. These implements, like the earliest human bones and skulls already described, are found in river- The Fist-Hatchet drifts and on river-terraces, where the higher deposits, left as the river cuts deeper into the soil, are the oldest, or in open loess stations on the plateaus between river valleys. Loess is fine loam that has been formed by glacial action and then carried and deposited by the wind in periods of dry climate. As we have no evidence of human habitations dating from this period, it is commonly assumed that the fist-hatchet men lived a nomadic hunting life.

Cave Men of the Middle Stone Age

We next find human remains in caves, sometimes at a depth of forty-five feet, the deposits reaching from floor to roof in successive layers which may alternate with those formed when the cave was tenanted only by beasts and which may extend beyond the stone age down to that of bronze. The cave men, however, are usually associated especially with the moist and colder climate of the last ice age in the pleistocene period, with which began what is often called the upper palæolithic or the middle stone age. In this epoch arctic animals such as the reindeer replaced in Europe the tropical animals which had been hunted previously.

Sub-Periods of the Old and Middle Stone Ages

The upper and lower palæolithic strata, or the old and middle stone ages, have been further subdivided into various cultures and periods which take their names from the places where the characteristic remains were first discovered. From Chelles in France is named the period of Chellean flints which seems to have been the warm and temperate interval between the last two glacial periods. But the finding of other flints, obviously more primitive than the Chellean variety, has necessitated the use of the term, Pre-Chellean, to denote the earliest stage of palæolithic or old stone culture. St. Acheul, on the borders of the Somme River, gives its name to the heavy Acheulean implements of stone which followed the Chellean. The name Mousterian, applied to the earliest deposits found in caves, comes from Le Moustier in France. Then follow the Aurignacian, Solutrean (from Solutré near the Saône where the men of the stone age had a great open hunting camp, and where bones of about one hundred thousand horses have been found in a wide circle), Magdalenian (from La Madeleine), and Azilian-Tardenoisean cultures or periods. The sequence of these periods is demonstrated partly by the evolution of flint implements, partly by evidence of geological and climatic change, and partly by superimposition in the same spot of layers representing different epochs and cultures. Thus, in the river deposits at St. Acheul we have not only Acheulean deposits but Chellean and Pre-Chellean deposits beneath them, and Mousterian, Aurignacian, and Solutrean implements above them. In a grotto in northern Spain are thirteen layers covering eleven periods from Acheulean times to the bronze age.

In the Mousterian period the fist-hatchet, after having been in use for thousands of years, finally gave way to the point, a more delicate implement made from a flake which had been chipped off and retouched on only one side. After this innovation, "cultural advance in Mousterian days" became "almost as portentously slow as ever it had been before." Thick human deposits in a cave on the island of Jersey are separated by a layer without human remains which appears to have been centuries in accumulating, for relics of one type of elephant are found above it and of a different type beneath it. Yet "one and the same type of flint instrument is found at every level alike; and the only development one can detect is a certain gain in elegance as regards the Mousterian point." It is hard to see how the Mousterians killed their big game with such delicate weapons. Doubtless they fitted their points to wooden spears and darts which have not come down to us. The bow and arrow, however, had not yet been invented. Nor have any lamps been found, although men by this time were probably acquainted with fire and lighted their caves with torches. We now, or perhaps back in late Acheulean times, first have evidence of burial of the dead, and consequently find skeletal remains in increasing quantity.

The Mousterian Point

With the Mousterian age is associated the Neanderthal type of man, of whom some thirty examples have been found. From these remains we infer a short, thick-set race, with broad shoulders, muscular chest, heavy hand, huge head but low forehead and protruding brow-ridge and primitive jaw, and "a cranial profile inferior to the lowest existing Australian races." The shins are short compared to the thighs; the knees are bent so that Neanderthal man must have been unable to stand quite erect. He seems to have had a habitual stoop, to have been clumsy and slow-moving, and to have squatted on his ankles much of the time. Yet this ungainly creature appears to have abandoned the fist-hatchet for the delicate Mousterian point and to have practiced ceremonial burial.

Neanderthal Man

Crô-
Magnons
and Cave
Paintings

Most persons would prefer to trace back their ancestry to the Crô-Magnons of the following Aurignacian period, which, however, seems to have been closely related to the Mousterian culture, since it immediately followed it and in many places occupied the same stations or settlements. The Crô-Magnons had a large brain and almost modern forehead, were long-legged, and, in some cases at least, quite tall. But the majority of Aurignacian men were under five feet, six inches. A few skeletons of about the same period, moreover, seem of a negroid type and are known as the Grimaldi race from the grotto where they were found. But the remarkable cave paintings and engravings of southern France and Spain have rather naturally been ascribed to the Crô-Magnons. They depict, often in colors, with fidelity, skill, and spirit, various animals such as bisons, boars, stags, and mammoths, with which the artist doubtless had an intimate acquaintance, and which he liked to draw as well as hunt, perhaps with the hope that his realistic picture might act as a charm and bring game to his cave, perhaps with the will that led eventually to the domestication of certain animals. We have preserved unbroken the stone palette on which some cave artist crushed his colors and numerous tools of the prehistoric sculptors: chisels, points, pickaxes, saws, chopping tools, and all sorts of planers and graving instruments. Extant works of scuplture from the Aurignacian period, however, are largely confined to corpulent female figurines which emphasize the parts of the body connected with maternity.

The Height
of Flint
Technique
and Ap-
pearance of
New Bone
Implements

In the Solutrean period, the art of flaking flints reached about its highest development in spear-heads and notched points, and needles began to appear. Henceforth we find objects made of materials other than stone, such as the ivory statuette of a mammoth. New races seem to appear such as the men of Brünn. In the succeeding Magdalenian period come many implements of bone such as the harpoon. Fishermen thus far seem not to have used nets and hooks but only harpoons and bait-holders. There was now much sculpture in reindeer horn, bone, and ivory, such as an ibex carved on a throwing stick,—a contrivance representing the first step of primitive man toward the gun barrel. Osborn says of such carvings, "Of all upper palæolithic work these decorative heads and bodies are, perhaps, the most highly artistic creations in the modern sense." Lamps are found in the La Madeleine stations, and similar ones are said to be still in use in that part of France today. Finally in the Azilian-Tardenoisean period palæolithic culture, or that of the old and middle stone ages, seems to decline in Europe; of bone implements we find only inferior harpoons and polishers, while decorative art is limited to the painting of characters on pebbles and geometric designs on stone walls.

The neolithic or new stone age is usually thought of as separated from the palæolithic by a break and some marked climatic change, and as the work of a different set or race of men. The palæolithic races are supposed to have become extinct or to have retreated to parts unknown. At any rate the neolithic men seem to have been of the same type almost everywhere, short and slender, with long skulls except that in the region of the Swiss lakes the broad-skulled Alpine type perhaps already predominated. Neolithic remains are found in Turkestan, Mesopotamia, Palestine, Egypt, Crete, and on the continent of Europe. There the stone age civilization persisted till a later date than in the orient, while in America the Indians were still in the stone age at the time of Columbus. The novel feature about the neolithic stone implements was that some of them were polished upon long flat slabs of sandstone instead of being chipped and flaked, but this innovation was not universally adopted. On the other hand, it was not very long before neolithic men began to make some use of metal.

The New Stone Age

It was therefore not the use of polished stone implements with a ground edge and handles that was the most important change from palæolithic times, but rather the appearance of pottery, the domestication of animals, the cultivation of food-plants, and in general the adoption of a more settled and civilized mode of life. Henceforth the archæologist ceases to rely mainly on the record of the rocks and the connected series of stone tools for his chronology, and finds his guide instead in the development of pottery, which at first is kneaded and shaped by hand without the potter's wheel and baked in the sun or open fire without oven or furnace. There is also gradual progress or decline in the decoration of the pottery with lines, designs, and colors. Stone is hard to break; clay is easy to mould. There is significance in this distinction. Human life becomes less hard; man begins to mould his destiny, to be constructive

Pottery More Important than Polished Stone

instead of destructive. As a result we see more progress in the relatively brief neolithic period than in all the many thousands of palæolithic years.

Among the most primitive centers of neolithic culture, at least in Europe,—although some interpret them as the last stage of palæolithic culture,—are those marked by the kitchen middens or heaps of shells and refuse along the shores of Denmark. In these are found broken pottery and skeletal evidence for the domestication of the dog, whose wolfish ancestors' noses were pleasantly attracted by the stench of the aforesaid refuse heaps, about which some of them lingered permanently, becoming habituated and devoted to human society. One wonders, however, if the custom of hunting with a pack of hounds originated from wolves following human hunters or from men following packs of wolves. Existing breeds of dogs seem to trace back to different wild ancestors who were perhaps domesticated in different parts of the world at different periods. Thus the black wolf of Tibet seems the forebear of all mastiffs, including the ancient Assyrian hound seen in the sculptures of Assurbanipal, the Molossian hound of the ancient street of tombs at Athens, and the Newfoundlands, Saint Bernards, bulldogs, and pugs of the present. We do not, of course, have any written records concerning the early domestication of animals, although some early sculptured reliefs from Egypt throw light on the subject. It must have been a very difficult and painstaking process, and it is noteworthy that after domesticating a few animals man has gone no farther in this direction. Indeed, the Egyptians tried to domesticate animals which are still wild. The dog was probably first domesticated because naturally the most affectionate and sociable, and of most service in hunting, which was so important to primitive man.

The neolithic men along the shores of Denmark almost certainly had boats. This thought leads us on to another evidence of new stone age culture, the lake village of dwellings supported on piles. The wooden piles of such settlements have survived to this day beneath the normal level of the water in some of the Swiss lakes, and can be seen when the water is at an unusually low level, as was the case again in 1921. They were first noticed in the winter of 1853–1854 and are the earliest wooden remains known. In one such settlement at Wangen there were some 50,000 piles, although these were not necessarily all driven in at one time. At Geneva stockades or break-waters were built to protect the village from waves when the lake was stormy. Boats that sank to the bottom have been found among the piles as well as many other remains including bones of the dog, ox, pig, goat and sheep. At the very bottom at St. Aubin on Lake Neuchâtel are many bones of wild animals showing that the inhabitants still relied on hunting, but as time went on they evidently used the domesticated animals more and more for their food supply. Grain spilt from the platforms of the lake villages and threads of flax indicate that they raised crops already, but probably by hoe culture and not yet by plough culture. These Swiss lake villages spread into northern Italy where remains of them are found in the Po valley in the form of over one hundred *terramare,* mounds formed by dykes which enclosed their artificial lakes and by the debris which gradually accumulated. Both these and the lake villages of Switzerland were inhabited into the bronze age.

All over Italy are other remains of neolithic habitations in the form of circular depressions containing fragments of tools and pottery. They are probably floors that were once covered by straw huts or wigwams of wicker-work daubed with clay, and are known as *fonde di capanne.* At Cnossus in Crete in 1923 a ground plan of a late neolithic house with a fixed hearth was discovered. Neolithic men used clay for other purposes than pottery and huts. Both in the lake villages and in Palestine, spindle-whorls have been found,—suspended weights of clay which were employed to twist the fibres of flax together into threads. The neolithic inhabitants of Eridu in Mesopotamia cut their crops with sickles of earthenware. In England and Belgium picks of deer-horn have been found with which the men of the new stone age mined for flints in the chalk. They often buried their dead in contracted postures and daubed them over with red paint. *Other Neolithic Habitations and Remains*

Two great inventions that seem to belong to the new stone age were the plough and the wheel. The plough, drawn by the domesticated ox, was a great advance in agriculture over the hoe in the hands of women. The heavier plough required the attention of a man. With the domestication of animals and introduction of plough-culture the distinction between nomadic, pastoral, and agricultural life came into existence. The first two great uses of the wheel were for transportation in carts *Invention of Plough and Wheel* and as the revolving potter's wheel in the improved manufacture of pottery. It seems to have been first so used in Elam or Egypt, and remained unknown in most of Africa and in the Americas.

Neolithic Trade and Stone Erections

There was increasingly wide trade as the new stone age wore on. Its culture spread to islands far from the mainland, and in the later Swiss lake villages we find beads made of amber from the Baltic. Crete traded by boats with Egypt and Cyprus before the end of the neolithic period in 3000 B. C. The close of the new stone age and the introduction of metal came of course at different times in different regions according as they were more or less advanced and in communication with other centers. There also is much difference of opinion as to the date and origin of the tombs and monoliths, and of the circles and avenues of great stones weighing many tons, which are found in western Europe. They are so numerous, and the great blocks so difficult to drag and erect in place, that they seem to imply a highly organized society. But Stonehenge in England, for example, has been attributed to the Celts and the men of the bronze age as well as to neolithic men.

Problem of the Transition to the Bronze and Iron Ages

The new stone age is commonly thought of as succeeded by the bronze age, but gold, silver, and copper were used before bronze, which is an alloy of copper with tin, and some now speak of a copper age as intermediate between the new stone and bronze ages. Others contend that iron would be known before bronze because it is easier to discover and work, and many African peoples appear to have passed directly from stone to iron tools. For the lands about the Mediterranean, nevertheless, it has been customary to place the bronze age before the iron age. We shall not treat of these ages separately, however, but shall presently trace the development of civilization after the new stone age at different leading centers beginning with ancient Egypt. But first we must treat of primitive custom and thought.

BIBLIOGRAPHY

For the earliest description of a lake-village see Herodotus, V. 16; for an ancient account of the origin of the dwelling house see Vitruvius, *De Architectura*, Bk. II, chap. I, Morgan's translation.

Atkinson, J. J. *Primal Law,* 1903.
Burkitt, M. C. *Prehistory,* 1921; reliable, but somewhat dry.

Childe, V. G. *The Dawn of European Civilization*, 1925.

Déchelette, J. *Manuel d'archéologie préhistorique*, 1910.

Haddon, A. C. *Evolution in Art*, 1914. *The Races of Men and their Distribution*, 1924.

Hobhouse, Wheeler, and Ginsberg, *Material Culture and Social Institutions of Simpler Peoples*, 1915.

Hoffman, W. I. *Graphic Art of the Eskimo*, 1925.

Keller, C. *Die Abstammung der ältesten Haustiere*, 1902.

Lubbock, Sir John (Lord Avebury). *Prehistoric Times;* a work which, like that of Sollas, has been found worthy of a new edition after a lapse of years.

MacCurdy, Geo. G. *Human Origins; a Manual of Pre-History*, 2 vols., 1924.

Mainage, Th. *Les religions de la préhistoire*, 1920.

Mason, O. T. *Origins of Invention*, 1901. *Woman's Share in Primitive Culture*, 1894; the author certainly does not underestimate it.

Morgan, J. de. *L'Humanité préhistorique*, 1921; English translation, 1925. *Le préhistoire orientale*, tome I, 1925.

Myres, J. L. *Dawn of History*, 1918.

Obermaier, Hugo. *Fossil Man in Spain*, 1924.

Osborn, H. F. *Men of the Old Stone Age*, 1915; a well organized, interestingly written, and finely illustrated book, but at times giving too great an impression of certainty.

Parkyn, E. A. *Prehistoric Art*, 1916.

Peet, T. E. *Stone and Bronze Ages in Italy*, 1909.

Perry, Wm. J. *The Megalithic Culture of Indonesia*, 1918.

Petrie, Flinders. *Tools and Weapons*, 1917.

Rau, Chas. *Prehistoric Fishing*, 1884.

Scott Elliot, G. F. *Prehistoric Man and his Story*, 1915.

Sollas, W. J. *Ancient Hunters and their Modern Representatives*, 3rd edition revised, 1924; a venturesome attempt to identify various existing peoples as survivals from the old stone age.

Starr, F. *Some First Steps in Human Progress*, 1901.

Tyler, J. M. *New Stone Age in Northern Europe*, 1921; the best single volume to combine with Osborn's on the old stone age.

Tyler, E. B. *Researches into the Early History of Mankind*, 1865.

Wilder, H. W. *Man's Prehistoric Past*, 1923.

Windle, B. C. A. *Remains of the Prehistoric Age in England*, 1904.

CHAPTER III

PRIMITIVE CUSTOM AND THOUGHT

The whole attempt of the savage to control the outside world, so far as it contained a theory or a doctrine, was based on magic.—W. I. Thomas

Inference from Uncivilized Peoples of the Present

THE material remains left by men of the stone age fail to enlighten us concerning many points. Not only are we puzzled as to the proper explanation of some of the extant remains; there is also the fact that much of their life and activity would not express itself in the use of such permanent objects, and that, in the period before written records, we are especially in the dark as to their thought and view of the world. This prehistoric gloom and mist we attempt to dispel and illuminate by a study of the uncivilized and savage peoples of the present. Since they are inferior to us in civilization—or so we, at least, confidently believe—it is natural to assume that they have failed to advance as our ancestors advanced, and that they consequently represent the earlier primitive stage of civilization and state of mind through which our ancestors once passed. If we find them still using stone knives, it is tempting to regard their dances, social institutions, and religious beliefs as further examples of neolithic culture. When we find an Eskimo today hurling a spear from a throwing stick as the hunters of the middle stone age did, it is tempting to take the Eskimo as a representative of early man in other respects. When we find North American Indians marking the passage of time by giving each year an individual name as the early Egyptians did, we are apt to conclude that the rest of their life has not progressed much beyond the stage which the ancient Egyptians had reached several thousand years ago. To a considerable extent the material side of the life of these uncivilized peoples of today seems roughly to correspond to the material remains which have reached us from the prehistoric periods.

It has therefore become customary to regard such barbarous

and savage tribes of the present as representative of early man and primitive man, and to regard many, if not most, of their customs, ideas, myths, and superstitions as survivals from the prehistoric and early period. But it is hardly probable that these peoples of America, Australasia, and Africa have remained for thousands of years in an absolutely arrested state of development, or even that they have been in their present habitats that long, or further have been distinct peoples. After all, the earth is a small place, man in all periods has apparently moved about a great deal, and good stories, rumors, nostrums, religious symbols, decorative motives, and handy devices have probably spread faster and farther than nomadic tribes and racial migrations. There is, then, always the question whether modern savages derive their institutions, stories, and superstitions directly from primitive custom and folk-lore, or whether these are not corrupt perversions of former borrowings from higher cultures, such as those of ancient Egypt, China, and India, or, as we are able to detect in some instances, from intercourse a few centuries ago with the Jesuits or other Christian missionaries. Instead of simply having failed to progress from a lower stage of civilization, savages may have retrogressed from a once higher state of culture. It is, therefore, none too certain that their customs and thought are those of primitive man, but if the study of these savage peoples does not convincingly dispel the prehistoric gloom, it does cast a dim and flickering light on the subject. And the numerous analogies and resemblances between various tribes and cultures, widely separated in space or time, do suggest a certain unity in human development the world over. Whether, strictly speaking, primitive or not, the customs and thought of the uncivilized peoples of today are very valuable for purposes of comparison with those of the past.

Language, music, and dancing seem to have been quite early human activities. The languages of uncivilized tribes of the present often have large vocabularies and elaborate grammatical and phonetic systems, and Sapir assures us that "many primitive languages have a formal richness, a latent luxuriance of expression, that eclipses anything known to the languages of modern civilization." I would suggest that gender, which seems to serve little purpose in several modern languages save to impose a burden on the memory, is a survival from a period when primitive magic and "animism" laid great stress upon the sexual relation, or at least upon the classification of objects as animate or inanimate, and it was thought important for practical purposes to distinguish the names of different classes of things very precisely.

Music and Dancing

A relatively high capacity for music is frequently found among peoples in the lowest stages of civilization. "Savages are highly susceptible to music, which excites them in the highest imaginable degree," sometimes causing them physical pain or making men "sick and unfitted for work for days together." This reminds one of Confucius, who was so affected by hearing a certain melody that he could not eat meat for three months. Savages also, like the ancient Greeks, think that they can cure disease by music. The most primitive music, however, "is no melody, but noise reduced to time." The longer and louder the noise, the better, while dancing is carried on to the point of physical exhaustion. Savages have a keen sense of rhythm, and harmony seems to be almost as old as melody. The association between music and dancing is closer and older than that between music and poetry. The choral or imitative dance and pantomime gave birth to the primitive drama before the origin of lyric or epic poetry. Lyric or emotional poetry probably was composed before epic or narrative poetry, but our earliest literary remains are often epics. There is difference of opinion whether the first musical instrument was the pipe, or a stringed instrument suggested by the hunter's bow, or a gong or sounding plate of stone, or a drum made of skin. In the early development of man as in the activities of other animals work and play are hardly distinguishable. For the ordinary savage continuous work is impossible unless it is accompanied by a rhythmic chant in unison with others.

Personal Adornment and Art

Savages give much time and attention not only to dancing but to their personal adornment. The stone palettes holding green face- and body-paint which have been found in the earliest predynastic Egyptian graves also show that the arts of the toilette, whether a token of civilization or barbarism, are at least no recent acquisition. Art in a higher sense, as the material remains of the stone ages have already shown us, is early as well as long in the course of fleeting time. And in the savage world today even the poorest and most primitive tribes devote themselves to art, "which," we are assured by one author, "civilized nations are coming more and more to regard from the height of their practical and scientific attainments as an idle pastime." To this it may be replied that all lasting and satisfying results of workmanship are art, and that all primitive arts were practical as well as æsthetic.

The savage or barbarian often has keen powers of observation and displays great skill in his customary industries and occupations. But his beliefs, theories, and stories are apt to seem childish and silly or illogical and mystical to civilized man. His experience is restricted, although it may be rich in certain particulars. His stock of ideas is small. He is naturally excitable and emotional, carrying on even an ordinary conversation in a high-pitched voice. He distorts facts by letting his imagination rather than his reason play with them. His entire education and frame of mind from infancy up has been preoccupied, not with a sound historical survey of all past, and a scientific estimate of all present phenomena, but with supposed occult forces and proceedings, and with the effort to divine the future. The savage is thus prone to look at everything from a mystical or superstitious standpoint. The very air that he breathes is, so to speak, filled for him with the poisonous gas of evil magic.

The Uncivilized Mind

We cannot tell just what early man's notions of personality were, and how far he thought of beasts and winds as beings like himself. Even civilized persons like to imagine or pretend that animals possess semi-human traits. Still more difficult to determine is the attitude of uncivilized man to such things as trees and stones. The worship, or at least the ceremonial cultivation and holding sacred, of such inanimate objects has been called by the rather absurd name "animism," much as a fat boy is called "Skinny." Modern writers, assuming that no one would worship anything but a spirit, assumed that savages believed there was a spirit in the stone. It is more likely that the savage at first believed in stones, or cherished certain particular stones for reasons best known to himself. Such a sacred object is called a fetish, and the use of, or belief in them is fetishism.

Animism and Fetishism

It is very difficult to draw a line between such "worship," or holding sacred of stones, herbs, animals, and other natural objects and phenomena, and the employment of these to work mir-

Magic Charms and Ritual

acles or magic because of their supposed occult virtue or magic force or *mana*. The use of these objects as amulets and charms, and the attribution to them of medicinal and miraculous powers, appear to have played a great part in the life of early man, as they do today in that of many savage tribes, as they continued to do in the medical and learned lore of many civilized peoples for a long time,—in China and India, indeed, until the present. When we read of the Thompson River Indians that "among the spirits peculiar to *shamans*, parts of animals or objects were not uncommon, such as the tail of a snake, the nipple of a gun, the left or right side of anything, and the like," we suspect that these shamans were originally magicians rather than priests or persons possessed by spirits, and that the conception of spirits among these Indians may not be very much older than their use of guns. The rattle suggests the venom of the rattlesnake, the nipple suggests the percussion cap which fires off the gun; it is the magic power or occult virtue rather than spirits in our sense of the word that is valued in such objects or parts of objects. Right is lucky, left is unlucky, and many such directions must be observed in magic. Perhaps one must face the east or turn one's back to the wind, or perform the operation at a specified time, such as the full moon, or repeat the rite or some part of it a certain number of times. In fact all sorts of rites and ceremonies may have to be gone through to secure the desired result. Certain persons, too, are believed either by natural gift or training to have greater magic power than others. These become "medicine men." The kit, or "medicine bundle," of such a magician is much the same sort of a collection as might be found in a small boy's pocket, only a little nastier:—"various small articles such as pieces of skin, small pebbles, quartz, animal or vegetable matter," prized, of course, because of the power they are supposed to exert as charms.

Magic and Medicine

As the terms, "medicine man" and "medicine bundle," which are today applied to such savage practitioners and their paraphernalia, indicate, the healing of disease and restoration of the sick to health are one of the chief aims of such magical procedure. The medicine man tries to scare away the disease by beating a drum and making a great noise, or maltreating the patient and giving him nauseous doses, or by spoken commands and abusive language. Thus words and incantations are thought to have great force. But the use of magic in medicine is not a sure sign of a belief that disease is possession by evil spirits. Today we do not so think of disease, yet we still speak of "getting rid of a cold" or ask a friend what he is "taking for *it*." The notion that a disease can be got rid of by magic transfer of it to some other animal or person seems early, and, like the theory of invisible demons possessing the patient, an interesting adumbration of the modern discovery of microscopic germs and bacteria which cause disease and are carried by tiny insects or in the air.

As these ways of contagion were unknown until recently, it is not surprising that savages often ascribe disease to the evil magic or sorcery of some enemy, and that some tribes to this day think that death is always caused by spirits or by evil magic. One widespread method of thus bewitching or secretly injuring an adversary is to make an image of him from wax or clay and then wound it or allow it to melt away before a fire. Or a crystal of quartz may be buried before the victim's threshold or in a path where he is sure to walk, or some other supposedly fatal charm may be concealed in his bed. *Sorcery*

Rain-making and weather prediction are other forms of magic among uncivilized peoples. Some have held that the original purpose of dramatic performances, which are quite general among primitive peoples, was to get something done by imitative action, which starts things going, as it were, like pouring a little water down a pump. Thus there were dances to produce rain, rites to regulate the sun's movements, dramas to drive away winter and bring in summer, phallic ceremonies to influence human generation, imitative pantomimes to cure sickness, and in religion imitation of the appearance, movements, and behaviour of the god in order to make the people feel his presence. Festivals like the Olympic games and classical Greek dramas still contained some suggestion of magic rite. Yet dance and drama are not merely imitative, they also stir emotion. Moreover, rain comes before imitation of it, and we have to experience summer before we can act summer. So the first origin of dance and drama would seem to be in sympathetic participation with nature. It rained and the people danced for joy, summer came and they played. Only at some later date would it occur to someone to dance as if it were raining in order to produce the rain-feeling and perhaps the *Rain-Making and Imitative Dancing: Magic and the Drama*

actual rain so needed for the crops.   Usually it takes a magician or actor to act like rain when it isn't raining; no one
else feels like it.   But man has a spontaneous tendency toward
gesticulation and movement, imitation and mimicry; and savages are perhaps especially fond of showy costumes and colors,
of dressing up and ef "make up."   If dance and spectacle
did not originate in magic, there is at least a connection between drama and magic, and between magic and acting.   Both
require imagination and a considerable amount of fiction, as
well as a considerable amount of fidelity to nature.   The same
holds true of mythology and literature, and indeed of most
forms of art.

Does Civilization Originate in Magic?   If therefore we agree with Plato that everything which deceives may be said to enchant, we shall have to assign magic a
fairly large place not only in primitive custom and thought
but also in existing civilization.   There has been a tendency
both to regard magic as characteristic of most sides of the life
of primitive man, and to think of civilization as originating in
magic or under the impulse of magic and then gradually growing away from this.   Thus music is said to have developed
from the incantation, law to have at first been largely magic
regulations; and magic has been regarded as the first stage both
of religious and scientific development.   In the case, however,
of the uncivilized peoples of the present, their industries—in
which they often display great skill—and daily occupations
seem in the main free from magic.

Taboo   Taboo has been called negative magic.   Anything may be
tabooed, either an object which one must not touch or even see,
or an action which is prohibited, or words which must remain
unspoken lest terrible calamity befall.   This conception of
taboo seems related to that of sanctity or mystery.   Sacred
objects must not be handled, mysteries must not be too curiously pried into.   It is said that some savages have died of
fright when they inadvertently violated some such prohibition.

Divination   We shall meet various forms of divination through the course
of civilization; some of the cruder forms are practiced by present savages.   All such invalid arts of forecasting the future
are to be classed as branches of magic.   This is illustrated by
the fact that one of the chief functions of the medicine man is
to discover or divine who has bewitched the patient.   Worship

of the sun or other heavenly bodies is likely to lead sooner or later to astrology.   It is well to remember, when boasting of our superior knowledge of the past or modern sciences, that former men were able to console themselves for these deficiencies with knowledge and sciences, as they thought, of the future.

Belief in spirits and even belief in one supreme deity or father are fairly common among uncivilized peoples today.   But the representations of these spirits in art or in the masks worn to impersonate them are generally quite unprepossessing to the civilized eye.   Guardian spirits of the living are often believed in as well as ghosts of the dead and various spirits in nature that affect the life of man.   The sounds made by ventriloquists seem at an early date to have been mistaken for spirit voices. *Belief in Gods*

Most peoples have their myths concerning their own past which they repeat or enact at their tribal initiation ceremonies and dramatic performances or at funeral celebrations.   They also have their fancies and imaginary stories about what the animals and plants are doing in the night or when we are not looking at them, and their cosmic myths explaining the creation of the world or the course of the sun and other celestial phenomena.   There are many resemblances between the myths of different peoples and different periods. *Mythology*

Social order and organization seems a side of life which early man developed sooner than others or in which we have failed to advance beyond him as far as we have in other phases of civilization.   The view that men once lived promiscuously in hordes and that the family developed only gradually, perhaps with settled life, has now been abandoned, and the family, usually monogamous, is recognized as the oldest human institution and "omnipresent at every stage of culture."   Westermarck holds that "marriage was transmitted to man from some ape-like ancestor, and there never was a time when it did not occur in the human race."   Lowie affirms that "on the very lowest cultural plane we frequently encounter matrimonial relations that would be rated exemplary by a mid-Victorian moralist."   Relationship is sometimes traced through the mother rather than the father.   This does not mean, however, that the mother rules the family, for it is her brother who inherits the property.   Some peoples call the sisters of the mother "mothers" and apply a term corresponding to our "aunts" only to the sisters of the father. *Social Organization: the Family*

Or they have a common designation for the mother's brother and the husband of the father's sister, and in other ways reckon or name relationships in different ways from ours.

Question of Paternal Power

The father or other head of the family, who in some tribes is the mother's brother, represents the wife and children, and among some peoples, such as the ancient Hebrews and Romans, has absolute and lifelong power over them.   But this is not universally the case among uncivilized peoples of today.   The present tendency is to reject the old patriarchal theory of the origin of the state from the power of the primitive father, who was represented as a jealous brute who ruled his brood of women and children by force until he grew old and feeble, and one of the boys, growing up, defeated him and took his place as lord and master bully.

Position of Woman and Relations Between the Sexes

In some of the rudest communities woman is surprisingly free, but her position is almost nowhere superior to that of man.   As warriors the males monopolize political power, and they usually hold most of the property.   Magicians, medicine men, and priests are usually males, who further maintain their ascendancy by secret societies.   The women do not display the same tendency to organize.   Economic activity is divided between the sexes.   Woman has a considerable share in primitive art and handiwork, and is said to be more given to music and dancing than man is.   But inventions and new processes are usually in the hands of males, who seem to manifest more progressiveness and creative ability.   In some tribes women perform tasks that are elsewhere confined to men, and *vice versa,* but in any tribe there is some line drawn between the work of the two sexes.   Uncivilized societies are given to elaborate marriage regulations and rules concerning the separation of the sexes.   Various groups are constituted, usually on the basis of relationship, with which one must marry or within which one must not marry.

Totemism

Totemism is a widespread system among existing uncivilized peoples, according to which society is divided into groups or clans.   Each of these has its own species of animal or other natural object, such as a plant or wind, which gives the group its emblem and name.   Often the members of the group believe or pretend that they are descended from or otherwise related to the animal in question, or that they share its peculiarities. The members of such a group do not intermarry.   Usually the totem is taboo; members of the group may not kill or eat their sacred plant or animal but should rather perform magic rites to multiply that species, perhaps dressing up to resemble the animal and imitating its actions and cries in a dramatic dance. Some think that worship of stones and trees and animals in later civilizations, for example, the black stone in the Kaaba at Mecca, the tree cult of the Druids, and the animal gods of Egypt, is a relic of totemism, but others regard such nature worship as quite distinct from totemism. Animal sacrifice would seem almost the opposite of totemism, since the totem is tabooed.

Such words as tribe and clan have been used so loosely and in such varying senses that it is difficult to define them. A tribe may be either a whole people living in union in a state of savagery or barbarism, in other words in a tribal state, or it may denote a political subdivision of the Iroquois or Athenians or Romans or any other people uncivilized or civilized. Clan carries more of a sense of kinship and common name for the members, but in medieval Ireland and Scotland clans were the only tribes. Recent ethnologists use *clan* as equivalent to *gens*, except that if children belong to the father's group, it is called a *gens*, while if the children join their mother's group, it is a *clan*. Thus a child always belongs to a different gens from its mother or clan from its father. Both gens and clan are supposed to be based on blood relationship and to be extensions of the family or kinship group, known also as the *sib*, but strangers are sometimes adopted into gens or clan. Members of sib, gens, or clan usually feel bound to avenge the death of a fellow member, they usually have a common name and perhaps totem, they usually must marry outside of their group. While the family is older than gens or clan, gentile and clan names seem to be older than family names. Phratries or brotherhoods are other common primitive groups. There are usually hereditary nobles and slaves. Men are often classified by their occupations, where these differ, so that gilds are of early origin. Within a tribe or people there are also local divisions such as villages. But primitive organization does not stop there, since uncivilized peoples show as strong an inclination to form clubs and secret societies as boys of twelve do. "We find the cooperative motive and the need for congenial companionship incarnated in a variety of forms among primitive peoples." The men are apt

Various
Social
Groups

to spend much of their time at a common club house.   Initiations into the tribe or secret fraternity or religious society are
often very painful and marked by such incidents as having a
front tooth knocked out.   The purpose is partly to impress the
youth with the seriousness of life and to "make a man" out of
him—the rites are often connected with the period of puberty;
partly to propitiate fortune or spirits and gain magic power;
partly to enforce the authority of the older men and of the
community.

Mutilation
and Other
Barbaric
Customs

Such painful procedure is indeed so frequent among primitive peoples that it is what comes first to mind when "barbaric
customs" are mentioned.   Mutilation is very common.   For
example, the Abbé Dubois wrote a century ago of a caste in
eastern Mysore in India, "in which, when the mother . . . gives
the eldest daughter in marriage, she is obliged to submit to the
amputation of two joints of the middle finger and of the ring
finger of the right hand.   And if the bride's mother be dead,
the bridegroom's mother, or in default of her the mother of the
nearest relative, must submit to this cruel mutilation."   Today
this custom has been softened; instead of being amputated the
two fingers are tied together and so rendered equally unfit for
use.   Some tribes flatten the children's skulls with a board into
a prescribed shape, or gradually elongate their women's necks
by an increasingly high collar of metallic rings, or in other
ways attempt to improve upon nature for the sake of appearance.   Sometimes, however, such practices seem not to be primitive but, as in the case of foot-binding in China, are said to
have been introduced in the course of civilized history.   Other
tribes practice human sacrifice, or devise cruel tortures for
prisoners in war and those found guilty in lawsuits.

Character-
istics of
Early Law

Early law, indeed, is usually harsh and seems to delight in
minute listing of penalties.   Good intentions and the motive
of the offender are little regarded; a penalty is fixed by custom
for a certain act or injury which it is supposed to follow as the
night the day, whether the act was malicious or careless or ac-
cidental or unintentional.   There is little legislating or making of new laws; ancient custom is supposed to prevail, and
everyone is supposed to be acquainted with it.   If a dispute
as to custom arises, it will probably be settled by the recollection of the elders.   The kindred or social group is held responsible for the deeds of an individual member and avenges him on

another group when he is wronged by one of its members. Compensation, or payment of the *wergeld* or blood price of the slain according to his rank, early appears, however, as an alternative to an unending feud. Sometimes such quarrels and other disputes are settled by single combat of selected champions. Inheritance is regulated by fixed rules of relationship, and a man may not leave his property otherwise. In deciding disputes it is customary for the parties to take solemn oaths and undergo magic rites or legal formalities and submit to religious tests or ordeals. Such disputes are more often heard and overseen by all members of the tribe or by the elders, than by a single man.

Primitive people are generally law-abiding and observe existing custom with great fidelity. They are very timid about trying anything new, and are also much afraid of being laughed at or socially ostracized. Public opinion thus has great force with them as well as with us. They especially defer to the attitude of their kindred—interpreted in a broader sense than our family. Often the old men have great influence and succeed in reserving certain privileges for themselves, but not always. Priests, magicians, chieftains in war, and kings also exert a varying amount of influence or power. The young are educated in the customs, religious, legal, and dramatic, of the tribe, and in its myths, as well as in its economic and military activities. There are recognized standards of tribal morality, a word which etymologically means simply approved custom. When savages today try to adopt our civilization or are considerably affected by it, their morals, being thus based on their own customs, naturally go to pieces.

BIBLIOGRAPHY

Bartlett, F. G. *Pyschology and Primitive Culture,* 1923.

Dixon, R. B. *The Racial History of Man,* 1923.

Frazer, Sir J. G. *The Golden Bough,* one volume edition, 1922.

Goldenweiser, A. A. *Early Civilization,* 1923.

Hankins, F. H. *The Racial Basis of Civilization* (forthcoming).

Keane, A. H. *Man, Past and Present,* revised and largely rewritten by A. H. Quiggin and A. C. Haddon, 1920.

Levy-Bruhl, *Primitive Mentality;* translated by L. A. Clare, 1923.

Lowie, R. H. *Primitive Society,* 1920; *Primitive Religion,* 1924.

Marett, R. R. *Psychology and Folk-Lore,* 1920.

Radin, P. *Primitive Man and his World* (forthcoming).

Robinson, J. H. *The Mind in the Making,* 1921.

Simar, T. *Étude critique sur la formation de la doctrine des races,* 1922.

Thomas, W. I. *Source Book for Social Origins,* 4th edition, 1909.

Wissler, Clark. *Man and Culture,* 1923.

Especially concerned with religion and folk-lore are:

Durkheim, E. *The Elementary Forms of the Religious Life,* translated by J. W. Swain, 1915.

Gomme, G. L. *Folk-lore as an Historical Science,* 1908.

Hopkins, E. W. *Origin and Evolution of Religion,* 1923.

McKenzie, D. *Myths of Crete and Pre-Hellenic Europe.*

Marett, R. R. *The Threshold of Religion.*

Reinach, S. *Cults, Myths, and Religions,* translated by E. Frost, 1912.

Spence, L. *An Introduction to Mythology.*

Toy, C. H. *Introduction to the History of Religions,* 1913.

On the origins of art, language, and music may be consulted:

Brown, G. Baldwin. *The Fine Arts,* 4th edition revised, 1916.

Bucher, K. *Arbeit und Rhythmus,* 1899.

Grosse, E. *The Beginnings of Art,* 1897.

Hirn, Y. *Origins of Art,* 1900.

Jespersen, O. *Language, its Nature, Development, and Origin,* 1922.

Rivers, W. H. R. "The Disappearance of Useful Arts," in *Festschrift tillegnad E. Westermarck,* Helsingfors, 1912, p. 109.

Sapir, E. *Language,* 1921.

Vendryes, J. *Language,* 1925.

Wallaschek, R. *Primitive Music,* 1893.

On the family and other social organizations there are:

Gennep, A. v. *L'état actuel du problème totémique,* 1920.

Malinowski, *The Family among the Australian Aborigines,* 1913.

Rivers, W. H. R. *Social Organization,* 1925.

Webster, H. *Primitive Secret Societies,* 1908.

Westermarck, E. *History of Human Marriage,* 5th edition, 1922.

Of the many treatments of particular peoples one or two are:

Dubois, *Hindu Manners, Customs, and Ceremonies,* 1816.

Lumholtz, *Through Central Borneo,* 1920.

Rattray, R. S. *Ashanti,* 1923.

Rivers, *History of Melanesian Society,* 1914.

Thurston, E. *Castes and Tribes of Southern India.*

Wissler, C. *The American Indian,* 1917.

BOOK II. DEVELOPMENT OF ANCIENT CIVILIZA-TION IN THE NEAR EAST

CHAPTER IV

ANCIENT EGYPT

(from before 4241 to 1350 B. C. and after)

And this his pyramid shall flourish; and this his building shall flourish unto all eternity.—Pyramid text of Pepi II

THE hot sun and lack of rainfall make of the regions both east and west of the Nile, deserts similar to Arabia and the Sahara beyond them. But the annual inundation of the river, with the rich loam that it brings down from the vegetation of the tropics, produces a long narrow ribbon of alluvial soil from the first cataract at Assouan to the delta deposited on the Mediterranean coast. From early times the Nile made communication by boat possible between all parts of the country. This fact and the advisability of common control of the inundation and regulation of irrigation, in time gave rise to union under one absolute monarch. The climate has preserved the remains and records of the distant past as almost nowhere else, and by its natural preservative properties encouraged the ancient Egyptians to further efforts in the same direction, such as the development of the process of embalming and mummification. **[Geography and Climate]**

The earliest pottery, found by sinking shafts deep into the Nile alluvium, may date from 13,000 to 15,000 B. C. and at any rate takes us far back into the stone age. The chronology of ancient Egypt is a difficult matter concerning which there is not yet complete agreement. It is customary to distinguish a predynastic period, before the land was united under one pharaoh, from the thirty-one dynasties into which Manetho, an Egyptian priest of the third century B. C. whose account is no longer extant, grouped the pharaohs down to his time. Some of his dynasties are difficult to discern from our sources, but those **[Chronology]**

35

that have been distinguished form a convenient means of dating the monuments without attempting to assign them an exact year according to our reckoning.   There is disagreement as to the date when Egypt became united under the First Dynasty and a list of year-names began to be kept which has been partially preserved on the Palermo Stone, an ancient monument now found in the museum at Palermo, Sicily.   About 3400 is now more generally accepted than the earlier date of 5000 or 5500.   If we adopt this shorter chronology, the Old Kingdom of the first ten dynasties, when the capital was at Memphis near the Delta, lasts from approximately 3400 to 2160.   It was followed by the Middle Kingdom or Feudal Age, and then by the New Kingdom or Empire with Thebes as the capital.   The New Kingdom or Empire may be dated more exactly from 1580 to 945, after which came a period of decline and foreign invasion and conquest.   The most famous dynasties were the Fourth or Pyramid-Builders (c. 2900–2750) of the Old Kingdom, the Twelfth (c. 2000–1788) of the Middle Kingdom, and the Eighteenth (1580–1350) of the Empire, when the pharaohs especially engaged in foreign conquest.   Our sources are naturally fullest for the Empire which is less remote in time.   "We shall probably never," in the opinion of Breasted, "be able to offer more than a sketch of the civilization of the Old and Middle Kingdoms, with a hazy outline of the general drift of events."

Pre-Dynastic Period

Among the graves which have been excavated, however, many are of the pre-dynastic period.   Their contents show us that the Egyptians were already using linen cloth, copper beads and bracelets, needles and chisels, while their flint knives were flaked with a precision and beauty found nowhere else in the neolithic age.   Barley husks in the stomachs of the buried corpses, grains of millet of a species no longer cultivated, and "wheat with ages of selective cultivation behind it," testify to the development of agriculture.   Domesticated sheep, cattle, and donkeys are already seen in a pre-dynastic relief on slate.   Glazed beads and amulets and green face-paint show how personal adornment and magic played their part in the civilization of early man.   From Egyptian myth and religion and from later local divisions we infer that before the union into one kingdom there were two rival kingdoms of upper and lower Egypt, and before this various smaller tribal or city states, each with

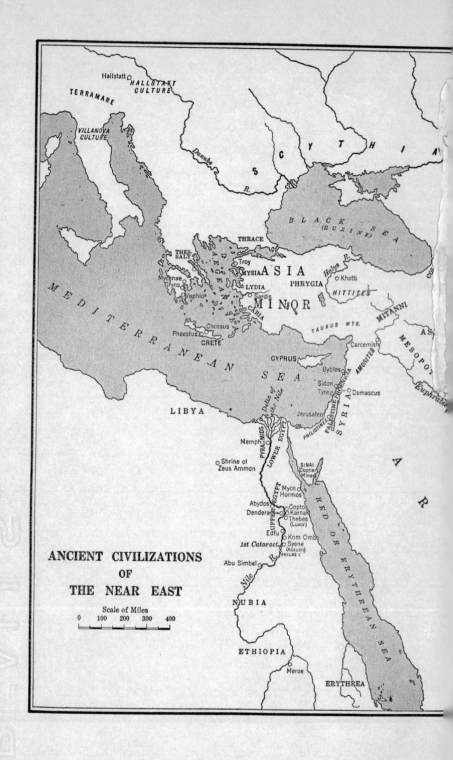

ANCIENT CIVILIZATIONS
OF
THE NEAR EAST

Scale of Miles

0   100   200   300   400

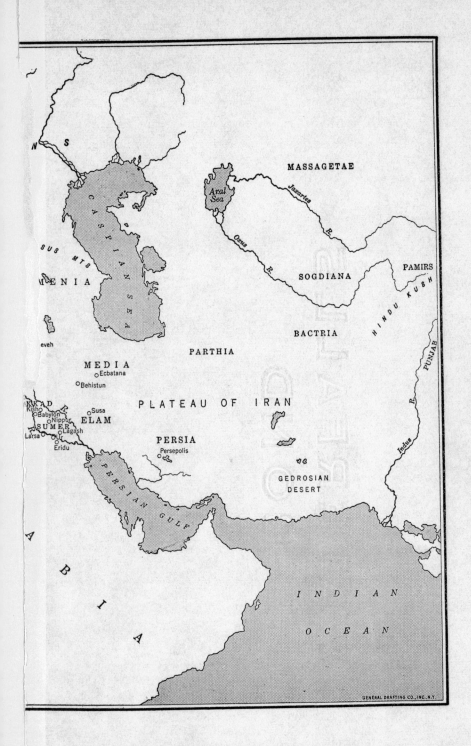

MASSAGETAE

Aral Sea

Jaxartes R.

SOGDIANA

PAMIRS

Oxus R.

BACTRIA

HINDU KUSH

CASPIAN SEA

SUS MTS

ENIA

PARTHIA

PUNJAB

MEDIA
○Ecbatana
○Behistun

PLATEAU OF IRAN

Indus R.

eveh

KKAD
Kisho
Babylon ○Susa
Nippur ELAM
SUMER
Larsa ○Lagash
Eridu

○Susa

PERSIA
Persepolis
○

GEDROSIAN
DESERT

PERSIAN GULF

A B I A

I N D I A N

O C E A N

GENERAL DRAFTING CO.,INC.,N.Y.

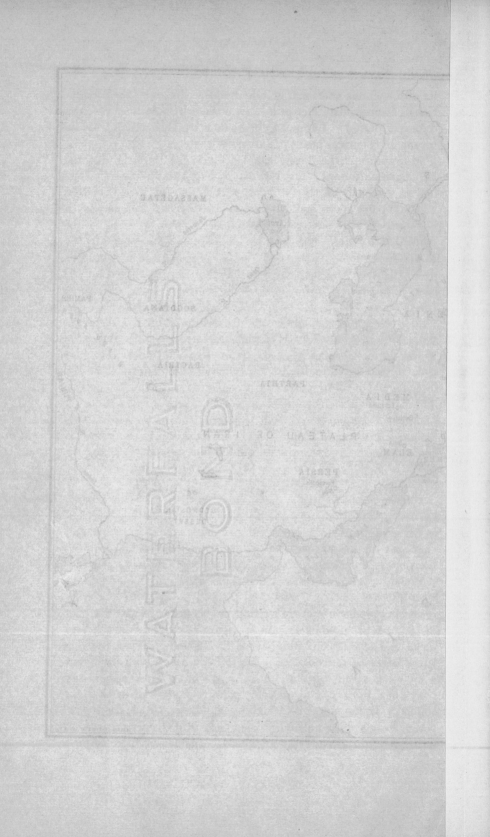

its own customs and local or tribal gods. In short, the foundations of subsequent Egyptian civilization were laid in the predynastic period. Later Egypt seldom equalled its pottery in technical resource, beauty, and good taste.

Many accept the date, July 19, 4241, for the origin of the Egyptian calendar. The Egyptians had a day of twenty-four hours, a month of thirty days, and a year of three hundred and sixty-five days made up of twelve months and five extra days which were regarded as unlucky. The division of the month into three ten-day periods seems traceable to the Middle Kingdom. Their year began on what for us would be July 19, when the star Sirius or Sothis first appeared on the eastern horizon simultaneously with the rising sun. This was furthermore about the time of the annual inundation of the Nile which meant so much to the prosperity of the land. Gradually this year of 365 days came to diverge more and more widely from the solar year and time of inundation of the Nile; then it began gradually to approach it again until after the lapse of about 1460 years the three were once more coincident. The Egyptians came to notice this fact, there is perhaps an allusion to it under the Fourth Dynasty, and in the second millenium b. c. three different sources give dates according to this Sothic era, from which the date 3400 has been inferred for the union of Egypt and the year 4241 for the introduction of the calendar.

The Egyptian Calendar

Carvings and paintings have come down to us from a much earlier period than any marks that at all resemble writing. Some even think that handiwork is older than language, and that man or his predecessor chipped flints before he acquired the power of articulate speech. At any rate drawing was earlier than writing, and the earliest form of writing seems to have been picture-writing. Pictures themselves of course convey ideas, but we have picture-writing only when the same fixed set of pictures are used over and over again to represent not merely ideas and objects but also words and sounds. Then the pictures begin to reproduce not merely what we see about us but what we say and think within us, and what we hear others say that they think. They become picture-signs and symbols of sounds. In the oldest written language known to us, the Egyptian hieroglyphic, we find this development from pictorial to written record already far advanced. Instead of there being a

Development of Writing

different picture-sign for every word in the language, the signs
for short words of one syllable were often used wherever the
sound which they represented occurred. Thus they became
phonetic symbols rather than pictures of things. Inasmuch as
vowel sounds were not depicted, some words of one syllable
would also represent a single consonant, thus giving twenty-
four signs denoting single sounds like our letters of the alphabet, except that they still had such shapes as birds, snakes, or
geometric figures, and so were less easy to write than our letters. Yet the ancient Egyptians never adopted these alphabetical signs exclusively and dropped the clumsier signs for
more complicated sounds and long words. Instead they continued to use the picture signs or ideographs too. Often they
would both spell out a word phonetically and indicate it pic-
torially. They usually wrote from right to left, sometimes in
horizontal lines, sometimes in perpendicular rows. As time
went on, the shapes of the hieroglyphs and styles of writing of
course altered considerably, and the Egyptian language itself
underwent such modification that the old style of writing did
not fit it very well any longer. When hieroglyphs were chiseled on stone monuments they were very carefully formed and
decorative in character. When written on wood or papyrus
they became simpler and more rounded in form, as in the style
known as literary hieroglyphic. The cursive or hieratic style
was still more hastily written, slurring over or abbreviating
and running together the hieroglyphs so that they ceased to
resemble pictures and became script. Finally this cursive style
was yet further abbreviated in the demotic or popular writing
of Greek and Roman Egypt, employed for business and private
correspondence. Egyptian thinking seems to have been limited
by the pictorial character of its language and to have been
graphic and without any abstract terminology. The ancient
Egyptian language closely resembles the Semitic group in
grammatical structure, but not in vocabulary. It was marked
by triliteralism, grammatical gender, lack of any special formation for adverbs, and scanty use of adverbial expressions.

Our Sources Funereal   We read the civilization of ancient Egypt chiefly in its tombs.
They came to be constructed of enduring stone, while the houses
of the living, even most palaces and public buildings, were made
mainly of sun-dried brick and palm trees and have long since
turned back into dust or mud. There is nothing to mark the

site of Memphis except its extensive necropolis, while from the Old Kingdom the most impressive remains are the tombs of the pharaohs in the shape of pyramids.   The earliest known forms of the temple and column are in the mortuary temples connected with these pyramids.   "The oldest chapter of human thought extant" is the Pyramid Texts, preserved in hieroglyphic at Sakkara from the Fifth and Sixth Dynasties. Within the tombs are found the first known doorways, corridors, courts, staircases, complexes of rooms, alcoves and recesses, pavements and wall reliefs, and decorated ceilings. These mark a great advance over the habitations of cave man or huts of neolithic men; yet we cannot quite call them the oldest extant living apartments, since they were intended for and tenanted by the dead.   Nevertheless this constant care of the ancient Egyptians for their dead has enabled their past to live again for us, so that they have in some measure attained that future life for which they planned so elaborately.

In the tombs of the pharaohs and the *mastabas* or private tombs of nobles, courtiers, and landowners which cluster about them, are sculptured and painted reliefs which supply most of our information concerning the occupations and daily life, agriculture and industry, boating, hunting, fowling, fishing with nets or spear, tax-collecting, family relations, games and amusements.   Here are pictures of musicians on harp and flute, lyre or lute; of nobles borne aloft in chairs resting on poles supported by the shoulders of their retinues; of dancers and mourners and tribute-bearers and prisoners-of-war; all with expressive Egyptian gesticulation of upraised or outspread arms with bent elbows and palms presented or averted.   Statues are being dragged along on sledges by men at the ropes.   Fields are being measured.   The pharaohs of the Old Kingdom had all their lands resurveyed every two years, probably because of the changes liable to result from the inundation.   The harvest is reaped with sickles or threshed and winnowed.   Cattle are branded, or we see the attempt made to domesticate antelopes and hyenas who are being fed in stalls.   Honey is gathered from hives.   Jewelers, potters at the wheel, cabinet-makers and shrine-makers, stone-masons, and various workers in leather, metals, and faience are shown at their tasks, or are bartering their products for food and animals.   Especially common is the representation of the deceased and his wife about to partake

Yet Represent Daily Life

of a last, or perhaps better, everlasting meal which their servants are preparing from a rich store. Or we find buried with the dead little mannikins of soldiers, or servitors bearing burdens on their heads, or baking, brewing, and performing other domestic tasks; and models of boats with upcurving prow and stern manned by crews, or of adzes, mattocks, and scourges, and other implements and articles of furniture. Economic life was fundamentally agricultural and without coinage, but there were skilled artisans, and there was trade not only up and down the river but by large sea-going ships in the Red and Mediterranean Seas.

Origin
of the
Pyramids

The pyramids of Egypt are probably the most impressive remains of the Old Kingdom and reveal alike its strength and its weakness. First we may note their stupendous size. The largest pyramid, that of Cheops, was 481 feet high (now 450), had a base with sides 755 feet long (now 746), and contained 2,300,000 blocks averaging two and a half tons in weight. Then there is the accuracy of their construction. The mean error in the four sides of the base just mentioned is only six-tenths of an inch, and that of the right angles but twelve seconds of one degree. A third consideration is the preparation, transportation, and putting in place of such heavy and hard material with the simple implements and devices of that period, such as copper saws and derricks of the well-sweep type, and with only human labor and domestic animals available for power. All these matters excite our amazement and bear mute testimony across the long intervening centuries to the vast power and resources concentrated in the hands of the pharaoh, to the systematic organization of government and economic life, and to the patient toil and skilled workmanship and concerted effort of the Egyptian people. The sepulchral chamber of the pharaoh was commonly below ground, and the pyramid proper was an erection over it. It is usual to trace its development from the heap of sand surrounded by a circle of stones which covered the graves of the late neolithic period. These were both walled in with sun-dried brick about the beginning of the First Dynasty. Somewhat before 3000 the sand-heap began to be enclosed in stone masonry with sloping sides. These earlier tombs, looking like very truncated pyramids, are known as mastabas and continued in use later for the lesser tombs of officials and nobles surrounding the pyramid of their Pharaoh.

The pharaoh Zoser of the Third Dynasty and his architect Imhotep took a long step toward the pyramid when they piled several successive mastabas one on the other in receding terraces to form a step pyramid. From this the change to the true pyramid with smooth sides of polished blocks converging to a single point was rapidly made. In fact, the whole process of development from what is commonly called the earliest stone masonry to the greatest pyramid of all, that of Cheops in the Fourth Dynasty, is said to have taken but one hundred and fifty years at most. We remember, however, the stone tombs of neolithic Europe for which rough blocks weighing from forty to three hundred tons were dragged from quarries miles away and stood up on end, while other huge slabs were sometimes placed horizontally on top of them to roof the intervening space. We wonder if these were crude efforts to imitate the obelisks and pyramids of Egypt, or if the latter were not the last and most successful stage in the primitive habit of erecting stones in tombs, circles, and avenues.

Much may be inferred from the pyramids. First is the patent fact that the pyramid proves that the square and right angle and four points of the compass were clearly comprehended then and durably presented for posterity. This very possibly led to the division of the year into four seasons, to the theory of four elements, and other such arbitrary human divisions of things into quarters. The pyramids further show the belief in future life and desire for immortality; and they make it quite evident that the Egyptian's motto was not the modern slogan, "Let's go," but the opposite, "Let's stay." Resting on the rocky plateau to the west of the river and secure from its inundations, and tapering from a broad base to a single point, they symbolize, intentionally or no, the structure of Egyptian society, resting on the land and people and centering in and supporting the power of the pharaoh. The pyramid was also the chief symbol of the sun god. The frequency of menacing human figures armed with stick or whip upon the Egyptian monuments, and the large percentage of fractured bones among the bodies that have been excavated, indicate that the average Egyptian's life or death was not a happy one, although it is well to remember that until quite recently any Egyptian peasant who paid his taxes without first submitting to a merciless beating was the laughing-stock of his neighbors,

Their Meaning

and that it was not uncommon for men to mutilate themselves in order to escape military service. The pyramids are commonly regarded as the product of forced labor under the lash of despotism, but they may have been more popular than we think. Building pyramids may have become a social habit; every child in Egypt may have played at building tombs and pyramids. At least babies are still regularly supplied with building blocks, although they usually prefer to hurl or drop them rather than to pile them up.

Long
Duration of
the Habit
of Building
Pyramids
Certainly the Egyptians were long unable to stop building pyramids. If it took them only one hundred and fifty years to arrive at the point where they could build the biggest and best one, it took them a thousand years to cease building pyramids. The term, pyramid age, is often applied to the five centuries from 3000 to 2500, but after a period of confusion and the end of the Old Kingdom we find the pharaohs of the Middle Kingdom and Twelfth Dynasty again building pyramids. This illustrates the weakness of Egyptian civilization, an excessive conservatism and increasing lack of originality as time went on. The pharaohs seemed no more able to cease from the fashion of building pyramids than birds do from the instinct to build nests. But let us not be too severe on the ancient pharaohs. When M. Clemenceau, visiting Egypt for recreation after the recent world war, pronounced the pyramids superstitious, puerile, and costly in human life and treasure, an Egyptian newspaper suggested that some medium get in touch with the spirit of Cheops and learn *his* opinion of the Treaty of Versailles. When we have learned how to stop wars and building forts and guns and battleships, we can more safely sneer at the pharaohs for not knowing how to stop building pyramids. Once it was built, a pyramid did little harm. Perhaps even in being built it gave work to the ancient unemployed.

Egyptian
Art
Egyptian art in general shares some of the characteristics of the pyramids. Connected with religion and the future life, it has a permanent and abiding character. It is at rest, dignified and durable, grave and solemn, massive and forceful and colossal rather than graceful or beautiful. As the pharaohs kept on building pyramids, so the same types persisted in Egyptian art through long ages.

Of other buildings than tombs from the pyramid age there is little left. The obelisk of the sun erected by King Nuserre of the Fifth Dynasty has totally disappeared, and the extant obelisks are of a later period. In a country where there is almost no rain, roofing is of little importance, and the usual sanctuary at this time seems to have been an open court surrounded by a colonnade. Enough fragments of these have survived to demonstrate that various forms of columns and capitals had been invented some two thousand years before the temples of classical Greece. While the valley temple of Khefren near his pyramid has only rectangular piers of stone, from the following Fifth Dynasty there are remains of three mortuary temples with fragments of granite palm-columns with round shafts and capitals shaped like bundles of palm leaves, of granite papyrus-columns, and of lotus-columns with bud capitals. The sixteen-sided pillar which eventually became fluted has been thought by some to be the original of the Doric column of the Greeks. The valley temple of Khefren is remarkable for being roofed. It had three aisles separated by two rows of piers and was lighted in a dim and mystic manner by narrow slits placed obliquely in the outer walls.

Early Temples: Origin of Column and Capital

The sculpture of the pyramid age largely consists of portrait statues of the deceased and scenes in relief representing their daily life. The work is realistic; the animals are well rendered; the human heads and faces are often finely done, but less care is bestowed upon the rest of the human form. Perhaps this is partly because very hard stone such as granite and diorite was so much employed. There are also, however, statues of wood and copper. In the reliefs various conventions soon came to prevail. The head is shown in profile, while the eye is drawn as if for a full face; the shoulders also face the spectator, but the lower part of the body is represented in profile. Perspective was not understood, and figures are not shown behind others but are depicted in full above them. Their postures and attitudes are monotonous and lack freedom. The reliefs were as a rule painted, and sometimes the sculpture consists merely in incising the outlines of the figures. The exteriors of buildings were painted as well as the walls and ceilings inside, and columns were often carved with reliefs and hieroglyphs in colors. But painting hardly existed as an independent art. Things were not colored according to nature but for decorative effect. Ideal statues of the gods are generally lacking; the deities shown in relief are commonly conventionalized

Sculpture and Painting

types and often have animal heads. Conventionalism set in especially after the Fifth Dynasty. Such small arts, however, as jewelry and faience, did not reach their height of tasteful delicacy until the Twelfth Dynasty.

Temples of the Empire

Sculpture declined rather than improved under the Empire, but from that period we begin to have large and well preserved temples such as those of Luxor and Karnak on the site of ancient Thebes, which had now become the capital. Across the Nile from it we find, instead of pyramids, other ruined temples and the numerous rock-hewn tombs of kings, queens, and nobles, of which that of Tutankhamen is the most recently discovered. These tombs are adorned with painted reliefs in which the future life and religious ritual play rather a greater part than in the mastabas at Sakkara of the Old Kingdom. In the temples a prominent feature is the pylons, a pair of sloping towers or masses of stone which stand on either side of the entrance and reach completely across the front of the temple, concealing the court behind them. Beyond the open court may be a vestibule leading into an impressive colonnaded hall. This last was roofed over, and its central portion or nave was lighted by openings above the lower columns which surrounded it. Beyond it were the sanctuaries of the gods and apartments of the priests. Or the temple might include several raised terraces. The private villa or palace of the feudal noble of the Middle Kingdom and Empire seems to have been a rather similar complex of courts, halls, terraces, and smaller rooms. Some temples, especially the great temple of Ammon-Re at Karnak, were added to by the rulers at intervals down into the Greek and Roman period, and have series of pylons, courts, and halls of columns. The largest columns in the temple at Karnak are nearly twelve feet in diameter and have capitals eleven feet high. These twelve huge columns are flanked on either side by a grove of sixty-one others only slightly inferior to them in size, and the total effect is one of grandeur outstripping the greatest of the pyramids. While the pyramid has practically no interior, here by using columns as supports a floor space of six thousand square yards was roofed over. But the massive columns themselves occupy a large fraction of the floor space. They are placed close together in order to support the stone blocks and slabs of the rafters and roof, and obstruct the view in every direction. Further architectural progress was re-

quired before the problem of roofing a vast interior can be said
to have been successfully solved. If Karnak is the greatest
and grandest, the best preserved and most complete temples
are naturally those built most recently, such as the temples of
Edfu and Kom Ombo, Dendera and Philæ, erected under the
Greek Ptolemies in the third and second centuries b. c. In the
main these temples imitate and continue the architecture and
sculpture of more ancient Egypt, but in details of sculpture, in
the capitals of columns, and in the greater symmetry of the
whole structure, they are apt to be affected by Greek art.

Egyptian monuments and works of art possess the merit of
seeming to grow out of, and to be part of, their surroundings
and material, but also have the defect of the seeming inability of
the artist to break free from these. A pyramid, sloping gradually away from the rock plateau on which it rests, is more a
miniature mountain than a building. The rock-hewn tombs
do not show above the surface of the ground. The open courts
of the temples neither entirely shut us in nor exclude nature.
The ponderous proportions of columns, lintels, and pylons keep
us more conscious of the rocky material of which they consist
than of such artistic form as builder or sculptor has added,
and a colossus like the sphinx seems a mighty boulder rather
than a portrait of a sovereign. Those figures that sit on the
ground, clasping their knees so that except for the head the
statue is little more than a polished cube with slightly rounded
corners, illustrate the same point. The best Egyptian sculpture is realistic and natural; on the other hand, it fails to
achieve the ideal. The ancient Egyptians could hoist huge
blocks aloft, tunnel far into a rocky cliff, or carve an obdurate
material like diorite, but their artistic ideas seem still limited by
their materials as well as by their traditions, conventions, and
precedents. Of course, the fact that dust or sand has half submerged their works of art, that time and weather have crumbled
them, and that their surface polish or paint has disappeared,
makes them seem more an integral part of the landscape than
perhaps was once the case, although the mud-brick villages of today which seem to spring from the soil are probably much like
those of the remote past. Once I wandered for hours in the
Egyptian museum at Cairo absorbed in examining richly inlaid
and elegantly fashioned furniture from ancient tombs and gaz-
ing at chiseled faces full of animation and dignity and charac-

Egyptian Art Dealt Mainly in Raw Materials

ter, as well as at cat- and falcon-headed deities and the portly shins and cylindrical ankles of many pompous pharaohs. But when at last I came to a single, graceful, delicate Byzantine capital of the Coptic period, how my heart leapt up in recognition of a power of design, a sense of form, and a capacity for beauty, such as either ancient Egypt never knew, or time has long since crushed to dust.

Origin of Egyptian Deities

We do not understand Egyptian religion well, although we know the names and conventional artistic representations and emblems of a number of their gods. The multiplicity of deities is to be partially explained by the survival of local and tribal worships as distinct cults, after Egypt had been united. Gods are often grouped in triads or trinities. It seems evident that some of the gods who were later represented in human form and clothing were originally fetishes or sacred posts, trees, and plants. Moreover, the various sacred animals, which later were kept in temples and carefully interred in cemeteries, and the animal heads of certain gods, may be a survival of primitive tribal totems. Other gods represent the sun and moon, earth and sky, or the powers of fertility and generation. Magic makes up a great part of the so-called religious texts, and it is well-nigh impossible to distinguish hymn and prayer from incantations and formulæ, occult virtues in nature from spirits, or religious worship and ritual from magical rite and ceremonial. The fact that some of the gods were represented as having lived on earth and as having made human inventions suggests that they originated from deified men. When Egypt came under one ruler, this pharaoh was reverenced even during his lifetime, if not worshiped as a god.

Pyramid Texts: Future Life and Mortuary Magic

The oldest extant religious texts, written on the walls of the passages and chambers of five pyramids of the Fifth and Sixth Dynasties (c. 2625–2475), are solely for the benefit of the deceased pharaoh; almost nothing of the sort is found in the tombs of the nobles of the same dynasties. The main object of these texts is to make the dead pharaoh live, and as this is contrary to nature, it has to be attempted chiefly through magic. Libations are poured to the tune of incantations in order to replenish the vital fluids in the dried-up corpse. By the liquid of the divine Osiris (i. e., the water of the Nile) the dead body is to be brought back to life, a conception somewhat like that of rebirth through baptism. The dead monarch in the sealed-up tomb is adjured to raise himself up to partake of "this thy bread, which cannot dry up, and thy beer which cannot become stale, by which thou shalt become a soul (*ba*),"—a passage which suggests the "bread of life" and "living water" of the New Testament, or bread and wine of the Eucharist some twenty-five centuries later. In the pyramid texts, however, these things are far from being merely symbolic, and the future life of the soul or *ba* is still represented as in many ways grossly material and apparently simply a pleasant continuation of the pharaoh's career here on earth. He must have "ten different kinds of meat, five kinds of poultry, sixteen kinds of bread and cakes, six kinds of wine, four kinds of beer, eleven kinds of fruit, besides all sorts of sweets and many other things." He "takes women from their husbands whither he wills and when his heart desires." Magic words, formulæ, and charms are provided in abundance to enable the deceased to pass the ferryman of the boat of the dead and the hell-hounds and porters and gates of the other world, of whom the Charon and Cerberus of Greek mythology are late copies, to mount the ladder to the sky despite the opposition of the gods, and to protect and preserve his body, name, and identity intact. The pyramid texts further include hymns and prayers and petitions and ritual to be performed by the living on behalf of the dead, and fragments of myths which remain for the most part obscure to us.

Under the Empire rolls of papyri, full of charms and incantations, were placed in the coffins of all who were able to afford them. Their contents are different from the pyramid texts. The title, Book of the Dead, has been applied to these rolls in modern times, although the contents vary in each coffin, and the rolls most frequently found are those containing "The Chapters of Going Forth by Day,"—series of incantations which permit the dead man to leave his tomb. Under the Middle Kingdom such matter had been written on the insides of the coffins themselves along with pictures which replaced the mannikins and models that were formerly put into the grave to serve the dead man. These "coffin-texts" of the Middle Kingdom form a transition between the pyramid texts and the rolls of the Empire. They are about half drawn from the former, while they contain chapters which we find again under the Empire.

Later Texts for the Use of the Dead

The Egyptian custom of embalming and wrapping up the

Mummies

dead bodies began in the old Kingdom.   The preparation of
a mummy became more elaborate under the Empire when the
costliest process lasted seventy days and was accompanied by
much magic ceremonial.   Modern examination of mummies has
sometimes, however, revealed evidence of fraudulent work on
the part of the embalmer or undertaker who, after removing
the entrails, stuffed the corpse with anything that came handy.
Nevertheless distant maritime expeditions were undertaken to
procure the resins and balsams for embalming and the wood for
coffins.   The poor had to content themselves with having their
corpses soaked in a solution of salt.   The Egyptians believed
that every man had a *ka* or double and guardian spirit who was
born with him and who lived on after his death to protect his
remains.

The Priests of Ammon
When Thebes became the capital in the Middle Kingdom and
Empire, its local god, Ammon or Amon or Amen, was identified
with the sun god, Ra or Re, and advanced to first place among
the Egyptian deities, as his vast temple at Karnak shows.   The
priests of the temple corporation became very wealthy in land,
cattle, and tenants or slaves, shared in the spoils of the foreign
conquests made under the Empire, and brought its last pharaohs more and more under their own control.   They are also
charged with having increased the amount of magic, superstition, and formal ritual in religion.   An earlier pharaoh, Ikhna-
ton, had tried to purify faith and practice by restoring the
simple worship of the sun as the one and only god.   The numerous deities and the confusion of magical practices could not be
got rid of so easily, however, and his effort failed.

Myth of Osiris
Egyptian mythology is in the main obscure.   It may be illustrated by the story of Osiris, which is fairly well known and
seems to have had a great and lasting influence.   Osiris, who
represents the Nile and the yearly reviving fertility of the
soil, is said in the myth to have once ruled Egypt well, until
he was murdered by his wicked brother Seth, who enclosed the
corpse in a chest which he cast into the Nile.   Isis, the widow
of Osiris, wandered the world over until she found the chest
and buried it.   But while she was visiting her son Horus,
Seth discovered and disinterred his brother's body, cut it into
pieces, and scattered them in every direction.   Isis again pa-
tiently sought out these and gave each burial, which is supposed
to explain the existence of tombs of Isis in different places.

When Horus grew up, he tried to avenge his father, and engaged in conflicts with Seth in which the latter wrenched out one of his eyes. Finally, according to the version of the myth that we are following, Horus either triumphed over Seth or forced him to divide the rule of Egypt with him, one taking the south and the other the north. Horus offered his lost eye at the tomb of Osiris who thereby became an immortal soul and ruled the region west of the Nile as king of the dead. We still use the expression "going west" of death. Thus the Horus-eye was for the Egyptians the symbol of self-sacrifice. The characters and incidents of this legend are duplicated or closely paralleled in the stories of many other times and peoples. The two brothers suggest Cain and Abel or Romulus and Remus. The wanderings of Isis are repeated by Innini going to the lower world to find her lost brother Tammuz in Sumerian myth and by Demeter seeking Persephone in Greek mythology. The chest, containing a human cargo, which is committed to the waves is another commonplace of folk-lore.

In order that we may not appear to do injustice to the higher aspects of Egyptian faith and worship, we may conclude our account of that religion by a quotation from the well known Egyptologist, Sir E. A. W. Budge, who believes that the Egyptian religion "closely resembled in many respects the Christian religion," and who says further: "When we consider the lofty spiritual character of the greater part of the Egyptian religion, and remember its great antiquity, it is hard to understand why the Egyptians carefully preserved in their writings and ceremonies so much which savoured of gross and childish superstition, and which must have been the product of their predynastic or prehistoric ancestors, even during the period of their greatest intellectual enlightenment. But the fact remains that they did believe in One God who was almighty and eternal and invisible, who created the heavens and the earth and all beings and things therein; and in the resurrection of the body in a changed and glorified form, which would live to all eternity in the company of the spirits and souls of the righteous in a kingdom ruled by a being who had once lived upon the earth, and had suffered a cruel death at the hands of his enemies, and had risen from the dead, and had become the God and king of the world which is beyond the grave." In these last clauses, which sound like allusions to the life of Christ,

The Higher Side of Egyptian Religion

Budge of course has in mind the story of Osiris.   In the literature of the Middle Kingdom there is also expressed a belief in the coming of a good pharaoh who will usher in a new age when right shall triumph and all men will be happy.

Literature and Learning: Medicine

The literary remains of the Middle Kingdom just mentioned are the oldest extant which are written in ink on papyrus. We possess fragments of stories such as the marvelous adventures of the shipwrecked sailor or the tale of the eloquent peasant.   There are collections of wise sayings, shrewd observations, and good advice, which show much the same standards in manners and morals, ideals of self-control and consideration for others, as prevail today.   Some interest is shown in the lower and laboring classes, and some pity for the oppressed. There are hymns to be sung responsively in praise of the pharaoh, census lists to form the basis of taxation, and some very elementary mathematical treatises.   Of medicine we have a few fragments from the time of the Middle Kingdom, but the four important papyri date from about 1600 to 1300 B. C. Magical procedure and formidable compound medicines occupy most of their space, although one contains surgical cases arranged in order from skull-cap to spine, and takes up first the symptoms, then a diagnosis of the case, then the treatment to be followed, if the case is not given up as fatal or hopeless. Examination of mummies by modern specialists has thrown considerable light upon the diseases and injuries from which they suffered.   It has not, however, found much evidence of skilful medical, surgical, or dental treatment of those complaints.   Astronomy and astrology seem to have been developing from an early date in Egypt, yet are difficult to trace in any detail.   No code of Egyptian law is preserved, and we have no legal documents until the Twelfth Dynasty, while the numerous contracts preserved are of the late Egyptian period.

Egypt and the Origin of Civilization

In this chapter we have been tracing not merely the peculiarities of Egyptian civilization but the origin of civilization in general.   Written records and literature, architecture and many of the industrial arts, reflective thinking and exercise of moral judgment, have made their appearance.   Articles of household furniture such as chairs and couches reached a point of development that has hardly been exceeded since, and our standards of right and wrong seem little different from those

THE CULT OF THE DEAD IN THE OLD KINGDOM
Above, the Sphinx and the Pyramid of Cheops; below, offering bearers.

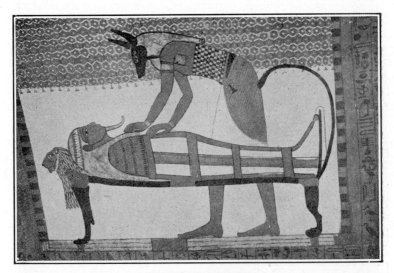

EGYPTIAN DEITIES

Above, in the sculptured relief from Karnak, Seti I of the 19th Dynasty is kneeling beneath a sycamore tree receiving his title from the god Touth; below, in the wall painting from the tomb of Prince Sennezem the god Anubis watches over the mummy of the prince.

of the Middle Kingdom. It must be kept in mind, however, that ancient Egypt had more time in which to develop civilization than has elapsed since. Boats with a strikingly close resemblance to those depicted on ancient Egyptian monuments are used to this day by natives of the interior of Africa and the East Indies, and bodies are still mummified, in islands of the Pacific, in a manner almost certainly derived from Egypt. The priority of the Nile valley in developing civilization is somewhat contested by another not very distant river valley, the Tigris-Euphrates, to which we shall turn in the following chapter.

BIBLIOGRAPHY

The most entertaining ancient account of Egyptian civilization is probably the second book of the Greek historian Herodotus in the fifth century B. C., but of course it is neither contemporary nor especially reliable.

Among leading modern writers on ancient Egypt are J. H. Breasted, Sir E. A. W. Budge, J. Capart, A. Erman, Elliot Smith, Maspero, A. Moret, and W. M. Flinders Petrie. We can list only a few of their works:

Breasted, *History of Egypt; History of the Ancient Egyptians; Development of Religion and Thought in Ancient Egypt; Ancient Records of Egypt,* 5 vols.; "The Origins of Civilization," in *The Scientific Monthly,* 1919–1920.

Budge, *Egyptian Magic; Egyptian Religion; Gods of the Egyptians; Egyptian Sculptures in the British Museum.*

Elliot Smith, *The Ancient Egyptians and Their Influence upon the Civilization of Europe,* 1911.

Erman, *Life in Ancient Egypt; Handbook of Egyptian Religion.*

Maspero, *Dawn of Civilization; Art of Egypt; Life in Ancient Egypt and Assyria; Popular Stories of Ancient Egypt.*

Moret, *In the Time of the Pharaohs; Kings and Gods of Egypt.*

Petrie, *Abydos; Ancient Egypt; Arts and Crafts of Ancient Egypt; Social Life in Ancient Egypt,* 1923; *Religious Life in Ancient Egypt,* 1924.

A few further suggestions are:

Baedeker, *Egypt,* 1914 (or later); a very serviceable hand book.

Bates, Oric. "Ancient Egyptian Fishing," in *Harvard African Studies,* I, 199–271, 1917.

Blackman, A. M. *Rock Tombs of Meir,* 1914.

British Museum, sets of postcards sold by, at one shilling a set; #33, Portrait Statues; #34, Egyptian Sculptures; #35, Mummies; #36, Coffins.

Hartmann, F. *L'Agriculture dans l'ancienne Egypte,* 1923.

Lexa, (Fr.) *La magie dans l'Egypte antique,* 1924, 2 vols.

Ruffer, Sir M. A. *Studies in the Palæopathology of Egypt,* 1921.

Steindorff, *Das Grab des Ti,* 1913, with over 100 plates.

Weigall, Arthur. *A History of the Pharaohs,* vol. I, "The First Eleven Dynasties," 1925; advances a number of new views.

Wreszinski, W. *Atlas zur altägyptischen Kulturgeschichte;* for illustrations.

CHAPTER V

THE TIGRIS-EUPHRATES VALLEY

(about 4200–2100 B. C.)

By the divine favor I am Hammurabi the exalted King, the worshiper of the supreme deity.—From an inscription of Hammurabi

THE Egyptian Empire at its height under Thotmes III reached Geography north-eastward across Syria, the region between the sands of Arabia and the Mediterranean Sea, to the Euphrates river and to Mesopotamia, the region between the Tigris and Euphrates rivers. This territory is also known as the Tigris-Euphrates valley or Land of the Two Rivers. It is bounded on the north and east by mountains. The most fertile part is to the south, where the two rivers approach close to each other and flow through an alluvial plain where they finally join and enter the Persian Gulf. This plain was called Shinar until the rise of the city of Babylon since when it has been commonly referred to as Babylonia. The rivers have kept changing their beds and forming new deposits of soil at the expense of the Persian Gulf. As in Egypt, there was not much rain, but the rivers made the plain exceedingly fertile if it was duly irrigated by a system of dykes and canals. To the east of the plain of Shinar and the lower Tigris was Elam, a land of mountains and fertile valleys where many early remains have been excavated. Farther up the Tigris to the north of Shinar was Assyria, a rolling plain which merged into the mountains to the east and north.

In the plain of Shinar traces of the ancient canals may still The be seen, and mounds which prove upon excavation to enclose Process of the ruins and debris of ancient settlements. Before the recent Excavation war, however, excavation was carried on here with greater difficulty than in Egypt. For instance, the site of Eridu was discovered in 1854 A. D. but, because of the unsafe condition of the vicinity, was not again visited until the British occupied the region during the war. Excavation there and at Susa in Elam have revealed settlements going back into the neolithic period and acquainted with agriculture and painted pottery.   Farther up the Euphrates at Nippur the University of Pennsylvania had been conducting successful excavations since 1893, but recently there have been discovered lists of eighteen dynasties before 2474 which were compiled at the temple in Nippur about 2300 and which seem to take us back to 4200 for the first dynasty. An astronomical tablet excavated at Kish in 1924 puts Sumerian and Babylonian chronology upon a firm basis as far back as 3000 if not still earlier.   These examples suggest that our knowledge of the ancient civilization in the Tigris-Euphrates valley has hitherto been less complete than our acquaintance with Egyptian remains, and that it will now be rapidly amplified and modified.   The first archæological discoveries, beginning in 1842 A. D., were of the sculptured reliefs and clay-tablet libraries of Assyrian monarchs who ruled only in the seventh century before our era.   While we have now worked back to far earlier periods, much of our information is still derived from the records preserved or revised by the Assyrian conquerors at the close of the ancient period.   The first Sumerian site to be excavated was that of Lagash at Tello from 1877 to 1900.   Our knowledge of Sumerian civilization was still largely based upon the finds from this single site, until the recent excavations at Kish and at Ur, from which interesting remains are now exhibited at the British Museum.

The
Sumerian
Language

In ancient times Semitic languages were spoken in Syria, the Tigris-Euphrates valley, and Arabia, and we have seen that ancient Egyptian was closely related to the Semitic group. But in the plain of Shinar the first written language was Sumerian.   It differed markedly from Semitic in its methods of forming and pronouncing words, and in having no gender.   It very early became a dead language which was preserved largely by the priests in religious writings, and most of the extant Sumerian texts contain words and even grammatical forms and usages that are evidently borrowed from the Semitic. On the other hand, the Semitic language was written in Sumerian characters which originally had been picture writing but had developed into a comparatively small number of ideographs and phonetic syllable signs, each of which may be taken in a great many different senses.   The form of writing is called cuneiform or wedge-shaped because the characters were made in clay with a stylus which left wedge-shaped impressions. The Sumerian signs were not well adapted to the Semitic sounds, and there seem to have been few determinatives or picture signs to help explain the syllabic ones, and no characters equivalent to the sound of a single letter as there were in Egyptian writing.

It is generally held not only that the people who originally spoke the Sumerian language were the first to develop a system of writing in the Tigris-Euphrates valley, but that most of the other advances in civilization following the neolithic age were their work. Sumer, the name for their territory, applies, however, only to a particular part of even the plain of Shinar, namely, to the region at the mouths of the river near the Persian Gulf as it was then. Here the Sumerians are believed to have reclaimed the marshes by irrigation, to have told time by year-names like the Egyptians but with a less convenient and regular lunar calendar which required frequent insertion of an extra month, and to have used a sexagesimal system of weights and numerals of which vestiges are still with us. Upon the monuments they are represented as short in stature but very broad across the shoulders, chest, and hips, and stocky and muscular. They do not have the fleshy nose and lips of the Semites, and appear to be further distinguishable by the fact that they are bare-footed, have shaven heads rather than bearded faces, and wear shaggy woolen skirts or kilts. We might take this costume as a hint that the climate about the Persian Gulf was once less torrid than it is now, were it not that Lord Curzon assures us that a modern Afghan would not shed his sheepskin waistcoat at the equator. The Sumerians had domestic animals and copper tools and weapons like the Egyptians of the same period, and the same word for split wheat; they were using wheeled carts and chariots before there is any trace of these in Egypt; but they appear to have given much less thought and care to the dead and the future life than did the dwellers along the Nile.

The Sumerians were not, however, without religion. Their very year-names often refer to religious events, and their religious literature had a lasting influence upon the Semites. Prominent among their remains are the ruins of the temples and towers from the tops of which they perhaps worshiped a god of the air or light, or observed the heavenly bodies. "We

Marginal notes:

Sumerian Civilization

The Temple and Tower

do not yet know the form or arrangement of an early Sumerian temple," but the towers were square, and the top was reached by an external stairway that wound about the four sides, which kept diminishing and receding by the width of the stairway. Thus the temple tower had somewhat the appearance of a stepped or terraced pyramid, and it seems to have been oriented to the four points of the compass. About the temple the life of the Sumerian settlement seems to have centred, and the office of king probably grew out of that of the high priest of the god. In the temple the local archives were kept, and it was a granary and storehouse not only for tithes and offerings and the revenues from its own lands, but from which the small farmer might borrow seed corn or provisions for his harvesters, from which the king too might borrow for public needs, and from which a townsman who had been captured by the enemy must be ransomed if he was unable to ransom himself.

Other Features of the Religion

The religious literature of the plain of Shinar, or that of Babylonia and Assyria which followed and continued it, consisted of the ritual of worship, magic incantations to repel evil spirits in this life rather than after death, prediction of the future from the movements of the heavenly bodies and the lives of sacrificial animals, and epics dealing with such themes as the creation and flood. Later these themes were combined in the Babylonian epic of the hero Gilgamesh and still later appeared again in the Hebrew *Book of Genesis*. It is to be remembered, however, that the Gilgamesh epic is known to us mainly through fragments preserved in the library of the late Assyrian ruler, Ashurbanipal. Leading Sumerian deities were Ea of Eridu, god of the sea and water and so a great purifying power; and Enlil of Nippur, storm-god and lord of ghosts and demons. Marduk, chief god of Babylon, and Ishtar, great mother goddess, representing fertility, spending half the year in the underworld, returning with spring and reviving vegetation, attained their prominence in the Semitic or Babylonian period. "The great nature-powers in Babylonia are, moreover, very curiously doubled with national or tribal or civic deities; and provided with consorts like a human monarch." On the top of the tower of Bel at Babylon was no image but a bed where a single woman selected from all those of the city slept alone with the god, a practice observed also in Egypt at the temple of Ammon in Thebes.

The towers and temple-enclosures at their bases and the cities generally were built of brick, not of stone like the pyramids and temples of Egypt. It is this crumbling brick which has made the city mounds that dot the plain. Perhaps because of this material, rather more use seems to have been made of the arch than in Egypt. Bricks in all ancient countries were much larger than ours; in the Sumerian period they commonly measured in inches 20 by 20 by 3½. Later in the history of the Tigris-Euphrates the size was reduced to 12 by 12 inches. Bitumen or asphalt was employed as mortar, glue, coating, and for various other purposes. Written records were chiefly inscribed upon clay tablets. Stone was scarce in the plain, but was used to some extent for inscriptions and for sculpture, which was rude compared to that of Egypt. It resembled Egyptian sculpture, however, in employing such a hard stone as diorite, in using black and colored stone for statuary, and in inscribing characters upon the sculptured figures. Wild beasts and monsters symmetrically grouped as in heraldic devices occur frequently, and there are human-headed bulls corresponding to the Egyptian sphinxes. Some fine metal work was produced, and the Sumerians were especially skilled in cutting stone seals, usually cylindrical in form so that they could be rolled over the soft clay tablets and leave an impression of the design engraved on them. This may be regarded as the earliest kind of printing. On one such seal are depicted a man and woman, or perhaps god and goddess, with a tree and serpent, suggesting the Biblical story of Adam and Eve. Inlay work is found, as in Egypt, but with use especially of shell.

Sumerian Art

The Sumerians seem to have been a warlike people. Their year-names often record military victories, weapons are among the most common emblems of their gods, and their reliefs show helmeted troops advancing in compact array behind serried spears and shields. Seemingly they were well disciplined and organized. The Sumerian cities fought with one another as well as against the Semites, and the kings of Elam kept attacking the plain of Shinar. The independent city state with its own temple, god, king, walls, and surrounding agricultural

War and Politics

district stands out more plainly in the remains and records of the Tigris-Euphrates valley and also of Syria than it did in Egyptian history. Such ancient city states were, of course, scarcely cities in our modern sense. The term is applied to a small local state with a single fortified and religious center.

Legal and Business Transactions   Many of the earliest clay tablets are legal contracts, deeds of sale and land transfer, and what may be termed business accounts. These remains, together with the economic uses to which the temple was put, indicate an active business life and fairly advanced legal development for a society so ancient and and still primarily agricultural. Fragments of Sumerian bodies of law have been recently discovered, and some of the provisions of the famous Code of Hammurabi are found to date back into the Sumerian period. Indeed, the debt of Semitic Babylon to the Sumerians may be stated in much broader terms. "For more than a thousand years before the appearance" of Babylon "as a great center of culture, the civilization it handed on to others had acquired in all essentials its later type. . . . If we except the spheres of poetry and ethics, the Semite in Babylon, as elsewhere, proved himself a clever adapter, not a creator."

Semitic Syria in the Copper Age   In Syria in the copper age towns came into existence with walls from thirteen to twenty-six feet thick, strengthened by occasional towers. In place of the rude huts of the neolithic age these towns had houses of brick and stone, for building stone was more available in Syria than in the plain of Shinar. Besides the fortifications we find such public works as a tunnel cut in the solid rock in order to reach a spring ninety feet underground. The center of town life seems to have been a high place where monoliths were erected and worn smooth by the kisses of worshipers or seekers after magic virtue, like the black stone of Mecca or the Blarney stone of Ireland. Beneath the high places are found jars containing the bodies of infants and children, a sinister reminder of the human sacrifice of children which the Phœnicians spread to Carthage and possibly even to central America. It is not easy to determine the age of these fortified Syrian towns; they perhaps go back to 2000 or 2500 B. c. Their inhabitants were the Canaanites, who in Palestine preceded the Hebrews, the Phœnicians, and the Amorites (Amurru),—all three Semitic peoples. Were they descendants of the neolithic inhabitants or had they

entered Syria from Arabia or elsewhere? They appear to have
been taller and more vigorous than the neolithic men, but this
improvement in physique might be due to the improved living
conditions of the copper age or to their eating more vitamins.

There is a strong inclination among certain ethnologists to
explain the origin of all the great races of the past by making them come from some place that no one would ever go to,
if one could help it, like central Asia. An additional reason
for regarding Arabia as the homeland of the Semites is that
they have long lived there and invaded other lands from it.
Yet we have earlier remains and records of them in Syria and
the Tigris-Euphrates valley. It is pointed out on the one
hand that the rolling stones seen in the mountain valleys of
Arabia leading toward the Persian Gulf show that these were
once well watered, while on the other hand it is argued that
Semitic civilization presupposes a desert origin and nomadic
life. But these two contentions seem mutually destructive.
Arabia is a more extensive region than one might infer from
some maps, and was to play an important part in later history.
On the other hand, the earliest inscriptions found there do not
antedate the sixth century B. C., and Arabia cannot be shown to
have been a great center of ancient civilization, which is our
interest rather than the problem of racial origins. Wherever
the original home of the Semites may have been, the earliest
traces of Semitic civilization are in Syria and Mesopotamia.
In the early history of Shinar we hear more of attacks from
the mountains of Elam than from the deserts of Arabia.

Was Arabia the Homeland of the Semites?

At first the Semites would seem to have been in the pastoral
stage and inferior in civilization to the settled, agricultural,
phalanx-fighting, wall-building, magic-word-speaking, picture-
writing, seal-and-stone-carving Sumerians. But they sooner
or later adopted the higher civilization and in the third millennium, if not earlier, occupied walled towns in Akkad, as the
northern part of the plain of Shinar was called in distinction
from Sumer. The walled town of Assur also was already in
existence in the region later named after it Assyria, but it was
still a small settlement, and the earliest remains appear to be
Sumerian rather than Semitic. There were centuries of struggle between Akkad and Sumer, traceable in an increasing
number of kings and gods with Semitic names. We will not,
however, confuse the reader with such royal appellations as

The Semites in Akkad

Luggalzaggisi, Lugalkigubniddu, or Sharganisharri. Fortunately the names of the cities were sometimes monosyllabic like Kish and Ur. Finally the Sumerian cities seem to have declined, although their language, religion, and economic life were continued elsewhere in the plain of Shinar. The power did not pass, however, to the Akkadians but to another Semitic dynasty from the Amorites of northwestern Syria. These fought for the plain with the Elamites, who had once more descended upon it from their mountains to the east.

Babylon Under Hammurabi

Babylon now became the chief city and ruling power in the plain, which we may henceforth speak of as Babylonia, and its inhabitants, whether Semitic, Sumerian, or Elamite, as Babylonians. Of its civilization at this time, about 2100 B. C., under King Hammurabi we are unusually well informed by the preservation of his code of laws and official correspondence, supported by a wealth of lesser documents, although of his capital nothing is left and little survives of the art of his time.

The Code of Hammurabi

The Code of Hammurabi was found at Susa, whither an Elamite king had carried it off, engraved on a block of black diorite with an accompanying bas relief showing Hammurabi receiving the laws from the sun god. Really, however, most of the code's three hundred provisions were neither revelations from the sun god nor new legislation by Hammurabi himself, but a compilation of established custom which had long since been reduced to written form and considerably improved and modified. Many of the characteristics of primitive law had disappeared as a result of this long development, and the law in many respects reflected and had become adapted to a rather advanced stage of economic life. Such tribal customs as marriage by capture and the feud were no longer recognized. Self-help had been largely replaced by the power of the king and judges, but the plaintiff still made his own plea in court, and there is no trace of advocates in Babylonia, although notaries drew up contracts and may have assisted the plaintiff in the written brief which he had to submit. Criminal accusations might be brought by private persons rather than by a public prosecutor, but inasmuch as one who charged another with a capital offense was liable to the death penalty himself if he failed to prove his accusation, it would seem that individuals would not often avail themselves of this privilege of prosecution. A locality or its magistrate was also sometimes held responsible for crime committed within its borders. Oath and ordeal were little employed, unless witnesses and documentary evidence were lacking. Thus a wife was allowed to clear herself by her own oath, if her husband accused her of adultery but had not caught her in the act, while if she was accused by common rumor, she must undergo the ordeal of water. Sale and other conveyances and transactions must have been attested by witnesses to be accepted in court. The principle of an eye for an eye and a tooth for a tooth was still maintained, and likewise the principle of family solidarity. Thus if a house collapsed through the fault of the builder and the owner was killed, the builder was put to death; while if the owner's son was killed, the builder's son was executed, though he was presumably in no way to blame for the accident. Penalties were still harsh, as where theft was punishable by death, or cruel, as when offenders were burnt to death, impaled, or had their hands or fingers amputated. On the other hand, a distinction was often made between blameworthy and unintentional injuries or those due to negligence and those due to accident, and exceptional cases were sometimes carefully provided for. The treatment of debtors was on the whole considerate compared to most legal systems of the past. Many of the appeals to Hammurabi were from the victims of extortionate professional money-lenders, if we may use that term when there was no coinage and when loans were made in kind. He showed no mercy to the creditors if their methods had been fraudulent.

There were three layers of society in the age of Hammurabi, when men by no means had equal rights or the same position before the law. At the top were those of greater worth who were entitled to exact retaliation for bodily injuries received, and who in other cases got larger damages or had to pay heavier fines. Next came a rather humble class who had to accept payment for their bodily injuries, while they were publicly scourged for their offenses, and who because of their poverty paid less in fees and fines. At the bottom were the numerous slaves who were the absolute property of their masters. Stealing slaves or harboring fugitive slaves was punished by death. The slaves, however, seem not to have had as hard a lot as might have been expected, and were sometimes set up in business by their masters or allowed to save a percentage and buy their freedom. Under some circumstances a slave

Social
Classes

might marry a free woman, in which case their children were free, and her dower could not be touched by the slave's master, who received only one-half of such property as the slave left when he died.

Position of Woman

The status of woman was very high. While concubinage was tolerated if the wife was barren, the rights of the wife and widow were well protected, and the woman had about equal rights in the matter of divorce. "The position of the married woman in the Babylonian community . . . was not only un-exampled in antiquity but compares favorably, in point of freedom and independence, with her status in many countries of modern Europe." Unmarried women of the upper class who took certain vows might engage in business and hold property. Wine-sellers were usually women, but this occupation seems to have been considered degrading and was forbidden to the upper class virgins just mentioned who were threatened with burning to death if they so much as entered a wine-shop.

Land System

Land remained the fundamental form of wealth, and many of the provisions of the code deal with such matters as irrigation canals, ploughing oxen, seed corn, crops, cultivation laws, mortgages, and the arrangements made between landlords and the cultivators to whom they had leased land or the herdsmen whom they hired. Animals might be hired by the year or the day. To encourage planting the date palm—which was perhaps even more important to Babylonia than the papyrus was to Egypt, since it yielded fruit, flour, wine, sugar, rope, and a light but tough wood for building—a tenant who would devote himself to growing a date plantation was freed from rent for it until the fifth year, when, if the result was satisfactory, he divided the trees with the owner, receiving half for his labor. Values were commonly stated in measures of grain; thus a shekel was 360 grains of corn.

Town Houses

That even in the city houses were only one story high is inferred from the provision that the builder is to be paid according to the amount of ground which the house covers. That the brick walls were thick is attested by the law, "If a man makes a breach in a house, they shall put him to death in front of that breach and they shall thrust him therein." Perhaps his ghost was thought to keep off other burglars. From other sources we learn that houses were usually let for a year, and the rent paid in advance twice a year.

Just as the landlord supplied his tenant with seed, cattle, and agricultural implements, so the merchant advanced to his agent goods or precious metal with which to trade abroad, and from which a profit of one hundred per cent was expected. Trade was by caravan or boats. The latter were very small. In trade down-stream inflated skins were often used to support rafts. They could then be deflated and brought back up the river packed compactly on the backs of donkeys. Grain or other property was deposited for safe-keeping in granaries or warehouses. In all such transactions witnesses were present and receipts were taken. This was also the custom when property was sold outright. *Commercial Transactions*

Workmen and contractors were held to strict standards of responsibility, as the case of the house-builder has already illustrated. If within a year of the launching of a boat defects developed, the builder must repair or rebuild it at his own expense. The boatman who hired a boat was responsible for it, but if it sank and he succeeded in refloating it, he need pay the owner only half its value. The man who hired an ox or ass was not responsible, if it was slain by a lion or by lightning or other cause beyond his control; in such cases the owner must bear the loss. A tenant who omitted cultivation for a year was penalized, and the peasant was responsible for damage done to the neighboring fields by failure to keep his dykes in repair or from letting the water run into his patch too long and overflow. While the right of private property was carefully protected, the laborer was also deemed worthy of his hire, and wages are often specified in the code. A surgeon who operated successfully received a fee varying in amount according to the rank of the patient, but might be punished by loss of his fingers if his lack of skill caused the death or loss of an eye of a man of the upper class. Probably, like the Egyptian surgeon we mentioned, he could refuse to operate if he deemed the case dangerous or hopeless. *Labor Held Responsible*

Of the poetical form of the Babylonian epic, if it had any, it is difficult for the English-speaking reader to get much idea, although it seems animated by a poetical spirit, much resembling in translation passages from our Old Testament. The story of Gilgamesh covered twelve tablets, each of which corresponded to a month of the year, and was so arranged that the episodes fitted the season. The Babylonian year began in the *The Babylonian Epic* spring, and so the sixth tablet, which told of the hero's rejection of the offer of marriage which the goddess Ishtar had made him, marked the end of summer. For this ungallant conduct Gilgamesh was afflicted with a painful disease and wandered about vainly seeking for some way to avoid the death which he felt approaching "when winter comes." Probably no modern novelist or playwright would venture to present so disappointing a love story and so unhappy an ending, but the Gilgamesh epic seems to have enjoyed a run of many centuries in the Tigris-Euphrates valley before it was buried in oblivion for as many more, until within the last hundred years it attained the new life which its hero sought in vain. If not the best seller, it is at least the oldest romance of them all. Many other episodes and narratives were interwoven with the main thread of the story. While often called a religious epic, it also deals with royal misrule, warfare, and adventure. It is likewise a cosmical and astronomical poem, and is true to universal nature, in harmony with whose light and shade its picture of human destiny is drawn.

Scientific Knowledge   While the first germs of scientific interest and observation of nature are thus inextricably mingled with myth and religion or with incantations and magic procedure, they are not on that account to be scornfully ignored. Painstaking observation of the time when the new moon first appeared in order to fix the calendar months and of the apparent movements of the other heavenly bodies has won for Babylonia the title of the mother of astronomy. It must have been long continued ocular observation of sun, moon, and stars, and mental reflection concerning what seemed their effects that caused the belief that their courses determined the periodical inundation of the rivers and seasonal winds, the fertility of the soil, prosperity or disaster to the crops, the king, and the city. Then this belief led to further continual observation of the heavens. It is difficult to discuss such a matter as the botanical knowledge of the ancient Sumerians or Babylonians because the names of herbs and plants have not yet been translated and identified. Can we say that they had no zoology when both their art and their religion show a much greater interest in animals than ours do? Can we deny to the first workers in copper, here or in Egypt, and to the inventors of bronze a very considerable advance for their times in metallurgy and mineralogy?

There are so many resemblances in the art, religion, govern- Common
ment, divination and magic, and economic life of the Nile and Share of
Tigris-Euphrates, and their respective advances in these direc- Babylonia
tions so coincide in time, that they seem to belong to the same in the
stage in the history of civilization.   In both we see the transi- History of
tion from the neolithic to copper age, from primitive drawing to Civilization
picture writing and then to phonetic signs, the introduction of
irrigation, the growth of absolute monarchy in close association with religion, the building of houses of bricks of clay, the
influence of the Semitic language.   It is difficult to believe that
these parallel developments went on quite apart without mutual
intercourse and influence, especially when we know that ships of
the Old Kingdom in Egypt visited foreign lands like Crete and
Phœnicia, and remember that the wares would be passed on farther than the traders penetrated.   At the same time both Egypt
and Babylonia had marked traits of their own, as England and
France have to this day although they have been in constant
contact for many centuries as well as subject to the unifying
forces of recent civilization.   Both Egyptians and Sumerians
were very conservative and made little change even in such
matters as costume for a thousand years or so.   Some of the
practices which thus became fixed by them not only were adopted
by other Semitic peoples like the Hebrews, as we shall note
later, but continued in the Greek or medieval world, or have
persisted to this very day.   For example, incense and holy
water are still employed in religious ceremonies.   The seventh
day is still specially observed.   We still build towers and battlements, although they are no longer of much utility.

BIBLIOGRAPHY

Bevan, *Land of the Two Rivers,* 1917.

Bonavia, *Flora of the Assyrian Monuments,* 1894, 98 illustrations.

Cruveilhier, P. *Les principaux résultats des nouvelles fouilles de Suse,*
   Paris, 1921.

Curtiss, S. I. *Primitive Semitic Religion Today,* 1902.

Handcock, P. S. P. *Mesopotamian Archæology,* 1912.

Harper, R. F. *Assyrian and Babylonian Literature,* 1901; *The Code of
   Hammurabi,* 1904.

Hilprecht, H. V. *Exploration of Bible Lands in the Nineteenth Century,* 1903; *The Earliest Version of the Babylonian Deluge Story and
   the Temple Library of Nippur,* 1910.

Jastrow, M. *Civilization of Babylonia and Assyria,* 1915; *Hebrew and
   Babylonian Traditions,* 1914; *Religion of Babylonia and Assyria,* 1898;

"Liver in Antiquity and Beginnings of Anatomy," in *Univ. of Penn. Medic. Bull*, Jan., 1908; "Medicine of Babylonians and Assyrians," in *Proceedings of Royal Socy. Medic., Sect. Hist. Medic.*, VII (1914) 109–76.

Jean, C. F. *La littérature des Babyloniens et des Assyriens*, 1924.

King, L. W. *History of Sumer and Akkad*, 1916; *History of Babylon*, 1915; *Letters and Inscriptions of Hammurabi*, 1891–1911.

Koldewey, R. *Excavations at Babylon*, translated by Agnes S. Johns, 1914.

Küchler, F. *Beiträge zur Kenntnis der assyr. Medizin*, 1902.

Kugler, F. X. *Sternkunde und Sterndienst in Babel*, 1907.

Langdon, S. *Babylonian Magic*, 1914; *Sumerian and Babylonian Psalms*, 1909; *Excavations at Kish*, vol. I, 1925.

Reimpell, W. *Geschichte der babyl. u. assyr. Kleidung.*

Robertson Smith, *Lectures on the Religion of the Semites*, 1907.

Rogers, *Cuneiform Parallels to the Old Testament*, 1912.

Sayce, *Social Life among the Assyrians and Babylonians*, 1893.

Schaeffer, H. *Social Legislation of the Primitive Semites*, 1915.

Thompson, R. C. *Semitic Magic*, 1908.

Weidner, E. *Beiträge zur babyl. Astronomie*, 1911.

THE VAPHIO GOLD CUP

Above, avenue of rams erected by Rameses II, Temple of Karnak; below, painting of horses and chariot from a tomb of the 18th Dynasty at Thebes in Egypt.

CHAPTER VI

ÆGEAN CIVILIZATION

(about 2500–1200 B. C.)

Nauticus exoritur vario certamine clamor;
Hortantur socii: 'Cretam proavosque petamus!'
—*Æneid*

WE must now sail with the Egyptian ships of the Old Kingdom
across the Mediterranean to Crete, a long mountainous island
forming the southern boundary of the Ægean Sea, and examine
the remains unearthed there of yet another type of civilization
from the same period of the third and second millenniums B. C.
The sites are not only in Crete itself but on the west coast of
Asia Minor, in the Greek peninsula, the islands of the Ægean,
and Cyprus. As the remains thus center chiefly about the
Ægean Sea, the civilization and the people responsible for it
are called Ægean. The people seem to have been a subdivision
of the Mediterranean racial type which is short, dark, and
long-skulled. They were slender and narrow-waisted and can
be distinguished upon the Egyptian monuments. Their language as yet remains unknown.

The Ægean Area and Race

The discovery of this prehistoric Ægean civilization began
only in 1870 when Heinrich Schliemann, a German business man
who was also an enthusiastic admirer of the Homeric poems
which he believed were based on actual events, excavated what
he thought to be the site of Troy. Here were found nine successive layers of ruins representing as many settlements through
the course of the ages from neolithic to Roman times, and telling their silent story of ups and downs of civilization,—invasion, war, desolation, abandonment, rebuilding. Schliemann
then turned to the homeland of Agamemnon, leader of the
Greeks in the Trojan War, and discovered the ruins of Mycenæ
and Tiryns. These sites showed that a high type of civilization had been evolved by about 1400 B. C., but the excavations in
Crete begun at Cnossus in 1899 by Sir Arthur Evans, the

Excavation of the Sites

67

British archæologist, revealed a still earlier and higher culture. These Cretan excavations are still in process, and meanwhile discoveries at other sites which we cannot list here have confirmed or further added to our knowledge of Ægean civilization.

Writing and Reckoning

No writen records had been found by Schliemann at Troy, Tiryns, and Mycenæ, but in Crete chests were found full of clay tablets. The writing on them has not yet been deciphered, though they appear to be tribute lists and inventories of stores. As yet we seem to have no remains of a purely literary character, although additional specimens of writing are continually being found. From them we infer that the Ægeans had a decimal system with numbers up to ten thousand.

Relation to Egypt and the Tigris-Euphrates

Almost from the first there appears to have been trade between Egypt and the Ægean, whose civilization was formed under Egyptian influence, and somewhat later contact with the Tigris-Euphrates through Asia Minor and Cyprus, whence copper was perhaps introduced. The same forms of stone vases and of hieroglyphs are found in Crete as in Egypt. From the Nile, too, were introduced such improvements as the potter's wheel and drain-pipes, while seal-cutting and writing on clay-tablets probably came from Sumer or Babylonia, although this later Cretan writing is linear and not cuneiform. In general the same development takes place from neolithic through the copper to the bronze age and from rude pottery and villages of sun-dried brick to flourishing cities and kingdoms as we have traced in the great, hot, fertile river valleys. Now, however, the process goes on in a region of mountainous islands and coast-lands where the climate, though sunny, was more moderate, and the plains were smaller and less fertile. Furthermore, while we find the same specialized handicrafts as in Egypt, we find these Ægean people possessed of original artistic power and freedom.

The "Second City" of Troy: 2500 B. C.

Ægean architecture yields early specimens of the castle and palace such as have not survived from that period in Egypt, Syria, or Shinar. The oldest considerable example is the so-called Second City of Troy, built on the debris of the neolithic settlement about 2500 B. C. It was about the size of a medieval castle which it resembled in other respects. Its walls were of sun-dried brick like the cities of the plain of Shinar, but it had a ramped approach, strong outer gates, then a narrow passage between parallel walls leading to an inner gate opening on a courtyard. Its chief inner apartment was of a sort not found in the palace of Cnossus in Crete which we shall presently describe nor apparently in Egypt or the Tigris-Euphrates region, namely a *megaron* or large hall isolated from the other rooms and having a central hearth and a plan similar to that of timber buildings found in central and northern Europe. Four columns forming a square about the hearth supported the beams of the wooden roof. This hall was the men's room where the chieftain and his followers gathered. In one of the gate towers was found a treasure of golden jewelry, indicating the existence of wealth and luxury in that region, whether the articles were made in Troy itself or are spoils taken by its robber barons from traders or from other settlements. The only weapons found were spears and axes, there were no swords or arrow-heads. Ornamentation was of the rude geometric sort.

In contrast to this stronghold there were excavated at Cnossus ruins of a very extensive but unfortified palace which seems to reflect the life of a period extending from 2200 to 1500, when it was destroyed by fire. Of course during these seven centuries it was often modified or rebuilt. It is a vast complex of corridors, courts, storerooms, chambers, colonnades, terraces, and staircases, for it was built on several levels descending a slope, and parts of it were four stories high. This maze of rooms and long passages, the pictures of bulls and bull-fights on the walls, and the frequent occurrence of the symbol of the double-axe, for which the Lydian word was *labrys*, suggest a connection between this palace and the Cretan labyrinth of Greek myth where King Minos kept the minotaur, a monster half bull and half man. From this legend and the fact that the place-name, Minoa, occurs frequently in the Ægean region, the adjective Minoan is sometimes applied to the civilization. The palace was built partly of stone, partly of small stones mixed with mud. The lower part of the wall was stone, and around its base ran a projecting ledge or seat of stone such as we find in some palaces of the Italian Renaissance or public buildings of today. The palace contained bath rooms and was well drained by channels cut in the pavement or by pipes of baked clay. There are a throne room, an olive press and great jars for storing oil and wine, altars and cult pillars, well shafts to admit air, windows, and folding and sliding doors. Some tiers of steps mounting to a platform from a paved court are

The Palace at Cnossus 2200–1500

perhaps for theatrical exhibitions or meetings of the court. Near the palace private houses clustered, well built of stone and plastered inside, and a paved street led up to the palace. Indeed, the course of the prehistoric road across the island from Cnossus to Phæstus has been traced at intervals. Pictures of the private houses show that these might be two or three stories high and had windows set one above another in regular rows as is the custom in most buildings today.

Tiryns

As the site of Troy was fitted for controlling or preying upon commerce between the Ægean and Black Seas or Europe and Asia at the narrow crossing of the Dardanelles, so Tiryns and Mycenæ at the head of the Argolic Gulf were well placed either to guard or molest intercourse between central and southern Greece or between Crete and the Gulf of Corinth. Tiryns was later than the second city of Troy but resembled it in its fortified character, its ramp by which the main entrance was reached and which forced an attacking army to expose their unshielded right side to weapons from the wall, its passage between inner and outer gates, its courtyard and megaron. It is both larger and better preserved than the second city of Troy. It included several other gates, a lower castle for the servants and stables, vaulted galleries and chambers along the inside of the walls, and a more palatial arrangement of the rooms in the upper castle. Besides the men's hall there were various other chambers, a bath, and women's apartments including a smaller hall for them. These inner residential portions were built of crude brick, but the outer walls, unlike the second city of Troy, were constructed of great rough blocks of stone with the chinks filled with smaller stones. This type of wall-construction is called Cyclopean masonry from the Greek tradition which ascribed the work to the mythical monsters or giants known as Cyclopes. These walls were about sixty-five feet high and twenty-six feet thick, and seemed to the late Greek traveler, Pausanias, as marvelous a work as the pyramids.

Mycenæ

Mycenæ seems to have become a flourishing city early in the second millennium, but the height of its power and most of the architectural features we are about to mention date after the fall of Cnossus from about 1400 to 1200 B.C. The wall surrounding the citadel or acropolis is of stones less roughly hewn and better fitted together than at Tiryns. Its famous lion gate has a sculptured design found in many other places,

namely, two lions standing on their hind legs facing each other
with their front paws resting on an object between them. In
this case it is a broad pedestal from which rises a column;
in others it is a mountain or chariot surmounted by a figure
of the great or mother goddess, whose worship and emblems
are found especially in Phyrgia and other parts of Asia Minor.
This, too, then serves to connect Mycenæ with Troy. Tombs,
which at Cnossus were late and of small account, are the most
noteworthy remains at Mycenæ. The shaft tombs, hewn per-
pendicularly in the rock, are enclosed by two concentric circles
of upright stone slabs covered with horizontal slabs like the
neolithic stone erections. A great profusion of solid gold
ornaments was found in the shaft graves. Then there are
seven bee-hive tombs, so-called because they are roofed with
concentric horizontal courses of which each projects beyond
the one below it, thus producing a false, conical dome. They
are all built underground and are approached by a long passage cut into the earth. The finest tomb is about fifty feet in
height and diameter, and its bee-hive roof was ornamented with
metal rosettes fastened by bronze nails at regular intervals.
The entrance to this tomb is surmounted by a huge lintel slab
which probably would weigh over one hundred tons and is larger
than that of the lion gate. The sixth city of Troy is noted for
its masonry and belongs to approximately the same period as
Tiryns and Mycenæ.

With a few exceptions such as the lion gate little monu- **Sculpture**
mental sculpture has been discovered in these sites, but some
of the statuettes and the relief work by vase-sculptors or goldsmiths which have been found are of the first rank as works of
art. Such are the head of a bull represented in high relief, the
pair of gold cups found at Vaphio in Laconia on which the
hunting and taming of wild bulls is depicted wth great vigor
and yet with the utmost delicacy of workmanship, the animated
carving on a stone vase of a procession of youths carrying
pitchforks and singing as lustily as if in a frieze by Donatello,
the ivory and gold female figure holding snakes in both extended
hands, and yet in features, form, and posture more natural,
graceful, refined, and European than Egyptian and Babylonian figures. To the modern eye, indeed, the detailed representation of a rather artificial, if not decidely modish and
even modern appearing, costume and coiffure, while showing

that Cretan ladies had skilful hair-dressers and dressmakers, seems rather inappropriate if the statuette is meant to represent the great mother goddess; and the face hardly displays, suggests, or inspires religious feeling. As against this well gowned goddess, the Cretan men are often shown nude like the later statues of Greek athletes or with only a loin cloth like the Egyptians. This statuette of the snake goddess and the Vaphio cups illustrate the extremes of Ægean civilization, which on the one hand had not forgotten the primitive stage of the domestication of cattle, and on the other hand had attained the wealth, the poise, and the artificiality of the court of a Louis XIV.

Pottery

Gracefulness of outline was characteristic of Cretan art from an early period when their stone vases, beautifully veined and wrought, surpass in this respect and in ornamentation and variegated color those of Egypt from which they are supposed to have been copied. Later the Ægeans displayed the same skill in clay pottery, moulding delicate vases no thicker than an egg-shell and inventing a lustrous black glaze or varnish which even acids cannot destroy and which continued in use in the Greek period. Then knowledge of its precise composition was lost, and it cannot be imitated today. Cretan and Mycenæan pottery passed through many changing though continuous styles and stages. The vase painters delighted in stripes and designs of brilliant colors, either in harmony or contrast, in spirals and curves, in motives from nature employed decoratively, including such marine life as sea-weed and the nautilus. There was nothing stiff or clumsy about such vase decoration; Cretan art was not rigid and at rest like the Egyptian; stem or leaf or tendril looks as if at any moment it might sway or bend or quiver in the air.

Fresco
Painting

The same brilliance of color and wealth of natural motives, background, and detail is seen in the fresco paintings. Remains of these exist at Cnossus in an abundance not to be found again until the last days of Herculaneum and Pompeii, for our knowledge of classical Greek painting is limited to literary sources and vase-painting. Nevertheless the fresco of the cupbearer at Cnossus or of the boy picking crocuses already seem to display some of the characteristic qualities of Greek art. Sometimes the frescoes depict the animated life of the pleasure-loving palace court, groups of ladies with deep blue robes and

jewelled necklaces, "gayly-adorned dames and curled gentlemen, standing, sitting, gesticulating vigorously, and flirting,"
or watching the combats of boxers armed with the cestus and
the antics of acrobats or bull-trainers of both sexes. These
seize the horns of the charging animals and turn somersaults
over them, suggesting the toreadors and bull-fights of the Mediterranean race to this day. Turning from the wall-paintings
of the palace to those in a private dwelling, explored in 1923
by Sir Arthur Evans and described in the *London Times*, we
find displayed in bright colors "vividly veined and banded"
rocks, "sea-weed or coralline and sponges, banded pebbles and
finely grained golden sand, argonauts and perhaps some kind
of medusa," many varieties of flowering plants such as "clumps
of crocuses, rose color and blue on undulating zones, orange
and white respectively, . . . madonna lilies and a very fine
white flower with long pointed petals, . . . more than one iris,
. . . flowering peas or vetches, labiates, stellate blooms, in one
case oddly combined with bell-shaped buds, flowering sedges,
ivy and other climbing plants, and briar roses, . . . olive
sprays, . . . branches bearing what look like egg-shaped plums,
red and yellow, . . . the jet of a fountain with falling spray,"
and monkeys "amidst exotic thickets."

In bronze we have a complete collection of kitchen utensils, a kit of carpenter's tools, and many instruments used
by other artificers. Bronze daggers are inlaid with gold to
show hunting scenes; a gaming board indicates another pastime.
Musical instruments have been found to the extent of pipes
and a lyre. A harp appears much earlier on a Sumerian monument. There seems to have been a system of weights and the
germs of a coinage, as we find ingots of bronze, ox-heads of
gold, and small pieces of metal in the form of double-axes.
Such objects indicate a well developed economic life, though
it was perhaps concentrated in the palace.

Bronzes and Other Miscellaneous Remains

Though the palace was unfortified, other indications of warfare are not absent. Besides the daggers and the Minoan
swords, which, with the pottery and other Ægean wares, are
found scattered about the coasts from Sicily to Syria, there
are found at Cnossus hundreds of bronze arrowheads and the
charred shafts of arrows. On a silver vase we see a city
besieged and Cretan bowmen and slingers, who were still noted
in Roman times, in action. A fresco in a private house shows

Warfare and Sea Trade

a Cretan leading what appear to be negro troops, although their waists are as tightly girded as his.   In later Greek legend King Minos of Crete was the first to establish a navy, conquer the pirates, and build up a great sea power.   Pictures of ships are not common, however, in Ægean art; those shown have a mast and low freeboard.   But the frequent representation of sea life and the wide distribution of Minoan works of art suggest trade and maritime affairs, and unfortified Cnossus would seem to have required naval protection.   When Cnossus was destroyed, some of the population seem to have gone by sea to Spain, others to Cyprus.   It is uncertain for any given period whether Tiryns, Mycenæ, and Troy were outposts of the Cretan sea-power, or hostile castles occupied by northern invaders.   It may be significant that no gold treasure remains at Cnossus, while a great deal was found at Troy and Mycenæ. Whether friendly or hostile, the other centers shared largely in the Ægean civilization, although parts of the Ægean area like Thessaly and Bœotia show only neolithic remains until perhaps 1600.   The Mycenæan remains from about 1400 to 1200 have been called inferior artistically but superior technically to those from the preceding periods.

Religion and Burial

We have already mentioned the most common religious symbol, the double-axe, and the chief deity, a nature goddess connected with mountains or sacred stones and pillars, and with snakes and doves who respectively represent the underworld and sky.   Upon a recently discovered gem the snake-goddess holds a sword in one hand and in the other a holy-water sprinkler such as the ancient Romans used, while on a stone vase a man holds the *sistrum* or musical rattle employed in the Egyptian worship of Isis.   Sometimes a youthful male god is associated with the goddess in a subordinate capacity.   There are many votive offerings and dedications.   The Ægeans had blood offerings but not burnt sacrifice, and in the tombs at Mycenæ there is little evidence of cremation.   The shrines and altars thus far discovered have been almost entirely in the rooms of palaces and houses, indicating royal and domestic cults but not temple-priesthoods.   The bee-hive tombs at Mycenæ may have been used in the worship of ancestral spirits, since the tomb proper was a square, dark chamber apart from the circular, domed structure.

BIBLIOGRAPHY

Bell, E. *Hellenic Architecture,* 1920, Chapter II.

Burrows, R. *The Discoveries in Crete,* 1908.

Evans, Sir Arthur, *The Palace of Minos,* vol. I, 1921.

Hall, H. R. *Ægean Archæology,* 1915.

Hawes, C. H. and H. B. *Crete, the Forerunner of Greece,* 1911.

Luke, H. C. *Handbook of Cyprus,* 1920.

Mosso, A. *The Palaces of Crete and their Builders,* 1917.

Tsountas and Manatt, *Mycenæan Age,* 1897.

CHAPTER VII

INNOVATIONS FROM THE NORTH

(1926–777 B. C.)

History knows no people of unmixed blood. Doubtless the Indo-Europeans in their common home were of various stocks.
—*G. W. Botsford*

Forecast   IN the second millennium B. C. three innovations altered the complexion of civilization, namely, the appearance of the domesticated horse, the Indo-European languages, and iron tools and weapons. All three came from the north into the regions considered in our three previous chapters, and were accompanied by southward invasions of new peoples in a nomadic, pastoral, or at least low stage of civilization. They seriously disturbed the existing states and previous civilizations. These then renewed their vitality for a time, either absorbing the newcomers or being adopted by them. Finally the older cultures succumbed, perhaps because of renewed attacks by fresh invaders, or unfavorable climatic change, or ruinous wars, or natural exhaustion and a failure to keep up with the new currents of civilization from a conservative attachment to their old ways. Meanwhile civilization upon the new bases developed in other areas by fusion of the invaders with the previously existing peoples and culture. Egypt, Babylonia, and Crete lost their supremacy, but much of their culture was passed on. The Mycenæans, Hittites, and Assyrians held the field for a time. Then Hindus, Iranians or Persians, and Greeks became the leading civilized peoples of antiquity outside of China, which must be reserved for separate treatment. Important literary remains are preserved in Indo-European languages from before and slightly after 1000: the *Rigveda* in archaic Sanskrit and the Homeric poems in Greek. The Greek poet, Hesiod, for whom the dates, 846–777, have recently been suggested for astronomical reasons also looks back upon our period.

The introduction of the domesticated horse and light swift-moving chariot revolutionized ancient warfare as the airplane bids fair to revolutionize modern warfare, but did not produce the sudden or sweeping change in the daily life of the people that the automobile has already wrought in some parts of the world.   Kings rode in chariots, and aristocratic knights might disport themselves on horseback, but the peasant continued to plough with his ox or plod along the path with his donkey, and merchants largely adhered to camels and asses as beasts of burden and to ox-carts as modes of conveyance.   In the Old Testament both Jeremiah and *Proverbs* mention the horse as prepared for battle and as rushing to battle, and a spirited passage in the *Book of Job* reveals the tremendous impression that this new fighting animal made upon both the art of war and the literature and thought of the time: *The Horse at First Used for War*

> Hast *thou* given the horse strength?
> Hast thou clothed his neck with thunder?
> Canst thou make *him* afraid as a grasshopper?
>   The glory of his nostrils is terrible.
> He paweth in the valley and rejoiceth in his strength;
> He goeth on to meet the armed men;
> He mocketh at fear and is not affrighted,
> Neither turneth he back from the sword.
> The quiver rattleth against him, the glittering spear and the
>   shield.
> He swalloweth the ground with fierceness and rage,
> Neither believeth he that it is the sound of the trumpet.
> He saith among the trumpets, 'Ha, Ha!'
> And he smelleth the battle afar off, the thunder of the cap-
>   tains, and the shouting.

Even as late as the *Book of Revelation* it is the four horses of the Apocalypse who bring death and destruction in their train.

The horse is first mentioned in cuneiform records as "the ass of the hill country."   It was introduced into Babylonia by the Kassites, who ruled there from about 1746 to 1169, and into Egypt by the Hyksos, who overran that country from approximately 1800 to 1600, when they were expelled.   It was with armies composed largely of war chariots and bowmen that the pharaohs of the Empire made their conquests.   In the Mosaic law the Hebrew king is forbidden to "multiply horses to him- *Brought into Babylonia and Egypt from the North*

self," or to "cause the people to return to Egypt to the end
that he should multiply horses." Lapis lazuli and horses became the two chief exports from Kassite Babylonia in return
for "Egypt's almost inexhaustible supply of Nubian gold." A
chariot in a cliff tomb of Egypt had fastenings of birch fibre,
a wood which grows only in northern latitudes, whence, therefore, the first horses and chariots seem to have come. We find
them represented also on vases of the Mycenæan period and frequently mentioned in the earliest hymns of the Aryan invaders
of India. Horse-shoeing with nails, however, was not introduced into Europe until the invasions of Asiatic mounted nomads during the late Roman Empire, although the invention
has been claimed for the Gauls. Various other methods of pro-
tecting the hoofs were employed in Egypt and elsewhere, but
the shoe-plates of bronze found in an Etruscan tomb were worn
only on mountain excursions. The domestication of the horse
was probably the work of nomadic peoples roaming the grassy
plains of eastern Europe and central Asia, and the invasions of
Egypt and the Tigris-Euphrates seem directly or indirectly
caused by the same agency.

First Traces of Indo-European Languages With these events seems also connected the introduction of
the Indo-European languages. The Hittites, who already had
raided Babylonia about 1926, had a language that was at least
in part Indo-European. The Kassites seem to have had one or
two Aryan gods. The names of the kings of the Mitanni, a
people appearing on the upper Euphrates about the middle of
the second millennium, appear to be Indo-European. The earliest settlement at Assur had been Sumerian, but the rulers of the
city in the period to which we have now come, who were looked
back upon by the later Assyrians as the founders of their
power, bore names which were at least unsemitic and somewhat
similar to those of the Mitanni. Some of the local rulers in
Syria who carried on a correspondence in cuneiform with the
pharaoh at Tell el-'Amarna also bore Iranian names. It is supposed that the plateau of Iran now became full of Indo-
European speaking peoples and that India was invaded by the
Aryans, as set forth in the *Rigveda*.

The Indo-European Hypothesis Such languages as Sanskrit, Iranian, Persian, and Armenian
in Asia, and Greek, Latin, Romance, Teutonic, Celtic, and
Slavic in Europe, have common characteristics and seem to form
one of the most widespread systems of human speech, differing

from the Semitic and other groups. In structure and inflexions Sanskrit is remarkably similar to Latin and Greek. Often the same word can be traced in several Indo-European languages; for example, seven is *septem* in Latin, *hepta* in Greek, *hapta* in Iranian, and *sapta* in Sanskrit. In the second millennium these languages appear to have been spread by migration and invasion all the way from Italy to India. There has been a great deal of not very profitable speculation as to the parent people and original homeland from which the first, simplest form of the Indo-European speech was spread abroad. It has been held that from those words which can be shown to be common to the various Indo-European languages in their earliest known forms we can reconstitute to some extent the vocabulary of the parent language or people, and from it infer the stage of civilization which then prevailed,—for example, that the horse, ox, sheep, dog, and pig were domesticated and that grain was grown. In short, life was not exclusively nomadic, but a combination of pastoral and agricultural economy requiring plain and upland in close contact. Hence one of the latest suggestions as to the cradle-land of Indo-European speech is the Hungarian plain and the adjoining areas of Austria and Bohemia. But the peoples who speak Indo-European languages are no longer at least one in race or physical appearance, and it is only the spread of languages that we can trace, not of a race or a civilization. The term, Aryan, is strictly speaking applicable only to the white invaders of India, who used the term to distinguish themselves from the black natives. In the last century what seemed striking resemblances between the myths and customs of different Indo-European peoples were noted, but more recent study of other peoples has shown that many of the myths and customs are even more widespread and so cannot safely be classed as specifically Indo-European. The Indo-European languages first brought with them destruction rather than civilization. But they early were marked by great bodies of literature.

The *Rigveda* seems to be the oldest extant literature in an Indo-European language and also in the history of India. It is primarily religious in character, consisting almost entirely of hymns, over a thousand in number, to the gods. These hymns were presumably the work of a number of priestly poets over a considerable lapse of time, as different hymns seem of dif-

Rigveda: Date and Authorship

ferent date and some are much superior to others in literary merit, while in general they appear to form a collection. The meters are simple and not yet definitely quantitative, consisting mainly of lines of eight, eleven, or twelve syllables. As these poems were sacred, they are thought to have been scrupulously memorized by subsequent generations and so to have been transmitted to us with remarkable accuracy from a period long before the introduction of writing into India. Estimates of their age vary greatly, however, the Hindus suggesting about 3000, while European scholars date the *Rigveda* somewhere in the second millennium. The recent *Cambridge History of India* does not favor a date before 1200 B. C.

Its Myth, Magic, and Religion

When this Vedic literature was first brought to the attention of western scholars at the close of the eighteenth century, it gave a great impetus to the comparative study of both philology and mythology, and many parallels were discovered between Vedic and Greek and Norse mythology. In the *Rigveda* the gods are perhaps least separated by personification from the natural forces and phenomena which they represent, although the hymns display the same power of vivid imagination and metaphorical fancy as the Greek myths. But they may have originated from incantations intended to make the forces of nature work for utilitarian purposes, or from more purely lyrical expression of sympathy with nature's varied moods and manifestations. About one-quarter of all the hymns are addressed to Indra, god of thunder. Nearly one-fifth concern Agni, the spirit of fire, who "wakes at dawn" and is produced daily by rubbing two sticks together, and then, as soon as he is born, devours his parents. What more natural than to sing an encouraging song either to yourself or the fire as you make it every morning? Or Agni is said to be produced by ten maidens, that is, by the fingers of the two hands which revolve one fire-stick against the other. There is even—as also in early Roman religion—a deity or good spirit of the furrow or ploughed earth, and the invocation of her may be regarded as a rite of agricultural magic. Plants too are frequently invoked, and their healing powers are praised, just as in the Gilgamesh epic the hero dived into the sea for a plant that would renew his youth but that was subsequently stolen from him by a snake. In the *Rigveda*, too, the snake appears more often than any other harmful animal. One hundred hymns are concerned with the making and offering of *Soma*, an intoxicating drink made from the juice of a plant. "We have drunk soma, we have become immortal, we have entered into light, we have known the gods." The storm-gods, "born from the laughter of the lightning," remind one of the Valkyrie.

They gleam with armlets as the heavens are decked with stars,
Like cloud-born lightnings shine the torrents of their rain.

The dawn goddess, Ushas, is a radiant and resplendent maiden like the Eos, or "rosy-fingered dawn," of the Greeks. The sun god, like Apollo, drives his horses and chariot and dispels disease. Varuna, perhaps the same name as the Greek Ouranos, or god of heaven, seems a more ethical and exalted conception of deity, representing cosmic and moral order, and is regularly prayed to for forgiveness of sin and guilt. Death and the future life, however, do not receive much attention, but heroes go off to a sort of Valhalla to revel with Yama, king of the dead.

Incidentally the hymns of the *Rigveda* supply a picture of the state of civilization of their authors. They would not, for example, repeatedly represent their gods as driving horses and chariots unless they were familiar with these themselves. The sacrifice of horses, too, was a prominent rite. The geographical allusions show that the Aryan invaders had then not penetrated into India much farther than the Punjab or land of five rivers. The Aryans were divided into different groups or tribes who fought with one another as well as with the black aborigines whom they were conquering and often enslaving, much as did the different tribes of Anglo-Saxons, who overran England, and the various Germanic peoples, who invaded the Roman Empire, two thousand years later. The Hindu word for caste means color, and even among the Aryans themselves the priesthood was perhaps already hereditary.

Civilization of the Aryans on Entering India

Cattle were a chief source of wealth and standard of value. Similarly the Latin word, *pecunia*, meaning money or property, is derived from *pecus*, meaning cattle. The conflicts in which the god Indra engaged were largely motivated by "desire of cows." But the cow was not yet sacred; the Aryans sacrificed bulls, were beef-eaters, and consumed much strong drink. Indeed, one might almost describe them as a crew of hard-drinking cattle thieves. Milk and clarified butter were among the chief foods. Life, however, was not purely pastoral. There was some ploughing, as the personification of Furrow has suggested; there were villages of wooden houses and fortified earthworks and stockades; most of the metals were known, and there were a few artisans such as the smith, carpenter, wheelwright, weaver, and tanner. The drum, flute, and lute were known as musical instruments, and there was much gambling with dice. The position of woman was higher than in later India; some of the hymns are by women. Marriage was sacred; the wife was more honored than later; the suttee was unknown. But the gods were predominantly male, and no desire for daughters is expressed in the *Rigveda*, where we find such sentiments expressed as: "The mind of woman is hard to instruct, and her intelligence is small," and "There are no friendships with women; their hearts are those of hyenas," or the grudging concession, "Many a woman is better than the godless and niggardly man." The political and legal institutions portrayed seem primitive.

Aryan Borrowings from Other Cultures

It is questionable to what extent the *Rigveda* reflects a fresh, independent, Indo-European or northern culture and to what extent it shows borrowings from the previous experience and thought of the ancient Near East. If the Aryans reached India by a slow progress across Asia Minor, Armenia, and the plateau of Iran, they might have become deeply affected in transit by Babylonian art, astrology, and mythology. A year of 360 days and twelve months suggests contact with the Babylonian calendar and sexigesimal system, while the two dogs guarding the path to the realm of the dead may be derived from Egypt. It has been suggested that Aryans from Mesopotamia brought into India the curvilinear form of temple *sikhura*, altering the conical mud huts of the Euphrates to a bamboo framework, and at the same time introducing millet, barley, wheat, and oil-seeds to enrich the agriculture of non-Aryan India. In short, much of Aryan civilization was not their own but had been picked up in the course of their wanderings. Even if they came to India not by way of northern Mesopotamia but through the Caspian area, they might have encountered an advanced stage of copper age civilization both in the northern Caucasus and Turkestan. The copper age civilizations of the third millennium wane, however, in the second. The period of the Hyksos in Egypt was one of confusion; of the long rule of the Kassites in Babylonia we know very little.

But in Asia Minor the remains of the Hittites attract our attention. Their first appearance in history was their raid into Babylonia about 1926; the height of their power was about 1272 when their king and chief priest signed a treaty of peace on equal terms with Rameses II of Egypt; after that they gradually declined before the rising power of Assyria. They were primarily an agricultural people, but had cities as fortified residences, and the land was held either by the king or by the citizens in common. Their power long extended over northern Syria, but their capital and chief site was Khatti, well to the north in Asia Minor where it lies due east of Troy but near the Halys river. In their most striking facial feature, the angular nose and retreating forehead, they resembled the modern Armenians. Yet some of their sculptured faces seem Greek, "others clearly Mongolian." Their art and religion seem to have most associations with the Ægean civilization. From Egypt and Babylonia they adopted both the hieroglyphic and cuneiform methods of writing. But their inscriptions and numerous tablets, which are now being deciphered and translated, contain Indo-European words and grammatical forms. They comprise, however, several other languages besides Hittite itself, and the Hittite empire seems to have included a medley of races and peoples. The Hittites seem to have been great horse-breeders, and the Semitic antipathy for the pig, a forest-ranging animal which was both freely eaten and employed in the holiest ceremonies by northern races, disappears in Asia Minor. The ladies of the royal family sometimes played a prominent part in state affairs and wrote letters to the pharaoh of Egypt.

Khatti was the largest city of Asia Minor in early times. The circuit of its walls was about three and a half miles; cyclopean masonry without mortar was employed; and the strengthening of the wall at intervals with towers, and the entrance gate flanked with towers and guard chambers, were features of military architecture passed on in turn to Assyria, Rome, and the middle ages. Moreover, the sculptured lions guarding the gate have been rather incongruously and thoughtlessly continued in such peaceful modern structures as museums and libraries, which might more appropriately display statues of calves, pigs, and sheep as contributors to the binding of their books and manuscripts. Except for some vigorous and real-

istic representations of animals in action, the Hittite sculpture
is not of a very high order, but it is rich in historical information. The mother goddess appears frequently; animal gods
are suggested when the worship of a bull is depicted, or goats
are shown wearing conical hats, or human deities are shown on
the backs of eagles and lionesses. The horse and chariot appear often; a covered wagon with four wheels may suggest nomadic transportation. Once we see stone masons working from
a ladder, and musicians playing the trumpet, bagpipes, and
guitar. The common male costume seems to be the afore-
mentioned conical hat, the hair worn ending in a pigtail or curl,
a short tunic belted at the waist, a vest with short sleeves, shoes
with turned-up toes much like the Turkish slippers of the same
region today. Women wore long pleated skirts, leaving the
breasts bare or wearing a tight-fitting bodice much like the ladies
of the Cretan palace. Their head-dress was "an upright flat-
topped bonnet with vertical supports." Sometimes the male
conical hat is shown with vertical flutings. Warriors always
carry daggers as side-arms and shields shaped like figure eights.
Their code contains more laws against stealing and unnatural
vices than that of Hammurabi, but also embodies penal reforms
and suggests a more wholesome family life than that of the later
Assyrians.

Introduction of Iron   Beads of hammered iron have been found in a pre-dynastic
grave in Egypt and some pieces of iron from the Fourth and
Sixth Dynasties in one of the pyramids at Gizeh and at Abydos.
These, however, are small, sporadic finds. The general introduction of iron in the ancient world seems to have come from
mines controlled by the Hittites in northern Syria or northeastern Asia Minor. The islands of Cyprus, Rhodes, and
Crete began to employ iron for jewelry about 1400. The
Nineteenth Dynasty (1315–1200) in Egypt received iron from
Syria; Assyria began to get it about the same time. Iron
weapons are found in Syria of the twelfth century, though
their great use was by the armies of the Assyrian Empire in the
subsequent period to be covered by our next chapter.

Indo-European Invasions of the Ægean and Italy   The Greek and Italian peoples of classical antiquity were being formed during the course of the second millennium by the
fusion of the peoples of Mediterranean race with northern invaders who poured in successive waves into those peninsulas.
As a result the prevalent languages in the following period are

found to be Indo-European. This change is first evidenced in the Ægean area by the Homeric poems and in Italy several centuries later by the earliest extant inscriptions in such tongues as Latin, Sabellian, Oscan, and Umbrian. The series of catastrophes which occurred in the Ægean region in the middle of the second millennium—the sack of Melos, Phæstus, Hagia Triada, and other sites as well as the burning of Cnossus—were very probably the work of these northern invaders, from whom the Ægeans fled in all directions. Some went to Spain or Cyprus; in the thirteenth century others joined the Libyans in ravaging the Nile Delta; in the twelfth century some migrated to the Syrian coast where they were known as the Philistines. The old Ægean culture continued for a time at Mycenæ, as we have seen, but then quite disappeared from view.

At some date between the thirteenth and tenth centuries the Indo-European Phrygians crossed the Hellespont from Europe into Asia Minor, and were later followed by another wave of Mysians who pressed them farther inland. This strengthened the Indo-European element in Asia Minor already evidenced by the Hittite language, but it weakened the Hittite power. *And of Asia Minor*

The Homeric poems supply our chief picture of the life of these northern invaders and the effect they produced upon Ægean civilization, and supplement the idea of early Indo-European literature, thought, and institutions which we derived from the hymns of the *Rigveda*. The *Iliad* and *Odyssey* are the oldest works of Greek literature, and it is uncertain just when they were composed, and how far they represent the accumulated activity of generations of minstrels or the skill of a single genius. Apparently they were for a time handed down orally, since the Cretan script appears to have fallen into disuse, and the phonetic alphabet seems to have not yet been introduced from Phœnicia. The time of the Trojan War and of the heroes of old of whom Homer—we shall continue to use the name for convenience—chants the tale, was supposedly long before his own period. But it was apparently of about the same stage of civilization, except that he imagines sumptuous and elaborate works of art like the palace of Alcinous and shield of Achilles, which archæology teaches us were not produced in his time but which he probably could not have imagined without seeing some surviving specimens of the Ægean art of the past. The descriptions of Trojan scenery and geography, however, *The Homeric Poems: Date and Authorship* are reasonably correct. They go to prove that there really had been a Trojan War, and that the poems were composed not far from Troy—perhaps at Smyrna or Chios where the combined Æolic and Ionic dialect was used—and somewhere between 1000 and 800 B. C.

Their Literary Quality

Both poems are epics in dactylic hexameter, a meter which cannot be employed in English as satisfactorily, but which has a very attractive swing and sonance in the more vocal Greek language. They are stories of fighting, not unlike the early French *chansons de geste* concerning feudal warfare, or of adventure and seafaring, somewhat similar to the Norse sagas. Thus the later products of other Indo-European literatures under feudal or unsettled conditions resemble these earlier poems and reflect similar conditions. Love stories and magic add to the interest, as do the devices of disguise and recognition. Along with primitive simplicity and heroic force goes an ability to touch the human heart. A deft power of imagination plays about the narrative like those colts begotten by the North Wind of the mares of Erichthonius, "which galloped over the tops of the flowers and brake them not, and over the crest of the ocean wave."

Religion and Moral Standards

The heroes are almost on a plane with the gods, who lead precisely the same kind of life as men, joining the fray of battle, hammering out armor, weaving clothing, building walls, and herding sheep. Conversely, even a swineherd, whose hut boasts neither chair, table, nor bed, is called godlike or divine. There is a tendency, however, to ascribe both ill and good fortune to the gods. Stormy human passions are mingled with more tender human sentiment, and there are exhibitions of generosity and selfish cunning, vengeance and relenting, brutality and chivalry, quarrels over the division of spoil, sulking and jealousy and deceit. Adultery is hardly censured, but the most touching scenes of family affection are presented. Military virtues are the most esteemed.

Social and Economic Life

Men lived in walled cities for better protection from hostile tribes and neighbors, but also tilled the soil, either ploughing a large field together or toiling under warrior lords who themselves oversaw the reaping of their domain lands. This indicates that once free and cooperative village communities were being replaced by serfdom and feudal and manorial lords, as later in medieval England and among the early Germans. This impression is borne out by these further facts. Along with the kingship existed folk courts where the effort was still being made to replace blood-feud by compensation for the slain. Unruly, high-spirited nobles and haughty, insubordinate, petty chieftains regarded themselves as quite the equals of kings and lorded it over the common people in the tribal assembly. Exploits of an individual against the mass are what both *Iliad* and *Odyssey* glorify; Achilles killed Trojans by the score, and chased them by hordes. Arts and crafts were in a low state. We hear of about the same occupations as in the *Rigveda*: wheelwrights, carpenters, smiths, curriers, goldsmiths, and potters, but each household as a rule supplied its own needs. Odysseus boasted that he constructed his own bridal bed, and one of Priam's sons made his chariot from wood which he himself hewed in the forest. Costly wares were seldom seen and were chiefly obtained from the Phœnician traders, although the *Odyssey* shows the Greeks themselves in repeated contact and conflict with the sea. Music and dancing already played much the same prominent part as in later Greek life. In general the rude life depicted or suggested much resembles that to be inferred from the *Rigveda* or from Tacitus' account of the early Germans before they invaded the Roman Empire. Yet the Homeric poems remained standard works throughout Greek history and formed a national Bible upon which everyone was brought up and which inspired artists as well as subsequent writers.

The bronze armor of Homer's Achæans, as the assailants of Troy are commonly called in the *Iliad*, their fondness for horse-grazing localities, their brooches and geometrical ornament, and their practice of cremation, all bear a close resemblance to the Hallstatt civilization of the upper Danube. This center is especially noted for its leaf-shaped sword which about the ninth century spread over a large part of Europe. We are also told that here developed first the riding of horses instead of driving them, but we suspect that any people who had before ridden asses would soon ride horses. The Hallstatt region gradually changed from the use of bronze to that of iron, but apparently at a later date than the introduction of iron in the Near East. The early iron age Villanova civiliza-

The Hallstatt Civilization

tion of north Italy was under its influence. The Homeric poems contain a few mentions of iron, which was apparently just coming into use.

Hesiod's Picture of His Own and Past Ages

Hesiod, although perhaps somewhat later than Homer, supplements the Homeric poems in more ways than one. He continues the epic form of poetry, though hardly the heroic content. His *Works and Days*, telling when and how to plough and sail, gives more direct information concerning the laborious life of the farmer, and reflects the belief in weather signs and lucky and unlucky days. His *Theogony* gives a more systematic account of the Greek gods and their supposed origin than the Homeric poems supply. Hesiod also gives an interesting, although brief survey of past ages of the world. This passage has usually been regarded as simply a fanciful myth, but it bears a certain crude resemblance to the classification of early ages adopted by modern scientific archæology. He not incorrectly regards his own as a degenerate iron age which had been preceded by an age of bronze. Apparently between these came an age of heroes and demigods, which may be regarded as corresponding to the period of the Homeric poems which were written, as we have seen, just as iron was begi_ning to replace bronze. Before the bronze age, however, in place of the old and new stone ages Hesiod has first a golden age when there was no war or work but an ideal climate which supplied every human need, in short, a sort of Garden of Eden or state of nature and age of innocence; and then a silver age, when extremes of heat and cold became noticeable and man required shelters,—circumstances which somewhat suggest the glacial period or middle stone age of cave man. In fact Hesiod says, "Caves were their dwellings and bowers and wattle huts." The latter habitations, however, would seem neolithic, a period further suggested by his saying that plough culture was now necessary in order to raise crops.

BIBLIOGRAPHY

Aigner, A. *Hallstatt*, 1911.
Bender, *The Home of the Indo-Europeans*, 1922.
Garstang, *Land of the Hittites*, 1910.
Hogarth, *Carchemish*, 1914.
Hrozny. *Die Sprache der Hethiter*, 1917; *Hethitische Keilschrifttexte*, 1919.

Iliad, English translation by Lang, Leaf, and Myers, 1907

Lang, A. *Homer and His Age,* 1906.

Leaf, W. *Troy, a Study in Homeric Geography,* 1912.

Macdonell, A. A. *Sanskrit Literature,* 1900 (out of print). Chapters II–VI.

Meier, H. *Die Bauern im Homer,* 1903.

Meillet, A. *Introduction à l'étude comparative des langues indo-européenes,* 4th ed., 1915.

Murray, G. *Rise of the Greek Epic,* 1911.

Odyssey, English translation by Butcher and Lang, 1906.

Ridgeway, Sir Wm. *Origin and Influence of the Thoroughbred Horse,* 1905.

Seymour, T. D. *Life in the Homeric Age,* 1908.

Zippelius, *Die geschichtliche Anfänge des europäischen Hufbeschlags,* 1903.

CHAPTER VIII

THE AGE OF ANCIENT EMPIRES

(c. 1580–485 B. C.)

Oh, where are kings and empires now
Of old that went and came?

New Semites NOT all the invaders of the ancient seats of civilization in the course of the second millennium were Indo-Europeans or from the north. The Hyksos who invaded Egypt seem to have been Semitic, and from this time on, at least, Semitic nomads from Arabia invaded the territories of their more settled kinsmen in Syria and the Tigris-Euphrates valley. The Old Testament represents the Hebrew patriarchs and tribes as in a pastoral and barbarous condition for some time after they entered Palestine. About 1400 another Semitic people, the Aramæans, began to appear in northern Syria, where Damascus may be regarded as their capital. Meanwhile the growing power of Assyria on the upper Tigris was in conflict with Babylon, which was further weakened by inroads of Semitic nomads from the Arabian desert.

The Assyrians The Assyrians continued the sequence of Sumerian and Babylonian civilization, employed the Semitic language, and resemble Semites when depicted upon the monuments. They took their name from their city and god, Ashur. In the previous chapter we saw that some of their early rulers were possibly Indo-European. Their later conquering monarchs too often displayed a ferocious cruelty, and even a tendency to boast of it, which reminds one of the ways of the later Asiatic nomads. So do their practice of building themselves new capitals in place of Ashur, and their custom of transplanting entire peoples. The sudden downfall of their power in 612 and disappearance of their name therewith from history, further bring to mind the fate of Attila and the Huns. When peoples are thus transplanted, it is a fairly safe conjecture that both the regions from which they are taken and those to which they are moved have been grievously depopulated and laid waste. The cruelty of the Assyrians may have some connection with the introduction of iron; sharp new steel knives and swords may have tempted them to flay their enemies alive and to lop off their hands and ears.

The introduction of the horse had ushered in an age of mobilization and distant conquest in which the Assyrians were far from having been the first offenders. Imperialism upon a notable scale may be said to have been launched by the Empire in Egypt (1580–1090), when the people stopped their patient piling up of pyramids for the pharaoh and engaged in arduous and exciting expeditions and campaigns in Nubia and Syria under his leadership. It was a questionable shift from construction to destruction. It is true that the imperialistic pharaohs were also great builders of temples, obelisks, and colossal statues; but the candle could not thus be burnt at both ends, and the new conquests could not be held indefinitely. When the Hittites withstood Rameses II in Syria, the Egyptian power had passed its zenith, and after 1090 Egypt itself was for the most part under foreign domination,—Libyan, Ethiopian, and so on. The Hittite power, which seems to have been a cosmopolitan empire including many peoples and languages, in its turn yielded to the Assyrian. The weakened condition of both Syria and Babylonia, where we have seen nomads from Arabia filtering in, gave Ashur a chance to develop, like Rome later, from a city state into an empire.

An Age of Military Imperialism

The period of greatest Assyrian success, although there had been earlier temporary conquests, was from 732 when Damascus, the key to Syria, was taken, to 612 when Nineveh, which had become the Assyrian capital, fell, and the days of Assyrian supremacy were forever at an end. In Egypt Psammetichus I (663–609) had already thrown off the Assyrian yoke with the the aid of the king of Lydia in Asia Minor and mercenary troops from the Greek cities. Other fresh peoples accomplished the downfall of Nineveh, namely, the Semitic Chaldeans who had earlier overrun Babylonia from Arabia, and the Manda or Medes. The latter were probably Indo-Europeans, although we do not know much about them, and some think that they have been confused with the Scythians. In any case, northern peoples known to the ancients as Cimmerians and

Wars of Mutual Destruction

Scythians had been making a great deal of trouble for Assyria and Lydia in Armenia and Asia Minor respectively. The Assyrians had destroyed Babylon, but Nebuchadnezzar, king of the Chaldeans from 604 to 561, made it a greater city than ever before, and fought against Egypt in Syria, carrying off the Hebrews into Babylonian captivity. Meanwhile the Medes were fighting in Asia Minor with the Lydians. Thus both the Medes and Babylon engaged in wars in the west when they should have watched the east.

Foundation of the Persian Empire

The Assyrian Empire had included Media and Elam to the east but not the great plateau of Iran. From it now issued a rapid conqueror, Cyrus, at the head of the Persians, a people more certainly Indo-European than the Medes. In 550 he seized the Median throne and capital at Ecbatana; in 546 he took Sardis in western Asia Minor and ended the reign of Crœsus, king of Lydia and proverbial for his wealth. Then for six years Cyrus was busied with eastern conquests in the direction of India. In 539 he captured Babylon with ease. Therefore he did not destroy it, and impressive ruins remain of Nebuchadnezzar's city. In 529 Cyrus died fighting against nomads in central Asia or northeastern Iran, the Massagetæ on the river Jaxartes. The Persians themselves fought somewhat in nomad fashion, depending chiefly upon archery and cavalry, as had the Assyrians before them. Moreover, the speed of the conquests just recounted, and the fact that entire peoples and kingdoms like the Medes and Assyrians dissolved and disappeared the moment their capitals were taken, indicate that by this time society was in a very loose and fluid state, and that there was not much settled civilization or durable government, or many walled cities left to check the march of royal armies and nomadic hordes. The successors of Cyrus added Egypt, Thrace, and some provinces of India to the vast Persian Empire, but failed in their attempt to conquer the cities of the Greek peninsula.

Assyrian and Persian Government

The Assyrian and Persian monarchs had great power, multitudes of men, and the resources of vast stretches of territory at their disposal, and could order great public works or monuments if they chose. For the most part, however, they devoted themselves to warfare, and their greatest ability perhaps lay in organizing huge military expeditions, for which the Persian kings required the subject peoples to furnish troops or ships, and not merely to pay tribute as the kings of Lydia and Assyria had required.   Sometimes they returned victorious; sometimes not.

> A king sate on the rocky brow
> Which looks o'er sea-born Salamis;
> And ships, by thousands, lay below,
> And men in nations:—all were his!
> He counted them at break of day;
> And when the sun set, where were they?

The king controlled the vast domains under his rule largely through the terror of their inhabitants lest he might lead his cruel hosts again to their destruction.   So with trembling they rendered their quotas and tributes.   The Persian rule, however, was milder than the Assyrian.   Over each large section of the empire the king placed a satrap who was often some member of his family or other person on whom he thought he could depend.   But royal agents or spies, known as the King's Eyes and Ears, were at hand to watch even the satraps.   Thus the Persian Empire was more centralized than previous empires, and the institution of the satrapy has been considered an important step in the history of political organization.   Messengers conveyed news and communications to the king by swift relays of horses such as the Tartar nomads later maintained across the whole breadth of Asia.   A royal road traversed Asia Minor and led from Mesopotamia up to the Persian capitals in the highlands.

This improved communication was beneficial to civilization. Rice and the peacock are said to have been introduced at Babylon from the west coast of India by sea during the sixth century, although the peacock may be referred to in an earlier Assyrian inscription of 738.   From India the Assyrians introduced cotton trees.   Darius (521–485), the most enlightened of the Persian kings, had his admiral Scylax return from the Indus river by sea, and completed a canal from the Nile to the Red Sea which the pharaoh Necho had begun but then abandoned a century before.   But the voyage of Scylax took so long that he had few immediate imitators, and the canal soon fell into disuse.   The vast Persian Empire gave opportunity for the diffusion of civilization, yet at most of the ancient centers there was decline.

Wider Communication

The Assyrians and Chaldeans Conserve or Destroy Rather than Create Civilization

Neither Assyrians nor Chaldeans can be regarded as great originators of civilization. They largely borrowed from the Hittites and Babylonians, and probably destroyed far more than they adopted. We are grateful to Nebuchadnezzar for rebuilding Babylon; to his successor, Nabonidus, for taking an interest in archæological finds which he records, sometimes inaccurately unfortunately; to Ashurbanipal for collecting and preserving many ancient records and books in his library. Nevertheless, the ruthless conquest of his predecessors had probably been responsible for the destruction of a far greater number. We must judge the previous civilization by the meager remains which escaped destruction through the age of invasion and empire. When Nineveh was destroyed, no one paid any attention to the 22,000 clay tablets of Ashurbanipal's library, which were not to be read again until our times. But the siege-tower and battering ram, which the Assyrians are said to have invented, continued their work of ruining cities and civilization to the time of Julius Cæsar and beyond.

Assyrian Sculpture

The chief remains of Assyrian civilization are sculptures. Architecture showed slight advance over the previous period. But the long series of bas reliefs, carved on alabaster or limestone slabs and setting forth in a profusion of successive scenes the conquests and hunting and court life of the various monarchs, must be admitted to be superior to anything of the sort preserved in Egypt. Since the later reliefs are considered superior to the earlier slabs, sculpture appears to have developed rather than retrograded under royal Assyrian patronage. The Assyrians are usually said to have excelled in the sculpture of wild beasts rather than human beings, but their representation of human faces is also not without merit and character in the case of smooth-shaven personages whose countenances are not masked and rendered meaningless by conventional beards. The bronze reliefs on the gates of Shalmaneser II (850) deserve particular mention as a first example of that type of sculpture which culminated over two millenniums afterwards in the famous bronze doors by Ghiberti in the baptistery at Florence.

Uncivilized Simplicity of the Persians

How little record of themselves the ancient Persians left may be inferred from the fact that we do not know their name for their own capital, which was later in the time of Alexander the Great designated by the Greek name, Persepolis, or city of the Persians. As a matter of fact, they were unaccustomed to city life or market-places or to any advanced civilization. Scylax was not a Persian but a Mediterranean sailor from Caria. Persian sculpture simply copied Assyrian; Persian colonnades were Greek; and the cliff tombs of the later Persian kings—Cyrus was not so buried—were hewn in the face of the rock like those of Egypt. For their god, Ormuzd, they adopted the symbol of Ashur, the god of Assyria. The simplicity of the Persian mind at this period may be seen from an inscription of King Xerxes (c. 485–465).

> A great God is Ormuzd, who hath created the earth, who hath created the heavens, who hath created man, who hath given to mankind the good spirit, who hath made Xerxes king, the sole king of many lords. I am Xerxes, the Great King, the King of Kings, the King of lands of many languages, the King of this great universe, the son of Darius the King the Achæmenian. Xerxes, the Great King, saith: By the grace of Ormuzd I have made this portal, whereon are depicted all the countries. Many other noble monuments there are in this Persia, which I have wrought, and which my father hath wrought. That which hath been wrought is good. All of it we have wrought by the grace of Ormuzd. Xerxes the King saith: May Ormuzd protect me and my empire. Both that which I have wrought and that which my father hath wrought, may Ormuzd protect them.

The early Persians are said to have been taught only three things: to ride, to shoot, and to tell the truth. The Greek historian, Herodotus, who tells us this, says further of the Persians, "Whatever things it is not lawful for them to do, these it is not lawful for them even to speak of: and the most disgraceful thing in their estimation is to tell a lie, and next to this is to owe money." They had already, however, begun to adopt the luxuries of the lands they conquered, and this softer mode of life in time brought about their military decline. Two sides of their original life mentioned by Herodotus are duplicated in Tacitus' account of the early Germans, another primitive Indo-European folk. Neither made images of gods or thought of their gods in human form as the Greeks did, and both were given to hard drinking, like the Aryans of the *Rigveda*, and to discussing important matters at such drinking-bouts but reserving final decision until next day when they were sober.

The religious beliefs and ethical standards of the Persians

are at least in part ascribable to the teaching of Zoroaster. Concerning his date and personality there has been much dispute, but the tendency now is to regard him as a real personage of the early sixth century B. C., of whose teaching portions are preserved in the *Avesta* or sacred book of the Persians and sole literary monument of ancient Iran.   The oldest existing manuscript of the *Avesta*, however, dates back only to 1258 A. D., and much of the work had been lost under Mohammedan persecution since the Sassanian period (227–641 A. D.) when it was compiled from older fragments.   As far as can be made out from this corrupt text, in which a few hymns seem to form the oldest kernel, Zoroaster was an abstract thinker who expressed himself rather obscurely, but who had the great idea that to be able to distinguish truth from falsehood is divine, and that man must strive to attain this goal by "good thoughts, good words, good deeds," and by the aid of the Holy Spirit or Great Wisdom and its six helpers,—Good Thought, Right Order, Excellent Kingdom, Holy Character, Health, and Immortality.   In the incessant, truceless struggle between life and death, light and darkness, good and evil,—opposing forces personified as Ahuramazda and Ahriman,—man should take an active and positive, not a quiescent and passive, part, and for this he will be held responsible at the final judgment.   Such ethical idealism was accompanied, however, by concrete advice to sow seeds and to till the earth, which perhaps represents an effort to turn a nomadic people to agriculture.   It was also accompanied by a great amount of ritual, purification, and detailed regulation of life, so that Zoroaster was later regarded as the founder of magic, and the Persian priests or *Magi* as the first magicians and astrologers.   Fire-worship and sun-worship were also associated with Zoroastrianism, and the emphasis upon the number seven in the *Avesta* suggests that the planets were still regarded as divine forces of light, although they had perhaps been for Zoroaster simply symbols in the struggle with powers of darkness, under which caption he seems to have classed many of the old gods.

In the extant *Avesta* burial of the dead is forbidden; instead the corpse must be exposed to be devoured by dogs and birds; yet the tombs of the Achæmenian dynasty to which we have referred indicate that burial was not strictly prohibited then. Herodotus explains, however, that the corpse was not buried until it had been torn by a bird or dog, after which the Persians covered the body with wax and buried it. In any case the custom differs from those dispositions of the dead which we have hitherto noted, and is probably a survival of nomadic life.

Traders and market-places were scorned by such a conqueror as Cyrus, and under the preceding Assyrian Empire trade had fallen for the most part into the hands of the Aramæans. They carried the products of Egypt, Syria, and Babylon eastward, while trade in the Mediterranean was largely in the hands of the coast cities of Phœnicia, such as Tyre, Sidon, and Byblos. The last named city exported so much papyrus that the name *byblos* or bible came to be applied by the Greeks to any book. In place of the simple galley rowed by twenty-five oars on either side the Phœnicians invented the bireme and then the trireme. Without increasing the length of the boat they somehow superimposed first a second and then a third row of oarsmen's benches, thus tripling the number of oars and speed of the vessel. How this was done has long since been forgotten. Coinage seems to have been invented in Lydia in the seventh century. The first coins were of electron, a mixture of gold and silver. Both trireme and coinage were adopted by Greek civilization.

Aramæan and Phœnician Commerce: Lydian Coinage

Tyre is not mentioned in the Homeric poems, and the name, Phœnicians or purple-folk, meaning those who traded, in the dye made from two molluscs, the *purpura* and the *murex*, is perhaps applied in the Homeric poems to Cretans rather than to "the men of Sidon," who are named separately. The purple dye itself was attributed to the Mæonians or the Carians of the southeastern Ægean. Heaps of the crushed shells of the molluscs may still be seen throughout the Ægean area, but the molluscs are also found as far north as the Black Sea and coast of Gaul and as far west as the Balearic Isles. The actual color varies in different places from black to blue, red, and violet. The molluscs can be gathered only in the fall and winter, and the dye must be extracted at once while they are still alive by blows with iron tools. But sailing was not possible for the ancients at that season of the year, so that it may be that the Phœnician colonies were an outgrowth of winter stations established for this purpose. They reached as far west as Sicily and as Carthage in northwestern Africa. The purple

Purple in Antiquity

dye was highly valued in antiquity, when wearing purple robes was considered one of the greatest luxuries and a sign of high social standing or even of royalty. Whether the early Greeks obtained this dye from the Phœnicians or not, they at first depended upon the foreign traders for most of their manufactured wares such as metal dishes and vases, ivory combs, and the common woolen garment known by the Semitic name, *chiton*.

Introduction of the Alphabet

The greatest service rendered by the Phœnicians and Aramæans was the exclusive adoption and dissemination of the phonetic alphabet. This reform was the work of hurried business men and not of leisurely priests or careful scholars. The Phœnicians have left no literature; it was the very fact that they had none that made it possible for them to start afresh. For business convenience they employed only twenty-two signs, which represented consonants and aspirates but not the vowels. It was this bare remnant, this mere debris, of previous systems of writing that was taken up by the new Semitic and Indo-European peoples and made the basis of all their literatures since. By about 1000 the Aramæans had borrowed the alphabet from the Phœnicians and spread it throughout the Assyrian Empire, while under the Persian Empire Aramaic was employed not only for private business purposes but in most governmental and official documents. The Persians furthermore used an alphabet of thirty-nine cuneiform characters. They do not seem, however, to have been a literary people; at least few of their inscriptions have survived. The remains have been chiefly important as enabling scholars to decipher cuneiform through study of Darius' inscription on the cliff of Behistun recording his victories in three languages: Persian, Susian, and Babylonian. Cuneiform writing even outlasted the Achæmenian dynasty, and the last known inscription in it dates from 80 B. C., by which time Aramaic had replaced all the other Semitic languages including even Hebrew in Palestine.

Its Spread to Europe

In the west the Ionian Greeks of western Asia Minor took over the alphabet from the Phœnicians with whom they traded, but used some of the characters to represent vowels, which were so frequent and important in the ancient Greek language. The alphabet, so-called from the names of the opening letters, *alpha* and *beta*, differed somewhat in the different Greek dialects, and the number of letters varied at different periods.

By about 700 it was in literary use, and the number of letters is usually reckoned as having been twenty-four. For their writing and inscriptions the Greeks long used only one form of letters, corresponding to our capitals and known as majuscules. From the Greeks the alphabet passed on to the Latins and other Italians, then to the modern European languages. Unfortunately this alphabet, which first denoted Semitic sounds, has never corresponded precisely to the sounds of European languages, so that today we have nine different pronunciations of the letter *a*, and a scientifically phonetic alphabet is still a thing of the future. Perhaps the stenographers' union will succeed some day in putting through this reform in some distant land, but at present even the cause of simplified spelling makes little progress in English-speaking countries. Alphabets have made possible cataloging and classifying in alphabetical order; such helps as dictionaries and other works of reference are hardly possible without such an arrangement, nor are typewriters and printing with movable types of much use in a language with a great number of different written characters.

The Old Testament tells us of a captivity of the Israelites in Egypt. Later the Assyrians led ten of the twelve tribes into slavery beyond the Tigris, and they never returned. Finally, the two remaining tribes were transplanted to Babylonia for a time by Nebuchadnezzar, but later returned to Jerusalem and resumed their national life. In their contact with the great monarchies and with the city-dwelling Hittites, Canaanites, Phœnicians, and Philistines they had acquired civilization, as the Old Testament makes evident. "There is no other body of documents in which you can so well trace the development of the race from nomad tribes down to completely developed industrial civilization." The Jews had survived the repeated sweep of invading armies through Syria, and developed an intense national, racial, and religious feeling, regarding themselves as a chosen people and their god, Yahveh, not as a tribal or local deity, but as identical with a divine Providence that overrules the whole world, all kings and peoples, all forces of nature—"The heavens declare the glory of God, and the firmament showeth forth His handiwork"—and the entire course of human history. Yet this vast, overseeing, divine Providence

Judaism and the Old Testament

would also be present to comfort and guide each trusting heart, as is evidenced by the twenty-third psalm and other familiar scriptural passages.

Its Relation to Previous Thought and Experience

Historians of religion no longer regard this development in religious thought as the work of the Hebrews alone, or as vouchsafed directly to them by God as his chosen people. Their religious development owed much to Egypt and Babylon, just as the Mosaic law was later than the Code of Hammurabi, and the Sumerian tales of creation and flood older than the biblical versions. But the Mosaic law was to have a long future influence; the Code of Hammurabi was carried off to Elam and rediscovered only a few years ago after a lapse of some three thousand years. So the Old Testament has been until recently in Europe and America man's chief, if not sole, source of information concerning the religious thought of the ancient orient, and even now that Egyptian and Babylonian documents have been published, it still presents that religious development in the most attractive form and that most suited to modern consumption. The writers of the Old Testament did somewhat the same thing with the mass of ancient religious thought and ritual as the Phœnicians did with all the hieroglyphic and cuneiform characters. They simplified and purified all this lore of the past, and put it into a convenient form which, like the alphabet, the common man could use.

Its Contents

Much of the Old Testament, written in a Semitic language, is poetry to compare with the *Rigveda* and Homeric poems, which are in Indo-European languages. It further contains an account of the early history of the world and mankind which long exerted great influence, other historical books concerning the Hebrews and their relations with surrounding states, a system of law and ritual, a collection of wise and philosophical sayings, and various prophetic books full of religious fervor and exhortation, of varied visions and imagery, of warning and lamentation as to contemporary conditions, and of high hope of better days to come. Thus its contents are varied, and it might be used to a certain extent as an encyclopedic manual, and often has been so used in times past. However, its chief importance is as a historical source, a literary monument, and an expression of religious thought and development. In all these three fields it remains a collection of documents of the first order.

From the wreckage of ancient Egyptian and Babylonian civilization Syria saved twenty-two letters and the conception of one God!

BIBLIOGRAPHY

Benjamin, S. G. W. *Persia and the Persians,* 3rd edition, 1891.

Bewer, J. A. *The Literature of the Old Testament in its Historical Development,* 1904.

Curzon, (Viscount) G. *Persia,* 2 vols., 1892.

Dedekind, A. *Ein Beitrag zur Purpurkunde,* 1906.

Dhalla, M. N. *Zoroastrian Civilization,* 1922.

Gardner, P. *A History of Ancient Coinage,* 1918.

Handcock, P. S. P. *Latest Light on Bible Lands,* 1913.

Huart, C. *La Perse antique et la civilisation iranienne,* 1925.

Jackson, A. V. W. *Persia, Past and Present,* 1906; *Zoroaster, the Prophet of Ancient Times,* 1899.

Jean, C. F. *Le Milieu Biblique avant Jésus-Christ:* tome I, "Histoire et civilisation," 1923; tome II, "La Littérature," 1923; tome III, "Les Idées religieuses," 1925.

Luke, H. C. and Keith-Roach, E. *Handbook of Palestine,* 1922.

Macalister, R. A. S. *Excavation of Gezer,* 1912; *The Philistines, their History and Civilization,* 1913.

Margolis, M. L. *Hebrew Scripture in the Making,* 1922.

Montet, Ed. *Histoire de la Bible,* 1924; "contains all it is necessary for a non-specialist to know."

Moulton, J. H. *Early Zoroastrianism,* 1913.

Ridgeway, W. *Origins of Metallic Currency and Weight Standards,* 1892.

Sayce, *Patriarchal Palestine,* 1912.

Smith, H. P. *The Religion of Israel,* 1914.

Sykes, General Sir Percy. *A History of Persia,* 2 vols., 1921.

BOOK III. CLASSICAL CIVILIZATION AND ITS DECLINE

CHAPTER IX

THE GREEK CITY STATE

(776–338 B. C.)

> There the sons of Athens set
> The stone that freedom stands on yet.
>
> —*Pindar*

Hellas and the Hellenes FROM the ancient empires of the Near East and its waning civilization we pass on in our next chapters to ancient Greece and Rome, and other cultures of the western Mediterranean. Hellenes, originally the name of a tribe in Thessaly, came to be applied generally by the ancient Greeks to themselves from perhaps the seventh century on, and Hellas included the whole range of their settlements throughout the Mediterranean basin and coasts of the Black Sea. They were thus conscious of their unity in language and civilization. The heart of Hellas, however, and the hearth of Hellenic culture was that Ægean area which had been the stage of the earlier Ægean culture represented by Cretan and Mycenæan art, and of the Homeric age which had followed the introduction by invaders from the north of an Indo-European language. These invaders, first apparently penetrating the Greek peninsula, had then conquered the islands and spread to the west coast of Asia Minor. For a time civilization declined, and the customs of the ruder invaders predominated; then from the seventh to the fourth century came one of the greatest developments of civilization in the world's history. Some would call it the greatest. It seems to represent a fusion of the strongest elements of both the Ægean and Indo-European cultures, the artistic ability of the former combined with the literary facility of the latter, and to both was added that philosophic pondering upon the

102

universe and life which manifested itself at this same period in Persia, India, and China. In the present chapter we shall note the geographical background, the economic foundation, the social and political organization of this ancient Hellenic or Greek civilization from about 776 (the traditional date for the founding of the Olympic games in which all Hellenes united every four years, so that the first Olympiad would be from 776–772), to the battle of Chæronea in 338 or the conquests of Alexander the Great in 336–323, when the Greeks were defeated by Macedon and Hellenic liberty merged into Alexander's empire.

We should guard against thinking of Hellas or ancient Greece as merely the Greek peninsula. Byron did well to emphasize

Influence of Geography

> The Isles of Greece! the Isles of Greece!
> Where burning Sappho loved and sung,
> Where grew the arts of war and peace,
> Where Delos rose, and Phœbus sprung.
> Eternal summer gilds them yet,
> But all except their sun is set.

Peninsulas that are practically islands are also frequent in the Ægean region, while the isles themselves are often separated only by the narrowest straits from one another or the adjoining mainland. Thus Hellas was a complicated coil of mountain and narrow coast with an equally complicated coil of gulf, bay, and strait. Mountains and sea combined to divide the land into small districts, whether islands, valleys, little plains, or narrow stretches of coast. Hence Hellas was especially adapted to the existence of many small independent tribes and city states, and we find great diversity of local dialects—Dorian, Ionian, Æolian, and others,—legends, and worships. This diversity was probably enhanced by the coming of the northern invaders in successive waves separated by considerable intervals of time, and by the persistence in many places of the previous population or its fusion in varied combinations with the newcomers. The Greeks were naturally led to a sea-faring life for these reasons. The sea offered the easiest means of communication between the different districts; in the clear air distant shores could be seen afar; there were many safe harbors; and the winds were regular. The climate was sunny but varied by mountainous altitudes and sea breezes, so that while Athens, for instance, becomes very hot in summer, only the southernmost part of the Greek peninsula has a semi-tropical climate. "Within a boundary of not more than two degrees of latitude the land of Greece reaches from the beeches of Pindus into the climate of the palm; nor is there on the entire known surface of the globe any other region in which the different zones of climate and flora meet one another in so rapid a succession." (Curtius)

Although the inland plateau of Asia Minor is melancholy and monotonous, and the north coast along the Black Sea somewhat lowering, "the scenery of the Ægean coast-lands is as bright and varied as that of Greece itself. . . . The sense of life and vigor is wonderfully quickened in the clear atmosphere and the bright light." (Ramsay) This west coast of Asia Minor, a plain watered by four considerable rivers, was more fertile than most of the islands and the Greek peninsula, where the streams were mere temporary mountain torrents and the soil, though varied, was rather barren. Today the condition is even worse because the surface soil has been washed off as a consequence of deforestation. Even in antiquity the supply of grain, the ancient Greek's chief article of diet, was inadequate for the population, which therefore had to work hard for a living and resort to trade, industry, and colonization. The vine and olive were staple products of the Hellenic world as of the Mediterranean basin generally. Metals were none too abundant and were often imported, but there were fine marbles at hand for building or sculpture and an abundance of potter's clay for Greek vases. The extent to which the scenery of ancient Hellas stirred the imagination of the Greeks is shown by their mythology and literature.

Trade and Colonies

Unproductiveness of the soil at home and overpopulation led the Hellenes to sail to distant lands to procure the commodities they needed or to find a market for their surplus manufactures. Thus the little city of Sicyon on the Gulf of Corinth imported copper from southern Spain for its metal working as early as the sixth century. The Hellenes also planted settlements in such new regions. The philosopher Plato tells us that "when men who have nothing and are in want of food show a tendency to follow their leaders in an attack on the property of the rich, these, who are the natural plague of the state, are sent away by the statesman in as friendly a spirit as possible; and this dismissal of them is euphemistically termed a colony." Indeed, whichever side was defeated in the frequent party strife within the Greek city states and driven into exile might well found, or take refuge in, some new settlement. As the period of the present chapter opens, the region that was being most densely colonized by the Hellenes was the island of Sicily and the coasts of southern Italy. This western Hellas, as it is often called, lay in the same latitude as the Ægean region, had a very similar climate, scenery, and vegetation; indeed, practically formed one world with it. It was as easy for western Hellenes to attend the Olympic games in Elis as it was for the Greeks of Asia Minor to do so. Greek settlements on the shores of the Black Sea supplied the other Hellenes with grain and fish, timber, metals, furs, and gold from the far north, perhaps occasionally with wares from the far east. Other centers of Greek colonization were in Cyprus, the Nile Delta, Cyrene,—where kings reigned, and where excavations have recently been successfully conducted by the Italians,—and on the coasts of Gaul and Spain. In general the Greek colonies kept to the coast but traded with the inland tribes. Thus the influence of Greek civilization was extended through almost the entire Mediterranean and Black Sea basin.

It was the usual practice for a Greek colony to have a mother city which granted it its charter, appointed it a leader, supplied it with sacred fire from the ancestral hearth, and in general arranged for its foundation as parents do for a daughter's wedding. But once founded, most colonies rapidly became politically independent, although ties of religion and kinship might keep alive a sentimental attachment to the home city. On the other hand, colonies sometimes became commercial rivals of the mother city and fought or allied against it. All this illustrates the tendency of each Greek city to be politically and economically an independent unit, ruling as much land around its walls as it needed for its support and was able to control. There were, however, tribes in Greece who had not developed city life, or there were simple neighboring villages which joined in some common worship and used a fortified hilltop as a common citadel. This latter practice, which we shall find also among the early Italians and Gauls, generally resulted eventu-

The Independent Polis or City State

ally in the development of town life. As trade and industry grew, town life became increasingly characteristic of the Hellenic world. But as a rule no state contained more than one city, or if it did, its government centred in one of these cities, which lorded it over the others. Municipal politics and national politics were one and the same. Indeed our very word, politics, comes from the Greek *polis*, meaning a city. Such a Greek *polis* would perhaps have a population of only a few thousands or even hundreds, and many of these might not be citizens, especially if the form of government were aristocratic or oligarchical, or if there were many slaves. The philosopher Aristotle preferred a small population so that every citizen might know the candidates for office, and so that foreigners might not creep in unawares as citizens. Even the smallest *polis* usually had some business life, however, and the scanty space within its walls was densely populated. The citizens were rather exclusive in bestowing citizenship on newcomers and maintained that all existing citizens were of common descent, although this was often a good deal of a fiction. But most of their families had lived there for a long time. Colonies were more ready than the older cities to grant citizenship to other Hellenes and even to the natives of the region where they settled, as these became hellenized. There was no distinction between church and state in the Greek *polis;* all citizens joined in the same religious worship, and this was under the charge of the magistrates and citizen body.

Forms of
Government
These city states went through a period of rapid political development characterized by the overthrow of the monarchy or feudal chieftains of Homeric days, the establishment of aristocracies of the leading families, or oligarchies of the newly rich, or timocracies of those substantial citizens who could equip themselves to serve the state as heavy infantry, or tyrannies founded by able and ambitious individuals who led the populace against the oppressive few. The tyrants usually checked the intense party strife and promoted the economic prosperity and culture of their cities. Sometimes practically all the freeborn native inhabitants secured a share in the government, and then it was called a democracy. Such political terms come to us from Greek usage.

The cities often fought against one another as the invading tribes had done before, especially as there was now the additional motive of commercial rivalry, and each felt free to levy tolls and dues on strangers or to make piratical attacks upon other ships than its own. On the other hand, some leagues were formed for commercial or religious purposes. While each city and locality had its own god or gods, legends, festivals, and other forms of worship, which explains why the religion of all the Hellenes taken together seems so polytheistic, many of these variants were of common origin. Moreover, there were sacred places and oracles which the peoples of different cities and tribes visited and consulted. The most famous oracle was that of Apollo at Delphi, and when the neighboring city of Crisa attempted to monopolize it, other Greek cities united to destroy Crisa and regulate the shrine in common. Other Panhellenic games than the Olympic were instituted in the sixth century. The interurban wars sometimes led to union, the chief city in a given area subduing the others and reducing them to villages and making their inhabitants either citizens or subjects of itself. Thus all the inhabitants of Attica became Athenians; the Spartans extended the Lacedæmonian state over all Laconia and Messenia but reduced the rest of the population to the position of *helots* (serfs) and *periœci* (townsmen without independent political rights); Syracuse destroyed the other Greek cities of southeastern Sicily, either enslaving their populations or admitting them into Syracuse as citizens.

Relations Between Cities: Wars and Leagues

We know the internal life of Sparta and Athens better than that of other ancient Greek cities. Sparta was a Dorian state of the conservative, military, and agricultural type. It profited by a warm climate, the fertile river valley of the Eurotas, and the iron mines of Mount Taygetus. Thus there were many men able to equip themselves with heavy armor and iron weapons. The town had no wall, it was a group of villages rather than a concentrated city area, yet no one dared to attack it. The Spartans lived a military camp life in the open, ate at public tables, and the individual citizen seems to have had no privacy and little home life. The elders and not the father decided whether the infant was physically fit to live. At seven he was taken from his mother and trained in camp life, military drill, foraging, gymnastics, endurance and self-repression, and a certain amount of music and poetry, perhaps largely of a martial character. Children were seen and not

Spartan Customs and Constitution

heard at Sparta, for any elder had the right to chastise them. The Spartans did not care much for speechifying anyway, but were noted for their laconic (from Laconia) witticisms and apothegms.   At twenty the youth joined a military fraternity and eating club, and entered the army.   Not until thirty, however, could he vote in the assembly, not until sixty was he eligible for election to the council of twenty-eight elders.   This predominance of old men helps to explain the conservatism of Sparta.   It retained its two kings throughout its history but added to them five ephors elected annually.   Every Spartan must marry, and the girls were given a gymnastic and athletic training which, in the opinion of the Greek writers, enhanced their beauty.   The position of women was relatively high at Sparta.   They enjoyed more freedom than the men, had little housekeeping to do, and took a part in the national customs such as beating copper kettles when a king died, marching unclad in processions like the boys, and singing choral songs in religious festivals.   Most Spartan customs, however, would seem survivals of the life of the savage tribe rather than an admirable advance in civilization.   And we must not think that the men and boys had an especially hard life.   A man's share of land was six times that of his wife.   The boys lived like boy scouts, which is just what most boys like.   The men spent their time in fighting, athletics, hunting, good eating, politics, and loafing at their clubs drinking wine and making jokes, which are just what most men like.   Trade and industry were in the hands of the *periœci* who also rendered military service in war. Agricultural labor was performed by the *helots*.   The Spartans were forbidden to use any except iron money, probably an instance of taboo, but they too often showed themselves susceptible to bribery.   They were trained collectively as a phalanx to stand their ground in war "with both feet fixed on earth, teeth biting lip," and not to flee "from any multitude of men," but "win the victory or lose their lives,"—to quote the exhortations of one of their poets.   They therefore surpassed any other Greek state in military reputation.

The Peloponnesian League

The Spartans were unable, however, to subdue rugged mountainous Arcadia to the north of them as they had subjected "fertile Messenia" to the west of them.   They therefore abandoned the policy of conquest for one of alliance with Tegea and other communities of Arcadia.   They also made treaties with

the peoples of Elis, with the cities, Sicyon and Corinth, where
oligarchies in sympathy with Sparta overthrew the tyrants,
and with the cities, Trœzen and Epidaurus, which feared the
power of Argos more than they feared Sparta.   Thus was
formed the Peloponnesian League whose members fought under
the leadership of Sparta, which thus outdistanced Argos, its
chief rival in the Peloponnesus, or southernmost part of the
Greek peninsula.   In fact, Sparta conquered the island Cythera
and the coastland Cynuria from Argos and embodied these in
her own territory.   Megara and Ægina joined the league before 500 and Athens at about that time.   Thus it began to
extend beyond the Peloponnesus, but it was never to succeed in
uniting all the Greeks.

The legendary hero and king, Theseus, was reputed to have
united all Attica under the rule of Athens.   The nobles then
substituted for the kingship nine annual archons and the council of the Areopagus.   When the phalanx was introduced, the
larger class who made up the heavy armed infantry came into
power with a general assembly and council of four hundred.
Then Draco wrote out the laws.   But the laws did not benefit
much the poorer classes who still lived mainly by agriculture.
With increasing population it became more and more difficult
to make a living off the soil of Attica, while the theft of a
vegetable or fruit was punishable by death.   The men of the fertile plain were well enough off; the men of the shore might eke
out a living by fishing and trading; but the men of the hills
had to mortgage their lands and were in imminent danger of
falling into the position of the helots at Sparta.

Political Development at Athens

At this juncture (594), the patriot, merchant, poet, and
philosopher, Solon, proposed a series of reforms that today
would make the opponents and advocates of socialism alike gasp.
Yet Solon himself was proud of having protected both parties.
His name has come down in history as the synonym for a wise
statesman and legislator, and his reforms probably helped to
make Athens the future center of culture that it became.   He
nullified the mortgages, freed those in slavery for debt, forbade
henceforth the lending of money on security of the person or
the sale by fathers of other members of the family.   He adopted
a free silver policy, that is to say, a lighter standard of silver coinage, for the Greeks made little use of gold coinage.
To keep down the price of food he forbade the exportation of

Reforms of Solon

agricultural products except olive oil, of which Attica had a surplus. To turn Attica from an agricultural into a manufacturing country he ordered every man to teach his son a trade and promised citizenship to skilled workmen who would settle at Athens. He encouraged the formation of business corporations and made the individual freer to dispose of his property as he chose. To put the law in the hands of the people themselves he instituted the popular courts, or perhaps rather revived and revised the primitive folk courts, admitted the poorer citizens to the assembly but left office-holding to the upper classes, and threatened with disenfranchisement anyone who did not take an active part in politics even to the point of taking sides in party strife and sedition. Far from emancipating women, Solon forbade them to go out nights, and, unlike the Spartan women, they were confined more and more to the home from that time on. The men and boys, on the other hand, spent most of their time away from home, the boys at school, the men in public, but their life was less military and their education was broader than the Spartan. Military training was only from the age of eighteen to twenty.

Through Tyranny to Fuller Democracy

The party strife continued despite Solon's reforms until in 560 Pisistratus, the leader of the hill men, became tyrant. He helped his followers, the poorer people, but also advanced the economic prosperity and culture of the city generally. Of his sons, however, one was assassinated and the survivor finally expelled in 510 by the nobles. The nobles then quarreled with one another, and the final outcome was a more democratic arrangement than that of Solon. Attica was divided into *demes*, and these were grouped in ten new tribes in such a way as to break up the old parties of hill, shore, and plain. To represent these new tribes there was a new council of five hundred, fifty being selected by lot from each tribe, and each fifty acting as *prytanes* or foremen for a tenth of the year. At first the popular assembly met once in each prytany; later there were four regular sessions devoted respectively to oversight of the magistrates, finance, religious matters, and foreign affairs. Other special sessions might be called. Ten generals, one from each tribe, were added to the archons and became the controlling force in war and foreign affairs, although the archons continued to assign cases to the popular courts and to perform other duties. To guard against a tyrant, the practice of ostracism was devised, by which once a year a majority could send any individual whom they deemed dangerous into exile for five or ten years. This of course also constituted a means by which the party in power could rid itself of the leader of the opposition or minority. As time went on, the Athenians elected most of their officials by lot. They also introduced pay for serving in the law courts, for attending the assembly, and for attending the theater, so that the poorer citizens could take the time from their work to perform these judicial, political, and religious duties. On the other hand, the wealthy citizen was assigned such honorable duties as equipping the chorus for a tragedy or comedy, or a trireme for the fleet. If he felt that someone else who had not been assigned such a duty could better afford it than himself, he could propose a complete exchange of property and duty with this person. Anyone could propose a law in the assembly, but he also could be punished for it afterwards if it turned out badly. Officials were examined upon entering and leaving office.

One chief criticism to be made of the Athenian popular assembly and courts is that they were somewhat lacking in detailed knowledge and technical training. So are many legislators and statesmen today, however, and the average Athenian was better informed than the average modern voter. Another criticism is that they were too easily swayed by oratory and subject to emotional reactions and mob psychology. In this respect they seem to have been no worse than aristocracies and oligarchies, and they were rather less greedy and factious. Athens produced abler leaders than Sparta, men such as Miltiades, Themistocles, Aristides, Cimon, and Pericles, but some of them were too ambitious or too tricky and deceitful— a little over-clever. As it turned out, the Athenians were too aggressive in foreign policy, and perhaps they had less sense of individual responsibility than the ruler under a tyranny. That least legitimate of Greek forms of government was often the most efficient in fact. *Estimate of the Athenian Democracy*

In the Athenian popular courts the greatest precaution was taken to prevent corruption of the jurors. Not only was the number of judges for each case or courtroom large, varying from 200 to 2500, but no *dicast* knew until the day came to which courtroom he would be assigned. The method of voting was also by secret ballot, so that no one could take vengeance *The Popular Courts* on a dicast for the way he voted.   The parties to the suit were supposed to plead their own cases, but there were clever speech-writers who would compose orations for them which would sound as if written by themselves.   When the law did not fix a penalty for the offense, both plaintiff and defendant would propose a penalty, and the jury had to take one or the other proposal.   The chief criticism that has been made of the Athenian courts is that when the government had difficulty in paying the dicasts, they were tempted to find persons guilty and fine them heavily so as to provide the wherewithal for their own pay.

Failure of Later Efforts Towards Greek Unity

The Persian monarchy had failed in its attack upon the Greeks of the peninsula, who were hard to get at and who showed themselves superior both in heavy-armed infantry and in seamanship.   Thereupon the Athenians, who had won the land battle of Marathon (490) without Spartan aid and had taken the leading part in subsequent sea-fights, broke away from the Peloponnesian League and put themselves at the head of a new Delian Confederacy.   It was composed of the Greeks of the Ægean islands and west coast of Asia Minor who had recently fallen under Persian rule and who were now being freed there-from.   This confederacy, in which at first each member had something like an equal voice, the Athenians rapidly trans-formed into an empire of their own and spent the surplus funds chiefly at Athens.   Such conduct caused revolt among their al-lies and discontent on the part of the other Hellenes, leading finally to the Peloponnesian War (431–404) in which Athens and its allies and Sparta and hers, including even numerous cities of western Hellas, fought for many years and greatly exhausted their resources.   In consequence Macedon, an al-most barbarous monarchy to the north of the Greek peninsula, ultimately gained the ascendancy.   Two later leagues, the Achæan and the Ætolian, combined a number of Greek cities for protection against Macedon.   But Sparta and Athens did not join them.   Moreover, these leagues were usually hostile to each other, their spheres of influence did not extend outside the Greek peninsula itself, and they both finally succumbed to the power of Rome.

Social and Economic Conditions

When Athens was at the height of its power, the total popula-tion of Attica was probably between 250,000 and 350,000, but about one-third were slaves, and there was also a large number

of resident foreigners or *metics,* for as Athens prospered she became less generous in bestowing the citizenship. The slaves
were well treated, worked together with citizens and *metics*
on temples, and were as well clothed as the poorer citizens.
Artisans such as smiths, potters, shoemakers, curriers, manufacturers of lyres and bucklers, leapt from bed at cockcrow to
go to work. There was considerable subdivision of labor. The
cook had his assistant, and separate slaves set the table and
went marketing, but pastry cooks were not yet distinguished
from ordinary bakers, as they came to be in Roman times. The
process of treating wool was subdivided between those who
washed it, those who plucked and combed it, the women who
spun it, and the fullers. Different cities specialized in the
manufacture of different kinds of cloaks, robes, and mantles.
Different workmen turned out men's and women's shoes or cut
and sewed the leather. In ceramics some specialized in human
and animal figures, others in lamps, others in bricks and tiles,
and different potters made different shapes of vases. Wages
varied from the three obols (about ten cents) which constituted
the daily fee of the Athenian juror to a drachma or two a day
(twenty to forty cents). A simple wheat or barley diet was
combined with a few greens, onions, garlic, or olives and oil for
relish, and with wine for a beverage. Most of the population
lived in very narrow quarters; a space perhaps twelve or eighteen feet square and divided into two or four rooms, opening
directly on the street. Often these were partly cut into the
native rock, which formed the floor and lower part of the walls.
These were carried up further in wood, crude brick, and tiles.
Herodotus noted the Egyptian custom of eating meals out-
doors but retiring indoors for less seemly necessities as the
direct antithesis of Greek custom. There was no sanitary
plumbing as in the palace at Cnossus.

The ancient Greek attitude towards the retail merchant and
middleman compared to the cultivator or artisan or shipowner
seems to have been normally one of silent contempt. Plato,
however, once spoke out, saying that no one would earn his
living in that way if he could help it. Plato, nevertheless, recognized that such middlemen were a convenience,
asking, "Supposing that a husbandman or an artisan brings
some product to market and he comes at a time when there
is no one to exchange it with, is he to leave his calling and

Retailers,
Capital and
Banking

sit idle in the market-place?"   In Athens such occupations were generally left to the resident foreigners, but they were subject to state surveillance and severe penalties.   For example, if a retail dealer in grain purchased more than fifty measures at a time, he could be put to death.   There were few very rich men in Athens, and its total private capital wealth was less than that of many individuals today.   The state owned such sources of wealth as the silver mines at Laurium.   Private banks now came into existence in addition to temples as places of safe deposit, and letters of credit were given.   But many people long preferred to bury their treasure.

Woman and the Family   Woman was restricted to the home at Athens, yet its civilization is reckoned much superior to that of Sparta where woman was freer.   Socrates dismissed his weeping wife and children in order to spend his last moments philosophizing with his male friends and disciples.   Sappho was the one poetess of note; the other writers and artists as well as philosophers were all men, though many of the statues are of women, and some of the noblest characters in the drama are female. The literature further lays much stress upon family ties, and the Greeks lavished much care and affection upon their children.   The exposure of infants was probably not common except in cases of illegitimate birth and of the deformed and idiotic, since parents usually wished to perpetuate the family and to assure future sacrifice at their tomb.   There was a celebration on the tenth day after the child's birth; the toys of Greek children have been preserved; if their parents could afford it, a slave accompanied them to and from school to shield them from any evil influence.   Like the Spartans the boys were trained in graceful manners, modesty, and music; they learned to read and write and to play the lyre; they memorized the Homeric poems, received physical education in the *palæstra*, and, if they were not given special instruction in public speaking and philosophy, could almost drink in these and art all around them.   From this cultured life in public the girls were excluded; little is known of their early training, but they married at an earlier age than the men.   Xenophon in his *Economist*, which should now rather be translated *Domestic Scientist*, represents a husband as instructing his fifteen-year-old wife in her household duties.   A woman in a well-to-do household had a number of servants and slaves to manage, and such matters

ARCHAIC
SCULPTURE
Left, archaic female statue from the Acropolis, Athens.
Right, Athenian woman of the 6th century B. C.

THE GREEK THEATER
Above, front seats for priests in the Theater of Dionysus at Athens;
below, the Theater at Epidaurus, dating from the 4th century, B. C.

to superintend as spinning, making of clothing, grinding of meal and baking of bread, and care of sick slaves.

Pericles in his famous funeral oration on the Athenian dead in the first year of the Peloponnesian War asserted that Athens was the school of Hellas, that her citizens had the ideal combination of physical and mental training, were not ashamed to work, and combined individual liberty with patriotic service of the state. "For we are lovers of the beautiful, yet simple in our tastes, and we cultivate the mind without loss of manliness." We next turn to this Greek cultivation of the mind and of the beautiful.

Athenian Ideals

BIBLIOGRAPHY

Ardaillon, E. *Les mines du Laurion dans l'antiquité,* 1897.

Bonner, R. J. *Evidence in Athenian Courts,* 1905.

Brandt, L. R. *Social Aspects of the Greek Life in the Sixth Century B. C.,* 1921.

Bury, J. B. *History of Greece,* 1913.

Dickinson, G. L. *The Greek View of Life,* 1910.

Donaldson, J. *Woman, her Position and Influence in Ancient Greece,* 1907.

Fairbanks, A. *Handbook of Greek Religion,* 1910.

Farnell, L. R. *Higher Aspects of Greek Religion,* 1912.

Fowler, W. W. *The City State of the Greeks and Romans,* 1904.

Freeman, K. J. *Schools of Hellas,* 1912.

Francotte, *L'industrie dans la Grèce ancienne,* 1901.

Fustel de Coulanges, *The Ancient City,* 1901.

Gardiner, E. N. *Greek Athletic Sports and Festivals,* 1910.

Glotz, G. *Le Travail dans le Grèce ancienne,* 1920.

Greenidge, A. H. J. *Handbook of Greek Constitutional History,* 1902.

Guiraud, *Études économiques sur l'antiquité,* 1900; *La main-d'œuvre industrielle dans l'ancienne Grèce,* 1900; *Les finances de cités grecques.*

Gulick, C. B. *Life of the Ancient Greeks,* 1903.

Hasebroek, J. "Zum griechische Bankwesen," in *Hermes,* 55 (1920) 113–73.

Herdst, P. *Le travail de la femme dans la Grèce ancienne,* 1922.

Holm, A. *History of Greece,* 4 vols.

Livingstone, *The Greek Genius and its Meaning to Us,* 1915.

Mahaffy, J. P. *Survey of Greek Civilization,* 1896.

Moore, C. H. *Religious Thought of the Greeks,* 1916.

Morgan, M. H. *Eight Orations of Lysias,* 1895; "Introduction."

Plutarch, *Lives of Illustrious Men.*

Preisigke, *Girowesen im griech. Aegypten,* 1910.

Seltman, C. T. *The Temple Coins of Olympia,* 1922.

Toynbee, A. J.   *Greek Civilization and Character,* 1923.

Ure, P. N.   *Origin of Tyranny,* 1922.

Wallon,   *Histoire de l'esclavage dans l'antiquité,* 1879, 3 vols.

Zimmern, A. E.   *The Greek Commonwealth,* 1911; a very interesting work, from which I have made some quotations in the foregoing chapter.

CHAPTER X

GREEK LITERATURE AND PHILOSOPHY

The simple, childlike frame of mind, the naïve way of looking at the world which the Greeks possessed, are irrevocably things of the past.—Herder

GREEK is perhaps the most beautiful and flexible of the Indo-European languages. The prominence of vowels makes it musical; the frequent use of particles enables it to express "fine distinctions and light shades of meaning." "No one who is a stranger to Greek literature has seen how perfect an instrument it is possible for human speech to be." Of the Homeric poems we have already treated. They represented an age of epic poetry. This was followed in the seventh and sixth centuries by a lyric age; in the fifth century dramatic poetry became the leading form of literature; while prose, historical, philosophical, and oratorical, began in the fifth century and became predominant in the fourth. The literary forms of course only roughly correspond to the centuries and overlap one another.

The Greek Language

Lyric poetry, strictly speaking, is that intended to be recited to the accompaniment of the lyre, though the flute often replaced the lyre. The expression is further extended to include all poetry in which the poet primarily expresses his own feelings and emotions, or even his opinions and reflections, as distinct from epic poetry, which tells a story, usually of the heroic past and in an objective manner, so that we have no clue to the personality of the author. The period of lyric poetry, in this sense, is from about 700 to 470 when it culminated in Pindar. The poets used various other meters than the dactylic hexameter of the epics, such as the elegiac and iambic meters. Some of the poems are much less truly lyrical than others, since anyone who composed any sort of a literary work in this period as a matter of course put it in metrical form. Prose writing did not begin until about the close of

Lyric Poetry

117

the sixth century B. C.   Before the invention of printing there
was a considerable advantage in composing in verse.   Not
only was it easier to memorize, but if, in copying it by hand,
one made mistakes, it was easier to catch them afterwards and
restore the right word or spelling which would fit into the
meter.   We must further remember that the music of the Greeks
was different from ours.   In singing they do not seem to have
exceeded the range of the normal speaking voice.   Measure and
quantity counted for a great deal both in poetry and music.
So it is probable that they could "sing" in their way with
fair success more of the poetry of the lyric age than we might
think.   In its broadest sense ancient Greek music included all
those intellectual arts presided over by the nine Muses.

The Lyric Poets

We know the names of a number of poets from these two
early centuries and something of their personalities and themes,
but for the most part we have only brief fragments of their
compositions.   These reflect the stirring life of the times, the
political parties and strife, reforms such as those of Tyrtæus
at Sparta and of Solon at Athens, barbarian inroads, colonization, and exile, or the more private joys of wine, women,
and song.   Some of the poetry is satirical, either at the expense of individuals or of the female sex.   We have fragments
by lawgivers, moralizers, and philosophers; by nobles, com-
moners, and courtiers of tyrants; by warriors, lovers, mourners,
and wine-bibbers.   Many of the poets employed the Ionic dialect, others used the Æolic or Doric.   Ionia, on the west coast
of Asia Minor, was a leading center of culture both in poetry
and philosophy in this early period.

Choral Poetry: Bacchylides and Pindar

The Dorians especially developed choral poetry to be sung
by the people in processions or choruses and accompanied by
dancing.   Its meters are more varied and intricate than those
of individual utterances.   Sometimes the chorus engaged in
dialogue with a single singer or its leader, which brings us to
the verge of dramatic poetry.   The two lyric poets of whose
work we have the most considerable remains are also among the
latest in time, Bacchylides of Ceos, who flourished about 476,
and Pindar of Bœotia, 521–441.   They composed a great
variety of poems, but are especially known for their odes of
victory in connection with the Greek national games, in which
they make much use of mythological allusion and a high-

sounding diction of compound words and "epithets like wrecked rainbows."

We have seen that dramatic dances and performances are almost universal among savage peoples, and that tiers of steps, which look as if they might have been seats for witnessing theatrical exhibitions, have been excavated in the prehistoric palace at Cnossus. But the earliest complete specimens of tragedy and comedy are those composed in Attic Greek for Athenian festivals of Dionysus, the wine god. Thus they were closely connected with religion and public life, drawing their subjects and characters from the myths, and being thought of, like primitive tribal initiations and assemblies, as something that all the citizens ought to attend. According to Aristotle's *Poetics*, which, aside from the dramas themselves, is our chief source of information concerning the origin of dramatic literature in Attic Greek, the drama developed from the dithyramb or choral ode to Dionysus. Costumes and dancing of the chorus long remained an important element in the success of a Greek drama, which was often named after the chorus rather than an individual character. In some of the comedies of Aristophanes the chorus represented birds, frogs, wasps, and clouds. The earliest Greek dramatists were called dancers rather than authors, actors, or playwrights. The addition of dialogue made the change from dithyramb to drama. Our word, "hypocrite," comes from the Greek word for an actor, but the original meaning of the Greek word was "answerer," that is, a person who replied to the chorus or its leader. The introduction of a second actor is ascribed to Æschylus, the earliest of the three great Greek tragedians; that of a third and fourth actor, to Sophocles.

Usually, however, there were not more than three actors or "answerers" or interlocutors in a drama. That is to say, there were not more than three speaking parts on the stage at once, although one actor might successively fill several parts. Masks were worn for this purpose, and the tragic actors, since they commonly represented gods or great personages, wore very thick-soled buskins and high headdresses to give them greater height and grandeur, and seem to have moved about with slow stateliness. Women's parts were taken by men. These devices show that little attempt was made at acting in our sense of facial expression and animated gesture, although the latter perhaps marked the dancing of the chorus. Battles and other such actions were not presented before the audience but were recounted in epic style by a messenger, who also commonly reported murders, suicides, and other shocking events. The chorus sang its odes and moved about in a full circle known as the orchestra or dancing-ground, which only in later Hellenistic and Roman theaters was reduced in size to a half circle. The Greek theater was in the open air. The actors, at first, entered the orchestra from a booth or tent which served as a dressing-room, while the audience sat on wooden seats on the hillside opposite. With the fourth century B. C. the encircling seats began to be built of marble, and the "scene," as the aforesaid booth had been called, became a permanent structure with a raised platform, upon which, in Roman times, the actors appeared. Behind this a high stage wall was erected, which could be used for a scenic, or at least an architectural background.

Greek Tragedy

A Greek tragedy dealt with violent death or some other sorrowful and terrifying theme and was marked by brevity and simple grandeur. The ending, however, does not always mark the climax of woe, but sometimes offers a solution or relief from the previous griefs and horrors. We have seven complete plays each by Æschylus and Sophocles, eighteen and a proportionally large number of fragments by Euripides who was the more copied and quoted by subsequent writers. Æschylus was perhaps the most sublime, conservative, high-sounding, and obscure of the three. Sophocles showed the greatest artistic skill in dramatic structure. Euripides was both the most intellectual and most pathetic, and introduced the love interest and something more akin to a plot. The Greek tragedies are in a sense finely conceived works of art, but the modern reader will find the three great tragedians mere tyros in many matters of stagecraft and psychological finesse. They made characters say things of themselves that would better have been said about them, or were guilty of anachronisms and other incongruities and improbabilities. There were intermediate steps yet to be taken before our conception of the drama was attained. Attic tragedy of the fifth century B. C. had something of the character of Grand Opera, or of a ritualistic church service, with music and choruses, readings and responses.

The comedies of Aristophanes, on the other hand, were more Aristoph-anes like a musical comedy of today or a farce and burlesque; lampooning the politicians, poets, and philosophers of his own time, and treating even gods and demigods with easy familiarity and broad humor. His method has often been compared to that of the cartoonist and caricaturist in our modern newspapers.

After all it is best to realize that the ancient Greeks were Euripides ancient Greeks, that most English translations of the Attic dramatists are unsatisfactory. In the case of Euripides, for instance, translators add to his words and detract from his thought. His wording is far from flowery, and he uses a few adjectives over and over again. But his simple and severe diction is something like those Elgin marbles from the frieze of the Parthenon, which achieve perfection with few chiseled lines and despite bare surfaces where the sculptor seems scarcely to have touched the stone. So a literal translation seems barren, awkward, and halting, while a literary or poetical translation makes one think of Minerva's helmet being replaced by modern millinery. The fact is that we must divest ourselves of over twenty-three centuries' accumulation of vocabulary, ideas, and experience before we try to translate Euripides. Really to appreciate his eighteen extant plays and numerous fragments we must see them, like some cluster of Doric columns that still stand amid the ruins of an ancient temple, against their own cloudless Attic sky. Thus viewed, they give us a remarkable picture of what people were thinking about, or what Euripides made them think about, and the various opinions which they held,—for his different characters express different views,—twenty-three hundred years ago. Religion, politics, war, social classes, the position of woman, family relations, and intellectual activity are constantly made the subject of sententious utterance or animated debate as in few modern plays. The economic side of life alone seems neglected. On the whole we form a very high opinion of "the scenic philosopher" and of the intelligent audiences who could appreciate such serious discussion and inquiry on the stage.

Confucius, in distant China, had edited the *Book of History* Herodotus and composed the *Spring and Autumn Annals* before Herodotus was born about 484 at Halicarnassus in southwestern Asia Minor. Yet there is some reason for leaving to Herodotus his customary title, the father of history. Not only is he the oldest extant Greek historian, but he was the first to apply the word "history," which in Greek meant "inquiry," to his work, thus introducing the ideal of historical investigation. His work would probably be held by most critics superior to the two Confucian classics and to the Babylonian chronicles in unity of design, fulness of treatment, and literary art. It is, at any rate, our first considerable example of Greek prose. The theme which Herodotus investigated was the recent great struggle between the Greeks and Persia and the rise and expansion of the Persian Empire which had led up to that struggle. He treated of the foundation of that empire by Cyrus, the early relations of the Greeks with the kings of Lydia before the conquest of Asia Minor by Cyrus, the Persian conquest of Egypt, Libya, and Cyrene, the expedition of Darius, king of Persia, through Thrace against the Scythians or northern barbarians, the revolt of the Greeks in Asia Minor from Persia, the consequent unsuccessful Persian campaigns in the Greek peninsula, and the famous battles of Marathon, Artemisium, Thermopylæ, Salamis, Platæa, and Mycale. To investigate this theme Herodotus traveled widely to the lands involved and, since their customs and civilization were little known to most of his Greek hearers, gave an account of them. In this connection he could sometimes state what he had seen, but as the events with which he was dealing had all occurred before he was born or while he was still a little child, he for the most part tells us simply what he has heard. Many of the tales that he tells were to be repeated by subsequent writers, and we may be almost equally sure that they had been told many times in the centuries before Herodotus. He says that he does not quite believe it all himself but that he must tell it. Indeed, very seldom can he resist the temptation of digressing from his main theme to tell an interesting or amusing anecdote. On the other hand, the reader of an ordinary history of Greece will note how much more dramatically the events begin to succeed one another when the modern author approaches the period of the Persian Wars and is caught in the flow of Herodotus' narrative. Herodotus has selected his materials, perhaps even violated the true chronological order, or modified details with an eye to the total effect. He does not take social forces enough into account, and makes too much of personal motives and of individual love and family affairs. He is too superstitious, and especially delights in tales

of ambiguous oracles which came true in unexpected ways.   He
holds up clever deceit and double-dealing, such as that of Themistocles, to the reader's admiration, and censures Aristagoras
"who in other respects acted cleverly and imposed upon him
well," but "in this point made a mistake, for . . . he . . . told
him the truth."   Yet it does not seem that Herodotus himself
is cleverly deceiving us in his History; he appears impartial
and ingenuous.   But the faults of superstition and deceitful-
ness are the more important to note because they were characteristic of his audience; he was simply giving the Greeks what
they liked, and we must keep in mind the mythology, popular
legends, and epic poetry from which he had to break away.

Thucydides, who thought that men were "too ready to re-   **Thucydides**
ceive ancient traditions" and "the tales of chroniclers who seek
to please the ear rather than to speak the truth," preferred to
write the history of his own time.   When the great Peloponnesian War between Athens and the Peloponnesian League
broke out in 431, he began to keep a record of it.   In 424 he
was so unsuccessful as one of the generals in the actual conduct
of the war that his suspicious fellow-Athenians sent him into
exile.   This enabled him, however, to travel, to devote all his
time to historical investigation, and to hear both sides.   He
seems to have sifted the evidence critically and usually to have
reached accurate conclusions.   Although he lived through the
war, and was recalled to Athens in 403 after its close, he did not
complete his account, leaving the last years (411–404) untold.
Thucydides indulged little in anecdote, and his account is more
sober than that of Herodotus.   He did not grasp the underly-
ing social and economic factors much more than had his predecessor, and he is not such easy reading on account of his more
condensed and involved style, which is more weighted with ideas
and less relieved by a sense of humor.   In this respect, and in
the many set speeches which he puts in the mouths of the leading men, he suggests the new learning and rhetoric of his time.
Thucydides boasted that his work would not be a momentary
popular success, but a possession for all time.   Von Ranke, a
celebrated historian during the nineteenth century, is said to
have read Thucydides' masterly account of the tragic Sicilian
expedition of the Athenians once every year.   It is to be regretted, however, that Thucydides devoted himself so exclusively
to the subject of warfare.   Doubtless that stirring theme most

absorbed the audience of his own day, but his work would have been of greater value for all time had he included more such glimpses of the civilization and ideals of ancient Hellas as those we catch in the Funeral Oration of Pericles. The history of Thucydides was continued from 411 to 362 in an inferior manner by Xenophon, another Athenian, who was exiled because of his leanings towards Sparta.

Oratory

Oratory and rhetoric seem to have received their first considerable development in the fifth century in Sicily, where we hear of Corax of Syracuse as the first teacher of eloquence, and of Gorgias of Leontini who wrote a rhythmical prose and who elaborated the period, or harmoniously divided sentence with carefully balanced clauses, carefully arranged phrases, and carefully selected words. Or two sentences might balance each other. Gorgias traveled about the Greek world and taught for some time at Athens. With its popular assembly and popular courts and large citizen body, Athens was a place where one would expect public speaking to flourish, and our extant specimens of Greek eloquence are largely by Attic orators of the fourth century. Lysias is of especial interest because he was a *metic* or resident foreigner and was not admitted to citizenship until 403 when he was about forty years of age, because he wrote speeches for others to deliver in lawsuits as well as some of his own, and because these speeches are not only skilfully adapted to the character of the person concerned but also deal with varied sides of the civilization of the times. Most famous of all the Attic orators was Demosthenes whose eloquence directed the unavailing struggle against the menacing power of Macedon.

Pre-Socratic Philosophy

Greek philosophy developed out of mythology and poetry. The first poets, Homer and Hesiod, were much concerned with theology and cosmology, with the gods and the universe. The first philosophers wrote in verse, telling the story of the evolution of the universe in epic style or musing over life's problems in reflective elegiacs or some other form of lyric poetry. But they began to reason, to seek a natural and rational, rather than supernatural and mythological, explanation why things are as they are. Aside from the seven sages, famous for their pithy precepts concerning the practical conduct of life, the Greek thinkers of the first period before Socrates were especially concerned with the problem of how the material world had come into being, and their first tendency was to explain it as an evolution from some one primal substance, which Thales of Miletus (640–548) held to be water, and Anaximenes (580–524) held to be air.   Anaximander, who came between these two in point of time, is reported to have taught among other things that men were first produced in fishes, and, when they were grown up and able to help themselves, were thrown out, and so lived upon land.   This doctrine is an amusing cross between the story of Jonah and the whale and the modern doctrine of the evolution of life on the edge of the land.   Pythagoras, who went from Samos to southern Italy, taught that number was the fundamental principle in the universe, and that life should be harmoniously regulated by music and mathematics.   The doctrine of perfect numbers, or magic numbers, is ascribed to him.   His followers in Italy formed political clubs and observed ascetic regulations.   This asceticism and his doctrine of the transmigration of souls may perhaps be ascribed to influences from India.   Xenophanes attacked Greek polytheism, holding that God was infinite, eternal, and unchangeable, and tending to identify God with the universe.   Parmenides argued that the whole universe is eternal and unchangeable, although he admitted that it seemed to change and wrote an account of this apparent evolution.   But he contended that change and motion were delusions of the senses.   Heracleitus, on the other hand, believed that the world, while eternal, was never at rest or the same but constantly changing.   In addition to the general theories which we are very briefly indicating, these thinkers are further credited with many particular views concerning nature or dicta dealing with philosophy and life.   They tended to be dogmatic, but also observed natural phenomena to some extent. Thales predicted an eclipse, and Xenophanes noted the existence of marine fossils high up on mountains.   Unfortunately we possess only fragments of their works and are largely dependent upon what much later writers said of them, which is sometimes none too reliable.

Empedocles, in the fifth century, claimed the power to work miracles like a god, and affirmed the existence of four elements, earth, air, fire, and water, from which all compounds are composed.   This beautifully simple explanation of nature, so easy for everyone to understand, persisted among men of science into the eighteenth century, and popularly into the nineteenth cen-

Elements
and Atoms

tury of our era.   Back in the fifth century B. C. we also find a
form of the atomic theory put forward by Leucippus and De-
mocritus.   Their atoms were indivisible particles, infinite in
number.   Instead of the varying atomic weights of which modern chemistry speaks, their atoms were supposed to vary in size
and shape, and to enter into varying combinations accordingly.
Everything in the universe was thought of as made up of such
atoms, and there was a theory of evolution to account for the
building up of things from them.   Anaxagoras then introduced
the conception of *Nous,* or directing intelligence, which had
brought order out of primeval chaos.

The
Sophists

In the later fifth century the sophists, as distinct from the
previous philosophers, represented a sceptical reaction against
the conflicting theories and general disagreement of past teaching.   This was combined with the teaching for fees of argu-
mentation and oratory, of dialectic and rhetoric.   In short, the
sophists gave the impression that nothing was absolutely and
universally true, and that it was less important to have convictions of your own than to be able to persuade others, to win
your case, to get the better of your adversary.   Man, said
Protagoras, is the measure of all things.   Nothing exists, argued Gorgias: or if anything does exist, it cannot be known;
or if it can be known, we cannot express our knowledge and
communicate it to others.   Thus the sophists turned attention
from the material universe to noetics and the problems of
thought and knowledge.

Socrates

Socrates resembled the sophists in rejecting the previous
philosophy and in reliance on argument and discussion as a
method.   But he scorned mere pretense and rhetoric, which he
regarded as an intellectual cosmetic.   He assumed the attitude
of a seeker for truth rather than a dogmatic teacher, appealing
to others for their ideas.   Nevertheless, his repeated questions,
objections, and irony soon convinced them that they did not
possess the knowledge or the definite ideas they had supposed.
It was not concerning the constitution or evolution of the
universe that he questioned them, but concerning such general
conceptions as justice, beauty, manliness, honor, and temper-
ance, which are supposed to serve as a basis for conduct.   Socrates' chief object, in other words, was to define and establish
moral standards, and to dispel loose hazy thinking on such matters.   If men only really knew what was right, he thought that

they would do it.   The Athenians, however, who did not appreciate his efforts to reform their thinking on life's fundamentals,
in 399 condemned him to death by drinking hemlock on a charge
of having corrupted the youth of Athens and denied the existence of the gods.   His dignified, uncompromising defense
before the democratic popular court, his refusal to entertain
schemes for his escape from prison, his saintly death, a martyr
to the great cause of free speech and free thought, discussing
philosophy to the very last with his followers:—these are portrayed with a master hand in the *Dialogues* of his disciple,
Plato.

Plato (427–347), of wealthy and noble family, was Socrates' Plato
pupil from his twenty-first to his twenty-eighth year.   Following the execution of his master he traveled to Megara, Cyrene,
Egypt, southern Italy and Sicily, and perhaps thus came under
the influence of oriental and Pythagorean thought.   Returning to Athens in 387, he transformed the Academy on the outskirts of that town from an athletic field into a school of
ideas—quite the reverse of the process going on in many American colleges.   With his original, imaginative, poetic genius, his
beautiful Greek style, his artistic dramatic presentation, his
lofty, aspiring, spiritual character, he almost combined philosophy and dramatic poetry into one, and is a successor of Euripides as well as of Socrates.   He did not, like Socrates, reject
earlier physical speculation, but combined previous theories with
daring fancies of his own and with echoes of oriental religious
teaching concerning the soul.   He continued the Socratic emphasis upon general concepts.   For Plato, for instance, the important thing in a statue was not the marble but the conception
worked into the marble by the artist.   The important quality
in a general was the degree of generalship that he displayed.
All particular instances of just conduct were mere manifestations of an abstract justice.   Different men are possessed by
the same ideas; the men die; the ideas persist and take hold of
other men.   Ideas for Plato are thus not merely states of consciousness but permanent realities, and finite things are real
only as they share in such perfect patterns or class types.
Man can best occupy himself in contemplation of these ideas
or idealism.   Philosophy, for example, may well begin with the
impassioned contemplation of beauty, and much attention was
given by Plato to æsthetics.   He spoke also of "the limitless

ocean of beauty," and advised his students to "beget in the beautiful." Aside from his more general theories, Plato's works abound in shrewd incisive remarks and flashes of insight, of which we cannot do better than quote a few. "The makers of fortunes have a second love of money as a creation of their own, resembling the affection of authors for their own poems, or of parents for their children." "Let early education be a sort of amusement." On the other hand, "Youth is the time of toil." However, "a freeman ought to be a freeman in the acquisition of knowledge," and, "knowledge which is acquired under compulsion has no hold on the mind." The following is a brief definition of the essential nature of magic that cannot be bettered: "Yes, said he, whatever deceives may be said to enchant." Finally let us quote, "That lie is the worst of which the liar is unaware, for it is inside the soul."

Hippocratic Medicine

The development of medicine in the Greek world as a secular profession, distinct from the priesthood and temples and allied with biological and physiological interest, is associated with the name of Hippocrates, about 460 to 377 B. C., whom Plato once or twice mentions. The Hippocratic oath is still taken by persons admitted to the practice of medicine. Some, at least, of the writings ascribed to Hippocrates are really of later date.

Aristotle

Plato's pupil, Aristotle (384–322), combined the scientific and philosophical spirit, and was also no mean historian, telling us much of the past development of Greek governments and of the origin of tragedy as well as of the views of earlier philosophers. He criticized Plato's theory of ideas as class types, holding that the universe is nothing substantial, that the essence cannot be external to the particular things of which it is the essence, that phenomena are not produced by ideas, and that individual things are alone real in the full sense of the word. Yet Aristotle as a philosopher continued to occupy himself quite largely with ideas. He summarized the principles of the art of logic in a form that was to hold the field for some two thousand years. His *Physics* was almost as theoretical as his *Metaphysics*, and his *Ethics* consisted largely in the right exercise of reason, although involving further a theory of the will. Aristotle also believed in the scientific study, observation, description, and classification of particular things, as his *History of Animals* shows us, and in collecting a mass of facts upon which to base conclusions.   In biology he was an accurate observer and acute classifier, and anticipated some modern discoveries concerning fishes.   In his psychological treatises he deals more with actual phenomena, such as sleep and waking, than with problematic matters like the divine origin and immortality of the soul, which Plato had set forth so appealingly. Aristotle's matter-of-fact, unimaginative, scientific style has nothing of Plato's poetic fire, but his works are a great storehouse of information and of training in thinking, and were to exert a tremendous future influence.

BIBLIOGRAPHY

Most of the Greek authors referred to in this chapter will be found in more than one English translation. There are also various histories of Greek literature by Jebb, Jevons, Mahaffy, Capps, Fowler, Symonds, and others. For the history of Greek philosophy the works of Zeller and Gomperz' *Greek Thinkers* are best. A few more specific references are:

Bakewell, C. M. *Source Book in Ancient Philosophy,* 1909.

Butcher, S. H. *Some Aspects of the Greek Genius,* 1916.

Cornford, F. M. *Origin of Attic Comedy,* 1914; emphasizes its relation to primitive magic. *From Religion to Philosophy,* 1912.

Easby-Smith, J. S. *Songs of Alcæus,* 1901.

Edmonds, J. M. *New Fragments of Alcæus, Sappho, and Corinna,* 1909; *Lyra Græca,* 1922.

Flickinger, R. C. *The Greek Theater and its Drama,* 1918.

Goodall, T. C. *Athenian Tragedy,* 1920.

Haigh, A. E. *Tragic Drama of the Greeks,* 1896.

James, H. R. *Our Hellenic Heritage,* 1921–24.

Kenyon, Sir F. *Greek Papyri, and their contribution to classical Literature,* 1918.

Patrick, M. M. *Sappho and the Island of Lesbos,* 1912.

Powell, J. U. and Barber, E. A. *New Chapters in the History of Greek Literature,* 1921; treats of recently discovered authors and works.

Ridgeway, W. *Origin of Tragedy,* 1910; would trace it exclusively to funeral rites.

Smyth, H. Weir. *Greek Melic Poets,* 1900.

Toynbee, A. J. *Greek Civilization and Character,* 1924. *Greek Historical Thought from Homer to Heraclius,* 1924; two volumes of translated extracts from Greek authors.

Windelband, W. *History of Philosophy,* 1895, Parts I and II.

CHAPTER XI

GREEK ART

We are lovers of the beautiful, yet simple in our tastes.

—Thucydides

Greek
Vases:
Their Uses
and Manu-
facture

CLASSICAL Greek art developed as a new growth after the dark ages of decline into which the Cretan and Mycenæan art of the Ægean world had disappeared. As practically the only remains of art in this region between 1000 and 700 are pottery decorated in the rude geometric style, we may treat first of the further development of Greek vase-painting. Whether plain or painted, Greek pottery was made to use, and not merely to look at. It has been well said that the Greeks had no bric-a-brac. Like so many material remains of the past, the Greek vases have been preserved especially in the sacred precincts of the tomb. They were employed, however, not only to hold the ashes or offerings, but to store food, wine, and oil, as table dishes, toilet receptacles, dedications at temples, prizes at athletic games, standard measures, and children's toys. At Athens the export of wine and olive oil seems often to have been economically combined with that of the painted vases used to contain those commodities. The shapes of the vases varied greatly with their purpose (for some standard shapes see the *Encyclopedia Britannica*, Eleventh edition, "Ceramics," page 713, Fig. 15). Potters and vase-painters are shown at work with their slaves or assistants on some of the vases. Sometimes the vases bear the signatures of their makers, who at Athens often seem to have been illiterate foreigners. The design to be painted was usually first outlined with a sharply pointed instrument. It is uncertain of what material the brush was made with which the painting was done, although for some very delicate and true straight lines a single bristle was perhaps used.

Develop-
ment of
Vase-
Painting

In the seventh and early sixth centuries the vase-painting was still archaic, but human and animal figures and oriental motives replaced the previous geometric decoration. Crete and the

130

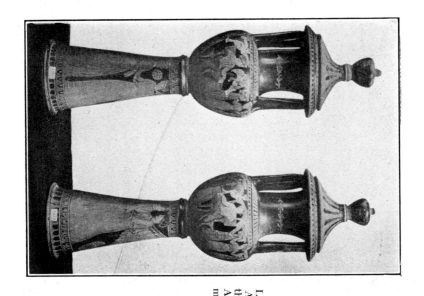

Left, nuptial vases, Athens; right, Stele from the Piraeus, an ancient Athenian funeral monument.

THE PARTHENON

Cyclades, Rhodes and Ionia in Asia Minor, Corinth in the Greek peninsula were now the centers of decorative art. At Corinth in the sixth century was developed the black figure style, in which the figures were painted in black upon a background of red or cream. Incidentally we may note that in the same century Corinth was one of the first Greek cities to mint coins with a beautiful series of designs. In the fifth century Athens became the great center of vase manufacture, and already before the Persian wars had developed the red figure style, in which the figures were left the natural color of the clay, and the background around them was filled in with the shining black. Meanwhile archaic stiffness and conventionality had been outgrown. The fifth century artists showed great improvement in drawing, composition, and decorative effect; and Greek vase-painting attained its period of perfection. As in Greek sculpture, so in vase-painting human figures soon came to predominate. At first they appear mainly in mythological scenes, but in the fifth century scenes from daily life are frequent. Usually each person and object is shown by itself in detached outline, and there is little background or perspective. After the defeat of Athens in the Peloponnesian War that city declined as a center of vase-painting. Most specimens of the fourth and third centuries are found in Sicily or southern Italy and are too florid and theatrical, with their gaudy colors, effeminate forms, even in the male figures, and excessively rich draperies. Then vase-painting died out entirely, much as stained glass later disappeared at the close of the middle ages. The vase-painters were not regarded in antiquity as either the social or artistic equals of the great painters such as Apelles and Protagenes. Since the works of the latter are not extant, we have to form our ideas of Greek painting mainly from the vases, although the aim in vase-painting was decorative rather than pictorial.

In the oldest building of the Hellenic or classical Greek period of which there are any remains, the *Heræum* at Olympia, the superstructure was of sun-dried brick and the columns were of wood. The change to stone came in the seventh century, while tiles for roofing were invented at Corinth. The stone at first employed was generally a soft lime-stone full of shells, known as poros-stone. Marble was introduced towards the close of the sixth century. The chief achievement of Greek

The Greek Temple

architecture was the temple, and the chief feature of the temple was the peristyle of sturdy, yet gracefully fluted, Doric columns around the four sides of its rectangle.   On the broad flat capitals of these columns rested the stone blocks of the architrave; above this strip of unadorned stone came the alternating grooved triglyphs and sculptured metopes of the Doric frieze so arranged that there were two triglyphs and two metopes for each column or intercolumnar space, then the cornice, and above it at either end of the rectangular temple the low triangular gables or pediments, commonly filled with groups of sculptured figures.   The interior of the temple, or *cella*, formed a smaller rectangular apartment within the colonnade, which often had a vestibule before and behind it and was lighted only through its doorway.   In the *cella* were the image and treasury of the god.   Temples were usually roofed with wooden beams which have disappeared; in most cases foundations and columns alone are left.   Of temples of the sixth century little is still standing; the so-called "Basilica" at Poseidonia or Pæstum or Pesto in southern Italy is the best preserved.

Proportion and Color

As anyone may soon convince himself by trying to make a good-looking drawing of a Greek temple, its beauty depends very largely upon its proportions: the relation between the height of a column and its diameter, the intercolumnar spaces which must decrease near the corners,—since the corner triglyph must come above the outer edge rather than the center of the corner column,—the depths of the shadows cast by the flutings of the columns, the projecting capitals and cornice. Another important consideration is the extensive employment of curved lines.   Not only are the columns themselves, the lower halves of their capitals, and the flutings channeled in them, all round, but vertically their shafts swell with a slight entasis, and many of the horizontal lines in the temple really curve slightly, giving a more graceful and less mechanical or rigid appearance.   In sixth century temples the shafts of the columns are apt to taper too rapidly to an unduly narrow neck just below the capital, while the underside of the capital may bulge excessively, or the columns may be placed closer together than they should be, and their capitals may project too far. Monolithic columns were employed in a sixth century temple at Corinth of which a fragment still stands.   Monoliths probably also stood above the sculptured drums which supported the shafts in the large archaic temple of Diana at Ephesus. Later the columns were usually composed of several drums which were channeled with flutings after they had been fitted in place. Where the rough poros-stone was used, it was commonly covered over with stucco, and, in any case, the surface of the temple was more or less painted, particularly the triglyphs and the backgrounds of the metopes and pediments. The best preserved ruins of Greek temples, dating chiefly from the fifth century, are to be found at Athens and Ægina, at Poseidonia, and at Girgenti (Greek, Acragas; Latin, Agrigentum) and Segesta in Sicily.

The finest and most celebrated of all Greek temples is the The Parthenon, built of marble on the Acropolis at Athens during Parthenon the age of Pericles in the years 447–438 by the architects Ictinus and Callicrates, and adorned with sculptures under the direction of Phidias. From a stylobate measuring 228 by 100 feet and reached by three steps each 20 inches high, rise 46 Doric columns, 34 feet in height, composed each of twelve drums, diminishing from 6 feet 3 inches to 4 feet 10 inches in diameter. Their flutings diminish in width but not in depth, thus producing a fine shadow effect. Along the four sides the metopes represented incidents from the siege of Troy and battles of the gods and giants, centaurs and lapiths, Athenians and Amazons. The sculptures of one pediment represented the birth of Athena from the brow of Zeus; of the other, the strife between Athena and Poseidon for the land of Attica. The Ionic frieze, encircling the outer wall of the *cella*, was over 500 feet long and a little over a yard high. It shows in low relief the procession at the Panathenaic festival. Youths are mounting steeds at the rear of the temple. Along both sides proceed horsemen, marching warriors, musicians, and youths leading sacrificial victims. On the front matrons and maidens approach from either side the magistrates and seated gods who await the arrival of the procession and the completion of the ceremony. Within the *cella* with its wooden ceiling was a statue of the goddess Athena some forty-two feet high.

The subsequent history of this great building is likewise of Its interest. Alexander the Great decorated the ends of its archi- Subsequent trave with splendid shields; the Roman emperor Nero affixed a History metal inscription. From about the fifth century A. D. it was variously rearranged to serve as a Christian church dedicated to the Virgin; in 1460 it was transformed into a mosque with a minaret at one angle. About 1670 some drawings were fortunately made and accounts published of it, for in 1687 when Count Königsmarck, in the service of Venice, attacked the Turks who had stored their powder in the Parthenon, a bomb fired by a German lieutenant ignited the powder and blew out the entire center of the building. Lord Elgin was permitted by the Turkish government in 1801 to remove most of the sculptures from the ruins to Great Britain, where they were subsequently purchased by the government for the British Museum, and remain to this day in London. Enough of the Parthenon, however, still stands, or has been restored to place, to make a very impressive sight.

Caryatids and the Ionic and Corinthian Orders

Human figures known as caryatids were sometimes used in place of columns to support an architrave, for instance, the giants between the engaged columns in the huge temple of Zeus at Acragas or the Porch of the Maidens of the Erechtheum on the Acropolis at Athens. The Ionic order, with its ornate base, its slenderer, less tapering shaft, and its capital of volutes, was invented in the fifth century, but in the Greek period was limited mainly to smaller buildings such as the Erechtheum and Temple of Wingless Victory on the Acropolis. The Ionic frieze, as we have already implied, is a continuous band of sculpture in relief. The oldest extant building of the Corinthian order, with its tall capital adorned with acanthus leaves, is the circular monument of Lysicrates erected at Athens in 335–334 with six engaged Corinthian columns. We have already described the open-air theater of the Greeks which they began to build of stone in the fourth century, from which time we have a good specimen preserved at Epidaurus. The stadiums for the games were similar structures.

Archaic Sculpture to About 480

The earliest Hellenic sculpture is of a crude and archaic type which seems to have no connection with the earlier Ægean art, but rather to have developed from the rough carving of a board, plank, log, or column. The human form and dress are only roughly indicated, the arms are held stiffly straight down at the sides, the face wears a fixed grin or attempt to "look pleasant" which is known as the archaic smile, the limbs are apt to be thick and heavy, seated figures are equally massive and are of one piece with their chair. The nude male form was a greater favorite with the Greeks than with the oriental artists. We have a series of statues of Apollo which at first resemble Egyptian pharaohs in their hair-dressing or wig, their squared shoulders, and thick calves and ankles, but gradually display increasing knowledge of anatomy, slenderness and grace of form, and approach to classical Greek features. From Egypt, too, the Greeks of Samos learned hollow-casting in bronze, although few life-size bronzes have reached us from any period of antiquity. There were also winged figures, sphinxes, and various animals, serpents, and monsters. Another noteworthy series of archaic statues is of draped females, generally with one arm bent at the elbow and holding in the palm of the extended hand some offering for the goddess. This extended forearm has usually been broken off, but the coiffures, faces, and delicate folds and embroidered borders of the robes of these sixth century ladies are represented with vividness and fidelity. Some of the faces wear a self-conscious smirk, but others have a dignified and modest beauty both of face and figure. Such statues are especially preserved for us on the Acropolis at Athens where, after the destruction wrought by the Persian occupation of 480, these, and the broken fragments of the earliest specimens of red-figured vases, were swept aside and were used to fill in and level the surface, when the Acropolis was enlarged and surrounded with supporting and protective walls. At Athens the sculptors at first worked in the soft poros-stone, then in marble. Traces of paint often are seen on Greek statues, proving that it was employed to adorn their sculpture as well as their architecture. In the course of a century or so, sculpture had made great strides, but the pediment sculptures of Greek warriors, executed for the temple at Ægina just after the Persian War, still show some archaic features and stiffness.

From the last three quarters of the fifth century we have names of artists of the first rank, but in the main, only Roman copies of their masterpieces, except for the Elgin marbles from the Parthenon and the funeral monuments at Athens. In the bronze charioteer at Delphi, however, we possess an original which forms an exception to the above assertion concerning the scarcity of bronze statues from antiquity. Critios and Nesiotes replaced the group of the tyrannicides at Athens which Xerxes carried off in 480, and there is preserved at Naples a

Specimens of Fifth-Century Sculpture

Roman replica of their work, except that an incongruous head has been placed on the body of Aristogeiton. Of the Discus Thrower and the Marsyas of Myron of Bœotia there are several later copies. Another famous sculptor of athletes, Polycleitus of Sicyon, is represented by the Doryphoros or Spear-Bearer, and Diadumenos or Fillet-Binder. He is also credited with an Amazon, but we have copies of two or three different types of Amazons who are always shown with short skirt and with limbs and one breast bare. Sometimes it is the right, sometimes the left breast, and sometimes the Amazon is wounded, sometimes about to pole-vault into the saddle. Winged figures are continued by the Victory of Pæonius, which has been pieced together at Olympia from fragments of the original. Of the broken statues from the pediments of the Parthenon the two finest pieces are probably the half-seated, half-reclining, nude male figure commonly called Theseus, and the group of three draped female figures identified as the Fates. Of other works attributed to Phidias, apart from the Parthenon, there are no good copies extant except perhaps some heads of Athena. The sculptured reliefs from Athenian tombstones which begin with the fifth century are in the main touching, yet dignified, representations of scenes of final leave-taking which illuminate Greek religion and family life as well as Attic sculpture.

Fourth Century Masterpieces

With the genius of Praxiteles, an Athenian sculptor of the fourth century, we feel fairly well acquainted, since the original of his Hermes was unearthed at Olympia in the later nineteenth century, while his Aphrodite of Cnidus, youthful satyr or "Marble Faun," and Apollo Sauroctonus, are known from copies at Rome. Of the work of his great contemporary, Scopas of the island of Paros, we know little except that his statues were deeply expressive of feeling and emotion. He superintended the sculptures of the tomb of King Mausolus of Halicarnassus (whence comes our word "mausoleum"), the fragments of which are preserved at the British Museum. Some of the reliefs may be by Scopas, but the statue of Mausolus, which has been pieced together from seventy-seven fragments, was executed by one of the architects, Pythis. We have fine copies of a statue of Peace Nursing Wealth by Cephisidotus, of the Apoxyomenos or athlete scraping oil and dirt off his arm by Lysippus, of a fourth century Aphrodite by an unknown artist, and of the wonderfully beautiful and touching relief of Orpheus, Eurydice, and Hermes. At Delphi the original may still be seen of three dancing girls grouped about a support, and a contemporary copy of Lysippus' statue of the victorious athlete, Agias. These do not exhaust the remains of fourth century sculpture but simply suggest a few that are especially pleasing to gaze upon.

The extension of Greek art to other lands through Greek colonies and trade may be illustrated by archæological discoveries in Scythia or the region to the north of the Euxine or Black Sea,—or, as we should say today, south Russia. Here is found an enormous number of works of Greek art, but of a different sort from those already described. Not a single good life-size statue has been discovered; on the other hand, this region yields almost our only specimens of Greek textiles and carpentry, and of the arts of inlaying and drawing on wood. The precious metals are employed with barbaric profusion; indeed, we have here an extension of Greek art to barbarians. Here, too, are preserved better specimens of decorative painting than elsewhere, but in its latest form which carries us on into the Hellenistic and even Christian periods.

Greek Art in South Russia

BIBLIOGRAPHY

Bell, E. *Hellenic Architecture*, 1920.

British Museum Sets of Postcards: XXVII, Types of Greek Vases; XXVIII, Select Antique Bronzes; XXIX, Greek and Roman Life; XXX, Frieze of the Parthenon.

Carpenter, Rhys. *The Æsthetic Basis of Greek Art*, 1921.

Collignon, M. *Le Parthénon*, 1909.

D'Ooge, A. L. *The Acropolis of Athens*, 1919.

Fowler, H. N. and Wheeler, J. R. *Handbook of Greek Archæology*, 1909.

Furtwängler (and Reichold, continued by Hauser), *Griechische Vasenmalerei*, 1900–1912.

Gardner, E. A. *Handbook of Greek Sculpture*, 1915.

Hekler, A. *Greek and Roman Portraits*, 1912.

Koldewey, R. and Puchstein, O. *Die griech. Tempel in Unteritalien und Sicilien*, 1899.

Lenormant, C. and Witte, J. D. *Élite des monuments céramographiques*, 4 vols., 1844–61.

Lethaby, W. R. *Greek Buildings*, 1908.

Minns, E. H. *Scythians and Greeks*, 1913.

Pottier, E. *Douris et les peintres de vases grecs*, 1908.

Powers, H. H. *The Message of Greek Art*, 1912.

Reisler. W. *Weissgründige attische Lekythen*, 1914.
Rostovsteff, *Iranians and Greeks in South Russia*, 1922.
Smith, A. H. *Sculptures of the Parthenon*, 1910.
Tarbell, F. B. *History of Greek Art*, 1896.
Walters, H. B. *History of Ancient Pottery*, 1905.
Weller, C. H. *Athens and its Monuments*, 1913.

CHAPTER XII

THE TRANSITION TO THE HELLENISTIC AGE

(336–146 B. C.)

Why may not imagination trace the noble dust of Alexander,
till he find it stopping a bung-hole?—*Hamlet*

THE expression, Hellenistic Age, is commonly applied to the years from Alexander's conquest of the Persian Empire to the Roman conquest of the eastern Mediterranean lands, or, since this Roman conquest was slow and gradual, until the beginning of the Christian era. The word, Hellenistic, in distinction from Hellenic, means less purely Greek, and indicates the extension of Greek civilization to peoples like the Macedonians and orientals. Thus in the sphere of language and literature we pass from Attic Greek to a less pure idiom called Hellenistic Greek, produced by persons who were not Greek trying to write in Greek and to speak Greek, or as a result of Greek intercourse with such people. Of course this spread of the Greek language and civilization had been going on all through the Hellenic period in the numerous Greek colonies in Thrace, along the coasts of the Black Sea, in Cyrene, and in Italy. The Persian kings had employed Greek artists, physicians, soldiers, and sailors. Greeks like Herodotus, Pythagoras, and Plato had traveled in the east and learned of its lore. But seemingly the movement was now carried on upon a larger scale, more especially in the orient and far inland. However, antecedents may be found of most features of Hellenistic civilization in the preceding period, and first we may note that even the political change was somewhat gradual and that Alexander's rapid conquest was not an entirely sudden or unthought of feat.

The Hellenistic Age

The great Persian Empire had sprung up like a mushroom overnight as the result of rapid conquest and might be overthrown in the same way. Back in 499 Aristagoras, who led the revolt of the Ionic cities of Asia Minor against Persia, had shown the Spartans a map of the royal road from the west

Weakness of the Persian Empire

coast of Asia Minor up to Susa, one of the Persian capitals, and had tried to persuade them of the ease with which an expedition of heavy armed Greek soldiers could penetrate to the heart of the Persian Empire and overthrow it at one blow.   He failed, however, to induce them to make this bold move, and for a century thereafter the Greeks fought Persia either on the defensive in their own peninsula or in a mild offensive along the coasts of Asia Minor.   But all the time the Greeks were proving themselves superior soldiers to the Asiatics, and in 401 Cyrus the Younger, a claimant to the Persian throne, hired thirteen thousand of them to form part of an army which he led from western Asia Minor as far as the neighborhood of Babylon.   Here they met the opposing army and were themselves victorious, but Cyrus was slain and his Asiatic troops were routed.   The few thousand Greeks, although their leaders were treacherously slain while negotiating with the enemy, elected new ones from their own number, overcame many hardships, and made their escape successfully through the mountain snows of Armenia to the Black Sea, where they found Greek ships and colonies.

Xenophon's Anabasis

The story of this expedition and retreat is told in the *Anabasis* of the historian Xenophon who had accompanied the expedition as a friend of one of the Greek commanders and who was elected one of the new leaders by the troops.   The *Anabasis* ranks with Cæsar's *Gallic War* as a leading military book of Greek and Roman times, and they have usually been the first books read by school boys studying Latin and Greek—a regretable emphasis upon the militaristic side of civilization.   Although himself an Athenian, Xenophon did not write pure Attic Greek and made slips in syntax.   In this respect, as well as in his cosmopolitan character and adventuring eastward, he already seems Hellenistic rather than Hellenic.

Decline of the Greek City States

The Greek cities continued too much at war with one another to unite in a vigorous offensive against Persia.   Other wars followed the Peloponnesian; the number of full-blooded and fully-equipped Spartans became seriously reduced; then Thebes, the chief city of Bœotia in central Greece, wrested the military supremacy from Sparta.   We have seen that the great merit of the otherwise rather slow and stupid Spartans had been that they were trained to stand in a continuous line protected by one another's shields and never yield ground at any cost, and that usually the result of this noble front and stand had been that the other side ran away first and was defeated. But the other Greeks had gradually been devising methods of circumventing this unyielding Spartan phalanx. Now Epaminondas, the Theban leader, put his best troops in a heavy column which advanced more rapidly than the rest of the Theban battle-line in order to attack the Spartans first. He led the column himself, and broke the Spartan line at one point on their right wing so that he could enfilade the greater part of the Spartans on their right side, which was unprotected by shields. The rest of the Spartan line, however, held its position as it was trained to do and calmly awaited the attack of the poorer Theban troops who were still approaching, drawn up in an oblique line *en échelons*. Meanwhile Epaminondas' column had broken through at the one point and now took the Spartans in the unprotected flank and rear just as the *échelons* were successively engaging their front, and rolled up their line in confusion and defeat. The Spartans might possibly have been defeated three hundred years earlier had someone only thought of this tactical movement sooner. But the human mind moves slowly at best, and the military mind still more slowly. Epaminondas' scheme had just one weak point; he had to lead the column personally, or it might have recoiled before the Spartan line. Consequently he was killed in his second victory, and both Thebes and Sparta lost the military supremacy.

A young Macedonian prince named Philip, who had been kept at Thebes for a time as a hostage, now rapidly made himself the master of the Greek peninsula. He is supposed to have learned something of Greek military methods and civilization during his enforced stay at Thebes. The Macedonian phalanx now replaced both the Spartan phalanx and the Theban column. But, as the poet Pope said, "A little learning is a dangerous thing." Philip deceived the Athenians more grossly than their own Themistocles, in days gone by, had hoodwinked the Persians and Spartans; he bribed one of the rival parties in each Greek city and purchased traitors as cleverly as the Persian king had ever done; he wiped out some thirty Greek city states and centers of civilization in Thrace and the Chalcidice and sold their entire populations into slavery; some twenty towns of Phocis were also destroyed, and their surviving inhabitants were scattered in villages. Reinforced by

Rise of
Macedon

these illustrations, the oratory of Demosthenes of Athens at last aroused a number of Greek cities to a united resistance. But it was too late, and Philip triumphed at Chæronea in 338 B. C.

Reasons for the Hellenic Failure

This event is usually taken to mark the close of the Hellenic period. The Hellenes who had repelled the hosts of Persia had been defeated by an army of Macedonians no larger than their own. But the Macedonians were a vigorous fighting race, akin to those northerners who had earlier invaded the Greek peninsula and formed the Hellenic race by fusion with the Ægean race. Philip understood conditions in Greece and was better situated to attack it than Persia had been. Moreover, certain qualities which the Greeks had shown all along now at last contributed directly to their ruin. First, the deceit and cheating which had been practiced by their leaders like Themistocles, and chuckled at by their historians like Herodotus, made the different city states and parties unable to trust one another even in a common emergency. A second weakness was the passion and violence and spirit of vengeance in their party politics within each city. A third defect was their extreme susceptibility to bribery and the consequent frequency with which acts of treachery were committed. Finally may be mentioned the selfish ambition of many of their leading men, who were always looking out for themselves rather than for the common weal. As a later Greek writer under the Roman Empire, Plutarch, put it: "For should a man except the achievement at Marathon, the sea-fight at Salamis, the engagements at Platæa and Thermopylæ, Cimon's exploits at the Eurymedon and on the coasts of Cyprus, Greece fought all her battles against, and to subdue, herself; she erected all her trophies to her own shame and misery, and was brought to ruin and desolation almost wholly by the guilt and ambition of her great men." The defect was not, as some modern nationalists have held, that the Hellenes persisted in retaining numerous little city states and would not unite into one strong nation; the defect was that the larger city states would not leave the smaller ones independent, and that ambitious individuals and factions would not subordinate themselves to the welfare of their city. Consequently the Greek city states had to yield the supremacy to the larger territorial and national state represented by Macedon.

Philip's greed for conquest was insatiable, and he prepared

to invade the Persian Empire. But this conqueror of others Career of
Alexander
the Great
could not control his own wild Macedonian court, and two years
after his victory at Chæronea he was assassinated at the age of
only forty-seven. His son Alexander, although but twenty
years of age, showed himself fully able to continue his father's
work of destruction and conquest. When Thebes tried to free
itself from its Macedonian garrison, he took the city by storm
and sold the inhabitants into slavery. Then with an army of
about 45,000 he traversed the entire Persian Empire from
Egypt, where the oracle of the god Ammon assured him that he
was a son of Zeus, to Sogdiana, where he fell in love for the first
time and married a native girl, Roxane, by a wedding ceremony
which consisted in their dividing a loaf of bread, and to the
Punjab in India beyond which his troops refused to follow him.
It would seem that his army must have been occasionally re-
plenished, since, despite great losses from war and privation, he
had enough veterans left to found numerous military colonies.
He almost of necessity assumed the absolute power and court
pomp of an oriental monarch and employed Persians as well as
Macedonians to govern his conquests. With despotic ruth-
lessness he put to death, sometimes with his own hand, various
individual associates and helpers who gave personal offense or
were charged with conspiracy or with misgovernment of the
provinces assigned them. He also violated the terms which
Philip had granted to the Greek cities. He remained, however, addicted to a practice which the Macedonians had in
common with the original Persians, namely, drunken carousals,
and suddenly died in 323 of a fever which was, perhaps, caused
by overwork rather than by hard drinking.

No contemporary account of Alexander has reached us, al- The
Impression
Left by
Alexander
though his Greek secretary kept a court journal, and some of
his generals wrote lives of him. The extant accounts, of which
those by Arrian and Plutarch are chief, were not written until
hundreds of years after his death. But his personality
seems to have made a great impression upon his contemporaries,
and the rulers who came after him long imitated him even in
such minor matters as his shaggy locks, habit of inclining his
head to the left, and reckless self-exposure in battle. Worse
was the fashion, which his adventurous career set, of distant
conquest by individual commanders in search of personal glory.
He also became a favorite hero of legend both in east and west

through the medieval period, when his name was especially associated with magic and occult science, with marvels of distant India, and with Aristotle. His name was given to a number of cities scattered through the conquered territory and occupied by Macedonian veterans; these subsequently became centers of Greek civilization in oriental lands. The chief Alexandria was in Egypt. It replaced Phœnician Tyre, whose inhabitants Alexander had sold into slavery, and became one of the most populous cities of the ancient world.

His
Relation
to the
History of
Civilization

It is doubtful if civilization profited more than it lost through Alexander's brief career. Aristotle had been his tutor, but most of the tales of his making scientific collections for Aristotle, as he traversed the orient, are probably later imaginings. Alexander was familiar with Greek literature and especially fond of the *Iliad*. Its primitive heroes were in about the same stage of semi-civilization as the Macedonians. Alexander's sparing the house of the poet Pindar alone of all the homes of Thebes was simply a silly gesture. He employed the great sculptor Lysippus to make statues of himself, but Lysippus could doubtless have found other, and possibly better, employment for his genius. Both Philip and Alexander, however, like the Persian kings before them, were more favorable to Greek culture than they were to Greek freedom; the Macedonians became more civilized, and Greek civilization continued to spread through the world.

The Break-
up of the
Persian
Empire

It is hardly proper to speak of Alexander's Empire, as has so often been done, for it was only a momentary conquest. What he really brought about was the break-up of the Persian Empire. When Alexander died, Roxane's son was not yet born, and a long struggle ensued between the various members of the Macedonian royal house and Alexander's other associates and generals. The last-named arranged various divisions among themselves, but the history of the time reads like a melodrama, and it was only after many years of murders, intrigues, marriage alliances, romantic adventures, and wars which kept the world turned upside down and no man certain what evil fate might not next befall him, that most of the claimants were killed off, and the political situation became somewhat clarified. As late as 282 three of Alexander's generals were still alive. Ptolemy, aged eighty-five, had recently retired from the rule of Egypt in 285; Lysimachus, aged seventy-nine, governed

Thrace: Seleucus, aged seventy-one, ruled from Syria to India. Each of these rulers also had a slice of Asia Minor. The fourth main kingdom was Macedon which had to content itself with a certain power in the Greek peninsula. These four were absolute monarchies based upon standing armies. Ptolemy had peacefully retired in favor of his younger son and thus founded a dynasty that ruled Egypt for three centuries. But the elder son whom he passed over went off to the court of Lysimachus, induced him to put his own son to death, and then joined Seleucus, who in 281 defeated and slew Lysimachus. Thus the kingdom of Thrace came to an end, leaving only three great monarchies. This enabled a great horde of Celts from the north to pour into Asia Minor and devastate it. In Asia Minor just before the defeat of Lysimachus his Greek treasurer had rebelled and seized the strong city of Pergamum near the site of Troy, thus founding an independent kingdom. Other small kingdoms which sprang up in Asia Minor with native rulers were Bithynia, Paphlagonia, Pontus, and Cappadocia. The invading Celts or Gauls finally settled down in the center of Asia Minor as the Galatians, to whom three centuries later St. Paul addressed his Epistle. Of Greek city states Byzantium, at the entrance of the Black Sea, and Rhodes, off the southwestern corner of Asia Minor, became with Alexandria leading commercial centers of the eastern Mediterranean.

The invading Celts had also overrun Macedon and had defeated and killed Ptolemy's aforesaid elder son after he had murdered Seleucus and was about to make himself king of Macedon. Both the Seleucid and Macedonian dynasties resumed their rule after his death, however. The Celts were halted at Thermopylæ by the Ætolians, a warlike people who now extended an old league of their own to include other Greek states and became the chief power in central Greece. Athens was henceforth important only as a famous center of culture. Sparta was overshadowed in the Peloponnesus by the Achæan League, and the Macedonian monarchy recovered considerable power there. In Crete independent republics fought with one another; the other islands of the Ægean were more interested in peaceful trade than wars, but piracy abounded, and the little island of Delos became a great slave-market. In the west the island of Corcyra was conquered by adventurers thrice within

Affairs of the Greek Peninsula and Western Hellas

ten years.   The Greek cities of Sicily and southern Italy were
conquered, sacked, and destroyed, or were occupied by tyrants
and bands of mercenaries who plundered them and killed off the
leading citizens.   Pyrrhus of Epirus, a knightly figure and as
a general comparable to Alexander, came to their rescue for a
time, but after he withdrew Rome and Carthage soon subdued
them.

Egypt under the Ptolemies

Of the greater Hellenistic monarchies we know Egypt under
the Ptolemies best.   They established a good understanding
with the Egyptian priests, added new courts and pylons to
the ancient temples, or built new temples in much the same style
as those of a thousand years before.   The best preserved ancient temple in Egypt, that of Horus at Edfu, was built in this
period.   The many finds of papyri that have been made of recent years in Egypt include documents which supply us with
more detailed information concerning the administration and
taxation of Egypt, both during the Ptolemaic and the following Roman and Byzantine periods, than for any other region.
The peasants were constantly watched by officials to make sure
that they kept steadily at work and that the government received its full share of the crops.

Spread of Greek City Life in the Orient

Although the Hellenistic monarchies were fundamentally in-
compatible with the ideals of the free city state, they in a way
encouraged the spread of Greek city life, since Alexander's
successors continued the policy of founding colonies of Macedonian soldiers and Greek traders or workmen in their domains.
The Seleucids were especially active in this respect, founding
Greek towns not only in Syria, but in distant Parthia, Hyr-
cania, and Bactria.   Usually these towns were allowed considerable powers of self-government.   The surrounding natives
gradually settled in them and thereby became Hellenized.   This
eastward migration of Greeks left many of the home cities, and
the Greek peninsula as a whole, depopulated.   In many ancient
Hellenic cities, says Mahaffy, grass grew in once busy streets,
and there were not enough men left to man the walls.   Presently Roman conquest by land, and pirate raids from the sea,
carried the decline further.

Hellenistic Capitals

The monarchs were apt to devote especial attention to their
capital cities, such as Alexandria, Antioch in Syria, and Pergamum.   These were carefully planned from the start for show,
and were not full of narrow, irregular streets or lanes like Ath-

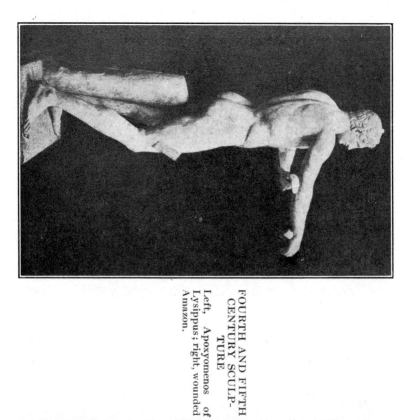

FOURTH AND FIFTH CENTURY SCULPTURE

Left, Apoxyomenos of Lysippus; right, wounded Amazon.

Above, the Hermes of Praxiteles; below, Hermes from Andros.

ens. At Pergamum the public buildings were grandly situated upon three successive terraces. At Antioch the streets were laid out in regular blocks of continuous houses, the sidewalks were protected by covered colonnades, and a very wide street, lined with colonnades, ran through the city from east to west for a distance of four miles. At night the streets were lighted by public and private lamps. Alexandria also rapidly became a very large city, not a small walled town surrounded by wild nature like those in the Greek peninsula. Greeks and Jews outnumbered the native Egyptians, and women and children circulated in its streets as they were not allowed or accustomed to do in Athens. There was great pomp at the court of the Ptolemies; elaborate shows and festivals were also provided for the city populace. The towering Pharos or lighthouse on the island at the entrance to the harbor of Alexandria was reckoned one of the seven wonders of the world; another was the Colossus of Rhodes, a great hollow metal statue of the sun god, 105 feet high, at the entrance to its harbor. Few men, Pliny the Elder tells us, could encircle its thumb with both their arms, and its fingers were larger than most statues. Rhodes contained one hundred other colossal statues, but none so large as it. It was thrown down by an earthquake fifty-six years after it was erected, and lay on the ground until 653 A. D., when the Saracens sold the materials, and these were removed.

In smaller towns like Priene in Asia Minor, the excavation of which has given us a complete plan of the streets and buildings of a Hellenistic town, the streets were also laid out at right angles, although Aristotle had recently advised that they be crooked so that enemies who forced their way in might not easily find their way about or penetrate to the center. Though Priene had only four thousand inhabitants, who lived largely by tilling farms outside its walls, it boasted two market-places, a theater, a gymnasium, a stadium, a sacred portico for public festivals and banquets, a town hall seating five hundred, and a number of temples. Water pipes ran to the houses, some of which also contained sanitary arrangements. By this time wages in the building trades had risen to two or three drachmas a day. Town life was apparently more comfortable and luxurious than before. The houses of the well-to-do were larger, and sometimes included a suite of rooms for a guest which he could enter or leave by a separate street door. Entrances to

Town and Family Life

Hellenistic dwelling-houses were commonly so placed that passers-by could not look into the interior of the house when the door was opened. In Ptolemaic and Roman Egypt, private houses were often from two to four stories high and sometimes had towers in imitation of the pylons of the temples. Even the old towns of Greece often took on a different aspect in this age. Sparta was now walled; Sicyon was rebuilt on a higher level. The papyri found in Egypt include private letters and business documents, and give us more insight than before into the family and private life of chance individuals from among the population at large.

Lot of the Lowly and Oppressed

While the homes of the rich were larger and finer, and the standard of living had in general risen, many cities developed a mob which lived wretchedly enough and was maintained partly by private bounty, partly at public expense. This continued to hold true under the Roman Empire, and indeed in the city of Rome itself. And while trade flourished and Greek business men prospered in oriental cities, the lot of the lower laboring classes seems not to have improved. Especially oppressed were the peasants on royal domains, on temple lands, and on the large estates of private holders who resembled feudal lords. Worst of all was the fate of those condemned to toil in mines. The ancient historian Diodorus thus describes the "labor of a vast multitude" in the mines of Egypt, Arabia, and Ethiopia under the Ptolemies. "The kings of Egypt condemn to these mines notorious criminals, captives taken in war, persons sometimes falsely accused, or against whom the king is incensed; and and not only they themselves, but sometimes all their kindred, . . . all bound in fetters where they work continually without being allowed any rest night or day," under the strict guard of barbarian soldiers speaking another language, and "at the very nod of the overseer who lashes them severely besides. No care at all is taken of the bodies of these poor creatures, so that they have not a rag so much as to cover their nakedness, and no man that sees them can choose but commiserate their sad and deplorable condition. For though they are sick, maimed, or lame, no rest nor intermission in the least is allowed them; neither the weakness of old age nor women's infirmities are any plea to excuse them," but they are driven with blows until they drop dead. Let us hope that Diodorus exaggerated,

and that his own attitude of compassion was more characteristic of the age than the king's cruelty.

Relations of the Mediterranean world with the Far East con- Trade with
tinued after the break-up of the Persian Empire during the India
following Hellenistic and Roman periods.   Of relations with
China we will speak further in a later chapter on China.   Alexandria became the chief mart for the trade with India, and
later its grain ships, famous in ancient times for their size,
brought Rome its food supply.   The canal which Darius is supposed to have constructed to the Red Sea seems to have soon
fallen into disuse.   Goods for India went up the Nile 328
miles, or twelve days' sail, to Coptos and were then carried
across the desert for six or seven days to Myos-hormos (Mus-
sel Harbor), a port on the Red Sea which Ptolemy Philadel-
phus had founded for the Indian trade in 274 B. C.   It was
then a long sail south to the mouth of the Red Sea, and a still
longer voyage to India by skirting the southern coast of
Arabia, and lands beyond.   About the beginning of our era,
however, a pilot named Hippalus, "by observing the location
of the ports and the conditions of the sea, first discovered how to
lay his course straight across the (Indian) ocean."   By leaving the mouth of the Red Sea when the monsoon was blowing,
it was possible to reach the nearest port on the west coast of
India in forty days.   Various things now found their way westward.   Rats seem to have been unknown in Egypt and Greece
before Alexander the Great.   Lucullus, who first carried the
Roman arms as far east as Armenia in 69 B. C., brought the
cherry-tree from the city of Cerasus, after which it is named,
in Cappadocia to Italy; the peach was introduced from Persia.

BIBLIOGRAPHY

Airian, *Anabasis of Alexander.*

Beloch, K. J. *Griechische Geschichte,* vol. III., 1922–1923.

Bevan, E. R. *House of Seleucus,* 1904.

Bouché-Leclercq, *Histoire des Lagides,* 1907, 4 vols.

Bouchier, E. S. *Short History of Antioch,* 1921.

Bury, Tarn, Tod, *The Hellenistic Age,* 1923.

Ferguson, W. S. *Greek Imperialism,* 1913; *Hellenistic Athens,* 1911.
    More recent treatments by an American than the following books by
    Mahaffy, an Irishman, and Holm, a German.

Holm, A. *History of Greece,* 1894–1898, vol. IV.

Luckhard, F. *Das Privathaus im ptolemäischen und römischen Aegypten,* 1914.

Mahaffy, J. P. *Empire of the Ptolemies,* 1897; *Alexander's Empire,* 1887; *Greek Life and Thought from the Death of Alexander to the Roman Conquest,* 2nd edition, 1896; written with vigor of style and freshness of thought.

Milligan, G. *Selections from the Greek Papyri,* 1910; brief translations of Hellenistic letters and the like, illustrating the social life.

Periplus of the Erythrœan Sea, translated by W. H. Schoff, 1912; our chief original source for ancient trade with the Far East.

Plutarch's *Lives of Alexander, Eumenes, Demetrius, Pyrrhus, Aratus, Agis, Cleomenes, Philopœmen;* immortal biographies of leading figures of the age.

Polybius; translated by Shuckburgh, 1889, 2 vols.; the ancient historian who is our chief source for the third and second centuries B. C.

Rostovtzeff, M. I. *A Large Estate in Egypt in the Third Century B.C.,* 1922.

Tarn, W. W. *Antigonos Gonatas,* 1913.

Torr, C. *Rhodes in Ancient Times,* 1885.

Wilcken, U. *Grundzüge der Papyruskunde,* 1912.

CHAPTER XIII

HELLENISTIC CULTURE

It is precisely in tracing the gradual diffusion of this civilization that lies the main charm of the period on which we are now entering.—Holm

THE spread of the Greek language and culture through the east and then to Rome is the leading feature of the Hellenistic age. If measured by Hellenic standards, this later culture may seem inferior or even decadent in some respects. But the Hellenistic culture was not merely a spreading of already existing civilization; it includes new developments and original contributions. It seems more modern in many ways than the culture of the preceding centuries. It was more cosmopolitan in character; less expressive of purely Greek ideals and attitudes; less a natural outgrowth of popular mythology and the activities and festivals of the city state; more the outcome of royal patronage. Yet its art and literature made a wider appeal to humanity at large. Sometimes they seem artificial compared to the instinctive artistry of the true Hellene, sometimes more natural than his artistic arrangement. Finally, this age continued scientific investigation in the spirit of Aristotle, and left for future ages a sure and solid foundation of mathematical method. One could hardly ask for more than this relatively brief and exceedingly troubled period has given us, and it is not surprising that it has so stirred the enthusiasm and imagination of some modern investigators that they have ascribed to it more than it really produced. It is not safe to assume that Hellenistic civilization made acquisitions and discoveries which were lost in the Roman period, or to ascribe all the good points in Roman writers who have survived to Hellenistic sources which have not survived, and all the bad points to the Roman writers themselves. It is true, however, that our knowledge of Hellenistic culture often is derived from Roman reference thereto or repetition thereof, and the one period shades imperceptibly into the other so that it is very difficult to distinguish Hellenistic from Græco-Roman culture.

New Comedy at Athens

Athens was still a great center of culture, although not so exclusively or predominantly as in the fifth century. But as the fourth century was giving way to the third, Athens was the scene of new developments of great importance both in literature and in thought. Comedy, in the sense that the word has been used ever since, now first took form, under the influence of the drama of Euripides in the preceding period. From his tragedies it took over the working out of a plot to engage the attention and interest of the audience, the introduction of the love motive or love story, and the humanizing of the drama. This New Comedy, as it is called in distinction from the Old Comedy of Aristophanes and from the Middle Comedy, which intervened between the two and of which we know little, dealt with private life and ordinary human beings, not with public questions and leading men. Whereas Aristophanes had coarsely burlesqued public life and caricatured familiar contemporary figures, the New Comedy gave a portrayal of manners and private society and a subtle delineation of character which are faithful not so much to that period as to human nature. The same tendency is seen in a series of sketches ascribed to the philosopher and botanist, Theophrastus, under the title *Characters*. Somewhat the same human types seem to have been presented in every comedy, as indeed they have been ever since. Philemon (c. 362–262) and Menander (c. 341–290) were the chief representatives of the New Comedy at Athens. Philemon is said to have possessed so keen a sense of the ridiculous that at the ripe age of one hundred he "literally died of laughter on seeing his ass eat figs."

Menander

Menander continued a prime favorite with the men of the Roman Empire. Plutarch wrote in the second century A. D., "Concerning new comedy there is no need of any long discourse. It is so fitted, so interwoven with entertainments, that it is easier to have a regular feast without wine than without Menander. Its phrase is sweet and familiar. . . . The sentiments are so natural and unstudied, . . . his poesy the most universal ornament that was ever produced by Greece." Plutarch much preferred Menander to Aristophanes, calling the latter "importune, theatric, and sordid in his expression," and objecting that he made all his characters talk alike, "and you would scarce discern whether he that is talking be a son, a father, a peasant, a god, an old woman, or a hero." Menander's style, on the other hand, "traverses many passions and humors," and is proportioned to every sex, condition, and age. Aristophanes appeals to the rude and vulgar; Menander, to the refined and educated. "And for what other reason in truth should a man of parts and erudition be at pains to frequent the theater but for the sake of Menander only? . . . To philosophers also and hard students (as painters are wont, when they have tired out their eyes at their work, to divert them to certain florid and green colors) Menander is a repose from their auditors and intense thinkings, and entertains their minds with gay shady meadows refreshed with cool and gentle breezes." The Latin poet, Manilius, paid the following tribute to Menander:

He composes amusing plays for the comic stage:
Impassioned youths, girls head over heels in love,
Fathers who're fooled, and slaves who're up to all tricks:
He who has made the life of his time live through all ages,
Beneath the polish of his speech intimate with his city,
Menander! who has mirrored life and put it on paper.

Until recently Philemon and Menander were known only from their clever sayings or fine lines as quoted by later classical authors and from the Latin adaptations of their comedies by Plautus and Terence. Now the papyri have revealed more considerable fragments of Menander's plays, though apparently not his best work, since compared to the foregoing eulogies of Manilius and Plutarch, "that little that we have discovered of Menander is a disappointment."

Menander was the friend of a cultured Athenian gentleman named Epicurus (371–270) who held that friendship was the sole tie worthy of men and who taught those who gathered in his private garden at Athens how to engage in the intelligent pursuit of happiness and how to enjoy the happy life of the intellect. When he died he left his garden to his friends. Epicurus rejected all the religious and superstitious beliefs of his day as tending only to frighten and disturb mankind. He adopted the atomic theory of the universe, explaining all phenomena as caused by chance mechanical contact and motion of the atoms, and even the mind or soul as simply a compound of finer atoms which would dissolve with death. Thus he rejected

Philosophy of Epicurus

belief both in ghosts and in immortality of the soul. If there were gods, he said, they lived happy lives apart from our world in the spaces between the various material worlds or universes, and certainly did not concern themselves with men. Why therefore should man concern himself with them? Let him enjoy himself and devote his intellect and will power to making himself happy. Such were the doctrines that Epicurus taught in the selfsame city where Socrates a century before had been condemned to death on a charge of teaching atheism. In the meantime philosophy had triumphed, and freedom of thought and speech now prevailed in Athens. The teaching of Epicurus brought a great feeling of relief to many minds of antiquity, and although his *Accepted Maxims* have not come down to us, we read "of the blessings conferred by that book upon its readers, of the peace, tranquillity, and independence of mind it produces, of the protection it gives against terrors, phantoms, and marvels, vain hopes and inordinate desires, of the judgment and candor it fosters and its true purging of the spirit, not with torches and squills and such rubbish, but with right reason, truth, and frankness." This quotation is from the essayist, Lucian, born in Syria in the second century A. D., but the Latin poet, Lucretius, of the first century B. C., in his *On the Nature of the Universe,* furnishes the best extant example of the Epicurean attempt to free the human mind from fear of death and of the gods by a glowing presentation of the atomic theory. Works of two other Epicureans have recently been brought to light at Herculaneum. One says that only by knowledge of natural science can men be freed from false notions and fears.

The Stoic Philosophy

Teaching at Athens at the same time as Epicurus was Zeno, a merchant of Cyprus who came there to study philosophy as many foreigners were doing, and then became himself a teacher in the Painted Porch (*Stoa Poikile*),—whence the name of Stoic for the school of thought which he founded and many subsequent thinkers elaborated. The Cynics, an earlier school founded by a disciple of Socrates, held that virtue was the only good. This principle they tried to impress upon the general public by openly showing their contempt for everything else,— worldly goods and comforts, rank and power. Of the Cynic Diogenes the story is told that he lived in a tub but liked his sun bath too, and that when Alexander the Great came to see him and, standing in front of him, asked if there was anything he could do for him, Diogenes replied, "Yes, get out of my light." There was much bitterness at this time over the unequal distribution of wealth and much satire at the expense of the rich, whom the Cynic Cercidas called "sepulchers of fat." Zeno adopted the Cynic protest against luxury and emphasis upon moral obligation, but gave it a different setting and expression. Taking the pantheistic view that the Universe is a living Whole, and adding the doctrine of Anaxagoras that it is animated by reason, he held that it was the duty of man, as a part of the universe, to conform his particular life to the whole and to live reasonably in accordance with natural law. Or, as a writer of the first century A. D., Philo Judæus, put it, "Since every city in which laws are properly established has a regular constitution, it became necessary for this citizen of the world to adopt the same constitution as that which prevailed in the universal world. And this constitution is the right reason of nature." This law of nature and harmony of the universe the Stoics were apt to identify largely with the regular movements of the heavenly bodies. Philo, for example, thought of the stars not only, like Plato, as divine rational natures, but as free-born citizens of the universe before the first human being had been naturalized. The Stoics therefore commonly were favorable to a belief in astrology and divination and fate in the sense of an unalterable order of nature regulated or designated by the planets. Yet their moral teaching at the same time committed them to the doctrine of freedom of the human will. It further was none too easy for them to explain the existence of evil—of disease, accident, crime, death, famine, and suffering —in a world supposed to be ruled by right reason. However, they were neither the first nor the last "good people" and moral teachers who have not been strictly logical, and the problem of the existence of evil has perplexed many. The Stoics held that evil need not trouble the good man or dispassionate sage, who should ignore it, not allow himself to be affected by it, or should overcome it and profit by it. When St. Paul said, "All things work together for good to them that love God," he was only varying Stoic doctrine, which might have been expressed as, "All things work together for good to those who live in accordance with Nature." The Stoics further held that every wicked man was a slave inwardly (since he did not conform to the law of nature), though outwardly he might reign as tyrant of a city or king of a country.   On the other hand, a slave by human law was as much a man and part of nature as his master.   "Nature has created all men free," wrote Philo Judæus seventeen hundred years before Rousseau.   The Stoics did not reject traditional religion but endeavored to accept the old myths as allegories of natural forces and law.

Common Ground of Stoicism, Epicureanism, and the New Comedy

The Stoic and Epicurean philosophies, in many respects, seem diametrically opposed, yet they had marked similarities. Both believed in a material and natural universe of which man was an integral part.   Both dealt with the problem of the conduct of his life by the individual at a time when the communal ideals of the ancient city state and the force of ancient custom were failing to satisfy and becoming exhausted.   As the new comedy dealt on the one hand with private life instead of public life and on the other hand appealed to humanity at large, so the Stoic substituted, for the narrow patriotism of the city state based on slavery, the conception of natural law and the brotherhood of mankind, while Epicurus, apparently rejecting not only all obligations of citizenship, but even family life and that love between the sexes which played such a large part in the new comedy, declared private friendship the only tie worthy of a philosopher.   On the other hand, both Stoics and Epicureans emphasized the importance of intellectual calm and of individual free will.   Both turned the attention from politics and worldly pleasure or pain to philosophy.   Political power was lost, but intellectual freedom was won.

Religion and Astrology

While philosophy largely took the place of religion for the educated, there were other influences at work.   The ancient tendency to worship the ruler as a god, which was resumed in the Hellenistic monarchies, possibly hurt religion more than it helped the ruler.   Euhemerus held that the old Olympian gods, too, were in origin simply deified men.   Oriental cults now spread more freely than ever before in the Greek world, and the influence of Buddhism probably began to be felt from India, since the rock edicts of Asoka (263–226) state that the Ptolemies and Seleucids have agreed to permit the introduction of Buddhism in their realms.   The Hellenistic age offers a hunting-ground to those in search of evidences of the indebtedness of Christianity to the cults of the preceding period. To it are traced back such conceptions as the representation of a leading and revealing god as a shepherd.   The Old Testament was in this period translated into the Alexandrine Greek dialect, "a clumsy, odd idiom." This version, known as the Septuagint, was the one chiefly cited by the writers of the New Testament and the early church fathers. And the Hellenistic Greek in which the New Testament is written is somewhat similar. At present the prevailing opinion seems to be that the art of astrology, in the elaborate form which takes into account all seven planets then known and the twelve signs of the zodiac, does not go back to early Babylon or Egypt but was a Greek development of this period, connected with the increased astronomical knowledge of Alexandria.

To Alexandria, then, and the literary and scientific studies which flourished there we next turn. Largely instrumental in the promotion of these was the famous Museum, founded apparently by the first Ptolemy towards the end of his reign. This first museum was not, like the art or historical or natural history museum of our day, a building in which paintings and other works of art or historical objects or specimens of animal and plant life were kept on exhibition. It was primarily an association of prominent scholars, poets, and men of letters, united under the leadership of a priest in the worship of the Muses, Greek goddesses whose cult was purely intellectual, without sacrifices, though with altars and statues. Ptolemy provided a temple to the Muses, courts, porticoes, gardens, and a common hall in which the poets and scholars had their meals together. Men of literary and scientific eminence were thereby attracted from all over the Greek world, were directly supported by yearly gifts or salaries from the king, and were provided with everything they needed for their researches.

The Museum at Alexandria

Especially important in this connection was the library, in which the Ptolemies tried to include a copy of every work of Greek literature. Manuscripts at that time were in the form of rolls of papyrus which the reader kept unrolling with one hand and rolling up with the other as he reached the bottom of one of the columns, which were placed side by side. The Alexandrian librarians regarded long rolls as inconvenient to handle and refer to, and hence divided many works of Greek literature into a number of rolls, which corresponded to the "books" into which they are still divided in modern editions. So the Ptolemaic library, of over half a million rolls of papyri, did not comprise that many works of Greek literature, or equal,

Its Library

in length of text, a modern library of half a million printed volumes. The Ptolemies were not the only kings of the time who collected large libraries; the rulers of Pergamum and Antioch followed suit, and Galen, the famous medical writer of the Roman Empire, tells us that when Attalus I (241–197), king of his native Pergamum, was bidding against the Ptolemies for books, persons who had valuable works for sale often tried to secure a higher price for them by interpolating passages and lengthening the work.

Philology
and
Literary
Erudition
The desirability of detecting such forgeries led to the critical study and editing of the ancient texts at Alexandria. Moreover, such marks of pronunciation as the Greek accents were now introduced. The Homeric poems were an especial object of study, and one surviving manuscript of the *Iliad* contains Greek notes selected from the commentaries of Alexandrian philologers, a name which one of them applied to himself. The great librarians of Alexandria were also poets, philosophers, or scientists of distinction. It is not recorded that any of them ever attended a library school, but they knew what was in the books of their library. One of them is said to have been appointed, because, when he disagreed with the other six judges of a poetical contest and furthermore selected the competitor who had pleased the audience least, he justified his choice by proving that the other competitors had all stolen or imitated their poems from past writers. So minutely was the literature of the past and its historical setting studied, that by the time of the Roman Empire a grammarian was expected to know offhand such matters as "the name of Anchises' nurse, the name and native land of the stepmother of Anchemolus, . . . how many years Acestes lived, how many flagons of wine the Sicilian king gave to the Phrygians." And Plutarch tells us that the grammarians proved from obscure passages in the Homeric poems that the heroes and demigods of that age shaved with razors and lent money for interest, and interpreted Homer's calling the night "quick and sharp" to mean that "the shadow of the earth being round, groweth sharp at the end like the body of a cone." Histories of literature and works of literary criticism also appeared. The latter was sometimes a bit rough. The poets, Callimachus and Apollonius, indulged in a literary controversy in the course of which the former called his pupil a pig wallowing in its own filth, while the latter called

his master a blockhead. Finally, dictionaries and grammars were made to assist in the study of language and texts. The first Greek grammar of which we know was that of Dionysius Thrax, about 120 B. C. It is still extant, and we can see that all Greek grammars since have been based upon it.

The poetry produced at Alexandria was apt to be pedantic and artificial, or antiquarian and didactic. The controversy just now alluded to between Callimachus and Apollonius had been whether the long epic was still adapted to their society, Callimachus holding that this new period called for a new style of short poems, while Apollonius composed an epic on the Argonautic expedition in which he, at least, displayed his antiquarian learning and asserted that he had authority for every statement. Aratus and Eratosthenes composed metrical astronomies. The latter not only embellished his poem with mythological incident, but also introduced a description of humble life among the poorer classes and a love story. These last two features became common in Alexandrian literature, and afforded a welcome relief to the life of the authors at court and in library. The portrayal of the passion of love—it was usually love at first sight—was the main concern of the Alexandrian elegy, from which the later erotic romance, or love novel, developed. The epigram, a few lines on any subject— a statue, a famous man of the past, a loved one—in which the poet endeavored to display his literary skill, was another form which continued a favorite into the Byzantine period. Of tragedy, in the Hellenistic period, we know practically nothing, but the *Mimes* of Herondas, discovered in modern Egypt, present a realistic picture of popular life, especially that of women, slaves, and children. Some of the scenes are laid at Cos in the Ægean. *[margin: Alexandrian Poetry]*

The only poetry of first rank produced at Alexandria was the *Idylls* of Theocritus, the first known writer of bucolic verse, describing in seemingly simple and artless style, but with exquisite skill, the idyllic shepherd life and scenery of his native Sicily. Though imitated by Virgil, the great Latin poet, and many others since, Theocritus has never been improved upon. His *Fisherman's Dream* had a great influence on all subsequent piscatory literature. *[margin: Pastorals of Theocritus]*

The chief scientific works preserved from this period are Euclid's *Elements*, the *Conic Sections* of Apollonius of Perga, *[margin: Euclid and Archimedes]* and some of the treatises of Archimedes.   The Greek way of writing numbers and calculating was so clumsy, more so even than the Roman numerals with which we are still familiar, that the Greeks made almost no progress in arithmetic.   But geometry had been developing since Pythagoras, and Plato had insisted that the young tyrant of Syracuse master it before he tackled political science.   Euclid now composed a presentation of elementary geometry which was as logical as Aristotle's textbook in logic and has been employed practically unchanged as a textbook in geometry until very recently.   He stated theorems in their most general form and in an exact, orderly, and convincing manner, but omitted any practical application and made no attempt to train the reader in original work.   Nor did he tell how the theorems were arrived at.   The story is told that when king Ptolemy asked Euclid if there were no shorter cut in geometry than through his *Elements,* he replied that there was no royal road to learning.   Modern democracy needs to realize that there is no popular road either.   Archimedes lived at Syracuse, 287–212, and was killed when the Romans took that city as he was intent on the solution of a mathematical problem.   For he, too, was primarily a mathematician, though his treatises are original investigations, not elementary textbooks.   Voltaire said that "there was far more imagination in the head of Archimedes than in that of Homer."   He calculated the value of π, determined the areas of such figures as the ellipse, parabola, and surface of a sphere, and the volumes of the sphere and of the solids formed by revolving an ellipse, parabola, and hyperbola.   His treatise on the equilibrium of floating bodies has reached us only in an Arabic version.   His mechanics are limited to statics and do not deal with dynamics.   He invented the water screw and military engines for Syracuse to use against the Romans; but his explanation of machines is based simply on the principle of the lever and extensions thereof.   Too often exaggerated accounts have been given of the invention or employment of machinery in the Hellenistic age.

Astronomy and Geography

Archimedes, and later Plutarch, casually mention that Aristarchus of Samos held the heliocentric theory, and moderns have often praised him wildly for this, although we know nothing more about it.   His only extant work is a clever calculation of the size and distance from the earth of sun and moon by measurement of angles and from the duration of eclipses. He came to the conclusion that the sun was 6918 times as great as the earth, and the earth twenty-seven times the size of the moon, and that the sun was 19 times as far from us as the moon is. Really the sun is 344 times as far away from the earth as the moon is. Hipparchus of Nicæa (161–126) set up an astronomical observatory on the island of Rhodes, invented the astrolabe and spherical trigonometry, made a catalogue of stars, discovered the precession of the equinoxes, introduced geographical longitude and latitude, and was called by the later astronomer, Ptolemy, the "father of astronomy." He seems to have had a leaning towards astrology, as Pliny tells us that "Hipparchus will never receive all the praise he deserves, since no one has better established the relationship between man and the stars, or shown more clearly that our souls are particles of heavenly fire." Eratosthenes (275–194), one of the librarians at Alexandria, computed the circumference of the earth with approximate accuracy by observing the shadows cast by the sun at Alexandria and at Syene, a place far up the Nile. He also wrote a history of geography, drew a map of the world, and suggested that India might be reached by sailing westward from Spain.

The scientists at Alexandria were permitted by the Ptolemies to dissect human cadavers and even to vivisect criminals condemned to death. Herophilus of Chalcedon was the leading name in medicine and anatomy, although Erasistratus might also be mentioned. Herophilus distinguished the nerves and held against Aristotle that the brain, and not the heart, was the center of the nervous system. He was the first to perform autopsies and to describe the *Torcular Herophili*, the *calamus scriptorius*, the duodenum, and the lacteals. He did not, however, as is sometimes stated, practically discover the circulation of the blood; he simply understood, as most ancient and medieval scientists did, that the blood is borne in streams to all parts of the body. He still cherished certain superstitions, such as that there were herbs which would heal a patient who merely trod on them. Similarly Theophrastus, the chief botanist of antiquity, included superstitious practices in plucking medicinal herbs. In the main, however, Theophrastus, like

Medicine and Botany

Aristotle, aimed to describe the normal course and condition of natural phenomena and to find a reasonable explanation for everything.

Master-pieces of Hellenistic Sculpture

Athens ceased in this period to be the chief productive center of Greek art, and our remains of sculpture are derived largely from cities of Asia Minor, such as Pergamum, Tralles, Ephesus, and the island of Rhodes. They include some priceless masterpieces. A marble sarcophagus has been preserved with colored reliefs showing Alexander at the battle of Issus and engaged in a lion hunt. To commemorate a naval victory of 306, one of the Hellenistic monarchs erected on an island in the northern Ægean Sea the Victory of Samothrace, a winged female figure at the prow of a ship with wind-swept draperies. The great frieze of the altar of Zeus at Pergamum, seven feet high and over four hundred feet long, is a turbulent and overwhelming representation of the struggle between the gods and giants. The defeat of the Galatians by the kings of Pergamum was commemorated in a series of bronze figures, of which a few marble copies remain. It may be doubted if the originals were superior to the existing group of the Gaul who kills both his wife and himself that they may escape capture, or to the single figure of the Dying Gaul:

> He leans upon his hand—his manly brow
> Consents to death, but conquers agony,
> And his drooped head sinks gradually low—
> And through his side the last drops, ebbing slow
> From the red gash, fall heavy, one by one,
> Like the first of a thunder-shower. . . .

The Laocoön group, representing the priest of Neptune and his two sons attacked by the two serpents sent by Juno, is ascribed by Pliny to three Rhodians. It was discovered in 1506, and pronounced a marvel of art by Michelangelo. It is probably a late Hellenistic work. Another celebrated group is that of the Farnese bull, found at Rome in the Baths of Caracalla in 1546, a Roman copy of the Hellenistic original. The Apollo Belvedere, a marble Roman copy seven feet tall of a bronze Hellenistic original, was for a time regarded as the perfection of Greek grace in sculpture, but now is considered somewhat showy and effeminate.

In this Hellenistic sculpture there is much depiction of

THE DYING GAUL

(Front and rear view.)

ROMAN BRONZES

Left, bust of Seneca, man of letters and Stoic philosopher; right, head of a statue of Hadrian, emperor and architect.

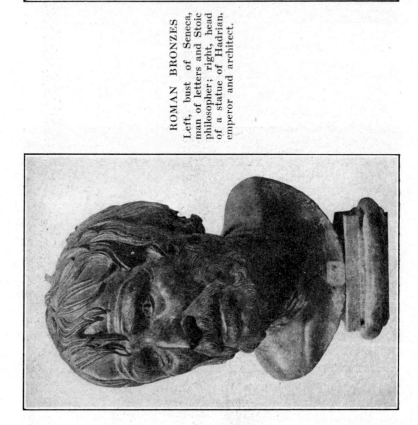

violent action and of pain and agony. There is also realism in place of idealism, and emphasis on emotion and expressiveness instead of, as before, on poise and beauty. This heightened dramatic effect perhaps reflects the influence of the theater. The artists have great mastery over their material, great technical skill, and accurate knowledge of human anatomy. Animals, plants, a rocky background, and other little details, to give verisimilitude, are introduced, suggesting the interest of the age in pastoral nature and natural science. Boëthus of Carthage was famous for statues of children such as his naked child struggling with a goose, his infant Æsculapius, and his boy extracting a thorn from his foot. Some think that this Hellenistic sculpture shows too great striving after striking effects. At any rate, it is different from the previous Hellenic art and has original powers and merits, if also defects of its own. Some motives in art, such as the symbolic representation of the sky by a half-length bearded man holding a mantle arched above his head, which we find repeatedly in later Roman and Italian Renaissance art, are traced back to the Hellenistic period. Hellenistic art became widely diffused through the eastern Mediterranean and even to Bactria and India; but then Roman generals concentrated much of it in Rome by despoiling Greek cities and bringing cart-loads and ship-loads of sculpture and paintings from all directions. Of the paintings we can say little, as they have not survived to our time except those from Roman Pompeii in the first century A. D. and recent finds in central Asia.

BIBLIOGRAPHY

In addition to the books listed at the close of the three preceding chapters, in which will be found discussions of the art, literature, and philosophy of this period, we may mention:

Allbutt, Sir T. Clifford. *Greek Medicine in Rome,* 1921, Chapter V.

Heath, T. L. *Aristarchus of Samos,* 1913; *Greek Mathematics,* 1922.

Heiberg, J. L. *Science and Mathematics in Classical Antiquity,* 1922, Chapters VII, VIII.

Neuberger, A. *Die Technik des Altertums,* 1921, 676 illus.

Ottley, R. R. *A Handbook to the Septuagint,* 1920.

Singer, Charles. *Greek Biology and Medicine,* 1922.

CHAPTER XIV

THE WESTERN FRONTIER OF ANCIENT CIVILIZATION

Shall we be a great people only in the sense in which Carthage was a great people?—*President Lowell*

Four Chief Cultures of the Western Mediterranean

BEFORE Rome brought the entire Mediterranean basin under its sway, there were in the western Mediterranean world four chief peoples and civilizations aside from the Greek colonies of which we have already treated. There was the Phœnician or Punic culture which had its center in Carthage in North Africa. There was the Etruscan civilization which centred in Etruria in Italy. There were the Italians, a name which for this period designates those Indo-Europeans who had invaded the peninsula of Italy and the race which resulted from their fusion with the previous population. Strictly speaking, however, the Greeks gave Italy its name from a minor tribe in the south called *Itali* who were *not* Indo-European, just as later the Romans gave Greece its name from a minor tribe in the northwest of that peninsula. Finally, there was Gallic civilization, which is to be similarly connected with the invasion by Celts from central Europe of the land west of the Rhine, and portions of Spain, Italy, and the British Isles. These regions lie in part beyond the limits of the Mediterranean basin and draw us on to northwestern Europe. Of the four civilizations just mentioned, the first two named were oriental and Mediterranean in their origin; the last two were in part of northern European antecedents. All seem to have been influenced more or less by the Greek colonies in their neighborhood. Thus we have a Hellenistic element in the west as well as in the east.

Economic Power of Carthage

The Phœnician colony, Carthage, founded perhaps in the ninth century B. C., became one of the greatest sea powers of history. It was situated at the best spot for anchorage in the great Gulf of Tunis and was near the richest grain district of North Africa. The expression, "North Africa" is here used to denote that portion of the continent between the Sahara desert and the western Mediterranean, and hence does not include Egypt.   In this North Africa Carthage reigned supreme, profiting by the decline of Tyre and Sidon to become independent.   It was cut off from the east by the Greeks, but extended its settlements, trade, and influence into Sicily, Sardinia, and Spain.   In Sicily its huge armies of mercenaries waged a long series of wars for the supremacy with the Greek cities through the fifth and fourth centuries.   We have to learn what little we can concerning Carthage chiefly from its enemies, the Greeks and Romans.   Thucydides declared Carthage superior financially to all the Greek states and second only to Persia, and even in defeat it was able to pay its heavy indemnities to Rome in advance.   The modern historian, Mommsen, estimated the city population of Carthage as perhaps 700,000.   The state was mainly supported by the produce paid by the subject Libyans, who were also liable to military service, or produced by slaves who cultivated the soil in chains.   The Libyans were the natives, apparently of the same race as the modern Berbers. There are indications of the existence of a public debt and token-money.   The Carthaginians had the reputation of being shrewd and unscrupulous traders who picked up a knowledge of foreign languages and ways readily and were willing to live abroad.   They put down piracy, but kept to themselves the knowledge of whatever geographical discoveries they may have made.   The high reputation of their navy seems scarcely justified in view of the defeats it suffered at the hands of the Greeks and Romans.   The form of government in this plutocratic metropolis is not well known, but was praised by Greek writers, and appears to have been a stable merchant-aristocracy like that of medieval Venice.

The Carthaginians seem to have possessed little originality in art, industry, or literature.   Most of the books they read were written by Greeks.   The only notable treatise by a Carthaginian of which we know was that of Mago on agriculture in twenty-eight books, which was translated into Greek and Latin and later into Arabic.   In art and industry the Carthaginians followed Egyptian and Greek models, but in such remains as have thus far reached us—excavations on the site of Carthage are still in process—display neither skill nor taste in their copying.   Their religion, with its cruel sacrifice of children and licentious worship of the goddess Astarte on the one hand,

Little
Original
Culture

and a monotheistic, spiritual tendency on the other hand, seems drawn from Syria. The latter tendency perhaps helped to make possible the later rapid spread of Christianity in North Africa.

Influence of Carthage on the Western Mediterranean

By hampering the development of the Greek cities in Sicily, and sooner or later destroying many of them, Carthage was partly responsible for the decline of civilization in western Hellas and for the rise of Rome, a city inferior in some respects to the Greeks in civilization. On the other hand, by fortified posts Carthage kept the nomad tribes out of North Africa, or took tribute and contingents of troops from them. By intensive agriculture she raised that region to a state of prosperity which enabled it to continue as civilized and cultured as any other Mediterranean land through the period of the Roman Empire, after which it gradually declined, until recently somewhat revived by French occupation. Even of the Spanish peninsula, which Carthage occupied for only a short time, Pliny could write nearly three centuries afterward, "Spain still sees the watch towers of Hannibal." The prosperity and decline of North Africa were paralleled by the fate of Carthage itself. Destroyed by Rome in 146 B. C., it was restored later, became the third city of the Roman Empire, and was permanently destroyed only in 697–698 A. D. by the Arabs, whose capital, Tunis, is less advantageously situated. By its trade and colonies Carthage promoted civilization in the western Mediterranean, and the inferior products of her artisans were perhaps as much appreciated by the barbarians to whom they were sold as the finer work of Greece or Egypt would have been. But the importance of Carthage in the history of civilization is primarily economic.

Etruscan Civilization Probably Derived from Asia Minor

Etruria, or Tuscany as it has been called for the last thousand years or so, is the region bounded by the Apennines, Tiber, and Mediterranean. Both names for the region testify to its connection with the Etruscans. This ancient people left numerous material remains and many inscriptions, but no one has yet succeeded in translating the latter. This very failure, however, indicates that their language was not Indo-European. Their customs, too, were in many respects peculiar; for instance, their week was of eight days, and their day began at noon, whereas the Greek day began at sunset and the Roman, like ours, at midnight. Various theories have been advanced as to their race and origin, and they have been connected with the Armenians, Basques, Canaanites, Egyptians, and Tartars. On the whole scholars are inclined to accept the statement of Herodotus that they migrated from Lydia in Asia Minor about 1000 B. C. Their art, industries, customs, and mode of burial are markedly different from those of other early peoples in Italy and on the whole suggest the ancient orient. This is particularly the case with their royal insignia, their long flowery robes with gaudy borders, their sandals and Phrygian caps. Unlike the Greeks, and other peoples of the west, they employed the round arch and vault at an early date. Their burial mounds rested on massive sub-constructions, or their tombs were cut into hill-sides with complicated series of interior chambers. Evil demons were prominent in their religion, their priesthood was numerous and powerful, and the elaborate divination by Etruscan *haruspices* from inspection of entrails of sacrificial victims or from thunder and lightning was perhaps derived from the liver divination and astrology of Babylon.

The Etruscans lived in cities, twelve of which formed a famous league. At first their wealth lay chiefly in raw materials, grain, timber, and metals, which they exchanged with the Greeks for finished works of art; later they cleverly imitated the Greek work in their own manufactures. For a time they had considerable sea power along the west coast of Italy and made a treaty with Carthage by which the latter received Sardinia, while they kept Corsica and control of the Tyrrhenian Sea between the islands and the Italian peninsula. After their defeat in 474 by Hiero of Syracuse their naval power appears to have declined. Their walled towns had impressive gateways such as Rome did not have until the days of the Cæsars. The Etruscans were greater engineers than architects, and their drains, bridges, and roads were superior to their houses and temples. Their tombs are not important architecturally, but the wall-paintings and reliefs with which they are adorned inform us concerning their social life and religion. They used horses and chariots—a fine bronze chariot is extant from the sixth century—and enjoyed a luxurious life with banquets, music, gay costumes, and animal pets. But their religion seems gloomy, brutal, and bloodthirsty like those of Assyria and ancient Mexico.

Etruscan Social and Economic Life

There was a lack of marble in Etruria, and its wooden temples offered less opportunity than the Greek temples for

Etruscan Art

sculpture.   The Etruscans nevertheless were exceedingly skilful in modelling and coloring terra-cotta.   The human figures
reclining on the covers of their sarcophagi are often as realistic
as waxworks.   We find two different physical types in the tomb
frescoes and the sarcophagus figures.   "On one side we see a
type with broad smooth forehead, high cheek bones, long slanting eyes, prominent nose, thin cheeks, and long chin, with lithe,
tall, slender bodies and a lively, expressive, almost sardonic
expression. . . . On the other hand, we see the type of broad-
faced, stolid, heavy-lipped and jowled people, with arro-
gantly placid and materially minded expression, with bull necks
and thick-set bodies" (Frothingham).   Lamps and dishes of
Etruscan bronze were sought after even in Periclean Athens,
and the Etruscan trumpet was famous.   The Etruscans delighted in gems and jewels, and were very skilful in soldering
minute globules of gold to form patterns on gold backgrounds.
More Etruscan than Greek mirrors are extant—both of course
were made of metal, not glass—but the designs outlined on the
backs of the Etruscan mirrors are either scenes from Greek
mythology or Etruscan subjects treated in Greek style.

Etruscan Influence on Rome

Until the invasion of northern and central Italy by the Gauls
in the fifth and fourth centuries B. C. crippled their power, the
Etruscans exerted a wide influence in the Italian peninsula,
spreading beyond the Apennines into the Po valley and Umbria
and southward into Campania.   The later Roman historians
were reluctant to admit that their city had long been under
Etruscan rule, but the situation of Rome on the Tiber or
frontier of Etruria makes this highly probable, and we can find
plenty of hints that such was the case even in the early legends
as told by the Romans.   Many of the names of the oldest and
noblest Roman families seem to be Etruscan.   Roman civilization, at least, was largely Etruscan in origin, and even the
Roman government took over from the Etruscans such forms
as the curule chair and the lictors who attended the magistrate.
To the Etruscans the Romans further owed their military organization, and the arts of fortification, engineering, drainage
and irrigation, and road paving.   Their first temples were in
the Etruscan style, and they probably derived the alphabet, as
well as the phalanx, indirectly from the Greeks through the
Etruscans.   The Romans also adopted the Etruscan methods
of divination and books of ritual for founding cities, placing

the town gates, taking the census, and even for the conduct of daily life.   To illustrate how long such mental habits persist in civilization we may note that in the Theodosian Code, a collection of imperial legislation made after the Roman Empire had become Christian, we find a law of 321 A. D. to the effect that, if public buildings are struck by lightning, the *haruspices* are to be consulted.   The Anglo-Saxon monk, Bede, in the eighth century translated, with some qualms it is true, a treatise from the Greek on divination from thunder, and in the thirteenth century astrology was still employed in regard to the fortune and founding of Italian cities.

While the Romans thus owed much of their civilization to the Etruscans, they spoke Latin, one of the Italian or Indo-European languages, and joined with the other tribes or towns of Latium in worship of Jupiter on the Alban Mount in the center of the plain of Latium, and in a defensive league under the leadership at first of a town called Alba Longa.   The Italy of that time was one of complicated ethnography and motley nationalities with a composite population of diverse races. However, a large part of the peninsula was occupied by tribes more or less closely related to the Romans or Latins.   There were, for example, the Hernicans, Æquians, Volscians, Marsians, Sabines, Samnites, and Umbrians.   There were many dialects besides Latin, for instance, Oscan, the speech of Iguvium, Sabellian, and Umbrian.   Many tribes, especially those who remained in the Apennines as mountaineers, were still in the pastoral stage.   Others, like the Latins, had settled in the plains and devoted themselves to agriculture.   They lived in towns or on occasion took refuge in citadels surrounded by long walls of immense polygonal masonry.   Thus in southeastern Latium, where in modern times hardly a person is to be seen because of the ravages of malaria and the neglect of irrigation or because of a more fundamental change in the climate, there were, in the eighth to fourth centuries, several hundred thousand inhabitants.   Many of these other towns were at first better fortified than Rome, but the latter was situated on the only navigable river and was the natural center of trade between the Latins and the Etruscans and in an advantageous position to profit by Etruscan influence.   Beginning from the fifth century inscriptions are extant in various Italian dialects.   The Italians were more numerous than either Etruscans or Car-

The Italians

thaginians, and so were likely to triumph over both, if they stopped fighting one another and united. Rome finally brought this about. The Sabellians, in the latter part of the fifth century overran Campania and much of Lucania in southern Italy, displacing the Etruscan and Greek powers in those regions and capturing such cities as Capua, Cumæ, and Poseidonia (Pæstum), famous for its Greek temples which still stand today. But the town rapidly lost its Greek language and customs. Elea, a stronghold of philosophy, alone held out against the Sabellians. The latter, however, adopted much of the Greek civilization.

Celtic Invasion of Gaul, Spain, and Italy

When the ancient authors spoke of Celts, they meant a tall, fair-haired race with blue or gray, not dark, eyes. Unfortunately they did not carefully examine and measure their skulls and tell us whether they were broad like the Alpine, or long like the northern European race. For various reasons we assume that these invaders from central Europe called Celts or Gauls, were of Alpine race and Indo-European speech. They established themselves firmly in Gaul, that is, the region between the Rhine, Alps, Pyrenees, and ocean, by about the seventh century. In the next century they took much of the Spanish peninsula from the Iberians, so that Herodotus noted the existence of Celts in what is now southern Portugal. In the fifth century they broke the Etruscan power in Italy and in 390 sacked Rome. The name, Galicia, still applied to regions in central Europe and Spain, has the same significance as Galatia in Asia Minor or as Gaul itself and shows how widespread was this Celtic expansion. These Celts would seem to have been closely related to the earlier Indo-European speaking invaders of the Ægean whom we saw depicted in Homer's Achæans, and to those who had entered the Italian peninsula in the previous millennium but had by this time become largely Mediterraneanized. In many of the territories overrun by these Gauls, they very likely constituted only a ruling military class rather than the bulk of the population, or else their physical characteristics were changed by the new climate. Thus, while successive waves of Celtic invasion are believed to have reached the British Isles, the dark complexioned peoples of western Scotland and western Ireland, although speaking Gaelic, are not strictly Celtic or of Alpine race. In Italy the Gauls soon receded somewhat, but the northern third of the peninsula was long occupied by them and was known as Cisalpine Gaul on this account.   What concerns us more, however, than the race or numbers of the invading Celts or the extent to which they fused with the previous populations is the civilization that prevailed in Gaul following their conquest and preceding the conquest of Gaul by the Romans under Julius Cæsar in 58–50.   This is of the more consequence because their characteristics and customs appear to have influenced the national traits and the civilizations of France and the British Isles to this day.

The Gauls before Cæsar were of quick intelligence though rather flighty, brave to the point of rashness but restive under rule and discipline, sociable, communicative, voluble, boastful and given to fits of blind rage.   Their military aristocracy combined generosity and ferocity.   The banquets given by the chiefs about a round table like that of King Arthur were marked by punctilious etiquette, athough the guests devoured their food voraciously from metal plates, drained a common cup, and amused themselves by watching mock combats, or became involved in real fights as a result of fancied insults.   All these characteristics are repeated in feudal France.   With their great leaf-shaped slashing Hallstatt swords the Celts swept everything before them in the fourth century.   Cæsar mentioned the use of the war chariot only in Britain, but remains of such chariots have been found in Champagne and Burgundy, and they are earlier mentioned in Cisalpine Gaul.   The swords and shields of the Gauls were highly ornamented.   They gave much attention to their dress and personal appearance, wearing long hair and mustaches, bracelets, collars, brooches, and other jewelry, brilliant colored cloths and gold embroidery.   They were clad in a mantle, pantaloons, and thick-soled shoes with high vamps called *gallicae* in Latin, from which our galoshes may be derived.   By the eve of Cæsar's conquest the aristocracy had, in large measure, overthrown the kings, and senates, somewhat like that at Rome, were the chief source of power.   There was also the personal band of comrades in arms, an association found further among the Iberians of Spain and Germans of the north.   Party strife existed in almost every state, and the mass of the people, excluded from a voice in the government, were ready to support individuals who were ambitious to restore monarchy.   Besides the slaves there were the poor and weak who had been forced to seek the protection of the power-

Gallic
Society

ful as the only way to secure their goods and persons, so that the majority of the population were in a state of clientage—a not uncommon condition among other peoples of antiquity and found at Rome itself. When the master died and his body was cremated, the slaves and clients were sometimes burned with him.

Government, Law, and Religion

Among the Gauls, as among many other ancient peoples whom we have considered, the small city state was the unit of government, although the land was covered with forests, and there were also isolated habitations and villages of thatched huts. The names of most of the tribes in ancient Gaul are still perpetuated in those of French towns: for instance, Treves represents the Treveri; Beauvais, the Bellovaci; Soissons, the Suessiones; Poitiers, the Pictones; Bourges, the Bituriges; Limoges, the Lemovices; and so on. The total population of Transalpine Gaul was perhaps five millions. There was both direct and indirect taxation, and the states had large public domains, but there was also private land ownership by individuals or families. In the family the father was supreme, and woman was subordinated. In marriage the wife brought a dowry, the husband contributed an equal amount, and the total sum went to the survivor. The Druids, or priestly class, like the Brahmans in India or the medieval clergy, controlled law and literature as well as religion, furnishing the bards of the time and determining land boundary disputes, inheritance, and criminal law. Their chief priest and power of interdict somewhat suggest the medieval papacy.

Towns and Economic Life

Cicero questioned if there was anything uglier in appearance than a Gallic town. The wall consisted of two rows of rough stone without cement and with the space between filled in with dirt. There were neither projecting towers nor crenelated battlements, though sometimes there was a moat outside the wall. There was considerable trade, and some states had coinages imitated from the Greek. The regions along the Atlantic coast developed many well trained sailors and serviceable vessels with flat keels, strong hulls of oak, and raised prows and sterns. In addition to the war chariot the Gauls had a variety of wheeled vehicles, some of which the Romans borrowed. Inoffensive travelers, like Pytheas, a Greek from Massalia (Marseilles) who about 330 B. C. gives us the first certain mention of Britain, were hospitably received and plied with curious questions to elicit interesting news and tales.

Gaul abounded in metals, and Britain was noted in antiquity for its tin mines, located in the southwest of the island just across the channel from Gaul. The Gauls were skilled metallurgists and perhaps first developed silver-plating and enamelling. Their ornamentation was still geometric. For a barbaric or semi-barbaric people they had already attained a fair degree of economic development, and their civilization was not merely a borrowed one.

BIBLIOGRAPHY

Besides the treatments of Carthage, the Etruscans, Italians and Gauls in the histories of Rome by Mommsen, Heitland, Tenney Frank, and others, we may mention:

ON CARTHAGE

Grant, C. F. and L. *African Shores of the Mediterranean,* 1912.

Gsell, S. *Histoire ancienne de l'Afrique du Nord.* Tome IV; *La civilisation carthaginoise,* 1920.

Khun de Prorok, (Count Byron) "Ancient Carthage in the Light of Modern Excavation," in *National Geographic Magazine,* April, 1924, pp. 391–423.

Moore, Mabel. *Carthage of the Phœnicians,* 1905.

Smith, R. B. *Carthage and the Carthaginians,* 1897; *Rome and Carthage,* 1883.

ON THE ETRUSCANS

Dennis, Geo. *Cities and Cemeteries of Etruria,* 1883.

Fell, R. A. L. *Etruria and Rome,* 1923.

Müller, Karl O. *Die Etrusker,* second edition by Deecke, 1877.

Poulsen, Frederik. *Etruscan Tomb Paintings. Their subject and significance,* 1922, translated by I. Anderson.

Randall-MacIver, D. *Villanovans and Early Etruscans,* 1924; a finely printed and illustrated account of the remains.

ON EARLY ITALY

Frothingham, A. L. *Roman Cities of Italy and Dalmatia,* 1910.

Peet, T. E. *Stone and Bronze Ages in Italy and Sicily,* 1909.

ON EARLY GAUL

Déchelette, J. *Manuel d'archéologie préhistorique, celtique, et gallo-romaine,* 1908–10.

Lavisse, E. *Histoire de France,* 1900, vol. I, part 2, first chapters on Gaul before the Roman conquest.

Siret, L. *Questions de chronologie et ethnographie ibérique,* 1913.

CHAPTER XV

ROMAN LAW AND GOVERNMENT

(753 B. C.–534 A. D.)

Old Cato used to say that the form of our government was preferable to other states, because in those there had generally been certain individuals who each formed his own state by his own laws and institutions, as Minos in Crete, Lycurgus in Sparta. . . . But our republic was not the invention of one man, but of many; nor formed in the life-time of one man alone, but gradually in generations and ages.—*Cicero*

Sources
and Legends
of Early
Roman
History

IT should be realized that the early history of Rome is very uncertain and largely mythical. The earliest Roman historian, Fabius Pictor, wrote his *Annals* in Greek about 200 B. C. There was no Latin literature worthy of the name until Ennius, an epic poet commonly called the father of Latin literature, who came from Calabria and was admitted to Roman citizenship in 184 B. C. Only fragments of their works are extant, and, except for such accounts by Greek historians as that of the first two Punic Wars by Polybius, the whole period before them may almost be regarded as prehistoric so far as Rome is concerned. Some laws were inscribed on stone, but mere fragments of these have been preserved. The archæological remains either indicate Etruscan influence, or are relatively late, or show no very high stage of civilization. They indicate, however, that there were settlements of a sort on the site of Rome at a very early date, and that gradually something like the general plan of the later city developed. We have, it is true, sections of the Roman histories of Livy and Dionysius of Halicarnassus, who both wrote just before the beginning of our era and who purport to set forth in detail the early history of Rome, which they carry down, in the books that have reached us, to 292 and 450 respectively. Their accounts were long accepted as essentially true. But while they may have written in good faith, it is evident that neither

of them really understood the early period.   They too unques-
tioningly copied the boastful funeral orations of Roman families in praise of their ancestors, real or imagined, and the clever
fabrications which Greek slaves and private secretaries had
concocted for Roman statesmen of previous generations who
were anxious to fill in the gap in their early national history
and to make out a glorious past for the great Roman republic
of their day.   These clever Greeks sometimes betray their
handiwork by transfering incidents from the pages of Greek
historians into the Roman past.   To a great extent Rome derived, not only its art and literature, but both its religious
mythology and its historical legends from the Greeks.   The
Romans doubtless had stories of their own concerning their
past, but these too were largely legendary, although they served
to inspire patriotism.   The account of the seven kings from
the supposed founding of the city about 753 to the change to a
republican form of government in 509 sounds not unlike the
Chinese narratives of their first emperors and the contributions
of each to the foundation of the social order and the advance
of civilization.   The sack of Rome by the Gauls about 390
makes it the less likely that records were preserved from before
that date, after which the city was rebuilt, and it became difficult to remember even its previous appearance.

The early Roman religion seems to have been a very crude
and primitive one.   It hardly rose to any conception of gods
or spirits, use of temples and images, or to any true attitude
of worship.   Neither hymns nor legends have come down to us.
"Where the Roman religion rises above fetishism, it does not
go beyond the lower stages of animism."   The main thing was
to repeat certain magic words and names, or to perform certain
ceremonies connected with the hearth-fire, door, and threshold
in order to safeguard family life and the home, or agricultural
magic to ensure good crops, or public rites to preserve the state.
Law and religion began together in Roman history; *ius civile*
being the maintenance of right relations between citizens, and
ius divinum being the similar maintenance of right relations
between the Romans and the mysterious world of nature or
the supernatural about them.   All vows must be exactly fulfilled like legal contracts; strict attention must be paid to all
omens, portents, and requirements of ritual.   This narrow,
legalistic attitude remained characteristic of the religion of

Relation of Roman Religion to Law and Government

the Romans, being only strengthened by their borrowing Etruscan divination and ritual, and little affected by their later adoption of Greek mythology. Thus their religion, while crude, testified to their strong sense of law and their respect for formalities, for obligations, for custom. Since their religion was primitive and, as time went on, became increasingly behind the times, they came more and more to adopt the attitude of observing merely the letter of the religious law. This also became true of their attitude to the civil law where, as we shall see, they pretended to continue the old rules and customs while really reading a new spirit into them. In religion, however, the new spirit did not seem to be forthcoming, until finally the empty shell of outworn paganism gave way to a new religious attitude from the orient and then to Christianity in particular. But the Roman government was so intimately connected with the old religious forms that it clung to them until a very late date.

The Family and Social Classes

In early Roman society the power of the father extended over the son even after he was married and over the son's wife and children. The father could punish, put to death, or sell into slavery. Inheritance, if the head of a household died without direct descendants, went back to his agnates, i. e., collateral relations in the male line from a common ancestor. The Roman law, however, permitted the adoption of sons, which was frequently resorted to in order to prevent a male line from dying out. The patricians, or heads of the most prominent families, could alone sit in the Roman senate and hold the chief priesthoods and magistracies. The plebeians, or common people, served in the army. Members of the same brotherhood or *curia* fought side by side, and occasionally met in the popular assembly, in which each *curia* had one vote.

Constitutional History of the Early Republic

When a republic was established, the military and political leadership passed from the king to two consuls who were elected annually. They constituted the chief executive and supreme magistracy, except in times of great emergency, when a single dictator was appointed. As time went on, new offices were added: quæstors in charge of the treasury, ædiles to superintend and police the streets, markets, and public works, a prætor to administer justice and civil law. These officials were annual like the consuls, but censors were chosen to take the census only every fifth year for a term of eighteen months.

They also let out contracts for collecting the taxes and for public works on a larger scale than those undertaken by the curule ædiles.   In taking the census they assigned the citizens to their proper tribes and classes, and might even drop from membership in the senate a patrician whose life they considered scandalous or who had showed himself lacking in devotion to the state.   It will be noted that the Romans appointed most of their magistrates in pairs.   Later the numbers of some officials were increased to four, ten, and so on.   Either magistrate could veto the action of his colleague or colleagues.   Aside from this there was little check upon the magistrates who had great power during their term of office.   The lictors, who attended the consuls with axes wrapped in bundles of rods, show that the magistrates could chastise the people at any time as a father might his son, and that they had power of life and death over the army in the field, although in the city the citizen had a right of appeal to the assembly.   Hence the Roman people were trained in strict obedience, well disciplined, docile, and deferential.   The senate, however, exerted a strong influence over the magistrates, since its members held their seats for life and had usually had previous experience as magistrates themselves.   Meanwhile a change had come about in the army. The Romans had adopted the phalanx and by means of the census had divided the people into centuries of heavy and light armed troops according to their property, which was still chiefly agricultural.   Voting in the popular assembly now also came to be by centuries, although the old form of voting by *curiae* was retained for certain ceremonial and religious purposes.   By this arrangement the more prosperous peasants became the heavy armed troops, and the vote of their centuries counted for more in the assembly.   A century of older men, too, although many of their number kept dying off and the others had ceased to fight, could still cast a vote of equal value to that of a full century of young recruits.   Thus the Roman government was, like the Spartan state, a conservative and military one in which landed property, rank, and age were potent.

Many of the plebeians, however, were not prosperous peasants but were being reduced to a state of clientage to the patricians, to whom they were losing their lands or falling in debt, and were being scourged or sold into slavery by their

Gains of the Plebeians

creditors. Throughout the history of the republic the agrarian question, or problem of the distribution of land, especially of new territory conquered by the Romans, and the question of debt, were recurrent problems. If we believe the ancient historians, the more prosperous plebeians seem at first to have sided with the more unfortunate, probably because the patricians had thus far refused to intermarry with any plebeians or to admit them to the magistracies and public priesthoods. The first concession that the plebeians were able to procure was special magistrates of their own, called tribunes of the plebs, who were to protect their fellow citizens against private oppression. They further presided at the meetings of a new popular assembly which voted by tribes instead of by centuries. As Rome added new territory to its immediate neighborhood, it organized the inhabitants into new tribes. In the third place, the tribunes of the plebs were allowed to listen to the deliberations of the patricians in the senate, to veto its proposed measures, then to veto also the actions of other magistrates. Meanwhile the plebeians had forced the patricians to write down the laws in Twelve Tables instead of interpreting custom to suit themselves. Later intermarriage was allowed between patricians and plebeians. Finally all the offices were opened to all citizens, and any Roman might attain the envied privilege of sitting in a curule chair and exercising *imperium*, or power.

Are Soon Nullified

But straightway a new upper class developed consisting of those who had held public office. and their descendants. As Rome with conquest and expansion became a great metropolis, capital, and center of trade, there furthermore came into existence an influential capitalist class, while the peasant farmers, who had been the backbone of the early republic, declined as a result of the many disastrous wars which had devastated Italy. They were replaced by a city mob, which the candidates for office and holders of office tried to keep in a good humor by spectacular shows and largesses of grain.

Rome Becomes Supreme in Italy

After a struggle of long duration with the other Latins against the various hostile peoples upon its borders, Rome, as the power of the Etruscans and Greeks in the peninsula declined and the invading Gauls receded northward, brought the rest of Latium under its leadership. It then proceeded to conquer the Samnites, who were the chief independent Italian stock left, and the few independent Greek cities of southern

ANCIENT FURNI-
TURE

Left, metal stand or ta-
ble; right, hot water
heater and bath.

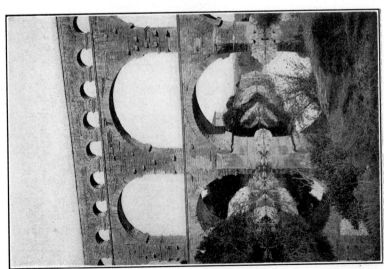

ROMAN ARCHED STRUCTURE

Left, aqueduct bridging a stream, the Pont du Gard near Nîmes; right, a ruined section of the amphitheater at Nîmes.

Italy that still survived.   The region north of the Apennines remained for the time being outside Roman control as Cisalpine Gaul.   Rome held the rest of Italy by planting military colonies of its own citizens here and there at strategic points and then gradually connecting these by excellent military roads. Here and there, too, Rome took over large tracts of land as public domain.   But to a great extent it left the other towns of Italy their own local government.   They were allies, bound to Rome by treaties which required them to furnish contingents of troops to aid Rome in war.   Many Italians were admitted to a partial Roman citizenship which did not include the right of suffrage (*suffragium*) but which did give such rights as freedom of trade (*commercium*) and intermarriage (*connubium*). Italy was to suffer severely during the second Punic War, when the great Carthaginian general, Hannibal, maintained an army undefeated for sixteen years (218–202 B. C.) in the peninsula.

For, having thus attained the leadership of Italy, Rome began in 264 B. C., a series of wars with Carthage which resulted in the acquisition of Sicily, Sardinia, Corsica, and Cisalpine Gaul, a free hand in the Spanish peninsula, and finally in the destruction of Carthage itself in 146 B. C.   In the same year, as the sequel to a series of wars in the Greek peninsula and Asia Minor, and to the annexation of Macedon (148), which had been one of the three chief Hellenistic monarchies, Rome wiped out the city of Corinth, which was, like Carthage, a commercial rival of the Roman capitalists.   This year further marked the end of Greek freedom, as the Romans forbade the Greek cities to form leagues or to establish democratic forms of government, although they left some towns independent under the rule of their wealthier citizens.   Rome next began to annex the small states of Asia Minor, the Mediterranean coast of Gaul, islands like Crete and Cyprus, and Syria, ending the Seleucid dynasty. Julius Cæsar added Gaul in 58–50 B. C. and made brief incursions into Britain and Germany.   Later under the imperial government, Egypt and the remaining Mediterranean coast lands and other northern provinces were added.   At the head of each province was a single magistrate from Rome, whose term was normally for a year only.   He had charge of Roman interests in the province, settled disputes between Roman citizens and provincials, levied troops, supported the tax-collectors, and ruled

Conquest of the Mediterranean World

with absolute power over such portions of the province as had been given no rights of local government.

Decline of the Republic

From the time that Rome began its great expansion outside Italy, it abandoned the policy of extending its citizenship even within Italy. Unless some form of representative government were worked out, it was obviously of not much use for persons who lived many miles from Rome to possess the right to attend a popular assembly in Rome, or to vote for magistrates there, especially since when they arrived they might find the assembly, or election, indefinitely postponed because of unfavorable omens, or on some other pretext. As no such representative form of government was worked out, the popular assembly naturally declined in importance and ultimately ceased to exist. Moreover, the senate had become the real governing power at Rome. Therefore the discontented element in Rome, the Italians who wanted the private and business rights of citizens rather than a vote, and the provincials who were oppressed by the generals, governors, tax-farmers, and speculators whom the senate sent out or permitted to prey upon them:—all these elements of discontent were ready to support any individual leader who promised reforms or, still better, having seized the power, performed them. Armies, too, would support their generals against the senate. Moreover, the agrarian question and that of debts were again troubling the body politic.

The Change to Imperial Government

Therefore after various civil wars, political intrigues, conspiracies, revolutions, massacres, and assassinations, the senate had to yield first place in the government to a single man who held office for life and whose power, as time went on, became increasingly absolute. This one-man power was in the eastern Mediterranean a natural continuation of the Hellenistic monarchies. The provincials received better treatment at his hands than before, and most of them were gradually admitted to the citizenship, that is, were "Romans" politically and legally as much as the inhabitants of the city itself. Neither had any longer a voice in the central government or took any active part therein unless asked to do so by the emperor; they simply passively shared in such benefits as the emperor, and the governors of the provinces whom he appointed, might bestow. But it is worth noting that after the first century A. D. almost every emperor came from the provinces. The emperor was worshiped throughout the empire as the oriental despots had been

worshiped in their kingdoms.   Secret and popular associations
were not permitted.   Cities that had been destroyed in the wars
of conquest, such as Carthage and Corinth, were now rebuilt
and repeopled, but the local municipal governments throughout
the empire continued to be aristocratic, governed by *duumvirs*
corresponding to the Roman consuls and a *curia* corresponding
to the Roman senate.   These wealthy office-holders embellished
their towns with fine buildings, or gave games and amusements
for the masses, or established charitable endowments, as the
emperors did for Rome and the empire at large.   By taking
charge of the grain supply, the emperors assured the large
population of Rome cheap food; they abolished the cruel underground prisons, or work-houses, of the republican period, and
passed laws to protect even slaves from ill-treatment by their
masters.   Greatest of all blessings were the peace, law, and
order which now generally prevailed within the empire.

The early Romans were a race of soldiers, and throughout The Army
their history to be a military conqueror seems to have been the
height of the individual Roman's ambition.   The republic had
been at war through most of its history, candidates for public
offices must have served in ten campaigns, most offices had their
military side.   Even those officials whose functions were really
civil liked to employ military trappings and insignia, as many
"desk officers" during the late world war liked to wear boots with
spurs and field uniforms.   While officials thus relished the flavor
of militarism, the common citizen soldier was subjected to the
sternest discipline.   The Romans soon improved upon the
phalanx by the legion, which was more flexible and easily *manipulated* by division of its heavy-armed troops into ten cohorts,
thirty maniples, and sixty centuries.   It is a remarkable fact
that although the ancient historians do little but narrate wars
and battles by land and sea, they do not describe even these military and naval matters scientifically and adequately, so that we
neither have a clear idea of how a trireme was constructed, nor
are we ever told just how the legion was manipulated.   Apparently the light-armed auxiliaries would engage in preliminary skirmishing before retiring between the maniples, which
then took turns in charging the enemy and retiring to recover.
Each soldier had two javelins to hurl from a short distance and
a short sword with which to thrust at close quarters.   One-third
of the maniples, usually those composed of veterans, were held

in reserve in case the attack failed. Another feature of the Roman army was its practice, when moving in hostile country, of building a fortified camp at each place where a night was to be spent. The square camp was surrounded by a trench and wall; the interior was laid out according to fixed rules so that each soldier knew his exact place. As the peasant farmers of the early republic gave way to the city mob, and as campaigns were carried on farther and farther away from Rome, often involving absence for years, it became necessary to employ a paid professional army. It was advisable for the general of such an army, if he wished to be popular and to continue successful, to allow his troops a little loot and license occasionally. Indeed, too many of the Roman commanders were intent on spoils for themselves.

The Army During the Empire

With the establishment of the empire the policy of further conquest was for the most part abandoned. About four hundred thousand troops, a small army compared to those recently maintained by modern nations of much less extent of territory, sufficed to keep order within the empire and to guard the frontiers, where most of them were stationed. These soldiers were chiefly volunteers who devoted the active period of their life to the military profession. Our word, "emperor," comes from the Latin *imperator*, meaning the commander-in-chief of an army. This suggests that the power of the emperor to some extent rested on the army. Unfortunately no permanent or regular mode of succession to the throne was worked out, so that there were apt to be armed struggles between rival candidates, and the troops would support the claims of ambitious generals. On the other hand, the troops were sometimes of assistance in ridding Rome of a bad emperor.

The Civil Law

The Civil Law, as written down in the Twelve Tables about 450 B. C., still contained many characteristics of early law such as self-help and the use of quaint symbolical verbal forms and ceremonial acts, and denoted a low state of economic civilization. Nevertheless the Roman citizens went on living under its provisions until 176 B. C. They were able to do so chiefly as a result of skilful interpretation of the provisions of this code by a class of trained jurists who developed out of the earlier priests and pontiffs. These jurists were usually men of wealth and rank who took no pay for their legal advice but gave it freely in order to gain a reputation which would secure

them advancement in public life. They were commonly consulted before the lawsuit was begun, were not committed to the
support of either party, gave impartial advice, and were accustomed to discuss moot points among themselves. Some of
them kept records of the cases in which they had been consulted and the opinions which they had expressed; thus a legal
literature began to develop. It was fortunate that in Latin
there were not two different words or ideas for what was legal
and what was right; *ius* meant right as well as law. Also the
old *ius civile,* while rigid in its formalities, was artistic in its
technicality and marked by very acute reasoning.

After the parties to a suit had consulted with one or more
of the jurists and had been advised how to bring their suit or
effect their object under the restricted system of the Twelve
Tables, they appeared before the prætor, who gave his final
interpretation of the law in the case and therewith settled it,
or else passed it on to a single *judex,* who was usually some
senator, to decide between the parties as to the disputed facts.
When Rome became the chief city of Italy and was thronged
with foreigners as well as citizens, it became necessary to make
some provision for the trial of suits in which foreigners were
concerned. Therefore in 242 B. C. another prætorship was
instituted for this purpose, the *praetor peregrinus,* as distinguished from the previous city prætor or *praetor urbanus.*
Since the Twelve Tables were exclusively for citizens, this new
prætor was free to apply new legal principles in disputes in
which foreigners were concerned through a formula of instruction to the *judex* who was to settle the case. It further
became the custom for the prætor at the beginning of his term
of office to issue an edict giving the rules by which he intended
to settle disputes. Each succeeding prætor would usually
reissue the edict of his predecessor with a few changes and additions that experience had shown to be desirable. Thus the
law was annually reconsidered and improved. The parties to
the suit could then select for themselves the particular formula
from the edict that best fitted their case, or, if none seemed to
fit it, they might induce the prætor to add a new formula to
the edict. As Rome added territories outside Italy, this same
method of law-building was employed by the governors of the
various provinces. Now, in this new legal procedure for foreigners the *praetor peregrinus* and the provincial governors of-

*Prætorian
Procedure:
Ius Gentium*

ten took suggestions from the previous customs of the foreigners or of the provinces, especially as some of this foreign law was better adapted to commercial and financial relations than the rather primitive law of the Twelve Tables. The Romans soon began to see that this new prætorian procedure, of which they could take advantage in suits with foreigners, was superior to the existing Civil Law which prevailed in suits between citizens. Therefore, by the *Lex Aebutia* about 176 B. C., they empowered the city prætor to send formulæ to the *judices* and to issue an edict which became the center of future legal development and was followed by the provincial governors. This new prætorian law and legal procedure, since it embraced the customs of foreigners and provincials, is known as the *ius gentium* (law of the nations) in distinction from the *ius civile*, and was appropriate to the change from a city state to a Mediterranean empire.

Writings of the Jurists

The law profited also by the reasoning of the Roman jurists, whose writings constitute the most original and constructive branch of Latin literature. Beginning with Sextus Ælius Pætus, consul in 198 B. C., whose work was later known as "the cradle of the law," this jurisprudence reached its height in the writings of Paulus, Ulpian, and Papinian about 200 A. D. These men had great command of the law of the past and were eminently logical in their legal reasoning. Moreover, they were not satisfied if in any case this logic led them to an inequitable result, but would turn back, re-examine their premises, and endeavor to establish a new principle which would lead to an equitable outcome in every case. The jurists took over from the Stoics the conception of natural law applicable to mankind at large, to fulfill which ideal, they considered, was the mission of the almost world-wide Roman Empire. Therefore relations between father and son, husband and wife, master and slave, were greatly improved. Papinian tried to uplift the law to a lofty ethical standard. Under the empire there were law schools with a course lasting six years, and these not at Rome merely but in such cities as Syrian Beirut. Although under the emperor Trajan (98–117 A. D.) the edict was permanently revised, the law continued to develop through new judicial decisions given as a result of appeals to the emperor. With the third century A. D., however, we have a sudden cessation of the names of great jurists. This is partly because

the emperors henceforth put everything forth in their own
names.   After the civil strife, confusion, and barbarian inroads of this third century, there was also a decline in the
quality of imperial legislation, which became less clear and
more rhetorical.   Moreover, the legal mind grew lazy and was
content to consult past authorities, and the tendency came to
be to reduce all law to a single code.   Theodosius II collected
the laws of his Christian predecessors in the Theodosian Code
in 438 A. D.

The Code of Justinian was a completer collection of all
imperial statutes, except that repetitions, contradictions, and
obsolete laws were omitted.   It was first issued in 529 and revised in 534.   Meanwhile in 533 Justinian's lawyers, headed
by Tribonian, had made a *Digest* of all Roman legal literature,
reducing some three million lines of writing to one hundred and
fifty thousand, arranged under subject headings similar to
those of the Code.   This work was henceforth to be the sole
authority; no one was to add to it or to write a commentary on
it; it was supposed to be self-explanatory.   Therewith the
living development of the Roman law ceased, but Justinian had
preserved it in a handy form for posterity.   He himself, nevertheless, found it necessary to make a few additional laws, known
as his *Novels*.   There has also come down to us a textbook for
law students, the *Institutes*, based on a similar earlier work by
Gaius.   Some of these earlier works have also been recovered,
but the law books of Justinian constitute our chief source for
the Roman law.

The Law Books of Justinian

This law was to have a great future influence.   Not only was
it continued in the Byzantine Empire of the middle ages, much
of it was administered under the name of Canon Law in the
ecclesiastical courts of the Roman Catholic Church.   The
courts not only judged the clergy but regulated for the laity
such matters as marriages, wills, sworn contracts, and the
prohibition of usury.   Roman law of a sort also persisted
among the peoples of Latin origin in western Europe, since the
invading Germans kept their legal customs for themselves only.
Beginning with the eleventh century, the study of Roman law
was revived on a large scale in the universities of Italy and
what is now southern France.   The glossators, as these medieval commentators upon the books of Justinian were called,
had shrewd legal instincts and worked out a practical system

Future Influence of Roman Law

suited to their own times.   It now became the custom for students to study both the Civil Law and the Canon Law.   The degree of J.U.D. (*Doctor utriusque juris*), or doctor of both laws, is still granted in European universities, while the LL.D., or Doctor of Laws, is a faint reflection of it.   It was men trained in both laws who filled the councils of the kings of France and England in the twelfth and thirteenth centuries and developed the Common Law in the latter country and the royal power in both.   The study and spread of Roman law received a further impetus in the fifteenth and sixteenth centuries in connection with the so-called Italian Renaissance or quickened interest in classical antiquity.   Finally, in quite modern times the various states of Europe, in their efforts to create a national law which they did not possess in place of the old local customs, were driven to make new codes covering the whole field of law.   In this task they made much use of Roman law as a unifying guide.   This process began with the Prussian Code of 1794 and the Code Napoleon; Austria, Italy, Spain, the Swiss cantons, and the Scandinavian countries, similarly codified their law; Germany spent from 1874 to 1900 in the process.

Future Influence of Roman Government   The Roman government, too, had a great future influence, and made a deep impression upon the human imagination. There were later attempts to revive the Roman Empire, such as the empire of Charlemagne, the Holy Roman Empire, Napoleon's assumption of the imperial office, and the Cæsarism or Kaiserism of the recent German Empire, not to mention the present ambitious dreams of Italy.   The organization of the Roman Catholic Church followed that of the empire closely. Modern patriots and contenders for republican forms of government in the seventeenth and eighteenth centuries made much of the examples and inspiration found in the pages of Livy and Tacitus.   The very names of Roman magistracies and governing bodies continued to be employed, as consuls, in the twelfth century towns of Lombardy and southern France, or senate, in the legislative assemblies of our own day.

BIBLIOGRAPHY

Abbott, F. F.   *Society and Politics in Ancient Rome*, 1911; *The Common People of Ancient Rome*, 1911.
Arnold, W. T.   *Roman Provincial Administration*, 1914.

Boak, A. E. R. *History of Rome,* 1921.

Bryce, Lord. *Ancient Roman Empire and British Empire in India,* 1914.

Buckland, W. W. *A Textbook of Roman Law,* 1921.

Cromer, Earl of. *Ancient and Modern Imperialism,* 1909, 2 vols.

Dill, S. *Roman Society from Nero to Marcus Aurelius,* 1905.

Fowler, W. W. *Religious Experience of the Roman People,* 1911; *Roman Ideas of Deity,* 1914.

Frank, T. *Economic History of Rome,* 1920; *History of Rome,* 1923.

Halliday, W. R. *Lectures on the History of Roman Religion,* 1922.

Hardy, E. G. *Some Problems in Roman History,* 1924; advanced studies on the administrative and legislative work of Julius Cæsar.

Heitland, W. E. *The Roman Republic,* 1909, 3 vols.

Holmes, T. Rice. *The Roman Republic and the Founder of the Empire.*

Hunter, W. A. *Introduction to Roman Law,* 1900.

Jones, H. S. *The Roman Empire,* 1908; a handy chronological survey.

Launspach, C. W. L. *State and Family in Early Rome,* 1908.

Lucas, Chas. P. *Greater Rome and Greater Britain,* 1912.

Marsh, F. B. *The Founding of the Roman Empire,* 1922.

Mommsen, Th. *History of Rome,* translated by Dickson, 1877; *The Provinces of the Roman Empire,* English translation, 1909.

Monro's translation of the *Digest* of Justinian, 1904–1909.

Morey, W. C. *Outlines of Roman Law,* 1914.

Muirhead, James. *Historical Introduction to the Private Law of Rome,* 1899.

Pound, R. *Readings in Roman Law,* 1914.

Reid, J. S. *Municipalities of the Roman Empire,* 1913.

Sohm, A. *Institutes of Roman Private Law,* translated by Ledlie, 1907.

Stephenson, A. *A History of Roman Law,* 1912.

Vinogradoff, *Roman Law in Medieval Europe,* 1900.

CHAPTER XVI

THE CIVILIZATION OF THE ROMAN EMPIRE

(31 B. C.–176 A. D.)

quanto plus est ingenii Romani terminos in tantum promovisse quam imperii.—Pliny the Elder

Extension of Civilization

THE Roman Empire to a large extent continued the same forms of civilization as had marked the Hellenistic period, and perhaps its chief accomplishment was in extending that culture westward and northward. The way, of course, had been paved for this by Carthage and by the Greek colonies planted at an early date on the coasts of Spain and Gaul. But the Romans moved the whole frontier of classical civilization north to the lowlands of Scotland, and the further banks of the Rhine and Danube. Dacia, a large tract north of the lower Danube, was the last province to be conquered and the first to be lost (106–270 A. D.), yet so thoroughly was it Romanized that even today its inhabitants are called Romanians or Roumanians, and the structure of their language is still Latin, although in vocabulary there are now three Slavonic for every two Latin words. It should be added, however, that in this case the original native Dacians seem to have been largely replaced by settlers from various parts of the Roman Empire. In Gaul, on the other hand, the Gauls themselves became slowly Romanized. It is less clear how far Britain was Romanized. The Roman system of roads, at least, was extended even to the province beyond the Channel. In general, internal peace, freedom of communication, trade, and residence between all parts of the great Empire, and resultant cosmopolitanism prevailed. Life became more comfortable, care-free, and cultured than ever before. There was not much to worry about except an occasional brigand, imaginary witches, ills predicted by astrologers, and the perennial problems of health, making both ends meet, and the future life.

The Greek and Latin writers of the early empire either satirized the luxurious city life of Rome with its newly rich who once had been slaves, its over-eating, and its neglect of true learning, or revelled in the history, art, and literature of the past, to which they had easy access in public libraries and numerous copies and reproductions. "For now," wrote Plutarch, "we repose altogether in the soft slumbers of peace; all our wars are at an end. . . . Now there is nothing of variety, nothing of mystery, nothing dangerous, but only bare and ordinary questions about small trifles and common things, as whether a man may marry, whether take a voyage by sea, or lend his money safely at interest." It is worth remembering, however, that men still kindled a fire "by rubbing together two pieces of wood," if there was no other flame handy from which they might light them. For life and society in the vast city of Rome read Juvenal, Petronius, and Martial; for travel through the empire, the Life of Apollonius of Tyana by Philostratus; for the attitude and ideas of the average "cultured reader," Plutarch and Pliny the Younger; for an amusing romance of magic, low life, and religious cults, *The Golden Ass* or *Metamorphoses* of Apuleius.

Social Life as Reflected in Literature

Despite the peace and prosperity the working classes and slaves still had a hard struggle for existence. "My master," says the Golden Ass of a gardener to whom he was sold, "was so very poor that he provided no straw nor even the least covering either for me or for himself, but lived contentedly under the shelter of a booth of leafy boughs. . . . My master and myself had exactly the same fare for supper and very scanty it was. It consisted of those ancient and unsavory lettuces which, when old age comes upon them and they have run to seed, grow so unreasonably tall that they look like brooms, while their fibres rot and are filled with a bitter muddy juice." As for the workers in a mill, "Good heavens! what stunted little men met my eye, their skin all striped with livid scars, their backs a mass of sores, with tattered patchwork clothing that gave them shade rather than shelter . . . their foreheads branded, heads half-shaven, ankles pierced with rings, . . . eyelids ulcerated."

Hardships of the Poor and Lowly

All manufactures were still handmade, which is the Latin meaning of the word, and were usually sold directly by the man who made them. The shops were small, and it was customary to bargain for goods. Each trade had its own street, or quar-

Industry and Business

ter, of the city.   Galen, however, tells us that most of the book-stores of Rome were located in the street of the Sandal-makers. Of the Roman gilds we do not know much, although they were supposed to have been founded by Numa, one of the early kings. Slaves were not admitted to them, and inscriptions have pre-served some lists of the members of gilds.   An occasional indi-vidual might, however, employ a large number of slaves in one sort of manufacture, and perhaps have the product sold by another slave from a separate shop.   Some manufactured ar-ticles, bearing the same firm names, are found widely distributed over the empire, showing that there was some mass production in such things as copper and bronze utensils, bricks, tiles, and glassware.   Puteoli, on the bay of Naples, was a great center of the iron industry as well as a busy port thronged with Syri-ans.   Business corporations were less common than today and were largely limited to tax-farming, but there were partner-ships, agencies, and share-taking in ships and voyages.   The Romans practiced bookkeeping and had shorthand writers, but of course no typewriters.   Although the Roman republic had degenerated into a plutocracy, the subject of money-lending is rather avoided or decried in the literature that has reached us, and there was already a strong feeling against making money simply by lending it—a prejudice which grew into a prohibition in the medieval church.

The Land System

We have mentioned the decline, in the late republic, of the small Latin and Italian peasant farmer, the military aristoc-racy of Gaul, the great estates of Asia Minor.   All Egypt was now a private imperial plantation.   The large landed es-tate became, it would seem, increasingly widespread through the empire.   Traces of Roman villas, as the country houses of the large landowners were called, are found even in Britain. At first these great estates were mainly cultivated by gangs of slaves, but as slaves became less abundant and were better treated, much land was given out to tenants or *coloni*.

Remains of Roman Buildings

Almost no buildings are left at Rome of the period of the republic, but the most impressive evidence that has come down to us of the widespread prosperity and civilization under the Roman Empire, consists in the many ruins of its buildings and other material remains.   These comprise roads that are still in use today, or that have sunk beneath the surface of the soil in spots no longer trod; foundations of private houses, or ground-plans of public edifices; pavements of rooms arranged in mosaic designs, or the still brighter paintings that adorned the walls; huge vaults of masonry and stately arches; crumbling walls overgrown with grass, moss, weeds, and shrubbery; arcades and colonnades; funeral monuments and sculptured sarcophagi; vast palace halls and domes; huge enclosures for the public entertainment; metal vessels and utensils corroded by the rust of centuries and perhaps fished up from the beds of rivers; or even an entire town or camp, preserved like Herculaneum and Pompeii by being buried in lava, or still standing untouched on the edge of the desert, like Palmyra in Syria and Lambessa and Timgad in North Africa. Such is some brief suggestion merely of the variety of Roman remains and the state in which we find them. Many more have yet to be unearthed. Excavations are still in process in the very forum of Rome itself, where there are many archæological strata, since later buildings were superimposed on the foundations of earlier edifices. In cities like London and Paris, whenever a new subway is built, or deep foundations are dug for an office building, something antique is apt to be discovered. The level of the ground has almost always risen about such ruins, so that a European may have a section of an amphitheater in his cellar, while those ancient monuments which still appear above ground do not appear as many feet above it as they used to. The roof also has usually fallen in or disappeared, although not so frequently as in the case of ancient Greek buildings.

For the Roman buildings were structurally superior to the Greek. By means of the round arch, the cylindrical vault, and the hemispherical dome of masonry, the Romans were able to span wide spaces or cover a considerable interior with a strong, permanent roof of stone or concrete. Their excellent mortar and cement also enabled them to build well in brick or rubble. Ancient building regulations required contractors to use mortar that was three months old. The round arch and vault exercised a strong horizontal thrust outward, to counteract which, thick supporting walls are required. Indeed, the Romans were apt to make their walls even thicker than was necessary. Their bricks were thin but measured 18 by 12 inches in length and breadth. Since they were laid flat, a wall eighteen inches thick would be only one brick in thickness. But Vitruvius, the leading Roman writer on architecture, tells us that brick walls can- *Their Structure* not support more than one story unless they are two or three bricks thick. By use of stone piers and partitions of rubble work, however, apartment houses of several stories were built at Rome, for, as Vitruvius says, "with the present importance of the city and the unlimited numbers of its population, it is necessary to increase the number of dwelling places indefinitely." Buildings of more than one story have recently been excavated at Ostia, the seaport of Rome. The average life of a party wall of rubble work was estimated as eighty years, and we are told that the fall of high buildings was frequent. Under Augustus, the first emperor, their height was restricted to seventy feet. It must be added that the Romans were not very skilful in wooden roofing, using heavy timbers as if they were blocks of stone, and seldom employing the truss. Glass was apparently not yet used in windows, although we hear how the emperor Caligula "burst into the principal building, and as soon as he had entered, he commanded the windows which were around it to be filled up with the transparent pebbles very much resembling white crystal, which do not hinder the light, but which keep out the wind and the heat of the sun." Mosaics made of bits of colored glass were set into arched roofs and domes as early as the first century A. D. Blown glass is not found in the Egyptian graves of the Ptolemaic period. It seems to have been invented at Sidon between 20 B. C. and 20 A. D., perhaps by Neikon and Artas whose names are blown into some of the extant specimens.

The Roman Forum   The forum or market-place, center of the public life of Rome, was an open area on low-lying ground between the hills of the city. Into it ran the sacred way followed by triumphal processions of victorious commanders; it was filled with temples, triumphal arches, and basilicas; above it on the Capitoline hill were the senate house and the temple to Jupiter, Juno, and Minerva, while on the Palatine were the huge palaces of successive Cæsars. Most impressive of the ruins that still overlook the forum are the three great vaulted recesses, each 74 feet wide by 56 feet deep, although they form only a third part of the Basilica of Constantine, built early in the fourth century A. D. Its other aisle and still loftier nave fell in an earthquake in 1348. Following the decline of Roman civilization, the forum became so buried in rubbish that parts of it were forty feet below the level of the ground, and cows were pastured above it until the nineteenth century. The emperors found it necessary to add other forums to the original one and to extend their building to other parts of the city, notably the Campus Martius, once a parade ground outside the walls.

The extensive use of arch and dome freed the Romans from horizontal lines and the rectangular ground plan. They were much given to circular temples and tombs. Greatest and best preserved of all such structures is the Pantheon at Rome, the main body of which consists of a great concrete dome 142 feet in diameter and rising to a point 142 feet above the floor. It is lighted by an aperture in its center thirty feet in diameter. It rests directly on a cylindrical wall twenty feet thick, further strengthened by relieving arches embedded in it, and carried up some distance above the springing of the dome. The portico of sixteen Corinthian columns supporting a pediment was erected in 27 B. C., but most of the building dates from the reign of Hadrian (117–138 A. D.) who was himself something of an architect. The dome was covered with gold-plated bronze tiles until 663. The bronze flowers that once adorned the square panels of its coffered ceiling and the bronze figures on the pediment outside have also disappeared. The bronze doors of the rotunda, which are over twenty-six feet high, are still in place and are both the oldest and finest in Rome.

The Pantheon

At Pompeii we see the narrow streets of the ancient town with the large, flat, hexagonal, paving blocks nicely fitted together, the narrow shops lining the street, the houses of the well-to-do also immediately abutting on the street, presenting a blank entrance wall pierced only by a door and perhaps a window for the porter, while the interior living rooms cluster about an open atrium or a second colonnaded courtyard and garden. Lambessa, situated 3600 feet above sea level, is our most perfect extant example of a permanent Roman camp, measuring 550 by 460 yards, with gates in the four sides, towers at the four corners and also along the walls. A town grew up around it, with the usual temples, triumphal arches, forum, theater, amphitheater, baths, and aqueduct. Timgad, built for the veterans of Trajan's Parthian campaign, was at an even higher level of 4000 feet, but on a somewhat smaller scale, being 370 by 340 yards. Nine parallel streets in each direction divided the town into square blocks.

Pompeii, Lambessa, and Timgad

The ancient Egyptians had built for the future life and the

Buildings
for Public
Utility and
Amusement

gods; the Greek games and theatrical performances were religious festivals and exercises. Now enduring works in stone were erected simply for the convenience and entertainment of the populace. To bring the people water there were aqueducts stilted high on series of arches, of which some of the finest remains are at Segovia in Spain, and the Pont du Gard near Nîmes in southern France. There were dignified or daring bridges, like those still visible at St. Chabas in southern France and Alcantara in Spain. There were basilicas to shelter their public gathering and concourse from rain or the glare of the sun. There were the great baths,—vast complexes of vaulted halls and open courts rather than single edifices,—where one might exercise or idle, as well as enjoy a warm, hot, cold, or vapor bath. It is now doubted whether the Romans heated their buildings by hypocausts as much as has been supposed; the walls and floors were left hollow rather for the purpose of dryness than to serve as flues for hot air. As a rule rooms were heated by charcoal braziers, while the water for baths was heated in metal kettles. "Hunting, bathing, gaming, laughing, this is the life!" says an inscription amid gaming tables inlaid on the forum pavement at Timgad, while an older epitaph ran, "The bath, wine, and love ruin one's health but make life worth living."

Amphi-
theaters

Then there were the exhibitions of wild beasts and gladiatorial combats in the amphitheaters, whose tiers of stone seats, sloping upward from the oval arena, were supported by a perfect honeycomb of vaulted passages, piers and arches, through which mounted the stairs to the upper tiers. The abundant entrances and exits made it easy to reach or leave any seat in a moment or two. This structure of the amphitheater, in which, rather in contrast to other Roman building, hardly an inch of space was wasted, can best be observed at Nîmes, where sections of the surface seats have disappeared, and the supports beneath stand revealed. Both this amphitheater and the Pont du Gard were built in part of huge blocks of stone placed together without mortar. The seats remain in most perfect condition at Verona, although there the exterior is not so well preserved as at Nîmes and other places. The huge Colosseum at Rome is in poorer preservation than these somewhat smaller structures, but we may note the ornamentation of its exterior, which was over a quarter of a mile in circumference.

ROMAN THEATERS AND AMPHITHEATERS

Above, the stage wall of the theater at Orange in the Rhone valley is 121 feet high, 338 feet long, and 13 feet thick; below, at Nîmes enough of the rows of seats are missing to disclose the structural arrangement.

TRIUMPHAL ARCHES

Above, the arch at Orange dates from the early first century A. D.; below, the arch at Reims, La Porte de Mars, from the fourth century A. D.

There were three stories of arches and between every two adjoining arches a column, making eighty Doric columns in the lowest story, eighty Ionic columns in the second, and eighty Corinthian columns in the third. Above this were eighty Corinthian pilasters and forty square windows in the alternate compartments.

This superimposition of different Greek orders and their combination with arches is characteristic of the Roman period, when, too, the purity and proportions of the Doric and Ionic capitals and columns were often lost. The Corinthian order was developed to a greater magnificence, as may be seen in the fifteen lofty columns which remain from the temple of Olympian Zeus at Athens of the reign of Hadrian, or in the smaller, yet wonderfully well preserved and proportioned, Maison Carrée at Nîmes, or in the Temple of Augustus and Livia at Vienne on the Rhone. *Roman Use of the Greek Orders*

The triumphal arch was a distinctive product of Rome. It served no useful or popular purpose but was simply a symbol of Roman empire. Yet with all our modern civilization and democracy we have been able to think of no better architectural monument with which to mark victories or arouse patriotism; in fact, in various modern capitals will be found mere copies of these ancient arches. Some of the finest Roman arches are those of Titus, Septimus Severus, and Constantine in the city itself, that of Trajan at Beneventum, that at Orange, and the Porte de Mars at Reims. In these monuments the Romans combined sculpture with architecture. The columns, too, of the emperors Trajan and Marcus Aurelius are covered with spiral bands of relief setting forth the incidents of their campaigns. The Vendôme column in Paris is a tasteless imitation of this form of art. *Triumphal Arch and Column*

It is in such historical bas-reliefs and in busts of the emperors and other portrait statues that the sculpture of the empire seems distinctively Roman rather than merely a continuation of the Greek. This Roman sculpture is at its best under the Flavian dynasty, 69–96 A. D. Of course sculpture in the Greek style also continued. There was great enthusiasm for the art treasures of the past together with much luxury in the art of the present. Why, asked a contemporary, do we travel over Asia and Africa and all Europe and the islands searching for pillars and capitals and architraves, and selecting them *Roman Sculpture: Other Luxurious Art* with reference to their superior beauty? Why do we inlay our beds with costly mother-of-pearl and variegated tortoise-shell? "Some beds are even made of solid silver or solid gold, and inlaid with precious stones, with all kinds of flowery work, and embossed golden ornaments."

Latin
Literature

While Greek remained the literary language of the eastern half of the empire, Latin became that of the western half. Already before the end of the republic Cicero, in his orations, essays, and letters, had developed a Latin prose style which has since been generally recognized as standard. Later in the same century under the first emperor, Augustus Cæsar, wrote Horace, born in southern Italy, the leading Latin lyric poet, and Virgil, born in northern Italy, the greatest Latin epic poet. Though much influenced by Greek models, Cicero, Virgil, and Horace were great masters of their own Latin tongue and also reflected the altered spirit of their own time. For example, although Virgil's *Æneid* begins like Homer's *Iliad* with the siege of Troy, he thinks of that event as belonging to a distant past and "now become common property throughout the whole world," so that even Æneas, fleeing from Troy, finds already in the palace of Dido at Carthage frescoes depicting the scenes of the siege, and exclaims:

> . . . What place now, Achates,
> What region of the globe is not full of our doings?
> Ah, Priam! Here, too, is his due meed of praise:

And then that famous line, too tender to attempt to translate,

> Sunt lacrimae rerum, et mentem mortalia tangunt.

We have already spoken of various other writers both Latin and Greek, of legal literature, and of the historians. To the last we must add the name of Tacitus. Besides narrating at length the first century of Rome under the emperors with republican rancor, he has left an admirable brief account of the civilization of the early Germans. Another historian, Ammianus Marcellinus, whose account of the years 353 to 378 has reached us, was the chief pagan Latin writer of the declining empire. By that time the style of Latin writing had generally become too rhetorical and artificial. The leading Latin writers of the fifth century were to be found in Gaul. When the barbarian invaders made life too uncomfortable in that region, some of these rhetoricians took refuge in Ireland, which lay entirely outside the Roman Empire, but evidently not beyond the reach of its civilization.

The scientific writers of the Roman Empire have too often been represented as quite inferior to those of the Hellenistic period. Yet we have far more scientific writing extant from the Roman Empire, and if a good deal of it, judged by modern standards, seems of inferior quality and interlarded with belief in magic and divination, it is not at all clear that much of the preceding Hellenistic science was any better. The little knowledge we have of many Hellenistic writers is drawn from what these later works of the Roman Empire say of them. Moreover, most of these Hellenistic writers had little future influence, whereas Pliny the Elder, Ptolemy, and Galen exerted a future influence comparable to that of Aristotle.

Science of the Roman Empire

Pliny came from Como in Alpine Italy. He perished in the same eruption of Vesuvius that buried Pompeii in 79 A. D. as he was rescuing others and trying to observe the natural phenomena from too close at hand. Pliny gave his work the attractive title, *Natural History*. While it was mainly a compilation, not only was he, as he himself says, the first single writer in either Greek or Latin to try to present nature entire, he was also, unless we except Herodotus, the first to write something like a history of civilization, or at least to supply us with the materials for, and even chapters of, such a history. We have no better source for the history of ancient customs, inventions, and arts. He not only has preserved for us great masses of the natural science and medicine of antiquity, but affirms that he adds many new points only recently discovered. On such a point as the need of a pure water supply, as the very aqueducts attest, the attitude was more enlightened in Pliny's time than in the first part of the nineteenth century, since he says, "It is generally admitted that all water is more wholesome when it has been boiled," on which his English translator of 1856 commented, "This is not at all the opinion at the present day." If it had been, however, the various cholera epidemics of the early nineteenth century might have been prevented.

Pliny's Natural History

The mass of ancient science and medicine presented in the *Natural History* is interlarded, as we have said, with superstitious practices and beliefs. Men were not yet able, as are

Magic and Science

chemists today, to extract from organic or inorganic matter salts, acids, and other chemical agents, and to test the action of these by repeated experiment. Instead they dealt with particular objects such as herbs, gems, and, in the case of animals, the various parts and secretions of the body, trying to cure diseases and perform artistic or industrial processes with these. Such individual objects, utilized just as they were found in nature, were known as simples. What strike us as absurdly marvelous properties were ascribed to some of these, and these properties were supposed to have been discovered by daily experience or were argued from analogy—the eagle can gaze at the sun, therefore its gall makes a good eye-salve. In all periods the sick, or those who imagine themselves sick, have been ready to try to cure themselves by all sorts of foolish notions; sometimes they further imagine that they have been cured by these means. In Pliny's day the causes of disease were ill understood, and strange relations of sympathy or antipathy were thought to exist between things in nature, like that love and hate which, the philosopher Empedocles had taught, combined or separated the four elements. Furthermore, there was much confidence in prayer and the power of words. This was found, not merely as today in religion and advertising, but in science and medicine. However, the recent great vogue in America of Coué's jingle warns us that for many there is still great comfort in the repetition of an incantation. Etiquette and ritual, too, then affected science and medicine as they still affect polite society and religion. For example, certain herbs must be plucked with the left hand, certain gems must be set or worn in a certain way to be efficacious. Or, no iron must be used in the operation, seven knots must be tied, the patient must do this or that, the object must not be allowed to touch the ground. Furthermore, times must be observed, a favorable hour chosen. Pliny was well aware that the science of antiquity was almost inextricably confused with such superstitious practices and beliefs, which he attributed to the *magi* or magicians, but he also makes it clear that these magicians, too, were investigating nature, and he himself proved quite unable to draw any sharp line between the scientific and the magical. He did have the courage, however, to omit from his book the elaborate compound medicines which we find in many other ancient medical authors, contenting himself with the virtues of simples. Pliny tells us that in his time "there is no one who is not eager to learn the future about himself and who does not think that this is most truly revealed by the sky," and there are not a few traces of astrology in his own pages.

Ptolemy, who bore the name of the Hellenistic kings of Egypt, where, however, he lived under the Roman Empire in the second century of our era, is our greatest authority on ancient astronomy and geography. Whoever may have originated them, all the leading achievements of antiquity in these fields are preserved at least through his labors. In both subjects he composed comprehensive works in a scientific form and with especial reliance on mathematical method. It is in this respect that his Geography is superior to that of Strabo, who wrote in Greek under Augustus, while Strabo tells us more of the physical geography and the past history of the places mentioned. Ptolemy, however, knew more concerning distant parts of Asia and Africa than either Strabo or Pliny. Astronomical observations had been gradually convincing the scientists of that time of the inaccuracy of the theory of Eudoxus and Aristotle that the earth was the exact center of concentric spheres, or heavens of the planets and fixed stars. It was now seen that at certain times, and in certain portions of their orbits, the planets were nearer to, or farther from, the earth than at others. But instead of abandoning the notion that the earth was the immovable center of the universe, and that the motion of the planets was circular, Ptolemy accounted for the observed irregularities and discrepancies by supposing excentric circular orbits. That is, he assumed that the earth was not exactly at the center of the planetary spheres—what he failed to note was that the sun is more nearly so. He also assumed a motion of the planets in epicycles about a moving center located in the circumference of their main circular paths. Such epicycles explained the apparent retrograde motion of the planets in the firmament and were really "reproductions of the earth's annual orbit transferred to each of these planets." One of Ptolemy's maxims was to adopt the simplest possible hypothesis consistent with the facts, or appearances, to be explained. In this case, however, he failed to adopt the heliocentric hypothesis, which it was left for Copernicus to introduce fourteen hundred years later. The Ptolemaic theory, although involving a complicated set of mathematical calculations, was supported by de-

Ptolemy

tailed observations and astronomical tables on Ptolemy's part, and fitted so nicely the apparent motions of the heavenly bodies, as men were then capable of observing them with the scientific instruments at hand, of which the astrolabe was the chief, that it long held the field.   Ptolemy's work, called *Syntaxis* in Greek, is better known by the name later Arabic writers gave it, The Great Work, or *Almagest*.

Astrology   One reason for clinging to the notion that the earth was in the center of the universe was probably astrological, the earth being thought of as different from the heavenly bodies, whose influences it was supposed to receive as it received their light. These influences altered with the changing movements and positions of the planets.   Astrology and astronomy had long developed together.   The desire to learn the future had been the strongest incentive to careful observation of the stars, which were thought of, if not as gods themselves, then as the supreme natural forces, or as God's chief instruments in ruling our inferior world of nature in accordance with those regular and orderly superior motions.   If the movements of those distant unknown spheres could be mathematically calculated and eclipses predicted far ahead, why could not phenomena here on earth also be calculated and predicted?   This attractive thought swept the world and scientists with it for many centuries.   Ptolemy himself wrote a work on nativities, predicting the course of a man's life from the horoscope at his birth.

Galen   Galen, who lived later in the second century than Ptolemy and came from Pergamum in Asia Minor, is the greatest name in Greek medicine after Hippocrates.   Indeed, he stands out as a much more distinct historic personality than Hippocrates. As his writings were far more voluminous, comprehensive, and detailed, and represent a further advance, he exerted a greater future influence.   He wanted to test everything for himself and was a great exponent of the experimental method, an enthusiastic and tireless seeker after truth.   He dissected many animals, thus learning much concerning anatomy; he investigated respiration, and proved that the arteries contain blood; in his medical practice he displayed remarkable powers of rapid observation and inference; he saw the need of exact measurement whether of weights or of the passage of time; sometimes he seems to have half-anticipated discoveries that were far in the future.   Yet his works contain some of that magic which we have noted in Pliny's *Natural History*, and he did not reject compound medicines as Pliny had done.

The attitude of such scientists to religious questions is of interest.   Galen, like Hippocrates before him, rejected the supernatural and miraculous in medicine.   On the other hand, he was inclined to argue from the structure of the parts of animals, which seemed to him marvelously adapted to their uses, to a divine maker and planner.   He thought that mere nature could not possess such wisdom.   As to the nature of God, he was uncertain, however, and also declared himself at a loss concerning the existence and substance of the soul.   He had some acquaintance with Judaism and Christianity, but regarded "the followers of Moses and Christ" as holding to "undemonstrated laws," and as going too far to the opposite extreme from the sceptical philosophy of Epicurus.   Galen would accept with Moses and Plato a divine creation of the world, not subsequent divine miraculous interference with natural law.   Pliny was more uncompromising.   For him Nature was enough.   "That is what we call God," although he also states that "it is God for man to aid his fellow men."   He ridiculed the deities of pagan polytheism and the hope of personal immortality, which he dismissed as "puerile raving," declaring that "all men, after their last day, return to what they were before their first. . . . What downright madness is it to suppose that life is to recommence after death!"

Science and Religion

The question naturally arises: was the imperial system of government, which gave one man absolute power, favorable to civilization?   Some of the emperors were not well educated, Hadrian was perhaps the sole genius among them.   Yet hardly any one of them can be said to have harmed civilization, which many of them did a great deal to promote.   This holds true even for some who had the worst reputation among their contemporaries for crime and vice, such as Nero, who was none the less a sincere patron of the arts and music.   Pliny dedicated his *Natural History* to the emperor, and Galen was well treated by the emperors but was slandered by his fellow physicians.   Moreover, the existence of the imperial government and the professional army left most men free to devote themselves to other sides of civilization than war and politics.   On the other hand, the question arises, could an artist, writer, or scientist

Was Imperial Government Favorable to Civilization?

make a real success and contribution to civilization without imperial recognition? And did not the emperors, as time went on, tend to take all the credit unto themselves and monopolize most activities so as to discourage individual effort and local or community enterprise? Furthermore, had not the source of Greek culture been the city state with its political independence, its local legends and religion, its public life? Did not the empire dry up that stream at its source? The Roman Empire was like the Roman mortar: it long cemented together the broken fragments of Egyptian, Syrian, Hellenic, Hellenistic, Punic, Italian, and Gallic civilization. There was strength in the arch and beauty in the mosaic. But Rome could not endow these past cultures with new life, and except in law and architecture, and to some extent in science, it failed to produce new creations of its own.

Decline of the Roman Empire: Economic Dry-rot and Barbarization

Be that as it may, it is generally agreed that after two centuries of peace and prosperity the Roman Empire began to decline, and that, having carried civilization to the barbarians, it gradually became slowly barbarized in its turn. Many barbarians invaded the empire, many were received within its frontiers as peaceful settlers, others were enrolled in its legions as warriors against their fellows, since the population of the empire no longer provided sufficient recruits. The emperors also found it difficult to get skilled labor and therefore made various occupations hereditary. It was hard to collect the taxes, so the wealthy governing class in the municipalities were made responsible for them and were thereby ruined financially along with the municipalities. It was hard to find slave labor, so a law was made forbidding tenants, or *coloni*, who had formerly been free, to leave their agricultural holdings, with the outcome that they became practically serfs, while the power of the great landowner again increased. Evidently there was depopulation among the original stocks of the empire, perhaps also exhaustion of natural resources. Was this the result of climatic change, of exhausted soil, of mosquitoes and malaria, of racial degeneration, or of sexual immorality and luxury? Whatever the cause, North Africa gradually fell back into a state of barbarism, and the Balkan peninsula, repeatedly overrun by invaders, has had practically no civilization since it was part of the Roman Empire. The British Isles, what are now France and Germany, and the Italian and Spanish peninsulas for a time seemed in the worst case of all, but recovered in a way which will be subsequently traced.

The city of Rome itself, although in 330 it ceased to be the imperial capital, and, following sacks by barbarian invaders in 410 and 455, lost most of its great population, experiencing the general decline of city life which occurred especially in the western half of the declining empire, nevertheless remained an impressive memorial of the civilization that was past and of "the grandeur that was Rome." A Christian clergyman from Gaul, visiting the ruined city about 1100, addressed it in the following verses:

Ruined Rome

There's nothing equal to you, Rome, though you're almost a total
    wreck;
But your fragments show how great you were when whole.
Long time has destroyed your pride, and in a swamp
Now lie the citadels of the Cæsars and temples of the celestials.

.   .   .   .

That city has fallen, of which, if I would say aught worthy,
I might say this, *Roma fuit!*—Rome has been!
Yet neither the succession of years nor flame nor sword
Could wholly wipe out this splendor.
Human effort could compose a Rome so great
That the efforts of the gods could not decompose it.

.   .   .   .

As much still remains as has fallen, so that neither
Can what now stands be equalled, nor what is ruined be restored.

Then the city is represented as replying to the poet and assuring him that it glories in its ruin, since it has turned Christian, exchanged the eagles for the cross, and become the see of Peter instead of the seat of the Cæsars. Since then the successors of Peter have added other impressive remains to those of the Cæsars, and Rome has become more than ever a center for the study of past civilization. In our next chapter we turn to this Christian Rome and to the problem of the effect of Christianity upon the course of civilization.

BIBLIOGRAPHY

The Latin authors mentioned in the chapter may be read in English translations. There are histories of Latin literature by J. W. Duff, H. N. Fowler, J. W. Mackail, W. C. Summers, and others. Chapters on science during the Roman Empire will be found in the works listed at the close of Chapter XIII and in the General Bibliography. Other suggestions are:

Bailey, C. *Legacy of Rome*, 1923.

Besnier, M. "Le commerce romain," in *Journal des Savants*, 1920.

Blümner, H. *Die römischen Privataltertümer*, 1911.

Bouchier, E. S. *Life and Letters in Roman Africa*, 1913; *Spain under the Roman Empire*, 1914; *Syria as a Roman Province*, 1916; *Short History of Antioch*, 1921.

Brock, A. J. *Galen on the Natural Faculties*, 1916.

Calza, "Æsthetics of the Antique City," in *Art and Archæology*, Nov., 1921 (with restoration of apartment houses at Ostia).

Charlesworth, M. P. *Trade Routes and Commerce of the Roman Empire*, 1924.

Clark and Geikie, *Physical Science in the Time of Nero*, 1910.

Davis, W. S. *Influence of Wealth in Imperial Rome*, 1910.

Dill, S. *Roman Society in the Last Century of the Western Empire*, 1906.

Haight, E. H. *Italy Old and New*, 1922.

Haverfield, F. J. *Romanization of Roman Britain*, 1912; *The Roman Occupation of Britain*, 1924; p. 171, "The Civilization of the Province."

Huelsen and Carter, *The Roman Forum*, 1909.

Krell, O. *Altrömische Heizungen*, 1911.

Lanciani, R. *Ancient Rome in the Light of Recent Discoveries*, 1888; *Ruins and Excavations of Ancient Rome*, 1897.

Laurie, A. P. *Greek and Roman Methods of Painting*, 1910.

Mau and Kelsey, *Pompeii, its Life and Art*, 1902.

Milne, J. G. *History of Egypt under Roman Rule*.

Platner, S. B. *Topography and Monuments of Ancient Rome*, 1911.

Ramsay, Sir W. M. *Studies in the History and Art of the Eastern Provinces of the Roman Empire*, 1906.

Rostovtzeff, M. *The Roman Empire: Social and Economic Development*, 1926.

Strong, Mrs. E. *Roman Sculpture*, 1911.

Waldstein and Shoobridge, *Herculaneum*, 1908.

Walters, H. *The Art of the Romans*, 1911.

Ward, J. *The Roman Era in Britain*, 1911.

Westermann, W. L. "The Economic Basis of the Decline of Ancient Culture," in *American Historical Review*, XX (1915), 723–43.

CHAPTER XVII

THE EFFECT OF CHRISTIANITY UPON ANCIENT CIVILIZATION

Thy true country is the heavenly Jerusalem; thy fellow citizens and thy compatriots are 'the first-born which are written in heaven.'—*Basil*

IN the ancient city state, religion and government had been indissoluble; therefore, when city states ceased to be self-governing, their civic religion declined, and the Church, as an institution distinct from the state, first appeared in connection with the rise of Christianity. The early Romans, when attacking other cities, were accustomed to offer the gods of those towns better treatment than they were then receiving, if they would cease to protect their native worshipers and allow them to be conquered by Rome. Hence the vast number of shrines and cults at Rome, the polytheism of the pagan Roman world as well as the Hellenic world, and the generally tolerant attitude of Rome toward other religions. But the other cities in a sense lost both their gods and their souls to Rome. Rome, however, made no compensating gain in religious development; her rites were formal; she came to have more confidence in her own Genius than in the earlier deities or supernatural forces. As her people ceased to engage in agriculture or fighting or political activity, their old rites of fertility and civic festivals ceased to have any meaning for them, and oriental cults, more suited to outworn civilizations and masses laboring under absolute monarchs, came in more and more. A religion was wanted that would "bind up the broken-hearted and preach deliverance unto the captive." *Decline of Civic Religion*

As we saw in speaking of Hellenistic culture, philosophy for a time tried to take the place of religion, showing the absurdities of pagan polytheism, offering natural science as a firmer foundation, inculcating higher moral ideas, teaching the individual how to attain peace and happiness. Many philoso- *Teachings of the Philosophers*

205

phers became popular preachers, ascetics, and missionaries. They urged men to abandon their evil ways and lead a righteous life. They subjected themselves and their disciples to bonds, floggings, and scarification with steel. But in general, philosophy did not succeed in winning the people, partly perhaps because each philosopher worked independently and had his own views. It prepared the way, however, for the coming religion by its destructive criticism of polytheism and by its positive influence favorable to monotheism through its emphasis upon the unity of nature.

Spread of Oriental Religions
The oriental religions which spread through the Roman Empire differed from philosophy in thinking of God as far removed from and above the world of nature and this life, and as approachable not through reason and science but through an authoritative revelation which had been made in the past or a present state of ecstacy induced by sacramental or ascetic practices. The truths of religion and secrets of divinity were thought to be beyond human comprehension and to be set forth only symbolically and apprehended mystically. Yet there was an equally strong tendency to believe that the Deity was concerned with human sufferings and anxious to save the individual from the evil of matter and of this life. To illustrate and enforce this point the Deity was often represented as having toward mankind the affection of a parent for a child, whether as Jesus conceived of his Father in heaven in the Gospels, or as Isis from Egypt and Cybele from Asia Minor were worshiped as a great Mother goddess who had herself been through grief and could sympathize with human woes. The present world with its natural processes and passions and selfish struggles was placed in opposition to God and regarded as evil. A future life in another world was promised to those who believed, who purified themselves from evil by penance and works of holiness, who partook of the sacramental mysteries. The way of escape from matter to immortality had to be revealed to mankind by some divine redeemer who had descended from the transcendent Godhead, had died to live again, and had instituted the mystic sacraments and symbols by which mankind could follow in the path of salvation. Some ancients sought initiation into several such cults in order to make the surer of their soul's salvation. The early Christian writers recognized the close resemblance between Christianity and other

oriental religions in such respects.   They ascribed it, however, not to a common background and evolution, but to the perverse ingenuity of Satan, who was thought to have made these partial imitations of the true religion in order to mislead souls into the wrong paths.   Satan, it may be added, long served theologians as a convenient scapegoat for anything that they were unable to explain otherwise.

Christianity was at first but one of these several oriental religions.   It arose in Palestine among the Jews, as the mysteries of Mithra came from Persia, the worship of Isis from Egypt, the cult of the Great Mother from Phrygia. Christianity was based on the previous religious experience of the orient and the Hebrews in particular as recorded in the Old Testament, but it added to this the career of Jesus, a more real and appealing figure than any other oriental redeemer, a personality loved and revered by many human generations.   It further included the miracles that he was believed to have wrought to demonstrate the power of God over nature, disease, and evil, his teaching of peace and love between men, and the acts and letters of some of his early followers.   After his death on the cross on the charge of trying to make himself king of the Jews, his disciples came to believe that he had indeed been the Christ and Son of God, had risen from the dead, ascended unto heaven, and would save whosoever believed on his name.   For the mere name of Jesus was long thought to have miraculous efficacy.   These new teachings are preserved in the New Testament.   It was written in Hellenistic Greek and often shows the influence of Greek literature and philosophy, as we should expect from the Hellenization of the eastern Mediterranean. *Rise of Christianity*

It is interesting to note how the early Christians impressed a superficial yet intelligent observer like the witty essayist Lucian in the second century.   Lucian himself, although born in Syria, was inclined to Epicureanism and scepticism, so that there is no danger of his allusions to the Christians being partial or unduly favorable to them.   He speaks of "their queer creed," and regards them as "misguided creatures" and "simple souls" who are easily imposed upon by impostors. While Lucian ridicules the Christians, he also testifies to their "general conviction that they are immortal for all time, which explains the contempt of death and voluntary self-devotion *Christians of the Second Century*

which are so common among them," and states that "the
activity of these people in dealing with any matter that affects
their community is something extraordinary," that they regard
themselves as "all brothers" and "despise all worldly goods,
regarding them merely as common property." This shows us
how the spirit of the Christian community was replacing that
of the ancient city. Lucian also alludes to their "orphans
and ancient widows," to their "sacred books," and to "their
forbidden meats," in which respect he perhaps confuses them
with the Jews or may have reference to meat sacrificed to
idols. Lucian further refers to their worship of Christ. "The
Christians, you know, worship a man to this day,—the distinguished personage who introduced their novel rites, and was
crucified on that account."

Spread of Christianity Despite Opposition

Jesus had not been accepted as the long looked for Messiah
by official Judaism, and others appeared before and after him
claiming to be Christ or the Son of God. Some of his disciples
remained at Jerusalem, others scattered outside Palestine,
spreading their new-found faith not only to Jewish communities
abroad, but to the Greeks and other peoples or "Gentiles."
Any person of either sex and any class was offered salvation.
This, indeed, was commonly true of the Greek mysteries and
the oriental cults, which were open to slave as well as freeman,
though sometimes not to both sexes. But Christianity, unlike
the other oriental religions, retained the Jewish characteristic
of not allowing its initiates to participate in any other worship,
not even in the public rites of their native city or the imperial
cult. This fact, together with the close association of the
early Christians with Palestine and the Jews, who had often
been in rebellion against the Roman Empire, made pagan
society and the usually tolerant Roman government hostile to
them. They seem to have been further criticized as unduly
superstitious, as dangerous teachers of pacifism and socialism,
and as enemies of existing society. But they thrived on persecution and martyrdom. In the fourth century the emperors
themselves became Christian, and the doom of dying paganism
and of other oriental religions was sealed. Christianity was
left without a rival to attempt the conversion of the northern
barbarians, who now began to obliterate the distinction between
the empire and their own territories. The philosophy of the
fourth century known as Neo-Platonism appealed only to the

cultured, while the empire was becoming barbarized. The Christian church succeeded in gaining an ascendancy over the barbarians and went on increasing in strength. "I recount," said Gibbon in his *Decline and Fall of the Roman Empire,* "the triumph of barbarism and religion."

Christianity did not so much cause the decline of ancient civilization as it did fill the void produced by that decline, supplying religious interest and comfort to replace economic, military, intellectual, and other worldly interests. As the barbarians came in because the population of the empire was depleted and its strength weakened, so religion occupied men's minds because other interests were ceasing to do so. It is true, however, that many conscientious Christians found classical literature too deeply dyed with pagan mythology and profane love, Greek sculpture too closely associated with idolatry. Yet Christians spoke Latin or Greek like other men, and such education as they received was for a long time necessarily classical. They of course read their own scriptures, but these gave moral and religious instruction rather than presented a body of knowledge or program of civilization. Therefore a large residue of previous civilization continued in Christian society, especially when the whole population of the empire in the fourth century rapidly followed the emperors in becoming nominally Christian. Such nominal adherents naturally kept much more of their worldly and even pagan ways than had the earlier converts. Greek gods were metamorphosed into medieval saints, and many rites of the pagan period continued under a Christian veneer. Christians who wished, like Basil, "to rid my soul of all sympathy with things on earth," withdrew to hermitages and monasteries, but the rest of the world went on in much the same old way. A feeling against marriage had long been developing among such sects as the Jewish Essenes, and Christianity can be held only in small part responsible for whatever effect the abandonment of family life may have had upon civilization. On the other hand, Christianity seems to have done much to reform the loose classical standards in matters of sexual immorality, and to soften ancient callousness towards human suffering. Lucian, for example, whose comments on the Christians we quoted above, found it laughable when a religious and philosophical impostor was forced to make good his promise of four years before to

Relation of Christianity to Declining Pagan Civilization

burn himself alive on a pyre at the Olympic games in order to show his contempt for death.   It is true that Christians were to burn heretics at the stake; but they did not regard it as a laughing matter.   It is, however, risky to generalize about such matters.

Patristic Literature

The best way to learn the mental outlook and interests of a cultured Christian of the later Roman Empire is to dip into the voluminous works of the church fathers or Christian writers of that time.   These consist of defenses of Christianity against the criticism of its opponents, onslaughts upon pagan worships, theaters, and the like, sermons and commentaries upon the Bible, moral and theological disquisitions, praises of virginity and asceticism, and long diatribes against heretical sects which existed within the church.   The reader may find the church fathers rather long and prosy, quoting the Bible and even Greek and Latin literature too frequently, and further-more too much like one another.   He may be surprised not to find more Christian joy and gladness, serenity and good-will in them.   But if he reads them attentively, he will find many informing bits as to the life and thought of those times, and will also recognize in those remote writings the lineal ancestors of most sermons that are preached today.   As classical Latin and Greek literature declined, this new patristic literature in both languages increased, and is our chief mirror for the civilization of several centuries.   There was some Christian poetry, but it was hampered by adherence to classical tradition and meter.

Early Christian Art

As the New Testament was written in Hellenistic Greek, so early Christian art is an outgrowth from Hellenistic and Roman art.   After the frescoes of Pompeii our remains of Roman painting are Christian from the catacombs of Rome and other cities of the empire and even south Russia.   These under-ground galleries were dug by burial associations of persons who could not afford individual graves and so purchased a plot of land together and then tunneled underneath it in suc-cessive levels which afforded space for a great number of in-terments.   Many of them are not Christian; for instance, recently remains of six thousand persons were found in two *columbaria* (or underground sepulchers) of the servants and freedmen of Augustus and Livia.   The Christian paintings found on the walls and ceilings of such catacombs are inferior artistically, and are interesting rather for the continuity with previous art which they manifest not only in decorative motives but in the retention of figures from pagan mythology such as Cupid and Psyche, Orpheus and Hermes. In fact, this last indicates religious as well as artistic continuity. The art tends to symbolism, although to say that Orpheus charming the animals by his music represents Christ winning over man's brutish nature by his love is a questionable assumption, since then we might have to hold that certain figures of Christ symbolize Orphic rites.

We find the nearest approaches to Christianity neither in the rationalism of Greece nor the orientalism of Rome, but in the heartfelt aspirations of Orphic and Dionysiac devotees. It was by no accident that the art of the catacombs repeated again and again the figure of Orpheus, or that the literature of the dark ages described the tragedy of Calvary in language borrowed from the Bacchantae of Euripides. (A. B. Cook)

More certainly Christian are the fish-symbol, the dove, lamb, and lamp. Scenes from the Old Testament, such as Noah in the ark, Abraham sacrificing Isaac, Moses bringing water from the rock (Mithraism, however, also had its rock of generation), and the story of Jonah, are used to suggest the doctrines and mysteries of the Gospel. Or the three Hebrews in the fiery furnace and Daniel among the lions commemorate the fortitude of Christian martyrs. It is interesting to find thus early, scenes from the apocryphal books of the Bible, such as the story of Susannah or Tobias with his fish in the presence of Raphael, which were later treated by the painters of the Italian Renaissance. The dominance of astrology in the thought of the time is attested by representations of seven persons breaking bread or eating fish instead of twelve disciples, thus making it the more likely that the latter number has reference to the signs of the zodiac. It would seem an influence of sunworship that the "venerable day of the Sun" was selected for Christian observance. Christian sculpture is found in metal relief upon church vessels, some of which are perhaps quite early, and on sarcophagi which date from the fourth and fifth centuries. For congregational purposes the Christians came to use the basilica, or, with the disappearance of paganism, temples were made over into churches. Bells seem to have been the Christian invention of St. Paulinus (354–431), bishop of Nola in Campania, whence bells were first named *nolae* and *campanae*, while the bell-tower or belfry is called *campanile* in Italian.

Church Organization

The first Christian communities expected the speedy second coming of Christ and the kingdom of heaven, shared their worldly goods with one another, were noted for their care of the poor and sick, and followed the guidance of the Holy Spirit as this expressed itself in prophesying by individuals. Great stress also came to be laid upon sacred symbols and acts and forms, such as the name of Jesus, sign of the cross, baptism, and the Lord's Supper. Local variation, which perhaps dated from the very foundation of the scattered communities by different missionaries with varying interpretations of the Gospel, and liberty in prophesying led, however, to sects and heresies. These and persecution by pagan society and the Roman government and the strong community spirit of the Christian brotherhood led in turn to the development of a firm distinct organization which we know as the church, thus separating religious from civic life. Yet the church organization was closely modelled after the structure of the empire in which Christianity found itself. There came to be a bishop at the head of the Christians in every municipality, an archbishop in every Roman province. As against this tendency to one-man government may be set various facts showing the more democratic side of the church, such as the use of the word, "brethren," for all members, or the derivation of our word "ecclesiastical" from the Greek word for a popular assembly, the church or *ecclesia* being the whole congregation of the faithful. Perhaps one reason why the emperors became reconciled to Christianity was that it ceased to organize itself in somewhat secret, communistic, popular societies and had recognized single heads in each locality through whom it could be controlled. In the west the bishop of Rome, or pope, gradually assumed a position of superiority to other bishops and archbishops, and as Rome was no longer the imperial capital after 330, he was relatively free from the imperial interference and domination that hampered the patriarch at Constantinople.

BIBLIOGRAPHY

The writings of the church fathers will be found in English translations in two great sets: *The Ante-Nicene Fathers*, edited by A. Roberts and J. Donaldson, and *The Nicene and Post-Nicene Fathers*, edited by H. Wace and P. Schaff. Of the almost innumerable books on the early church and religious conditions during the Roman Empire, only a few of the more recent publications can be mentioned.

Allard, P. *Histoire des persecutions*, 1892, 5 vols.

Bigg, C. *The Church's Task under the Roman Empire*, 1905.

Bussell, F. W. *Religious Thought and Heresy in the Middle Ages*, 1918.

Case, S. J. *Evolution of Early Christianity*, 1914.

Charles, R. H. *Apocrypha and Pseudepigrapha of the Old Testament in English*, 2 vols. 1913.

Clemen, Carl. *Primitive Christianity and its Non-Jewish Sources*, English translation by R. G. Nisbet, 1912.

Conybeare, F. C. *Myth, Magic, and Morals*, 1910; *History of New Testament Criticism*, 1910.

Cumont, F. *The Mysteries of Mithra*, English translation, 1903; *Oriental Religions in Roman Paganism*, 1911.

Duchesne, L. *Early History of the Christian Church*, 1909–1912, 2 vols.

Flick, A. C. *The Rise of the Medieval Church*, 1909.

Glover, T. R. *Conflict of Religions in the Early Roman Empire*, 1909.

Goodspeed, E. J. *Story of the New Testament*, 1918.

Harnack, A. *Expansion of Christianity in the First Three Centuries*, 1904–05. 2 vols.

Hodgson, Mrs. G. *Primitive Christian Education*, 1906.

Jenner, Mrs. H. *Christian Symbolism*, 1910.

Jones, M. *The New Testament in the Twentieth Century*, 1914.

Kidd, B. J. *History of the Church to A. D. 461*, 1922, 3 vols.

Labriolle, Pierre de. *History and Literature of Christianity from Tertullian to Boethius*, 1925.

Lake, Kirsopp. *Landmarks in the History of Early Christianity*.

Lamberton, C. D. *Themes from St. John's Gospel in Early Catacomb Painting*, 1908.

Legge, F. *Forerunners and Rivals of Christianity*, 1915, 2 vols.

Leigh-Bennett, E. *Handbook of the Early Christian Fathers*, 1920.

Loisy, A. *Les mystères païens et le mystère chrétien*, 1919.

Nunn, H. *Introduction to Ecclesiastical Latin*, 1922.

Patterson, L. *Mithraism and Christianity*, 1921.

Ramsay, Sir Wm. *The Church in the Roman Empire before 170 A.D.*, 1894; *St. Paul the Traveler and Roman Citizen*, 1903; *St. Luke the Physician*, 1908; *The First Christian Century*, 1911.

Robertson, J. M. *The Historical Jesus*, 1916.

Sihler, E. G. *From Augustus to Augustine*, 1923.

Swete, H. B. *Essays on the Early History of the Church and the Ministry,* 1918.

van den Bergh van Eysinga, *Radical Views about the New Testament,* 1912, English translation by S. B. Slack.

Workman, H. B. *Evolution of the Monastic Ideal,* 1913.

CHAPTER XVIII

BARBARIAN INVADERS

(Huns, Germans, and Slavs)

There were his young barbarians, all at play.—Byron

IN the present chapter our attention is to be claimed by
the barbarian peoples to the north and east who were connected with the decline and fall of the Roman Empire, and
have played a large part in the history of both Europe and
Asia ever since. They divide into three great groups, the
mounted nomads of central Asia, and the Slavic and Germanic
peoples of Europe.

Central Asia, that is to say, the regions between Siberia Central Asia
on the north and China, India, Persia, and Arabia to the south,
is in the main a series of plateaus and deserts where, during
most periods of history, life has been possible only for hardy
nomads. Enumerating from east to west, this area comprises
Manchuria, Mongolia, Eastern Turkestan, Turkestan, and the
Khirghiz steppe about the Aral and Caspian Seas. From this
area the nomads naturally overflow into Europe in the Russian
steppes north of the Black Sea. Tibet and the Himalayas
intervene between India and Mongolia, but from Turkestan
invaders may enter the Indus valley by crossing the plateau of
the Pamirs or "roof of the world." From the Pamirs the
ancient Oxus (Amudarya) river flows to the north-west to the
Aral Sea, while to the north-east, south-east, and south-west
respectively radiate the Alai, Karakoram, and Hindu Kush
mountain ranges. Across the Pamirs passed the ancient trade
routes from China to the west, and today the boundaries of the
Chinese, British, and Russian empires meet at this point.
The prevailing winds for many centuries have denuded Mongolia of its surface soil. In the Caspian-Aral basin deserts of
sand or gravel likewise prevail. The Caspian itself, although
an inland sea, is salt, and so are the steppes near it, showing

that evaporation exceeds the amount of rainfall; in this region there are few fertile spots.

Life of the Nomads

To support life and avoid the extremes of heat and cold which characterize these regions, the nomads have both summer and winter camping stations, leaving the south as its scanty pasturage dries up with the approach of summer and seeking the better-watered grass steppes of southern Siberia until deep snows begin to cover them. This hard life of continual transit produces desperate fighters who have to spend much of their time on horseback in order to round up their herds and cover great distances in search of pasture. Their horses are small but of a very hardy breed, and can cover great distances at a stretch. From fermented mares' milk the nomads make the nutritious drink called kumiz or koumiss. Besides horses they often keep sheep, goats, and sometimes camels or cattle. As to the honesty and hospitability, the immorality and cruelty of these nomads there seems to be and to have been difference of opinion. Their uncleanliness is more generally admitted, especially in winter when they are confined to their tents. All civilized nations whose borders they have harried have invariably looked upon them with disgust and fear as hopeless barbarians who must be kept out, and they have been very slow to adopt a settled life and little amenable to civilizing influences. But when once they had determined to invade, it was not easy to keep them out because of the rapidity of their movements on horseback. They were perhaps especially likely to succeed in overruning a region which was sparsely populated or already beginning to decline in fertility or civilization. Having once overrun such a region, they were apt to complete and seal its ruin.

The Ural-Altaic Languages

The present peoples of central Asia for the most part speak languages of the Ural-Altaic group. The name, Ural-Altaic comes from the Ural Mountains which form the boundary between Europe and Asia and the Altai Mountains, which separate Mongolia on the northwest from Siberia. The languages of this group are now, at least, by no means confined to the region between these two mountain systems, but are spoken also by the Manchus in Manchuria and northern China, the Turks in Asia Minor, and the Finns in Finland. The four chief divisions of the Ural-Altaic languages are the Finno-Ugrian, Turkish, Mongol, and Manchu. All are agglutinating and attach suf-

fixes to roots which remain unmodified; all are apt to put the
object rather than the subject first in a sentence; but some seem
more developed or altered by outside influences than others,
and there are marked differences between them. For instance,
the numerals are entirely different in Turkish, Mongol, and
Finno-Ugrian.

Most of the peoples who today speak Ural-Altaic languages
are also primarily of the Mongoloid physical type. This of
course does not hold true of the fair Finns who are northern
Europeans of the white race, nor of the Turks in Asia Minor
and Thrace who have so intermarried with white women that
they have become largely European in physique. But the
Khirghiz of Turkestan seem of closely allied stock to the
nomads of Mongolia, having the Mongoloid features of long
trunks but short limbs, square build and inclination to corpulence, broad head and face, high cheekbones, flat nose, small
mouth and small black oblique eyes—in which respect, however, they resemble the Chinese rather than the Mongols and
Manchus whose eyes are set horizontally. They further have
small hands and feet, black hair and scanty beard, while their
complexion, although sometimes fair, is usually sufficiently
swarthy or dirty to entitle them to rank as of the yellow-brown
race or races. Most of the ancient and medieval mounted
nomads from central Asia were probably of the same stock
or not distantly related to it. However, the Indo-European
invaders of early India perhaps entered it by way of Turkestan, although they may have come by way of Asia Minor,
Armenia, and the plateau of Iran. As late as the eighth century A. D., Iranian was spoken almost on the edge of China,
and some Indo-European nomads are still found in central
Asia. Such names as Tartars (or, Tatars) and Mongols have
been very loosely employed by various writers; the population
of central Asia has very possibly shifted a great deal with
the passage of centuries; and there have been great sweeps of
migration and conquest in which the tribal name of the leaders
has been carelessly applied to all those who were swept along
in their train. Thus such words as Turks and Tartars have
had little fixed meaning. Furthermore, languages of common
origin have more and more diverged, while physique has altered
with change of climate and location, or different types have
amalgamated by living under the same conditions and inter-

*Mongoloid
Physique*

marrying.   But on the whole the evidence seems to favor the
view that the Hiung-nu and other troublesome tribes on the
northern frontier of ancient China, and the Huns who in 372
A. D. crossed the Volga and threw Europe into confusion, were
about such Asiatic nomads as may still be found in central
Asia.   Whether the Scythians who invaded India at the beginning of our era were of similar origin is less certain.

Relations of the Nomads with China   Probably because of the Mongoloid characteristics which
these nomads have in common with the Chinese and also be-
cause of longer direct contact with them, China seems to have
had the greatest success of any land in gradually absorbing
many of them and at the same time maintaining its own civilization against their infiltration.   However, we shall argue
in a later chapter that its civilization has suffered from them
in the long run, and we may note now that the language of
northern China has been deeply affected by Tartar influence.
The Chinese early cultivated archery and horsemanship, either
because they had themselves once been mounted nomads or in
order to meet the nomads with their own style of fighting.
Five or six nomad tribes had already established themselves in
China in the days before Confucius, and he said that but for
Duke Huan who defeated them, "we should all have been but-
toning our coats on the left side."   Of the Hiung-nu, the building of the Great Wall against them, and their successful
entrance into northern China after the Han dynasty, we shall
speak presently.

The Huns take Europe by Surprise   Europe was much less accustomed to these Asiatic nomads,
and their crossing the Volga in 372 took the western world
by surprise.   The contemporary Roman historian and retired soldier, Ammianus Marcellinus, spoke of them as "a race
of men, hitherto unknown," who suddenly appeared "as if they
had risen from some secret recess of the earth," and who, "like
a whirlwind . . . were ravaging and destroying everything
which came in their way."   He described them as "savage beyond all parallel, . . . without beards and without any beauty,
. . . of great size and low-legged, so that you might fancy them
two-legged beasts, or the stout figures which are hewn out in
a rude manner with an axe on the posts at the end of bridges."
This westward sweep of the Huns was probably caused by a
period of even greater aridity in the Caspian basin than prevails today, since walls built against them in the fifth and

sixth centuries can now be traced under water as far as eighteen miles from shore. This extreme aridity probably forced many of the nomads to seek other pastures. A similar dry spell ruined Chinese Turkestan, where the Turfan basin had at the beginning of our era been flourishing and densely populated.

Before the Huns reached the Roman frontier they came in contact with other barbarians, between the Volga and Danube, who seem for the most part to have been either Germans or Slavs. These early Germans were the direct ancestors not only of the present Germans and Austrians but of the Scandinavians and Dutch, and to some extent of the English, Flemish, and Swiss. Although many of the Swiss speak German, they are physically rather of the Alpine type. The Slavs are today represented not only by the bulk of the population of Russia, but in Latvia, Lithuania, Poland, Czecho-Slovakia, Jugo-Slavia, and to some extent in the other Balkan states. Both Germans and Slavs spoke Indo-European languages and were taller and fairer than the Mediterranean peoples. But while the Germans had long skulls and were of Nordic race, the square heads or round skulls of the Slavs mark them as of Alpine stock. Both peoples engaged in agriculture to some extent, unlike the Asiatic nomads, but the Germans seem to have had more domestic animals and greater knowledge of metals. At first living in the bronze age around the southwestern end of the Baltic from perhaps 1500 to 500 B. C., they gradually expanded southeastward and southwestward, adopted the Hallstatt type of civilization, and entered the iron age. The Roman Empire had not been able to conquer them east of the Rhine, and the river Vistula was apparently the boundary between Germans and Slavs at this period. In the third century A. D., German tribes known as Goths had migrated southeast to the shores of the Black Sea, and the Roman Empire had been forced to abandon Dacia, the region north of the lower Danube, to them. Thus, along Rhine and Danube and from the North Sea and Baltic to the Black Sea, German tribes lined the Roman frontier and intervened between Roman civilization and the Slavs, who were indeed as yet totally unheard of.

But Roman writers like Julius Cæsar (about 50 B. C.) and Tacitus (*Germania*, 98 A. D.) briefly yet accurately described the Germans. Moreover, their own laws, first written down

Germans and Slavs

Customs of the Germans

from the close of the fifth century A. D. on, and their own literature, in its written form of still later date, give a retrospective view of their life, although after it had been considerably altered by more or less contact with Roman civilization and by their conversion to Christianity. This last, for example, obliterated their heathen religious ritual and left their laws almost entirely secular. Apparently their original religion and mythology was much like that of other Indo-Europeans, as may be seen by comparing Norse and Icelandic literature with the *Rigveda* and Homer and Hesiod. Their social organization and customs were not especially peculiar to themselves but much like those of other uncivilized and primitive peoples, especially the Celts. They had the kinship group or sib in addition to the family, and a voluntary union of fellow warriors devoted personally to a leader and commonly known by the Latin name *comitatus*, meaning a band of comrades. There were both nobles and slaves among them. Blood-feud between sibs was largely replaced by compensation or payment of the *wergeld* of the slain, which varied in amount according to his rank. Perhaps their most outstanding trait was individual liberty, although they had the usual respect of primitive man for custom, so that even after invading the Roman Empire they long kept their own laws in opposition to the Roman law. Their laws were much like early law in general. Their women were allowed no little freedom, however, and the son became free from the father's authority as soon as he received his arms in the assembly of free warriors. Even before their conversion to Christianity the authority of the heathen priests seems not to have been great. Royal power developed mainly through contact with the Roman Empire.

Their Conversion to Christianity

Why and how the Germans were so easily converted to Christianity is somewhat of a puzzle, but the fact that many of them had been converted before the break-up of the Roman Empire was of great advantage to the church. The Goths in the Crimea were represented by a bishop at the Council of Nicæa in 325, and a little later Ulfilas translated the Bible into Gothic. At first the Germans generally adopted Arianism, a form of Christianity which within the Roman Empire was regarded as unorthodox, although professed by many, especially in the east.

Barbarian
Invasions
and Over-
throw of
the Roman
Empire

Since the reign of Marcus Aurelius (161–180) who had had to take the field against them for a number of years, the Germans had been threatening the Roman Empire and either invading it, peacefully settling within it, or serving in the Roman armies as soldiers. The result, as we said in an earlier chapter, was the gradual barbarization of the empire. In the third century it had seemed about to go to pieces, but had recovered and was holding the Germans in check when the sudden advance of the Huns drove the Germans west and south across the Roman frontiers. This movement began with the West Goths who received permission to cross the Danube and settle within the empire in order to escape from the Huns. The latter had forced a people of doubtful race called the Alani to join them, had defeated the East Goths, and had thrown all central Europe into confusion. The West Goths became angry at the treatment they received from Roman officials and profiteers, and in 378 at Adrianople in Thrace, fighting together with some of the Huns who had somehow crossed the Danube too, they so decisively defeated and killed the emperor Valens that Ammianus Marcellinus already in the fourth century regarded the Roman Empire as overthrown.

Henceforth the Balkan peninsula swarmed with barbarians. Some, like the West and East Goths, eventually moved on to Italy, Spain, and Gaul, but they were succeeded by the Bulgars, another group of the Asiatic nomads, and by the Slavs— two peoples who have remained as a permanent element in the peninsula. The barbarians were not able to take Constantinople, however, and the easternmost provinces of the Roman Empire were further protected by the existence of the strong Persian kingdom of the Sassanids to the east as a buffer between them and the onsets of the nomads from that direction. On the other hand, various German tribes broke across the Rhine into Gaul, or even traversed Spain and settled in North Africa, as was done by the Vandals, or descended upon the coasts of Britain, which had been abandoned to its fate by the Roman troops. When, however, the Huns under the lead of Attila invaded Gaul in 451, the West Goths joined with the Roman commander Aëtius in making a successful stand against them in the battle of the Catalaunian Fields or Châlons. Never again were the mounted nomads of central Asia to come so far west. German stock began to rise again.

The German
Kingdoms
and Their
Civilization

Since the reign of Diocletian (284–305), the imperial office had usually been divided between two co-emperors, one in the east and one in the west. After the battle of Adrianople the western emperors were for the most part weaklings who hid themselves at Ravenna on the Adriatic coast of Italy, and in 476 the imperial office ceased in the west. Its place was taken by German kingdoms, of which the chief were those of the Vandals in North Africa (439–534), of the West Goths in Aquitaine and Spain (419–711), Burgundians in the Rhone valley (419–534), East Goths in Italy (493–555), Lombards in Italy (568–774), and of the Franks on the lower Rhine. The Franks began their conquest of Gaul under Clovis (481–511) and reached their greatest extent under Charlemagne (768–814), who attempted to revive the imperial title. From about 450 to 600 Angles, Saxons, and Jutes were invading Britain, but their little kingdoms did not coalesce into one England until the time of Alfred the Great (871–901) and his immediate successors. Celtic culture still held out unconquered in Brittany, Wales, the Scottish highlands, and Ireland. Of these various peoples the Goths and Vandals adopted Roman ways to some extent. Franks and Anglo-Saxons were less acquainted with, and less favorable to, Roman civilization, but they were converted to orthodox Roman Catholic Christianity instead of being Arians like the Goths and Vandals. Towns decayed; economic life became stagnant and largely agricultural. Little has reached us from these kingdoms in the way of art and letters; Boethius sought consolation in philosophy, and others retired to monasteries. Nevertheless the condition of the Germans and of the Roman provincials whom they had conquered was superior to the state of the central Asiatic nomads and the poor Slavs whom they conquered.

Asiatic
Nomads and
the Slavs

Of the Huns under that name we do not hear much more after the death of Attila in 453. The nomadic Bulgars gradually fused with the Balkan Slavs into the present Bulgarian nationality. About 545 Chinese sources begin to mention Turks in central Asia, who presently defeated the Ephthalites or White Huns (so-called presumably because they were nomads who were not of yellow race) in the Oxus river basin on the northeast frontier of the Persian kingdom. As yet, however, the Turks did not trouble the west. But another division of Asiatic nomads known as Avars entered the Hungarian plain in the later sixth century and until the eighth century exercised a wide dominion over the surrounding regions. Charlemagne defeated their declining empire, and late in the ninth century they gave way to the Magyars or Hungarians of the present day. This wedge of Asiatic nomads in Hungary served to separate the northern Slavs from those of the Balkan peninsula. Slavic settlement in the Balkan peninsula seems to have taken place especially during the seventh century. In the north a little later the Bohemians and Poles revolted from the Avars and founded dynasties of their own. As the Germans had moved west, the Slavs had followed in behind them, occupying the region between the Vistula and the Elbe which once had been held by the Germans, and thus separating the Scandinavians from the other Germans.

With the close of the eighth century the still heathen Northmen, or Norwegians, Danes, and Swedes, began their period of expansion, attacking the rest of Europe from the sea, rowing far inland up the rivers all along the coast, and repeatedly crossing Russia from the Baltic to the Black Sea. Indeed Russia takes its name from them, since *Rōs* is Slavic for Swedes. They ruled over principalities there, and also sold many of the wretched Slavs in slave markets of the south. They broke up the Frankish empire. In particular they colonized Normandy, which takes its name from them, the northeastern half of England, which was called the Danelaw because the customs of the Danes prevailed there, and various outlying portions of the British Isles such as the Shetlands, Orkneys, Hebrides, Isle of Man, northernmost counties of Scotland, and certain ports in Ireland. In the eleventh century Normans overran southern Italy and Sicily, where they established a kingdom during the twelfth century which may be regarded as the latest of the kingdoms founded by German invaders in the Mediterranean world.

Invasions of the Northmen

BIBLIOGRAPHY

Czaplicka, M. C. *Turks of Eastern Asia,* 1918.
Gjerset, K. *History of the Norwegian People,* 1915.
Grant, M. *Passing of the Great Race,* 1916.
Grimm, J. *Teutonic Mythology,* 1882.
Guerber, H. A. *Myths of Northern Lands,* 1895.

Gummere, *Germanic Origins,* 1892.

Huntington, E. *Pulse of Asia,* 1907.

Keary, C. F. *The Vikings in Western Christendom,* 1891.

Kerner, R. J. *Slavic Europe, a select bibliography,* 1918.

Mauver, *The Vikings,* 1913.

Niederle, L. *Manuel de l'antiquité slave,* 1923.

Pumpelly, R. *Explorations in Turkestan,* 1908, 2 vols.

Radosavljevich, *Who are the Slavs?* 1919, 2 vols.

Revel, Jean. *Histoire des Normands,* 1918–1919, 2 vols.

Schevill, F. *History of the Balkan Peninsula,* 1922.

Schwarz, P. *Iran im Mittelalter,* 1910.

Stein, M. A. *Ancient Khotan,* 1907.

Williams, Mary. *Social Scandinavia in the Viking Age,* 1920.

BOOK IV. CIVILIZATIONS OF THE FAR EAST

CHAPTER XIX

INDIA TO BUDDHA

> . . . living a life of rich and fine feeling, . . . contemplating nature and their own lives and purposes in rituals, pictures, poems, and songs. This kind of culture the East, I think, has always had in a finer sense than the modern West.
> —*G. Lowes Dickinson*

LEAVING for a time the European West, where the Roman Empire was breaking up, barbarians coming in, and Christendom making preparation for a later revival of civilization, we shall consider in the next few chapters the origin and development of civilization among the leading Asiatic peoples of the Far East. This will at first take us far back in time to the beginnings of Indian and Chinese cultures, while for the sake of continuity we shall carry their story on even somewhat beyond the point which we have thus far reached in the west. We shall then note certain new civilizations appearing in the Near East—Byzantine, Persian, and Arabic—which present a fusion and transformation of Hellenistic, or late-classical, and oriental elements. These cultures kept civilization alive during the early middle ages while it was at a low ebb in the west, and had much influence upon the revival of civilization in the west which will thereafter claim our attention.

Eastward Ho!

India is a sufficiently distinct portion of the earth's surface, having well marked physical boundaries in the Indian Ocean on the south and on the north high tablelands and mountain ranges, of which the Himalayas are the chief. The shape of the area so enclosed may be roughly described as two triangles having a common base on the Tropic of Cancer. The other two sides of the northern triangle are the Ganges and the Indus river basins. The southern triangle, whose west side is the Malabar coast along the Arabian Sea and whose east side is the Carnatic along the Bay of Bengal, extends south through

Geography of India

225

rather more degrees of latitude until its sides meet at a sharper point almost at the equator. The Indo-Gangetic plain in the north is the most fertile and populous part of India, including several hundred thousand square miles from sea to sea, with a breadth varying from about one hundred to three hundred miles. The moist monsoon blowing in from the tropical waters of the Indian Ocean condenses against the lofty Himalayas and swells the streams of the Ganges. The Indus and Brahmaputra have their sources north of the Himalayas, along whose northern slopes they flow a long distance in opposite directions before breaking through into India on the northwest and northeast, thus stealing drainage from central Asia for the benefit of northern India. The sun-baked plains of the Punjab, however, seem, like the plateau of Iran and central Asia, to be drier now than in antiquity. Thus the Saraswati, spoken of in the Vedas as a mighty river flowing seaward, now disappears in the sands of the desert. The lower course of the Indus is without tributaries and bordered, like the Nile, by deserts where men have to dig two or three hundred feet through rock for water. The desert to the east of the Indus, and the forest to the west and south of the Ganges, bring us to the base of our southern triangle, the Deccan or peninsula of India. The Deccan is a much older land area than the Himalayas which are, geologically speaking, but a recent uplift. It more closely resembles Arabia, South Africa, and western Australia in being a plateau with steep walls rising not far from the coast, with, however, a number of deltas on the east coast.

Climate and Products

India as a whole has a hot and enervating climate. The north is somewhat cooler in "winter," while the peninsula is hot without intermission. At present it is estimated that about one-fifth of India is jungle and four-fifths cultivated. Of this cultivated area one-seventh bears two crops annually, but sometimes the rainy season ends too early, with resultant drought and famine. Over a century ago the Abbé Dubois, who spent much of his life like a native in India, regarded the climate as having a universally debilitating effect, which not only enfeebled the mental faculties and moral stamina as well as the physical constitutions of the Hindus, but also affected the very beasts, of which the elephant and tiger alone displayed much vigor. He found that the meat there had little succulence, the game a poor flavor. "Vainly would one search for a good

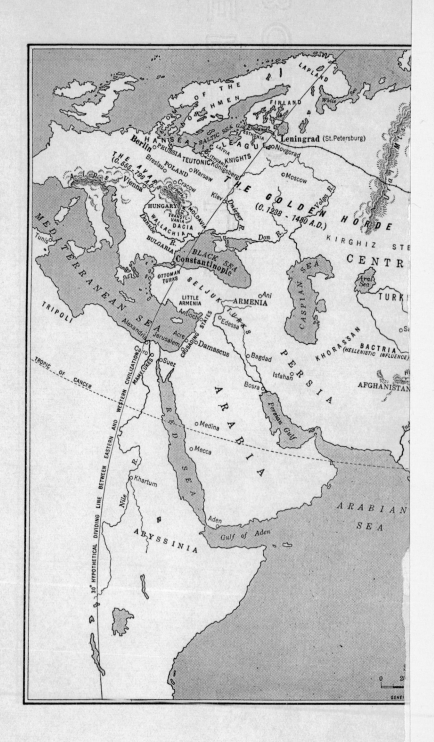

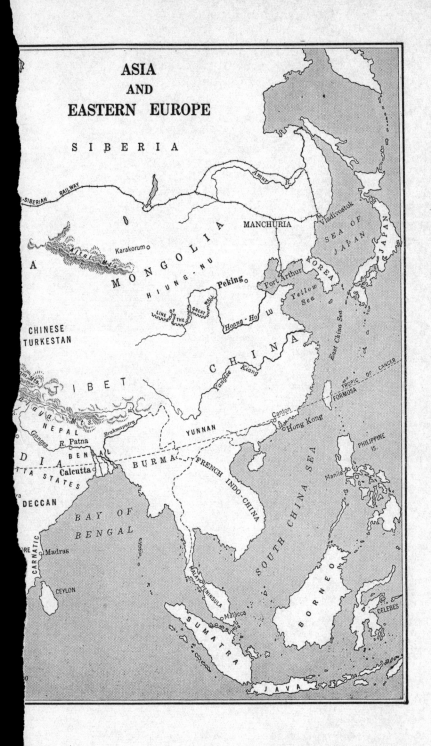

ASIA
AND
EASTERN EUROPE

SIBERIA

TRANS-SIBERIAN RAILWAY

Amur R.

MANCHURIA

Vladivostok

SEA OF JAPAN

JAPAN

Karakorum

MONGOLIA

HIUNG - NU

Peking

Port Arthur

KOREA

Yellow Sea

A

Altai Mts.

CHINESE
TURKESTAN

LINE OF THE GREAT WALL

Hoang - Ho

Lu

CHINA

East China Sea

TIBET

Yangtze Kiang

FORMOSA

TROPIC OF CANCER

Himalaya Mts.

NEPAL

Brahmaputra

YUNNAN

Canton

Hong Kong

PHILIPPINE IS.

Ganges

R. Patna

BENGAL

Calcutta

BURMA

FRENCH INDO-CHINA

Manila

DIA

STATES

DECCAN

BAY OF
BENGAL

SOUTH CHINA SEA

BORNEO

CARNATIC

Madras

CEYLON

MALAY PENINSULA

Malacca

SUMATRA

JAVA

CELEBES

hare or partridge." The green stuff, roots, and fruits were also for the most part "insipid and tasteless, and do not possess half the nutritive value of those grown in Europe," while with two or three exceptions the indigenous flowers had no scent, and the trees and shrubs were generally covered with thorns and prickles. On the other hand, there were plenty of poisonous plants, snakes, reptiles, birds of prey, insects and vermin. The air was almost everywhere damp and unhealthy; the water, brackish and unpleasant to taste. There is today, however, an abundance of fish in both sea and rivers, while the domestic fowl first came from India or Burma. Sugar, too, seems to have been known in India before it was introduced to other lands; the Sanskrit *sharkara* appears to be the earliest form of the word. We may also recall the great reputation which India had in classical and medieval times as the home of medicinal herbs, potent drugs, spices and aromatics, although the credit for these belonged partly to the spice islands in the East Indies or to other neighboring lands.

Indeed, India is said to have no distinctive flora of its own but a composite blending of vegetation from Persia, Siberia, China, and the Malay peninsula and archipelago. In view, however, of the great antiquity of the Deccan land area, this assertion is not wholly acceptable. Despite India's imposing northern barrier it has not been cut off from the rest of the world, since ancient and much frequented trade routes have crossed the Himalayas by passes higher than the topmost peaks of the Alps—over 18,000 feet above sea level. Moreover, invaders have been frequent from the time of the Aryans. We shall not recount all these invasions at the times of their occurrence; of some of them no record has been preserved. But their lasting effects can be seen in the diversity of races and languages in India today. *Relation to Other Lands and Peoples*

The oldest aboriginal inhabitants are probably represented by the short black men with almost negro noses who have been crowded south into the Deccan as various invaders occupied the north. Some speak Munda languages, which were once widespread in northern and central India, perhaps also in the Malay archipelago and Australia. More of them speak Dravidian languages, which include the four literary languages of the south. Both of these groups of languages are steadily losing ground to Aryan speech, and hold out chiefly in hill *Variety of Races and Languages* country and jungle on, quite appropriately, the oldest geological formation. The Indo-Chinese and Tibetan languages, numbering over ninety, were brought in by invaders of yellow race, but are spoken by only a small fraction of the total population. Besides three Iranian tongues on the northwest frontier, there are now twenty-three varieties of Aryan speech. These Aryan languages are employed by over two-thirds of the population. This of course does not mean that all these people are descendants of the Aryan invaders, who were of white race. Many black peoples have adopted Aryan speech, while the majority of the population are a fusion of Aryan and non-Aryan stock. There are also various other racial mixtures, such as Turko-Iranian, Scytho-Dravidian, and Mongolo-Dravidian. The present Mohammedan population represent invading peoples who have mingled with the previous inhabitants, and are partly of Arab, partly of Persian, partly of Mongoloid descent.

The Later Vedas

Religion and literature continued as the prominent features in the civilization of India in the period following the *Rigveda*. The *Samaveda*, dealing particularly with the ritual of the *soma* sacrifice, is based upon the earlier *Rigveda* from which it draws large extracts. In the *Yajurveda* the invading Aryans have new tribal names and have moved the center of their civilization farther eastward into the Ganges valley. New ceremonies and forms of worship also appear, such as snake-worship which was previously unknown to the Aryans. Religion further appears to grow mechanical and over-elaborate, and to become less spontaneous; there are sacrifices which last over a year and require the participation of many priests. The influence of the new environment and even of its cults and aborigines becomes deeper; a more settled daily life is reflected; cities are now mentioned. The language and grammar of the *Atharvaveda* are of a later date than the *Rigveda*. Its vocabulary contains more common words. It especially reflects popular life and customs in its many charms and spells to be employed against beasts and diseases, enemies and demons, or to obtain peace, long life, and good luck, especially in gambling. It advises the use of herbs, and has been called the oldest literary monument of Indian medicine.

Brahmanas and Upanishads

Later than the *Atharvaveda*, but for the most part composed before the time of Buddhism, are the *Brahmanas*, theological treatises in prose which embody mythology as well as further discussion of sacrificial rites. The use of prose is probably a sign that writing had been introduced, making it no longer necessary to compose in a verse form which could be readily memorized. The alphabet was perhaps first introduced on the southwestern coast by merchants from the Red Sea or Persian Gulf, and thence gradually spread north. The so-called *Forest Treatises* lead on to the *Upanishads*, which represent the last stage of the Brahmanas and are partly prose, partly in metrical form. They contain a greater amount of metaphysical speculation, attempting to attain correct knowledge of the universe and the divine principle, or world-soul, or absolute power, which animates and dominates the universe and gives unity to all existence. The sage renounces the world and retires to the forest to think things out, or holds secret conferences (*upanishads*) with his disciples.

This philosophy of the Upanishads will be found to compare favorably with the beginnings of ancient Greek philosophy at practically the same time. There are, indeed, close resemblances between them, as in the doctrines of pantheism and of the transmigration of souls. Sometimes, at least, the thinking of the Hindus seems more advanced, subtle, and abstract, less childish and crudely expressed than the Greek. There were said to have been no less than sixty-three different schools of philosophy in Buddha's time. The Hindus were already grappling with the problem of individual consciousness; some of them displayed a scepticism which we do not find in Greece until the sophists of the fifth century B. C. The founder of this Hindu sceptical school held that mental operations were performed mechanically and did not prove the existence of an individual soul. One of the Upanishads holds that after death there is no consciousness because the duality of being and cognition, of mind and matter, upon which consciousness is based, ceases after death. Another teaches that true knowledge will reveal the identity of the individual personality with the spirit of the universe, and so remove fear of death. A third holds that this sense of union with the world-soul can be best attained by freeing the mind as far as possible from material limitations or the bonds of natural phenomena—for instance, in such a state as that of dreamless sleep.

The feeling also became widespread that this ideal mental

Ancient Hindu Philosophy

Jainism

state could be best attained by mortification of the flesh, abstention from all material joys, and meditative contemplation. Such asceticism was strongly emphasized by Mahavira, the founder of the religion known as Jainism, but while he tortured himself in order to acquire holiness, he showed great consideration for all other living beings. Indeed, the Jains were animists, believing in the existence of souls in various objects. For a time they went about stark naked, and so were perhaps the originals of the Gymnosophists, or naked sages of India, famed in Greek and medieval legend.

Career and Teaching of Buddha   Siddhattha Gotama (c. 568–488 B. C.), a contemporary of the founder of Jainism, tested the ascetic life and found it wanting. A member of a clan on the lower slopes of the Himalayas at the edge of what is now Nepal, he led, like St. Francis and many other saints, a life of pleasure and worldly prosperity in his youth. At the age of twenty-nine he abandoned all this, including his wife and new-born babe, and for six years gave himself over to penance. It was only after he had renounced this mode of life in its turn that peace, serenity, and spiritual satisfaction came to him at last as he meditated and agonized under the shade of the Bo tree, like Elijah under the juniper tree, or Luther when he found in the doctrine of justification by faith the satisfaction he had failed to secure from monastic life. Gotama now felt himself an enlightened one, or Buddha, and proceeded to teach to others his Eightfold Path or Aryan Way. It reminds one of the Great Wisdom and its six helpers of Zoroaster and of the Tao, or Way, of the Chinese religion, Taoism. A great quest for the right way of life seems to have swept over all Asia, from the Yellow to the Black and Red Seas, in the sixth and seventh centuries before our era. Buddha rejected the entire Vedic sacrificial system with all its magical ceremonial, and substituted a method of self-control which called for incessant intellectual watchfulness against evil and low desires, useless or sensual cravings, and sluggish stupidity, and for constant practice of right views, right aspirations, right speech, right conduct, right livelihood, right effort, right mindfulness, and right rapture. This was not all. Buddha resembled the Jains in wishing not to harm any living creature, and he urged his followers to cultivate unbounded love towards all. "And with that feeling as a basis we will ever be suffusing the whole, wide world with thought of love far-reaching, grown great, beyond measure, void of anger or ill-will." All other forms of doing right "are not worth the sixteenth part of the emancipation of the heart through love." It was this gospel of righteousness, self-mastery, and love towards others that Buddha, with his beggar's bowl in his hand, went about proclaiming by word of mouth and largely in personal conversation for the rest of his life. He taught in Pali, the language of the people, and the oldest Buddhist literature is in this language.

As time went on, many supernatural details were added to Buddhism, which became more like the other beliefs and practices of India. Opposed by the Brahmans, it finally yielded to Hinduism in India, and is found today chiefly in Ceylon, Tibet, China, and Japan. From a strenuous exercise in righteousness and love by each individual it was transformed into a collection of miraculous tales, a worship of serene, superior, saintly beings, who are supposed to have devoted themselves to the salvation of their fellows, and into support of Buddhist temples and monasteries. After all, everybody cannot enter a monastery, or go about begging with a bowl, or think of nothing else than righteousness and love, or the economic foundations of society would come to a sudden smash. Confucius, the Chinese contemporary of Buddha, knew better how to shape his teachings to the requirements of his native state and society, both present and future. But Buddhism had more of the missionary spirit, as its spread to other lands shows. For a time it was a great force and inspiration in the literary and artistic activity both of India and China, while its monasteries in deserted central Asia have recently revealed precious relics and records of the civilization of the past.

Future of Buddhism: Its Relation to Civilization

Positive science, as well as speculative philosophy and theosophy, was making some start by about the time of Buddha, although the dates are uncertain. In the later Vedic literature appears evidence of detailed astronomical observation in the distinguishing of twenty-seven or twenty-eight "mansions of the moon," or divisions of the circle of the zodiac, named after groups of stars or constellations in which the moon appears on successive days. The physicians, Atreya and Susruta, perhaps lived in the sixth century B. C. They had a fair knowledge of the structure of the human skeleton, although there was a tendency to enumerate 360 bones, including teeth

Ancient Hindu Learning

and nails, probably from an astrological desire to place one under each degree of the zodiac or day of the year. One modern scholar holds that Susruta is simply a corruption of Hippocrates through the intermediate form, "Bukrat." A work by Apastamba, of the fifth or fourth century B. C., would indicate that Hindu geometry developed at first independently of Greek influence. The elaborate ritualistic regulations for constructing the altar, and dissecting the animals offered in sacrifice, perhaps led to this development of geometrical and anatomical knowledge. About 500 B. C. the treatise of Yaska concerning words in the Vedas and the language of his time, may be taken as marking the beginning of a scientific study of grammar and philology. Some authorities would date back that far the existence of an alphabet so scientifically constructed that it has remained unmodified since, consisting of forty-six letters representing all the sounds and arranged in order as follows: vowels, diphthongs, consonants, labials and dentals.

BIBLIOGRAPHY

Cantor, M. "Ueber die älteste indische Mathematik," in *Archiv für Mathematik und Philosophie,* 1904, on Apastamba.

Das Gupta, *History of Indian Philosophy,* 1922.

Eliot, Sir Charles. *Hinduism and Buddhism,* 1921, 3 vols.

Havell, E. B. *History of Aryan Rule in India,* 1918.

Hoernle, A. F. R. *Studies in the Medicine of Ancient India,* 1907.

Hopkins, E. W. *Ethics of India,* 1924.

Hume, R. E. *The Thirteen Principal Upanishads translated from the Sanskrit with an outline of the philosophy of the Upanishads and an annotated bibliography,* 1921.

Kaye, G. R. *Indian Mathematics,* 1915; or see article by him in *Isis,* II, 326 ff.

McCrindle, J. W. *Ancient India as described by Megasthenes and Arrian,* 1877.

Macdonell, A. A. *Sanskrit Literature,* 1900, Chapters 7, 8, 15.

Macnicol, N. *Indian Theism; from the Vedic to the Muhammadan period,* 1915.

Rhys Davids, T. W. *Buddhist Birth Stories; Buddhist India,* 1903; *Dialogues of the Buddha.*

Saunders, K. J. *Epochs in Buddhist History,* 1924; the Haskell lectures.

Smith, V. A. *The Early History of India* (600 B. C. to the Mohammedan conquest), 1904; fourth edition, 1925.

Trotter, L. J. *History of India,* 1894; Introduction.

Winternitz, M. *Geschichte der indischen Literatur,* 1908, 1913, 2 vols.

CHAPTER XX

INDIA FROM ABOUT 500 B. C. TO 800 A. D.

The sacrifice of knowledge is superior to the sacrifice of wealth, for action is wholly and entirely comprehended in knowledge.—from the Mahabharata

INDIAN chronology continues almost as confused and uncertain after Buddha as before him. Yet, as the later Vedas, Brahmanas, and Upanishads reflected a distinctly later period in the development of Indian civilization than that revealed in the *Rigveda*, so we reach a still later stage in the *Sutras* ("threads"), manuals of instruction arranged systematically in short sentences. Some are in prose, some in meter. While the earliest perhaps date back to the sixth or seventh century, they in the main supply a picture of the period following Buddha and extending to about the second century B. C., although some authorities would date certain Sutras as late as the third century A. D. These works, representing the point of view of the Brahman class, may be supplemented and checked for the same period by early Buddhist literature. Of about the same date as the latest Sutras are the two great Hindu epics, the *Mahabharata* and the *Ramayana*, while the law books, which take much of their substance from the Sutras but employ the same language and metrical form as the epics, probably begin with the first centuries of our era. All these works seem to reflect essentially the same civilization, although they mirror it in different ways. Then we pass on to the golden age of Sanskrit literature from about 400 A. D. to 800 A. D.

Magic ceremonial, and minute regulations concerning religious ritual, continue to play a prominent part in the Sutras, perhaps even increase in amount. In making a clay pot for use in the sacrifices, for example, one must mix with the clay the black hairs of an antelope. Or a husband who wishes a male child should stuff his wife's nostril with pounded

The Chief Literary Sources

Magic Ritual

233

shoots of the banyan tree.   Such instructions remind one of
the contents of Pliny's *Natural History* a little later in the
Roman Empire.   Whether they are primitive magic borrowed
from the black peoples of India or a common Indo-European
heritage, or are the product of perverse ingenuity on the part
of the Brahman priests, or indicate an interchange of religion, superstition, and science between the Hellenistic and
Hindu areas, or simply denote the world-wide prevalence of
magic, is not easy to determine.

Sacramental
Occasions

Some thirty-three sacramental occasions were distinguished
in the life of the individual from birth to marriage.   For
instance, on the tenth day following the birth of the child,
just as at Athens, it was given its name, including a secret
name known only to its parents in order to protect it from
witchcraft.   At the age of three another very solemn ceremony was enacted; the child received the tonsure and had his
first hair-cut.   At sixteen the boy's first shave was a sacramental proceeding.   Marriage was about the only sacrament
in which the female sex had a share.   The groom took the
bride by the hand, she stepped on a stone to attain firmness,
they took seven steps together and together partook of sacrificial cakes, as Alexander and Roxane were married by dividing a loaf of bread.   The groom then conducted the bride
to his house where she sat on the hide of a red bull and held
in her lap the son of a woman who had borne only living male
children; after nightfall he pointed out the polar star to her,
and they exchanged vows of loyalty.   All the dead were cremated except infants; the Brahman's staff, the warrior's bow,
the cultivator's goad, were broken and thrown onto the funeral
bier; but although some writings of the time encouraged the
voluntary death of the widow, the suttee was not yet a general
custom.

Learning
and Student
Life

One tradition states that the Sutras dealt with six main
subjects: religious ritual, which we have just been illustrating;
astronomy, none of the Sutras concerned with which have survived; and the four related fields of phonetics, meter, grammar,
and etymology.   Some historians are very sceptical as to the
antiquity of Hindu science, holding that its mathematics and
physical science were borrowed at a late date from the Greeks.
There is room for difference of opinion, since many names of
prominence may be dated almost anywhere between the sixth

century B. C. and the fifty century A. D.   We, however, have already mentioned some of them as probably of the period immediately following Buddha.   The grammarian Panini was perhaps about 300 B. C.; the medical authority Charaka according to Chinese testimony was a royal physician around the first century A. D.   He and Susruta were translated into Arabic in the eighth century A. D. and were much cited as authorities thereafter in the Latin world as well.   The study of law is attested by the various law books.   Student life in general receives considerable attention in the Sutras.   The student was supposed to spend twelve years in the study of the Vedas, during which time he was a sort of apprentice, sleeping on the ground and begging food and gathering fuel for his master. For children between the ages of five and sixteen some fourteen sciences and sixty-four arts are listed in a late sutra.   Besides more serious studies, they include gymnastics, dancing, sword-stick exercise, playing on musical glasses, cock-fighting, and teaching parrots and starlings to sing.

At first most states were small; in the republics the members of the warrior aristocracy or ruling clan assembled in a common hall to transact political business; in the monarchies the king was supposed himself to belabor thieves with a cudgel. He was withal something of an autocrat, and, if not actually regarded as supreme landlord of his entire kingdom, at any rate had the disposal of the forest or unoccupied land and received a tithe of their produce from all the peasant cultivators.   Similar was the position of the chieftains of clans in Celtic Ireland far away across two continents. *Kings and Clan-Republics*

The fundamental social group and local settlement were the joint family and the village community.   The family might include not only the grandparents, but married sons and their wives and children.   Every prosperous family usually included household slaves.   The members of the family enjoyed their patrimony in common, so that individual ownership and inheritance scarcely existed.   Almost everyone lived in villages. In the sacred books towns are ignored or condemned, although there were some in existence.   No directions are given for the performance of rites in towns, and their influence was considered contaminating, like that of a visit to a foreign land. Each village had its headman and attended to its own local economy.   Holdings were sometimes redivided, or redistributed, *Joint Family and Village Community* perhaps once in a generation. The villagers cooperated in irrigation, and the ditches for this purpose commonly formed the dividing line between their individual holdings. One neatherd usually tended all the cows of the village.

Economic Life and Gilds

Economic life, aside from agriculture, was naturally not as highly developed as were religious ritual, magic lore, grammar and literature. There were professional money-lenders, but most persons hoarded their capital, such as it was. A metal currency, however, was replacing the practice of barter and the older standards of value, such as the cow or the measure of rice. There were as yet no bridges over the rivers, only ferries, though there was trade both by boat and caravan. The pilots and guards of caravans seem to have been organized. We hear both of competition and partnerships between merchants. Craft gilds also are mentioned in the literature of the period, such as smiths, weavers, painters, woodworkers, and leatherdressers. The leaders of such gilds are represented as influential personages whom the king had to take into account. One seems to have entered a gild through apprenticeship, the apprentice boarding with his master. There was, in fact, a strong tendency for the son to continue in the trade of his father, and so for the gilds to become hereditary castes. Often they constituted separate villages whither the people resorted to buy of them. Or if found in towns, they each occupied a distinct street or quarter, as seems to have been the practice of gilds in all times and places.

Growth of Caste

The development of caste received somewhat of a check from the spread of the teaching of Buddha with its love towards all the world, humility and kindliness, and rejection of many of the pretensions of the Brahmans. In the literary romances, princes in disguise lead the life of the lower classes without apparently suffering pollution, and Brahmans are sometimes found engaged in manual occupations or business without exciting especial remark. On the other hand, the old orders of priests, warriors, and people are on the whole still maintained —a warrior's wergeld is a thousand head of cattle, a common freeman's is one hundred—except that agriculturists and gildsmen now form distinct groups of the people. Hired laborers rank, if anything, rather lower in the social scale than the slaves. There is perhaps an increasing fastidiousness manifest in the matter of food; particular people, for example, disdaining any that has a hair or an insect in it, or that has been touched by the foot of a crow or by certain other persons. Such persons would include non-Aryans, those who eat refuse, misers, or even physicians, jailers, and policemen, who come into frequent contact with criminals and the diseased.

The language of both the great epics is not Vedic but a popular form of Sanskrit developed by the poets into a poetic medium. The *Mahabharata*, with two hundred thousand lines, is the longest poem in existence. The original epic kernel, which seems to have had as its plot the rivalry between two clans, involving court intrigue and a tense gambling contest as well as warfare and vengeance, has been enormously enlarged by the addition of other episodes and the introduction of a great mass of didactic matter, which is religious, cosmic, philosophical, legal, and social in character. Two armies halt on the verge of battle while a philosophical disquisition in eighteen cantos is recited. The *Ramayana* may also be described as a court epic. It employs practically the same meter, verse-tags, similes, tales and fables, and reflects essentially the same stage of civilization, although its verse is somewhat more polished, and it alludes to a more advanced form of architecture. Rama, its hero, loses his faithful wife but finally recovers her after slaying many giants and demons and receiving timely aid from his ally, the king of the monkeys. Many ideal women also appear in the *Mahabharata:* one follows Death until he restores to her the husband whom she had married despite a warning that he would live only a year, an interesting variant on the Orpheus and Eurydice, or Alcestis and Heracles, myths of the Greeks.

The Hindu Epics

With these epics began the development of profane or secular Sanskrit literature, for which the epics furnished a model both of language and form. Like the epics this literature continued profuse, moralizing, and full of marvels, but was very strict in its observance of the rules of literary form. For the most part it was metrical; even the law books were in verse; but prose was employed to some extent in the drama and in fables, romances, and fairy tales. The meters, always quantitative, are most varied and complicated. The golden age of classical Sanskrit began with the Gupta empire in 319 A. D. India's greatest poet was Kalidasa who probably flourished early in the fifth century A. D. The writers show great powers

Further Development of Sanskrit Literature

of observation and description, tender or deep emotion. Literary refinement and displays of skill were sometimes indulged in to an excessive degree, so that we have not only much indulgence in alliteration, figures of speech, puns, and verbal conceits, but compound words which, in one case, run to one hundred and twenty syllables, or half-lines and whole stanzas that, if read backward, are found to be identical with the preceding half-line or stanza. About 800, by the use of ambiguous words and phrases, a poet performed the feat of telling the stories of the two great epics simultaneously. All this at least shows that a vast amount of time, pains, and interest was given to literature.

Sanskrit Drama

The best period of the Sanskrit drama was from the fifth to eighth century A. D. Its origin is suggested by the derivation of both the words for an actor and a play from the word to dance. Many plays are extant, also elaborate directions concerning dramatic composition in treatises on poetics. The dialogue is in prose, men of the upper class speaking Sanskrit, women and men of the lower classes speaking Prakrit; but there are numerous lyrics in many meters. After a prologue invoking divine favor on the audience, and an introductory dialogue between the stage-manager and one or two of the actors concerning the play, comes the play itself in from one to ten acts. During the course of an act the stage is never left vacant by the actors, nor the locality changed. There are sometimes interludes between the acts. The plot is usually a love story and always ends happily, though it may be only after much romantic and fabulous adventure. Magic and magicians figure prominently, but love of nature and a natural background also appear constantly, while the dramatists are skilled in character-painting. It is the rule not to represent anything painful or indecorous, though intoxicated persons are sometimes introduced to amuse the audience. The court jester plays somewhat the same part as the Shakespearian clown. Such stage devices are employed as the writing of a letter and the play within the play. Medieval India seems to have had no buildings designed especially as theaters.

Chronological Retrospect

We now turn back to trace the evolution of art during our period, and inasmuch as the works of art may be associated with rulers rather more than can the works of literature, we may first briefly note two or three political landmarks. Fol-

By Elmendorf, from Ewing Galloway, N. Y.

By Cowling from Ewing Galloway, N. Y.

CAVE TEMPLES OF INDIA

Above, Karli Cave Temple, general view of the interior; below, Elephanta Caves near Bombay.

Above, panorama of the Great Wall in China; below, the triple arched stone pailu in the grounds of the Hall of the Classics, Peking, China.

lowing the invasion of India's borders by Alexander the Great and amid the confusion produced by the break-up of his empire, a new Hindu dynasty, the Maurya, established a widespread empire. Chandragupta, its founder (c. 315–291), was a robber chieftain who established a kingdom in the Ganges valley with Patna as his capital and then conquered the Punjab from Seleucus. His grandson, Asoka (263–226), claimed authority from Afghanistan to Madras and from Nepal to Ceylon. The next great event was the invasion of India in the first centuries A. D. by the Scythians from the northwest, who conquered about one-fifth of the peninsula but were rapidly Hinduized so that they do not seem to have interfered seriously with the development of civilization. Later came the Gupta dynasty to which we have already referred as perhaps beginning in 319 A. D., although Indian history from 1 to 500 A. D. is obscure. Of the Dravidian south, before 1000 A. D., we have even less information than for the Aryan north, as native annalists were equally lacking, and the south was untouched by foreign invasion or intercourse. It appears to have been rich and prosperous and, as its artistic remains indicate, not inferior to the north in culture. Many inscriptions are found there, but very few of them are earlier than the seventh century A. D. The presence of Roman coins in India attests the trade between India and the Roman Empire. No coins are found of Roman emperors of the third century A. D., a period of confusion in the west, but Roman or Byzantine coins of the fourth, fifth, and sixth centuries are abundant; even copper coins are found as far east as Bengal where no earlier coins have been discovered. This evidence of a lively interchange of trade was perhaps due to the intervening prosperous Persian monarchy of the Sassanids at that time.

The Hindu emperor Asoka became a convert to Buddhism, in consequence of which he erected a number of colossal stone pillars, adorned with carvings, to mark holy sites. He also issued a number of humanitarian and philanthropic edicts, which, inscribed upon these pillars or cut in rocks and caves, have come down to our time. These constitute our earliest extant specimens of Hindu writing and are among our earliest examples of Indian art. Persian wording is detected in the edicts. Asoka turned from conquest to the promotion of peace and the protection of all living beings. Instead of tak-

Asoka and Buddhism

ing animal life in hunting, he now led his court on pious pilgrimages.   He planted shade trees, dug wells, and built rest houses along the highways for the benefit of his people.   Asoka encouraged the spread of the Buddhist faith, although he further enjoined religious toleration, which indeed has always been characteristic of India.   "Even upon the forest tribes in his dominions His Majesty has compassion," we read in one of his edicts, while in another he asks, "And what is the object of all my exertion?   Simply to acquit my debt to living beings, that I may make some of them happy here, and that hereafter they may attain to heaven."

Art of
Asoka's
Time

Recent investigation of certain statues, such as those of two rulers of the fifth century B. C., and inscriptions, tends to show that some extant specimens of Indian sculpture may be dated before the Maurya dynasty, but in the main the story of Indian art has to begin with the reign of Asoka.   The earliest surviving memorials of Buddhism were erected by him or his successors, and there is no trace of stone architecture in India before his reign.   The monolith shafts of his pillars, usually of polished sandstone and some thirty feet in height, are sometimes set up hundreds of miles from the nearest quarries.   They are surmounted by carved lions or saints, and often there is sculpture on the capitals.   It was not yet customary, however, to make images of Buddha.   Architecture is represented in this period by the *stupa*, which, like the pyramids of Egypt, seems a development from the earthen mound.   The Great Stupa, which was repeatedly enlarged after Asoka's time, was a solid hemispherical mass of masonry, within which relics have been found imbedded, about one hundred feet in diameter, set upon a cylindrical plinth some fourteen feet high, which formed an elevated path upon which worshipers could walk around the stupa.   The stupa was flattened on top to form a terrace, on which there was erected an altar and a series of stone umbrellas rising one on top of the other to a height of a hundred, or even several hundred, feet.   The plinth or base was encircled by a rather complicated fence or railing of stone, of which the pillars, bars, coping-stones, and especially the entrance gate, were elaborately carved and adorned with sculptures in relief.   The curved lines and bars of this fence and its gate suggest that it was originally built of wood, or even bring to mind the work of the wheelwright. The early Buddhist tales speak of wooden architecture only. No painting is extant from the time of Asoka.

Indian sculpture was derived from Hellenistic art, but took on characteristics of its own, introducing the vegetation of the jungle and such native animals as the elephant, making the human figures soft, round, and supple, sometimes depicting fantastic demon forms, and taking its subjects from Hindu mythology or Buddhist legend. The representation of Buddha seated with his feet beneath him became common after the beginning of our era and spread from India to Tibet, China, Korea, and Japan. Indian sculpture continued a long development for many centuries, displaying "inexhaustible invention and boundless patience" as well as great richness, variety, and mastery of technique. Noteworthy are its ornamental design, its use of light and shade in reliefs, the grouping of the figures, their individual attitudes and gestures, and the very accurate execution of the less fleshy parts of the body, such as the hands. *Further Development of Sculpture*

Indian architecture is not much more than sculpture. Not only are the surfaces of temples completely encrusted with reliefs of gods, demons, men, and animals, with geometric decoration, niches, canopies, columns, and pilasters, so that there is scarcely any flat or free wall space. The most famous temples and monasteries are really not buildings, since they were not constructed of building materials brought to the spot, but were hollowed or chiseled entire out of the living rock. One of the earliest, and also the largest and finest of these rock-cut or cave-temples is that made at Karli, forty-five miles from Bombay, in 78 B. C. Inside it looks much like a Christian cathedral, having three portals, a vestibule, a nave separated by columns from aisles on either side, a rounded apse with ambulatory aisle, and a semi-circular roof that looks like a barrel vault. Moreover, it is lighted by a great open horseshoe shaped arch over the portal which somewhat resembles the medieval rose-window. But it does not compare in size with the great medieval cathedrals, measuring only 126 by 45½ feet. The ambulatory aisle encircles a cylindrical drum on which is a dome surmounted by a relic casket and wooden umbrella, much like the stupa already described. The bases of the columns are vase-shaped, perhaps because the earlier *Subsequent Indian Architecture* wooden posts were stood in vases to protect them from the white ants. The shafts are here octagonal; in other cases they are square, sixteen-sided, or cylindrical; the capitals have complicated designs including kneeling elephants. Some later temples, like that of Kailasa at Ellora, begun about 760 A. D., were completely cut out of the rock both within and without, so that their entire exteriors could be seen, not merely the façade or entrance, as in the case of the cave temples. These exteriors, too, were elaborately sculptured. They are marvels of patient art, no doubt, but somehow they seem to have been executed for show rather than use. The lavishness of detail is too intricate; the sculpture runs riot, jungle-like. Pagodas and pavilions were other common forms of buildings. The finest temples are found in southern India. The horseshoe arch seems to have originated in India.

Buddhist Painting

Buddhist paintings are known rather from examples preserved in central Asia, China, and Japan than in India itself. They are distinguished from the other paintings of China, not only by their repeated representation of sacred persons and scenes, which to a large extent tend to become set types, but also by their brilliant decorative coloring and especially by their lavish use of gold. These features probably originated from India where the dimly lighted cave temples call for such treatment. Whether Buddhist painting was, like Indian sculpture, influenced strongly by Hellenistic art, or whether the haloes and nimbuses, which early Christian art has in common with Buddhist art, and the frequent use of brilliant color on a gold ground in Byzantine mosaics denote a Buddhist influence on the west, are interesting questions but are difficult to answer from our lack of Hellenistic painting.

BIBLIOGRAPHY

Barnett, L. D. *Antiquities of India*, 1913.

Buddhistic Records of the Western World, ed. Beal, 1906.

Burgess, J. *Cave Temples of India*, 1880; and other special studies. *History of Indian Architecture*, 1910; a revision of Fergusson's work, 2 vols.

Cambridge History of India, Vol. I, 1922; plates at close of volume illustrate the earlier art.

Coomaraswamy, A. K. *Medieval Singhalese Art, mainly as surviving in the 18th century*, 1909.

Faure, E. *Medieval Art,* English translation, 1922; chapter I on India has 37 illustrations.

Fergusson. *History of India and Eastern Architecture,* 1910, 2 vols.

Foucher, A. *L'Art gréco-bouddhique du Gandhâra,* 1918; *Beginnings of Buddhist Art,* translated by L. A. and F. W. Thomas, 1917.

Havell, E. B. *Ancient and Medieval Architecture of India,* 1915; *Indian Architecture,* 1913; *Handbook of Indian Art,* 1920.

Hopkins, E. W. *The Great Epics of India,* 1920.

Jayaswai, K. P. "Statues of two Saisunaka emperors (483–409 B. C.)," in *Journal of the Bihar and Orissa Research Society,* V (1919) 88–106; "Another Saisunaka Statue," (518 B. C.) *Ibid.,* 550–1.

Ketkar, S. V. *History of Caste in India,* 1909.

Kramrish, Stella. *The Vishnudharmottaram (Part III) a treatise on Indian painting,* 1924, 59 pp. A translation of the chief Indian text dealing with painting. "For the student of art generally, and of Indian art in particular, this is one of the most important books that has appeared in recent years."

Monahan, F. J. *The Early History of Bengal,* 1925; deals with the history, institutions, inscriptions, and art of the Maurya period.

Ray, P. C. *History of Hindu Chemistry,* I, 1902; II, 1909.

Rea, A. *South Indian Buddhist Antiquities,* 1894.

Records of Buddhistic Kingdoms, ed. Legge, 1886.

Records of Buddhistic Religion, ed. Takakasn, 1896.

Ridgeway, W. *Dramas and Dramatic Dances,* 1915; pp. 131–149 on the *Ramayana* and *Mahabharata* with full page illustrations.

Smith, V. A. *Asoka: the Buddhist Emperor of India,* 1901; *History of Fine Art in India and Ceylon,* 1911; *Early History of India from 600 B.C. to the Muhammadan Conquest,* 1914.

Vaidya, C. V. *History of Medieval Hindu India,* 1924.

Vidyabhusana, S. C. *History of the Medieval School of Indian Logic,* 1909.

CHAPTER XXI

CHINA TO CONFUCIUS

There was a time when a culture or perhaps a succession of of cultures in eastern Asia made such contributions as silk, tea, paper, gunpowder, the compass, block-printing, folding fans, umbrellas, wheelbarrows, and a long list of other complexes now worldwide.—*Wissler*

Geography of China

CHINA is separated from India by mountain ranges and deep valleys, while the dreary tablelands of Tibet and Mongolia have, on the whole, effectually secluded it from the rest of the world. It lies for the most part in the temperate zone, although the very southernmost provinces along the Si-Kiang (Western River) are partly south of the Tropic of Cancer. The oldest center of Chinese civilization seems to have been farther north in the valleys of its two chief rivers, the Yangtze-Kiang and Hoang-Ho (Yellow River). All these rivers flow from west to east. There are many high mountains in the west and south, and Chinese artists have always delighted in mountain landscapes. In the northeast the two great rivers have through the centuries kept forming a great Deltaic plain. The fertility of north-central China is further increased by the loess formation; dry winds blowing half the year from the plateau of Mongolia denude it of its surface soil and deposit this in China, while the returning monsoons from the southeast moisten the deposits and hold them there. The vegetation is very varied, and the name, Flowery Kingdom, is well deserved. Today China supports almost exclusively by agriculture a population about three times that of the United States, although its area is only half as great. The standard of living in China is of course much lower. Many of its mineral and other natural resources are hardly touched, although the Chinese in each locality have mined its coal and iron from early times, and its people may still be enjoying them when we have exhausted ours. The long coast line and

244

navigable rivers have been favorable to communication by water. Traders from the Indian Ocean founded a colony at Shantung about 675–670 B. C., while enterprising Chinese merchants reached the coast of Africa before the tenth century of our era.

The Chinese are probably a mixed race, but an old one. At least in all their literature there is no trace of a foreign origin. However, some other aboriginal peoples are contained in the present extent of China, having been absorbed by the expanding Chinese. The Chinese are of yellow race; they are short like the Japanese and Koreans; their skulls and faces are round; they have prominent cheek bones; their eyes are set obliquely, are almond shaped and usually black; their hair is coarse, lank, and invariably black; their beards come late and are scanty; they have small hands and feet, and a tendency to corpulence. Their language is very terse and concise, with short words and short sentences. It is monosyllabic and uses relatively few sounds, so that different meanings are attached to the same syllable and are distinguished by the tone in which it is uttered. This prevents the Chinese from expressing emotion in his utterance, and may give foreigners the impression that he is less emotional than is really the case. Furthermore, the language is neither inflected like the Indo-European group, nor agglutinated like the Ural-Altaic group, which comprises the Mongols and Manchus, who physically somewhat resemble the Chinese, and in medieval and modern times have invaded China and supplied its ruling dynasties. But Mongolia and Manchuria were not parts of ancient China.

The People and Language

China is our best existing example of uninterrupted, incessant civilization with a continuous culture from Confucius, or long before him, to the present. This culture repeatedly proved deep-rooted enough to survive the blighting incursions of the central Asiatic nomads. In this successful preservation of their past culture the Chinese apparently became too conservative in more recent centuries, and ceased, for a time at least, to progress and to originate, being content to hold their own. Now they stand face to face with our western civilization, which some of them are ready to adopt and which some of us are eager to force on them. Will the ancient Chinese civilization go by the board, or will a fusion of the two civilizations result, and the Chinese, recovering their old inventive

Continuity of Chinese Civilization

power, work out something new without breaking completely from the old?

This incessant continuity of civilized society in China and the density of population, at least in recent times, have tended to wear things out and use them up. China is not strewn with unoccupied ruined sites or the discarded remains of past civilizations. In art the Chinese have preferred the picturesque to the monumental, in social life the ceremonial to the material. They worship their ancestors with continued funeral rites rather than with enduring tombs. China is not a graveyard like Egypt; it is an ancestral home. Although stone is plentiful in most parts of China, brick and wood seem always to have been preferred to it as building materials. Whether for such reasons as these, or for other reasons that may come out as we proceed, at any rate the fact is that China possesses few ruins or other archæological remains. The oldest buildings do not antedate the eleventh century A. D. Recent discoveries have chiefly been on the outskirts of China proper in Buddhist monasteries in desolate central Asia or at abandoned frontier stations along the Great Wall—places where there has been no subsequent wear and tear of civilization to efface them. In north China there was excavated a collection of bone fragments inscribed with archaic, mystic characters, which are probably the responses of diviners and may date back to 1100 B. C. The oldest works of art that have survived are archaic bronze vessels from the prehistoric period of the Shang and Chow dynasties (c. 1766–255 B. C.) which "have a certain savage monumental grandeur of design," and are decorated with simple geometrical patterns or with figures of animals and monsters. The characters inscribed upon them also suggest a primitive stage of culture, and they are richly colored with the rust of centuries.

If archæological evidence is scanty, on the other hand China has the fullest and most consecutive historical records of any country. In China history and historians have always been prized. The questions that used to be set in the competitive examinations for official positions were largely historical. What is more, they dealt with the history of civilization— such matters as improvement in agriculture and currency—as well as politics and the art of war. There was a board of historians to record the deeds of each emperor. In fine, China is "the paradise of the historian," and what may be called historical romances fill the place which epic poetry occupies among other peoples. Most accounts of the earliest period sound quite mythical and are probably late inventions. Panku, the first man, who fashioned the world out of chaos with his adze, lived millions of years ago. He was followed by ten cycles of sovereigns, some of whom, like the first king of Athens, were half-snake or half-fish, or, like the gods of Egypt, had animal heads, or, like the seven legendary kings of Rome, are credited with varied advances in civilization and the introduction of existing customs, or, like the Old Testament patriarchs, were extremely long-lived. Thus the thirteen Celestial Emperors reigned for eighteen thousand years each. The first reliable date is afforded by a solar eclipse on August 29th, 776 B. C., which, as it happens, was also the traditional year for the first celebration of the Olympic games by the ancient Greeks, a date sometimes taken as the beginning of their calendar.

The oldest extant historical record appears to be the Book of History, a collection of historical material supposed to have been put together by Confucius himself and applying to the period from about 2400 to 700 B. C. Even it is suspected of being more of a moral and edifying romance than a critical collection of texts. Its first chapter tells of the glorious reign of the emperor Yao who arranged the calendar; chapter two concerns the emperor Shun who worshiped one God with prayer and sacrifice, made tours of inspection and held periodical examinations of his officials, established penalties tempered by mercy, and created governmental departments of forests, of the care of animals, of music, and of religious observances. In the third chapter we hear of Yu who gained the throne by draining off a great flood; "but for Yu we should all be fishes." Other chapters give details of geography, tribute from adjacent countries, royal speeches to the troops and announcements of victories, and proclamations such as that against drunkenness from the twelfth century B. C. *The Confucian Book of History*

From all this we derive a fairly accurate picture of early Chinese civilization. The legendary contributions of various rulers may not be in correct chronological order, but we see how far civilization had advanced by about the time of Confucius. Such institutions, or inventions, as the imperial form *Its Picture of Early Chinese Civilization* of government, its chief territorial subdivisions, observation of the stars, regulation of the calendar, the use of fire and dwellings; marriage, social conventions, ancestor-worship; geomancy, knowledge of the medicinal properties of herbs, irrigation, agricultural and musical instruments; writing characters with a brush of frayed bamboo dipped in varnish, in place of the still earlier means of record and communication by knotted cords and notched sticks; the board of historians, the first temple of bricks, the manufacture of silk, carts and barges, banners and uniforms, mediums of exchange, weights and measures, public schools:—all these are thought of either as having existed from time immemorial, or as having been invented long, long ago by the earliest emperors.

Chinese Writing

The invention of writing is ascribed to a four-eyed individual who got the idea of the Chinese characters from observation of bird-tracks. At this discovery, we are told, heaven rejoiced and hell trembled, or, to translate more literally, "The sky rained grain, and demons mourned by night." Some of the characters are pictures of the object represented, Chinese being the only language in which such pictographs survive. Others are ideographs, but the great majority are phonetic. Where the same character, or syllable, has different meanings, determinative signs are added.

Early Social and Political Regulations

We hear that under the Chow dynasty (about 1115 B. C.) candidates for public positions were examined in the six arts of archery, horsemanship,—two which are somewhat suggestive of a nomadic origin—writing, reckoning, music, and ceremonial. This last branch, an all important one from the Chinese standpoint and doubtless a good antidote for any nomadic instincts or yearnings, is elaborated in great detail in the *Book of Rites,* which is reckoned one of the Five Confucian Classics, although actually dating from the Han dynasty about the beginning of our era, and in another work which was long coupled with it as the sixth classic but is no longer included in the Confucian Canon, namely, an account of the government of the empire under the aforesaid Chow dynasty. It gives not only innumerable details of sacrificial rites, such as we have seen develop in India, and elaborate directions for all sorts of divination of the future, but also equally rigid regulations for the emperor and his court, and minute instructions for the government of the people. These rules are justified as promoting order and stability in state and society, good manners and morals among the people. They probably originated, however, in magic ceremonial and taboo intended to preserve the tribe from disaster. Many despots in other lands have resorted to a similarly stiff court etiquette in order to impress their subjects with a due sense of their own greatness. The Chinese view was that the emperor should also be an example to his people, and in certain respects at least he was held responsible for their welfare. Thus when they suffered from famine, he was supposed to starve himself. This was perhaps originally an act of magic atonement, a sacrifice intended to satisfy and avert the famine rather than an attempt to make the emperor feel for the suffering of his people. There was also a special official to reprimand the emperor for any unseemly conduct, a public remonstrator who mingled with the people to observe and correct their faults, and a mandarin who saw to it that no man remained unmarried after thirty.

The imperial palace was a walled enclosure within which were the dwellings of the emperor, empress, concubines, staff of eunuchs and other servants; the reception halls, temples, ministerial offices, archives, treasuries, storehouses, and shops or workrooms for weaving the silk and hemp used by the court. The six chief departments of government, presided over respectively by mandarins of heaven, earth, spring, summer, autumn, and winter, may be described as dealing with personnel, revenue and agriculture—the chief tax was on land, which was theoretically all the property of the emperor as in Egypt,—rites and ceremonies, military matters, justice, and public works. There were maps of the nine provinces which then constituted the empire, showing the sacred mountain of each, its chief rivers, lakes, and economic products. There was to be a census every three years and a careful apportionment of the soldiers which each family must supply for the imperial army, but the science of statistics would appear to have been as yet in a very rough state indeed, since we are assured that one province had five men for every two women and that another had two women for every man,—hardly credible ratios. The common people were classified in nine groups: grain producers, gardeners and fruit-growers, woodmen, keepers of livestock and poultry, artisans, merchants, women engaged in mak-

Depart-ments of Government and Classes of Society

ing clothing, domestic servants, and a miscellaneous group. Slavery seems never to have existed in China to any great extent.

In the time of Confucius, and the centuries immediately preceding, the imperial authority had declined. Feudal lords, who nominally held their posts under the emperor, were ruling over practically independent states and engaging, as is the wont of feudal lords of all times and places, in frequent warfare with one another. This period is depicted in the *Spring and Autumn Annals* of Confucius, a terse chronicle of his own feudal state of Lu from 722 to 479 B. C. It consists of a few brief entries under each year recording such matters as the births, deaths, and marriages of the rulers of Lu and neighboring states; the chief battles and invasions; and such portents or disasters as floods, droughts, and famines, eclipses, comets, and earthquakes. This bare and meager record is accompanied, however, by a brilliant picture of feudal life and society, warfare and intrigue, heroism and adventure, in the shape of a commentary upon it by one Tso, which, except that it is in prose, bears somewhat the same relation to the *Spring and Autumn Annals* as the *chansons de geste* of feudal France bear to the Carolingian annals of the Frankish period. In it we read of alliances and feats of arms, jealousy and treachery, assassinations and poisonings, flights and pursuits, forced marches and night attacks made by troops who were gagged to insure silence. A flag of truce was sometimes used for purposes of parley, but when it came to actual battle, quarter was rarely given, and the ears of the slain were commonly cut off. Men went into battle with banners and streamers flying, to the sound of horns and gongs, drums and cymbals. There were archers, charioteers, and men armed with sword, spear, and shield, iron hooks, clubs shod with iron, and daggers. If another work on the art of war really dates from the sixth century B. C., the importance of drill and discipline, tactics and strategy, was already recognized in the feudal period.

The oldest Chinese poetry is lyric, not epic, consisting of the *Book of Odes*, a selection of some three hundred popular ballads and folk songs made by Confucius from previous poetry as far back as the second millennium, but chiefly from the feudal age. They are in rhyme; various meters are used; but the usual line is one of four words. It was customary for the

heads of the feudal states to forward at intervals to the central
government specimens of the popular ballads of their localities, from which the imperial musicians might pass judgment
as to the manners and morals of the regions concerned, and
which were taken as fair samples of the effects produced by
the government of the local dukes.   Thus these poems reflect
the life and thought of the time, except that the moral Confucius has possibly been careful not to include any that might
offend against the proprieties or seem too vulgar.   The written
language was already much like the literary language of today.

The people lived in houses with walls of plaster and pressed *Popular
Life and
Institutions*
earth, thatched roofs, and earthen floors pounded hard and
strewn with dry grass.   At first they sat on mats, but presently had chairs and tables.   They ate well cooked food from
dishes and plates of pottery and drank spirituous liquors.
Clothing was of silk for the well-to-do, homespun for the poor;
they wore shoes of leather.   To this day the Chinese hate nothing worse than getting wet, and the umbrella was introduced at
an early date.   The fundamental institution in society was
and has remained the family with great authority of the father.
But the Chinese are very fond of babies.   The married son
continued to live under the paternal roof and authority.
Women were always under male authority, either of father,
husband, or other male head of the household.   Private religion consisted of worship of ancestors and such household
spirits or magic powers as those associated with door or
threshold, hearth or kitchen-stove, courtyard, cultivated land
and crops.   The feudal lords in many cases attempted to
reduce the people to a state of serfdom; consequently the
emperors from an early date encouraged or countenanced
popular local government in opposition to the feudal lords.
Villages, townships, and wards chose their own headmen
and made their own regulations or followed their old customs in matters of police, taking the census, and assessment
of taxes.   How far back the Chinese gilds go seems problematic,
so we shall leave these democratic, but strictly speaking illegal
or at least extra-legal, associations, which have been so all-
powerful in Chinese industry and commerce, for later comparative treatment in connection with the gilds of medieval
Europe, since the two constitute our best known examples of
the gild system.

Currency
and
Measures

The Chinese at first bartered goods like the ancient Egyptians, then used shells for currency, then pieces of stamped silk, linen, or deerskin, then circular disks of copper perforated with a round hole, and finally "cash" with square holes and inscriptions as at present.   The grain of millet, which with rice constitutes the food staple of the majority of the population today, was the unit of measures from inches and feet to pints and quarts.   The decimal system was in use from the first: ten millet grains placed end-ways making an inch, ten inches a foot, ten feet a *chang,* and so on.   The one exception was the pound which consisted of sixteen ounces as with us, and was represented by a rude axe-head.

Divination
and
Medicine

Interest in natural and mathematical science was shown in the star-gazing and search for medicinal herbs, and in the arithmetic and music, to which we have already referred.   But the amount of astronomical knowledge possessed by the ancient Chinese and the question whether they borrowed from Babylon are disputed matters.   As astronomy was combined with astrology, so objects in nature were often scrutinized with a view to discovering the future, as in the observation of the fissures made in the scales of a tortoise when they were scorched by fire.   Confucius not only recorded omens and portents in his *Spring and Autumn Annals,* but set great store by the *Book of Changes,* which seems originally to have been a set of geomantic figures for predicting the future, although later it was supposed to contain the key to the mysteries of the universe and to political and moral problems.   But scepticism concerning witchcraft and sorcery is sometimes displayed in the early Chinese histories.   In the science of medicine diseases were classified by the four seasons: headaches and neuralgic pains went with spring; skin diseases, with summer; fevers and agues, with autumn; throat and lung complaints, with winter.   Drugs were distinguished as derived from animals, minerals, herbs, trees, and grain; each of these five classes included five flavors.   Sweet medicines were thought to nourish the flesh; acid, the muscles; sour, the bones; salt, the blood-vessels; and bitter, the general vitality.   It was known that the heart pumped blood to all parts of the body, and a skilled physician was supposed to be able to distinguish between twenty-four and seventy-two varieties of the pulse, although there were no accurate time-pieces.

Of all the learned men and teachers of that time Confucius, "the most sagely ancient Teacher, the uncrowned King," was to have the greatest future influence on Chinese civilization. He was of illustrious lineage, but his father was past seventy when he was born and died when he was only three, leaving the family in poverty. Confucius was compelled to do many kinds of work, thus gaining valuable practical knowledge of the arts. As a child he is said to have been fond of playing at ceremonies. At nineteen, like Buddha, he married; at twenty-two began to teach, and was gradually surrounded by an increasing number of disciples. Some of his famous sayings in the field of pedagogy are: "When I have presented one corner of a subject, and the pupil cannot of himself make out the other three, I do not repeat my lesson. Learning undigested by thought is labor lost; thought unassisted by learning is perilous. He who has heard the truth in the morning may die in the evening without regret. Let poetry be the beginning, manners the middle, and music the finish." Confucius underwent no sudden conversion like Buddha but was constantly improving his mind by study and fixing his moral convictions. Late in life he gave the following résumé of his inner development: "At fifteen I had my mind bent on learning; at thirty I took my stand; at forty I was free from doubt; at fifty I understood heaven's decrees (signs in the sky?); at sixty I never relapsed into any known fault; at seventy I could follow my own inclinations without going wrong." Slow but sure, he impressed his ideals permanently upon the Chinese people.

In China at this time, as in India, many sages and ascetics were withdrawing in despair or disgust from the disorderly and corrupt society of the feudal states, and were seeking solace in philosophy or religion. But Confucius refused to withdraw from the world. "With whom," he asked, "should I associate but with suffering men?" He accordingly wandered from state to state seeking a prince who would give him a free hand to institute the reforms he had at heart and to reestablish "right principles" through the kingdom. He held that the people were naturally docile and well-behaved, that you could not pay them to steal, were it not for the greed of the upper classes, that their conduct would straightway improve, once they had a model ruler. Society would become orderly, wholesome, and prosperous, once things were called by their right

Confucius: 551–478 B.C.

His Effort to Reform the State and Society

names and people observed in deeds the full meaning of what
they accepted in words, once filial piety was duly observed and
the respect for one's superiors that goes with it, once the past
and its lessons were held reverently in mind, once right principles were distinctly enunciated and understood, and the people
were trained for a little in manners and ceremonial.   For "all
virtues have their source in etiquette."   Yet Confucius also
affirmed, "Simplicity accompanies true virtue, which is seldom
associated with a plausible tongue and fascinating expression."
It was perhaps fortunate that Confucius never found the favorable opportunity to execute his program of political and
social reform, which might have failed in practice in a particular instance, with fatal results to his reputation and future
influence.   As it was, the number of his disciples kept increasing; all the Five Classics, or oldest extant specimens of Chinese
literature, are associated with his name—the *Book of History*,
the *Spring and Autumn Annals*, the *Book of Odes*, the *Book of
Changes*, and the *Book of Rites;* his sayings and ethical teaching are preserved in other works by his disciples such as the
Analects and *Great Learning*.   These have become the component stones in China's true Great Wall against barbarism,
—literature, history, philosophy, and moral character.

**Not a
Religious
Teacher** Confucius was not a religious leader or the founder of a
religion.   We are told that there were four subjects which he
never discussed: fairy tales, feats of strength, outrageous
crimes, and the gods.   Far from claiming any divine mission
or revelation, he avoided speaking of the supernatural, or death,
or a future life.   "While you cannot serve men, how can you
serve spirits?   While you do not know life, what can you
know about death?   To give one's self earnestly to the duties
due to men, and, while respecting spiritual beings, to keep aloof
from them, that may be called wisdom."   Such were the answers he gave, when questioned about such matters, and he succeeded in making his position so clear that even after his death
his disciples did not claim divinity or divine inspiration for
him.   It would seem to be due in considerable measure to Confucius personally, as well as to the climate and the practical
character of the Chinese, that religion has had so much less
hold in that country than in India.

**But a Moral
Philosopher** Confucius was rather a philosopher.   There is an intellectual element in his sayings which is absent in those of most

religious teachers. He required mental capacity of his disciples; "the superior man" was his frequent, if not favorite, theme. If some of the sayings ascribed to him carry instant conviction, suffusing one's entire being as light spreads through glass, it is because they are so sane and sober, so true to life, yet so perfectly in accord with justice, rather than because of any emotional appeal, religious thrill, or call to self-sacrifice in them. He gave "heart-iness" or cordiality as his watchword, but interpreted it thus, "What you do not like when done to yourself, do not do to others. You should love all but cultivate friendship only with your equals; spend the rest of your energy in improving your mind. If you employ a man, trust him; if you don't trust a man, don't employ him." Lao Tzu was teaching his followers to requite evil with kindness; this was too much for Confucius' sense of justice. Then what will you requite good with? he asked. When a feudal lord boasted that his people were so honest that a son would testify against his father if the father had committed theft, Confucius refused to approve this breach of filial piety. "With us," he replied, "the father screens the son, and the son screens the father; that is real integrity."

We are struck by resemblances to the teaching of Confucius *Greece and China* in the Greek philosophers, Socrates and Plato, a century later. Socrates also held that men would do the right if they knew it. Plato put the problem whether a son should bring his father to justice, if the father commits a murder, and used the expression, "straight thinker," similar to the Chinese, "straight man." Giles finds other reasons for thinking that "Greece must have had early relations with China"; namely, the "notable similarity" in their houses, "their domestic customs, their marriage ceremonies, the public story-tellers, the puppet shows which Herodotus says were introduced from Egypt, the street jugglers, the games of dice, the game of finger-guessing, the water clock, the music system, the use of the myriad (ten thousand), the calendars, and in many other ways."

Lao Tzu means the old philosopher. Like Socrates, and *Lao Tzu, the* unlike Confucius, he never wrote out his teachings. He seems *Old Sage* to have been something of a mystic and to have delighted in paradox. He had none of Confucius' confidence in governmental action or desire to revive the imperial power as exercised by the virtuous monarchs of old. Lao Tzu apparently felt that Chinese government was too paternalistic, that it would be better to leave the people alone. "I do nothing, and the people become good of their own accord," is a saying ascribed to him. He also did not share Confucius' confidence in study and intellectual superiority. "Abandon wisdom and discard knowledge," he is reported to have said, "and the people will be benefited a hundredfold." He also declared that if there was less education, there would be fewer thieves. Thus he had even greater faith than Confucius in the natural goodness of mankind and believed that educated leaders were not needed. Some of the sayings attributed to him are very much like those of Confucius, for example: "Wit is exhausted by many words," and "If you do not quarrel, no one on earth will be able to quarrel with you." In other ways his teaching seems more like Christianity than that of Confucius, especially his counsel to requite evil with good. He also said, "Mighty is he who conquers himself," and "Put yourself behind, and you shall be put in front." He not merely preached universal kindness, self-control, and humility, but went to the extent of advising inaction, affirming that by doing nothing everything could be done. By this, however, he perhaps meant something like our common proverb, "All things come to them that wait," or the promises in the Bible that the meek shall inherit the earth, and, "But rather seek ye the kingdom of God; and all these things shall be added unto you." Lao Tzu, however, had no intention of trying to tell exactly what he did mean. "Those who know, do not tell; those who tell, do not know. The way that can be walked upon is not the eternal way. Follow diligently the Way in your own heart, but make no display of it to the world." The secret of this Way, he declared, could not be imparted to others even by those who understood it themselves. Perhaps his meaning was that each person should live in the way that was natural to him. He had great faith in letting nature take its course. Tao means not only the Way, but the order of the universe, the revolutions of the heavens, the succession of the seasons, the unchanging course of nature. If man could live in accord with this, he too might become immortal.

Taoism

The religion known as Taoism aimed to follow this path to spiritual purity and eternal life, but sometimes indulged in experiments of alchemy or tried to discover an elixir of life.

Later it suffered many other superstitious additions. Somewhat like Zoroastrianism, it conceived of a struggle between two opposing forces or contending halves of the universe, represented on the one hand by light and warmth, spring and summer, life and productivity, and the gods; on the other hand by darkness and cold, fall and winter, death and decay, and malignant specters. These evils afflict the wicked and avenge wrongs done the innocent, while the gods and kindly influences protect the good. The good are those who shape their lives in harmony with the order of the universe, conduct themselves correctly with reference both to the gods and evil spirits, and study the writings of the sages of old and the imperial almanac which instructs them as to lucky and unlucky days. Taoist priests today are mainly occupied in exorcizing demons by magic amulets, charms, spells, words, and characters, by rites and noisy processions, and by beating or wounding themselves or the patients, who are supposed to be possessed by the demons.

Philosophy continued to flourish among the successors of the Old Sage and Confucius. Mencius (372–289) spread the Confucian doctrines, taking middle ground between other philosophers who were maintaining extremes of altruism and egoism. He somewhat departed from strict Confucianism in maintaining that the people were the most important element in the state, that "heaven sees as the people see; heaven hears as the people hear," and that "killing a bad monarch is no murder,"—a view in which he anteceded Mariana by two thousand years. He further declared that there was no such thing as a righteous war; demanded universal education and free trade: attacked trusts and profiteers: and advocated taxation of non-producers or a single tax on land. A still earlier Chinese economist had been Kuan Chung, a merchant of the seventh century who became prime minister. Chuang Tzu was the leading Taoist philosopher of the fourth and third centuries and master of a beautiful literary style. Somewhat paradoxically perhaps, like Lao Tzu before him, and like Nicholas of Cusa in western Europe in the fifteenth century A. D., he maintained the coincidence of contraries, questioning if there was any distinction between positive and negative, subjective and objective, right and wrong, life and death. One night Chuang dreamt that he was a butterfly. Afterwards

Philosophy after Confucius

he wondered whether he had then really been a man dreaming that he was a butterfly, or whether he was not now a butterfly dreaming that he was a man.   More positively, Chuang lauded the life led by "the pure men of old."   Such paradoxical statements as we have quoted naturally encouraged sophistry, however, which flourished in ancient China as well as in ancient Greece.   Hui Tzu, whose writings would fill five carts, held that there must be feathers in the new-laid egg, since they appeared later in the chick; that either a motherless colt never had a mother, or, if it ever had one, was not motherless; that fire is not hot, it is merely the man who feels hot; that you can never reach the end of a stick by cutting it into halves; that one and one make three, since they are two separately and one together.

Chinese Architecture   Although extant remains of Chinese architecture do not begin until the eleventh century of our era, the literary records show that in the fifth and fourth centuries B. C., it was essentially the same as today, except for the later incoming of Buddhist influence.   The arch was known, though little used. Most buildings were only one story high with horizontal lines accentuated and the roof serving as the main architectural feature.   It was often double or triple, rested on wooden columns, and was ornately carved, sometimes with fantastic monsters, or adorned with lacquer and glazed colored tiles. Special types of architecture are the memorial gateway, square stone tower, and brick pagoda of thirteen stories.   Pagodas are perhaps subsequent to the introduction of Buddhism into China.

BIBLIOGRAPHY

Allan, C. W. *Makers of Cathay*, Shanghai, 1909.

Ayscough, F. and Lowell, Amy. *Fir-Flower Tablets*, 1923.

Bashford, J. W. *China: an Interpretation*, 1919.

Budd, Charles. *Chinese Poems*, 1912.

Cordier, H. *Histoire générale de la Chine*, 1920, 4 vols.

Dawson, *The Ethics of Confucius*, 1915.

Doré, F. J. *La thérapeutique et l'hygiène en Chine*, 1920.

Doré, H. *Researches into Chinese Superstitions*, 1915–1923.

Giles, H. A. *Chinese Biographical Dictionary*, 1898; *Gems of Chinese Literature*, 1884; *History of Chinese Literature*, 1901; *Musings of a Chinese Mystic*, 1911.

Griffis, W. E. *China's Story*, 1922.

Groot, J. J. M. de. *The Religion of the Chinese*, 1910.

Haines, C. R. "Ancient Chinese Poetry," in *Edinburgh Review*, April, 1924, pp. 358–376.

Hirth, F. *Ancient History of China*, 1908.

Latourette, K. S. *The Development of China*, 1920; 3rd ed., 1924.

Laufer, Berthold. *Jade, a study in Chinese archæology and religion*, Chicago, 1912; and many articles in periodicals such as "Some Fundamental Ideas of Chinese Culture," in *Journal of Race Development*, V (1914) 160–174.

Lee, M. P. *Economic History of China*, 1921.

Legge, J. *The Chinese Classics*, 1861–1876, 6 vols.

Leong, Y. K. and Tao, L. K. *Village and Town Life in China*, 1915.

Martin, W. A. P. *The Lore of Cathay*, 1901.

Parker, E. H. *Ancient China Simplified*, 1908; *China: her history, diplomacy, and commerce*, 1917; *Studies in Chinese Religion*, 1910.

Richards, L. *Comprehensive Geography of the Chinese Empire*, 1908.

Russell, Bertrand. *The Problem of China*, 1922.

Smith, A. H. *Chinese Characteristics*, 1900; *Proverbs and Common Sayings from the Chinese*, 1914; *Village Life in China*, 1899.

Stein, Sir M. A. *Serindia*, 1921, 5 vols.

Susuki, D. T. *A Brief History of Chinese Philosophy*, 1914.

Waley, Arthur. *A Hundred and Seventy Chinese Poems*, 1918; *More Translations from the Chinese*, 1919.

Werner, E. T. C. *China of the Chinese*, 1919; *Myths and Legends of China*, 1922.

Williams, E. T. *China Yesterday and Today*, 1923.

CHAPTER XXII

CHINESE CULTURE PERFECTED

(The Han, T'ang and Sung Dynasties)

In China, of which kingdom the government and arts, without commerce with, or knowledge of ours, surpass our examples in several excellent features, and of which the history teaches me how much greater and more various the world is than either the ancients or we have been able to penetrate. . . .—*Montaigne*

The First Emperor

THE feudal age in China was finally brought to a close by a military genius, Shi Hwang-ti, who towards the close of the third century B. C. once again united the Chinese under one strong imperial power, and hence is often called "the First Emperor." He began the Great Wall along the northern frontier to keep out the Tartar nomads of Mongolia, but this first wall, which was continued by the Han dynasty, seems to have been simply an earthen rampart. An old saying describes the Great Wall as the ruin of one generation (which was forced to labor on it) and the salvation of thousands following. The First Emperor united the provinces by roads and canals, erected public buildings which have since entirely disappeared, and introduced a good copper coinage. He sent a fleet to search for islands off the coast. The one destructive measure attributed to him is the Burning of the Books, whether with the motive of extirpating Confucianism, or with the idea of stimulating more original literary composition by removal of all past models and perhaps of turning over a new leaf generally. Only works of agriculture, medicine, and natural divination were to be spared. Many scholars are said to have been put to death for concealing books, and only a few manuscripts of the Confucian classics were preserved by hiding them in the walls of houses. After this emperor had died, many passages from the old books were restored from memory, but forgeries also seem to have replaced many of the lost works.   At the death of the First Emperor the population of China is said to have been 13,700,000.

The First Emperor was followed by the Han dynasty which gave China four centuries of peace and prosperity.   To this day the Chinese call themselves "sons of Han."   Either at the beginning of this dynasty, or earlier in the third century B. C., were created officials known as the Eyes and Ears of the emperor who were much like the officials of the same name in the Persian Empire.   They traveled about as inspectors, receiving complaints and appeals from lower officials or from the people; they might denounce other officials to the emperor; finally they acted as censors who might criticize the conduct of even the emperor himself.   He, however, might disregard their criticism and advice, or degrade them from their office. We saw in the preceding chapter that officials with somewhat similar functions were ascribed to the earlier Chow dynasty. Other interesting officials were those instituted in 110 B. C. to buy up commodities in times of abundance and low prices in order to sell to the people at reasonable prices in times of scarcity, as Joseph had done under the Pharaohs in Egypt. Under the Han dynasty filial piety and integrity were required of the candidates who took the competitive examinations for public positions.   In addition to the traditional six arts of archery, horsemanship, ceremonial, music, writing, and reckoning, they might now be examined in civil law, the art of war, agriculture, revenue, and geography.   A census in 156 A. D. gave the population of China as 50,000,000.

Han Dynasty: 206 B. C. to 221 A. D.

In the third century B. C. the invention of the hair brush, with which the Chinese are exceedingly skilful, revolutionized both painting and the art of writing the Chinese characters. Illustrated manuscripts seem to have been produced in China earlier than the Roman Varro's *Imagines* which has sometimes been called the first illustrated book.   Paper was invented by Ts'ai Lun in 105 A. D., and ink took the place of varnish as a writing material.   The invention of the water-mill is ascribed by Chinese records to Tu Yü, 22–84 A. D.   Strabo, however, states that king Mithridates had one in Asia Minor in the previous century.   The Han dynasty was further marked by such progressive measures as abolition of the custom (which continued among the Tartars and Mongols) of burial of slaves

Inventions

with the dead master, and shortening of the period of mourning for parents from twenty-seven months to the same number of days. In modern times the longer period again became the rule.

Expansion Westward

In the second century B. C. the Chinese Empire made a great extension of its territory to the west, wresting Turkestan from the Hiung-nu, as the Mongols or the Huns were called in the Chinese writings of that time. The Great Wall was soon extended to guard the line of communication with this western region. In its watch towers have been found by recent explorers many military orders, accounts, and letters of soldiers which date back as early as 98 B. C. Central Asia was also penetrated by civilization from India; settlements were made along the river beds; and fields and orchards were irrigated by canals. Perhaps because of a drying up of the climate, these regions were abandoned in the early centuries of our era. Only scattered oases now remain to mark once fertile areas. The Chinese soldiers hated their life on this desolate frontier, but it probably promoted a rich trade with distant countries. And this occupation of Turkestan made possible Chinese borrowing from Hellenistic civilization and the introduction of Buddhism from India into China.

Hellenistic Influence

This Greek influence seems to have come in through intercourse with the kingdom of Bactria. In a Buddhist shrine, recently discovered in central Asia on the borders of China, are frescoes that seem the work of Hellenistic artists. Chinese music to this day closely resembles that of ancient Greece. The explanation seems to be that at the time of which we are now speaking Chinese music was reformed under Greek influence. In 104 B. C. the Chinese adopted Meton's cycle of nineteen years which harmonizes the lunar and solar year, and much of their astrology may have been derived from Hellenistic sources at this time. Alchemy, which became so cultivated by the Taoist priests, is said to have been introduced from Greek sources, but it is not certain that works of alchemy were composed in Greek much earlier than the third century A. D. The making of wine from grapes was borrowed from the west at this time, and disappeared in China again two or three hundred years ago. The water-clock was another innovation from the Hellenistic world. There was interchange with the Iranians and Persians as well as the Greeks. The great Chinese traveler,

Chang K'ien, brought back alfalfa and the vine from western Asia. China was also expanding southward under the Han dynasty. After the conquest of the province of Yunnan in 111 B. C., betel nut trees were introduced in the imperial gardens.

Buddhism was introduced from India about 65 A. D. and was to survive in China longer than in India itself. Our knowledge of ancient Buddhist temples and monuments in India is largely indebted to the accounts of Chinese pilgrims who braved the perils of intervening mountains and desert to visit the holy homeland of their faith. By the time Buddhism reached China it had undergone considerable transformation. Great stress was laid upon the prospect of universal salvation in a pure dreamland in the west with pavilions and terraces, a presiding Buddha, and a host of angelic musicians. With this went worship of Bodhisattvas, beings who had earned the final bliss of Buddhahood but had renounced it until the deliverance of the whole world should be accomplished. The White Buddha, or Ta-mo, reached southern China in 520. When summoned before the emperor, he offended him by preferring wisdom and purity to good works. In retiring to Lo-yang he is said to have crossed the swollen tide of the Yangtze-Kiang on a reed. The incident has been a favorite theme of Chinese poets and painters ever since. "There he spent the rest of his life, teaching that religion was not to be learned from books, but that man should seek and find the Buddha in his heart." But since then most Buddhist priests, or bonzes, in China have ceased to be either teachers or preachers. "The Buddhist liturgies have been written out in Chinese characters which reproduce the sounds of the original Indian language, and these the priests learn by heart without understanding a word of the meaning." Buddhist themes dominated Chinese art for several centuries following the decline of the Han dynasty.

Buddhism in China

We have still to speak of art and literature under the Han dynasty itself. Its pottery was "extremely rich in fine shapes," all of which seem to have been turned on the wheel. The pottery is also marked by skilful glazing. Among extant specimens are a model of a farm shed with a rice-pounder, a model of a grain-tower which might almost be called our earliest grain elevator, a mastiff, a well with pulley and water-bucket, a pottery stove with a bronze kettle. Among the bronzes

Pottery, Sculpture, and Painting to 400 A. D.

there are many small solid figures of animals, and mirrors ornamented with Hellenistic designs. From 400 to 960 the bronzes declined greatly both in quantity and quality. From the second century B. C. some spirited, incised stone reliefs are extant. We have other sculpture such as an ornamental brick moulded to represent a gateway, but the Chinese genius lay rather in painting than in sculpture. The earliest paintings on whitened walls and panels of wood have disappeared. Extant paintings are generally executed in water colors on woven silk, less often on paper. In the second century A. D. we get the names of individual artists, while landscape painting is added to portraiture and historical subjects. The oldest extant Chinese painting is probably a scroll, now preserved in the British Museum, ascribed to Ku K'ai-chih of the fourth century A. D. It is worth noting that it deals not with a religious subject but with common daily life, including a family group and a toilet scene. The human figures shown are drawn with great delicacy in fine line, their attitudes are very natural, the grouping is well planned. All this shows that painting had already been evolving for centuries. This painter, Ku K'ai-chih, is supposed to have excelled in portraits, and would add a scenic background fitting to the character of the person portrayed.

Poetry Between Confucius and the T'ang Dynasty

After the collection of odes made by Confucius, the next poetry of which we hear began about 300 B. C., when the poets commenced to employ a sort of free verse. The lines often did not rhyme, and the meter was irregular, lengthening or cutting short the lines to suit the thought or mood of the poet. His aim was so to carry his audience away by the flow of his language and poetical imagery, or by his simplicity, naturalness, and depth of feeling, that they either would not notice, or would not be offended by, the somewhat rough form and wild measure. But since the second century B. C. most poets have employed either an old seven-word meter, or a five-word meter which was developed during that century. There were several poets of high rank during the later Han dynasty; then followed a period of still greater productivity with some loss of naturalness and originality; from 557 to 618 a period of literary decadence intervened until the great poets of the T'ang dynasty. The poetry, like the painting, deals with the affairs of this life, its humor and pathos, love and war, beautiful ladies and gallant soldiers, finding often in common incidents the impulse to reflection or feeling. Only the lover whose sweetheart has died of grief, and the soldier who bids farewell to his wife for maybe the last time, express interest in or hope of a future life.

Of post-Confucian philosophy we treated in the previous chapter. Ssu-ma Ch'ien, 145–87 B. C., the father of Chinese history, became the model for all the official dynastic histories which have been penned since. His great work ran to over half a million words, comprising not only annals, biographies, and chronological tables, but monographs dealing with subjects of importance for the history of civilization, such as religion, rites and ceremonies, music, natural philosophy, waterways and commerce, the calendar and astronomy. In these last matters he was naturally closely interested as hereditary grand astrologer since the death of his father in 110 B. C. At the beginning of our era Lady Tsao composed *Rules for Women* with which the church fathers, Solon, or Shakespeare would have heartily agreed, but which the suffragette or "flapper" of to-day would put right back on the shelf or consign to the ash can.

The Father of History and Lady Tsao

With the end of the Han dynasty China broke up into three kingdoms, and internal wars became chronic. Then the Hiung-nu or northern nomads, whom the Han dynasty had with difficulty held back along the wall and in Turkestan, renewed their invasions. Henceforth the history of the period becomes very confused, with independent states or even imperial dynasties in the north founded by the successful nomads. This period of Chinese history roughly coincided with that of the barbarian invasions in the west which overthrew the Roman Empire.

Political Confusion, 221–589 A. D.

While most of Europe remained in the throes of barbarian invasions, and for a time gave little sign of reviving civilization, which had already so seriously declined in the later Roman Empire, China soon righted itself from the confusion which had followed the decline of the Han dynasty, and maintained the development of its civilization without serious break. The brief Suy dynasty (590–618) did good service in defeating Koreans and Tartars to the north and the Uighurs to the west in central Asia, thus laying the foundation for the glorious age of culture under the T'ang (618–907) and Sung (960–

Continued Progress of Civilization under the T'ang and Sung Dynasties

1280) dynasties. As both these dynasties declined greatly in their later years, the most flourishing periods of civilization are the first century or two of either. For a time the T'ang dynasty extended the Chinese Empire to the Caspian Sea and frontier of Persia. Ambassadors were received from the states of northern India, the Mohammedans, and Constantinople. Chinese maps of west and central Asia have been reconstructed which were of an even earlier date. In the seventh century Persian *Magi* or fire-worshipers, Manicheans, and Nestorian Christians, all found a refuge in China; but Jews do not seem to have appeared there until the twelfth century. In the eighth century Kao Hsien-chih led ten thousand troops of poor quality and morale across the Pamirs and Hindu Kush to the successful conquest of Yasin and Gilgit—an exploit surpassing Napoleon's and Hannibal's crossings of the Alps, or the retreat of Xenophon's ten thousand through Armenia.

Poetry

The T'ang dynasty is especially noted for its poets. Over a thousand might be named, and when in 1707 by imperial order an anthology was made from their voluminous works, it included some 48,900 poems. The poetry of this period became the accepted model thereafter. The five and seven word stanzas now became standard, all words were classed for poetical purposes as even or oblique in tone, the order of the occurrence of these tones in the stanza was fixed. In their lives, which are reflected in their verse, the poets seem to have gone to one or the other of two extremes, and were either recluses in mountain monasteries or Horatian-Byronic-like good-livers and deep-drinkers. One was so retiring that he hid under the bed when the emperor came to visit him in his mountain retreat. On the other hand, Li Po, who stimulated his angelic muse with the wine cup, met his end by leaning out of his boat to embrace the reflection of the moon in the water, while the wandering Tu Fu—"For thirty years I rode an ass"—proved by his sudden demise that it was really possible to eat too much roast beef, at least when a great deal of white wine was taken with it. The early emperors of the T'ang dynasty instituted the Hanlin, "Forest of Pencils," or literary academy which lasted into the twentieth century. Greater stress was now laid upon excellence of literary style in the competitive examinations for public office. Some, however, ascribe to the following Sung dynasty the introduction of the *wen chang*, or polished essay, as a test for office-holding. It has been described by the Chinese themselves as "a clever contrivance adopted by a former dynasty to prevent the *literati* from thinking too much." From that time the official class and the *literati* have been practically indentical in China. The poets of the Sung dynasty maintained about the same high level as those of the T'ang dynasty, perhaps with somewhat less freedom. Many tales of demons and specters which are still current in China may be traced back to the Sung dynasty.

Buddhist painting of the T'ang dynasty has to be judged mainly from later Japanese copies and from the many paintings which adorn the "grottoes of the thousand Buddhas" in central Asia, dating from the fifth to the eleventh centuries. Wu Tao-tzu of this period is ranked as the greatest of Chinese painters, but no genuine work by him is extant. Han Kan set a standard in his depiction of horses. There were noted schools of landscape painting. The iconoclastic emperor, Wutsung (841–847), who closed temples and monasteries and ordered Buddhists and representatives of other foreign religions to leave the country, was partly responsible for the loss of this art. Some sculpture is extant, such as spirited cave-reliefs, a more than life-size statue of the deity of Compassion, and a large statue of a Lohan, or apostle of Buddha, seated on the ground. This last is made of white pottery with colored glaze for the draperies. The brief space of time between the T'ang and Sung dynasties was marked by some great painters, famous for their birds and flowers. *Art of the T'ang Dynasty*

Buddhist sculpture continued under the Sung dynasty. There was also a more realistic and truly national school which represented deified historical personages in a very natural manner. But painting continued to be the leading art of the Chinese, who believe that "a picture is a voiceless poem." Landscape painting, often of a wild, romantic type, now attained a height which has never been surpassed anywhere. Chinese painting is generally linear and in light water colors, avoiding the appearance of solidity or relief. Shadows, reflections, and linear perspective are ignored. The Sung artists often sketched in ink,—perhaps the most characteristic kind of Chinese painting. Much was left to the imagination and to sentimental suggestion. The Sung painters succeeded in communicating to, or arousing in, the onlooker something of their *Art of the Sung Dynasty* own passionate love of nature, delight in it, and feeling for its deeper meaning and mystery. These are pictures such as one would never tire of, for they make no pretenses and do not obtrude themselves. There is a delicate reticence to their exquisite perfection; they are always setting one thinking and drawing the fancy on. All sorts of animals are shown in their natural haunts; the philosopher muses in the moonlit forest; the fisherman idles in his boat on the water's surface; there are mountain scenery and mists.

Porcelain

The oldest extant porcelain is of the Sung dynasty, although it had probably been developing for some centures. The date of its first manufacture is sometimes given as 300 A. D. The earliest reference to glazed ware is under the Han dynasty; we have already spoken of glazed pottery from that time. In making porcelain the Chinese fired the clay to a very high temperature, producing glazes and varieties of pottery which were unknown in other lands. A Mohammedan traveler in the ninth century tells of a fine clay from which the Chinese make vases so transparent that water can be seen through them. Imperial porcelain works were established about 1000 A. D. which are said to have at one time employed a million people. The kilns were largely destroyed by the rebels in 1850, so that in 1900 there were only 160 kilns and 160,000 workmen.

Progress of Invention

The inventiveness of the Chinese had continued, it would seem, despite the decline of the Han dynasty and incursions of nomads. It is possible to infer from their records that the Chinese made discoveries at an early date which our civilization has acquired only comparatively recently and which they themselves seem in some cases to have lost in the meantime. But such inference is not always justifiable. Thus the early stories of a magic south-pointing chariot are not sufficient proof of the existence of the mariner's compass. However, in the fourth century occurs the earliest notice of a carriage fitted with a machine to record the distance traveled; in the fifth century the Chinese ceased to kick a ball stuffed with hair and substituted the modern football in the shape of an inflated bladder covered with leather; about the sixth century they devised block printing, though such printed books did not supersede manuscripts until the tenth century; in the seventh century they employed the system of identification by fingerprints and used something of the nature of gunpowder in fireworks; in the early ninth century they had bills of exchange, while paper money became quite common after the middle of the twelfth century. Movable types of baked clay are said to have been invented by an alchemist in the eleventh century. Wang Chen was printing with movable wooden types in 1314 and devised a revolving table with many boxes to bring the different characters within easy reach. Movable bronze types were used in Korea later. Movable types were, of course, less labor-saving to the Chinese than to people with only twenty-six letters to print; the ordinary font of a modern Chinese newspaper printed with movable types includes from six to seven thousand characters. The art of refining sugar was learned from India under the T'ang dynasty; the Chinese had no ancient character to represent sugar but called it stone-honey because the crystals looked like little stones.

Foot-binding for girls is believed to have started only in the tenth century, a painful process which enabled them for the rest of their lives to wear tiny shoes only three or four inches long. The flower-boats with their "fatal beauties" and seductive music date back to the T'ang dynasty. The Empress Wu of that dynasty admitted women to the competitive examinations for public office, but an emperor had already made the experiment in the third century. This empress wore a false beard, like Queen Hatshepsut in Egypt, and was as vain as Elizabeth of England. It was not enough to compliment her by saying that she was as fair as the lily, or as lovely as the rose; one must say that the flowers were as fair or lovely as she. After she had long ruled the land with a rod of iron, and had in 696 entitled herself God Almighty, she was in old age deposed, and the rightful heir restored. The position of woman at this period is further illustrated by a lawsuit in 999 when the judge reversed a will under which a father had left his daughter seven-tenths of his property on condition that she rear his son. The judge gave the son seven-tenths, while the daughter received only the three-tenths that the will had given to the son.

Position of Woman

In the latter part of the eleventh century the prime minister Wang An-Shih introduced reforms that illustrate the financial, social, and agrarian conditions. There was to be a resurvey of all lands, the soil was to be taxed according to its fertility, not according to the number of cultivators; the government

Reforms of Wang An-Shih

was to make advances and loans to needy cultivators, or supply them with seed and tools.   They were to be allowed to pay their taxes in kind from their produce, while an income tax paid in money was to be substituted for the forced labor of the poor on public works.   Once again the plan was tried of having the government purchase superfluous produce in one district for use in other districts, where it was needed, or for storage against time of famine.   Younger sons were liable to military service, but the farmers were allowed to use the cavalry horses during times of peace.   Wang further sought popularity with the farmers by appearing even in the imperial presence with dirty clothes, hands, and face.   But too frequent wars incensed the farmers by taking away the horses; property-owners generally regarded his measures as too socialistic; and they were finally all annulled.

Philosophy of Chu Hsi

The philosopher Chu Hsi (1130–1200), who won the third or final degree in the competitive examinations at the early age of nineteen, was successful in his official career and turned out an immense amount of literary work.   As a commentator on the Confucian Canon, he was superior to the earlier commentators of the Han dynasty in that he always gave the same interpretation to the same word wherever it occurred.   He rejected the conception of a personal God as suggestive of arbitrary caprice and wilfulness, interpreting the Chinese word for God as signifying nothing more than abstract right, an interpretation which Chinese scholars have accepted ever since.   He believed in the reign of a uniform, unvarying system of natural law throughout the universe.

Influence of Chinese Civilization and of Buddhism in Japan

The earliest known inhabitants of Japan were the Ainu, who now scarcely exist as a separate people but are a large factor in the present racial composition of the Japanese.   They were in the neolithic stage of civilization and for several millenniums remained in undisputed possession of the entire archipelago. In the centuries just before and after the beginning of our era, Mongoloid races seem to have entered the southwestern extremity of Japan by way of Korea and to have gradually pushed the Ainu further and further north and east.   By about the tenth century the conquest of the Ainu of the main island was completed.   The Japanese language is related neither to the Ural-Altaic group nor to the Chinese, but is of an independent family comprising also Korean and Loochooan.   The civilization of Japan, however, was long largely derived from Mongoloid or Chinese sources.   The earliest metal armor in Japan, of about 800 A. D., is like that of central and eastern Russia—lands which of course the Asiatic nomads penetrated—while other customs resemble those of Mongolia.   The higher forms of civilization, however, came mainly from China, although often by way of Korea.   They were introduced especially in connection with Buddhism.   Writing was introduced from China through Korea about 500 A. D., but for a long time remained a trade secret of gilds descended from Chinese or Koreans. In 588 Korea sent over Buddhist relics, priests, ascetics, sculptors, and architects.   The departments of state administration under the T'ang dynasty were imitated by the Japanese government.   In the eighth century, when the imperial court ceased to be migratory, the new capital imitated the Chinese method of laying out the streets, and contained fine residences. The costume of the upper classes became very elaborate, but the mass of the people remained little affected by the new culture from the continent.   On the other hand, the spread of Buddhism was perhaps of greater aid than forcible conquest in the final assimilation of the Ainu.

BIBLIOGRAPHY

Bishop, C. W. "Historical Geography of Early Japan," in *Geographical Review* XIII (1923) 40–63; and "Geographical Factor in the Development of Chinese Civilization," *Ibid.*, XII, 19–41.

Brinkley, F. *Japan and China, their History, Arts, and Literature,* 1903.

Bruce, J. P. *Chu Hsi and his Masters,* 1923.

Bushell, S. W. *Chinese Art,* 1909.

Carter, T. F. *The Invention of Printing in China and its Spread Westward,* 1925.

Chavannes, E. "Les livres chinois avant l'invention du papier," in *Journal asiatique,* 1905.

Fenellosa, E. F. *Epochs of Chinese and Japanese Art,* 1912.

Hobson, R. L. *Chinese Pottery and Porcelain,* 1915, 2 vols.

Laufer, B. *Chinese Pottery of the Han Dynasty,* 1909.

Munro, N. G. *Prehistoric Japan,* 1911.

National Geographic Magazine, Feb., 1923; well illustrated article on the Great Wall.

Obata, S. *Works of Li Po done into English Verse,* 1922.

Pier, G. C. *Temple Treasures of Japan,* 1914.

Roerich, G. *Tibetan Paintings,* 1925.

Simcox, E. J. *Primitive Civilizations*, 1894; vol. II is entirely devoted to "Ownership in China."

Smith, D. E. "Chinese Mathematics," in *Scientific Monthly*, 1912, 597–601.

Stein, Sir A. *Ruins of Desert Cathay*, 1912.

Waley, Arthur. *An Introduction to the Study of Chinese Painting*, 1923; *A Hundred and Seventy Chinese Poems*, 1919.

Wieger, Léon. *Histoire des croyances religieuses et des opinions philosophiques en China*. 1917.

CHURCHES AT RAVENNA

Above, the Basilica of S. Apollinare in Classe; below, S. Vitale, an example of concentric plan.

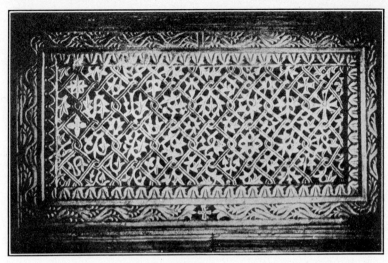

Left, capital from S. Vitale, Ravenna; right, open-work marble screen from S. Vitale.

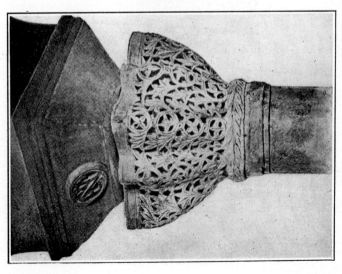

BOOK V.

MEDIEVAL CIVILIZATIONS OF THE NEAR EAST

CHAPTER XXIII

BYZANTINE CIVILIZATION

Find what interest one may in medieval Byzantium,—and it is full of instruction,—still it is a tale of what had reached its zenith, of what was past its best strength, a tale of decadence postponed with skill and energy, and yet only postponed.—*Henry Osborn Taylor*

". . . the autumn glory of Byzantine art. . ."—*Percy Dearmer*

THE adjective, Byzantine, is derived from Byzantium, the name of the original Greek colony on the site of the city of Constantinople. That city took its name from the first Christian Roman emperor, Constantine the Great, who enlarged and rebuilt it in 326–330, making it his capital instead of Rome and excluding pagan worships from it. In a sense Byzantine civilization began therewith; for it continued the past Greek culture, was Christian in character, and centred about the city of Constantinople. At first no doubt it was a small beginning and did not seem especially distinctive; the Roman Empire as a whole and its declining economic prosperity and culture continued. Officials, workmen, artists, and men of letters probably left Rome in large numbers for the scene of new activity and employment, never to return. As Greeks had poured into the Rome of Augustus to labor there, so now we have a reflux from Rome to the east; Greece folds back on itself. Latin for a considerable time continued to be the official language of the imperial government at Constantinople, although eventually the Greek tongue prevailed even in the Roman specialty of government. The culture and civilization of the eastern Mediterranean had of course been Greek all along. But now the Græco-Roman period yielded to the Byzantine, just as the Hellenistic had merged into the Græco-Roman. Therefore,

Meaning of Byzantine

273

as the empire gradually goes to pieces in the western Mediterranean and in western Europe, we may cease to speak of it as the Roman Empire and call what was left of it, the Byzantine Empire.   It is true that it did not call itself that; even the inhabitants of Constantinople called themselves Romans.   And some historians, who have wished to emphasize the fact that it was an unbroken continuation of the Roman imperial government, have preferred to call it the Later Roman Empire or the Eastern Roman Empire.   But these are ambiguous titles, as the former is often applied to the declining empire of the third and fourth centuries in distinction from the more prosperous early empire of the first two centuries, while from 280 to 476 the empire was usually divided into eastern and western halves. Some have called it the Greek Empire, but if we call its culture Greek too, we do not sufficiently distinguish it from earlier Greek civilization.   Byzantine civilization further grew out of early Christian culture, received oriental influences, even betrays something of the barbarism which surrounded and penetrated it.   In fact, Byzantine is the only adjective generally used for the civilization of this empire, so it is the handiest and clearest to apply to the empire as well, although it is rather paradoxical to use the term Byzantine for a civilization which began only after Byzantium had ceased to exist under that name.   However, that is just what has been done.

A Brief Outline of Byzantine History

The Byzantine Empire varied a great deal in size at different epochs.   We saw the first century of barbarian invasion reduce the authority of the emperor at Constantinople to little more than his Asiatic provinces and Egypt.   Then Justinian, 527–565, the greatest of all the Byzantine emperors, more or less reestablished the imperial power in the Balkan peninsula, and reconquered Italy from the East Goths, North Africa from the Vandals, and some of the coast of Spain from the West Goths. But most of these conquests proved of short duration.   Moreover, with the spread of Mohammedanism from Arabia in the seventh century the Byzantine Empire was reduced to Asia Minor and not much more than the islands and coasts of the Balkan and Italian peninsulas.   Bulgarians and Slavs held the interior of the one; Lombards, that of the other.   Gradually Constantinople lost all its possessions in Italy; in the Balkan peninsula it would expand for a time at the expense of the barbarians, then contract again; the same was true of its relations

with the Mohammedans in Asia Minor.   In the tenth century
the Byzantine Empire was the prey of Armenian and Slav.
Around the year 1000 came a period of expansion and prosperity, then from the eleventh century the Turks threatened
the Byzantine Empire with extinction.   The crusades from the
west staved off the Turks for a while, but in 1204 the westerners
did irreparable damage to the past works of art by their sack
of Constantinople, and parceled out the Byzantine territories
among themselves.   In 1261 a Greek dynasty was set up again
in Constantinople, but its jurisdiction was limited to the immediate neighborhood.   In the course of the fourteenth century the Ottoman Turks took away all its outlying territory;
in 1453 the city itself finally fell into their hands.

The Byzantine emperors maintained great pomp at their
court, perhaps to impress the barbarians with whom they had
to deal both within and without their territories.   Their armies
were largely recruited from the surrounding barbarians; even
the imperial office itself was more than once attained by someone of humble peasant birth or barbarian origin, who had
gradually worked his way up in the palace guard or offices.
The administration had been well reorganized by Justinian.
Blinding, however, was a common form of punishment which
cannot be regarded as much of an improvement upon Roman
crucifixion.   As time went on, the oriental element became more
marked, and the successive emperors came from regions farther
and farther east,—Phrygia, Isauria, Cappadocia, Armenia.
Syria was for a time more prosperous than it had been under
Roman rule; "new towns and villages covered the face of the
country, cultivation was pushed far out into the desert"; then
it suffered greatly in the wars between Persia and the Byzantine Empire, and was conquered by the Mohammedans in 634–
636.   The Byzantine ruins in Syria still surpass those of
earlier times.   The saying, "all roads lead to Rome," no longer
held true in the Byzantine Empire, when Constantinople became the center of all military and commercial communication.
In Asia Minor, for example, a complete revolution had taken
place in the system of roads and of the forts defending them by
the time of Justinian, who organized everything so skilfully
that subsequent emperors simply maintained his arrangements.
There was also a distinctly Byzantine type of fortress, no
longer resembling the Roman military camp but perched on a

Government
and Or-
ganization

precipitous height, like the medieval castle in the west a little later. Any place which was made the see of a bishop after 530 was usually a fortified hill town of this type.

The Eastern or Greek Church

The eastern or Greek church gradually became distinct, diverging in customs and doctrine from the western church under the papacy. The Byzantine emperor and the patriarch of Constantinople refused to recognize the superiority of the pope, who for his part would not yield to the emperor even when Rome was in Byzantine territory. Today the Greek priests have their own vestments. The interiors of their churches are often small and differ in appearance from those of Roman Catholics. The ecclesiastical calendars also differ. The Balkan Slavs were converted to the eastern form of Christianity in the ninth century; the Russians, at the close of the tenth century. In both cases this was largely due to the translation of the Scriptures into the Slavic languages. The populace of Constantinople, who were allowed no share in the absolute power of the emperor, became keen partisans in theological disputes, which sometimes led to popular outbreaks. There were also religious factions throughout the empire, especially so long as Syria and Egypt remained parts of it with independent patriarchs at Antioch, Jerusalem, and Alexandria. In Syria and Mesopotamia the sect of Jacobites were prominent, founded by a Jacob or James who became bishop of Edessa in 541. They were an offshoot of the earlier Monophysites who had contended that Christ possessed only one nature, the divine. The Nestorians, founded by Nestorius, a Syrian patriarch of Constantinople who was deposed in 431, went to the opposite extreme, holding that there were not merely two natures but two persons in Christ, namely, the divine Word and the man Jesus. They further objected to ornamentation in churches. Persecuted in the empire, they found a refuge in the Persian kingdom, and even spread to China.

Copts and Armenians

The Copts in Egypt were Monophysites. After the Council of Chalcedon in 451 they had little to do with the orthodox eastern church, becoming still more distinct after Egypt was conquered by the Mohammedans. Coptic is a continuation of the ancient language of Egypt; it has now died out and survives only in the church liturgy, but for a long time there was much Christian literature written in it. Copts were therefore at first the native Egyptians in distinction from their Greek or

MOSAICS AT RAVENNA
Above, the Mausoleum of Galla Placidia; below, procession of saints
along the side wall of S. Apollinare Nuovo.

APARTMENTS IN THE ALCAZAR, SEVILLE

Arabic conquerors. Later the name came to be confined to the Egyptian Christians, a native ceasing to be a Copt if he embraced Mohammedanism. Armenia had always been disputed territory between Romans and Parthians, or between Byzantines and Persians or Mohammedans, and was at times an independent kingdom, especially from the ninth to the eleventh centuries. From the beginning of the fifth century it had its own church organization, distinct from Greek official Christendom, under a *catholicus* and hereditary priesthood who continued the animal sacrifices of the previous pagan period. About 400, too, the Armenian alphabet was invented, and the Bible and Greek and Syriac fathers were translated into the Armenian tongue. Ani, now a mass of deserted ruins, in the eleventh century was a city with some two hundred churches and a population of one hundred thousand.

Constantinople was the heart of the Byzantine Empire. Although again and again invaders appeared under its very walls, it was practically impregnable. Thus it rendered a double service to civilization, first keeping invaders in the Balkans out of its Asiatic provinces, then keeping invaders of Asia Minor out of Europe. It further kept trade open between the Mediterranean and the Black Sea with its vast hinterland. Even today there are few ports through which as much shipping passes as goes through Constantinople. In the early Byzantine and medieval period it practically monopolized the commerce of Europe, the Mediterranean, and the Near East, and even traded with China. Skilled workmen both in early medieval Europe and the Mohammedan world were largely drawn from the Byzantine Empire. Thus its economic and artistic dominion was far more extensive than its political power. Constantinople became the most populous city of the Mediterranean basin, perhaps for a time of the world, and was so crowded that the height of buildings had to be regulated. The populace, as might be expected, was very cosmopolitan in character. Foreign merchants were subjected to strict regulation. Slavery existed, but about 800 the iconoclastic emperors freed the peasantry from serfdom, recognizing only slaves or fully free peasants. In the following period, however, there was a tendency to revert to serfdom. Combats with wild beasts were continued for a time in this Christian city, and there were many theaters, but what most excited

The City of Constantinople

the people were the chariot races, on Sundays in the Hippo-
drome. The people took sides according to the colors of their
favorite charioteers, such as the Blues and the Greens. These
sporting factions sometimes, like the theological sects, covered
political parties or even engaged in rioting. At the Hippo-
drome the mob even dared to express its dissatisfaction with
the government or emperor.

Byzantine
Literature
and
Learning,
Especially
Medicine

Byzantine literature was a continuation of declining ancient
Greek or Hellenistic literature and of Greek patristic literature. As the Roman amusements and spectacles were continued at Constantinople, as Justinian preserved the legal
literature of Rome in a condensed form, so the ancient classics
were treasured and imitated, quoted and inventoried. Past
Greek medical writings were digested in much the same fashion
as the Roman law; there is also some evidence of continued
progress in the field of medicine. In the sixth century Aëtius
of Amida in Mesopotamia and Alexander of Tralles in Asia
Minor described diseases not before mentioned in Greek medicine or suggested new methods of treating familiar complaints
and new medicines, while Paul of Ægina in the seventh century
composed his compendium "with great originality and independence." All three made innovations in surgery. Moreover, their works are superior to those of Galen and of classical
authors generally in orderly presentation and systematic arrangement, for the Latin and Greek authors of the classical
period were apt to be rambling and discursive. Aëtius is even
the first to speak of the use of a drying oil in painting, stating
that nut oil forms a protective varnish over encaustic or gild-
ing. Alexander of Tralles seems to have been the first Greek
medical writer to mention rhubarb and tape-worms, and to
venture to open the jugular vein. He ingeniously stopped
nosebleed by blowing fuzz into the nostrils through a hollow
reed, and dislodged foreign objects from the ear by having the
patient sneeze with nose and mouth stopped up. The medical
and legal work came before 650, when a barren period ensued
until 800. Then the ancient literary classics were again extensively studied, while we have some lively historians who
wrote of their own times. But the chief new developments were
in ecclesiastical writing, especially church poetry, and in vulgar Greek, for the language of the people gradually diverged
from the obsolete literary Greek of the classics. There seems

to have been little in the way of invention except the mysterious Greek fire used in sea fights to burn the enemy's ships.   Greek ceased to be so universally the literary language of the eastern Mediterranean as it had been in the Hellenistic and Roman periods.   There was much writing in Syriac, Armenian, and Coptic.   In the later centuries of the Byzantine Empire, after Arabic and medieval Latin learning had developed, works were translated from Arabic or Latin into Greek, as well as from Greek into those tongues.   But at first the borrowing was from Greek into Arabic and Latin.   On the whole Byzantine literature served chiefly as a storehouse of ancient Greek literature and transmitter of ancient Greek learning.

Byzantine art was more creative and distinctive.   At the same time it was indebted to Roman and oriental as well as Greek sources.   Roman architecture had hardly shared in the general decline of ancient civilization, but had continued its development to the verge of the final barbarian invasions. These edifices of the late third and fourth centuries already contained the germs of much later developments.   The erection of Byzantine churches gave a new turn to this architectural activity.   Byzantine buildings were apt to have thinner walls, airier roofs, greater admittance of light, slenderer columns with more graceful capitals, than the previous Roman buildings.   This was partly due to superior structural skill and feeling for beauty of line.   But possibly more fragile Byzantine buildings have survived because they have been kept in better repair through the centuries owing to their being constantly used for purposes of worship.   Another feature is decoration of the interior by brilliant color in various materials: stucco, marble slabs and columns, but especially mosaics.   In general there is more evidence of attention to the interior of buildings than ever before.   Early Christian symbolism continued to affect Byzantine art, but there was also a tendency to tell the Bible story plainly in sculpture or painting.   The figures, human or animal, are often quite crudely outlined, though usually skilfully placed with a view to decorative effect. There now came in a new wealth of beautiful ornamental patterns and decorative designs such as Greek art had not known. Much of this was Coptic from Egypt, but perhaps Persia was its ultimate source, since some of the designs seem drawn from textiles such as Persian rugs.   As one example of these

Byzantine Art: General Characteristics

decorative patterns may be mentioned the formal vine-scroll enclosing birds and beasts in its windings, which is employed alike in mosaic, stone sculpture, and ivory carving.

Byzantine Capitals and Mosaics

A new Byzantine type of capital for the column was the double capital with impost block. It seems to have first appeared at Ravenna in the old Basilica Ursiana of 370–384. The lower capital came to be variously carved with the new wealth of delicate design, while the upper impost block which supported the arches was usually left severely plain except perhaps for a cross or monogram. Such Byzantine capitals must be counted one of the most graceful and beautiful, yet at the same time dignified and almost mystic, creations in all the long history of art. The ancient Greek capitals of the colonnades about a temple exterior had been too exposed to the weather to be thus intricately carved and undercut. The Byzantine capitals are protected indoors, where, too, the more subdued light is favorable to effects from light and shade. The mosaics which now fill dome, apse, or side walls, instead of being pavements on the floor, are pictures constructed of little cubes of colored or gilded glass which are fixed in place in a cement covering against the brick or stone wall. In the dome alone of the church of St. George at Saloniki it is estimated that there are thirty-six millions of these little glass cubes or *tesserae*, each of which had to be set independently in its place. "Mosaic is a noble form of the pictorial art which is beyond us today, with its glittering lights, its soft, dusky shadows, its depth of color, its majesty of vision and vastness of design. The painting of the thirteenth century sprang out of it." (Dearmer.)

Famous Extant Buildings

The largest, finest, and most famous of all Byzantine churches, perhaps of all churches, is the great domed church of St. Sophia at Constantinople, erected by the great emperor Justinian (527–565) who is further noted for his law books. Although somewhat modified and marred, both inside and outside by the Mohammedan Turks since 1453, and in danger of collapse from lack of recent repair, it still stands. We still have, too, the description of the contemporary Procopius testifying to the new splendor and sublime religious effect of this unwonted interior of the house of God. Here architecture solved the problem of a grand, well-lighted, beautifully decorated interior as never before. Next to it in excellence come various smaller buildings erected in the fifth and sixth centuries at Ravenna in northern Italy close to the Adriatic, the retreat of the last Roman emperors in the west and the capital of the East Goths and of Byzantine Italy after Justinian reconquered it. Here are the Catholic Baptistery, an octagonal brick building with a dome made of a double spiral of tapering terra cotta tubes fitted into one another and embedded in mortar, the tomb of the empress Galla Placidia in the form of a Latin cross, the concentric church of San Vitale (of which the central octagon is surrounded by a lower, but two-storied, aisle), and the two rectangular columnar basilicas of Sant' Apollinare in Classe (the port of ancient Ravenna) and Sant' Apollinare Nuovo. All these buildings are wonderfully adorned with mosaics which include representations of Justinian, his empress Theodora and their attendants, stately processions of saints and virgins, and a symbolic representation of the Transfiguration. The early Christian basilicas at Rome are somewhat less well preserved or have been modified subsequently. Byzantine ecclesiastical architecture may also be traced in southern and central Gaul, perhaps in Spain, and certainly in the important stone churches of Armenia from the seventh to eleventh centuries.

Byzantine stone sculpture and ivory carving are mainly executed in one plane rather than modelled in the round or relief. As we have implied in speaking of the capitals, the figures are deeply undercut to bring out light and shadow. Both in stone sculpture and metal jewelry there is much fragile-looking, pierced work. Some beautiful openwork marble window screens have been preserved at Ravenna. The iconoclastic movement in the eighth century resulted in much destruction of art in the east and the exclusion of statues and images from the churches. Icons in the form of pictures were finally permitted, although a medieval Latin writer tells us that the Greeks paint the human figure only from the waist up, "that all occasion of vain thoughts may be removed." These paintings were often in enamel and richly bejewelled, even to the cruel cross. Inlaid gold jewelry seems to have been introduced from the east in the fourth century. The covers of manuscripts of the Gospels and reliquaries were often enamelled in cells marked off by gold bars or set with root of emerald and sapphire or table garnets and colored pastes.

Sculpture, Painting, Jewelry, Enamels

As the mention of covers implies, manuscripts were now shaped, folded, bound, and paged like our printed books instead of like the rolls of Hellenistic libraries. This new method prob-ably developed in Egypt and is especially associated with Chris-tian literature. By the fourth century A. D. the codex form of manuscript had replaced the roll entirely. A close resem-blance has been noted between the mosaics and the illuminations in manuscripts of the Bible, which has led some to hold that the artists worked under the instructions of the theologians and that art was bound by ecclesiastical tradition. At least the paintings were rather stiff and stately, with important per-sonages centred, in frontal position—this perhaps a heritage from Roman imperial art,—and often of larger size, while it became customary to place mosaics of certain themes in cer-tain parts of the church. Both early Christian and Byzan-tine paintings were usually executed in tempera. The later impoverished Byzantine Empire could not afford such magnifi-cent churches as had been erected in Justinian's time. We have more jewelry, too, from the fourth to seventh century than later. But from the tenth to twelfth century was the great period of Byzantine enamels. From paintings in Cap-padocian churches and from Greek psalters of the tenth and eleventh centuries perhaps came the more circumstantial, real-istic, and pathetic representation of the crucifixion which the Italians adopted in the thirteenth, the French in the four-teenth and fifteenth centuries. In the Balkans and Morea (the ancient Peloponnesus) Byzantine painting flourished once more with considerable freedom of experimentation between 1261 and 1453.

Byzantine Influence on Other Lands

Already we have touched on Byzantine influence on lands beyond its political boundaries through its art, its trade, and its Christian missions. In the orient the Arabs took over much of its civilization. The civilization of the Balkan peoples and of Russia in the middle ages was derived almost entirely from Constantinople. In Italy Venice, especially after Ravenna fell to the Lombards in 751, began its development as a great trading center under Byzantine control and in close connection with Constantinople. Sicily and southern Italy long felt the Byzantine influence and even received a further accession of immigrants from the Greek east. Ravenna has been called "the half-Syrian city on the Adriatic"; at Rome monks and merchants from Syria and Egypt occupied permanent quarters; from 685 to 741 five popes were Syrians, four Greeks, and only one Roman. The oldest Christian building preserved in Gaul, the baptistery of St. John at Poitiers, "proves how completely Byzantine influence had permeated all the west." Moreover, "all Christian inscriptions of Gaul long continued to be written in Greek."

Since 1453 the Ottoman Empire of the Turks has succeeded to the geographical and political position of the Byzantine Empire. The Turks have held not only Constantinople but, until the last century, Roumania, practically all the Balkan peninsula except for Venetian holdings along its coast, and, until the recent war, more of Asia than the Byzantine Empire held at its height. Even in Europe a considerable part of the population became Mohammedan, though the eastern church continued. Asia Minor and Mesopotamia were largely given over to nomads, with the consequence that economic productivity and civilization further declined, although the Turks appropriated some features of Byzantine and western civilization, notably military ones.

The Ottoman Empire as a Continuation of the Byzantine

BIBLIOGRAPHY

Andréadès, A. M. *History of Hellenic Public Economy* (in Greek), 1918; pp 337–624 deal with the Byzantine period.

Bareilles, B. *Constantinople, ses cités franques et levantines,* 1918.

Bliss, F. J. *Religions of Modern Syria and Palestine,* 1912.

Bréhier, Louis. *L'art byzantin,* 1924; fully illustrated.

Brightman, F. E. *Eastern Liturgies,* 1896.

British Museum Guide to Early Christian and Byzantine Antiquities, 1921; a very informing manual.

Bury, J. B. *The Later Roman Empire,* 2 vols., revised ed., 1923; a standard historical work on the earlier centuries of the Byzantine Empire.

Cattaneo, R. *Architecture in Italy from the Sixth to the Eleventh Century,* English translation, 1896.

Dalton, O. M. *Byzantine Art and Archæology,* 1911; an authoritative work.

Davis, W. S. *Short History of the Near East,* 1923; a brief manual.

Diehl, Ch. *Byzance, grandeur et décadence,* 1919, *History of the Byzantine Empire,* 1925; a summary treatment in 149 brief pages.

Diehl, Le Tourneau, Saladin, *Les monuments chrétiens de Salonique,* 1918.

Ebersolt, J. *Constantinople byzantine et les voyageurs du Levant,* 1919.

Finlay, G. *History of Greece from its conquest by the Romans to the present time,* 1877, 7 vols.; reprinted 1906 in Everyman's Library **as** *History of the Byzantine Empire.*

Foord, E. A. *The Byzantine Empire,* 1911.

Fortescue, A. *The Orthodox Eastern Church,* 1911, 3rd edition.

Freeman, *Historical Essays,* Third Series, the sixth essay on the Byzantine Empire at pp. 235–282.

Gelzer, H. *Byzantinische Kulturgeschichte,* 1909.

Harrison, Frederic. *Byzantine History in the Early Middle Ages,* 1900; and "Constantinople as an historic city," in his *Meaning of History,* 1908.

Jackson, T. G. *Byzantine and Romanesque Architecture,* 1913, 2 vols.

Jerphanion, Guill. de. *Les églises ruprestres de Cappadoce,* 1924–1925, 2 vols.

Krumbacher, K. *Geschichte der byzantischen Literatur,* 1897; the standard work on the subject.

Laurent, J. *L'Arménie entre Byzance et l'Islam depuis la conquête arabe jusqu'en 886,* 1919.

Lynch, H. F. B. *Armenia: Travels and Studies,* 1901, 2 vols.

Millet, G. *L'Ancien art serbe, les églises,* 1919; *Recherches sur l'iconographie de l'évangile,* 1916.

Oeconomos, L. *La vie religieuse dans l'empire byzantin au temps des Comnènes et des Anges,* 1918.

Procopius, *Of the Buildings of Justinian,* English translation by A. Steward, 1896; an intensely interesting contemporary account.

Sammné, G. *La Syrie,* 1921.

Schevill, F. *A History of the Balkan Peninsula,* 1922; a brief manual.

Schlumberger, *L'Epopée byzantine,* 1890–1905, 3 vols., illustrated; **and** other works.

Tafrali, O. *Thessalonique, des origines au XIVe siècle,* 1919.

Vogt, A. *Basile I et la civilization byzantine,* 1908.

CHAPTER XXIV

PERSIAN AND ARABIC CIVILIZATION:
MOHAMMEDANISM

That vast empire which may almost be said to have been
flung in the faces of the Arabs, to be picked up with the minimum of effort, by the rival empires of Persia and Rome. . . .
—*Sir Thomas W. Arnold*

The Arab mind, on the other hand, is clear and positive, and
the Arabic language nervous, virile, and rich both actually
and potentially. The old Arabs were an acute and observant
people. . . .—*E. G. Browne*

WE have seen that the Roman and Byzantine empires were
protected on the east from the attacks of Asiatic nomads by
the revived Persian kingdom under the Sassanid dynasty, 226–
651 A. D. Berthold Laufer is even of the opinion that Persia
under the Achæmenians and Sassanids was the center of the
world's very highest civilization, "playing in the cultural development of lands about her a part whose importance we
are only just beginning to understand." The reign of Chos-
roes I, 531–579 A. D., marked the golden age both of Pahlavi
literature and Mazdean religion. Unfortunately the Byzantine Empire, like the Roman before it, became involved in a
series of wars with this powerful Persian kingdom which were
disastrous to both sides, making it possible for the Arabs to
overthrow Persia and greatly reduce the Byzantine Empire.
This made it easy later for Mongols and Turks to invade
southwestern Asia and even Europe by way of Asia Minor.
Peace and alliance between Constantinople and Persia would
have been a priceless boon to civilization; the deserts of the
Near East might still be blossoming like the rose.

    Under the Sassanids, although Christian sects which were
persecuted in the Byzantine Empire were welcomed as a matter
of policy, the religion of Persia was still Zoroastrian. A little
earlier an offshoot from it, known as Mithraism, had spread

Margin notes:
Rule of the
Sassanids in
Persia:
226–651 A. D.

Religions
from Persia

285

over the Roman Empire and for a time had been Christianity's most dangerous rival. In the early years of the Sassanid dynasty Mani or Manes had again presented the doctrine of two great contending powers, the good and evil, in a form called Manicheism, which invaded the Roman Empire. Later it revived as a Christian heresy in the twelfth century in medieval Europe, while fragments of Manichean manuscripts have in recent years been discovered in central Asia and western China. Divination and sorcery were also much practiced in Persia. Today, almost the sole survivors of Zoroastrianism are the Parsees of India, whither they fled from Mohammedan persecution centuries ago. Living chiefly in Bombay, they are among the wealthiest, best educated, most philanthropic, and most kindly to women of the many peoples of India. They still neither bury nor cremate their dead lest they defile earth or fire, but expose the bodies to vultures on the tops of "towers of silence." Within ten minutes the birds leave nothing but bare bones.

Persian Art   It is not easy to distinguish between what the Persian kingdom borrowed from Rome or Constantinople, and what the Byzantine Empire borrowed from it. The greatest architectural relic of the Sassanid monarchy is a huge hall 163 feet long by 86 feet wide and 95 feet high. It dates from 550 A. D. and still stands in ruined condition on the site of the ancient Persian capital, Ctesiphon. It has an elliptical vault rather crudely constructed of brick; the side walls slant inward. There seem to have been no windows; the external decoration is very clumsy. All this is quite simple and crude compared to such a structure as St. Sophia. Yet some hold that the later Saracenic architecture derived from Sassanid Persia the gypsum arch, adorned with honeycomb cells and suspended pyramids like stalactites. Some Sassanian sculpture is preserved beneath the rock-hewn tombs of the ancient Achæmenian Persian kings which is more valuable for its representation of royal costume than for its artistic merit. What Persia excelled in then and since was conventionalized flower and leaf design, decorative painting, colored inlay, painted tiles, costly earthenware, exquisite embroidery. Most extant specimens of such work, however, together with Persian rugs and illuminated manuscripts, are of the later Mohammedan, rather than the Sassanid, period.

From desert Arabia, whose vast area compared to adjoining
regions should be carefully noted, a great wave of invasion
was now about to pour forth into Syria and the Tigris-
Euphrates valley under the unifying stimulus of a new religion
proclaimed by the prophet Mohammed (c. 570–632 A. D.).
The Arabs, although then still to a large extent nomadic, especially the Bedouin tribes, were of course Semitic and entirely
different in physique and language from the Mongoloid, Ural-
Altaic nomads of central Asia. Before Mohammed they had
some towns, trade, wealth and luxury; they were grouped in
clans and drew social distinctions; such social evils as slavery,
polygamy, and sexual immorality existed. But they lacked any
central political organization, were not yet unified in religion,
while the different tribes varied considerably in barbarism or
civilization. The chief thing that united them even then was
the Arabic language and poetry.

Arabic is a concise language, clear and strong in expression,
and rich in fitting and "finely differentiated words" for
natural objects, suggesting that the Arabs had acute powers
of observation. Their poetry, we are told, "flew faster than
arrows across the desert." The oldest poems extant were
perhaps composed about a century before Mohammed. Even
by that time the poets, although illiterate, had become such
masters of their craft, that this pre-Islamic poetry has been
regarded by Moslems ever since as setting the highest standard
of excellence. Quantitative meters and rhyme were both employed; the usual form of verse was a monorhymed ode of
from twenty-five to one hundred lines. In this poetry the
Arabs drew a somewhat idealized picture of themselves as
fierce and bold, but also generous, hospitable, truthful, and
chivalrous bandits. This poetry passed from mouth to mouth,
and we hear of a man who could repeat 2900 pre-Islamic odes
from memory.

Mohammed was good-looking and rather fastidious in matters of personal cleanliness. He had some business experience
and knowledge of life but almost no book education. He was
of an affectionate and kindly disposition, of delicate health and
very nervous temperament, very devout, much given to fasts,
vigils, and religious meditation. He became subject to seizures
during which he was believed to be divinely inspired and which
resulted in the revelations, or teachings, that are partially pre-

served in the *Koran*. This collection of his utterances was
made two years after his death and is about two-thirds as long
as the New Testament. At first he had only a few followers
in his native city of Mecca, but he also preached to the pilgrims who came annually to visit the *Kaaba*, a cubical building containing sacred objects. When his followers were ill-
treated at Mecca, he accepted an invitation to come to Medina,
and from this *Hegira*, or flight, in 622 A. D., the Mohammedans date their era. Their year, unlike ours, is the Semitic
lunar year of only 354 days. Mohammedans call themselves
Muslimin, or Moslems, their faith Islam. Both words carry
the idea of surrender to Allah, the one and only God, "the mer-
ciful, the compassionate." "All believers are alike in their
utter subjection to the unapproachable divine majesty." Mohammed denied the divinity of Christ, although granting that
Jesus had been a holy man and prophet. Strictly speaking,
Islam possesses no church organization and no priesthood.
Mohammed attacked idolatry, to which many of the Arabs had
been given. He enjoined prayer five times daily, a religious
gathering every Friday, fasting during one month of the year,
and, when possible, the annual pilgrimage to Mecca. Holding
up before his followers a vivid picture of the day of judgment
and future reward and punishment, he gave them various moral,
social, legal, and hygienic injunctions. They were no longer
to seek revenge but forgive injuries, give alms, treat slaves
and women somewhat better, not expose infants. While Mohammed permitted some practices upon which we frown, such
as polygamy, it may be noted that the Koran does not ex-
plicitly order that women cover their faces, much less decree
the prison life of the harem. He insisted that Moslems keep
their teeth clean, and abstain from alcohol as well as pork.
In time innumerable sects developed in Islam just as they have
in Christendom.

Moham-
medan
Conquests

The ideal of Islam was a brotherhood without dissension or
injury. At Medina, however, Mohammed found it difficult to
support his followers until he allowed them to attack and
plunder unbelievers—in particular the Jews of Medina and
merchants of Mecca. This prospect of pillage attracted many
of the Bedouins of the desert to his side, and in 630 he re-
entered Mecca in triumph. He died two years later but had
already begun incursions into Byzantine territory. Indeed,

the country of nomads is so sparsely populated that probably foreign conquest is the only way to draw them together. Within twenty years after Mohammed's death the Arabs had conquered Syria, Egypt, and the entire kingdom of the Sassanids. By 669 they were before the walls of Constantinople, Carthage fell in 697–698, in 711–713 the Spanish peninsula was occupied except the extreme, mountainous, northwest coast. Only in 732 were the advancing Moslems checked in central Gaul by the Franks at the battle of Tours. Thus their empire stretched over three continents from the Atlantic to India and south almost to the equator. Later it was to invade India and spread through the interior of Africa and the lands adjoining the Indian Ocean. Camp cities of Arabs in the conquered territories led a semi-nomadic life, supported by tribute which the conquered unbelievers were forced to pay them. Apart from this, many Christian sects were less persecuted under Arabic rule than they had been by their orthodox Christian rulers. But no unbeliever was allowed to live in Arabia itself.

General direction of affairs was in the hands of a single caliph, or successor of Mohammed. After the first four caliphs, "who followed a right course," came the more worldly Ommiad, or Umayyad, dynasty (661–750) which transferred the capital from Medina to Damascus. In 750 the Abbasids, a Persian dynasty, moved it again to Bagdad. There also came to be many emirs or independent Moslem chieftains. A fugitive Ommiad thus established himself in Spain, where his descendants finally resumed the title of caliph so that there was a Caliphate of Cordova, as well as of Bagdad. Various independent states also arose in North Africa, where in modern times we have Morocco, Tunis, and Algeria. The Fatimite dynasty, 909–1171, claiming descent from Mohammed's daughter Fatima, established there a third caliphate which, after 969, transfered its capital to Cairo in Egypt. *Government*

The Caliphate was "the outgrowth of conditions that were entirely unfamiliar to the Arabs." Many problems arose for which the Koran offered no solution, since it had never envisaged them. To meet these new problems developed the Traditions, supposed to be utterances of Mohammed himself or of his intimate companions which had not been included in the Koran but handed down orally, and which were "embodied *The Traditions and Religious Learning* in authoritative compilations during the third century of the Mohammedan era." These were reverenced as of almost equal authority with the Koran. The Koran itself neither represents nor is favorable to a high degree of civilization, and bigoted or narrowly conservative Moslems hold that it, with perhaps the Traditions, contains all that a Moslem need know or ought to know. It is true that it is the function of the learned to interpret these books, but the narrow Moslem would confine learning to religious interests.

Civilization under the Caliphs

Ibn Khaldûn, an Arabic historian of the fourteenth century, asserted that every land conquered by the Arabs was soon ruined, that they could not govern satisfactorily, and had little aptitude for the arts. The chief contributors to civilization and leading scientific writers under their rule, were usually not genuine Arabs. But they wrote in Arabic, which spread all over the Mohammedan world, so that we find Spanish Christians imitating the Arabic style and neglecting Latin. Many of the caliphs were broad-minded patrons of civilization who made no distinction between Christian and Moslem, or Greek, Persian, and Arab. The Arabic civilization was a composite and cosmopolitan one, drawing contributions from India and Constantinople, Persia and Spain and Egypt. The reigns of the Ommiads at Damascus were "the genuinely Arab period in the history of Islam, . . . full of color and life and light, love and song, battle and feasting." But even during this period, as Macdonald goes on to say, "The great theologian of the Greek Church, John of Damascus, held high office at the Umayyad court, and al-Akhtal, a Christian at least in name, was their poet laureate."

Economic Aspects

City life continued to flourish in the Mohammedan world. Great new metropolises were created in Bagdad and Cairo with various quarters and suburbs of the court and resident foreigners, countless streets, lanes, alleys, gates, bridges, markets, wharves, warehouses, bazaars. There were shops of artisans and booksellers, mosques, synagogues, Christian churches, jails, cemeteries, orphan and insane asylums, hospitals, schools and colleges, public baths, assembly halls for poets. The oldest university now existing in the world, and in which instruction has always been free, was founded in 988 at Cairo when the caliph converted the mosque of el-Azhar to that purpose. Cordova was another great city with, we are told, one hundred thousand homes and three thousand mosques. Other towns of Moslem Spain, though smaller, were busy centers of commerce or manufactures. Silk and carpets were now woven in Spain as well as in China and Persia; cotton was introduced into Europe; and in the eighth century factories were established in the east, at Samarkand and Bagdad, to make paper from rags, an industry learned from the Chinese. Paper was not used in the Christian west until centuries later, however.

The trade and travel of the Mohammedans was almost world-wide. They had many trading stations on the west coast of India and supplied China with steel weapons and armor, or glass-ware, cotton, dates, rose-water, sugar, and camphor. Many Moslem coins have been found in the Baltic coast-lands. The situation of the peninsula of Arabia, extending southward between the Red Sea and Persian Gulf far across the Tropic of Cancer to the Indian Ocean, brought it from an early date into relations with equatorial Africa and other lands bordering on the Indian Ocean. Egyptian records seem to show that Arabs were active in Africa in the second millenium before our era. The *Periplus of the Erythræan Sea*, written in the first century A. D., speaks of the east coast of Africa, even south of the equator, as under Arabian sovereignty and of "large ships" that go there with "Arab captains and agents, who are familiar with the natives and intermarry with them, and who know the whole coast and understand the language." These traders were of course from the south coast of Arabia, not from the nomadic Bedouin tribes of the interior. It is therefore not surprising that with the spread of Mohammedanism the Indian Ocean became almost an Arabic lake. Alberuni, who was "almost the only Mohammedan scholar who ever took the trouble to learn Sanskrit," wrote in 1031 A. D. his *Inquiry Into India*, giving much information concerning Hindu customs, literature, and science.

Of works of Arabic learning the commentaries on the Koran, collections of Moslem tradition, biographies of Mohammed, and other religious or historical literature are of less interest to us than their science and medicine. Sometimes they translated the Greek authors in these fields not directly from the Greek but through Syriac or Aramaic versions. Some Greek works are preserved only in Arabic versions. Upon these authorities the Arabic writers commented, or made compilations

Trade and Travel

Arabic Science and Medicine

from them, or partially based upon them new works of their own in the same fields.   They not infrequently employed the experimental method.   They further seem to have learned something from India, as in the case of the Hindu-Arabic numerals, an advance in mathematical reckoning and record comparable to the phonetic alphabet in literature.   Algebra shows by its very name its Arabic origin.   In alchemy experiments were made and some new chemicals were discovered.   Al-Hazen's work on Optics marked an advance on any known previous work in that field.   In astronomy the Arabic writers supplemented Ptolemy by new tables based on their own observations such as those of Al-Zarkali.   Jewish and Arabic travelers enlarged geographical knowledge.   Medicine was much cultivated. The treatment of the insane among Mohammedans seems to have been more enlightened than among Christians, who were apt to regard them as possessed by demons or as amusing clowns and possible prophets.   Rasis, a Persian, Isaac, a Jew, and Avicenna, another Persian, were leading medical writers in Arabic.   The ten parts of Rasis' chief work dealt with the following matters: (1) introduction to medicine and discussion of anatomy; (2) temperaments, humours, physiognomy and how to select slaves; (3) diet and drugs; (4) hygiene; (5) cosmetics; (6) rules and medicines for travelers; (7) surgery; (8) poisons; (9) treatment of diseases, arranged in order from head to feet; (10) fevers.   It was a common practice of Arabic men of learning to give their treatises flowery titles such as *Meadows of Gold* or *The Highest Degree of Wisdom,* which suggest little as to the specific subject.   Often the works themselves are of a correspondingly rhetorical or mystic and romantic character.   Moreover, occult science, divination, and necromancy were in favor, although sometimes writers expressed scepticism concerning even alchemy and astrology.   Two writers in Arabic of the twelfth century who, like those already mentioned, had much influence on western Latin learning, were Averroës and Moses Maimonides, the latter perhaps the leading medieval Jewish philosopher.   Both were born at Cordova, although the family of Maimonides had to flee when he was a child from Moslem persecution by the fanatical Almohades in Spain, so that he spent most of his life in Cairo.   Both were noted commentators on Aristotle, although Maimonides tried to reconcile Aristotle with the Jewish faith, while Averroës did not allow the Koran to affect his interpretation.   Both also wrote on medicine, astronomy, and other subjects.

The Koran forbade the artistic representation of living be- Moslem Art ings as idolatrous, but permitted use of color and ornamentation in the form of geometric and conventional designs, whence the use of the word "arabesque" for such decorations.   Wood carving and metal work were often beautifully done.   The architecture of Mohammedan mosques, of tombs such as those of the caliphs at Cairo, of palaces such as the Alhambra at Granada and Alcazar at Seville, most of which were not built until the later middle ages, is largely borrowed from other lands and periods, but also has features of its own such as the minarets, slender towers from which the muezzin summons the people to prayer.

If we ask why the Mohammedan world is today much less Why the civilized than our own, whereas the Arabic world of the early World of middle ages was far in advance of the barbarism of western Uncivilized Christendom at that time, the answer is that less civilized Today peoples have kept invading Mohammedan territories, such as the Almoravides and Almohades in Spain and the Turks in the Near East, and that Mohammedanism has been extended to uncivilized peoples such as those just named and the tribes of interior Africa.   It must further be said that the Arabs, Persians, Syrians, and Egyptians failed to advance very much the state of civilization with which they began in the seventh century.   There has been more progress since in the west, and perhaps climate or change in climate has been responsible for a decline in energy of the southern Moslem lands.

BIBLIOGRAPHY

The works on Persia already listed at the close of Chapter VIII for the most part apply also to this period.

Arnold, Sir T. W.   *The Caliphate,* 1924; its history both in theory and practice.

Bliss, F. J.   *The Religions of Modern Syria and Palestine,* 1912, Chapters 4–6.

Blunt, Lady Anne and W. S.   *The Seven Golden Odes of Pagan Arabia,* 1893.

Browne, E. G.   *Arabian Medicine,* 1921; four lectures on the subject.

Bussel, F. W.   *Religious Thought and Heresy in the Middle Ages,* 1918, pp. 361 ff., on Islam, its sects and philosophies.

Caetani, L. *Annali dell' Islam* and *Studi di Storia Orientale;* two works by "the greatest living historian of Islam."

De Slane. *Histoire des Berbères d'Ibn Khaldoun;* a new edition of this French translation of "the first author of a naturalistic and sociological history of civilization," (born Tunis 1332, died Cairo 1406) in 5 vols. is announced for 1925–1926.

Dozy, R. *Spanish Islam,* translated by F. G. Stokes, 1913.

Faure-Biguet, G. *Histoire de l'afrique septentrionale sous la domination musulmane,* 1905.

Goldziher, I. *Aspects of Islam,* translated by K. E. Chambers, 1915; *Mohammed and Islam,* translated by K. C. Seelye, 1916.

Goodrich-Freer, A. *Arabs in Tent and Town,* 1924.

Hogarth, D. G. *Arabia,* 1922.

Huart, C. *L'Histoire des Arabes,* 1912, 1913, 2 vols.

Hurgronje, C. S. *Mohammedanism,* 1916.

Lane, E. W. *Arabian Society in the Middle Ages,* 1883.

Lane-Poole, S. *Speeches and Table-Talk of the Prophet Mohammed,* 1905.

Lyall, Sir Chas. *Ancient Arabic Poetry,* 1885.

Macdonald, D. B. *Muslim Theology, Jurisprudence, and Constitutional Theory,* 1903; *The Religious Attitude and Life in Islam,* 1909.

Mann, J. *Jews in Egypt and Palestine under Fatimid Caliphs,* 1920, 1922, 2 vols.

Margoliouth, *Mohammed,* 1905; the best one volume biography.

Nicholson, R. A. *A Literary History of the Arabs,* 1914; *Studies in Islamic Poetry,* 1921.

Muir, W. *The Life of Mohammed from original sources,* revised edition, 1912.

Noeldeke, T. *Geschichte d. Qorans,* 2nd ed., 1909, 1919.

Palmer, E. H. *The Koran* (in English translation), 1880.

Rivoira, G. T. *Architettura musulmana: sue origini e sviluppo,* 1914.

Robertson Smith, W. *Kinship and Marriage in Early Arabia,* 1903.

Sachau, E. *Albiruni's India* (in English translation), 1888; a work of a high intellectual level for its time (1031 A.D.).

Smith, E. D. and Karpinski, L. C. *The Hindu Arabic Numerals,* 1911.

Westermarck, E. *The Moorish Conception of Holiness,* 1916.

Whishaw, E. M. *Arabic Spain,* 1912.

Zwemer, S. M. *Arabia, the Cradle of Islam,* 1900.

BOOK VI

REVIVAL OF CIVILIZATION IN THE WEST

CHAPTER XXV

WESTERN EUROPE IN TRANSITION

A recent writer on the history of education wittily suggests
that successive investigations keep pushing the "dark ages"
so much further and further back that they will probably
ultimately cover no time whatever.

DURING the centuries, usually described as medieval, which followed the decline of classical civilization and of the Roman
Empire in the west, as the successive and repeated inroads of
barbarians gradually ceased, there came a time when decay
and stagnation began to yield to vigor and enterprise, when
the old was transformed into the new, and when a distinct, western civilization began to develop, of which our present civilization, whether European or American, although altered from
it in many ways, is nevertheless a direct outgrowth. Just
when this time came is a difficult question. It was once the
fashion to postpone it until the so-called Italian Renaissance
and Protestant Reformation at the close of the fifteenth and
opening of the sixteenth centuries. But that date is much too
late and is further misleading because the Italian Renaissance
was in part an attempt to bring back ancient civilization, while
the Protestant movement was in part an attempt to bring back
early Christianity, and both these attempts were in these respects counter to the fundamentally new and distinctively northwestern character of the true development that was going on.
In this book we have retained the customary usage of the
word medieval for matters comprised between the fifth and
fifteenth centuries, whether Byzantine, Arabic, or western European; and we shall apply the expression, "early modern
times," as usual to the period from the fifteenth to eighteenth

Evolution of a Distinctly Western Civilization

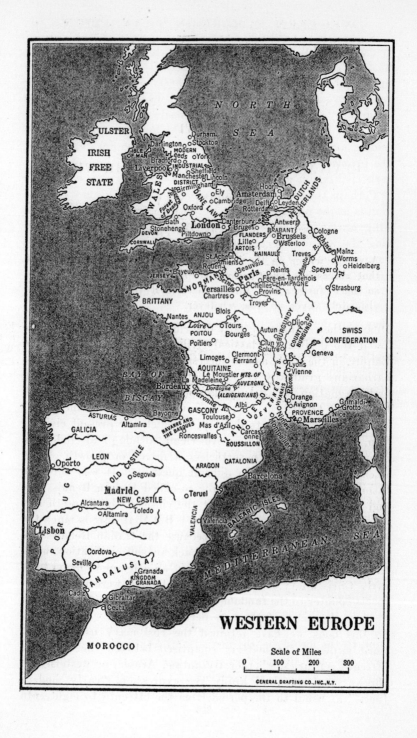

WESTERN EUROPE

Scale of Miles

0   100   200   300

GENERAL DRAFTING CO., INC., N.Y.

centuries. But I hope to convince the reader that modern western civilization really began in the middle of the middle ages, and on the other hand that western civilization has altered more since the eighteenth century than before it. In other words, one might make a plausible argument for a new period of history to include from the middle of the so-called middle ages to the eighteenth century. But for the present the problem is to find that time in the middle ages when western civilization may be said to have made its new start.

Perhaps the best date for the first stirring of this new civilization is in the tenth century, after the Northmen, Saracens, and Magyars had ceased to vex western Europe. Soon after that time the western world of Latin Christendom may be said to have permanently assumed the offensive and begun to expand. In the tenth century various dukes and counts and bishops were erecting castles, albeit as yet of wood rather than stone, for defense. That is, they were taking their stand. Furthermore, they were developing feudal states and relationships out of the wreckage of the Frankish empire of Charlemagne. In other words, they were beginning at the bottom to rebuild society. In the tenth century come our earliest recorded medieval instances of peasants attempting to escape from serfdom. In other words, ambition and freedom began to stir even the lowest classes and common people. When Alfred the Great died in the first year of the tenth century, he left England uniting in one kingdom against the Danes and Anglo-Saxon culture reviving. A decade later the Northmen on the continental side of the Channel were assigned Normandy, where they settled down and developed a high type of civilization for those times. In 955 the Saxon, Otto, defeated the Hungarians at the Lechfeld; in 962 he was crowned emperor at Rome. In 987 the Capetian dynasty began to reign in the north of France. Town life was reviving in northern Italy; Venice cleared the Adriatic of pirates and received privileges at Constantinople at the close of the tenth century; a few years later in 1015 Genoa and Pisa expelled the Saracens from Sardinia. It is true that in Lombardy architecture is said to have sunk to the lowest depths in the tenth century. Schools, too, were few and far between. But perhaps this was just because that was the very period of the growth of the towns, whose struggles for independence from their bishops may have

Perhaps Began in the Tenth Century

halted culture for a time until the first raw and disruptive period had passed. The foundation about 910 of the monastery of Cluny in Burgundy with complete independence from feudal or royal or episcopal—except papal—control heralded the rise of a more highly educated clergy, and the independence of intellectual and spiritual leaders from local or worldly domination or interference.

Tenth Century Culture

Writers were not numerous as yet in the tenth century; the Latin poets generally continued the empty rhetoric of the preceding period. Nevertheless the dramas of the nun Hrosvita are the first extant in Latin since those of Seneca in the first century. Widukind and Liutprand now wrote the history of their own peoples or times in a much more animated and intelligent manner than the annals of the earlier Carolingian period. Arabic words and influence are already evident in a western manuscript of the tenth century. Gerbert, who visited the Spanish peninsula, wrote mathematical works, and became acquainted with the new Hindu-Arabic numerals except zero, ended his career as pope Sylvester II (999–1003). Earlier in his busy life he wrote to a correspondent, "I am eagerly collecting a library; and as formerly at Rome and elsewhere in Italy, so likewise in Germany and Belgium, I have obtained copyists and manuscripts with a mass of money and the help of friends in those parts. Permit me to beg of you also to promote this end. We will append at the end of this letter a list of those writers we wish copied." Meanwhile the modern European languages were evolving. Notker Labeo (c. 950–1022), a monk of St. Gall, translated works of Aristotle, Boethius, and Martianus Capella from Latin into German, as Alfred had translated Boethius, Orosius, and Gregory into Anglo-Saxon. We obtain some idea of the transition from colloquial Latin to the Romance languages by comparing the Strasburg oath of 842 with the *Song of Roland* (*Chanson de Roland*) of the early twelfth century. This feudal French epic in assonanced decasyllabic lines was accompanied by other folk epics, which lie back of our own modern civilization just as the Homeric poems preceded the culture of classical Greece: *Beowulf* in alliterative Anglo-Saxon verse in a manuscript of about 1000 A. D. but composed no one knows how long before, and the German *Nibelungenlied*, which was not written down until about 1200. The Benedictine monk, Guido of Arezzo (c. 995–

CARCASSONNE

The medieval fortifications, dating chiefly from the 12th-13th centuries, were restored by Viollet-le-Duc in the 19th century.

Left, peasant warming himself at a fire in February, from the portal of Amiens Cathedral; right, armed knight and horse taking a fall, from a miserere in the choir stalls, Lincoln.

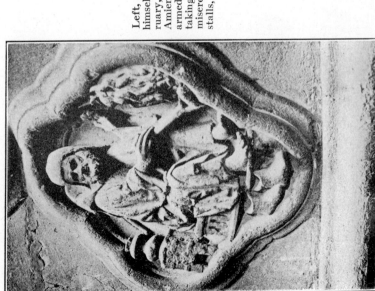

1050), invented the method of staff-notation which is still employed in music. We do not know as much as we should like of the tenth century; the progress, especially in culture, becomes more manifest in the eleventh and twelfth centuries, but while the list of its forward tendencies just given is perhaps more suggestive than overwhelming, it is to be further noted that it was not accompanied by the set-backs and disasters which we should have to mingle with the names and achievements of any previous century since the decline of Rome and the invasions of the barbarians.

We may therefore restrict the expression, Dark Ages, which once was erroneously applied to the entire medieval period (i. e. c. 400–1500), merely to the early part of it. Even it is perhaps dark more in the sense that we lack information concerning much civilization during it than that we are sure it was an age of ignorance and backwardness. Indeed, it must be recognized that even the centuries from the fifth to the tenth contributed not a little to the formation of the civilization of the following period; only these seeds often did not come to harvest until later. We shall now turn back to consider them. *The "Dark Ages"*

The new culture combined Latin and northern characteristics, resulting from the fusion of Latinized Roman provincials and invading northern races. The Latin language and the Christian church long served as unifying forces, quite as important as, if not quite commensurate with, the bonds of international finance and rapid communication which perhaps more enmesh than unite the warring nationalities of our day. But Celtic and Teutonic folklore, legend, custom, and ideals now came to the surface in civilization as they had not done under the Roman Empire. The very conditions of a more northern climate gradually imposed changes on a civilization that had emanated from the Mediterranean. The infusion of new blood and the vigorous physique of the northern invaders aroused again the declining Mediterranean stocks to new accomplishment in civilization. *Latin-Northern Character of Medieval Civilization*

Literary studies still flourished in Gaul as nowhere else in the last century of the declining Roman Empire. Sidonius Apollinaris, bishop of Lyons, continued his literary correspondence with cultured landlords of the senatorial aristocracy despite the annoying presence of greasy, butter-fingered, Burgundian giants with yellow hair at his very elbow. Many of *Contribution Made by Ireland* the rhetoricians of Gaul fled, however, from the invading barbarians to distant Ireland, although it lay outside the limits of the Roman Empire.   St. Patrick was carried off from Britain and sold in Ireland as a slave; he escaped in a trading vessel, but subsequently returned as a missionary.   About the same time tribes of "Scots" from north Ireland crossed the North Channel and founded the kingdom of Dalriada in what was later named after them Scotland, while refugees from Britain, which was being overrun by German tribes, crossed in such numbers to the westernmost peninsula of Gaul that it was named Brittany after them.   Thus there was activity, migration, and navigation in such regions as were left to the Celts.   Ireland as converted by Patrick was largely monastic, yet in these monasteries was preserved rather more Latin culture than now existed elsewhere and even some knowledge of Greek.   In the sixth century missionaries went forth from Ireland to the other British Isles and to the continent, establishing many monasteries among the German tribes which were still pagan or which had relapsed again into that state.   Most early medieval manuscripts which are still extant in continental libraries were the work of these Irish monks or of persons whom they trained.   The extant literature in Old Irish is entirely religious in character.   The manuscripts are noteworthy for their illuminations.   This form of painting was developed from decorative writing with elaborate initial letters.   The ornamentation was borrowed from the patterns of textiles such as plaits, bows, knots, and zigzags, or from those of metal work such as spirals and nail heads; or utilized geometrical figures, crosses, chequers and lattices, and other designs involving animal and human forms.   Composition, sense of color, beauty of design, and play of fancy are all manifest.   Until the Carolingian period of the eighth and ninth centuries the Irish monks constitute the sole original school of illumination in the west. As Coptic Egypt devised new types of art in the Byzantine area, so Irish monasticism made its new contribution to western civilization.   Thus a land which had never been included in the Roman Empire restored something of culture to lands that had once been parts of it, and spread civilization to other regions, like Scotland and Germany, which had lain outside it.

Contribution Made by the Monks   The monks in general, as well as the Celtic monks in particular, must be given credit for preserving and spreading something of civilization during the dark ages. Persons who retire from the world to devote their lives to religious contemplation would not usually contribute much to such an end. But in seeking mountain and forest fastnesses or establishing missions among barbarian peoples, the monks carried something of civilization with them to these new sites. Although they spent most of their time in religious exercises and devotions, rather than in study or in copying manuscripts, nevertheless, aside from a goodly number of bishops, the names of most writers which have reached us from the period are those of monks, while most of the manuscripts that have been preserved from that time were kept in monasteries. Amid the barbarian invasions and economic distress of these centuries monasteries were almost the only institutions which could support a man who devoted his hours to art, study, writing, or thought. Such a man can hardly support a family in our prosperous and enlightened age; at that time he could not support himself, but the monastery could support him. The monks won the esteem of the outside world; their holy peaceful life awed even the blood-stained barbarian warriors; they harmed no one; they befriended the poor; their monasteries were convenient stopping places for travelers—even for royalty. Therefore they received many gifts and legacies, and often came to own extensive lands. Their food and clothing were very simple; their common mode of life was inexpensive; their direction by a single head or abbot under rules of strict obedience was intelligent and efficient, and likely to result in better agriculture and industry than was just then found elsewhere. In short, while some monasteries were mismanaged, others were the most business-like institutions of their time, and, in the decay of town life, were even among the chief centers of population. Their successful organization was in considerable measure due to the spread of the Benedictine Rule, which was composed in 529 at Monte Cassino in Italy by St. Benedict of Nursia and was gradually adopted throughout the west, although the Celtic monks long retained their own Rules. The Benedictine Rule was a sensible set of regulations for the control of a monastic community, and, while breathing the spirit of religious devotion, did not encourage the excessive asceticism and individual self-mortification which had often characterized both the Christian and Buddhist orient.

Contribution
Made by
the Papacy

During the early middle ages the authority of the pope, or bishop of Rome, kept increasing in the west. The distant Irish monks and British clergy were for a time cut off from relations with Rome and developed different customs, but later they gradually returned to papal control. The spread of the Benedictine Rule owed much to the support of Pope Gregory the Great (590–604), who also sent missionaries to the Anglo-Saxons in England, increased the papal patrimony or lands in Italy, exerted much political influence there, and developed the authority of the pope over other bishops. By virtue of his writings he ranks as one of the four great Latin church fathers. In the eighth century the papal missionary, Boniface (Winfrith was his original Anglo-Saxon name) completed the conversion of various German tribes east of the Rhine which had been initiated by the Irish monks, reformed the Frankish churches, received the submission of their bishops to Rome, and instituted a new dynasty, the Carolingian, among the Franks by crowning in 752 Pepin, son of that Charles Martel who in 732 had checked the Mohammedans between Poitiers and Tours. The Franks then aided the pope against the king of the Lombards, who had conquered Ravenna from the Byzantine Empire and was threatening Rome. Pepin and his successor, Charles the Great or Charlemagne, donated certain districts in Italy to the papacy, and these formed the foundation of the later Papal States there. In 774 Charlemagne made himself king of the Lombards; in 800 the alliance of papacy and Franks was further cemented by the coronation of Charlemagne as emperor at Rome.

Contribution
Made by
the Franks

The Franks were not much more than rude warriors, and it is dubious if their dominance was of much service to civilization. However, they saved western Christendom from the Asiatic nomads in the persons of the Avars to the east and from the Arabs who invaded Gaul from Spain. And they supported orthodox papal Christianity. Charlemagne conquered the Saxons on the continent and brought them into the Christian fold. Although he killed a great many in the process, those surviving contributed not a little to subsequent civilization, as the names of Otto and Widukind in the tenth century have already shown. Charlemagne was an energetic, efficient ruler who tried to improve the organization of his government and the administration of the laws, and to secure a better educated clergy. There was some culture at his court, although he himself could not write, and under his successors. Then his empire disintegrated, and the attacks of the Northmen did not spare even the monasteries.

But when the Northmen had been converted, the last conflict between the northern Teutonic peoples and Latin Christianity was over, and until the time of Luther the two worked together in the upbuilding of civilization. The Northmen were a vigorous sea-faring people of stalwart physique who appear to have aroused western Christendom from a state of agricultural lethargy and economic isolation into which the earlier invaders and their victims had alike gradually settled down. But we must not think of them as too poverty-stricken, since for a time they seem to have had gold with which to buy off the Northmen. There had been an increase in the amount of precious metals from mines in the eighth century in the regions which we now call Alsace, Bohemia, and Hungary. The Northmen established ports; they traded with Russia, the Byzantine Empire, and the Mohammedan world, and learned something by that contact. They explored northern waters beyond the Arctic Circle to the North Cape and White Sea, and went west across the Atlantic to Iceland, Greenland, Labrador, and "Vinland"—wherever that may have been. Thus a new world of the north, with which the Greeks and Romans had had little or nothing to do, became an integral part of Christian Europe and added its contribution to the formation of a new civilization. The Northmen were also great rulers of other peoples. Besides their principalities in Russia and the kingdom of Southern Italy and Sicily may be mentioned the Norman conquest of England in 1066 by William, duke of Normandy. Not all the Northmen were rulers. The mass of them reinforced the Nordic, Teutonic strain in the population of the British Isles, Gaul, and Italy, and the trait of individual liberty. Indeed, while the first, cruel invaders from Scandinavia were largely pirates, outlaws, and adventurers, they were followed in the later ninth century by more peaceful settlers who wished to escape the tyranny of chieftains at home who were developing into the kings of Denmark, Sweden, and Norway.

There had been tendencies towards feudalism in the declining Roman Empire and again among the Franks before the Carolingian dynasty. In the course of the ninth century

Contribution Made by the Northmen

Contribution Made by the Feudal Lords

Charlemagne's empire broke up into a number of small feudal states, or perhaps it is more accurate to say that there were thousands of petty lords contending for power. There was poetic justice in this outcome. Charlemagne's successors had quarreled over the division of his territories among themselves and had failed to give protection against the Northmen and other invaders. The localities therefore turned to their dukes or counts or bishops or other local magnates, who often defended them stoutly. Charlemagne had really tried to do too much for those times; he had tried to be king of the Lombards as well as of the Franks; he had taken their native duke away from the Bavarians. Even in those times it was possible by careful action and good fortune to unite under the rule of one king a not too large area that possessed natural boundaries and a certain geographical and racial unity, such as England, Norway, Sweden, or Denmark. It was not possible for one ruler to hold together and govern with success regions both east and west of the Rhine and both north and south of the Alps. Charlemagne and Otto might make the experiment; their successors could not maintain their position; the real power remained in the hands of the feudal lords. A good deal has been said against these feudal lords; they have been called cruel, oppressive, bellicose, uneducated, plundering, blasphemous bullies. But there is something to be said for them, too. If they weren't born fighters, they were certainly trained fighters; and what is more, they did their own fighting, unlike modern kings, diplomats, premiers, representatives of the people, financiers, and owners of newspapers who force or arouse others to do their fighting for them. Those knights furthermore gave fighting most of whatever glamour it has had since. And they were builders, as their castles show. No doubt building a castle was as great a burden on the people of a feudal state as building five million dollar battleships is on the people of a modern national state. But it is an equally good indication of enterprise and civilization; and it certainly lasted longer than a battleship does, and didn't shoot off natural resources into thin air as naval guns do. We think a battleship superior because it can blow a castle into smithereens, but the castle was a work of defense, not an engine of destruction, although it might shelter robbers. The region about the famous fortress of Carcassonne enjoyed unbroken peace under its count for about three hundred years from the time of Charlemagne to the accession of the House of Barcelona in 1067. No modern nation has enjoyed such a long interval from war. Perhaps in other ways the work of those feudal lords has proved more enduring and conserving than ours will. At any rate they possessed energy, they made the people work, and the ruins of their castles still cover western Europe by the hundreds. Some of them were cruel and blasphemous; yet when Pope Urban II preached the First Crusade in 1095, three hundred thousand men denied themselves and took up their cross, and the main strength of the host was in its knights and feudal lords.

We have seen that for several centuries after the decline of Roman civilization in the west commerce was in Byzantine hands, and that architecture and other works of art were Byzantine in style and origin. During this same period Byzantine medical writers and Greek theologians were translated into Latin, and Arabic influence in learned works becomes apparent in the Latin west as early, as we have said, as the tenth century. In Spain and Sicily there was ample opportunity for westerners to profit by Arabic accomplishment. Such influence, and the translation of works from Greek and Arabic into Latin, grew apace in the eleventh, twelfth, and thirteenth centuries. But the west put its own mark on what it borrowed. It made omissions and additions in the writings; it took what interested it and would serve its purpose. *Byzantine and Arabic Influence*

The importance of the Christian church at this period has already been repeatedly suggested. Bishops and monks were as essential to that time as capital and labor are to our economic civilization. In the game of chess the bishop ranks as a major piece along with king and queen, castle and knight; the bishop's church is the cathedral of the diocese; only the town that has a cathedral ranks as a city. Bishops were among the chief patrons of learning as well as of ecclesiastical art; they were so prominent that their successions and terms of office form one of our surest methods of dating in the medieval period; they were great local potentates and landholders, and often the right-hand men of kings. Moreover, divided as western Europe became into small feudal states and lordships, the ideal persisted of one united "City of God" and Christian community. Pilgrims and clergy passed freely across Alps, *The Medieval Church and the Ideal of One Christian Community*

Pyrenees, and sea.   In the eleventh century, if not before, the church struggled to mitigate the evils of feudal warfare and to introduce a Truce of God over week-ends and at other holy seasons.   The popes even aimed at a world-state under their supremacy.   Such efforts were to prove none too successful. But through penance the clergy regulated the morals of the barbarians.   The ecclesiastical courts, which dealt with questions of birth, baptism, legitimacy, marriage, divorce, oaths, contracts, wills, and usury, probably settled more lawsuits than did the feudal courts.   The magnificent response made to the pope's appeal for a crusade showed that the ideal of a Christian community was a living one among feudal nobility and common people as well as clergy.

BIBLIOGRAPHY

Bede, *Ecclesiastical History of England,* translated by A. M. Sellar, 1912.

Burr, G. L.   "The Year 1000," in *American Historical Review, VI* (1900) 429–439.

Drane, A. T.   *Christian Schools and Scholars,* 1881.

Joly, H.   *The Psychology of the Saints,* translated by G. Tyrell, 1898.

Joyce, P. W.   *Old Celtic Romances,* 1861; *Social History of Ancient Ireland,* 1914; *Story of Ancient Irish Civilization,* 1907.

Judson, W. H.   "Hrosvitha of Gandersheim," in *English Historical Review,* III (1888) 431-457.

Ker, W. P.   *The Dark Ages,* 1904 (Periods of European Literature).

Latouche, R.   *Histoire du Comté du Maine pendant le X⁰ et le XI⁰ siècle,* 1910.

Marsfield, M. F.   *Castles and Chateaux of Old Burgundy,* 1909.

Orton, C. W. Previté.   *Early History of House of Savoy,* 1912.

Plummer, C.   *Life and Times of Alfred the Great,* 1902.

Poux, (Joseph) *La Cité de Carcassonne. . . . Les origines . . . ,* 1922; the result of painstaking original research on the spot.

Poupardin, R.   *La royaume de Bourgogne (888–1038),* 1907.

Smith, L. M.   *Early History of the Monastery of Cluny,* 1921.

Thompson, A. H.   *Military Architecture in England during the Middle Ages,* 1912; a scientific treatment.

Zimmer, H.   *Celtic Church in Britain and Ireland,* 1912; *Irish Element in Medieval Culture,* 1913.

Works on the Northmen will he found listed at the close of Chapter XVIII.

CHAPTER XXVI

THE EUROPEAN LAND SYSTEM AND ARISTOCRACY

I will swynk and sweat and sow for us both,
And labor for love of you all of my lifetime,
In covenant that you keep Holy Church and me
Safe from wasters and wicked men who would destroy us.
— *Words of Piers the Ploughman to the Knight*

THE peasant is the basis of the European land system. The majority of persons engaged in cultivating the soil in the various countries of Europe today have had ancestors similarly engaged for many past generations. Thus there is, and has been, a peasant class with a distinct point-of-view and limitations, yet with a skill in husbandry acquired through long experience and perhaps with a physique superior to that of city dwellers. Old superstitions and folklore, old words and customs persist longer among the peasants. During the decline of Roman civilization and the barbarian invasions, this class had sunk lower in the social scale until the majority of the cultivators of the soil were unfree. *(The Peasant)*

In the middle ages the peasants quite generally lived in village communities and cultivated their fields more or less in common. Whether this was because they had been grouped under a single lord ever since their ancestors were slaves on a Roman villa, or because they had once been equal freemen in a German community or Celtic clan or Slavic *mir*, is disputed. At any rate they ploughed the arable land together and kept their cattle in a common pasture. Boston Common and similar commons in other old towns of the United States are a relic of this institution. The peasants also fed their swine or collected their fuel from the same woods. While they thus worked together, they ploughed a certain amount of arable land for the exclusive use of their master and pastured his cattle and pigs along with their own. They shared a common fund of agricultural knowledge and profited or suffered from one another's improvements or mistakes. *(Common Fields and Cultivation)*

307

Open Fields,
Scattered
Holdings,
Fallow

The arable land lay in great expanses, devoted one to spring wheat, one to winter wheat, another to rye, and so on. These were known as open fields because no fences separated the holdings of the individual peasants within these fields, although the common pasture might be fenced in to keep the cattle from straying. Although the peasants ploughed and perhaps harvested together, each had his own strip of land stretching long and narrow across the great ploughed expanse. From the produce of his own strip he must support his family as well as pay his further dues to his lord. His strip was marked off from those of other peasants on either side of it, not by a fence, but merely by omitting a furrow between them, or by dyking up a balk or ridge which would serve as a path to reach the strips. Each peasant would normally have a strip in each of the crops then under cultivation; in other words, his holdings were scattered through different open fields. The arable lands were allowed to lie fallow and recover their fertility either every other year or every third year. While some fields were lying fallow, others were of course being cultivated, and the fallow fields were sometimes used as pasture.

Exceptions
to the
Foregoing
Statement

This arrangement was not universal, varying in different localities. Where the soil was poor and the population was too scanty for village communities, there would be isolated, independent farms cultivated by individuals. Where the soil was very fertile, as in the valley of the Garonne, it would be given no rest. In the Garonne valley in the thirteenth century agriculture was already commercialized and modern. Where the population was very dense, the peasants would resort to manuring, irrigation, and more intensive cultivation in order to provide enough sustenance for all. In some regions they already knew how to raise artificial meadows of clover, lucerne, and sainfoin. Vineyards and orchards were often walled. When new regions were opened up for settlement, consolidated individual holdings were often offered by the landlords to attract settlers. Or perhaps this was done because the new settlers came as individuals rather than in communities.

Inheritance
and Divided
Holdings

The rules for inheritance of real property varied for different regions and classes of people, but even the unfree passed on the use of their strips of land to their children, who paid a fine to the master in recognition of his claim. If there were no direct heirs, the land reverted to him.   He also could prevent the daughter of a serf from marrying the tenant of another lord.   Among the peasant class equal division of the father's holdings among the children was often the practice. Hence some holdings became minutely subdivided.

The lord exercised various powers over his peasants according to their degree of freedom or dependence.   His share of the lands, called *demesne* or domain, was tilled by their labor, and they might have to perform other forced labor for him. They further must pay him a part, usually varying in amount according to the amount of land they held, of their crops and young animals; they must pay fees for use of the winepress, flour mill, swineherd, blacksmith, and so forth.   The lord also held a local court which administered the rural economy and settled their disputes.   This court they must attend and serve, but the income from it went to the lord.   Thus our village community was a little world by itself with a lord of the manor, as such a unit of settlement and jurisdiction is commonly called in English, at its head.   A recent road-map of southern England will still be found thickly strewn with green patches bearing the names of manors or of commons.   Because the lord lived in a manor house superior to the huts or thatched cottages of the peasants, the builders of pretentious apartment houses in America have adopted the ridiculous practice of naming them So-and-So Manor, although of late there perhaps has been a certain analogy between the rapid raising of the rent by the landlords of such establishments and the arbitrary exactions of the feudal lords from their serfs.

The Lord of
the Manor

Of serfdom there were varying degrees.   Absolute serfs were little more than agricultural slaves or human beasts of burden who had the additional burden of supporting their families. The villein or *villanus*, that is, man of the villa or manor, commonly held a virgate or yardland of about thirty acres, which was only one-quarter of the hide or holding of the earlier Anglo-Saxon freeman.   Cottagers held very little land, and must have experienced great difficulty in ekeing out a living.   Most tenants on the manor were customary tenants; that is, they had no written deed or title to their land and no definite contract with the lord as to the services and payments which they owed him, but all these matters went accord-

Degrees of
Serfdom and
Types of
Tenure

ing to the custom of the manor.   In contrast to this were the freemen in England with a freehold title to their lands and without personal obligation to a lord.

Emancipa-
tion of the
Peasants
in Certain
Regions
In the twelfth and thirteenth centuries there was a great emancipation movement among the peasantry, especially in what is now France, where they were raised from serfdom. This was usually done in return for a substantial payment, while for the future the peasants still owed various rents and services to their lords, who also maintained a certain superior jurisdiction over them and their land.   But such rents and services were now definitely stipulated and fixed in amount. In some cases groups of peasants formed rural communes entirely independent of any lord.   This remained about the state of affairs down to the French Revolution of 1789, when the last vestiges of feudalism were abolished.   German settlers east of the Elbe also did not pay their lords much more than a money rent.   In fact, there was a general tendency to commute services and payments in kind for money payments. Moreover, from the twelfth century on, the amount of coined money in circulation greatly increased; consequently its purchasing power grew less.   Thus the peasants gained and the lords lost by the change to money payments.   The lords were therefore inclined to increase their demands again, or to encroach upon the common lands.

Feudal
Relations
Between
the Lords
Since the feudalism of this period is known in more detail than that of ancient Egypt, Homeric Greece, Confucian China, or feudal Japan, we have reserved until now a description of the relations existing between the feudal lords.   They held fiefs from one another as overlords, vassals, or sub-vassals, and were distinguished further by such titles as duke, earl, count, viscount, baron, castellan, and knight.   Almost everyone held some land, or other form of fief, from and under someone else as his lord, and then in his turn had one or more vassals holding fiefs from him.   These vassals of his would be in the position of sub-vassals to his lord.   Almost any source of honor or profit might be infeudated, but landed estates and governmental offices and jurisdictions were the most usual forms of fiefs.   The fief was hereditary and passed on to the vassal's oldest son or was divided among his sons, but the lord or original donor retained rights over the fief and the new vassal or vassals.   Each new incumbent of the fief must kneel before

his lord, render homage and pledge fidelity to him, and pay a relief varying in amount according to the size of the fief, in the possession of which he was therewith confirmed. He must thereafter on occasion attend his lord's court, follow him in war, or help him in other ways that had been agreed upon in the first place or were customary and generally understood. He must make presents or payments to his lord on certain occasions such as the knighting of the lord's oldest son or the marriage of his oldest daughter. If there were no direct heirs, or the vassal proved disloyal, the fief reverted, or was forfeited, to the lord who gave it. These customs were analogous to those by which the peasant held of his lord, but the vassal was usually of noble rank like his lord, rendered only honorable service, and was not subject to menial tasks, manual labor, or servile restrictions.

The fief was commonly thought of as noble land involving knight-service; even a king might hold a province as a fief from another king. But between the large estate or considerable office held as a fief by the noble and the small holdings of the peasant came intermediate stages in which ordinary freemen held plots of land, or certain rights and income derived from land, by a sort of feudal relationship midway between the military service of the knight and the economic exploitation of the villein. The whole system became very complicated but was hardly more so than the economic relations between banks, trust companies, corporations, stockholders, bondholders, mortgage companies, insurance companies, and the owners or occupants of office buildings and apartment houses today. The Domesday Survey of 1085 in England and the feudal register of the counts of Champagne for the years 1172–1222 illustrate feudal relations under two different sets of conditions. In England, where a strong king had just given out all the land afresh, there were 1400 tenants-in-chief who held directly from him as their lord, although their lands varied in amount from one or two manors to hundreds of them. They subinfeudated portions of their fiefs to 8000 other lords of the land. The counts of Champagne held the twenty-six different castellanies which comprised their feudal possessions from ten different overlords; namely, the Holy Roman Emperor, the King of France, the duke of Burgundy, two archbishops, four bishops, and an abbot. The counts had in their turn subinfeudated these castellanies to 2017 vassals of their own.

Castles and Armor

The military strength of the feudal lords lay in their knightly training, their heavy armor, their fighting on horseback, and in their castles. The castle is the chief surviving monument of feudalism and of European aristocracy, an impressive symbol of the strong local independence which then prevailed. One of our earliest sources of information concerning feudal life is the so-called Bayeux Tapestry, a long strip of embroidered linen of the later eleventh century setting forth consecutively, somewhat in the style of a moving-picture film, the Norman conquest of England with the previous adventures of Harold and Duke William of Normandy on the continent. Here we see knights in hauberks of interwoven ring mail,—a single garment that reaches only to knee and elbow and can be put on or pulled off over the head, but so heavy that servitors carry it by thrusting a pole through its sleeves and resting the ends of the pole on their shoulders. The helmet is a stiff cone with nose-guard projecting in front and a hood of link mail hanging behind to protect the neck, while the cheeks are left bare. The shields are kite-shaped. The offensive weapons are sword, lance, and battle-ax for the knights, but archers also are shown participating in the battle of Hastings. Harold, while William's guest or captive on the continent, performs the heroic exploit of dragging two Normans from the quicksands, for which he is later "given his arms," or knighted by William on the field of battle. The castles of the continent shown on the tapestry are for the most part wooden erections on earthen mounds, but William built rectangular keeps of stone to hold conquered England. That there is already a certain feudal formality or etiquette, is indicated by the method of surrendering a castle. Its lord from the battlements extends the keys on the tip of his outstretched lance; William, mounted on horseback, receives them on the point of his spear, from which also flutters a pennon.

We cannot here trace all the developments in armor but may note that by the fifteenth century knights were completely encased from top to toe in plate armor. It was not until the seventeenth century that royal artillery really battered down the stone castles, or that they were dismantled, or were transformed entirely into residential palaces. In the same century pikemen still wore armor, and Cromwell's cavalry regiment could appropriately be named "Ironsides" by that dashing cavalier, Prince Rupert. Still later both James II and Marlborough wore armor when their portraits were painted. During all the intervening period various additions and changes had been made in the castles, in the style of their towers, in the comfort of their residential portions. Therefore the different parts of castle ruins today usually represent structures of different centuries. Common characteristics are the selection of as precipitous, impregnable and commanding a site as possible; the surrounding of the castle by a moat as well as a very thick wall; the projection of the upper part of the walls or towers out over the base, and the jutting out of towers to enfilade the wall; the presence of only narrow slits or openings in the outer wall and crenelated parapets or battlements along the roofs; the especial strengthening of the entrance by drawbridge, portcullis, and gate-towers; the provision by postern gates or secret passages for retreat, or for sallies against the foe. But castles are of all shapes, sizes, and arrangements. These remarks apply also to the fortifications of the walled towns of the middle ages.

Lords and vassals met at one another's courts where they entertained one another. From this beginning many subsequent social functions have evolved. Hunting and mock fights were the chief pastimes of the men. In early feudal literature women are seldom mentioned or are roughly treated, but gradually a certain attention to the other sex, as well as defense of Christianity against heathen and Moslems, became recognized as part of the social ideals comprised in the word chivalry. This word comes from *cheval*, the French for horse, and so denotes the life of knights. It was as if all the owners of automobiles should gradually formulate a set of high ideals, a code of honor, and a series of social conventions which would distinguish them. Courtesy, or court manners, also came to be regarded as important. The boy was first trained as a page in the feudal household, and then as a squire on the field of battle, before he was dubbed a knight. *Feudal Society*

The church was a great landholder in the middle ages and has continued to be in some Roman Catholic countries such as Spain. It received many legacies and gifts, and as the succession of bishops and abbots never ceased, such lands never *The Church as a Landlord* reverted to the original donors. The church, however, sub-infeudated a large amount of its lands to feudal lords who might otherwise have taken them without so much as "by your leave." At the time of the Domesday Survey churchmen held about three-tenths of the soil of England. The church further received tithes from the lands of the peasants. The church-men generally were good landlords, and for a time their serfs seem to have been more prosperous and better treated than others. But the churchmen were also conservative and in-clined to cling to their property rights. At the time of the emancipation movement of the twelfth and thirteenth centuries they were sometimes less willing to free their serfs than were other lords, who, however, emancipated more from enlightened self-interest than from humane motives.

Failure of Later Peasant Revolts

After this early emancipation movement had ceased and the democratic trend in the towns, of which our next chapter will treat, had also run its course, the peasants again found their condition becoming unsatisfactory and revolted at various times in various parts of western Europe. The ruling classes suppressed these revolts with vehemence until the French Revo-lution. The destructive pestilence known as the Black Death in 1348 upset the economy both of France and England, who were also then engaged in the wasting Hundred Years War. The French countryside suffered so from this war that in 1358 an uprising occurred known as the Jacquerie from Jacques or Jack, the common name for a peasant. The English Peasants' Revolt of 1381 was caused by the continuance of serfdom and by hostility to the clergy and to parliament, which had tried to keep down the wages of hired laborers and yet had imposed new taxes upon them. In Scandinavia and in central European countries like Poland and Bohemia the peasant cultivators of the soil seem to have fallen more and more under the power of the landed nobility in the later middle ages. The German peasants became especially dissatisfied toward the close of the fifteenth century, when a series of revolts ensued without suc-cess. On the contrary, the peasants were to be reduced to an even worse condition as a result of the devastating Thirty Years War (1618–1648).

Separation of the Peasant from the Soil in England

However badly off the peasants were in other parts of Eu-rope, they at least retained possession of their lands. In England, however, it early became the practice of cottagers,

MEDIEVAL STONE CASTLES

Above, ruins of Landshut on the Moselle; below, the interior of the Donjon, or, residential portion of the castle of the counts of Flanders at Ghent, a Romanesque structure of the 12th century.

TOWN WALLS

Above, Perugia, Porta S. Angelo; below, Rothenburg, portion of the
wall near the Rödertor.

and those who had little land of their own, to work for others
for wages.   The lords cultivated their domain lands largely
in this way.   During the confusion produced by the Black
Death many serfs seem to have run away from their manors;
at any rate there was now a large class of wandering, land-
less agricultural laborers.   The lords, too, seized the opportunity to be rid of their customary tenants, leasing out large
plots of land for such terms as fifty years to middlemen who
cultivated it by hired labor.   They also began to enclose or
fence in what had before been open fields, and to pasture sheep
there.   Even where the open fields remained, the peasants
gradually ceased to cultivate their strips in common.   This
change was under way by the sixteenth century in England.

On the other hand, in France as late as the middle of the
nineteenth century a scholar could write, "A thirteenth century peasant would visit many of our farms without much as-
tonishment."   By a more recent writer we are told that from
1500 to 1850 the peasant constituted the great social problem
of Europe.   The landed aristocracy also persisted in practically all parts of Europe long beyond the limits usually set
for the feudal period.   Even in England where by 1500 the
legal jurisdiction of the lord over the villein had practically
disappeared, the "squirearchy," or country gentry, still formed
the bulk of the ruling class in the eighteenth century.   In
France the *noblesse* retained certain feudal rights until the revolution.   Prussia had its *junkers* into the nineteenth century,
while in Russia the entire medieval land system persisted.   The
soil was cultivated by village communities by the three-field system, with common lands and an occasional redistribution of
the strips of the peasants, who before the abolition of serfdom in 1861 were bound to the soil and must work three days
a week for their lord.

Persistence of the Peasant and the Landed Aristocracy

BIBLIOGRAPHY

Works on castles are listed at the close of the previous chapter.

Belloc, H.   *The Book of the Bayeux Tapestry,* 1914.
Cornish, F. W.   *Chivalry,* 1901.
Curschmann, F.   *Hungersnöte im Mittelalter,* 1900.
Curtler, W. H. R.   *The Enclosure and Redistribution of our Land,* 1921.
Dean, Bashford.   *Handbook of Arms and Armor,* 1915.

Fage, R. *La propriété rurale en Bas-Limousin pendant le moyen âge,* 1917.

Fordham, Montague. *A Short History of English Rural Life,* 1916.

Foulkes, C. *Armor and Weapons,* 1909.

Fustel de Coulanges, *The Origin of Property in Land,* 1891.

Gonner, E. C. K. *Common Land and Enclosure,* 1912.

Gray, H. L. *English Field Systems,* 1915.

Hasbach, *English Agricultural Laborer,* 1908.

Hewitt, J. *Ancient Armor and Weapons in Europe,* 1855–1860, 3 vols.

Hone, N. J. *The Manor and Manorial Records,* 1906.

Latouche, R. *La vie en Bas-Quercy du quatorzième au dix-huitième siècle,* Toulouse, 1923; an interesting study of a secluded and backward rural district.

Meller, W. C. *A Knight's Life in the Days of Chivalry,* 1924.

Moore, M. F. *A Classified List of Works relating to English Manorial and Agrarian History—to the year 1660,* 1912.

Peake, Harold. *The English Village,* 1921.

Prothero, *English Farming, Past and Present,* 1912.

Reymont, L. *The Peasants,* 1924, 4 vols.; a novel describing the lives of Polish peasants, which won the Nobel prize in 1924.

Seebohm, F. *The English Village Community,* 4th ed., 1890.

Seignobos, C. *The Feudal Regime,* translated by E. W. Dow, 1902.

Slater, G. *English Peasantry and the Enclosure of Common Fields,* 1907.

Tappan, E. M. *In Feudal Times,* 1913.

Usher, A. P. *The History of the Grain Trade in France, 1400–1710,* 1913.

Vinogradoff, *Growth of the Manor,* 1905.

CHAPTER XXVII

THE REVIVAL OF TOWN LIFE

The immensely larger scale of modern city-growth calls for a purely sociological and statistical treatment, whilst in the medieval city of five thousand one can take in the wood without losing sight of the trees. The superior concreteness of medieval communities and the wealth of accessible material ought to make the study of them one of the finest instruments of historical training as soon as the rapidly accumulating facts begin to be constructively handled by the scientific imagination.—*G. Unwin*

WHEN, where, how, and why did town life revive in western Christian Europe after the decline of the Roman Empire with its civilization, and after the invasion or infiltration of Asiatic nomads, Germans, and Slavs, none of whom had been accustomed to town life? We have noted that the Franks and Anglo-Saxons came to lead a rather stagnant, inland, agricultural life, but that the Northmen founded ports and stimulated trade, and that apparently by the tenth century town life was reviving in northern Italy. Previously the chief trading towns had been in southern Italy and were more connected with the Byzantine Empire than they were representative of developing western civilization. There had been many flourishing towns in Spain under Mohammedan rule as early as the eighth and ninth centuries. But war and confusion followed, and these towns were not absorbed into Christian Europe until considerably later, by which time they had somewhat declined or had been outdistanced by towns in other lands. Nevertheless, the rise of chartered towns in the Christian kingdoms of the north of the Spanish peninsula such as Leon and Castile, began in the tenth century. On the whole in western Christian Europe the towns in northern Italy, or Lombardy and Tuscany, were the first to become noticeable, the richest, the most populous, and the most independent politically. Such of course is no longer the case, but then the Mediterranean Sea

When and Where?

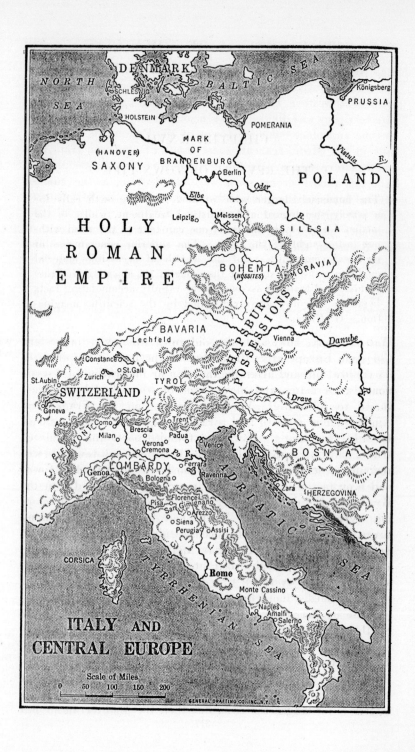

ITALY AND CENTRAL EUROPE

was the chief waterway, while Italy was the best situated of the three southern European peninsulas for overland trade with northwestern Europe. In Lombardy practically the entire territory was divided between some thirty-six towns. Next in time and place came the towns of the Provençals and Catalans in the Mediterranean coast lands of southern Gaul and northeastern Spain. In Gaul further north, the people and land of almost every town were divided under the rule of several lords in the eleventh century, but the twelfth century was marked by the growth of union and by more or less independence on the part of the townsmen. In Germany east of the Rhine, in the Baltic region and Scandinavia, in Holland north of the Rhine, and in England it was only from the thirteenth century that there was notable growth of towns.

Because of the lack of records for the early period of town growth it is impossible to give a satisfactory detailed explanation of why and how this occurred. Some towns occupied the sites of Roman towns, but it is often questionable if town life had gone on continuously in the meantime. The towns of Lombardy corresponded to the Roman municipalities more closely than did those of Gaul, where only about one town out of six occupied a Roman site. In England there was even less connection between the towns of the Roman and medieval periods. Increasing population, rise of native industries and of a native merchant class, security gained by building walls and town fortifications at a time when central government and police protection were lacking, and the tendency of communities to form independent local governments of their own to supply this lack, were other causes, explanations, accompaniments, and incidents or modes of the growth of towns. They developed from over-populous or crowded manors, about castles or monasteries, where fairs were held, at churches whither many pilgrims resorted, at fords, or harbors, or other convenient places. From the confusion that followed the disintegration of Charlemagne's empire and the inroads of Northmen, Magyars, and Saracens arose not only the castles of the feudal lords, but the walls of the medieval towns. **Why and How?**

There was a close connection between the rise of towns and the emancipation of peasants in the twelfth and thirteenth centuries. Serfs might now run away to towns unless their masters offered them better terms, while free labor in the towns **Relation of the Rise of Towns to the Emancipation of the Peasants**

began to show its economic superiority to servile labor elsewhere. Looking at the matter another way, if lords were ready to improve the social status of the peasantry, still more would they be ready to grant privileges and charters to the traders and artisans of the growing towns. Finally, when towns began to become independent governments, various little villages of peasants imitated them and became rural communes owning no lord.

Rights of Townsmen

Not all towns, by any means, were independent or self-governing. Some were granted only a certain share in their government and were still under the rule of a lord, or, if the town was at all large, different lords controlled different sections, or quarters, of it. Thus the local count might govern the *bourg*, while the bishop was supreme in the *cité*. Even if the town did not govern itself, the townsmen were apt to be in a superior position to the peasantry. Not only did they suffer less from war and devastation, they were generally freer from exploitation by a lord. At first he might grant freedom and privileges of travel only to merchants and might force the artisans to work for him on his premises a part of their time. Gradually they too became free socially and economically, and in many cases acquired political power. Before we go on to speak of this, however, let us note the general economic relation of the medieval town to the outside world.

Relation to the Outside World

Although not quite so isolated a unit and little world by itself as the manor or purely agricultural community and large estate, the medieval town was to a large extent self-centred. It depended upon the immediate vicinity for its food-supply; hence in most cases it did not have a large population. Communication was slow and poor; political and economic connection with other towns or with distant regions was slight. Most of the household articles, clothing, and furniture required by the inhabitants were made by hand in the town itself and were sold directly by the maker to the consumer. Goods from other towns were taxed as only goods from foreign countries are taxed today. These were much the same sort of conditions as still prevail in the orient and as had prevailed in all towns up to this time, whether in Greece, Babylonia, or China, except for a few great cities like Athens, Rome, and Constantinople to which cereals had been brought by ships from a distance.

Wars and Leagues

Like the city states of ancient Greece, the independent Italian towns fought with one another, or formed the Lombard League to resist the Holy Roman Emperor as the Peloponnesian League had resisted the Persian kings.   Once the danger was over, they both fell to fighting among themselves again. The towns north of the Alps were less aggressive and more inclined each to mind its own business.   In medieval Germany, however, the lack of other strong government led the towns of the Rhine to league together for a time, while towns and rural cantons of Switzerland banded together in a confederation that grew into a permanent state.   In northern Germany the cities formed a Hanseatic League which through the fourteenth and fifteenth centuries monopolized the trade of the Baltic and North Seas, holding the economic fate of Denmark, Norway, and Sweden in the hollow of its hand.

Share of Towns in Representative Assemblies

Where there was a strong king or feudal lord, the towns were willing to send representatives to the assemblies which developed in most of the feudal states of western Europe, such as England and Denmark, Artois and Normandy, Brittany and Burgundy, Aragon and Catalonia.   These representative assemblies, which granted taxes and agreed to changes in the laws, were an outgrowth of the feudal court of the lord and his vassals.   They commonly consisted of three "estates,"—clergy, nobility, and towns.   Sometimes, however, there were variations, as in the four estates of the Cortes of Aragon where greater and lesser nobles formed separate estates, or the two houses of parliament in England where the upper clergy and greater nobles joined in the House of Lords, while the knights of the shire went with the burgesses in the House of Commons. Once or twice simple free peasants as well as townsmen sent representatives to the French Estates-General.   Later, as the power of kings and the size of kingdoms increased, these representative assemblies, with the signal exception of the English parliament, were disregarded, and either disappeared or lost their influence until the French Revolution and subsequent democratic revolutions in other European countries, which then revived representative government.   But it first originated from the feudal court, the church council and synods of the clergy, and the corporate personalities of the medieval communes.

When the townsmen, acting as a body, took the government

of their town into their own hands, they called themselves a commune. In some towns, like those of Lombardy, the local nobility took a prominent part in the first formation of the communes, in which the lower classes had little share. In other towns, like those of northern France, the commune was rather a popular revolt against the feudal nobility. Once established, some town governments, like Florence and Siena, developed in the direction of democracy, admitting the poorer working classes to citizenship and to office, while others, like Venice, hardened into aristocracies and oligarchies. In general more and more persons were admitted to a share in the government until the thirteenth or fourteenth century; thereafter the control passed to the richer citizens. Although the medieval towns (to some extent) copied one another, there was the greatest variety in their constitutions. In the twelfth century boards of consuls headed the communes both in northern Italy and Mediterranean France. In the thirteenth century as a result of the party strife, family quarrels, and street fights which kept the Lombard communes in continual turmoil, a single official called a podestà, was introduced to maintain order impartially between the factions. He was elected annually, but could not be an inhabitant of the city. Several cities of Provence introduced the same office. From the thirteenth century on, ambitious individuals in the Italian cities tended to seize this power and to hold it permanently, so that many despotisms were established. In the north an elected mayor or burgomaster usually was the chief official. That he was sometimes personally called to account, is shown by a tablet in the old town of Provins, famed for its medieval fairs, which still marks the spot where, in the year 1279, the citizens massacred their mayor. There were also various boards, councils, and other town offices. "In our old communes," writes Maugis of these towns of northern France, "democracy has never been a political reality, but it was in large measure a social reality, if by that one understands, not utopian equality, but the system best fitted to assure each human being the highest degree of self-respect, of material security, and of moral dignity."

Each town had its own laws or local customs by which it was governed and by which the inhabitants settled their private disputes. The following are a few of the 552 laws of Teruel in Aragon in 1176 A. D. Law 113 provides that an official shall inspect measures every week. Law 282 deals with the offense of spitting or throwing water out of a window on a man. In fourteenth century Florence, it may be remarked in this connection, it was forbidden to keep flower-pots on window ledges but not to empty slops out of the window, and in fifteenth century Paris, when Louis XI was drenched in this manner on his way to early mass by a student who arose before it was light to study his lessons, instead of being enraged at the incident he made the industrious scholar a chaplain. Law 284 penalizes anyone who throws stones at another's door. Law 290 regulates the use of the public oven for baking bread. Law 291 concerning the public bath, provides that men shall have the use of it on Tuesday, Thursday, and Saturday; women, on Monday and Wednesday; Mohammedans and Jews, on Friday; while on Sunday, in reverence of the Lord's resurrection, the bath shall not be heated. No one is to pay more than one obol for bath service; servants and children bathe free. The bath-keeper is penalized if he does not supply plenty of water and other requisites, and there are further penalties for theft of the bathing utensils, or property of the bathers. German towns in the fourteenth and fifteenth centuries had four, eight, eleven, thirteen, fifteen, seventeen, or twenty-nine public baths each, while that jolly old sot, King Wenzel, had the borders of his German Bible adorned with pictures of bath-tubs and bathing-girls.

Law 294 concerning mills is seven pages long, regulating such matters as water rights in detail, while laws 296 and 297 have each four pages on gardens and vineyards respectively. Burning at the stake is the penalty for such crimes as adultery, sorcery, and sodomy. This cruel punishment was all too common at that period; Dante had to flee from Florence to avoid it. Law 402 prescribes a money fine for "anyone who hits a man with an egg or bottle or cucumber." Law 420 legislates against evil-smelling latrines. Law 425 regulates lawsuits between Christians and Jews. Law 436 gives directions concerning the standard or banner of the town council. Law 453 concerning the sale of beasts provides that the buyer may return the beast within three days if he finds it not to be in good condition. Law 459 provides that hired laborers shall work until the bells ring for vespers in the parish churches. In hunting, law 463 awards the animal or bird to the person who started it, no matter who may have killed it.   Law 465, returning to the subject of hired laborers, provides that if the employer does not pay them promptly at the close of each day, the judge shall fine him double the amount.   If a workman, or serf, strikes his master, he loses his pay and right hand; a nurse or chambermaid who strikes her mistress is similarly treated.   If the lord strikes his servant, he must pay a fine; even if the hired laborer works badly or dishonestly, the employer may not strike him but only discharge him.

Various laws follow concerning shepherds, cowherds, goatherds, inn-keepers, and traveling salesmen.   Contractors for buildings must complete the work or refund double what they have received to expend upon it.   False work, if detected in time, must be done over, or, if damage results from it, the builder must restore double.   Law 518 fixes the price for shoeing a horse, mule, or ass.   Regulations follow concerning goldsmiths and silversmiths, shoemakers, tailors, weavers, dyers, fullers, wine-merchants, wool-sellers, potters, butchers, and fishmongers.   Law 536 penalizes those who deny or curse the saints, or who spit insultingly at the sky.   Hanging is the penalty for one who dishonors the king, and anyone who sells goods at a higher price than usual when the king comes to town is also punished.

Industrial and Social Life of the Gilds

Until the eighteenth century practically every manufactured article was still made by hand and quite commonly was sold directly by the maker to the consumer.   Persons working at the same trade usually lived in the same street and in many towns were organized into gilds for mutual protection.   To enter a gild one became an apprentice as a boy; learned the trade in the house of a master-workman; then, after a few years of working for wages as a journeyman, and after producing a masterpiece, set up as a master-workman.   These three stages were similar to those of page, squire, and knight in the feudal system, or of undergraduate, bachelor of arts, and master of arts in the university.   Indeed, the Italian name for craft gilds was *arti;* the Latin name, *universitates.*   They were also spoken of as mysteries because they kept their processes of manufacture secret.   Usually one was not allowed to work at the trade in question unless he belonged to its gild.   This monopoly, however, did not lead the gild to attempt a great profit, as the ideal of a "just price" prevailed.   On the other hand, the gilds maintained high standards of quality. The gild often supplied its members with raw materials at cost, and commonly regulated hours and conditions of labor. It was more likely to forbid night labor than to agitate for a short working day, since most of its members wished to work long hours in order to make and sell more goods. However, counting Sundays and other holidays, there were eighty or more days a year on which no work was done, and sometimes the artisans quit work early in the afternoon on the day before the holiday. The gilds almost always secured a share in the town government; they also were little governments in themselves, with officials, statutes, treasury, and a court for the settlement of disputes. The gilds gave mystery plays, held banquets on the day of their patron saint, aided members' families when in distress, attended their baptisms, marriages, and funerals, burned candles or paid for masses to be said for their souls after death. A master-workman usually could keep but one or two apprentices at a time, which ensured individual attention for them and a good chance to become master-workmen in time themselves. From the fourteenth century there was a tendency for the gilds to become oligarchical and hereditary, it being easier for the son of a master-workman to become a master-workman than for the ordinary journeyman to do so.

The mining gilds of Saxony and Bohemia have been praised for their care of the health and welfare of the miners. In England the right of mining iron in the Forest of Dean was restricted to the corporation of free miners with itinerant forges who were resident in that forest. The lead miners of Alston Moor, Derbyshire, and the Mendips, who had already been long established by the thirteenth century, were granted various privileges by the king such as the right to prospect anywhere, to take what timber they needed, and to hold proprietary rights in their mines, although the king took his share. They held courts every three weeks, while the tin mines or Stannaries of Cornwall and Devon held parliaments of their own as well as courts. In Spain a curious voluntary organization was the Mesta, a great corporation composed of migratory owners of merino sheep who led their flocks back and forth over a network of wide sheep tracks from southern to northern pasturage from 1273 to 1836, when the Mesta was abolished

Some Special Gilds

and dissolved. The sheep, however, still feed in both the northern and southern pastures, but are now transported in three-decker railway cars.

Passing of the Gild System

English gilds and self-governing towns began to show serious decline in the sixteenth and seventeenth centuries, partly because the crown confiscated all their property which had been used for religious purposes, partly because of the increase of individualism and capitalism. The central government, however, in the Statute of Apprentices of 1563, attempted a nation-wide regulation of industry modelled on that of the local gilds. The industrial revolution of the eighteenth century introduced the factory system in England, but on the continent the gilds did not cease in France and the Low Countries until the French Revolution, and not until the middle of the nineteenth century in Spain, Portugal, Italy, Germany, and Austria. The system of apprenticeship still persists in some skilled trades.

Chinese Gilds

It is noteworthy that the Chinese gilds of today are very similar to those of medieval Europe and probably have been so for many centuries. They manage their own affairs in democratic fashion, elect their own officials, and discourage their members from resorting to the ordinary law courts and magistrates. All industries, except agriculture, are organized in gilds. They regulate commercial matters, such as the rate of interest and of exchange, without consulting the government. Persons who practice a craft without belonging to the gild have to obey it none the less. They pay tolls to it and seem to exist on suffrance. The Chinese gilds limit the number of apprentices, and have some connection with a temple, where they burn candles and meet if they have no gild hall, just as medieval gilds met in the chapter-house of the cathedral before they built their gild halls. The Chinese gildsmen also have dinners, contribute to one another's funerals, and give theatrical representations. Sometimes the journeymen strike for higher wages—usually with success. At the opening of the twentieth century four-fifths of the clothing of the lower classes in China was still supplied by domestic spinning and the weaving of cotton on hand-looms, while almost every province made its own supply of paper, bricks, and earthenware. Artistic and industrial processes are sometimes the monopolies of certain families who keep them secret.

We have already incidentally mentioned some of the chief

medieval economic pursuits, or articles of trade and manufacture, but may add a few others.   Marseilles was noted for
its leather, trading in Morocco leather from North Africa.
The herring fishing in the Baltic and North Seas was very important when everyone went without meat on Friday.   The
combined effect of changes in ocean currents which had brought
the herrings, and of the Protestant Revolt in northern Europe,
was one of the chief causes of the decline of the Hanseatic
League.   Whales became much better known in the middle ages
than in antiquity, and were hunted in the Bay of Biscay by
the Basques, Asturians, and the men of Bayonne.   There are
many Spanish words in the whaler's vocabulary.   Gascony
supplied the British Isles with most of their wine.   The crafts
of Paris about 1300, included such specialized occupations as
farriers, cutlers, locksmiths, makers of knife-handles, copper-
smiths, beaters of brass, of tin, other workers in tin, wire-
drawers, makers of copper lamps, seal makers, different men
making nails and rivets, pins, buckles, clasps; tailors, hatters,
glovemakers, beltmakers, shoemakers, slipper-makers, cobblers,
stocking-knitters, hosiers, button-makers, sheathmakers, comb-
manufacturers, carpenters, masons, plasterers, mortar-makers,
potters, porringer-makers, glass-makers, beadmakers, jewelers,
goldsmiths, workers in gold thread and gold leaf, workers in
wax, toymakers, tanners, furriers, manufacturers of various
textiles, and many other artisans.

Before the thirteenth century money was scarce, credit
hardly existed, capital as an economic force was insignificant.
There was plenty of landed property, otherwise labor was the
chief force.   There was no war between labor and capital; the
gilds blended employers and employees in one harmonious whole.
It was felt by the church and the Christian conscience at this
time, that it was not right to take another's money unless in
return for goods or labor of the same value.   If one took all
the trouble and risk to import goods from abroad, certainly
one was entitled to sell them for more than one paid for them
in order to recompense oneself for one's time and labor.   But
to demand payment of interest on a loan in addition to repay-
ment of the principal was condemned as receiving more than
had been given.   For a time, therefore, Jews, who charged
high rates of interest, were the chief money-lenders.   They
also gave letters of credit and bills of exchange payable by

Jews in other countries or towns.   With the thirteenth century, however, many Christian townsmen began to have surplus capital which they did not care either to invest in land or give to the church or to the poor.   In Flanders cloth-merchants bought up wool in England and dyes in France or from Italy with their surplus capital, and then employed whole gilds of weavers and other master-workmen to produce the cloth for them.   Later similar clothiers developed in England.   They bought wool when it was cheap—often before it had grown on the sheep, later gave it out to poor people to spin for low wages, then to others to weave, pocketing most of the intermediate profits themselves.   In Italy Venice launched a public debt as early as 1171, showing that there were many citizens with capital to lend to the state, and Lombards and Tuscans established banking firms which did not charge the borrower interest or usury—Oh, no!—they simply charged for the labor of bringing the money to him or of changing their foreign coins into his native currency, or charged damages if he did not repay them in time for them to oblige another customer by a similar Christian loan.   These firms also collected the papal income from foreign lands, keeping what they could get above an agreed amount, or speculated in English wool.

Fairs, Trade Routes, and Law Merchant   As yet there was, however, little dealing in futurities; the actual goods were commonly bought on the spot.   Fairs were held at certain seasons, either in towns or the centers of agricultural districts.   Perhaps the most noted were the fairs of Champagne at Troyes and Provins, where Italians met the Flemish merchants.   Trade-routes were, for a time less by sea than by river and pilgrim-routes, as the vessels were small and the tolls charged by feudal lords along the rivers were preferable to the ravages of pirates and storms on the main.   But with the fourteenth century the Italian cities began to send fleets around the Spanish peninsula, while the ships of the Hanseatic League from the Baltic met them in Flanders.   The Venetian, Marco Polo, who himself spent many years in China in the thirteenth century, tells us that the merchants of the rival city of Genoa had begun to navigate the Caspian Sea, carrying ships across from the Black Sea.   Already in the twelfth century the Jewish traveler, Benjamin of Tudela, tells us that twenty-eight different Christian states, such as Genoa, Pisa, Amalfi, Tuscany, Lombardy, Sicily, Apulia, Roussillon, Catalonia, Aragon,

Navarre, Saxony, Flanders, Hainault, Poitou, Anjou, Burgundy, and Provence, had each at Alexandria its own walled enclosure, market-place, warehouses, church, baths, taverns, and bakery.   At fairs and in business relations between merchants of different cities the Law Merchant usually was followed.   It was a set of customs worked out by the Mediterranean cities, which has had much influence on modern admiralty law, and such matters as agency, brokerage, bookkeeping, trademarks and the protection of a firm's name.

A medieval town was usually not too large to be taken in at a glance as one approached it from a distance, especially as its situation on a hill or slope, and its encircling wall, topped by towers, helped to set it off clearly.   Medieval writers with considerable justice described their cities as very beautiful, although they seem to us also somewhat quaint.   They may be studied not only in what still stands of them today but in various representations of them in illuminated manuscripts and Italian paintings, or their topography may be worked out from old plans and tax-lists.   The chief public buildings were the churches, belfry tower and town hall, and gild houses.   The dwellings often rose in tiers, perhaps surmounted by the massive bulk of the cathedral and its lofty spires.   The streets, as in the ancient city, were intended more for pedestrians than for vehicles.   They were often narrow and crooked, or degenerated into mere flights of steps, or passed under arches and houses.   Projecting upper stories, public fountains, signboards and wayside shrines further complicated the crowded scene. The layout of the streets was determined by that of the gates to which the chief streets ran, and by the site, or by the fact that formerly independent settlements had grown together into one large town.   In new towns which were opened up to settlers the streets were laid out more regularly.   But medieval men never sacrificed convenience for regularity; they knew better than to have two streets cross in the center of a public square; in their market-places the streets entered at the corners, and traffic proceeded around the outside of the square so that the center was undisturbed for meetings, markets, and so forth. Street cleaning and lighting, sanitation and sewerage, would seem unsatisfactory to us, but soon attained about as good a state as they were to attain until the last century.   And when we read of the filthy condition of medieval streets, let us remem-

Appearance of the Medieval Town

ber that this was limited to organic matter largely; that they did not have the debris of cheap, factory-made articles strewn about, as we have torn, dirty newspapers, battered tin cans, and scrap iron; that there was nothing so ugly as railroad tracks running through their towns; that chemical and mineral refuse from factories and iron-works did not pollute earth, air, and drinking-water; and that they sometimes legislated against the smoke nuisance, although they used coal on a much smaller scale than we. Therefore, while their streets may have smelled worse, they probably looked much better than ours. A smiling countryside was within a short walk from any part of town, and was visible from the windows of some of the houses.

Houses and Furniture

The artisan's shop commonly occupied the ground-floor front of his house, with perhaps a courtyard and kitchen behind, and living rooms above. The tendency was to have each house fit the individuality of its occupant, to have a few good-sized rooms rather than a number of tiny ones, and to place windows so as to admit the maximum of light rather than to look well from the outside, although they usually achieved that end too. It is surprising how many houses have been preserved from as early even as the twelfth and thirteenth centuries. Naturally they do not look nearly so attractive now as they did when new. Paris in the thirteenth century had "houses several stories high with beautiful plaster fronts." Furniture was apparently scanty but substantial. A four-poster bed curtained for privacy, since it was often placed in the living room, and to keep out drafts, an oaken chest at its foot for clothing, a table, either permanent or ready to be set up on trestles, some forms or benches, tapestries, curtains, and other hangings to cover these and the walls, a chair or two, and some stools or cushions, were the commonest articles. In Cologne, the wills of the burghers show us that "gaily colored cushions, all embroidered with the arms of the house . . . seem to have existed in dozens. Clothes and chattels pass on and on in indestructible succession from generation to generation." The floor was generally strewn with rushes. But there might be figures sculptured in the stone or wood of the home within or without.

Daily Life: Food and Manners

Medieval men were great eaters and deep drinkers. They seasoned the food with hot spices and washed it down with copious draughts of beer, ale, or wine. Coffee was not introduced, even at Venice, until the close of the sixteenth

Left, towers of rival noble families at Bologna erected about 1109–1110 A. D.; right, the town hall of Oudenarde, erected in 1525–1529.

MEDIEVAL STREETS
Left, the Shambles, York; right, Rue du Bourg, Chartres.

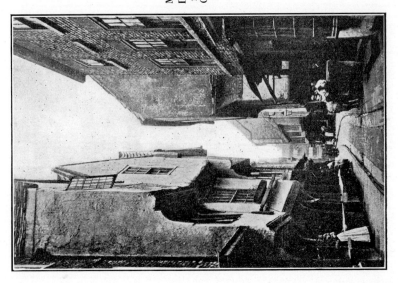

century; tea came into use in England only in the later seventeenth century. This is a thirteenth century description of a dinner party:

First the food is prepared; at the same time the guests are assembled; chairs and also stools are required; in the dining room tables are set, and the table furnishings are arranged and adorned. The guests are placed with the host at the head table, but they do not sit down at table before the hands of the guests are washed. Next the host's children, and then the servants are grouped together at table. Spoons, knives, and salt cellars are first placed upon the table. Loaves of bread and cups of wine are presently added. There follow many and varied courses; the butlers and waiters serve each person diligently. The guests joyfully engage in vying with one another in pledging toasts; they are cheered with viols and citharas; now the wines and now the courses are renewed; they divide and share with one another the dishes which happen to be opposite them; finally the fruit and dessert are brought in. When dinner is finished, the table furnishings and remains of food are carried away, and the tables are set aside. Hands are again washed and wiped; thanks are returned to God and to the host; for the sake of good cheer the cups go round again and again. When these features of the dinner are over, the guests either are offered couches for some rest, or are allowed to return home.

With this may be contrasted the picture in the fourteenth century poem, *The Vision of Piers the Ploughman*, of

. . . prisoners in pits and poor folk in cottages,
Charged with children and the landlord's rent.
What they save up by spinning, they spend in house rent,
And on milk and meal to make porridge with
To satisfy their children who cry for food.
They themselves, too, suffer much hunger
And woe in winter time, waking in the night
To rise up out of bed and rock the cradle,
To card and comb, to patch and wash,
To rub and reel, and to peel rushes;
So that it is painful to read, or to show in rhyme,
The woe of these women who dwell in cottages,
And of many other men who suffer much woe,
Going hungry and thirsty in order to dress respectably;
And who are ashamed to beg, and will not let it be known
What they need from their neighbors at noon and at evening.

To such people, the poet goes on to say, bread and small beer are a banquet, cold meat and cold fish taste as sweet as roast venison, and on Fridays and fasting days a few mussels are a feast for them.   Calendars of the months in manuscripts and the sculptures on the cathedrals show us, however, that to the peasant "January was the month of feasts and rest," when "Janus seated in person at the family table opened the medieval year with mirth and jollity."   The preceding description of a dinner party showed us that the good old custom still prevailed of the servants eating in hall with their masters.   But the lot of the handmaid was hard, as the following account by the same author shows:

She is assigned to the more laborious and demeaning tasks, she is fed with coarser food, she is clad in meaner clothing, she is oppressed by the yoke of servitude, . . . is afflicted with scoldings, is bruised by rods and beatings, is oppressed by varied and conflicting vexations and anxieties, is scarcely permitted to breathe amid her miseries.

Apparently in France, England, and Germany striking a servant was not forbidden as it was at Teruel in Aragon.   Such "slaveys" may still be found in Dickens' novels depicting nineteenth century conditions.   A medieval medical author tells us that serfs and handmaids are especially subject to enuresis, since they go about with bare feet and insufficient clothing and become thoroughly chilled.   One of the characters in *The Vision of Piers the Ploughman* "crept into a cabin for cold of his nails."

The medieval Italians were more moderate in food and drink than the northerners and more refined in manners.   Already in the twelfth century the German bishop, Otto of Freising, described the Lombards as possessing "something of Roman culture and civilization," and "the elegance and refinement of Latin speech and manners."   A writer about 1300 A. D. thought that by that time the Italians had made a great further advance since the time of Otto.   "In those days," he writes, "the manners of the Italians were rude.   A man and his wife ate off the same plate.   There were no wooden-handled knives, nor more than one or two drinking-cups in a house.   Candles of wax or tallow were unknown; a servant held a torch during supper.   The clothes of men were of unlined leather; scarcely any gold or silver was seen on their dress." Forks were not mentioned in the foregoing account of the dinner party, but that supercilious son of Gascony, Piers Gaveston, foster-brother and playmate of Edward II of England, ate pears with a fork in the early fourteenth century. His example was not widely followed: both Queen Elizabeth in the sixteenth century and that very model of majesty, Louis Quatorze, in the seventeenth century, disdained to employ forks. Such indoor games as chess and playing cards were introduced in the middle ages, the former from Persia and India. In their face-cards and pieces they still reflect the feudal court or society, the Indian elephant and chariot as chessmen being transformed into the bishop or castle, while the horseman or knight remained the same.

Medieval philanthropy and charity were profuse and kindly, but, we are apt to think, were unsystematically organized and unscientifically administered compared to our present arrangements. Thus in fourteenth century England the insane are represented as wandering witless and without money, but with a good will, through many wide countries. "And so we ought to receive and help them when they come." On the other hand, a modern French writer speaks with pride of the glorious past of charitable institutions in Burgundy, and finds that practically all the hospitals now existent in Burgundy have come down from the middle ages. "Our benevolent societies take the place of almsgiving societies; our mutualities replace their brotherhoods; our departmental chest for aid to sufferers from fire succeeds, after a long interval, to the chest of the Provincial Estates; our free medical attendance had its forerunners in the fifteenth century. We have met (in the middle ages) the placing in the country of foundlings, orphan asylums, maternity hospitals, public kitchens, rural banks, advances on crops. . . ." In German Cologne the "middle-class burghers seem to have been imbued with the idea that convents, soup-kitchens, pilgrims' rest-houses, lepers, the sick and infirm, lunatics, and even poor girls in need of marriage portions were their peculiar care." *Medieval Philanthropy*

We may well conclude this chapter on economic and popular life in the middle ages by a list of practical inventions made at that time which have rendered life more comfortable or labor more efficient, or have aided art and letters. The first known mention of windmills occurs in a Norman charter of 1105. *A List of Medieval Inventions*

Navigation was helped by the invention of the rudder and the mariner's compass.   Home life was improved by the chimney which keeps the heat in and lets the smoke out, by window glass which lets the light in and keeps the wind and dust out, and by plumbing, or soldering underground pipes with lead instead of tin.   Vision was enlarged by eye-glasses and magnifying lenses which were ultimately to be developed into the telescope and microscope.   Warfare was altered by gunpowder and cannon.   Industry profited by the improved apparatus of the alchemists, the new dyes and chemicals which they discovered, and by the use of coal.   By 1300 practically all the English coal-fields known today were being worked to some extent.   The fine arts were affected by the flying buttress, the ribbed vault, stained glass, oil painting (clearly described by Theophilus about 1100), and engraving (about 1440).   The invention of mechanical clocks for the first time enabled man to mark the passage of time with fair accuracy, while their clock-work may be regarded as the forerunner of most subsequent machinery. Mirrors of glass were another medieval invention.   Printing with movable types, invented in the fifth century, greatly stimulated literature and learning, but has come in our day to be somewhat debased to commercial and popular uses.   We have already suggested the steady evolution that went on through the period in such things as armor and castles.

BIBLIOGRAPHY

Abram, Miss A. *English Life and Manners in the Middle Ages,* 1913.

Boissonade, P. *Le travail dans l'Europe chrétienne au moyen âge,* 1921.

Blok, P. *History of the People of the Netherlands,* 1898, I, 215–51.

Britten, F. J. *Old Clocks and Watches and Their Makers,* 1899; 5th ed., much enlarged, 1922.

Brown, H. F. *Venice,* 1895.

Butler, W. F. *The Lombard Communes,* 1906; their political history and constitutional development.

Coulton, G. C. *Social Life in Britain from the Norman Conquest to the Reformation,* 1918; an excellent selection from the original sources.

Courteault, H. *Le Bourg-Saint-Andéol,* 1909.

Davidsohn, R. *Geschichte von Florenz,* Bd. 4, in two parts, 1922–1925; the town government, gilds, and economic life.

Davis, H. W. C. *Medieval England,* a new edition of Barnard's *Companion to English History,* 1924; beautifully illustrated.

Doren, A. *Das Florentiner Zunftwesen vom 14–16 Jahrhundert,* 1908.

Espinas, G. *La vie urbaine de Douai au moyen-âge,* 1913, 4 vols.

Fidel de Moragas i Rodes, *L'antigua Universitat de Valls*, 1914.

Garnier, J. *Chartes de communes et d'affranchissements en Bourgogne*, 1918, 994 pp.

Giry and Réville. *Emancipation of Medieval Towns*, English translation by Bates and Titsworth, 1907.

Green, Alice S. *Town Life in the Fifteenth Century*, 1894, 2 vols.

Hessel, A. *Geschichte der Stadt Bologna von 1116 bis 1280*, 1910.

Heyd, W. *Histoire du commerce du Levant au moyen-âge*, 1923, 2 vols.; a standard work.

Heywood, Wm. *A History of Pisa*, 1921.

Jacobs, J. *The Jews of Angevin England*, 1893.

Jusserand, J. J. *English Wayfaring Life in the Middle Ages*, 1890.

King, W. *Chronicles of Three Free Cities*, 1914.

Klein, J. *The Mesta*, 1920.

Koebner, R. *Die Anfänge des Gemeinwesens der Stadt Köln*, 1922, xxiv, 606 pp.

Kuske, Bruno. *Quellen z. Gesch. d. Kölner Handels u. Verkehrs. im Mittelalter*, vols. 1 and 3, 1923; vol. 2 previously.

MacGibbon, D. *Architecture of Provence and the Riviera*, 1888; illustrated and well written, good for remains of small towns and castles.

Mackay, D. L. *Les hôpitaux et la charité à Paris au XIII⁰ siècle*, 1923.

Marez, M. G. des *La première étape de la formation corporative*, 1921.

Martin-Saint-Léon, E. *Histoire des corporations de métiers*, 3rd ed., 1922.

Navarro, F. A. *Al Fuero de Teruel*, 1905; statutes of a Spanish town.

Palumbo, M. *I comuni meridionali*, 1910.

Pirenne, Henri. *Medieval Cities; their origins and the revival of trade*, 1925; a brief book of 249 short pages.

Poëte, Marcel. *Une vie de cité. Paris de sa naissance à nos jours. I. La jeunesse. Des origines aux temps modernes*, 1924.

Power, Eileen. *Medieval People*, 1924. Six individuals are portrayed as types of medieval life.

Rogers, Thorold. *Six Centuries of Work and Wages*, 1890; a much cited authority.

Salzmann, L. F. *English Industries of the Middle Ages*, 1913; new ed., 1924; full of interesting specific facts.

Sapori, *Le compagnie dei Bardi e dei Peruzzi in Inghilterra nei secoli XIII e XIV*, 1923.

Schaube, Adolf. *Handelsgeschichte der romanischen Völker des Mittelmeergebiets*, 1906.

Schevill, F. *Siena; the story of a medieval commune*, 1909.

Sedgwick, H. D. *Italy in the Thirteenth Century*, 1912, 2 vols.

Sorbelli, A. *Il comune rurale dell' Appennino emiliano* (14th–15th centuries), 1910.

Villari, *First Two Centuries of Florentine History*, 1901, chap. 6.

CHAPTER XXVIII

LEARNING, EDUCATION, AND LITERATURE TO THE INVENTION OF PRINTING

Mens humilis, studium quaerendi, vita quieta,
Scrutinium tacitum, paupertas, terra aliena,
Haec reserare docent multis obscura legendo.
—Bernard Silvester

Medieval
Latin

ALTHOUGH the Roman Empire and classical civilization had declined, Latin long remained the language of the church and of all educated persons. Grammar meant the study of the Latin language and literature; a grammar school was where these were studied. The popular idioms were for a long time incapable of expressing abstract thought. The vernacular literatures, except in so far as they reflected folk legends or the popular life of the time, derived most of their plots, information, and ideas from works in Latin. "The finest and most profound books of the middle ages were not, and could not be, translated." In the course of the Roman Empire most of the population of its western half had come to speak a colloquial form of Latin from which the various Romance languages have developed. The book Latin was therefore not difficult for such persons to learn and to write. While it remained much more like the classical Latin in word formation than did the popular speech, it constantly enriched its vocabulary, and in word order and method of thought became more modern in character, so that it is usually easier for us to translate than the ancient style. Medieval Latin can therefore scarcely be called a dead language; it was rather a living, universal language such as scholars vainly sigh for today; and many new technical words were invented to supply the scientific, philosophical, and theological defects of the ancient Latin.

Rhythmic
Prose and
Latin
Poetry

Sermons and theological works from the time of the early church father, Tertullian, were much given to "a highly ingenious prose rhetoric, based mainly on antithesis and balance in phrasing, the use of alliteration, rime, and punning,"—

336

medieval writers were very fond of puns—"and of various other formal devices derived ultimately from the Greek rhetoric of Gorgias and his successors." Moreover, instruction in letter-writing (*ars dictandi*) was given in medieval schools "in a more or less formal or ornamental style." As early as the eleventh century the documents emanating from the papal chancery became distinguished by rules of balance and cadence based on accent rather than meter. Through the twelfth century this regularity of rhythm steadily improved, and the "beauty and delicate euphony of the sentences thus produced" was imitated in the schools and in the chanceries of other courts. In the case of many medieval Latin works a full translation would seem dry and tedious to a modern reader, but the men of science are usually clear and direct in their utterance. "Naturally Christian Latin poems reflect classic phrase and pagan commonplace and reminiscence"; poetry has continued these features to some extent even to this day. But rhyme was introduced; great hymns were written such as *Dies Irae, Stabat Mater,* and some ascribed to St. Bernard; on the other hand, there were satires on the clergy and rollicking drinking and love songs. Already in the twelfth century the religious dramas *Antichrist* and *Adam,* the one in Latin verse, the other in Anglo-Norman, are remarkable for their stage-directions, lively dialogue, and character portrayal. On the whole, however, medieval Latin prose surpassed medieval Latin poetry.

Except for the ancient papyri most manuscripts are of the medieval period. Even the ancient classics have for the most part been preserved through this medium. Many works written during the middle ages still remain in manuscript and have not yet been printed or even studied. It is very likely that when they have been more thoroughly examined and interpreted we shall know more of medieval civilization. Medieval manuscripts were generally written on parchment or sheepskin instead of papyrus until the fourteenth and fifteenth centuries, when paper came into use. In the early medieval centuries the change was made from capital letters, such as are found in Greek and Latin inscriptions, to small letters, but in the best chirography each letter was written separately much as if we should "print by hand." We cannot here go into the various styles of handwriting and shapes of letters which are of aid in dating and placing the manuscript. The behest,

Medieval Manuscripts

"Mind your p's and q's," very likely dates back to the medieval abbreviations when a *p* might stand for *pro, prae, per, or pri-*, and a *q* for *quis, qui, quae,* or *quid,* according as it had a line or dots above, below, or through it.   Such abbreviations came to be employed a great deal, either as a result of note-taking by students, or to save the time of copyists, or to economize the rather expensive parchment.   This last was the especial reason for crowding the letters close together in the long works of the thirteenth century.   Perhaps the handwriting of the twelfth century is best to read; in the fourteenth and fifteenth centuries one finds more scrawling and illegible flourishes. Many manuscripts consist of several, or even as many as sixty or seventy, different treatises bound together, which may be the works of quite different authors on different subjects.   Often a new work begins immediately after an old one ends without even commencing a new page, and although there may be an illuminated initial or rubric, these also occur at the opening of new chapters and so are no sure sign of the beginning of a new treatise.   Often, too, the maker of the manuscript has copied only such parts of the works in question as were of interest or use to him.   Or he may have inserted new ideas and observations of his own in a work by another author.   These might first be in the form of marginal notes or glosses, but the next copyist might embody them in the work.   For such reasons it is necessary to consult many manuscripts in order to determine the correct and full form of a text and to avoid the errors, or interpolations, of individual copyists.   It is essential to know the opening and closing words, or *Incipit* and *Explicit,* of a treatise in order to identify it, since many manuscripts give no titles or name of author.   On the other hand, some manuscripts are not only written beautifully and with great accuracy, but are supplied with full tables of contents, title, preface, and other means of identification.   In general, works in medieval Latin are well arranged; often they are systematic presentations of a subject intended either as a textbook or as lectures for students.

Popular
Education
in the
Middle
Ages

The common notion that in the middle ages education was only for a favored few, and that the clergy were the only learned class, is quite erroneous except perhaps for the early medieval centuries.   Around the year 800 Charlemagne had difficulty in securing even an educated clergy.   But by the first half of the eleventh century we find a poet reproaching well-to-do Germans for not sending their sons to school, pointing out that in Italy "all the youth are bade to sweat in schools," and that only the Germans think it needless to educate a person unless he is going to enter the clergy. The Lateran Council of 1102 provided for free education of the children of poor parents in cathedral schools. By the thirteenth century towns, as well as monasteries and cathedrals, had their schools. Villani, writing of Florence in the fourteenth century, gives the number of boys and girls learning to read as from 8000 to 10,000. There were 1000 to 1200 boys in six schools learning to use the abacus and arithmetic, apparently with a view to entering business life. In four other high schools were some 600 pupils studying grammar and logic. In England many grammar schools date from before the Norman conquest (1066), and Leach estimates that before the Protestant Reformation there was a grammar school for every 5625 people, whereas in 1864 the ratio was only 1 to 23,750. In medieval France there were separate elementary schools for boys and girls both in town and country. Boys entering the mechanical arts would go from the elementary schools to apprenticeship in the gilds, which served as a technical training. Those entering the liberal arts would go on to grammar school and university and become school-teachers themselves or doctors, lawyers, and clergymen.

It is true that Latin learning and education were rather closely associated with the church, which offered a satisfactory sort of position and mode of life for one who wished to devote himself to thought, reading, and writing. Owing to the importance of the church courts and canon law, a large percentage of lawyers were then numbered as clergy; a great many more persons were enrolled in monasteries, or religious orders; canons, chantry priests, and other holders of ecclesiastical benefices swelled the number; while at many universities the student body were classed as clerics. Thus, even if it were true that the clergy were the only learned class, we should have to remember that the clergy were much more numerous then than now. Great scholars and scientists became bishops or even popes. One who studied a great deal was not expected to pray so much; prayer might be a little preferred as free from all possible admixture of worldly pride and ambition, but

Relation of the Church to Learning

study was also esteemed as a good work, excellent in the sight
of the Lord.   There was some feeling, and even legislation,
against the practice of medicine outside their monastery by
monks vowed to celibacy, yet every monastery had its medical
books and medical chest, and the friar orders of the thirteenth
century gave much attention to the sick.   Astronomy, which
dealt with the heavens, was regarded as closely related to theology, which dealt with God.   Medieval authors commonly open
or close their works with devout phrases, but sometimes these
are well-nigh the only indication of a relation between learning
and religion.

**Theology
and Logic**

Theology, which had especially occupied the attention of
patristic literature, remained the supreme subject for a clergyman to study, but should—it was felt—be founded on a careful survey of other fields.   At first, it is true, theology did not
concern itself with much more than the Bible and writings of
the fathers.   Yet one must not only study grammar in order
to read these authorities, one must study logic in order to draw
correct conclusions from them.   Syllogisms and disputations
therefore became the order of the day.   Abelard (1079–1142)
in his *Sic et Non* showed that there were many theological
questions still open to discussion by listing conflicting views
of the fathers on some 158 points.   Hugh of St. Victor (1096–
1141) in his *Didascalicon* told the medieval student what to
read and how to read it, classifying the various arts and
sciences, mechanical and liberal, theoretical or practical.
Abelard and Hugh have been called the founders of scholasticism, of which more anon.

**History and
Other Social
Sciences**

The writing of history at this period showed a tendency to
interpret the past as the working out of the divine plan in the
world, and to begin with Adam protoplasm and end with a
full description of the last judgment.   Not all histories were
of this type, however, especially when men of the Italian towns
began to write them.   The attitude of most medieval historians was uncritical and credulous.   Social science was
written largely from an ecclesiastical, or at least Christian,
standpoint.   In political philosophy and discussion theocracy,
church and state, empire and papacy bulked large, or counsels
of perfection were administered in a fatherly way to "Christian princes" until the time of Machiavelli (1469–1527).   The
advice of the pseudo-Aristotle to Alexander, however, which in

thirteenth century Latin translation became perhaps the most popular book of the middle ages except the Bible, is rather an exception. Economic theory was largely ruled by such ideals as those of a just price and no usury.

More curiosity seems to have existed as to theological and natural than as to social problems. Abelard said that "the master-key to knowledge" was "to keep asking questions"; an English contemporary of his with a similar name, Adelard of Bath, wrote *Questions about Nature.* The acute questions put in medieval books are perhaps their best feature; the attempted answers to them are often less satisfactory. For the answers, men turned either to past written authorities, many of whom were now translated from Greek or Arabic into Latin, or to experience, or attempted to reason out the matter by the exercise of logic. But personal experimentation was another method that was not neglected, especially in the field of natural science. The interest in science cannot be called purely secular, as knowledge of nature was supposed to lead on to knowledge of the Creator, and natural science to be a useful preliminary to theology. However, there was interest in this world and curiosity concerning natural phenomena for their own sake. Moreover, such studies as medicine and Roman law, while often pursued by clergy, were primarily secular.

Constant Questioning

Science proceeded to a large extent along the lines already indicated in the ancient period by Aristotle, Pliny, Galen, and Ptolemy, but it made further advances in these directions. Superstition was still confused with science as in the past, but such superstition assumed a more scientific guise, and we hear a good deal of "natural magic." Astrology, too, became more natural and less fatalistic. That inferiors, or objects upon our earth, which was thought of as a sphere occupying the lowest, or central, point of the universe, were ruled by the superior bodies was generally accepted as a fundamental law of nature. Past authorities such as Aristotle, Galen, and Ptolemy were sometimes criticized or corrected, and there was an increasing tendency to rely on observation and experimental method in scientific investigation. Such experimentation, however, often aimed at magical or marvelous results. But our list of inventions has shown that solid results of practical value were also achieved; there was furthermore progress in pure science.

Scientific Progress

The advances of the Arabic world in arithmetic and algebra

Mathematics
and
Astronomy

were appropriated and continued. Leonard of Pisa, early in the thirteenth century, explained the Hindu-Arabic numerals to the Latin world more fully than Gerbert had done. Roger Bacon spoke of ten or twenty years being spent in the study of mathematics by the men of his day. Thomas Bradwardine, who wrote his *Speculative Geometry* in 1344, became archbishop of Canterbury five years later. Another Englishman of the fourteenth century, Richard Suisseth, called the Calculator, was ranked among the ten "rarest wits that ever appeared" by Scaliger and Cardan in the sixteenth century. In fourteenth century France Nicholas Oresme devised the use of co-ordinates and fractional exponents, in addition to translating works of Aristotle into French and writing on economic questions. Reform of the calendar was urged; indeed it was already considered by the popes. Astronomical tables were freshly calculated which corrected those of Ptolemy and subsequent Arabic astronomers.

Progress
Beyond the
Aristotelian
Physics

In physics there was increased knowledge of such matters as vacuums, syphoning, perspective and optics. We have already mentioned mirrors, lenses, and clock-work run by weights: all very important inventions for the future of scientific apparatus. Jordanus Nemorarius in the thirteenth century wrote an important work on weights and falling bodies. Men did not rest content with Aristotle's physical theories. His account of the rainbow was modified by Albertus Magnus, but it remained for Dietrich von Freiberg about 1304 to give the "first satisfactory account of the rainbow in Latin." Aristotle's incorrect explanation of the motion of projectiles was refuted at the University of Paris, where the science of modern dynamics may be said to have been engendered before 1350.

Geography

We have already suggested the increased geographical knowledge of this period in mentioning the voyages of the Northmen and travels of Marco Polo. The Latin world also absorbed much of the knowledge of distant lands possessed by Arabic writers who had traversed the vast extent of Mohammedan territory. It was appropriate that a descendant of the Northmen, Roger, ruler of Sicily, should have set an Arabic geographer, Edrisi, to work upon a book which, when completed in 1154, was superior to any previous work. Roger had said to him, "I want a description of the earth made after direct observation, not after books." The incident is a fine illustration of the fusion, in medieval civilization, of Nordic and Mediterranean, Teutonic and oriental elements, and of new discovery. This new discovery went on after Edrisi. Not until the thirteenth century was it known that cinnamon comes from Ceylon where it is native; the Greeks and Romans thought it came from Arabia and East Africa which do not produce it; the Arabs and Persians called it "Chinese bark," probably because they received it from Chinese traders. Italian sailors in their *portolani* charted the Mediterranean and its coasts with an accuracy unapproached before, giving us our first true maps in the modern sense of the word. The Madeiras, Canaries, even the Azores, seven hundred and fifty miles out to sea, had been visited and charted before 1351, when the Laurentian *portolano* also shows something approaching the true shape of Africa.

About 1305 Pietro dei Crescenzi (c. 1233–1320) wrote his *Liber cultus ruris* which has won him the title of "the father of modern agriculture." After serving as a judge at Bologna and as podestà in many Italian cities he retired in 1299 to his country estate where he composed his book, which remained the standard volume on the subject until 1600. By that time it had run through some sixty Latin editions and had been translated into many modern languages. *Agriculture*

The pursuit of alchemy, or the attempt to transmute metals, both encouraged and retarded the development of chemistry. Alchemy, however, became more scientific in its methods than ever before, while the majority of writers on nature held fairly sensible views as to the possibility of transmuting other metals into gold. Collections of "colors," "waters," and other recipes, industrial or medical or magical, were numerous and sometimes embodied new chemicals. In the thirteenth century Roger Bacon defined alchemy as the science "of the generation of things from the elements, and of all inanimate things, such as the elements and humours, single and compound, ordinary stones, gems, marbles, gold and other metals, sulphurs, salts, dyes and colors, oils, bitumen, and countless other things." The recipes of the alchemists for coloring metals were practicable; in fact, about the same methods are still employed. *Alchemy*

Medicine was much studied in the middle ages at such universities as Salerno, Montpellier, Padua, and many works were written: accounts of drugs in alphabetical order, treatments of *Medicine* disease in top to toe order from baldness and headache to chilblains and gout, works on the pulse and urine analysis, bathing and diet, anatomy and surgery. Amid much discussion based on scientific theory which has since been abandoned, and much repetition of diagnosis and remedies hallowed by the authority of the past, these works contain shrewd observations based on personal experience and conjectures prophetic of later discoveries. Peter of Abano, for instance, three centuries before Harvey's discovery of the circulation of the blood, was asking the leading question, "Are the arteries dilated when the heart is and constricted also when it is?" In the practice of medicine there were municipal physicians, cleanly hospitals, clinical instruction, greater knowledge of contagious diseases and more measures to prevent infection than in antiquity. Henry of Mondeville in the early fourteenth century was a pioneer of antiseptic surgery; dissections of human cadavers are provided for in the statutes of Italian Universities of the same century; in the fifteenth century two Sicilian surgeons were celebrated for their skill in plastic facial surgery, repairing mutilated noses, lips, and ears.

Rise of Universities   It is important to realize the enthusiasm for learning of every sort that prevailed in the eleventh, twelfth, and thirteenth centuries: the fame of teachers in towns of Gaul north of the Alps, the vogue of the medical translations and adaptations from Greek and Arabic of Constantinus Africanus (c. 1015–1087), the rush of students of the revived Roman law to Bologna, the crowds that thronged the lecture room of Abelard, the wanderings of intellectual pilgrims like Adelard of Bath from England to Greek and Arabic lands in search of new learning, the activity of devoted translators in the Spanish peninsula and Sicily. As this enthusiasm for learning became widespread, the numerous wandering teachers and students began, like members of all other occupations of the period, to organize themselves for mutual protection in gilds, or *universitates*, from which our modern universities are directly descended. At first somewhat migratory, these educational institutions gradually became permanently located at centers such as Bologna, Paris, Oxford, Cambridge, Toulouse, and Naples, and were granted privileges by pope or kings. By the sixteenth century there were about eighty of them. Before the invention of printing instruction was largely oral, consist-

ing of lectures and disputations.   Manuscripts could be purchased of booksellers, but students often made their own copies.

The term, scholasticism, is applied to the teaching, thinking, Scholas-
ticism
and writing done in these medieval schools by the schoolmen.
In especial it denotes their systematic, somewhat cut-and-dried
method of stating a question or problem, defining its terms,
citing authorities on both sides, meeting the opposing arguments, and so gradually arriving at some conclusion.   This
was not, however, the sole method employed; we have already
noted the experimental and mathematical methods.   Scholastic method was more especially characteristic of philosophy
and theology, although sometimes employed in medical and
scientific works.   In point of time scholastic philosophy succeeded patristic literature, and was at its height from the
twelfth to fourteenth centuries.   Scholasticism was not merely
the study of the works of Aristotle, although Albertus Magnus
(1193–1280) and Thomas Aquinas (1225–1274), who may perhaps be respectively ranked as the greatest natural scientist
and the greatest theologian of the Latin middle ages, made
extensive use of his works which they attempted to combine
with Christian thought.   But Albert also laid great stress upon
experimental method.   Medieval authors were very prolific,
although they had neither typewriters nor printing-presses.
The works of Albert fill thirty-eight large volumes; those of
Aquinas, thirty-four.   Scholasticism continued in printed books
and university curriculums even into the seventeenth and eighteenth centuries, while recent years have seen a Roman Catholic
"neo-scholasticism."

Meanwhile, in the twelfth and thirteenth centuries, popular Icelandic
and
Provençal
Literature
literature in vernacular languages had been blossoming forth
in two regions which today one would hardly expect to be hot-
beds and cradles of culture, namely, Iceland and the south of
France, representing respectively the Teutonic languages
and spirit of the north, and the Romance languages and culture
of the Mediterranean.   The *Eddas* or poetry of Iceland disclose Norse mythology to us, the prose Sagas deal with viking
adventure; both reveal the moods and forces of northern nature and scenery.   The troubadours of the south, wandering
lute in hand from castle to castle and court to court, addressed
their songs especially to the ladies, introducing into literature,
and through literature into the manners of daily life, those

notions and habits of chivalry, courtesy, romantic love, and superficial consideration for women which have persisted to our day, although one recent writer speaks with distaste of "that sentimental gallantry which comes to us as a heritage of the middle ages and which progressive women themselves repudiate as prejudicial to their dignity as human beings." The troubadours loved nature as well as woman, and besides love poetry composed songs of battle and revenge, funeral laments, satires and burlesques, or poetical dialogues, contests, and debates of an intellectual and somewhat scholastic character.   They also contributed greatly to the advance of the modern literatures in poetical form by wide experimentation with new and difficult meters and intricate rhymes.   Yet the language in which this experimentation was carried on, the sweet and musical Provençal, has long since disappeared from written literature.   It was less like the other northern dialects from which modern French has developed than it was like the speech of Catalonia in Spain and of Lombardy in the Italian peninsula—regions which were further closely associated in town governments and in art.   But Provençal was enough like all the Romance languages derived from Latin to affect profoundly the national literatures of France, Italy, Spain, and Portugal.   Its influence spread to England through the Norman French kings and nobles and the later Angevin court, to Germany through the *minnesingers*.

Other Medieval Literary Forms

Meanwhile in France had developed the *chansons de geste* or feudal epics, paralleled in Castilian by the *Poema del Cid* with a local Spanish hero.   The fusion of these rougher romances with the more refined lyrics of the troubadours and their imitators, then produced the courtly epic and sentimental romance, while the influence of Latin learning often provided plots and heroes from antiquity or digressions introducing matter of social, historical, theological, or scientific interest. A more popular element appears in the animal epic, such as *Reynard the Fox*,—though it, too, is in part based on a Latin poem of the twelfth century, *Ysengrimus*—in the *fabliaux*, or short tales in verse, often satirical and redolent less of feudal than popular life, and in the mysteries and miracle plays. Vernacular prose writing in French began in the thirteenth century.   Dante (1265–1321) made the Florentine dialect the literary language of Italy, setting forth somewhat too gloomily

MEDIEVAL HOUSES

Above, a well, preserved house of the thirteenth century in Chartres, now used as the post-office; below, medieval arches in the Piazza S. Pellegrino, Viterbo.

WOODWORK, WIN-
DOWS, AND FURNI-
TURE IN THE OLD
HOUSES OF CAEN
AND LE MANS

and mystically many of the thoughts of the time in his great epic, the *Divine Comedy*.

The twelfth and thirteenth centuries were the great period of this medieval or early modern literature. In the early thirteenth century the religious wars and persecution of heresy in southern France largely destroyed the society of the troubadours, although it perhaps accelerated the spread of their poesy to other lands. Colder winters and less fertile summers in the fourteenth century wiped out the settlement of the Northmen in Greenland, and perhaps chilled the genius of Icelandic literature, whose period of productivity is the twelfth and thirteenth centuries. The *chansons de geste* and *fabliaux* also declined with the early fourteenth century. In Italy, however, Petrarch's odes and sonnets and Boccaccio's tales carry us on past the middle of the century, while in England Chaucer did not die until 1400. Indeed in Italy Lorenzo de' Medici (1449–1492) revived the interest in Italian literature, and the romantic epic continued to be popular with Pulci and Boiardo in the fifteenth, and Ariosto and Tasso in the sixteenth century. During the fourteenth and fifteenth centuries much work was done in the field of music, which became more complicated and technical. John Dunstable, "the father of English harmony," died in 1453.

As for Latin literature, in their eager pursuit of logic and theology, of metaphysics, law, and medicine, of mathematical and natural science, the medieval scholars gradually came to neglect *belles lettres* and the amenities of literary discourse, to which in the twelfth century not a little attention had been given. But then a reaction ensued, and with the fourteenth and fifteenth centuries, especially in Italy, began a revival of classical authors who had been hitherto neglected, accompanied by an intensive, sympathetic study of Latin and Greek literary style, grammar, history, art, geography, mythology, and general civilization. Scholastic Latin of the fourteenth century was generally worse than that of the thirteenth; there was, therefore, the more reason for a reaction, such as that in Italy, toward purity of classical Latin style. Scholastic method, too, had already asked most of its questions over and over, had exhausted its authorities and arguments. Sometimes, however, the classical enthusiasts were unfair to medieval Latin; for example, in reviving the quantitative prosody of ancient

Period of Medieval Vernacular Literature

Humanism

times they came to judge everything by that standard and could see no beauty in the rhythmic medieval style, which we described above, for the reason that they failed to note that it was based on accent rather than quantity. The humanists who revived the classics thus were so called because they regarded their studies as of much greater human interest than the dry abstract disputations of the schoolmen. Until recently Latin and Greek as thus studied have been known as the humanities. Really the studies of the humanists were just as bookish as those of the scholastics and were even more antiquarian, artificial, and doctrinaire, since they dealt with a culture that was dead and gone, which they could not hope to resuscitate except in ghostly form, while it put them out of touch and tune with their own immediate past. Today we have in turn abandoned the humanities as dead languages and useless culture; the tendency is to study only subjects "of present interest," such as sociology, psychology, political science, economics, modern languages and literatures, the modern novel, the modern drama, natural science. Perhaps it is now too late for us to reach our roots down where they belong into medieval civilization, but could we do so, we should draw strength and nourishment from knowledge of the past beneath us as well as from the intellectual atmosphere of the present about us.

True Relation of Medieval to Renaissance Culture

So out of touch and tune with the Christian centuries before them did intellectuals become in early modern times, that the notion finally came to prevail that these medieval centuries had been dark ages without civilization worthy of the name, that civilization had revived only with the "Italian Renaissance" of the humanists. But the revival of civilization dates rather, as we have seen, from the tenth century. Some sides of medieval civilization declined in the course of the fourteenth and fifteenth centuries, it is true; others went on without a break or any great change. For example, the mathematical and scientific writings and experiments continued their gradual evolution comparatively independent both of scholasticism and humanism. Daily life in country and town remained about the same until the eighteenth or nineteenth century.

Greek Introduced into the Curriculum

A new feature was the effort to place Greek beside Latin as a language with which every cultured person must be familiar. This came about only slowly, as many of the earlier humanists were merely Latin scholars, while others had only a little Greek.

On the other hand, a scholastic like Peter of Abano had been familiar with Greek back in 1300. Greek came to occupy a large place in the curriculums of schools and universities from the sixteenth through the nineteenth century.

Printing with movable metal types, invented shortly before 1450, as the outcome of a series of experiments going back to 1400 or earlier, for some time continued to employ the abbreviations which had characterized the manuscripts. "The invention of printing reduced the cost of books by fully one-half." Reading and bibliographical knowledge now gradually replaced oral methods and memorizing in education and literature. "The less pains the eyes take in reading a book," says a seventeenth century writer, "the more liberty the mind hath to judge of it." As it now became easier to obtain an accurate, proof-read copy of almost any work, while a passage in a work could be found, or the whole work could be read, more quickly than before, there was less merit in simply ascertaining and setting forth what the ancients had said and more demand for originality and variety. On the other hand, it became possible and profitable to issue printed matter of purely temporary or popular interest, and various forms of periodical and ephemeral publications gradually arose. Printing-presses have, of course, developed greatly in size, complexity, and mode of operation from the first small presses worked by hand. Victor Hugo said that the sun of Gothic art set behind the printing-press. It is indeed true that humanism and printing were accompanied both by developments and decay in the realm of art and of taste for art. In our next chapter we have to note the glorious rise and zenith of Gothic art which had preceded its decline.

Printing with Movable Types

BIBLIOGRAPHY

It would take too long to list English translations of various medieval works or histories of national literatures containing chapters on the middle ages. Some other books are:

Bédier, J. *Legendes épiques,* 1909–1913, 4 vols.

Bulfinch, T. *Age of Fable, Age of Chivalry, and Legends of Charlemagne,* 1913.

Carter, Thomas F. *The Invention of Printing in China and its Spread Westward,* 1924.

Chambers, E. K. *The Medieval Stage,* 1903, 2 vols.

Diepgen, Paul. "Die Bedeutung des Mittelalters für den Fortschritt in der Medizin," pp. 99–120 in *Essays on the History of Medicine presented to Karl Sudhoff on the occasion of his seventieth birthday*, ed. C. Singer and H. E. Sigerist, 1924.

Guiraud, J. *L'eglise romaine et les origines de la renaissance*, 3rd ed., 1904.

Haskins, C. H. *The Rise of Universities*, 1923; brief, three lectures; *Studies in the History of Medieval Science*, 1924.

Husik, J. *A History of Medieval Jewish Philosophy*, 1916.

Jourdain, C. *Excursions historiques et philosophiques à travers le moyen âge*, 1888; very informing and suggestive studies; especially may be recommended those on the education of women, teaching of Hebrew, and beginning of economics in the middle ages.

Lawrence, W. W. *Medieval Story*, 1912.

McCabe, Joseph. *Abelard*, 1901.

McLaughlin, E. T. *Studies of Medieval Life and Literature*, 1894.

Mallet, C. E. *A History of the University of Oxford*, 1924, vol. I.

Monnier, P. *Le Quattrocento*, 8th ed., 1924, 2 vols.

Mortet, Chas. *Les origines et les débuts de l'imprimerie d'après les recherches les plus récentes*, 1922.

Mullinger, J. B. *The University of Cambridge from the earliest times to the decline of the Platonist movement*, 1873–1911, 3 vols.

Munro, D. C. *The Medieval Student*, 1895.

Norton, A. O. *Readings in the History of Education; Medieval Universities*, 1909.

Paetow, L. J. *The Arts Course at Medieval Universities*, 1910.

Paris, G. *Medieval French Literature* (Everyman's Library), 1903.

Pater, W. *The Renaissance: studies in art and poetry*, various eds., 1873, 1910, etc.

Poole, R. L. *Lectures on the History of the Papal Chancery*, 1915. *Illustrations of the History of Medieval Thought*, 1920.

Rait, R. S. *Life in the Medieval Universities*, 1912.

Rashdall, H. *Universities of Europe in the Middle Ages*, 1895, 3 vols.

Ribera, Julian. *La Música de las Cantigas*, 1922; these are shown to bridge the gap between medieval and Muslim music, perhaps even to furnish a key to the lost music of ancient Greece; "these Galician hymns in honor of the virgin are last echoes of love-melodies gathered in Bagdad to please Harun ar-Rashid."

Saintsbury, G. E. B. *The Flourishing of Romance and the Rise of Allegory*, 1897.

Sandys, J. E. *History of Classical Scholarship*, 1903–1906, 3 vols.; 3rd ed. of vol. I (covering to the end of the middle ages), 1921.

Smith, Justin H. *The Troubadours at Home*, 1899, 2 vols.

Thorndike, Lynn. "The Study of Western Science of the Fourteenth and Fifteenth Centuries," in *Medical Life*, vol. 32 (1925), 117–27.

Trench, (Archbishop). *Sacred Latin Poetry*, 2nd ed., 1864.

Updike, D. B. *Printing Types; their history, forms, and use*, 1922.

Voigt, G. *Die Wiederbelebung des classichen Altertums*, 3rd ed., 1893.

SPEYER
CATHEDRAL

An example of Rhenish
Romanesque. Views of
arched windows and col-
onnades high up above
the tree-tops.

CATHEDRAL TOWERS

Left, St. Ouen, Rouen; right, Norman tower, Canterbury

Wulf, M. de. *History of Medieval Philosophy*, 1909. *Philosophy and Civilization in the Middle Ages*, 1922.

For further bibliography of books published before 1917 see L. J. Paetow, *Guide to the Study of Medieval History*, 1917, part III, "Medieval Culture."

CHAPTER XXIX

MEDIEVAL ART

The unerring medieval instinct of style.

Art the
Supreme
Expression
of Medieval
Civilization

MOST writers fail to treat impartially and with true insight the period with which our last few chapters and the present one are concerned. Some are swept away by romantic enthusiasm for its ideals. Some display their ignorance by their neglect or vague disparagement of it. Others collect material to prove that its realities often fell sadly short of its ideals, or minimize its more distinctive qualities, by imitation and recovery of which some have thought that our age and civilization might profit, by arguing that human nature is essentially alike in all times. Thus modern economists urge that the members of the medieval gilds were really just as selfish as modern capitalists or members of labor unions, or contrast the full dinner-pail of today with the frequent famines of the medieval centuries. As against the hero-worship of St. Francis and Thomas Aquinas which we meet in some books, modern churchmen uncover the seamy side of medieval monasticism, inquisition, or worship of the saints. Modern liberals question whether medieval towns were ever truly democratic and complain that the church prevented freedom of thought. There is some truth in these and similar contentions and there is more or less evidence to substantiate them, though in part they are uneasy efforts to justify our own pot by calling other kettles black. But one feature of medieval civilization can bid defiance to disparagement. It has no seamy side; outside or inside it is equally honest, equally beautiful. Its foundations are as solid as its aspirations are lofty. It is medieval art.

Its Basis
was Honest
Work

Today we have almost lost even the definition of art. Before me is a modern book which, in addition to the æsthetic quality, emphasizes as utilitarian motives in primitive art the elements of information, propitiation, stimulation, and magic efficiency. But what about the element of work? In the middle

352

ages art and work were not divorced. Every apprentice looked forward to the production of a masterpiece. Barons and bishops were builders, the towns were picturesque, the books were beautiful. If a smaller percentage of the population could read and write than today, a larger percentage could draw and appreciate design. The genius of the middle ages can be better seen in the little carved plaques by the *Portail des Libraires* of the cathedral at Rouen—to call them grotesques only shows how unnatural art has since become—than in the tomes of Aquinas or Alain de Lille. Recent archæological and scholarly disputes whether the great cathedrals were more the work of the clergy or the communes, and whether medieval art was a popular product or the expression of a few leading personalities, do not affect the more fundamental fact that both clergymen and workingmen enjoyed their jobs more and put into them more of themselves, more of nature, and more of truth— as they saw it—than they do today. The result was medieval art.

It is perhaps somewhat of an exaggeration to say that we cannot make even a good copy of a medieval cathedral or other work of art, since we often catch ourselves admiring as a bit of medieval genius a statue, chimæra, or arched corbel-table which was really restored or rebuilt in the nineteenth century. Even archæologists have been so deceived. Still, one wonders if the medieval originators would have been thus taken in. Kingsley Porter, even after adducing several such instances of archæologists having been deceived by restorations, flatly declares, "Modern workmen cannot reproduce nor copy Gothic work." More serious than this charge, however, is the fact that they do not originate an art of their own. Our artists are apt to be Bohemians, living in an artificial world of their own, in revolt from the civilization about them instead of giving it artistic expression. Our employers of art are largely animated by considerations of profit or show. They count the cost of a building they are erecting, lop off some of the architect's ideas at the last moment, and seldom accept any attempt to make an edifice attractive in appearance except on the side facing the street, which of course proves that the decoration there, like the architect's ideas, is no integral or essential feature of the building but only for show. On the other hand, a small fortune will be expended to secure personal possession

Difference Between Medieval and Modern Art

of a single easel painting in order that no one else may look at it. All this has to be mentioned to convince the reader that art in the past was not the same thing as "art" now. Medieval men did not care so much about owning works of art as they did about making them. We boast of "creative chemistry"; they had creative art. They built walls and castles with considerations of defense, abbeys and cathedrals with purposes of worship in mind rather than of profit and show. But they did not think that because a thing was to be useful, therefore it need not be attractive. This, of course, is not saying that every medieval building or object is attractive.

Relations Between the Romanesque and Gothic Styles

Of castle and armor, town-halls and towers, houses and streets, manuscripts and illuminations, we have treated in previous chapters, so that we may now center our attention upon architecture, sculpture, and painting as revealed in the churches. The Gothic cathedral was the greatest, most inclusive, most comprehensive work of art of the middle ages, perhaps of all civilization. But it is to be remembered that medieval art owed not a little to the beautiful Byzantine art and the impressive remains of Roman building. Their influence, however, was strongest in Italy and Southern France, whereas the greatest Gothic cathedrals are found in the north. The Gothic style seems to have originated especially in the north of France, although it perhaps successfully combined elements that had been experimented with elsewhere; for example, the solution of the problem of stone vaulting by use of diagonal ribs came from Lombardy. Others urge oriental influence or Roman models and suggestions. As a whole, however, the Gothic cathedral was in a new style, worked out in the twelfth century, perfected in the thirteenth, preceded and accompanied by the Romanesque style, which was more in the nature of a continuation or revival of Roman and Byzantine building and of the earlier Christian basilicas at Ravenna, Rome, and elsewhere. Romanesque was also a progressive and experimental art; otherwise we should not have Gothic developing from it. While Romanesque is a fairly satisfactory name as indicating a resumption or outgrowth of Roman art from about 1000 in the west, Gothic is of course an absurd misnomer, since the Goths had disappeared from history five or six centuries before. It is useful mainly to remind us how little understood the middle ages were in early modern times when the name was given. But it has stuck, become a glory rather than a reproach, and it now seems too late to change it. Some would call the style French, because the purest specimens are found in what is now northern France. This too would be an anachronism, since France and Frenchmen as we understand the words hardly existed when this art began, and it was not national but universal. We might distinguish Romanesque and Gothic as Mediterranean and northern medieval architecture.

The usual ground plan for a church in the west came to be the Latin cross. The long nave with its two or more lower side aisles resembled the rectangular basilica, but at its further end on either side opened two transepts, usually of the same width and height as the nave and with side aisles of their own. Beyond the transepts the main body of the church continued as the choir, commonly with a rounded east end, or apse, which very likely would be covered with a half dome. The side aisles might continue along the choir to terminate in chapels or to meet behind the high altar, forming an ambulatory beyond which might be radiating chapels, disposed in a semicircle about the apse and ambulatory. Thus something of the concentric plan was also preserved. Romanesque churches sometimes had a choir at either end of the nave. Sometimes the floor of the choir was higher than that of the nave, raising the clergy and singers above the congregation as on a platform and making room for a crypt beneath the choir. In Gothic churches this feature was generally dropped as detracting from the impression of sublime height which the interior gave.

The Ground Plan of a Cathedral

Romanesque basilicas of the eleventh century already had lofty naves (Speyer and Worms, 105 feet; Mainz, 90 feet; Durham, 70 feet; Ely, 62 feet) and still loftier towers. These naves consisted of two parallel walls of thick masonry, pierced however by series of round arches one above the other much after the manner of a Roman aqueduct or the outer wall of a Roman amphitheater. The arches directly above the floor opened into the aisles; if the aisles were high and had a gallery, another series of arches would open into it; the next row of arches corresponded to the space above the side-aisles and their lean-to roof; the highest series of arches contained windows, also round arched, letting light directly into the nave above the side aisles. Most of the decorative effects in the building, aside from sculpture, were attained by use of round arches.

Problem of Attaining Loftiness with Round Arches

But the round arch is necessarily twice as wide as it is high, and so is not well adapted to give the sensation of aspiring height.   If rows of round arches are superimposed one on another, the horizontal rows impress one more than the vertical superimposition.   If a single round arch connects two tall parallel lines or columns at the top, as in a tower, it looks stilted, and the termination of their upward movement is too abrupt.

Problem of the Stone Vault

It is not always easy to say whether at first a flat, relatively light roof of wood covered the space between the two lofty, impressive, parallel walls of the nave, or whether they were designed originally to support a stone vault.   Certainly in most churches the roof was not yet vaulted.   Where it was, the round-arched barrel-vault exerted an outward thrust that required thicker, solider walls and a consequent diminution of window space.   This problem gave the builders much concern. They could without much difficulty arch over in stone the lower and narrower side aisles, which pressed against the lower walls of the nave on one side and could be strengthened by external buttresses at the points of stress on the other outer side.   But to build a durable, indestructible stone vault across the wider, loftier nave whose upper walls had no outward support,—that was another matter.   The perishable nature of the timber roof may be inferred from the fact that there is hardly a single one from the thirteenth century left.

Gothic Structure: the Ribbed Vault and the Flying-Buttress

These problems were solved by the use of the ribbed vault, the flying-buttress, and the pointed arch.   The vault of masonry is so constructed that its weight is borne by ribs or arches of stone which carry this weight off to certain points only of the side wall.   Consequently this side wall needs to be thick only at these points and need not be solid and massive throughout its length.   The vaulting is usually done in sections corresponding to the arches along the side wall, each unit including a pair of such arches on either side, or a single arch spanning about the same space as two did before.   Diagonal ribs crossing in the center of each section carry the weight and stress off to the four corners, the same points to which the open arches bring the weight of the side walls.   Manifestly these points require to be heavily buttressed, so now an external support was invented for them in the flying-buttress, which in a graceful arc bridges the space above the roof of the side aisle and braces its other end against the solid buttress, on which it

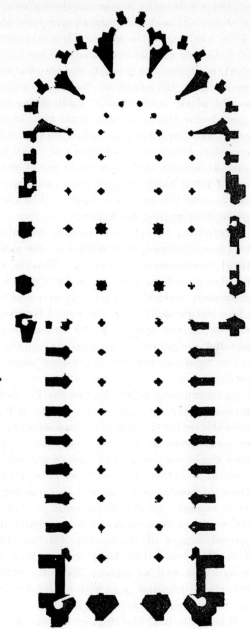

GROUND PLAN OF
REIMS CATHEDRAL

Interior dimensions:
total length 455 feet,
width of nave 98 feet,
height 125 feet.

is clamped down by a superimposed pinnacle or canopied statue of stone. This solid buttress lower down also receives the thrust of the vaulting of the aisle. Thus economy, firmness, and unity of structure are simultaneously secured. The same columns or clusters of columns inside that carry the weight of the side walls receive also the stress of the aisle vaults and a little of the weight of the main vault. Each flying-buttress meets two diagonal ribs that converge from two adjoining sections of the vault, and the entire stone skeleton is tied together. The whole gigantic structure is composed of small blocks fitted together, just as human society is made up of many small individuals, not of great blocks weighing tons and costing tremendous labor and loss of life to put in place. The Gothic cathedral was a triumph of brains, not brawn.

The Pointed Arch

Moreover, the pointed arch is introduced in vault, flying-buttress, windows, open arches of the side walls, and architectural memberment generally. This is a double gain. The pointed arch brings the weight of the vault and superstructure down more vertically on the supports and does not exert so much of an outward stress as the round Roman arch. Moreover, it carries the eye upward better and unites the tops of two long parallel uprights more gradually and harmoniously. Finally, it is less rigid and far more diversified, since the ratio of its height to its breadth may be infinitely varied. The pointed arch had been known long before this to the Persians, Copts, Arabs, and was employed in what is now southern France as early as the eleventh century. But the "masons at first had clearly no idea of what could be done by means of the pointed construction; they employed it only as a sort of makeshift, in places where no amount of cramping could make a round arch do service." Only in Gothic architecture was employment of the pointed arch brought to perfection both in structure and adornment. These improvements resulted in greater actual, as well as apparent, height of the interior (Reims, 125 feet; Amiens, 139 feet; Beauvais, 158 feet). The clearstory windows became broader as well as higher, filling the entire space between the structural ribs and piers with brilliant expanses of stained glass set in elaborate stone tracery.

Beautiful Unison of Gothic Structure and Ornament

The structural skeleton, or better, the living muscular frame of the Gothic cathedral is not concealed, as in the steel framework of a modern building, by outer walls of brick or stone.

Above, Le Mans cathedral; note the difference between the nave (11th-12th centuries) and the transepts and choir (13th-14th-15th centuries); below, Reims cathedral after the German bombardment showing the structural skeleton. The lower part of the cathedral is concealed by the ruined buildings in the foreground.

ROMANESQUE AND
GOTHIC INTERIORS
Left, Durham (Norman) ;
right, apse of Limoges.

It stands forth boldly to view, a thing of beauty and strength to the eye, corresponding faithfully outside to its interior arrangements, clothed with sculpture and architectural detail only as a lithe body and perfect figure may be covered with fair flesh and hair. Sculptured saints, gargoyles, carved pinnacles, delicate and airy colonnades spring from the gray walls as naturally as buds and leaves do from the boughs of a tree in springtime. No other buildings ever blossomed forth like these. The very ground plan of such a church, though seen on a small scale, is a design of great symmetry and beauty. How much more stupendous the actual elevation!—the two great towers supporting the west end of the nave, the three receding portals which open into nave and aisles between the great buttresses of the towers, the sculptured screen above, the stately succession of buttresses along the sides of the nave, the impressive transepts with central spire (or *flêche*) over the crossing, the curve of the apse supported by converging buttresses, surmounted by chimæras or angels, and surrounded by chapels and aisles rising in successive stages! Every side of the church has its own special attractions and features; from every angle of observation we get new views of the diversified, yet unified, whole. Or if we enter by one of the west doors in front, how it seems as if we had stepped into another world! How the impression of solemn grandeur grows as we pass from vestibule into long-drawn aisle; as we come out from the aisle beneath the loftier vault of the nave; as we walk down the long nave, whose side walls keep repeating the poem of Gothic in great, rhythmic, lofty sections of pier-arches, triforium, and clearstory; as we proceed to the spreading spaciousness of the transepts, with great rose windows high above us to the right and left that remind us to look back at that radiant west window behind us! In the choir are perhaps higher lights and more exquisitely executed columns and carvings, in the apse a great flood of light from the concentrated windows of the east end, in the ambulatory and chapels solemn stillness with new vistas of the whole. Only outside do you see the form of the cross outlined in the loftiest lines of the roof of the main body of the building, and even there the towers rise high above the cross; inside it is all heavenly crown. Or would be, if the windows were still filled with their blazonry of thirteenth century glass, and if the interior were freed from execrable altar-pieces, transparencies, and monuments of the Baroque, Jesuitical, and modern periods.

The cathedral has been compared to an art or historical museum because of the many minor and subsidiary works of art or mementos of the past which it contains. This comparison, although intended to be complimentary to the cathedral, really does it an injustice. In the museum we are constantly being reminded that all the things we see come from other places where they really belong, and the collection is apt to make a bewildering, heterogeneous impression. In the cathedral everything—except the later, tasteless additions—was made exactly for the place it occupies and sinks its individuality in the glory of the whole. Here we may see every kind of sculpture in almost every sort of material, ideal or natural, dignified or humorous, soul-expressive as Greek sculpture was not for all its beauty, human or animal, angelic or diabolical, realistic or symbolic, suggesting the story of Christian legend or developing decorative forms from foliage and flowers. There are statues in the round, scenes in relief, medallions, panels. All this is carved anywhere and everywhere from the same stone as the church itself is built, or on alabaster reredos, bronze door, or wooden choir seat. There are funeral monuments, tablets of brass, sculptured marble pulpits, baptismal fonts, fine old candlesticks, wrought iron work of gates and grilles, and many other treasures.

The statues of the medieval cathedrals were usually painted like those of the Greek temple. Medieval sculpture began in the Romanesque period not only in the south of what is now France, but in the Spanish peninsula, where the carved capitals of cloisters are both "the loveliest product of the period," and "the most valuable kind of document concerning contemporary social conditions," representing the life of different classes and occupations. The cathedral portals perhaps contain the richest, most serious and instructive material for the study of medieval sculpture. In the concentric arches above are rows of patriarchs, prophets, confessors, martyrs, and virgins looking down upon the sacred scenes represented in the three strips of sculpture filling the tympanum of the arch above the doorway, while below, on either side of the entrance, are larger statues of the saints, "great figures breathing deathless serenity." Beneath these may be medallions containing realistic representations of the signs of the zodiac and the occupations of the different months of the year.   The effect of this sculpture grows on the beholder.   "Features that at first seem archaic and crude assume an almost celestial radiance: drapery which seemed stiff and conventional is seen to fall in folds of the most exquisite grace; and the very distortion of anatomy seems to lend added dignity and charm" (Porter).

We must leave the reader to read elsewhere concerning the various regional styles of Romanesque and Gothic, such as Norman and Early English, or the peculiar merits of particular cathedrals.   No two churches are alike; often the same cathedral combines different styles in parts built at different periods. Among the best are Notre Dame of Paris, Chartres, Amiens, Reims, but there are many others.   Sunny Italy and Spain preferred small windows and solid buttresses; yet their cathedrals are exceedingly magnificent, sumptuous, and ornate.   English Gothic churches had less lofty naves than those in the north of what is now France, but longer choirs and sometimes more delicate detail.   After the thirteenth century there were such later Gothic styles as the *Rayonnant* and *Flamboyant* in France, the Decorated and Perpendicular in England.   In the fifteenth century were built the two largest medieval cathedrals, Milan and Seville, both in Gothic style.   Before that century closed, however, the Italians had begun to revive classical architecture and sculpture in sympathy with humanism. These more gradually supplanted Gothic in other countries.

Variations in the Style of Architecture with Place and Time

Pictorial art was represented in the medieval period by stained glass which largely took the place of mosaics, by illuminations in manuscripts, by frescoes on the walls of churches, by splendid tapestries.   After the thirteenth century painting and sculpture, especially in Italy, became more independent of ecclesiastical architecture—so that we visit Italian churches more to see their pictures than to see the churches themselves— and more realistic and accurate in their representation of the human form and of the world about them.   At the same time the old-fashioned illuminators and cathedral sculptors lose their inventiveness, contact with nature, and ideal strength, introducing the pathetic and painful.   Hence as humanism gradually replaced scholasticism in learning, so Italian painting, sculpture, and architecture gradually replaced Gothic, introducing more "human interest," for example, in paintings of

Independent Development of Italian Painting and Sculpture

the Holy Family, or Madonna and Child.   But such artists of
the fourteenth and fifteenth centuries as Giovanni and Andrea
Pisano and Ghiberti still owed much to the Gothic; the vast
dome by Brunelleschi (1377–1446) for the cathedral at Florence is as much Gothic as Renaissance; and "the spirit of Botticelli is essentially medieval."   The church continued to be
the chief employer of the artists; the subjects were for the most
part still professedly, at least, ecclesiastical; the inspiration of
a Fra Angelico or a Perugino was still largely spiritual.   For
a long time the names of the Italian, and more particularly the
Florentine, artists have been immortalized through Vasari's
Lives of the Painters, while their Romanesque and Gothic predecessors have been forgotten.   This is now ceasing to be the
case, and we no longer feel obliged to view the history of medieval art from the shaky standpoint of the Italian Renaissance.
Indeed, some would go so far as to hold that Giotto (c. 1266–
1337) terminated rather than initiated a great period.

Illustrated
by the
Works of
Donatello

However, it is the new developments that we have next to
note.   In sculpture Donatello (1386–1466) will serve to
illustrate the change.   While his wonderful St. George still
breathes the spirit of medieval chivalry and saintliness, his
frieze of boys running and laughing reflects not much more
than animal spirits, however skilful a specimen of bas relief
it is.   His bust of Niccolo da Uzzano and equestrian statue of
the mercenary general, Gattamelata, are portraits of contemporaries.   His funeral monument for the pope introduced
classical architecture and sculpture; his David is the first nude
bronze statue cast since Roman times.

Progress of
Painting

The painters even of ecclesiastical themes and Madonnas
tend to reproduce the features of their Italian models rather
than to achieve ideal saintliness, and they depict contemporary
costume, Italian scenery, and classical buildings.   They show
an improvement in knowledge of anatomy, of perspective and
foreshortening—in general in technical excellence.   After a
period of rapid production and many great masters—some in
Flanders as well as in Italy—the climax in painting and sculpture is reached in Leonardo da Vinci (1452–1519), the greatest genius, Raphael (1483–1520), the greatest painter, and
Michelangelo (1475–1564), the greatest sculptor of the period.
It is the opinion of Monnier, however, that there is more Hellen-
ism in a medal by Pisanello, marble of Donatello, or mythology

of Botticelli than in all the work of Raphael and Michelangelo. The Italian artists were quite commonly versatile masters of all the fine arts and precocious in the early manifestation of their genius.

The changes in painting soon affected glass windows, into which perspective, classical architecture, and brilliant colored enamels were introduced. But the sixteenth century lost both the good taste and the mosaic effect of the thirteenth century windows, which had been composed of small bits of glass held together by leads which formed the outlines of the figures in the design, whereas now the glass was painted in larger square sections or panes, which subdivided the picture arbitrarily so that a lead might bisect a limb or face. In other words, the picture was not fitted to the window. It is not surprising that the taste for stained glass soon waned and that it became practically a lost art.

Decline of Stained Glass

BIBLIOGRAPHY

Adams, Henry. *Mont St. Michel and Chartres*, 1913; a favorite book of the cultured reader.

Anderson, W. J. *The Architecture of the Renaissance in Italy*, 4th ed., 1909.

Berenson, B. *The Central Italian Painters of the Renaissance*, 1909; *The Florentine Painters of the Renaissance*, 1909; *The North Italian Painters of the Renaissance*, 1907; *The Venetian Painters of the Renaissance*, 1894.

Bode, W. *Florentine Sculptors of the Renaissance*, 1909.

Bushnell, A. J. de H. *Storied Windows*, 1914.

Cram, R. A. *Heart of Europe*, 1918; and other works.

Crowe and Cavalcaselle, *History of Painting in North Italy from the Fourteenth to the Sixteenth Century*, 1912, 3 vols.; *A New History of Painting in Italy*, 1908–1909, 3 vols.

Cust, A. M. *Ivory Workers of the Middle Ages*, 1902.

Dalbon, Ch. *Les origines de la peinture à l'huile*, 1904; with bibliography of previous works.

Dehio, G. *Geschichte der deutschen Kunst*, vol. II (1250–1500), 1921.

Enlart, C. *Manuel d'archéologie française depuis les temps mérovingiens jusqu'à la renaissance*, 1919–1920, 2 vols.; standard.

Freeman, L. J. *Italian Sculpture of the Renaissance*, 1901.

Gardner, A. *French Sculpture of the Thirteenth Century*, 1915.

Humphreys, H. N. *Illuminated Books of the Middle Ages*, 1849.

Hutton, Edward. *The Cities of Spain*, new edition, 1924.

Jackson, T. G. *Gothic Architecture in France, England, and Italy*, 1915, 2 vols.

Kemmerich, M. *Die frühmittelalterliche Porträtplastik in Deutschland*, 1909.

Mâle, E. *Religious Art in France in the Thirteenth Century*, 1913; *L'art religieux de la fin du moyen âge en France*, 1922; both are charmingly written, full of ideas, and show the relation of art to thought.

Moore, C. H. *The Development and Character of Gothic Architecture*, 1904; an important definition and delimitation of the term "Gothic."

O'Reilly, E. B. *How France Built Her Cathedrals*, 1921; sympathetic.

Porter, A. K. *Medieval Architecture*, 1912, 2 vols.; *Lombard Architecture*, 1917, 3 vols.; two important studies.

Reinach, S. *Répertoire de peintures du moyen âge et de la renaissance*, 1905.

Reymond, M. *Brunelleschi et l'architecture de la renaissance italienne au XVᵉ siècle*, 1913.

Ruskin, J. *Modern Painters, Mornings in Florence, Stones of Venice, Bible of Amiens*, etc.

Scott, G. *The Architecture of Humanism*, 1914.

Sherill, C. H. *Stained Glass Tours in France*, 1908.

Sirén, Oswald. *Toskanische Maler im XIII Jahrhundert*, 1922, 130 illustrations.

Symonds, J. A. *The Renaissance in Italy*, vol. III, "The Fine Arts."

Vasari, *Lives of the Painters*, translated by Blashfield and Hopkins, 1907; translated by G. du C. de Vere, 1912–15.

Viollet-le-Duc, E. *Dictionnaire raisonné de l'architecture française du XIᵉ au XVIᵉ siècle*, 1854–1868, 10 vols.; a great work.

Witkowski, G. J. *L'art profane à l'église, ses licences symboliques, satiriques et fantaisistes*, 1908.

CHAPTER XXX

CRUSADERS AND MONGOLS

(The Rival Expansion of Latin Christendom and Asiatic Nomads,
and Civilization in the Far East Since)

The real barrier between East and West is a distrust of each
other's morality and the illusion that the distrust is on one
side only.—*Robertson Scott*

In a previous chapter we briefly adverted to the expansion of
Christendom which occurred after the tenth century and to the
crusades. We have deferred fuller treatment of these matters
until now in order to set them over against a further expansion
of the nomads of central Asia which checked Christian Europe
for a time and apparently held back civilization generally.

In the course of the eleventh century Normans conquered
southern Italy and Sicily from Byzantines and Saracens. In
the Spanish peninsula, after surviving a period of weakness
and disorder in the ninth century, the Caliphate of Cordova
finally in 1036 broke up into a number of small Moslem republics and principalities. The little Christian states of the north
then began to expand. In 1085 Alfonso VI of Castile and Leon
took Toledo in the center of the peninsula, while 1095 may be
regarded as the date of the foundation of Portugal as a separate state. Hosts of fanatical Moslems from North Africa,
first the Almoravides, later the Almohades, resisted the Christian advance. In the twelfth century monks, knights, military
orders, and crusaders from Christendom beyond the Pyrenees
aided the expansion of the Christian states. By the middle
of the thirteenth century only the little kingdom of Granada,
along the southern coast, was left to the Moslems, who succeeded
in retaining it until 1492.

Christian Expansion in Spain and Italy

In the northeast during the twelfth century German colonists
displaced the Slavs in the region between the Elbe and Oder
rivers. In the thirteenth century they expanded into Silesia,
Pomerania, and east of the Vistula into Prussia. The Order of

German Advance Eastward

365

Teutonic Knights and the Hanseatic League of towns spread Christianity, German influence and trade along the east coast of the Baltic to the Gulf of Finland. Poland and Lithuania became Christian but resisted the German influence. In the fifteenth century they reduced the power of the Knights. Bohemia, which had been converted to Christianity in the tenth century, in the next became a part of the Holy Roman Empire. Her kings often encouraged German colonists, although the majority of the population remained Czech. Austria expanded eastward in the late twelfth and thirteenth centuries. The Magyars of Hungary, who became Christian in the later twelfth century, introduced Flemish and German settlers in Transylvania to the east of Hungary as a buffer against the Petchenegs (or Patzinaks), a Turkish race on the lower Danube. Such German settlers seem to have been more industrious and capable than the natives. They had better ploughs, superior methods of agriculture, and knew how to reclaim waste land. Obviously, too, the land was becoming over-crowded in the west.

The Seljuk Turks

Of the Turks, both Seljuk and Ottoman, we have had occasion to speak in connection with the Byzantine Empire. Both were originally nomadic peoples from central Asia. After the eleventh century the caliph at Bagdad became a mere puppet in the hands of the Seljuks. Until the recent establishment of a republic and secularization of Turkey a Turkish Sultan was the real head of the Mohammedan world. The Turks had accepted Islam after their conquest of Persia. This made them only the more ready to wage war on Christendom. After their victory at Manzikert in Armenia in 1071 over the Byzantine Emperor, they gradually transformed Asia Minor into a desert by their nomadic life there. Against the Petchenegs who had invaded Thrace the emperor Alexius (1081–1118) was more successful, expelling them from his territory.

The Crusades

The crusaders from the west had for their main object the recovery of the Holy Sepulcher in Palestine, where the Turks had been interfering with the pilgrims. The western hosts did not wish to tarry and try to expel the Turks from Asia Minor for the benefit of the Byzantine Empire. Indeed, they found the march across Asia Minor from Constantinople difficult enough; and after the first two crusades they generally abandoned the land route and went to Syria or Egypt by sea. The

Above, tympanum of central portal, Laon; below, statues of central portal, Notre-Dame, Paris.

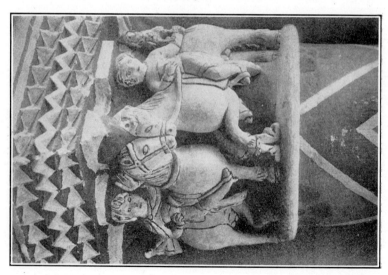

Left, 12th century capital, Angers; right, stone carving, Lincoln.

First Crusade was proclaimed by Pope Urban II in a speech at Clermont-Ferrand in 1095, when he decreed that "if anyone through devotion alone, and not for the sake of honor or gain, goes to Jerusalem to free the church of God, the journey itself shall take the place of all penance." Crowds of the common people in town or country were stirred to take the cross by popular preachers, but started too soon, were poorly equipped, and got little farther than Constantinople. The carefully prepared feudal hosts who reached that city later by various routes from divers parts of western Europe were more successful. In 1099 they took Jerusalem after a siege of two months. They also established a row of Christian states stretching from the Euphrates along the east coast of the Mediterranean to an arm of the Red Sea. It was hard to hold these distant regions against Turkish attack, since few westerners cared to remain there permanently. Hence military religious orders were founded for that purpose. Gradually, however, these territories were lost to the Turks again; the later crusades were failures, athough increased privileges were offered to attract crusaders; finally, after almost two centuries, Acre, the last Christian stronghold in Syria, fell to the Moslems in 1291.

The effect of the crusades upon western civilization has often been stated in very exaggerated terms. It may be doubted if they contributed to civilization much more than other wars. *Relation of the Crusades to Civilization* Perhaps they contributed indirectly to the growth of communes and monarchies by exhausting the energy of the feudal lords, but if so, did this result in any net gain to society? Intercourse with the orient and Mohammedan world no doubt went on during the crusades, promoting civilization, bringing to the west new food and relishes—garlic, watermelons, spices; spicy stories, too, and new ideas. Such intercourse, however, had been going on before the crusades through pilgrimages to the Holy Land or constant communication with Moslem culture in Spain and Sicily. Trade between the Italian cities and the orient was established in connection with the crusades, but these cities had earlier traded with Constantinople, and after the last crusading stronghold was lost, they kept their trading stations in Mohammedan countries. The Roman church, especially the papacy, seemed to gain great prestige and authority through the crusades. Many eastern Christians both in Europe and Asia were now received into the Roman

Catholic church. Then the popes carried the matter too far, directing crusades not only against heretical sects in western Europe but against mere political enemies of the papacy there, until Marsiglio of Padua in the *Defensor pacis*, 1324, could accuse the papacy of being the chief upsetter of the peace of Christendom. Certainly the crusades of the thirteenth century against the Albigensians in southern France, and those of the fifteenth century against the Hussites in Bohemia, were ruinous to civilization in those regions. Even the crusades proper were a dubious relief in the Byzantine Empire, which they overthrew in 1204, destroying many works of art in Constantinople. The empire was restored in 1261 in a much weakened form. The crusades did serve to hold the Turk somewhat in check for two centuries from 1095 to 1291.

The Mongol Invasions and Empire of the Great Khan

Meanwhile new Asiatic nomads swept in from the east in the persons of the Mongols, who had been united by Jenghiz Khan (1206–1227), and proceeded to conquer a vast empire. In 1215 Innocent III was holding at Rome the Fourth Lateran Council, most widely attended of all medieval ecclesiastical assemblies, marking both the height of the papal power and the greatest extent of Latin Christendom, which then stretched from Greenland and Norway to Syria. In that same year the Mongols took Peking, having broken through the Great Wall. By 1222 they had crossed the whole breadth of Asia and began to invade eastern Europe. For a time they were resisted with the aid of the Bulgars and Magyars, but in 1238 they took Moscow; in 1240 they sacked Kiev, Cracow, and Breslau; in 1241 they thoroughly ravaged Hungary and the Balkans. From these regions they soon withdrew. Nevertheless, the civilization of central and eastern Europe, which had given signs of promise in the twelfth century, had suffered a great set-back at their hands. A detachment known as the Golden Horde held most of Russia under its domination until 1480. Meanwhile the Mongols had terribly devastated Persia. In 1258 they sacked Bagdad and brought its caliphate to a close. They entered Syria, but were driven out by the Mamelukes from Egypt. The Mamelukes were a body-guard of the Egyptian Sultan, composed of slaves and captives in war, who had recently seized the throne. Since all the vast territories overrun by the nomads acknowledged the rule of one Great Khan, who was sometimes a man of considerable shrewdness and enlightenment like

Kublai Khan (1259–1294), trade with the Far East was for a time somewhat facilitated, especially by the more northerly overland routes. Western Christendom for a time had hopes of converting the Mongols or of using them as allies against Islam and the Turks.

A new group of Turks now began to make themselves obnoxious, namely, the Ottomans, who still constitute a world problem. They are first heard from in the territory in northwestern Asia Minor immediately opposite Constantinople and the Dardanelles. In our chapter on the Byzantine Empire we have seen how they overthrew it, taking its place and long controlling large territories in southeastern Europe and southwestern Asia. They did not enter Africa until 1517, when they stormed Cairo and occupied Egypt and Tripoli. Although they had many able Sultans, great military capacity, and fanatical devotion to Islam, most sides of civilization have declined under their rule. They were usually not hostile to trade, but there was little production in their territory. Although their naval wars with such Christian powers as Spain and Venice in the Mediterranean were probably no more destructive than those of preceding centuries, certainly pirates and corsairs did not appreciably decrease there.

The Ottoman Turks

For a time the expansion of the Ottoman Turks eastward into Asia was checked by a renewal of the Mongol invasions under Timur (1336–1405), or Tamerlane, whose terrible devastations and slaughter completed the ruin of civilization in Persia, Mesopotamia, Syria, and Asia Minor. He also ravaged a portion of India, including Delhi. Persia recovered a measure of prosperity under Shah Abbas I the Great (1586–1628) who defeated the Turks at Basra in 1605. He made Isfahan, his capital, an attractive city with a royal square which was one of the most imposing in the world. Isfahan never recovered from its sack by the Afghans in 1722 and is now in sad decay. In general the regions ravaged by Tamerlane have been thinly populated and at the mercy of nomadic peoples ever since. Eastern Europe also long remained backward and oriental in character. It had, of course, been repeatedly overrun by Asiatic nomads before the Mongols came, but it had gained something from both Byzantine and western civilization and might have progressed further, had it been left unmolested. Western Christian Europe was now put

Tamerlane and the Nomadization of Western Asia and Set-back to Civilization in Eastern Europe

on the defensive against the Turks, who repeatedly threatened central Europe and even the western Mediterranean. Western Europe turned to the sea-routes for compensation. After the fifteenth century Christian expansion was mostly in the new world of the western hemisphere, or missionaries went by sea around Africa to India and China.

Mongols, Mings, and Manchus in China

What was the effect of the nomadic expansion upon civilization in the Far East? Since the glorious age of the Sung dynasty and the Mongol inroads of the thirteenth century, Chinese civilization may on the whole be said to have done little more than hold its own, remaining in a medieval stage until recent contact with western civilization. The Mongols were expelled in 1368, after which the native Ming dynasty reigned until 1644. Then China was overrun by new nomads from the north, the Manchus, whose foreign dynasty reigned until the recent establishment of the republic.

India under the Moguls

Timur's devastation of northern India in 1398 was followed, over a century later, by the more permanent foundation by Baber in 1526 of the Mohammedan empire of the Great Mogul (i. e. Mongol, although actually, like Timur himself, probably of Turkish race). His capital was at Delhi in the north, with a loose suzerainty over the entire peninsula. Gradually this empire decayed owing to internal weakness, the rise of the native Mahratta states in western and central India, and the development of British rule in the eighteenth and nineteenth centuries.

Kublai Khan and Akbar

The most enlightened Mongol ruler of China was Kublai Khan (1259–1294), with whose luxurious court and efficient government Marco Polo was much impressed. The most enlightened Great Mogul of India was Akbar (1556–1605). These were two great reigns, no doubt, though exaggerated estimates have too often been made of their civilizing influence. Both Kublai and Akbar deserve credit for staying the depredations of their nomadic followers, for recognizing the value of higher civilizations with which they came into contact, for employing able men regardless of race or religion, and for generally efficient rule. But a single despot, however benevolent, cannot revive or create civilization through a vast area; what he is apt to do is simply to concentrate enough of what is left of it about his own person to make a brave show. Even the cruel Timur had an impressive court at Samarkand where he amassed the spoils of cultures that he had uprooted. Kublai was more constructive. To him are credited the Grand Canal, River of Locks, and Transport River, which together provide some 650 miles of water communication between Peking and Canton. Yet he still regularly made the annual nomadic migration to his summer camp in Mongolia. Similarly, long after Akbar there were lesser chieftains who pitched their tents nomadlike in the square before the Mogul's palace at Delhi, "those petty sovereigns having an insuperable objection to be enclosed within walls." Akbar himself had taken delight in the sport of making tame antelopes fight each other, and a century later the Great Mogul still encouraged the Tartar sword exercise of severing a dead sheep with one stroke of the blade.

The hearts of the Chinese and Hindus were not with such monarchs, still less with inferior members of their dynasties. Localism and conservatism have been the natural reaction against such foreign rule and intrusion. A drawing closer of the lines of caste has been the Hindu reply. "Surely it is something that in a country conquered for a thousand years the doorkeeper of a viceroy's palace would feel his race too good to share a cup of water with the ruler of all India." The strength of Chinese local institutions, of the family and ancestor worship, of the gild which controls industrial and business life without governmental support or interference, has preserved Chinese civilization amid repeated invasion and misgovernment. This great stability was long accompanied by excessive conservatism, lack of communication with other parts even of China itself, and mistrust of all foreign ways and ideas. For this past attitude the Chinese were less to blame than their uncongenial Mongol and Manchu invaders. Indeed the Earl of Macartney, in the eighteenth century, believed that the Chinese were ready to adopt European improvements, but that the Tartar government, fearing their subjects' taste for novelty and sagacity in adopting European methods, made it a policy to "impress them with an idea of their own sufficiency and undervalue foreign inventions."

Residue of Localism and Conservatism

Much beautiful architecture in India dates from the Mohammedan period. The Moguls erected tombs, mosques, and palaces at their capital cities of Agra and Delhi which combine the features of Hindu and Moslem art. Especially famous is the Taj Mahal, a magnificent marble mausoleum for his favorite

Magnificent Architecture in Squalid Cities

wife erected by Shah Jehan (1628–1658).   It stands on a great
marble platform 313 feet square with four minarets rising at
the corners.   The building itself is octagonal within and without, surrounded by pointed or keel-shaped arcades, surmounted
by a great bulbous dome over the central chambers and by four
lesser domes.   It is richly ornamented with mosaics and ara-
besques.   Bernier, who described Delhi and Agra just after
Shah Jehan's reign, was astonished at the contemptuous manner in which Europeans in the Indies spoke of these beautiful
towns.   He admitted, however, that the brilliant appearance
of the shops in European towns was wanting here; that, apart
from those of the palace, "workshops, occupied by skilful artisans, would be vainly sought in Delhi"; that most of the
dwelling houses were small ones of mud thatched with straw,
whereas Paris in the seventeenth century consisted "of three or
four cities, piled one upon another, all of them containing numerous apartments, filled, for the most part, from top to
bottom."   And whereas in Paris seven or eight out of every ten
persons seen in the streets would be "tolerably well clad and
have a certain air of respectability, in Delhi for two or three
who wear decent apparel there may always be reckoned seven
or eight poor, ragged, and miserable beings."   There was almost no middle class.

Hindu
Social
Conventions
and Position
of Woman

The social conventions and the position of woman had by
this period at least diverged greatly in east and west despite
the bond of Indo-European origin.   About 1800 the Abbé
Dubois noted that "laws of etiquette and social politeness are
much more clearly laid down, and much better observed by all
classes of Hindus, even by the lowest, than they are by people
of corresponding social position in Europe."   On the other
hand, "what we call love-making is utterly unknown amongst
the Hindus.   The playful sallies, the silly jokes, the perpetual
compliments, and the eager and unlimited display of attention
in which our youth are so profuse, would be looked upon as insults by any Hindu lady, even the least chaste, that is, if they
were offered to her in public. . . . To inquire after a man's
wife, too, is an unpardonable breach of good manners."   And,
"if a European lady is seen taking a gentleman's arm, even
though he may profess the profoundest respect for her, nothing
would persuade a Hindu that she was not his mistress."   On the
other hand, "A Hindu woman can go anywhere alone, even in

the most crowded places, and she need never fear the imperti-
nent looks and jokes of idle loungers." It will be noted that our
manners have somewhat modified from those of France in Dubois'
time, yet in the main the contrast still holds. A recent missionary points out that "a westerner would suffocate in a room in
which Hindus would delight to spend a night," and repeats
Dubois' statements that a mother-in-law is not permitted to
appear in the presence of the husband, that the wife waits on
the husband at meals and takes the leavings, and walks several
paces behind him in the street. The Hindus are opposed to
the education of women, while a very recent writer asserts
that "the higher castes still regard the masses as little better
than beasts, and these depressed classes still acquiesce in their
dependence and show little sign of throwing off their social
degradation."

Under the Mongol, Ming, and Manchu dynasties the amount Chinese
of Chinese poetry kept increasing, but the T'ang and Sung Drama and
standards were not improved upon, there was little new develop- Fiction
ment. The drama, however, seems to have come in under the
Mongols. Chinese fiction began in the thirteenth century and
reached its height in the seventeenth. Chinese actors are often
called "Apprentices of the Pear-tree Garden," because in the
eighth century an emperor of the T'ang dynasty founded an
academy of that name to give choral or operatic performances.
True stage-plays for the people are first heard of in the thirteenth century. The Mongol dynasty was the great period
of dramatic activity with some eighty-five names of authors
known, of whose plays a selection of one hundred has been preserved. Modern Chinese plays follow this past model. Most
of the actors still come from Peking and are trained from child-
hood to contort both face and body. Women's parts, usually
played by men, are the best acted and paid. The first known
Chinese novel, *San Kuo Chih*, was historical, dealing with the
stirring times of the declining Han dynasty. *Hung Lou Mêng*,
perhaps the greatest novel of the seventeenth century, is described as "a creation of a very high order" with an "intricate
and original plot" and a "startlingly tragic dénouement."
Each of its more than four hundred characters stands out as
"a distinct personality, drawn with marvelous skill."

Beginning with the Ming dynasty (1368–1644), elaborate
ornamentation and somewhat excessive grace and elegance have

Over-
Elaborate
Art of the
Ming
Dynasty

replaced the simple dignity of the art of the earlier periods. In bronze work, for instance, there was improvement in technique and workmanship, but the majestic, if crude, grandeur of the old bronzes was lost in a wealth of decoration. Painting also lost in directness and became rather too complicated. We have to judge Chinese furniture entirely by specimens from the time of the Ming dynasty or later. The work of the sixteenth and seventeenth centuries seems the more artistic; greater mechanical skill is evidenced in the eighteenth century. At that time the Earl of Macartney wrote of the Chinese, "They have tables, couches, and chairs, loosely covered with rich carpeting, but they have no bureaux, commodes, lustres, or looking-glasses."

Oranges and
Shams

The artificial character which then seems to have taken possession of Chinese civilization did not escape the sharp eyes of contemporaries, if we may judge by the following diverting passage from a writer of the Ming dynasty:

"I saw oranges exposed on a fruit-stand in midsummer, and sold at a fabulous price. They looked fresh and tempting, and I bought one. On breaking it open, a puff of something like smoke filled my mouth and nose. Turning to the seller I demanded, 'Why do you sell such fruit? It is fit for nothing but to offer to the gods or to set before strangers. What a sham! What a disgraceful cheat!'

" 'Well were it,' replied the fruit-seller, 'if my oranges were the only shams.' And he went on to show how we have sham soldiers in the field, sham statesmen in the cabinet, and shams everywhere. I walked away silently, musing whether this fruit-seller might not be, after all, a philosopher who had taken to selling rotten oranges in order to have a text from which to preach on the subject of shams" (from Martin, *Lore of Cathay,* pp. 122–123).

The Chinese soldiers, however, were not always shams, since in the eighteenth century they were still capable of performing such a feat as marching two thousand miles across the plateau of Tibet and defeating the warlike inhabitants of Nepal in northern India on their own soil.

Effect of
the Manchu
Invasion

The Manchu invaders, who finally established their dynasty in China in 1644, imposed the pigtail upon the conquered male population, but after four years withdrew the edict by which they had forbidden the practice of binding the feet of girls—

VAULTING AND WOODWORK

Above, diagonal ribs carrying vaulting, from the church of Madeleine,
Vezelay; below, grotesque from Lincoln cathedral.

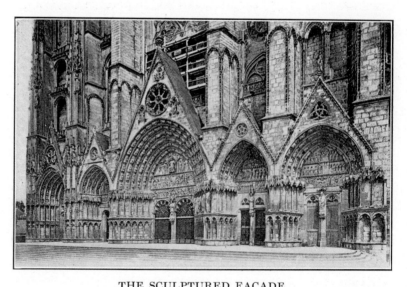

THE SCULPTURED FAÇADE

Above, sculpture over the portals of the Romanesque church of Notre-Dame-la-Grande, Poitiers; below, the portals of Bourges cathedral.

although the Manchu women continued not to bind theirs. The Manchus had agreed from the first that there should be no Chinese concubines in the imperial palace. They made an effort to keep their own language and to have all the important Chinese works translated into it. The regulations of the imperial academy early in the twentieth century still prescribed two presidents, two librarians, and so on, one Manchu and one Chinese in each case. But the Manchu language had become practically obsolete in Peking even before the overthrow of the dynasty. The invaders still filled public offices by the system of competitive examinations, but a disproportionately large number were reserved for the Manchus, who competed for these only among themselves and not with the Chinese. During the eighteenth century there were two long and prosperous reigns of able emperors, but toward the close of the Manchu dynasty everything in China seemed to have run down. How far the new Chinese Republic will remedy this condition, and whether it is true that the Chinese have lost their originating power and become merely clever copiers of others, time will tell.

Already in the seventh and eighth centuries of our era feudalism was taking a strong hold on Japan. The final stages of the conquest from the aboriginal Ainu were carried out by a warrior aristocracy. The mass of the population, ceasing to fight, had become serfs on large estates which belonged to Buddhist temples, nobles, and high officials. When the northern and eastern parts of the main island were subdued, they became tax-free estates of the nobles who had conquered them or who reclaimed them by serf labor. The mass of the peasants was shifted to these tax-free lands. The system of communication broke down between the tenth and twelfth centuries; feudal warfare was frequent from the twelfth until the seventeenth century. The great Buddhist monasteries became fortresses. The sovereigns were often weak minors under the power of feudal administrators, like the later Frankish kings of the Merovingian dynasty and their Carolingian mayors of the palace, who initiated a similar feudal period in western Europe. The Japanese aristocracy gave much attention to costumes and uniforms. At one time there were some twenty-six different kinds of head-gear denoting as many social grades. Again, the men wore several suits of clothes at once so that the overlapping colors contrasted, or powdered and rouged their faces

Feudal
Japan

like women.   Armor was elaborately decorated by the twelfth century, but swords were not until the fifteenth.

From the eleventh century a native style in painting developed and excellent sculpture in wood, although wooden masks for theatrical performances had been used even earlier.   The earliest Japanese literature was historical, dating from the seventh and eighth centuries.   Early in the eleventh century two ladies, one in a sort of novel, the other in a book entitled Pillow Sketches, gave a very detailed and realistic picture of the society of their time.   From the fourteenth to the seventeenth century, was in general a dark period for Japanese art and letters, although some dramas and new Chinese schools of painting marked the fifteenth century.   From 1615 to 1864 Japan became free from feudal and civil warfare, as the nobles were required to spend every alternate year at the capital where they maintained family mansions.   Kowa Seki, born in the same year as Sir Isaac Newton, is said to have invented the binomial theorem independently.   The seventeenth century was also a period of renaissance when Japanese traditions and ancient styles were revived, and when further innovations were made from China.   Lacquer work was advanced to an excellence surpassing even the Chinese.   Great skill was displayed in block color-printing, which was perhaps introduced from the western world like tobacco.   From the seventeenth century also date the popular stage and a school of painters who represented the life of their own times.   In the two following centuries naturalistic painting came in.   The Japanese have shown themselves extremely deft and skilful workers in the arts in modern times.

BIBLIOGRAPHY

Archer, T. A. and Kingsford, C. L. *The Crusades*, 1895.

Aston, W. G. *Shinto (The Way of the Gods)*, 1905.

Beazley, C. R. *Dawn of Modern Geography*, 1897–1906, 3 vols.; an elaborate original treatment and standard work.

Bernier, F. *Travels in the Mogul Empire, 1656–1668*, ed. V. A. Smith, 1914.

Cesconsky, Herbert. *Chinese Furniture*, 1922.

Chamberlain, B. H. *Things Japanese*, 1890.

Curtin, J. *The Mongols in Russia*, 1908; *The Mongols: a History*, 1908.

Gibbons, H. A. *The Foundation of the Ottoman Empire*, 1916.

Giles, H. A. *China and the Manchus*, 1912.

Harrison, E. J. *Lithuania, Past and Present,* 1922.

Harzer, Paul. *Die exakten Wissenschaften im alten Japan,* 1905, 39 pp.

Kennedy, P. *History of the Great Moghuls . . . 1398–1739,* 1905.

King, G. *A Brief Account of the Military Orders in Spain,* 1922.

Krey, A. C. *The First Crusade,* 1921; our chief original sources for it brought together in translation.

La Jonquière, *Histoire de l'empire ottoman,* 1914, 2 vols.

Lodge, R. *The Close of the Middle Ages,* 1901; purely political history.

Martin, F. R. *The Miniature Painting and Painters of Persia, India, and Turkey, from the 8th to the 18th century,* 1913, 2 vols.

Moreland, W. H. *India at the Death of Akbar; an economic study,* 1920.

Munro, Prutz, and Diehl, *Essays on the Crusades,* 1903; suggestive studies.

Oaten, E. F. *European Travelers in India* (15th–17th centuries), 1909.

Page, Curtis Hidden. *Japanese Poetry; an historical essay,* 1923.

Parker, E. H. *A Thousand Years of the Tartars,* 1895.

Piggott, J. F. *Music and Musical Instruments of Japan,* 1893.

Wright, J. K. *Geographical Lore of the Time of the Crusades,* 1925.

Yolland, A. B. *Hungary,* 1917, Chapters 7, 8, 9, 10.

Yule, Sir Henry. *The Book of Ser Marco Polo,* 3rd edition revised by Cordier, 1903, 2 vols.; also in the Everyman library. *Cathay and the Way Thither: being a collection of medieval notices of China,* revised ed. by H. Cordier, 1913–1915, 3 vols.

Zimmern, Helen. *The Hansa Towns,* 1889.

And further chapters in books on India, China, and Japan already listed at the close of previous chapters.

BOOK VII.   EARLY MODERN TIMES

CHAPTER XXXI

THE RISE OF MONARCHY, INDIVIDUALISM, AND CAPITAL IN WESTERN EUROPE

Two things produce a nation—a rich inheritance of memories and the desire to preserve those memories.—E. M. Hulme

General Character of Early Modern Times

AFTER the revival of civilization in the west which has been outlined in the previous book there appears to have been a falling-off in enterprise and prosperity. The reader should beware of regarding the period of early modern times, upon which we now enter, as one of wholesome, steady progress and general happiness. From the time of the first great outbreak of the Black Death in 1348 to the late seventeenth or even early eighteenth century Europe was constantly plague-ridden, with the result that the population was kept down, and all sorts of human activities were subject to continual interruption from the pestilence. From the Hundred Years War (1337–1453) on, general wars convulsed Europe, civil and religious struggles on a large scale being added to those of rival kings and nations. Old local centers of civilization lost their former prosperity as well as their independence. Relatively few new buildings were erected. Popular political and social institutions ceased to develop. The educational situation was often very discouraging. Disruptive changes such as the rise of monarchy, individualism, and capital, and the religious breach and secularization added to the distress. At the same time there were great developments, such as the discovery of the new world and new sea routes to the east, the flowering of national literatures, and the progress of science. But the economic prosperity of this period was largely confined to certain western powers like Holland and England which profited by the change in sea routes and colonial possessions. And there was something hard, unwholesome, narrow, artificial about much of the civilization between the fifteenth and eighteenth centuries.

Through the middle ages the ideal prevailed of one Christian community or city of God, and the historian's guiding interest was to present the past as the working out of a divine plan, first through God's chosen people, the Hebrews of the Old Testament, thereafter through the progress of the Christian Church.   In modern times the patriotic historian has largely confined his attention to a glorification of the past of his own nation which he has tacitly, at least, regarded as God's chosen people.   Even the impartial historian has too often found his chief interest in the rise and conflict of the different present nationalities, which he would actually try to trace back or to put back into the medieval or even the ancient period.   But the nations of today are not the nations of yesterday, and we have no assurance that they will be the nations of tomorrow. In the twelfth century the true nation or "people" seems to have been the small feudal state such as Normandy, Brittany, Piedmont, or Bavaria, or the independent city such as Venice. Each had its own language, customs, and past tradition; even to this day their inhabitants are spoken of and think of themselves as Normans, Bretons, Piedmontese, Bavarians, and Venetians.   They may read as school children in a little textbook that was published in Paris that they are Frenchmen or in a modern newspaper that they are Italians or Germans.   The memories that cling to the very soil, and the traditions that long passed from mouth to mouth are more local and near. Frenchmen, Italians, and Germans are much later breeds, built up by conquest and aggression, by incorporating discordant elements and stifling local liberties and aspirations.   The recent treaty of Versailles has attempted to restore to life certain suppressed nationalities like the Poles and Lithuanians, to reduce to normal size certain bloated nationalities, and, unfortunately, to inflate others still further.   Bloated nationalities are those which have gobbled up and swallowed other nations or which are puffed up with patriotic oratory, propaganda, press agitation, and self-esteem.   One feels a mischievous desire to stick a pin into them, but the explosion would be something terrific.   Our purpose here is rather to place them against their true background by setting forth first the politi-

Nationalities: Medieval and Modern, Bloated and Suppressed

cal conditions of the preceding medieval period and then the gradual emergence of a different state of affairs, especially from the fifteenth century on.

Four Chief Factors in Medieval Government

Most modern nations have grown up about monarchs or about oligarchies expressive of capitalistic enterprise. In a medieval state there were commonly four chief elements: the king or other head of the state, the feudal lords, the church, and popular or local institutions. The power of the head of the state was limited by feudalism both in theory and practice. Feudal theory was that the power of the lord was based upon, and limited by, a contract expressed or understood between him and each of his vassals; that they had duties to him, and he to them; that if either violated his part of the bond, the other was thereby freed from his obligation. In practice kings had to rule subject to feudal limitations and largely by feudal methods. When the barons forced King John of England to sign Magna Carta (1215), they were simply making him agree to such a contract in writing, and its detailed provisions will be found to be largely feudal in character. The innumerable charters granted in this period to monasteries, merchants, and towns express or extend the same principle. The church, with its own courts of law, officials, synods and councils, existed everywhere as a sort of state within a state,—or better, the states of the medieval period existed as states within a church. Sometimes the church sided with the feudal lords against the king, sometimes with the king against the feudal lords. Nationalist historians have generally held that the church on the whole supported the growth of monarchy; perhaps their view is none too reliable. Certainly they have given far less attention to the popular or local institutions of the middle ages than to the rise of the monarchies. How important such popular institutions really were, has already been illustrated in showing that the economic life of the period was almost wholly local in conduct and control, that even distant trade with other continents was not carried on between nations, but by towns such as Venice and Genoa which were independent sovereign states. Indeed, as late as the sixteenth century the credit of the German Free Cities was much superior to that of "poor and dishonest national governments," and they would readily dispose of their bonds at five per cent when great monarchs like Charles V and Francis I found it hard to borrow at ten or twenty per cent.

WORKS OF DONA-
TELLO
Left, Niccolo da Uz-
zano; right, Amorino.

PORTRAITS
Left, old man
and his grand-
son, by Ghir-
landajo; right,
Lucrezia Cri-
velli (?) by
Leonardo da
Vinci.

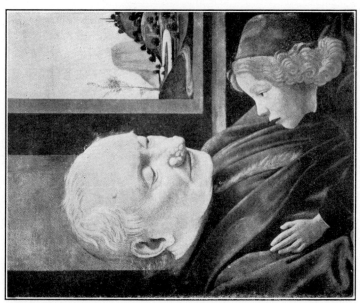

Yet the ideal of one united Christian community was strong, Empire and Papacy and also the recollection of the Roman Empire. These two thoughts are combined in the name, Holy Roman Empire, applied to the state that resulted from the coronation of the Saxon, Otto I, at Rome in 962 A. D.   While the emperor might claim to be supreme overlord of all western Christendom, his real authority was confined to the regions lying north to south between Saxony and Rome, and east to west between Bohemia and Burgundy.   Even there his power was very limited.   The Lombard communes, for instance, became practically independent at an early date.   Moreover, the emperor found a rival for the headship of the Christian world state in the pope, whose court at Rome transacted ten times as much real business in the way of government as did the emperor, who in fact hardly succeeded in establishing any permanent organs of government at all.   Pope and not emperor initiated the crusades; more monarchs admitted that they were vassals of the pope than paid homage to the emperor; the papal diplomacy was far superior to the imperial arms.   Naturally pope and emperor came into frequent conflict, not however so much over the question of world empire—in that respect the emperor did not have a chance —as over such questions as whether the emperor should have any control over the clergy in his own territories or whether he should be allowed to establish a strong government in the Italian peninsula.

The papacy decided that the latter would be dangerous to Disunion of Germany and Italy until the Nineteenth Century its own position at Rome and succeeded in totally ruining the House of Hohenstaufen which attempted it.   After an interregnum from 1256 to 1273 the subsequent emperors were weak, seldom ventured south of the Alps, and failed to keep order even in their German territories, where the Swiss Confederation, Hanseatic League, and other petty states and local courts looked after themselves.   The net result was that what we now call Italy and Germany remained disunited groups of states until the last century.   Even Switzerland, although from 1499 it was practically independent of the Holy Roman Empire, did not have a real federal government until the nineteenth century. For three hundred and fifty years it was a mere league of local states, any one of which could make separate alliances with foreign countries.

England and France, however, were already assuming form. England

The amalgamation of originally independent Anglo-Saxon tribal kingdoms which had been effected by Alfred and his successors as they recovered the lost territory from the Danes, had begun to fall to pieces again, when William the Conqueror reduced the whole to submission with brutal thoroughness and organized it with rare intelligence, although necessarily largely on a feudal basis, linking up local and popular institutions with the central government. Under successors who pursued the same policy, a national legal system resulted,—the English Common Law. It was another foreign monarch, fresh from Anjou, Henry Plantagenet, who did most towards instituting this national legal system, and his lawyers were trained in Roman and Canon Law. Natives would have kept their local customs. For the most part the Norman and Plantagenet kings gave a strong government, strong to the point of oppression and extortion. Consequently the opposition to them had to be kingdom-wide or national to hope to succeed. It expressed itself in Magna Carta in 1215 and later in the parliament which represented all England. Wales was conquered by the English king, quite against the wish of its inhabitants, towards the close of the thirteenth century, but was not represented in parliament until the sixteenth century. Since 1603 Scotland had the same king as England, but the Act uniting the two kingdoms into one Great Britain was not passed until 1707. Ireland, gradually occupied, lost, and reconquered, has never been a willing partner and now is again—at least in part and in name—a "Free State."

France   From 987 to 1108 the Capetian kings cut a sorry figure compared to the great feudal lords in what is now France. However, at Paris they had an advantageous situation with a surrounding region rich in varied natural resources. Until 1328 their direct male line was continuous with few minorities, an immense advantage in a period when so much depended on family alliances and personal feudal relationships. They seem to have maintained harmonious relations with the church. After 1108 there were several rulers of great individual ability under whom the royal domain and influence were greatly augmented. The French kings pursued the policy of "Divide and rule," seldom dealing with their subjects as a whole but treating each province differently and negotiating with it separately. The Estates General met infrequently unless the king was absent or a minor, and displayed very little independence. In the fifteenth century the king began to collect taxes, to maintain a standing army, and to enact laws, independently of the Estates General,—things which the kings of England could not do without the consent of parliament. But the policy of "Divide and rule" also maintained the old medieval nationalities, and at the Estates General of 1484 "France" was only one of six regions which voted separately, the others being Normandy, Burgundy, Aquitaine, Languedoc, and Provence. Brittany and Alsace-Lorraine were added still later. Most of these regions remained practically independent nations with their own laws, customs, taxes, tariffs, and system of government. The division of what we now call France into such provinces continued until the French Revolution. Even the French language was not introduced in the provinces of the *Midi*, or south of France, until between 1450 and 1600.

After more or less standing still and maintaining the *status quo* from the mid-thirteenth to the mid-fifteenth century, the various kingdoms of the Spanish peninsula, with the exception of Portugal, suddenly coalesced at the close of the fifteenth century. Ferdinand of Aragon married Isabella of Castile and Leon; in 1482 they brought the church in Spain under the control of the crown; they completed the conquest of Granada in 1492; Ferdinand annexed Navarre to Castile after Isabella's death in the early sixteenth century. What was then called Spain did not end there. Sardinia had belonged to Aragon since 1297; Sicily and the Kingdom of Naples had been more or less connected with it; both they and the Duchy of Milan were ruled by the Spanish king in the sixteenth and seventeenth centuries. Spain at that time further gained great treasure and possessions in the new world and seemed a great military power in European affairs, but its component parts were far from being contented, even in the Spanish peninsula itself. The Moors were repeatedly persecuted and finally driven out of the peninsula. Catalonia and Barcelona revolted against King Charles I (1516–1556); they have been revolting against the Spanish government again today. From 1580 to 1640 Portugal was annexed by Spain, but then recovered its independence. Such instructive facts illustrate the transitory, shifting, evanescent, kaleidoscopic character of political and national boundaries.

The Spanish Peninsula

The
House of
Hapsburg

Ferdinand and Isabella had no sons. Their oldest daughter married a member of the Austrian House of Hapsburg. Her son, Charles, became both King Charles I of Spain and Emperor Charles V of the Holy Roman Empire. From his paternal grandparents he inherited Austria and the Tyrol—with prospects of Milan and the kingdoms of Bohemia and Hungary which were realized in 1526—and the Netherlands and a county of Burgundy which is now embedded well within the borders of France. Indeed, he fought several wars with the kings of France, and this rivalry of France and the House of Hapsburg forms the key to the political history of Europe in the sixteenth and seventeenth centuries. But we will not turn the key for fear that we would find nothing inside. Suffice it to say that Charles' brother succeeded him as emperor and as ruler of Austria, Bohemia, and Hungary, thus constituting the modern state of Austria-Hungary, while his son Philip II kept all the Spanish possessions that we have already enumerated and also the Netherlands and county of Burgundy. Thus there were henceforth two branches of the Hapsburg family, the Austrian and the Spanish; they were thereby enabled to make twice as much trouble. The Netherlands proceeded to revolt against Philip, and the Dutch portion finally made good its independence.

Rise of Individualism and Capital

It would be a very questionable generalization to say that in all respects the modern period has given greater prominence to the individual than the medieval period gave. Just at present we are so committed to mass production and education of the masses that we are hardly in a position to boast of our individuality. On the other hand, feudalism, for example, was notoriously individualistic; the bond between the lord and each of his vassals was personal, while modern government is territorial. It has been repeatedly stated that, while the knights were great individual fighters, the feudal armies lacked discipline and cohesion. On the contrary, the self-abnegation of the medieval monk, without personal property or family, trained in obedience and humility, may be contrasted with the reliance on the individual conscience supposed to have been introduced by the Protestant Reformation. But what we wish more especially to note now is the growth in connection with the rise of capital of a spirit of individual gain in economic life, which seems in rather sharp contrast with the common cultivation of open fields and the gild life of the middle ages.   Just as certain kings and dynasties, whether through superior ability and organization, or luck, inheritance, lack of scruple, and disregard of popular rights, emerged triumphant from the medley of feudal states with large acquisitions of territory, so certain individuals came up from the peasants or townsmen, with large acquisitions of land or capital similarly obtained, to form a new middle class or *bourgeoisie*.   They left the mass of peasants, artisans, and shop-keepers reduced to a worse state comparatively than before, whether through misfortune, disinheritance, inferior ability, or too strict and blind adherence to old methods and ideals.   However, in so far as capital was now employed more productively than before, the general wealth and standard of living would tend to rise.   And as facilities were provided for everyone to invest his savings or accumulated wealth productively, many could share directly as well as indirectly in the advance.   But from the fifteenth to the eighteenth century there were still relatively few such persons. Gradually this new class which controlled capital was to reduce even the clergy and nobility to positions of minor importance in society.   Such is the economic and social history of several centuries in a nutshell.

A few specific illustrations of the change may, however, be added.   In fifteenth century England the letters of the Paston family show a somewhat coarse, unattractive household of ordinary freemen accumulating considerable landed estates and holding high offices.   At the same time the Wars of the Roses were exterminating the old nobility, while a middle class family even ascended the throne in the persons of the Tudors. In France courtly, chivalric, cultured figures and open natures, like Charles the Bold of Burgundy and King René the Good of Anjou and Provence, succumbed to the machinations of the ill-clad, stealthy, miserly, cruel Louis XI.   Common cultivation of the soil was ceasing in England, as we saw, by the sixteenth century; on the continent the life of the peasants was less affected.   But already in the thirteenth century we saw capitalistic banking firms in Italian cities, and there were capitalistic cloth merchants in Flemish towns before the rise of the clothiers of England.   Of the rich individual a good French example of the fifteenth century is Jacques Cœur of Bourges, where his magnificent Gothic mansion may still be seen.   He

Some Examples

was a silversmith and banker, an owner of both ships and mines; he revived the commerce of French Mediterranean ports with the Levant, was interested in the paper and silk industries, and was the chief financial support of the French monarchy. In sixteenth century Germany the banking house of Fuggers was a leading instance of the merchant princes. Its members were descended from a fourteenth century weaver.

Relation of Renaissance Culture to Monarchy and Individualism

The culture of the Quattrocento and Cinquecento, or period of the so-called Italian Renaissance, was much affected by the forces which we have been outlining. In Italy it was the age of the despots, ambitious individuals who seized the government of cities formerly ruled by communes. Many of the humanists were too self-centred, or wrote rather more fulsomely adulatory dedications to their princely patrons than had before been customary, although individuals had written for patrons a good deal in the twelfth and thirteenth centuries. In art, all over western Europe, representations of individual donors began to figure in stained glass windows and religious paintings as they had not done before, sculptured funeral monuments grew more pretentious, and the painting of individual portraits became common. The popes themselves were among the worst offenders in this respect; the frescoes of the Sistine Chapel and Stanze of Raphael reflect and flatter their personal pride. Often the faces of heroes of sacred legend are really portraits of Julius II or Leo X. Indeed, the faces in sixteenth century art cannot compare in fineness of character with those of the thirteenth century sculpture, and, as a rule, do well to conceal their features behind beards. Was this the fault of the artists, or had there been a general falling off in human character and ideals? Bishop Stubbs was of the opinion that "the sixteenth century, as a century of ideas, real, grand, and numerous, is not to be compared with the thirteenth century. The ideas are not so pure, not so living, nor so refined. The men are not so earnest, so single-hearted, so lovable by far."

For royal and private palaces the revived classical or Renaissance architecture came to be preferred to the Gothic, until today the latter seems to us essentially ecclesiastical. Well it may, compared to the neo-classical or Renaissance churches like St. Peter's at Rome or St. Paul's in London, with their suggestion of the architecture of pagan temples. The architects of this new style aimed in the case of a palace or great house at presenting a grand front, a regular well-proportioned exterior, while within there was a grand staircase, a long sombre picture gallery, and some cheerless rectangular apartments of state with stuccoed ceilings but no thought of comfort or convenience. On the other hand, illuminations in manuscripts, engravings in books, tapestries, enamels, furniture,—all such things had become more elaborate, refined, and true to life in the later middle ages and sixteenth century, or at least more in accord with our present notions of how such things should look. Modern museums, for instance, always seem to put on show fifteenth and sixteenth century illuminated manuscripts in preference to twelfth and thirteenth century ones.

It is a noteworthy point that the voyages of discovery of the fifteenth and sixteenth centuries, to which we turn in the next chapter, were largely carried on by ambitious individuals like Columbus and directed or supported by monarchs like John II of Portugal or Queen Isabella of Spain. Columbus came from an Italian trading city, Genoa, but sought support for his enterprise from one monarch after another. Many other navigators and cartographers of the age of discovery were from Italian cities but entered the service of the western monarchies as individuals. Some improved their position, others wrecked their fortunes in the new enterprises. The capital for Columbus' first voyage was not supplied entirely by the Spanish monarchs but in part by private capitalists, the Pinzon brothers of Palos. The communal gilds, the independent towns, had almost no share in the new movement. Thus it was the new modern nationalities that profited by the great extension of trade and territory which was to follow, that gained a new sense of self-consciousness by their rivalry with ships and settlers flying the flags of other monarchs, by their feeling of contrast to the strange lands beyond the seas which they visited, or their feeling of superiority to oriental and aboriginal races of a different color than their own, who fell such easy victims to their force and guile. Individualism was equally heightened in the adventurers and settlers who broke away from the conventions and institutions of their home communities to seek their own fortunes or realize their own ideals in an unfamiliar environment, to which each must adapt himself as best

Relation of the Voyages of Discovery to Monarchy and Individualism he could with less help or hindrance than before from the experience or habits of society.

BIBLIOGRAPHY

Bennett, H. S. *The Pastons and Their England,* 1922.

Brun, A. *Recherches historiques sur l'introduction du Français dans les provinces du Midi,* 1923.

Cotta, J. G. *Zur Entstehung des Kapitalismus in Venedig,* 1905.

Cuvelier, Joseph. *Les origines de la fortune de la maison d'Orange-Nassau, contribution à l'histoire du capitalisme au moyen âge,* 1921.

Deroisin, H. P. *Mémoire sur Philippe le Bel et les origines de la société moderne,* 1912.

Dunbar, C. F. *Theory and History of Banking,* 2nd ed., 1901.

Gairdner, J. *The Paston Letters,* 2nd ed., 1901.

Goris, J. A. *Étude sur les colonies marchandes méridionales (Portugais, Espagnols, Italiens) à Anvers de 1488 à 1567: contribution à l'histoire des débuts du capitalisme moderne,* 1925. Despite its particular title, this work has been hailed as "the most important contribution yet made to an understanding of European commerce as a whole in this critical period of its development."

Hashagen, J. "Calvinism and Capitalism on the Rhine," in *Schmollers Jahrbuch,* vol. XLVII (1924); the article is a part of his book on Rhenish Protestantism and Rhenish civilization.

Hayes, C. J. H. *Essays on Nationalism,* 1926.

Heaton, H. *Yorkshire Woollen and Worsted Industries,* 1920.

Hewins, W. A. S. *English Trade and Finance in the Seventeenth Century,* 1892.

Holdsworth, W. S. *A History of English Law,* 3rd ed., 1923.

Huizinga, J. *The Waning of the Middle Ages,* 1924.

Sombart, W. *Der moderne Kapitalismus,* 4th ed., 1921, 2 vols.; *The Quintessence of Capitalism,* 1915, is a translation of his *Der Bourgeois.*

Unwin, Geo. *Industrial Organization in the Sixteenth and Seventeenth Centuries,* 1909.

CHAPTER XXXII

NEW CONTINENTS AND SEA ROUTES

. . . That of the world least part to us is read;
And daily how through hardy enterprize
Many great Regions are discoverèd,
Which to late age were never mentionèd.

—*Spenser*

IN our chapter on Latin learning in the middle ages we have already spoken of the very considerable advances made in geographical knowledge before the fifteenth century. In the thirteenth century Europeans were able to cross Asia to the camp of the Great Khan at Karakorum or to his Chinese capital at Peking. Before 1351 they had sailed hundreds of miles out of sight of land into the Atlantic and charted the Azores, for the mariner's compass had been known since the twelfth century. The Basques had doubtless pursued the black whale far beyond the confines of the Bay of Biscay. In 1424 sailors from Bristol began to go to Iceland for stockfish "by needle and by stone." When in 1425 the herring began to spawn in the North Sea, the Dutch Netherlands began to rival the Hanseatic League. Through the fifteenth century the Portuguese kept edging southward along the west coast of Africa until they first crossed the equator and then in 1487 rounded the Cape of Good Hope, so named because they expected soon to reach the desired shores of India. Various Portuguese and English seamen were also sailing westward into the Atlantic in search of good fishing or islands to which they might lay claim.

Exploration and Discovery from the Thirteenth to Fifteenth Century

The voyages of Columbus, who is commonly credited with the discovery of America in 1492, should be regarded simply as one further step in this exploration of new seas and coasts which had been going on for some time and was bound to lead soon to the discovery of America. It is now disputed whether his purpose at the start was to reach the East Indies and Cathay by sailing west, or simply "to discover and appropriate" for the Spanish sovereigns, Ferdinand and Isabella, "certain islands

Voyages of Columbus

389

and mainland in the Ocean." Soon, at least, he convinced himself that he had reached the outskirts of China and India, and he died in that belief. His voyages brought Spain first into the American continents and led to Spanish preemption of most of the new world. But as Portugal had already been exploring the Atlantic for a century or so, it was necessary for Spain to come to some understanding with her. In 1494 it was agreed that Spain might annex all new discoveries lying beyond a meridian 370 leagues west of the Cape Verde Islands. All new lands east of this were reserved for Portugal, who thereby was able to lay claim to Brazil.

Further Exploration and Discovery in the Western Hemisphere The return of Columbus from his first voyage with natives and reports of abundant gold in the new regions promptly stimulated many other navigators to similar voyages of exploration and discovery, if they were not engaged in them before. Of many of these voyages perhaps no report has survived whatever; indeed, few of the great discoverers left personal narratives. Almost all the originals of the maps charted by these early expeditions have been lost, although almost immediately afterward we have new world maps by geographers in Europe which are evidently in part based upon such charts. But these circumstances make it difficult to tell how new lands got their names and who discovered each first. Our information, for example, is very scanty concerning the voyages of John Cabot and his sons, Venetians in English service. On his first voyage in 1497 he appears to have reached the coast of Labrador, but we know indirectly from Portuguese archives that a Portuguese named Labrador made some voyage of discovery between 1490 and 1495. There were at least eight voyages to the coasts of South America between 1498 and 1502. In 1513 Balboa "stared at the Pacific," while Ponce de León landed in Florida, thereby initiating Spanish exploration of the interior as well as of the coast of North America. The expedition of Ferdinand Magellan, a Portuguese mariner sailing under the Spanish flag, was the first which is known to have circumnavigated the globe. Starting in September, 1519, with five old vessels, untrustworthy crews and captains, he encountered long calms, terrific storms, intense cold, disease, mutiny, and famine. It took him five weeks to pass through the straits at the southern extremity of South America which have since borne his name and so enter the Pacific. It was 1521 when he reached the Philippines, where he met his death in a fight with the natives, but his one remaining vessel regained Spain in September, 1522, after almost three full years' absence.

The Spaniards also explored the Pacific coasts of both North and South America, and led various expeditions into the interior. It was eight years (1528–1536) before the four survivors of Narvaez's inland expedition of three hundred men, which had started at Tampa Bay in Florida, reached the Gulf of California. Cortés had conquered Mexico from the Aztecs (1518–1521); Pizarro, Peru from the Incas (1532); Coronado visited the Grand Canyon in 1540, and the next year De Soto discovered the Mississippi. Towards the close of the sixteenth century both the Dutch and English were at war with Spain and Portugal, and directed voyages of trade, plunder, and exploration both to eastern and western seas. They sought in vain to shorten the distance to the Far East by searching for a northwest passage through the continent of North America to the Pacific, or a northeast passage which would lead around Europe to China. In the early seventeenth century they both planted colonies in North America. As maritime powers they proved superior to Spain and Portugal and gradually gained control of the seas. Cape Horn was first rounded in 1616 and named from the Dutch town, Hoorn, whence the expedition had sailed the previous year. France, which was often at war with Spain in the sixteenth century, attempted various settlements from the St. Lawrence to Florida during that period. They were without lasting success until the seventeenth century, when the French occupied the basin of the St. Lawrence and the Great Lakes. Germans were also active in the Atlantic until the Thirty Years War (1618–1648) checked the economic development of Germany.

Because of Columbus' conviction that he had reached the orient by sailing west, the natives of America came to be known as Indians and the islands which had been discovered as the West Indies. Many of the Indian tribes in North and South America were in a state of savagery which has already been sufficiently described in our chapters on the stone age and primitive custom and thought. Others, although they too still used stone knives and arrowheads and practiced barbarities, had distinctive, in some respects highly developed, civilizations. The chief cultures of this kind were those of the Aztecs and their predeces-

Aboriginal
American
Civilizations

sors in Mexico, the Incas and their predecessors in Peru, and the Mayas in Central America.   The Aztecs, who were migratory in the twelfth century of our era, founded the city of Mexico about 1325 and established a bloodthirsty military domination over the surrounding tribes.   The earlier culture of the Toltecs in Mexico can be traced back to the eighth century.   The first of the Incas ruled about 1134 A. D., but the great expansion of their power began only about a century before its overthrow by Pizarro.   There had been a long development of art before them, and they were in many ways inferior to their various predecessors.   When the Spaniards entered Yucatan in the sixteenth century, they found already deserted and in ruins those cities and stone buildings which are our chief source of information concerning the aboriginal civilization of Central America.   The Old Empire of the Mayas seems to have existed approximately during the first seven centuries of our era, although the earliest dated monument goes back to about 200 B. C.   Three artistically illustrated manuscripts are all that remain of Maya literature.   As this volume is being published, the Mason-Spinden expedition of 1926 is discovering new sites and remains of Maya civilization along the coast of Yucatan.

Question of Origins   There is a general resemblance between these various cultures which points to a common origin, and in many ways their civilization seems an importation from Asia.   Especially striking is what seems the representation of an elephant with a mahout in one of their works of art.   The present inhabitants of northeastern Asia show signs of racial connection with the American Indian, making it probable that man entered America at a relatively late date by way of Siberia and the Aleutian Islands.   It is tempting to connect the ancient Peruvian system of knots for keeping records and the wampum belts of the North American Indians with the use of knotted cords which Chinese historians say preceded written characters.   It is impressive to find both Mayas and Toltecs building pyramids, the latter worshiping the sun disk, the former orienting their structures according to the four points of the compass, building platforms and sunken courts like those of Persepolis and Cnossus, vaulted ceilings like the bee-hive tombs at Mycenæ, or carving fantastic façades like those of Hindu temples, and surrounding the base of the pyramid with a sculptured wall as the Hinda stupa is

PALACES OF THE FIFTEENTH AND SIXTEENTH CENTURIES

Above, Palazzo Consiglio, Verona, erected 1476–1493; below, Palazzo
Farnese, Rome, of the sixteenth century.

FIGURES OF THE REFOR-MATION

Left, portrait by Holbein of Erasmus, the Christian humanist accused of bringing on the movement; right, portrait by Raphael of Leo X, pope when the revolt began.

enclosed by a fence. We also wonder if the use of hieroglyphs and picture writing sprang up independently or was suggested by the old world. Some would hold that such a practice as the use of the zero in Yucatan could not possibly have spread there from India. But the Polynesians who traverse great distances in their canoes seem to have migrated from India. Asiatic culture may have spread to America by similar agencies straight across the Pacific. There is a close resemblance between the food-stuffs of Polynesia and America, but possibly this transference was the work of early European navigators.

The Mayas had a remarkable calendar and method of dating, which seems to go back as far as 613 B.C. Their year of 365 days they corrected by adding 25 days in the course of every 104 years. Instead of twelve months they had eighteen of twenty days each; this left five extra days just as in ancient Egypt. They further employed a 260 day cycle wherein each day could be distinguished by the use of twenty names and thirteen numbers. The Mexican cycle of 52 years was similarly distinguished by use of thirteen numbers and four names corresponding with the belief in four elements—earth, air, fire, and water—and four ages of the world, which were to end respectively in an earthquake, a storm, a conflagration, and a deluge. The Chinese, Mongols, and Tibetans have a similar cycle of sixty years by combining the names of twelve animals, like our signs of the zodiac, with those of five elements. Mayan astronomers especially observed the planet Venus; Peru had its poetical astrologers; in Mexico the child's horoscope was taken at birth by a "sun-calculator," and to be married a pair must have compatible horoscopes. *Chronology and Astronomy*

Perhaps the most impressive feature of American art was the megalithic masonry. Of the remains of Maya architecture we have already spoken. The Incas, whose stone city of Machu Picchu situated high up in the Andes has recently been rediscovered, cut and fitted together the stones with great skill and accuracy, building walls of beautiful masonry. Especially noteworthy for its sculpture was the earlier widespread and highly developed Tiahuanco II culture (200–900 A.D.), which combined human or animal forms and ritualistic or mythological motives in fantastic and complicated conventionalized designs. These are also seen both in textiles which excite the admiration of modern workers and in pottery of many colors. The latter *Art* displays increasing skill in modelling until the most graceful shapes occur under the Incas. In America the pyramids were commonly terraced or stepped, and truncated, with a temple or altar on the flat top. Those of Mexico were larger than those of the Mayas but were built of adobe bricks with concrete facings instead of a core of rubble encased with cut stone. That of Cholula covered nearly twice as much ground as the Egyptian pyramid of Cheops, though it was not so high or so regular in shape. Although remaining in some respects in the stone age, the Aztecs and others not only worked gold and silver but mined copper and tin and combined them into bronze. They displayed considerable skill in the mechanical arts. Great stores of gold and silver were taken by the greedy Spanish conquerors both in Mexico and Peru. A collection of numerous articles of armor and ornament, all of gold, excavated in 1920 in the mountains of Ecuador and now preserved at the University of Pennsylvania, is said to be the most important treasure that has been found in South America since the Spanish conquest.

Economic Life

The Incas are sometimes said to have surpassed the Europeans of their time as cultivators and engineers, but this assertion seems a bit exaggerated. However, they maintained roads over the mountains with post-houses in places where none are found today. In Yucatan may be seen remains of paved highways, reservoirs, and underground cisterns lined with stone and cement to preserve the water supply during the dry season. Ownership of land was tribal, not individual. The Aztecs had ditches for irrigation, and supplied the royal palace with water by a channel of hewn stone carried on a huge embankment. Yet they had no plough-culture; instead they used sharply pointed sticks, wooden shovels, and hoes with bronze blades. They had, however, currency of a sort in the shape of cocoa beans, pieces of copper, and quills of gold-dust. Moreover, there were traveling gilds of merchants who made distant expeditions. The Incas had no words for buying and selling, although their vocabulary permitted them to distinguish varying degrees of drunkenness with great accuracy.

Morals and Religion

Among the Aztecs only the aged were allowed to drink freely; young men who got drunk were clubbed to death, and tipsy flappers were stoned to death. Both in their religion and administration of justice the Aztecs seem to have been about the most unfeeling people known to history with the possible exception of the Assyrians.   Slanderers were punished by singeing their hair to the scalp with a pine torch; one who stole gold or silver was flayed alive and sacrificed to the god of the goldsmiths and silversmiths; children were gently corrected by holding their faces over the fumes of burning chillies.   On the tops of the truncated pyramids the Aztec priests slashed open the breasts and tore out the hearts of human victims whose bodies were then eaten.   There were festivals when infants with painted faces and paper wings were sacrificed, or when men were flayed and others danced in their skins.   A common representation in art is that of a priest or worshiper making a blood sacrifice to his god by drawing through his tongue a long cord pierced at frequent intervals with thorns.   "Among the devotees were some who offered their lives upon the sacrificial altar joyfully and gloriously that the demands of the ritual be fulfilled." Such self-torture, or disregard of the lives of others, might be accompanied, however, by moral instruction, for the Indians generally had their own standards of conduct to which they conformed better than did the Spaniards who came among them. The Caribs of the West Indies were cannibals but detested theft and would say when one of them missed something from his hut, "Some Christian has been here!"   Both in Mexico and Central America a sacred or royal game of ball was played with a rubber ball in a court.   The object was to throw the ball through one of two rings somewhat as in the present game of basket-ball.   The Incas regaled themselves with bards and dramas.   The Mayas had masks of both gods and animals, wore elaborate head-dresses and long hair, liked perfumes, tattooed and painted the body, pierced ears and nose with ornaments, chipped and inlaid their teeth,—as did the Mexicans —flattened their infants' heads with a board to a sugar-loaf profile and made them squint because they regarded that as beautiful.

The voyage of Vasco de Gama (1497–1499) from Lisbon to Calicut and back with a valuable cargo of spices and gems was the first of which we know between Europe and India by the all-sea-route around Africa.   This new route provided a cheaper method of transport; avoided various reloadings, profits of middlemen, and customs duties; and broke the monopoly of far eastern trade that Mohammedan and Mediterranean traders

Portugal's Commercial Empire

had been enjoying in favor of the enterprising little power on the Atlantic at the southwesternmost corner of Europe. The Portuguese foresaw that they would have to fight with the Mohammedans for control of the Indian Ocean. In 1505, Almeida was sent out to oppose the Mameluke sultan of Egypt, over whom he won a complete naval victory in 1509 at Diu on the west coast of India. On the way home he perished in a skirmish with the Hottentots of South Africa. Albuquerque, who came out from 1508 to 1515, attempted to control coasts as well as sea, and entertained such ambitious, not to say visionary, projects as stealing the bones of Mohammed and turning the Nile into the Red Sea. By occupying Ormuz he bottled up the Persian Gulf, but he failed to take Aden at the mouth of the Red Sea. Ormuz, by the way, which in 1300 had been transferred from the mainland to an island to escape the Mongols, once had fine buildings and 40,000 inhabitants, but has been in ruins since the rapid decline of its prosperity in the early eighteenth century. Under Albuquerque's lead the Portuguese pressed on to Malacca on the Malay peninsula and to the Moluccas or Spice Islands themselves, with which direct trade was thus established. In such wise Portugal speedily founded a great maritime empire with possessions on both sides of Africa, in Brazil, in India, and in the East Indies. By 1517 a Portuguese fleet of eight ships reached China. The Portuguese also penetrated to Japan. They were allowed to establish a permanent trading station in China only when it became well understood by both sides that there should be no conquests.

Cruelty of
the Times

Sailors of this period were apt to be a rough lot, little better than pirates. Most European settlers adopted an attitude of sovereign scorn and pitiless hostility towards the natives which was strangely combined with a truculent desire to convert them to Christianity. In these respects the Portuguese were not the least offenders, displaying a ferocious crusading spirit, especially at the first. Vasco da Gama captured a ship bearing pilgrims to Mecca, three hundred and eighty men with many women and children. After removing the money and goods that were on board, he "burned the ship and all the people on board with gunpowder." Albuquerque slew every Moslem in Goa, man, woman, or child. At Malacca he allowed the Mohammedans in the fort to escape on condition that they surrender some Portuguese deserters, whose lives he promised to spare but whom he deprived of their noses, ears, right hands, left thumbs, and pulled out their hair by the roots.

Missionary priests were included from the first in the trading posts that the Portuguese established in the east.   Many of them were noble, devoted men such as Francis Xavier, one of the founders of the Society of Jesus, who visited India, Malacca, the Moluccas, and Japan, but died before he could enter China. He fasted and scourged himself, longed for martyrdom, had ecstatic visions, baptized converts till his hands ached, said mass while the altar shook from earthquakes.   He vainly tried to induce the pope to change Lent in the east to a time when the fish did not rot so fast.   Sometimes the Portuguese tactlessly carried their opposition to heathen religions to absurd lengths. When a famous relic supposed to be the tooth of Buddha was captured in Ceylon and brought to Goa, a native rajah offered an enormous ransom for it, but the archbishop pounded it to dust, burned the powder to ashes, and threw the ashes into the river.   All this had no result except to enrage the Buddhists, whose priests presently discovered that the captured tooth had been a false one, and that they still retained the true relic in their possession.   In fine, the Portuguese had no such general success in converting the natives of the Far East as the Spaniards had in Central and South America.

Missionary Activity

The Chinese learned some astronomy from the Jesuits who improved their instruments for them; the Polynesians probably picked up some notions from traders and missionaries which, surviving in perverted form, are today regarded as primitive; but on the whole little lasting impression was made by Europe or Christianity at this time upon the orient.   Indeed, the China of that day had little to learn from westerners as to the arts of civilization.   Garcia da Orta, writing at Goa about 1563 on the drugs and simples of India, grew indignant at authors who spoke of the Chinese emperor as "a barbarous king."   You can tell them, he said, that the king of China is one of the greatest sovereigns in the world.   "The merchandize from there consists of silver bedsteads, richly worked services of silver, silk woven and unwoven, gold, musk, pearls, copper, mercury, vermillion, and porcelain twice the value of silver." He said that 431,200 pounds of silk came to Goa and Cochin

Impression Made upon Europeans by Chinese Civilization

every year from China.   In short, "In the grandeur of the kingdom, in the number of the people, in the excellence of its polity and government, and its wealth, it exceeds every other country in the world."

Portuguese
Policy
of Royal
Monopoly
India at this time was divided into many independent kingdoms, so that the Portuguese did not find it difficult to establish trading posts with garrisons.   But their policy of enlarging these colonies by intermarrying with the natives proved a failure.   Moreover the early spirit of patriotic enterprise and devotion to the king at home, who controlled the entire eastern trade as a royal monopoly, gave way to corruption on the part of the officials and their subordinates.   The Portuguese kept secret their geographical discoveries and their charts, soundings, and logs concerning the route around Africa.   Other European nations who wished spices or African slaves came to Lisbon to buy them, but were allowed to go no farther.   In thirty years Lisbon trebled in population, with negro and Moorish slaves outnumbering the freemen.   Portugal really had too small a population to hold and develop so great an empire.

Dutch and
English
India
Companies
Dutch and English sailors, by serving in the crews of Portuguese vessels, learned the secrets of the new route.   In 1580 Portugal passed for sixty years under the rule of the king of Spain who was preoccupied with many other matters so that the Portuguese maritime empire was somewhat neglected.   Moreover, as even the port of Lisbon was now closed to the Dutch, who had revolted against Spain and were waging war against her, and as they were usually victorious on the sea, they began to make voyages to India on their own account.   English buccaneers were likewise preying upon Spanish commerce or engaging in the slave trade.   The depredations of these Elizabethan seamen finally forced Spain to declare war upon England, but the Spanish Armada to invade England in 1588 turned out a complete failure.   English merchants had also been forming various companies for trade with Turkey, Russia, the Baltic, Guinea, and the Barbary coast of the Mediterranean; while in Holland the citizens of Amsterdam, Rotterdam, Delft, and Zeeland had formed several small companies for the far eastern trade.   Such competition had its risks and disadvantages, however,   Therefore, about 1601 the sole privilege of trade with the Indian Ocean was given for twenty-one years

to the Dutch East India Company, supported by the leading municipal governments, with a capital equivalent to two and a half million dollars, and with power to make treaties with the natives, appoint governors, employ troops as well as armed ships, and build forts as well as establish trading posts. Twenty years later the Dutch West India Company was organized to extend Dutch trade and power in Brazil and Spanish America. The English East India Company, established in 1600, was at first a much smaller affair, with only $150,000 capital and empowered only to trade, not to engage in any military or political activity. During its first few years the members of the company invested as much or little as they chose in each voyage and divided its profits accordingly, which varied from 95 to 235 percent. Later the company became a true joint stock one. The Dutch and English soon quarreled in the east. As the former were then the stronger, the English company had to keep away from the Spice Islands and confine its activities mainly to stations on the coast of India. Gradually it built up a very profitable trade with that vast land and population, and then interfered increasingly in Indian politics, laying the foundations of later British rule in India.

Portugal still retains a few relics of her former maritime empire: the Cape Verde Islands, Guinea, Mozambique, Angola, a port or two in India and elsewhere. The Dutch later lost many of their possessions, chiefly to England, but retain important islands in the East Indies. The early Dutch navigators also visited many places which were not then permanently occupied and which in the late eighteenth and early nineteenth centuries were re-discovered and annexed to the British Empire. Thus in 1636 Tasman, sailing from Mauritius, reached the islands of Tasmania and New Zealand, and explored the northern coast of "New Holland," now called Australia. By virtue of Magellan's having first visited them, the Philippine Islands were occupied by Spain. Often in the seventeenth and eighteenth centuries sailors asked to be left behind on some of the balmy, delightful South Sea islands to pass the rest of their lives in indolent ease.

Present Remains of the Portuguese and Dutch Eastern Empires

Westerners had had considerable trade or communication with the Far East, and even knowledge of it, before this period; but never had there been such direct, steady, and protracted relationship, nor had the southern coasts of Africa and remoter

Effects of the Voyages of Trade and Discovery upon Civilization

regions of the Indian Ocean and Pacific been so visited, at least from Europe. Above all never had man sailed about the globe and circumnavigated continents in such wise. The nomad now had to yield the palm completely to the navigator; sea-power took the lead in the world's affairs. In the fifteenth century the Portuguese and Spaniards employed caravels, light and for those times fast sailing vessels with raised overhanging bow and stern, for deep sea sailing and long voyages. Columbus used a vessel of only 230 tons burden, 128 feet long with a beam of 26 feet; the vessels of Vasco de Gama were somewhat larger but of the same type. The voyages of discovery and the foundation of trading companies stimulated shipbuilding. Vessels of as much as 1600 tons were built in the sixteenth century. Science was broadened by a more accurate knowledge of eastern plants and drugs, by the discovery of new flora and fauna all over the world, by astronomical observations taken from the other side of the earth, and by an enormous extension of geographical knowledge. New diseases and novel climatic conditions stimulated the medical art. New states successively rose to power; colonial and maritime empires were built up; great economic organizations took shape. Literature soon felt the influence of the new lands and seas which so stirred the imagination and spirit of adventure. Art seems to have been less affected, although there are signs of the influence of India and the ocean in the exuberant *Arte Manuelina* which takes its name from the reign of Manoel I of Portugal (1495–1521). The late seventeenth century saw a widespread love for oriental art and wares in Europe—porcelain, textiles, lacquered screens, chests and cabinets—and the Chinese also copied western originals. A regrettable accompaniment of the growth of sea-power and opening up of new lands was "the enhancement of pride, prejudice, indolence, and extravagance, and the development of an earth-hunger, a commercialism, and a greed for wealth which has found satisfaction in the plunder or exploitation of native peoples and the robbery of European rivals." Deplorable also, says Shepherd, were "the gross immorality inseparable from contact with racial servility or inferiority, the unfortunate status of the half-breed, the unfairness and cruelty practiced upon slaves or otherwise 'backward' folk, and the callous injustice of 'contracts' into which 'natives' have been inveigled." This reproach may also be applied to some extent to the process of Europeanization of the American continents to which we now turn.

Columbus had not been able to control the Spanish colonists whom he took out to the West Indies. Finally, he was himself superseded and sent home in chains. Jealous intrigues, or open disorder and feuds also followed the conquests of Mexico and Peru. But gradually things settled down into the quiet, regular life of permanent settlement, and we find Spain with a great colonial empire, while Spanish civilization and Roman Catholicism were spread over large areas of the New World. By 1600 there were more than 160,000 Spaniards in America, where they occupied some two hundred settlements. In the West Indies Spanish planters had at first exploited native labor to the point of slavery and even extermination. Although the ravages of disease added their toll, more deaths probably resulted from overwork under abusive European masters than had resulted from the bloody sacrifices of the Aztecs over the same length of time. The Dominican, Las Casas, finally secured the abolition of such Indian slavery about the middle of the sixteenth century, although the planters continued to purchase negroes from Africa from slave-traders. By 1600 in the various Spanish possessions in America there were about five million natives gathered in villages, for the most part at least nominally Christian, and more or less under the influence of European civilization. There are, however, to this day in South America wild tribes in a low state of savagery, if not cannibals. Europeanization was most apparent in the city of Mexico which in 1574 had a population of 15,000 Spaniards and 150,000 Indians. It contained handsome public buildings, churches, monasteries, hospitals, printing presses, a high school for boys and girls, and a university—all this before there was a single English-speaking settlement in North America. Through these regions the Spanish language spread as Arabic had spread through the Mohammedan world, and there came to be many children of mixed race. Roman Catholic missionaries, especially the Jesuits, were more successful than the Protestants later in converting the natives. In North America not only did Spanish missions spread north into California, but French missionaries penetrated to the Great Lakes and Mississippi valley.

The natives, however, were not more Europeanized than were

Things
Borrowed by
European
Settlers
from the
American
Indians

the European settlers Americanized by the new country which became henceforth their environment.   Even in North America, where relations between the Indians and Europeans were so often hostile, the latter kept the Indian place names and learned from the Indian how to smoke and chew tobacco, to grow maize and squashes, to swing in a hammock, to make maple sugar, to use canoe, snowshoes, and toboggan, chocolate, vanilla, sarsaparilla, quinine, arrowroot, red pepper or chillies, potatoes, tomatoes, peanuts, and many other plants, foods, and medicines.

British
Colonies
in North
America

The settlements in America which turned out of most importance to the future of civilization were not made until the seventeenth century, when Protestants from England, Sweden, and the Netherlands founded colonies along the Atlantic seaboard north of Spanish Florida and south of French Canada. The Swedish colony on the Delaware was absorbed by the Dutch on the Hudson, who in their turn were conquered by the British. Although under the British flag, the American colonies received settlers from various other European countries: Germans in Pennsylvania, French Huguenots, Moravians, and Finns. Thus immigration from other than English-speaking peoples prevailed from the start.   In New England, however, the settlers remained almost purely English.   These North American colonists under the British flag generally dispossessed the Indians or bought them out.   They lived their own life apart from the natives, which was a reflection of the civilization of their home countries modified by their new environment. Largely founded by trading companies or individual proprietors, the colonies at first commonly had charters and somewhat resembled the feudal states and self-governing towns of the middle ages.   But they displayed new life and a strong tendency to take the government into their own hands, with ideal schemes of representation in some of the Quaker colonies, and a healthy local government in the case of the New England "town meeting."   The home government, becoming somewhat concerned at this tendency to self-assertion alike in political, economic, and religious matters, gradually transformed most of the colonies into royal provinces with governors appointed by the Crown, and attempted by acts of trade and navigation to restrict their commerce and shipping to British channels. Such acts were largely violated by the colonists who wished to trade freely on their own account, and their representative assemblies were repeatedly at logger-heads with their royal governors.   Social ranks were by no means absent in the colonies, though some were more aristocratic in their government than others.   They also varied in their religious inclinations, some being Puritan, others Episcopalian, others Quaker, and in their degree of religious toleration, in which Rhode Island under the influence of Roger Williams' ideal of religious freedom and Maryland under Roman Catholic proprietors, the Calverts, set a shining example.

BIBLIOGRAPHY

Almeida, F. de   *La découverte de l'Amérique*, 1913.

Anderson, R. C.   *Treatise on Rigging* (probably written between 1618 and 1637) edited by, in *Society for Nautical Research, Occasional Publications*, I, 1921.

Babcock, W. H.   *Legendary Islands of the Atlantic*, 1922.

Beazley, C. R.   *Life of Prince Henry the Navigator*, 1897.

Bensaude, J.   *L'astronomie nautique au Portugal à l'époche des grandes découvertes*, 1912; *Histoire de la science nautique Portugaise à l'époche des grandes découvertes*, 1914–1915, 4 vols.

Beuchat, H.   *Manuel d'archéologie américaine*, 1912.

Bingham, Hiram.   *Inca Land*, 1922; and other similar works.

Bourne, E. G.   *Spain in America*, 1904.

Capiten, L. and Lorin, H.   *Le travail en Amérique avant et après Colomb*, 1914.

Cheyney, E. P.   *European Background of American History*, 1904.

Chinard, G.   *L'Amérique et la rêve exotique*, 1913; *L'Exotisme américain dans la litt. franc. au XVIe siècle*, 1911.

Cook, O. F.   "The American Origin of Agriculture," in *Scientific Monthly*, 61, 492.

Danvers, F. C.   *The Portuguese in India*, 1894, 2 vols.

Day, C.   *The Dutch in Java*, 1904, pp. 39–125.

Fiske, John.   *The Discovery of America*, 1892, 2 vols.

Frampton, J.   *Joyful News out of the Newe founde Worlde*, 1577; (a translation of the *Historia Medicinal* of Nicolas Monardes); "a good account of all its most valuable vegetable productions."

Heawood, E.   *A History of Geographical Discovery in the Seventeenth and Eighteenth Centuries*, 1912.

Jayne, K. G.   *Vasco da Gama and His Successors*, 1910.

Joyce, T. A.   *Mexican Archaeology*, 1914; *Central American and West Indian Archæology*, 1916.

Lannoy, de and Van der Linden.   *Histoire de l'expansion coloniale des peuples Européens: Portugal et Espagne*, 1907.

Larsen, S.   *The Discovery of North America Twenty Years before Columbus*, 1925; deals with Danish northwest expeditions made at the suggestion of Portugal,—"interesting but often far from convincing."

Markham, Sir C. R.   *Incas of Peru,* 1910.

Martin, J. P. O.   *The Golden Age of Prince Henry the Navigator,* 1914.

Means, P. A.   "A Survey of Ancient Peruvian Art," 1917, in *Transactions of the Connecticut Academy of Arts and Sciences,* XXI, 315–442.

Merriman, R. B.   *The Rise of the Spanish Empire,* 1918–, 4 vols.

Morris, H. C.   *History of Colonization,* 1908, 2 vols.

Nadaillac, De.   *Prehistoric America,* 1885.

Nance, R. M.   *Sailing-Ship Models,* 1924.

Opisso, A.   *La conquista de Africa,* 1911.

Payne, E. J.   *History of European Colonies,* 1889.   *History of the new world called America,* 1892–1899, 2 vols.

Ravenstein, F. G.   *Martin Behaim, His Life and His Globe,* 1908.

Saville, M. H.   *Goldsmith's Art in Ancient Mexico,* 1920.

Shepherd, W. R.   "The Expansion of Europe," articles in *The Political Science Quarterly,* 1919, pp. 43–, 210–, 392–; an important survey.

Spinden, H. J.   *A Study of Maya Art,* 1913; *Ancient Civilizations of Mexico and Central America,* 1917.

Stevenson, E. L.   *Christopher Columbus and His Enterprise,* 1913; *Portolan Charts,* 1911; and other works on maps and globes of the age of discovery.

Synge, M.   *A Book of Discovery,* 1913.

Van Loon, H. W.   *The Golden Book of the Dutch Navigators,* 1916; thrilling true stories of adventure.

Vignaud, H.   *Le vrai Christophe Colomb et la légende,* 1921; and other works.

Warshaw, J.   *The New Latin America,* 1922.

Wissler, C.   *The American Indian,* 1917.

CHAPTER XXXIII

RELIGIOUS CHANGE IN EUROPE: SECULARISM

We went . . . with officers and souldiers and . . . we pulled
down two mighty great angells with wings, and divers other
angells, and the four evangelists and Peter with his Keies
over the chappel door, and about a hundred Cherubims and
angells and divers superstitious letters in gold.

—Dowsing the Iconoclast

In the sixteenth century came a great religious change. For
many centuries in western and central Europe there had been
but one church which everyone, being baptized in infancy,
joined as a matter of course, whose services in all parts were
usually conducted in the Latin language, at whose head was
the pope at Rome. Now considerable areas of territory or sections of the population broke away from this general communion, affirming that their own creeds and forms of worship
were alone truly Christian, or were read out of the Roman
church and excommunicated by the pope and his supporters.
Several causes may be suggested for this. First the rise of
modern nationality with its self-complacency and hatred of foreign nations in contrast to Christian unity. It is true that
feudal states and medieval towns had been distinct nations in a
sense, with a germ of danger to the church in the secular spirit
of the towns. But feudalism was ever shifting, its personal
bonds were often international, and these feudal states and independent towns were each too small seriously to affect the
whole. Second, the wealth and power of the church and the
privileges of the clergy, which stirred qualms in the conscientious and spiritually-minded, provoked the wrath of reformers
and revolts of the socialistic, and aroused the cupidity of laymen who were intent on increasing their own privileges, wealth,
and power. Third, the gradual failure of the church to re-
strain such selfish individualism, to satisfy the poor and needy,
the sick and suffering, the oppressed and unfortunate, that it

Causes of the Protestant Revolt

405

was their friend and supporter,—or to stop wars. Fourth, the church was losing its hold on the intellectual class and the leaders of thought. Fifth, as a natural sequel or accompaniment of this, there was an increasing number of persons, some of them clergy, who did not believe as the church did, or who were indifferent in the matter of religion. At first, of course, such persons disagreed with the church on a few points, but then other persons disagreed on a few additional points, or on the same points they disagreed with other reformers as well as with the church. Thus already in the sixteenth century there were formed various religious bodies who all regarded themselves as the church of God. As time has gone on, the number of persons has greatly increased who do not agree with any church, or who question revealed religion in any form.

Protestant Views

On this more strictly religious side those who broke with the church of Rome may be said to have criticized it in three chief respects: the position of the clergy, the doctrine of sacraments, and various religious practices. They refused to recognize the papal power, indeed sometimes they rejected the episcopal office generally and had no bishops; they usually reduced the sanctity and authority of the priest, whom they preferred to call by some such name as pastor, elder, or minister; they abolished celibacy of the clergy, monasticism, and asceticism.

Sanctity of the priest was a conception associated especially with his office in administering the sacraments. Those who broke with the church as a rule assigned the sacraments a place of less importance and significance in the religious life than they had come to occupy in the medieval church. The mass, for instance, ceased to be the central feature of religious worship in the Protestant and Reformed churches; the sermon tended to take its place. Private confession to one's priest or pastor, and performance of penance assigned by him were also generally abandoned. In place of seeking spiritual comfort and assurance of soul salvation through performance of the sacraments and other "good works," Martin Luther (1483–1546) put forward the doctrine of justification by faith.

Many popular religious practices were condemned as superstitious or as bordering upon idolatry and savoring of pagan customs of the past, for instance: pilgrimages to holy places, masses for the dead, worship of the Virgin and saints, preservation of the relics of the saints, and observance of saints' days or other holy days than the Lord's Day. Various features of the old church ritual were also censured as idolatrous, especially by the more extreme Protestants. In place of all this Protestants were urged to pray, to read the Bible, of which printed translations could now be multiplied, and to "go to church"—a formality which was still felt to possess much efficacy—where they could now hear service in their own national tongue and take part therein.

More positively, much stress was laid upon the spiritual life and "inner man," as opposed to outward "good works," ecclesiastical ritual, and the aggressive interference of the church as an institution in matters which had hitherto been regarded as its concern, but which today are considered primarily political, economic, social, or scientific. The ultimate result was the loss by the clergy of temporal power, possessions, and jurisdiction, the separation of art and drama from religion, of science from theology.

This decisive break in the sixteenth century had been led up to by various thinkers, heresies, and efforts at church reform in the later middle ages. The German mystics had emphasized the inner, spiritual life. Occam had implied the incompatibility of scientific thought and theology. Wyclif had wished to restrict the clergy to purely spiritual functions and to subordinate them to the state. These movements may be said further to have displayed an increasingly national character. The Albigensians, who had been crushed by a war of extermination in the early thirteenth century, had represented the culture of Languedoc, which largely passed away with them. The Waldensians were also primarily of the *Midi*. Wyclif, a fourteenth century forerunner of Protestantism in England, was spokesman of a national opposition to the papal temporal claims and financial exactions. His follower, Huss, whom the Council of Constance burned at the stake, became the national hero of Bohemia, where the Hussite Wars of the fifteenth century were in large measure a struggle between Czechs and Germans. The need of reform in the official system of the church had been felt ever since the papacy, in the mid-thirteenth century, triumphed over the Holy Roman emperors by a very questionable use of military force and what amounted to wholesale bribery by bestowal of church offices and revenues. In the early fourteenth century it looked as if the pope had broken the

Heresies and Efforts at Church Reform of the Later Middle Ages

power of the empire only to fall under the domination of the French king.   The residence of the pope at Avignon from 1309 to 1376 was objectionable to many Christians and a confession of weakness on the part of one supposed to be bishop of Rome. The great schism between rival popes and colleges of cardinals which followed from 1378 to 1417 increased the demand for reform in church government.   Several general councils were held for that purpose but accomplished little, as the popes resisted the attempt to impose reforms upon them.   What was more noteworthy was that voting in the councils was now by nationalities, and that the papal court escaped the unpleasant prospect of general and thorough-going reform by separate negotiations with kings.   The monarchs of France and Spain had secured about what they wanted before the Protestant Revolt opened; the rulers of England and the German principalities had failed to do so; that is one explanation of the throwing off of papal control in those countries.   In the later fifteenth and early sixteenth centuries the popes succeeded in reestablishing themselves firmly at Rome, which they made a great center of art and learning.   Yet the handwriting had already appeared upon the wall; the rule of the papacy was not finished, but its kingdom was to be divided.

Leading Protestant Reformers

The monk, Martin Luther, struck the spark which ignited the Protestant Revolt in Germany, when on All Saints' Day, 1517, he issued his Ninety-Five Theses against the preaching of indulgences to secure funds for the building of the church of St. Peter at Rome.   He questioned the power of pope or church to act for God or Christ in absolving from guilt or penalty for sin.   On the other hand, the ecclesiastical authorities objected that his doctrine of Justification by Faith, which already found expression in these theses, was heretical.   He found that in large measure German public opinion was in sympathy with him, and was led on to reject the whole papal power and much of the sacramental system, and to organize Lutheran churches under the supervision of the heads of the local German states.   We must regretfully add not only that Luther showed no more sympathy with the building of St. Peter's than he did with the indulgences, but that Renaissance architecture and Protestantism combined have sounded the knell of ecclesiastical art, if not of art in general.   The Protestant movement in Switzerland began with the preaching of Zwingli at Zurich in

1519. It almost broke up the Swiss Confederation, as some of the towns and cantons remained Roman Catholic. In the religious wars which were now to upset Europe for almost two centuries Swiss mercenaries often took a decisive part, but they served for pay rather than from religious zeal. The leading French reformer was John Calvin, whose *Institute of Christianity*, first issued in 1536, became the most influential single work on the Protestant side. John Knox was the leader in Scotland, where Calvinism took the form of Scotch Presbyterianism. His characteristic treatise, *Blasts of the Trumpet against the Monstrous Regiment of Women*, illustrates the fact that the Protestant spokesmen were inclined to be a trifle noisy, and that the position of women was not likely to be improved under the new dispensation. Luther had a more genial temperament than Knox, yet he once said, "If women bear children until they become sick and eventually die, that does no harm. Let them bear children till they die of it; that is what they are for."

Calvin's conviction of human sinfulness and depravity was so strong that he made salvation entirely a matter of divine election. His followers carried this doctrine of predestination to the extent of maintaining that the exact number and identity of persons who were to be respectively saved and damned, whether men or angels, had been irrevocably determined before the foundation of the world. Such doctrines did not take the joy out of life quite so completely as might be expected, however. Their holders took a certain grim satisfaction in asserting them, and still ate and drank with hearty appetites; it gave them a thrill and feeling of moral responsibility to think that they were God's elect, mean instruments chosen to work out His glorious purpose. They even spoke, somewhat inconsistently, of "making their election sure." And it was not entirely unsatisfactory to reflect that anyone with whom you did not agree was probably one of those condemned to be damned. However, the Calvinists have a reputation for austere morality and opposition to worldly amusements and any popular customs which they thought savored of paganism, such as maypoles. Their strict observance of Sunday somewhat compensated for their abandoning medieval asceticism and observance of other days. The Huguenots in France and the Puritans in England and America were Calvinists. In general those churches which are called Reformed or Presbyterian rather than Lutheran, such as

Calvinism and Presbyterianism

the Dutch Reformed or the Scotch Presbyterian, emanated from Zwingli, Calvin, and Knox. Most of these religious bodies developed in opposition to the existing political rulers as well as to the pope, and would fight for their faith. Furthermore, the Presbyterian form of organization, which rejected the episcopal office and instituted representative assemblies in which elders chosen by the congregations participated as well as clergymen, was not consonant with monarchy. A Scotch presbytery, remarked the sapient James I, "agreeth as well with monarchy as God and the devil."

Nationalization of the Church

After a struggle with the Stuart kings Presbyterianism was recognized as the established church of Scotland. The formation of the Dutch Reformed church was accompanied by the successful revolt of the Netherlands from the rule of Philip II of Spain and the rise of the Dutch Republic. In the various Lutheran countries, too, we have distinct state or national churches. The Church of England is the most outstanding instance of nationalization. Henry VIII, who had previously written against Luther and had been hailed by the pope as "Defender of the Faith," in 1534 broke off all connection of the church in England with the pope, not because of any sympathy with Protestant doctrine but because the pope could not, or would not, grant him a divorce and because he wished to increase his revenue at the expense of the clergy. Parliament declared the king supreme head of the church in England, a title softened to supreme governor under Elizabeth. All the monasteries were dissolved and their property confiscated, shrines and religious foundations were despoiled. As the nobles and leading land-owners and men of property shared in the spoil, the Roman Catholic cause was lost. On the other hand, Protestant views, for which Wyclif and his followers, the Lollards, had earlier laid the foundation, took strong hold in England among the people and clergy, and the main question became whether the church should remain episcopal or become Presbyterian. After civil war and a brief experiment with Presbyterianism and Puritanism in the middle of the seventeenth century, it finally remained Episcopalian. Gradually other forms of worship and church organization came to be tolerated, as has also come to be the case in other countries.

Growth of Religious Toleration

It has been said that toleration was not born of the reformers, yet was the child of the reformation. The very fact that the leaders of the Protestant Revolt, Luther, Zwingli, and Calvin, had differed irreconcilably in their views of such a fundamental matter as the Eucharist, or Lord's Supper, meant that there would be perpetual disagreement between different individuals and religious bodies, and that within each nation there would be not only a distinct national religious organization but any number of other dissenting bodies.   It has been said of England during the Civil War just referred to, that the principle of the individual conscience and interpretation of Scripture "shattered the Puritan church in the hour of her victory into a hundred sects and destroyed the whole system of Protestant dogmatics" (Slater).   We have not dwelt much on religious persecution and intolerance in this book; Roman Catholic rulers continued for a time to burn Protestants as they had burned heretics in the past, and Protestant rulers executed Roman Catholics as traitors; Calvin burned Servetus.   Gradually this ceased, though we are none too sure that there has been any great net gain therefrom to individual liberty or freedom of thought. Present legalized punishments—we omit lynchings—are less excruciating, but the spirit of intolerance has perhaps simply been transferred to other fields, from justification by faith to evolution, from Socinians and Quakers to Socialists and Pacifists, from Anabaptism to Bolshevism.

The violent intolerance and religious wars of the age of the reformation were in part due to the fact that it, too, touched men's pocket-books, that it was no mere religious movement or theological quarrel, but an attack upon a venerable institution which had affected and been intertwined with every side of human life.   Therefore the Protestant Revolt involved serious economic and social as well as political changes, as we may briefly illustrate.   Luther put through the Reformation in Germany partly by his *Address to the German Nobility* which appealed to their selfish interests by attacking the financial exactions of the papacy and by proposing to promote industry through abolition of pilgrimages, religious vagrancy, and holidays.   On the other hand, he was painfully surprised when a general peasants' revolt accompanied his Protestant Revolt as a corollary.   He hastened to disown it and advise its suppression by the sword.   Such measures as the disappearance of ecclesiastical courts, the confiscation of monastic property, and of many other past religious endowments, had very serious

Economic and Social Accompaniments of the Religious Change

economic and social consequences which were seldom for the better, at least immediately. The life of the gilds suffered, the landlords who replaced the monks were intent on making money, treated their tenants less leniently, did nothing for the poor and suffering of the neighborhood. Religious persecution drove forth colonists to the New World, or skilled artisans migrated with the secrets of their crafts to other countries of Europe. England in the seventeenth century laid the foundations of her future industrial leadership by learning for the first time, from religious refugees from the continent, such arts as the weaving of silk and linen, ribbon-making, the manufacture of plate-glass, canvas and sail-cloth, combs, buttons, jewelry, baskets, needles, parchment, hats, watches, mechanical toys, engraving and book-binding.

The Catholic Reformation

Menaced by the rapid spread of Protestantism, the Roman Catholic church made haste to put its house in order and to attempt to regain lost ground. The Council of Trent (1545–1563) reformed the abuses at the papal court, lessened the number of appeals to Rome from the localities, restored more independent power to the other bishops, and forced the local clergy to attend more faithfully to their religious duties. On the other hand, the council reaffirmed practically all of the doctrines and practices of the medieval church that the Protestants had called into question, and so shut the door against any prospect either of religious union or of progressive development within the church of Rome. The papal inquisition was revived to suppress heresy in Italy,—the Spanish inquisition of the same sixteenth century was under royal control. An Index of forbidden books was instituted. The *Spiritual Exercises* of the Spaniard, Ignatius Loyola, for the religious novice and his father confessor, was a book on the Roman Catholic side corresponding in importance to Calvin's *Institute* for Protestants. It detailed a method—almost a drill, for Loyola was an ex-soldier—by which one might attain conviction of the truth of catholic doctrine and religious peace. Loyola founded a new religious order, the Society of Jesus, or Jesuits, trained to strict obedience and subordinated to the pope, who were of immense assistance in recovering lost ground in Europe through their excellent schools, and in winning new ground in America and Asia by their fearless missionary activity. The chief reproach made against them is that they engaged too much in political intrigue; for they were often the private confessors of great personages.

The whole Reformation movement, whether Protestant or Roman Catholic, whatever its religious value may have been in the form of a quickening of the spiritual life or of missionary zeal, can scarcely be regarded as beneficial to civilization, except perhaps in the long run. The period was too filled with wars of religion, or at least so they were called, although often at bottom they were due to political and economic causes. Protestants must shoulder the blame for a long series of heart-sickening acts of vandalism and iconoclasm which destroyed vast quantities of the wonderful sacred sculpture and stained glass of the middle ages. It is hard to understand how any devout person could smash figures so expressive of the spirit of devotion, still less boast of it afterwards. Yet even at the Council of Trent the complaint was made that the Gothic artists had scandalized the faithful by their childish superstitions. Mural and detached medieval paintings which had existed by thousands in England almost entirely disappeared. Monastic libraries were destroyed, and whole collections of invaluable manuscripts were annihilated in the effort to destroy the medieval church service books. The Puritans opposed the theater and drama.

Effect of the Reformation on Civilization

In England educational endowments were often confiscated by the greedy government of the Reformation period with the result that in the seventeenth century education became confined to the upper classes, while the masses "sank into deeper and deeper ignorance." The reformers, however, usually favored education. In Scotland John Knox set forth the ideal of "an elementary school for every parish, a grammar school for every market town, and a university for every city." But the Jesuit schools showed that emphasis upon education was not a monopoly of the Reformed churches. As a matter of fact, the period of the so-called Renaissance and Reformation was not marked by a great increase and development in popular education or school facilities. Often a single new humanistic college or Protestant school took the place of several medieval schools which had decayed. The schools of the sixteenth to eighteenth centuries often had to put up with old buildings which in the middle ages had been used as hospitals and pesthouses. The old towns had suffered so from recurrence of

No Marked Advance in Education

pestilence, royal taxation or economic interference, and religious wars, that they could no longer support their municipal schools or colleges and were glad to turn the responsibility over to the Jesuits, who in many cases simply filled a gap rather than offered superior instruction. Furthermore, there seems to have been a diminishing demand for education from the people. Courses were shortened and made simpler and easier. These evils were in large measure due to the times rather than to the classical revival or religious change. On the other hand, they make it evident that those movements are not to be credited with any great improvement either of popular education or local prosperity.

Not a Popular Movement

Indeed, the Reformation was not a popular movement, nor was it allowed to become one. We have seen that the German Peasants' Revolt was disowned by Luther. The Anabaptists were generally abhorred not merely because of their views on baptism, but because of their sympathy for the down-trodden, their opposition to a state church, and their supposed leanings towards communism. The populace gained nothing economically or socially, much less politically, by the Protestant Revolt. Along with the abolition of pilgrimages and religious fraternities, and the reduction in the number of religious holidays went the loss of much of the popular life and good old customs of the past. The Reformation was accompanied, however, by a certain popularizing of theology, which was now extended to laymen of the upper middle class who could read the Bible for themselves and comprehend a doctrinal sermon.

Question of Enlightenment, Morality and Ideals

Protestants often think that their faith has led to greater enlightenment and progress, but this is more probably due to the advance of modern science. If a list of great modern inventors, men of letters, and scientists should be made out, it would be found that they were about equally of Protestant and Roman Catholic origin. It is true that the Protestants rejected many "idolatrous superstitions," but they long remained as firm believers in witchcraft and a personal devil as the Catholics. "The Reformation had no permanent discernible effect on moral standards," is the conclusion of a recent impartial historian of the period, Preserved Smith, who adds, "That the majority of clergymen (whether Catholic or Protestant) were morally unworthy is the melancholy conviction borne in by contemporary records." Indeed, it was the opinion of the martyred Protestant, Latimer, that the Reformation in England had been followed by a wave of wickedness. Another recent historian, Slater, writing of the Civil War in England between Puritans and Parliament on one side and King Charles I and the Church of England on the other, states that "the noblest Puritans and the noblest Cavaliers mostly died in battle or were ruined by the sacrifices which they made for their respective causes. Half-hearted partisans survived,"—time-servers, and the unprincipled, unscrupulous, or indifferent. "Then, too, a subtle degeneration of character occurred in those partisans who were driven by party spirit into bitter enmity"; while the miseries and devastation of war, and the subsequent military despotism of Cromwell's major-generals, "tended to sicken ordinary men of all pretense at high principle and lofty ideal, and to usher in a period of gross materialism." This, however, was in its turn followed by such revivals of religious interest as the Methodist and Evangelical movements of the late eighteenth, and the Tractarian movement of the early nineteenth, century.

But there we have perhaps the chief influence of the age of the Reformation upon civilization; namely, that civilization henceforth becomes more secular in character, and that the church ceases to be the leader in civilization. The very tendency to make of religion a purely spiritual matter of the "inner life" favored this outward secularization. Shakespeare gives us a sign of the times when he represents Falstaff as buying a horse in St. Paul's cathedral. When we hear that not only were there horse-dealers in the north aisle, but usurers in the south aisle, we realize that the church has indeed lost its grip of the situation, and that the modern world of business is being ushered in. Charles II of England gave voice to the new spirit that was in the air when he remarked that "Presbyterianism was not a religion for gentlemen." What new force would take the place of the church? The dons at Oxford are said to have tried to dissuade Robert Boyle, a son of the Earl of Cork, from the study of chemistry by the same argument that Charles II used against Presbyterianism, that it was not a study for gentlemen. But Charles was glad to found the Royal Society in 1660 and Greenwich Observatory in 1675, and he recommended for membership in the former a mere shopkeeper who had produced a meritorious scientific work. Thus

More Secular Character of Civilization Henceforth

while the day of the united church had passed, science was coming to include men of all ranks. We turn our attention to its progress in the next chapter.

BIBLIOGRAPHY

Calvin's *Institute* and Loyola's *Spiritual Exercises* may be had in English translations.

Bax, E. B. *The Social Side of the Reformation in Germany*, 1894–1903, 3 vols.

Beard, C. *The Reformation in its Relation to Modern Thought and Culture*, 1885.

Crouch, J. *Puritanism and Art*, 1910.

Crue, F. de *Anne de Montmorency*, 1889.

Grisar, H. *Luther*, translated by E. M. Lamond, 1913–1917, 6 vols.

Hashagen, J. *Der rheinische Protestantismus und die Entwicklung der rheinische Kultur*, 1924.

Janssen, J. *History of the German People at the Close of the Middle Ages*, translated by A. M. Christie, 1896–1910, 15 vols.

McGiffert, A. C. *Protestant Thought before Kant*, 1911.

Macmillan, K. D. *Protestantism in Germany*, 1917.

Marcks, Erich. *Gaspard von Coligny: sein Leben und das Frankreich seiner Zeit*, 1904–.

Murray, R. H. *Erasmus and Luther: Their Attitude to Toleration*, 1920.

Pastor, L. *History of the Papacy from the Close of the Middle Ages*, 1902, 6 vols.

Plummer, A. *The Continental Reformation*, 1912.

Romier, Lucien *Origines des guerres de religion*, 1913–1914, 2 vols. *Le royaume de Catherine de Médicis*, 1922, 2 vols. These two works are superior to previous treatments of the French Wars of Religion.

Sedgwick, H. D. *Ignatius Loyola*, 1923.

Sichel, Edith. *Catherine de' Medici and the French Reformation*, 1905; *The Later Years of Catherine de' Medici*, 1908.

Smith, Preserved. *Life of Erasmus*, 1923.

Symonds, J. A. *The Renaissance in Italy: The Catholic Reaction*.

Thompson, J. W. *The Wars of Religion in France*, 1909.

Troeltsch, E. *Protestantism and Progress*, 1912 (English translation).

Van Dyke, Paul. *Catherine de' Medici*, 1923.

Wace and Buckheim. *Luther's Primary Works* (in English translation), 1883.

Walker, Williston. *John Calvin*, 1900.

CHAPTER XXXIV

SCIENCE IN THE SIXTEENTH AND SEVENTEENTH CENTURIES

If we have to name a year for the end-point of medieval science we would select 1543, when appeared two fundamental modern works based on the experimental method, the *De fabrica corporis humani* of the Belgian Andreas Vesalius and the *De revolutionibus orbium caelestium* of the Pole Nicholas Copernicus.—*Charles Singer*

THE name of Leonardo da Vinci (1452–1519) is sometimes given as high rank in the history of science as in that of art. The sketches in his notebooks have been interpreted as indicative of scientific knowledge beyond his time and of modern inventions.   It is more likely that they are representative of his time, that many other minds were pursuing like germs of new scientific theories or groping after new appliances.   Certainly the great experimental painter but continued that close observation of nature, that ingenious inventiveness, that alliance between practical mechanical arts and natural experimental science, which had characterized the artists and artisans of the twelfth and thirteenth centuries.   Many of his scientific theories and ideas were suggested by his reading in authors of the thirteenth and fourteenth centuries, while in some respects his thought had not advanced as far as theirs.   For it should be kept in mind that the same books on natural science which had been read in manuscript in the twelfth, thirteenth, and fourteenth centuries were now read in printed editions in the fifteenth, sixteenth, and seventeenth centuries.   It is, however, the new contemporary contributions that we would now examine.   The higher sides at least of civilization have probably been advanced mainly by the work of a comparatively few individuals, and we shall consider the further scientific advance of the sixteenth and seventeenth centuries in terms of the work of certain individuals.   Again it should be remembered that we could not name here all those who contributed, even if we knew who they were, and that those whom we name profited by the labors of others, or are representative of a general effort and advance in which others shared.

Agricola and Metallurgy

Agricola (1494–1555), or in German, Bauer, is usually called the founder of modern metallurgy and mineralogy, but what he put into print was largely based upon practices in mining and smelting that had been going on in Germany for several centuries, and there were other writers on metallurgy contemporary with him. However, his *De re metallica* was the leading work. The production of steel by the puddling process was now first described, and methods of estimating the approximate amount of metal in the ore. By-products were utilized which had been previously neglected. The separation of gold from silver by nitric acid is said to have first been carried out on a large scale in Venice about 1500, although such experiments had of course long been carried on by the alchemists.

Paracelsus and Pharmaceutical Chemistry

Paracelsus Theophrastus Bombast von Hohenheim (1493–1541) also had learned much practical chemistry from the miners as well as natural magic and occult science from the abbot, Trithemius. He stirred the medical world of his day by attacks upon tradition and upon contemporary physicians and apothecaries, composing many works, not in Latin but in a vigorous Swiss-German, although various works of dubious authorship are also ascribed to him. He combined fantastic imagination with original insight; his name, bombast, has come to denote an inflated style of writing. He led the wandering life of the medieval student and searcher after truth in different lands, and retained any number of erroneous notions such as that animals discover marvelous remedies by natural sagacity. His chief new contribution was to attempt to employ chemicals as drugs. Instead of using herbs or parts of animals in a state of nature, or various compounds of these, he tried to get certain essences from natural bodies. He further realized that the operations of the human body in health or disease involved chemical change. This connection of pharmacy and chemistry, or application of chemistry to healing, came to be known as Iatro-Chemistry and had great, if not dominating, influence for the next century or so. Ambroise Paré (1517–1590), however, improved the practice of surgery.

Palissy

Palissy (c. 1510–1589) was a rare example of a practical

craftsman breaking into the circles of the learned and making valuable scientific investigations and suggestions. First a wandering apprentice in the trade of glass painting, then the inventor of a new type of glazed pottery, he collected a museum of natural history with which he illustrated the lectures that he gave before distinguished audiences at Paris (1575–1584). His works in French advocate scientific agriculture, show much insight into chemistry, and in discussing fossils and the orgins of rocks and springs forerun the development of geology two centuries later. "I am . . . only a simple, humble-minded, ill-educated handicraftsman," wrote Palissy, "but I read in the book of the heavens and the earth more than all the books of the philosophers could tell me." It is doubtful, however, if his acquaintance with the books of the philosophers was sufficient to justify him in venturing on so sweeping an assertion.

Copernicus (1473–1543)—it is disputed whether he was of Polish or German descent—did not publish his new theory of the motions of the planets until the year of his death. It was that the earth revolved about its axis from west to east and with the other planets moved about the sun. In other words, the heavens as a whole are not revolving about the earth in a direction opposite to the movement of the planets, and the earth is not the center of the universe. This new theory was slow in finding acceptance because the opposite Ptolemaic theory had so well accorded for centuries with the repeated observations of astronomers. Also it was a blow to astrology, which had represented the earth at the center of the universe receiving the radiation of influences from the various heavens, stars, and planets encircling it, which we have seen it had been customary to call "superiors." Both the Roman Catholic and Protestant churches took the ground that the Copernican theory was contrary to the Bible. In this connection it is interesting to note that Copernicus had been a canon, and even general vicar and visitor of the diocese during an episcopal vacancy, and that he had been allowed to dedicate his *De revolutionibus* to Pope Paul III. Copernicus' definition of weight is also noteworthy: "I regard weight as the natural tendency of matter in the smallest objects to unite itself into a whole and a spherical whole." *The Copernican Theory*

The church moves slowly in accepting new ideas. Today the Copernican theory is unquestioned. Since the thirteenth century, at least, computists had been pointing out the need of re- *The Gregorian Calendar*

forming the Julian calendar, which made leap year occur a
little too often. Finally in 1582 Pope Gregory XIII introduced the needed change which was generally accepted except
in lands belonging to the Greek or Russian church and in some
countries which had rejected the papal authority. England,
for example, did not accept the reformed calendar until 1751.
All this gives us reason to believe that in the course of time
those religious bodies which now oppose the theory of evolution
will cease to do so.

Mathemat-
ics, Physics,
Astronomy,
and
Geography
of the
Sixteenth
Century
In mathematics algebra and trigonometry made progress in
the sixteenth century. The mathematicians of the time would
set problems for their fellows to solve, or challenge the others
to discover the same solution as they themselves had reached
but had announced only in anagrams and enigmas. Rhæticus,
so named from Swiss Rhætia, his native land, devised trigono-
metric tables; John Napier, of England, perfected logarithms;
Vieta and Stiefel invented mathematical symbols. Tartaglia,
Cardan, and others extended the theory of equations and introduced the conception of imaginary quantities. Gilbert
(1540–1603), with his experiments with magnetic bodies, was
perhaps the most noteworthy physicist before Galileo and a
forerunner of the later study of electricity. He stole some of
his thunder, however, from the thirteenth century treatise of
Petrus Peregrinus. Tycho Brahe (1546–1601), a Danish astronomer, made a series of careful observations in his island
laboratory, which was unusually well equipped for that period
with large, specially made quadrants, clocks, and celestial
globes for recording the exact position of the stars at an exact
time, and with a printing press and a workshop for making
apparatus. The Flemish geographer, Mercator (1512–1594),
made a terrestrial globe and a celestial globe that were regarded
as superior to any before, and advanced scientific geography
in other respects. His method of projecting the earth's surface on a flat map is still much employed.

New
Scientific
Instruments
Indeed, about 1600 or shortly thereafter, a number of sci-
entific instruments were either invented or came into general
use, which have made close observation and exact scientific
measurement possible as never before. The telescope was now
ready for use by Galileo, who first heard of it in 1609, and by
Kepler, who explained the theory of the instrument in 1611.
Air thermometers were devised by Galileo in 1597, Scarpi in

1600, Drebbel in 1609, and Santorio in 1610; also hygrometers were constructed to measure the amount of moisture in the air. The barometer was employed in Torricelli's famous experiment (1644) with the tube filled with mercury, by means of which he produced a vacuum and determined the weight of the atmosphere. The mercury thermometer was not perfected until about 1725 by Fahrenheit. Huygens introduced the pendulum clock in 1657. The micrometer was invented in 1639 by Gascoigne. Harvey in 1628 in setting forth the circulation of the blood wrote, "Nay, even in wasps, hornets, and flies, I have, with the aid of a magnifying glass, and at the upper part of what is called the tail, both seen the heart pulsating myself, and shown it to many others." The first compound microscope was probably made in 1590 by the Dutchman, Zacharias Jansen. The Neapolitan, Porta (1540–1615), devised the *camera obscura*, or magic lantern, so called quite appropriately, since his chief work was entitled *Magia naturalis*, and he clung fondly to almost all the superstitions of past science.

Porta was instrumental in founding the Natural Academy of Naples in 1560, and later became a member of the Academy of Lynxes at Rome, so called because their intellectual insight was supposed to penetrate the obscure secrets of nature, as the eye of a lynx was supposed to see through solid walls. Other scientific societies were founded in the course of the seventeenth century at Florence, London, and Paris—the two last under royal patronage. In this connection it should be realized that, while we may have occasion to mention the discovery of this or that man in this or that particular field of science, scarcely a scientist of this period was a specialist in a single field merely, much less in only a section of a field as today. Tycho Brahe, for example, had his chemical laboratory as well as his astronomical observatory; Copernicus thought out his new theory of the heavens while practicing medicine; Fabricius of Aquapendente discovered both a variable star and the valves of the veins, of which last he made wonderfully beautiful and accurate drawings.

Scientific Societies

Learned periodicals are a natural accompaniment of scientific societies. In 1682 the *Acta eruditorum* of Otto Mencke of Leipzig aimed to summarize and review all new works produced in Europe, and by 1700 almost every department of

Learned Periodicals

learning in Germany had its own periodical. To this day periodical literature is most highly specialized in Germany. The oldest modern periodical, however, is the French *Journal des Savants*, which started publication in 1665.

Biology and Anatomy Before Harvey

In biological science the chief work of the sixteenth century on animals was by Gesner (four volumes in 1551–1558 and the fifth in 1587), on plants by Cesalpino (in 1583) who, some have contended, understood the circulation of the blood before Harvey. Vesalius of Brussels in 1543 gave a great impetus to further advance in anatomy by his criticism of Galen's description of the human body. Berengario da Carpi had already in 1521 denied the existence of the rete mirabile below the brain and of pores in the sinus. He is also said to have been the first to describe the vermiform appendix. Pierre Belon (1517–1564) examined some two hundred species of birds anatomically. After further advances, such as that of Fabricius of Aquapendente above mentioned and the full description of the lesser circulation by Servetus and Colombo in the sixteenth century, came the work of Harvey.

Discovery of the Circulation of the Blood

Harvey (1578–1657) pointed out that Fabricius did not rightly understand the use of the valves in the veins which he had discovered. Harvey showed that they opened towards the heart, not away from it, and that "it is manifest in opposition to commonly received opinions that the diastole of the arteries corresponds with the time of the heart's systole." On the basis of such reasoning as this, nine years of experiment, ocular demonstration by ligatures of veins and arteries, and frequent vivisection, Harvey held that the blood was pumped from the left side of the heart through the aorta to all parts of the body, whence it returned through the veins to the right side of the heart, and then through the lungs to the left side. Harvey furthermore was no mean embryologist and made some approach to the cell theory. Sir Thomas Browne, himself a doctor of medicine whose *Inquiry into Vulgar Errors* (1646) exposed many pseudo-scientific superstitions of the past and of his own time, acclaimed Harvey's discovery as greater than that of America. It first made possible a science of physiology; "the whole conception of feeding of tissues, of respiration, and of glandular activity took on a new form." It was, however, for a time disputed, especially at Paris, until in 1673 that enlightened monarch, Louis XIV, established a chair of anatomy "for the propagation of the new discoveries." It remained for Malpighi (1628–1694) with the microscope to find the capillaries by which the blood passes from the arteries to the veins.   Meanwhile three other anatomists had discovered the vessels which supply nourishment to the blood: in 1622 Asellius traced the lacteals which carry nutritious matter from the intestines to make fresh blood; in 1647 Pecquet found the thoracic duct which conveys the blood-making fluid to the large veins; in 1649 Rüdbeck investigated the lymphatic vessels in other parts of the body.

Harvey and the new anatomy are often represented as in direct opposition to Galen, but they rather continued the experimental spirit and devotion to truth of the great ancient, whom Harvey constantly cites, usually with approval, in his treatise on the circulation.   It should also be understood that Harvey himself still cherished many notions which science has since shown to be incorrect, as that "grubs and earthworms . . . are engendered of putrefaction and do not preserve their species," that "garlic applied to the soles of the feet assists expectoration," that "nature always does that which is best," that man is a microcosm or universe in miniature, and that vital and animal spirit may be distinguished in the human body. Harvey was an interesting personality.   He was very fond of the new beverage, coffee, but also drank freely of alcoholic liquors on occasion.   No one knows whether he was a Roman Catholic or Protestant.   He was physician to both James I and Charles I, to whom he dedicated his *De motu*, comparing him to the heart or sun of England.   At the battle of Edgehill in the Civil War he had charge of the royal children who later became Charles II and James II.   Some of his treatises yet unpublished were destroyed by the parliamentary soldiers when they ransacked his rooms in Whitehall palace in 1642.

Harvey's Further Characteristics

An important advance made in botany in the late sixteenth and seventeenth century was the development of a scientific terminology and nomenclature.   Cesalpino and Jung (1587–1657) took the first steps in this direction.   In the previous medieval herbals there were many illuminations depicting plants in colors, but often these were more artistic or odd than readily recognizable, and accurate technical words in which to describe the details of the plants were largely lacking.   Gaspard Bauhin in his *Pinax*, 1623, employed a binomial nomenclature for

Progress Toward Scientific Nomenclature in Botany

plants, though the great work of Linnæus in scientific terminology came only in the eighteenth century.

Galileo

Galileo (1564–1642) was the most creative mind of the period in physics and astronomy. Born in Pisa of Florentine family, on the same day that Michelangelo died at Rome, he was for a time apprenticed to a cloth merchant of Florence, then studied medicine at Pisa, but ultimately turned to mathematics and mechanics. Through the influence of Guido Ubaldi Marchese del Monte (1545–1607), who was himself a physicist of repute, Galileo obtained professorships at Pisa and Padua. He especially advanced the knowledge of dynamics, investigating the resistance which solid bodies offer to fracture, the cause of cohesion, the oscillation of pendulums in particular, and motion in general, whether uniform, naturally accelerated, or violent, such as that of projectiles. "To give us the science of motion," wrote the contemporary Venetian historian and champion of free thought, Fra Paolo Sarpi (1552–1623), "God and Nature have joined hands and created the intellect of Galileo." When Galileo procured a telescope in 1609, or rather constructed a superior one for himself, he began to make new astronomical discoveries at a feverish rate that finally cost him his eyesight four years before his death. "He has," says the notice by the publisher of one of his works in that same year, 1638, "discovered the four satellites of Jupiter, has shown us the true character of the Milky Way, and has made us acquainted with spots on the Sun, with the rough and cloudy portions of the lunar surface, with the threefold nature of Saturn, with the phases of Venus, with the physical character of comets. These matters were entirely unknown to the ancient astronomers and philosophers."

Galileo and the Inquisition

As early as 1597 Galileo wrote to Kepler, the German astronomer, that he had for years been an adherent of the Copernican theory and had collected data in support of it which he feared to publish lest it bring upon him the same ridicule. He was destined to meet with more serious opposition. About the time that his observations with the telescope were deepening his conviction of the truth of the Copernican theory, the Inquisition declared that theory contrary to the Bible and heretical, and forbade anyone to teach it as truth. This setting up the Bible as authoritative in natural science is perhaps more modern than medieval.   Alexander Neckam (1157–1217), for example, although himself an abbot, explained that Adam's body was composed of all four elements and not merely of earth as the Book of Genesis might seem to imply, and that its statement, "God made two great lights," concerning the creation of sun and moon, "follows the judgment of the eye and the popular notion," but is not accurate, since of course the moon is not one of the largest planets.   The church in Galileo's time did not adopt so sensible an attitude towards the Ptolemaic and Copernican theories.   Galileo outwardly acquiesced but made visits to the papal court at Rome in vain efforts to have the prohibition of the Copernican theory removed.   In writings which he managed to get permission to print he showed the error of the Ptolemaic theory and advanced strong arguments for the Copernican, although always adding as a matter of form that the Copernican theory must be wrong since the theologians so pronounced it.   Thus he spread the Copernican theory.   The Inquisition finally decided that he had gone too far; in 1633 he was summoned to Rome and, while persisting that he had not taught the Copernican theory, made complete submission.   He probably was not actually tortured, although he was once reminded that he might be if he did not tell the whole truth, for as usual the object of the inquisitors was to obtain a confession from the accused.   There is no authentic evidence that he muttered, "But it (the earth) does move," after his recantation. He was assigned a light penance, which his daughter seems to have performed for him, and was confined in residences for a time, rather than put in prison.   But he was kept under surveillance for the rest of his life, and there were two inquisitors present by his bedside at his death.   He resumed, however, his researches with the telescope until he became blind, and ventured to publish at Leyden in 1638 a work which the inquisition would not allow him to print in Italy.

Meanwhile Kepler's laws of planetary motion had been announced in 1609 and 1618.   They are to be regarded as a further refinement and substantiation of the Copernican hypothesis.   They state that the orbits of the planets are ellipses of which the sun is at one focus, that as the planet moves in its orbit its radius vector to the sun sweeps over equal areas in equal times, and that the square of any planet's periodic time is

Kepler's
Laws

proportional to the cube of its mean distance from the sun. Despite his scientific achievements Kepler still made astrological predictions.

Chemistry to Boyle

Chemists continued their activity in the seventeenth century. Van Helmont (1577–1644) seems to have introduced the term "gas"; Hooke and Mayow suggested the existence of such a substance as what we now call oxygen but failed to discover or segregate it; Glauber (1604–1668) discovered the salt which bears his name, or sulphate of sodium. Robert Boyle (1627–1691), seventh son and fourteenth child of the Earl of Cork, in 1660 discovered his law that the volume of a gas varies inversely with the pressure, and in 1661 in *The Sceptical Chemist* questioned "the experiments whereby vulgar Spagyrists" (i. e. the followers of Paracelsus) "are wont to endeavor to evince their Salt, Sulphur, and Mercury to be the true principles of things." He protested against considering chemistry simply with a view to the preparation of medicines, as physicians did, or to the improvement of metals, as alchemists did, and wished to view the subject more broadly from the standpoint of natural philosophy. He clearly described the nature of chemical action, or change, but held that there is one primary matter, and so was not entirely unfavorable to the possibility of transmutation.

Sir Isaac Newton

Sir Isaac Newton (1642–1727), born the year that Galileo died, was a creative mathematical genius like Archimedes. Already, in 1665–1666, he had discovered the binomial theorem, the method of tangents, and the direct method of fluxions. He demonstrated the compound nature of white light and concluded that rays which differed in color also differ in refrangibility. In 1687 he published the *Principia*, clarifying the basic principles of mechanics and setting forth his general theory of gravitation. It may be briefly expressed thus: Every particle of matter in the universe attracts every other particle with a force varying inversely as the square of the distance between them, and directly proportional to the product of their masses." The simplicity of this universal law for all matter, whether the apple dropping from the bough or the rotations of flaming worlds far away, made a great impression upon the thought of the time. It was taken as the great model of natural law in electricity and other fields. Its purely mathematical consequences, we are told, were drawn with an increasing success "un-

PAINTINGS BY
MICHELANGELO
AND RAPHAEL

Left, detail of decorative
figure from the frescoes
of the Sistine Chapel;
right, the Vision of Ezek-
iel, now at the Pitti
Gallery.

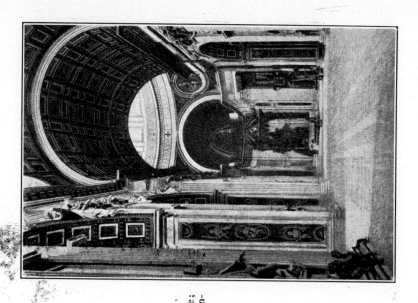

ST. PETER'S
ROME

Left, view of the dome;
right, view of the in-
terior.

paralleled in any other domain of science," while by analogy and experiment it was extended to other fields. Even more than the Copernican theory or astronomical discoveries of Galileo did it destroy the foundations of astrology. The planets and other heavenly bodies, far from being living rational beings, or from controlling all terrestrial phenomena by their complicated motions, were themselves subjected to a simple mathematical formula and were found to act just as all other matter acts. Nor could their periods and orbits be taken any longer as evidence of a great, intricately devised, divine design, since they all conformed to a simple mechanistic principle and needed no supernatural switchman to keep them in their tracks. Furthermore, men began to wonder if some simple formula could not be discovered to account for the seeming disorder of human society, or to reduce those chaotic political and social relationships to an order like that of the natural world. And it was perhaps not entirely a coincidence that the widespread introduction of machinery in the world of industry and travel followed soon in the wake of this mechanistic formula for the material universe as a whole. As for Newton's further career, in 1690 and 1701 he represented the University of Cambridge in Parliament; he also held other political offices; from 1703 he was president of the Royal Society.

While Newton was thus subjecting the remote celestial spheres to a simple law, investigators with the microscope were revealing new worlds as unforeseen as Galileo's numerous discoveries with the telescope had been. One of the first books published by the Royal Society of London was Robert Hooke's *Micrographia*, in 1665. Describing the view of the tail of a tadpole through the microscope, Leeuwenhoek (1632–1723) wrote, "A sight presented itself more delightful than any mine eyes had ever beheld; for here I discovered more than fifty circulations of the blood in different places, while the animal lay quiet in the water, and I could bring it before my microscope to my wish." Leeuwenhoek made many microscopes himself as well as examined through them a world of minute beings hitherto invisible and unknown. In 1675 he discovered protozoa; in 1683, bacteria or microscopic plant organisms; and he was the first to describe the human spermatozoön. He demonstrated the existence of Infusoria in the presence of the Royal Society of London. He disproved the belief in spontaneous

Discoveries with the Microscope

generation of various animals by showing that fleas came from eggs, not sand, and that there were embryo eels in the body of the female. "For my part I hold it equally impossible for a small shell-fish to be produced without generation and for a whale to have its origin in the mud." Swift, learning somehow of Leeuwenhoek's discovery that a minute parasite fed on the pupa of the flea, wrote:

> So Naturalists observe, a flea
> Has smaller fleas that on him prey;
> And these have smaller still to bite 'em
> And so proceed *ad infinitum*.

Swammerdam (1637–1680) had already, in 1658, discovered the blood corpuscles of the frog, although his observations were not published until later. He also showed that insects and lower animals were not simpler in structure, as Harvey for one had taught, but that the minute animals, too, had brains and heart, nerves and muscles, stomach and intestines. Malpighi (1628–1694) also studied the anatomy of insects through the microscope, describing the internal structure of the silkworm, for example, and the air tubes to every part of its body. The excretory organs of insects are named Malpighian tubes after him. He worked himself into a fever and inflammation of the eyes, but, to quote his own words, "Nevertheless, in performing these researches so many marvels of nature were spread before my eyes that I experienced an internal pleasure that my pen could not describe."

Political Philosophy

The political thinking and writing of this period was in a way becoming scientific and based upon reason, historical research, or contemporary observation, although it showed a bias in favor of absolute monarchy, or at least of the national state, just as the previous period had been largely influenced by the ideals of the church. The Florentine Machiavelli (1469–1527), famed especially for *The Prince*, a manual instructing the Italian despots how best to gain their ends without much regard for the means, showed shrewd insight into the practical politics of his time and coolly adopted a purely political standard. He enforced his reasoning by contemporary or historical examples. The Frenchman Bodin (1530–1596) showed a curious combination of old and new views. In his *Method for the Easy Understanding of History* he expounded the theory of human progress which was such a favorite of recent times until the great war. In his *Republic* he defended absolute monarchy, such as had developed in France, as the best form of government, contending that it should be supreme over parliaments, estates, gilds, and communes. The sovereign should make the laws and be unrestrained by them. Bodin earnestly defended private property, but opposed the taking of interest on capital on the ground that it would encourage speculation and make a few men too rich. His emphasis on the influence of climate and geography was accompanied by a belief in astrological influence, and he maintained the existence of sorcery and witchcraft. He upheld nobility, scoffed at equality, and regarded women as unfit for anything except household cares; yet he regretted the revival of domestic slavery in Europe in the sixteenth century, where it had ceased to exist since the emancipation movement of the twelfth and thirteenth centuries. The Dutchman Grotius (1583-1645) in *The Law of War and Peace* founded the science of international law, a subject for which there was a crying need, now that one church was no longer recognized and that kings were asserting unrestrained power over increasingly wide territories and coming into constant conflict with one another. The Englishman Hobbes (1588–1679) in *Leviathan* justified the state as essential to peace and civilization on the ground that man, if left to himself, is unsocial, guided solely by self-interest, and an enemy of every other man. He believed that the state originated in an agreement of the people, or social contract, but that once established it should have supreme authority in all matters and should control even church and individual conscience. The form of sovereignty which he preferred was hereditary monarchy.

Our two centuries were marked by much industrious and scholarly work in the collection and publication of historical materials from the middle ages, mainly however for their ecclesiastical interest, and somewhat affected by Roman Catholic and Protestant bias. The Benedictine monk, Mabillon (1632–1707) is perhaps as good a single example as we could select. He was a scholar of vast erudition, especially at home· in the period from the seventh to eleventh century, and practically the founder of the science of diplomatics, or the scientific study of documents. The church authorities did not always allow him to publish the whole truth, against which restriction he

Historical Scholarship: Mabillon

protested, pointing out that it would only afford the enemies of the Roman Catholic church a further ground for complaint.

Metaphysics of the Seventeenth Century: Descartes

The great names in philosophy are found in the seventeenth rather than the sixteenth century. At its beginning Francis Bacon (1561–1626) lent the weight of his literary and legal reputation, his official position and noble rank to the advocacy of impartial and systematic scientific research and investigation of nature by the inductive method, holding that the human reason can accomplish nothing when left to itself. Subsequent philosophers, however, were far from entirely abandoning metaphysics. Descartes (1596–1650), it is true, agreed with Bacon that one must start with an attitude of sweeping doubt as to all assertions of past scientists and authorities. This readiness to doubt was very essential in ridding science of the many magical details and superstitious assertions which were still confused with it. But Descartes then proceeded to make self-consciousness the foundation of his whole philosophical system. *Cogito, ergo sum,*—"I think, therefore I exist"—of that much at least he felt certain. Indeed, he went on to argue that "whatever I am clearly and distinctly conscious of is true." He trusted reason more than the senses. He also stressed the importance of mathematical method as Bacon had not; indeed, he invented—or re-invented—analytical geometry. With Descartes the discussion of substance took a leading part in metaphysics. He held that mind and body were independent substances and failed to explain their interaction satisfactorily. Was he perhaps somewhat influenced towards this view by the fact that "some of his most fruitful ideas dated from dreams and his best thinking was habitually done before rising"? Tragi-comic was the end of this philosopher who was "always fond of his bed," for when he accepted a call to the court of Christina of Sweden, that capricious queen insisted upon his giving her lessons in mathematics at five A. M. in the depth of winter, and he died of a cold contracted in consequence.

Spinoza and Leibnitz

Spinoza (1632–1677) had even more confidence than Descartes in the power of the human reason, which he believed to be the eternal part of the soul. Mere general and abstract ideas, however, he mistrusted as vague and valueless. He held that mind and body were the same substance considered under different attributes of thought and spatial extension. Everything is both body and spirit; substance, nature, and God are identical. Thus Spinoza's philosophy was pantheistic. He explained away free will as an illusion of consciousness, arguing that if a falling stone were conscious, it would imagine that its fall was the result of its own decision. Leibnitz (1646–1716), a publicist and librarian with a command of all fields of learning like that of the Alexandrian librarians of old, revised the ancient atomic theory somewhat as Spinoza had revived pantheism. Leibnitz denied the reality of matter, space, and time. For him substance was active force. In place of physical atoms he introduced the conception of immaterial and non-spatial monads. Each monad represents the universe, but each represents it differently, and they do not affect one another. There is, however, a continuity in nature and a conservation of force, and a stream of consciousness in the human mind where ideas can arise only from ideas. Body and mind are like two clocks which run independently but keep the same time.

Less subtle and profound, perhaps, but seeming more practical and comprehensible to the ordinary common sense was the philosophy of John Locke (1632–1704), who may be said to have dissected the human intellect. Descartes had argued that the idea of God, a being more perfect than man or nature, could not come through the senses and must be innate and implanted in the human mind by God himself. Locke in his *Essay concerning Human Understanding* (1690) held that all ideas are received through sensation and built upon it by subsequent reflection; that all knowledge comes from experience, and that the particular and concrete is perceived before the general. Man is superior to the brute in his faculty of abstraction and forming thoughts, which he communicates to his fellows by language. The external world is real, but many things exist which our senses fail to note, and our senses cannot tell us the true inner nature of bodies. Much of our knowledge is only probable, and there are matters above human reason like the resurrection of the dead. That revelation was not contrary to reason Locke endeavored to show in *The Reasonableness of Christianity*, which he was amazed to find some regard as directed against Christianity. His *Letters on Toleration* urged religious freedom for all except atheists and those sects which were themselves intolerant (if strictly interpreted, this would still have excluded most of them), and are to be connected with the Toleration Act passed at the same time by the English

Philosophy of Locke

parliament for all except atheists, those who did not believe in the Trinity, and Roman Catholics. In his *Treatise on Civil Government* Locke urged that the chief power should reside in a representative legislature. His *Thoughts Concerning Education* urged sympathetic development of the pupil's individual capacities rather than the attempt to transfer a certain amount of knowledge to him. We have mentioned these works by Locke in some detail because his views were to be so influential in the following eighteenth century as our subsequent chapter on the Age of Reason will show.

BIBLIOGRAPHY

Allbutt, Sir T. C. "The Rise of the Experimental Method in Oxford, Ninth Robert Boyle Lecture," reprinted at back of his *Greek Medicine in Rome*, 1921, pp. 491–525.

Conway, B. L. *The Condemnation of Galileo*, 1913.

Crew, H. and DeSalvio, A. *Dialogues concerning Two New Sciences by Galileo Galilei*, English translation, 1914.

Gunther, P. T. *Early Science at Oxford*, 1921–1925, 4 vols.

Harris, D. F. "The Man who discovered the Circulation of the Blood," in *Popular Scientific Monthly* (now *The Scientific Monthly*), May, 1913, pp. 453–67; "Anthony van Leeuwenhoek, the First Bacteriologist," in *The Scientific Monthly*, XII (1921) 150–160.

Hoover, H. C. and L. H. *Agricola, De re metallica*, English translation, 1912.

Lieb, John W. "Leonardo da Vinci, natural philosopher and engineer," in *Journal of the Franklin Institute*, June–July, 1921.

McCurdy, E. *Leonardo da Vinci's Note Books*, 1923; "arranged and rendered into English with Introductions."

Ornstein, Martha. *The Rôle of the Scientific Societies in the Seventeenth Century*, 1913.

Robertson, J. M. *The Philosophical Works of Francis Bacon*, 1905.

Rohde, Alfred. *Die Geschichte der wissenschaftlichen Instrumente vom Beginn der Renaissance bis zum Ausgang des 18 Jahrhunderts*, 1923, 119 pp., 139 illus.

Shipley, A. E. *The Revival of Science in the Seventeenth Century*, 1914.

Singer, Charles. *The Discovery of the Circulation of the Blood*, 1923; a lucid treatment.

Stimson, Dorothy. *The Gradual Acceptance of the Copernican Theory of the Universe*, 1917.

Taylor, Clara M. *The Discovery of the Nature of the Air and of its Changes during Breathing*, 1923.

CHAPTER XXXV

NATIONAL CULTURES

(Italian, Spanish, Portuguese, Dutch, and Elizabethan)

We gaze and turn away, and know not where,
Dazzled and drunk with beauty, till the heart
Reels with its fulness; there—forever there—
Chained to the chariot of triumphal Art,
We stand as captives, and would not depart.

—Byron

THE cynical Machiavelli had permitted himself one patriotic touch in urging the member of the Medici family to whom he dedicated *The Prince* to crown his achievement of despotism by expelling the foreign domination from Italy, quoting the verses of Petrarch:

Brief will be the strife
When valor arms against barbaric rage,
For the bold spirit of a bygone age
Still warms Italian hearts to life.

Italy under Spanish Influence

This, however, was not to be until the nineteenth century. For the present, with Spain in control of Sicily, southern Italy, Milan, and the Tuscan ports, society as well as politics became quite Spanish in character. Military life was exalted; princes secluded themselves from their subjects; enterprising burghers bought titles and turned into indolent Spanish nobles; the peasants were over-taxed, land went out of cultivation, brigands abounded, and Lombardy suffered from frequent campaigns and Spanish garrisons; the black Spanish garb replaced the gay Italian colors. "Venice and Genoa were spared, the one as a bulwark against the Turks, the other as a state bank for Spain." In 1571 in the naval battle of Lepanto, Venice, the pope, and Spain decisively defeated the Turkish fleet and checked the progress of Islam in the Mediterranean. Italy remained the financial center of Europe whose leading banks were

433

those of Venice and Genoa until in 1609 the Bank of Amsterdam was founded. Double-entry bookkeeping was not invented in 1494 as has often been asserted. Although described in a book printed in that year, it seems to have been in use since the thirteenth century.

End of the Italian Renaissance

Italy also continued a center of culture, much visited by foreign tourists and collectors, although the so-called Italian Renaissance had nearly run its course. Humanism spread to other countries but was almost exhausted in Italy itself, where the attitude of the Catholic Reformation, with its censorship of books and art, was less favorable to culture than that of the popes of the later fifteenth and early sixteenth centuries had been. Of the great masters of that time Michelangelo lived on until 1564, but the efforts of other artists to imitate his genius resulted in over-emphasizing his peculiarities to the point of faults rather than in further progress. No great Italian painter was born after the death of Raphael in 1520 except at Venice, which had a score of painters of the first rank. At Florence in 1571 died Benvenuto Cellini, sculptor, goldsmith, and silversmith, but now best known for his autobiography, full of the spice of adventure and artistic temperament. It remained in manuscript form, however, until 1730. In 1574 died Vasari, an artist himself but more celebrated for his appreciative lives of the previous painters. Tasso (1544–1595), last and greatest of the Italian writers of the romantic epic, was insane and broken in health in later life, and died at Rome before he could be crowned poet laureate.

The Academic, Baroque, and Rococo Styles

With Palladio (1518–1580) we reach the strictly classical type of Renaissance architecture, a frigid academic style based largely on the book of the Roman, Vitruvius, yet also not without grandeur and impressive proportions. The banqueting hall of Whitehall palace in London, completed by Inigo Jones in 1622, exactly as high as it is wide and twice as long, is the best English example of this style. Inigo Jones also built the earliest academic church in England in 1631. The sixteenth century further witnessed the introduction of Italian landscape gardening, by which palaces of brick, stone, and stucco were set off by cypresses and clumps of ilex, green lawns and terraces, pools and fountains. St. Peter's church was not finished until 1626, and the later alterations in plan, made after the death of Michelangelo who had completed the great dome, did not improve it. Even the dome is illogically constructed, with "buttresses formed of coupled columns vigorously applied to the drum where there is no thrust," and "ribs appliquéd on the surface of the cupola itself in such a manner that, far from gathering or relieving the structural strain, they merely increase it by so much added weight" (Porter). The interior is in a pseudo-Roman style of architecture which fails to bring out its great size, and is covered with surface decoration inappropriate to a church. The façade is baroque, a style which especially marked the architecture and sculpture of the seventeenth century. It may be described as severe and grandiose, ostentatious and theatrical. Bernini (1598–1680), an architect and sculptor who also wrote and staged plays, was its leading exponent. His work may be seen at its best in the great colonnade which he erected around the piazza in front of St. Peter's in 1665–1667, and which is more imposing than the church itself. "No baroque artist had much regard for his medium," mixing up colored marbles with copper, lead, and tin. We wince at the sight of twisted columns, or pillars composed of alternating cubical and cylindrical sections, or rounded pediments and arches of which the centers are broken, or missing entirely. Baroque sculpture is too agitated and florid, with diagonal lines, disordered draperies, sculptured clouds and sunbeams, saints striking attitudes, angels toe-dancing, and disgustingly realistic or stagy representations of sacred story and religious experience. The Baroque in turn gave way, especially in the eighteenth century, to the Rococo style, which was less heavy and more elegant but also more fantastic and exuberant in surface decoration. It was dainty but artificial, and did not mean anything or bear any close relation to structure. "All interiors were conceived more or less in the mode of a lady's boudoir." A word should be added concerning the artistic pottery of the sixteenth and seventeenth centuries: Italian majolica, old French faience, and the tin-enamelled earthenware of Delft. Tapestries in the seventeenth and eighteenth centuries became too florid, pseudo-classical, and allegorical.

In music Palestrina (1524–1594) gave unsurpassed expression to the religious service of the Roman Catholic church, and marks the high point reached by several centuries of experimentation in choral counterpoint. Orlando Lasso (Roland Delattre), a Belgian who worked at the court of the duke of

Music and the Opera

Bavaria at Munich from 1557 to 1594, showed great range and originality. He is especially noted for his humorous music. Grand Opera may be said to have begun in Italy in 1600, when the first public performance was given at Florence in the Pitti palace on the occasion of the marriage of Henry IV of France and Mary de' Medici. In the same year at Rome was presented a dramatic oratorio, "The Soul and Body." The first opera house was built at Venice in 1637. The Opera was originally intended to revive the ancient Greek drama with its accompanying music and dancing. Italian opera reached its peak of literary excellence in Metastasio (1698–1782), famous also for his Ode to Nice or *La Libertà*. The themes of his lyric dramas, however, are all classical. Others composed the music for these operas, but his words and meters are wonderfully musical in themselves. He wrote at Naples, Rome, and longest at Vienna at the Austrian court. This was also the age of famous violin makers of Cremona, Brescia, and Venice, of organ builders, and of great singers. The pianoforte was not invented until the early eighteenth century, by Bartolommeo Cristofori.

From the *Commedia Dell' Arte* to Goldoni

The popular stage was occupied through the seventeenth century by the *Commedia dell' Arte*, in which the actors were masked and always took the parts of certain stock characters with traditional costumes, such as Harlequin and Pantaloon, the doctor, the soldier of fortune, and the soubrette. The conversation was commonly improvised, though there was a scenario or skeleton plot to be followed. Somewhat similar was the French pantomime with its typical characters such as Pierrot. In the eighteenth century the *Commedia dell' Arte* degenerated into horse-play and was supplanted by the light comedies of Goldoni (1707–1793) which mirror admirably the surface life of the Venetian society of his day.

Economic Decline of Spain and Portugal

The prosperity and greatness which Spain and Portugal derived from the treasure of Mexico and Peru and the royal monopoly of trade with the East Indies did not prove lasting. Both nations were somewhat spoiled by their sudden riches and ceased to be economically productive at home. The Spanish persecution of Jews and Moors tended further to deprive the country of industrial skill and business ability. Many other enterprising citizens had gone out to the new colonies. Therefore, as the Dutch and English gradually took away the sea power from Spain and Portugal and supplanted them as colonial and commercial empires, the peninsular states, losing revenue from the carrying trade and exploitation of their colonies, were thrown back on their undeveloped internal resources and entered upon a state of decline. This was hastened by the fact that proud Spain persisted in maintaining an expensive foreign and military policy on the continent of Europe, while Portuguese interests suffered during the sixty years that Portugal was under Spanish control (1580–1640). Even before that, as we have seen, the royal monopoly of the oriental trade had prevented the growth of private business and individual effort, and had led to inefficiency and corruption on the part of the officials.

Portugal, moreover, had perhaps somewhat exhausted itself by the maritime and colonial efforts which it had for a time put forth, surprising from so small a nation. These glorious exploits of the past in various quarters of the globe were set forth in the *Lusiad*, a national epic published in 1572 by Camoens, who had twice been banished from the court at Lisbon, first for making love to a high-born lady and later for his part in a street affray. During the former exile he lost an eye in a naval fight at Ceuta; during the latter he spent seventeen years of adventure, persecution, and distress on the coasts of India, China, and Africa. The popularity of his epic is believed to have preserved the Portuguese language during the sixty years of Spanish occupation, when the court spoke Castilian. *The Lusiad of Camoens*

By the early seventeenth century, after the death of Philip II, Spanish society was badly demoralized; the court was luxurious and ceremonious, while the people were in misery. These marked contrasts were especially noticeable at Madrid, the capital. Here the showy, heavy palaces of the nobles, filled with curios and works of art, were surrounded by filthy streets and the mud huts of the masses. The upper classes indulged in extravagant dress, in much idle walking up and down or promenading,—what Charles II of England later called sauntering—and in gossip, badinage, and scandal. Religious processions and ceremonies were also frequent; the people were exceedingly superstitious. This corrupt society is reflected in the literature of the time, picaresque novels, romances of roguery, and other fiction. There we meet a great variety of *Demoralization of Spanish Society* beggars and cheats, office-seekers and hangers-on at court, and practitioners of vice and crime,—persons who are as picturesque in books as they are unpleasant in real life. Yet Madrid was full of pleasure-seekers from all parts of Europe, and the Spanish court set the style for high society generally. Anne of Austria, daughter of Philip III of Spain, wife of Louis XIII from 1615 to 1643, herself regent of France from 1643 to 1661, is said to have introduced there the ways of the Spanish court—manners, games, words, dishes, as well as Spanish dress, authors, and actors. Molière followed Spanish models; later Dumas imitated the Spanish novel of adventure. Philip III (1598–1621) and Philip IV (1621–1665) were rather weak personalities who left affairs largely in the hands of their favorites or ministers. In the middle of the century Portugal revolted successfully; Catalonia, Andalusia, and Naples, unsuccessfully.

Cervantes, Lope de Vega, and Calderón

The three leading Spanish authors of the seventeenth century were Cervantes (1547–1616), Lope de Vega (1562–1635), and Calderón (1600–1681). The former's *Don Quixote* appeared in 1604–1605 and 1615. It is a satire on the old romances of chivalry and marks the disappearance of the knightly and religious spirit of the past. Lope de Vega wrote an enormous number of plays, sometimes dashing off an entire drama in the course of a day. Over four hundred survive, to show his great facility and inventiveness of plot and incident, his mastery of dialogue, and his diverting gaiety. Although he wrote tragedies and historical dramas, his special new contribution was "the cloak and sword play," in which the main motive was gallantry. He is also noted for his comic characters and power of parody. Calderón, who succeeded Lope as dictator of the Spanish drama, possessed great lyrical gifts as well as mastery of stage craft, but was somewhat inferior to Lope in knowledge of character and passion, being more ideal than natural. Loyalty to the king, avenging one's personal honor, and devotion to the church are prominent characteristics of his dramas, of which some of the best are religious mysteries celebrating the Eucharist.

The Spanish Theater

By the close of the sixteenth century strolling players were visiting all the villages of Spain. Both boys and women played the female parts. The two theaters at the capital were courtyards enclosed by houses from the windows of which nobles might look on through grated windows without themselves being seen. In front of the raised stage at one end of the enclosure were seats for men only, and behind these came cheaper standing room. Women were accommodated in an enclosed gallery on the left known as the *cazuela* or "stew-pan." Performances for the court were given at the royal palace, but Philip IV liked to go masked and incognito to the ordinary theaters and look on from a private room in one of the adjoining houses, "vigilant for any new beauty who appeared on the stage or in the *cazuela*."

This was the great period of Spanish painting, marked especially by the work of Velasquez (1599–1660) and Murillo (1618–1682). Both were born at Seville in southern Spain, but Velasquez worked chiefly at Madrid as court-painter for Philip IV, of whom he painted many portraits, while Murillo remained in Seville painting saints, cherubs, and Virgins of the Immaculate Conception for religious brotherhoods, orders, and churches. They also executed landscapes and genre paintings depicting the common life of their time. Velasquez is noted for his "silvery brilliancy" and "startling power of creating true breadths of light and space"; Murillo for his "spirit of purity" and three different manners distinguished as "cold," "warm," and "misty." Their masterpieces are to be seen especially in the Prado Museum at Madrid. In the same city may be seen the bronze statue of Philip IV on horseback, which, although nineteen feet in height, is ranked among the finest of equestrian statues. El Greco (1550–1614) is esteemed as a forerunner of the modernists. Renaissance architecture in Spain was often in the plateresque style, a florid imitation of silverwork. *Velasquez and Murillo*

In the paintings of Velasquez we see the costume of the seventeenth century cavalier: a wide-brimmed hat, often adorned with plume or feathers; elaborate collar or ruff and cuffs; long hair, mustache, and the Vandyke beard; the cape or cloak, and jacket or coat, often belted; the sword or cane; the loose knee breeches, stockings or gaiters, and spurred heels. The ladies wore immense hoops and farthingales, long-waisted bodices, and frizzed their hair and rouged their faces very freely. Little children were pompous, stuffy replicas in miniature of their elders. *Costume of the Seventeenth Century*

The years between 1575, when William the Silent founded the University of Leyden, and 1688 when his descendant, the *The Golden Age of the Dutch Republic*

Stadtholder, William of Orange, sailed for England to become its king, have been called the Golden Age of the little Dutch Republic, a confederation of seven provinces. This was a period of economic prosperity as an accompaniment and result of the successful struggle for independence from Spain and for world-wide trade and maritime power. Antwerp at the close of the middle ages had supplanted Bruges as the Venice of the north and, owing to its carrying trade with Lisbon and Cadiz, surpassed Genoa and Venice themselves. A hundred ships entered and cleared its port daily; a thousand foreign firms had offices in its streets before 1566. Then, since it was located in the provinces which remained under Spanish rule, it lost its population and trade in the wars with Spain. Its place was taken by Amsterdam, the metropolis of the Dutch Netherlands. After the middle of the seventeenth century English rivalry deprived the Dutch of much of their carrying trade, and three naval wars against England and three land wars against Louis XIV of France further weakened them. But in the meantime the Netherlands produced many scientists, philosophers, and makers of scientific instruments, as our last chapter has illustrated. Of the great painters of the seventeenth century Rubens and Van Dyck were Flemish and connected with Antwerp, but Rembrandt (1607–1669), master alike of religious, portrait, and landscape painting, whose magic brush found beauty everywhere, transmuting objects into pictorial effects and with Velasquez founding impressionism, was Dutch, being born at Leyden and dying at Amsterdam. W. Vandevelde the younger (1633–1707) excelled in depicting "calm seas and shipping," and also executed many paintings of sea-fights between the Dutch and English. During this period education was widespread, there was much writing in the Dutch language, and no little culture among women of the middle classes. The form of government should not be thought of as democratic, however. In each province the fundamental units were municipal councils which were in the hands of a burgher oligarchy, while the merchants of Amsterdam had a preponderating influence in the central councils.

Dutch Freedom and Cosmopolitanism

One of the chief glories of the Dutch Netherlands was that their free political constitution, religious toleration, and uncensored printing-press made that little country the refuge of advanced thinkers from many lands and of varied views. There

Descartes found twenty years of quiet in which to think out his philosophy. There the Portuguese Jewish family of Spinoza had fled. Although he was expelled from the Jewish community for his heretical thinking, he still found a refuge in Holland, supporting himself by grinding optical lenses. There Locke's patron, Shaftesbury, founder of the Whig party, fled from the Tory reaction and died in 1683, while Locke himself stayed in Holland until the Revolution of 1689 in England. Switzerland offered a similar haven to political, religious, and intellectual refugees, but was a somewhat less cosmopolitan center, since it lacked Holland's intercourse by trade and exploration with distant lands and foreign climes.

Although England became an economic enemy of the Dutch Netherlands, she learned not a little from them. If market-gardening was introduced under Elizabeth rather from Flanders than Holland, and if the religious refugees from Spanish persecution in the Netherlands who enriched Elizabethan industry were also mainly from the portion of the Low Countries which is now Belgium, it was "largely through the skill of Dutch engineers and laborers" that English marshes were drained. Moreover, the Dutch knew how to build canals, dykes, and embankments long before the English. Charles I had Van Dyck paint his portraits; the Commonwealth borrowed new methods of taxation from the Netherlands in the form of the excise and monthly assessment; and Charles II introduced the Dutch pastime of yachting. The Bank of Amsterdam (1609) antedated the Bank of England, which was in fact instituted in 1694 by the Dutch king of England, William III. Dutch customs continued in America long after the colony of New Amsterdam had become New York, and its patroons had become British subjects.

In England the confusion and distress occasioned by the break with the church of Rome, the transfer of monastic lands and other religious property, the weakening of gild and manor, and the financial difficulties of Henry VIII, began to disappear by the reign of Elizabeth (1558–1603), when a period of rather general prosperity and contentment ensued for "merrie England." The queen reformed the debased coinage, vagabondage and pauperism were held fairly well in check, the Statute of Apprentices dealt with the labor problem of those days. Bold seamen scoured the main in all directions and enriched

Marginal notes:

Dutch Influence in England and America

The Elizabethan Age

England by their plunder and gains, however ill-gotten these may have been at the expense of other countries and peoples or however destructive to others' property and personal liberty.

Luxury and Show: Euphuism

The age was one of luxury and show. Although the queen was economical, even parsimonious in many ways, she and her courtiers were extravagant in dress and entertainments. This continued in the next reigns. The royal favorite, the Duke of Buckingham, when he went to Paris in 1625 to escort Henrietta Maria to wed Charles I, had twenty-seven "rich suits embroidered, and laced with silk and silver plushes." One white satin velvet suit with diamonds was estimated to be worth eighty thousand pounds sterling, while a purple suit adorned with pearls was valued at twenty thousand pounds. This of course makes no approach to the luxury of the present day when the wife of an ordinary business man, in going down the elevator from an apartment to a taxicab, may be robbed of a necklace worth $125,000, another worth $65,000, a bracelet valued at $35,000, another at $11,000, and various rings worth from $5000 to $20,000. Servants, however, were more easily had then. Buckingham took with him the same number of cooks as of suits of clothes, and six or seven hundred other servants. Englishmen who traveled in Italy returned home with foreign airs, and the upper classes in general tried to copy the polite refinement of the Italians or the etiquette of the Spanish court. Talk has always been cheap, and was indulged in with great wordiness, affectation, and far-fetched, pedantic circumlocution in the polite circles of various lands at about this time. In Italy Marino (1569–1625) was the great exponent of his style, and its other practitioners were called *Marinisti* after him; in England we hear of "Euphuism," a name derived from John Lyly's *Euphues* (1579); in France the *Précieux*, later satirized in Molière's *Les Précieux ridicules*, spoke and wrote in this artificial and exaggerated fashion.

Elizabethan Literature and Drama

In the later reign of Elizabeth and that of James I, English literature attained to better things than this, and poured forth copious streams both of poetry and prose which made the period one of the greatest in all literary history. There were pastorals and sonnets, songs and lyrics, comedies and tragedies. There were translations from Greek, Italian, and French of high worth, but greatest of all the translations was the King

PHILIP IV
OF SPAIN
Two paintings
by Velasquez.

VELASQUEZ
AND
MURILLO

Left, Beggar
Boy, by Mu-
rillo; right,
L'Infante Mar-
guerite, by Ve-
lasquez.

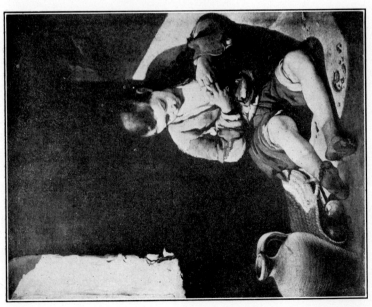

James' version of the Bible. There were histories, sacred and profane, Foxe's *Book of Martyrs*, Hooker's *Ecclesiastical Polity*, Hakluyt's account of the voyages of English navigators, Bacon's *Essays*. Spenser's *Færie Queene*, which still follows somewhat in the footsteps of medieval romance, is a poem whose merits perhaps only poets can fully appreciate. More popular in character was the drama, which about one-third of the population of London attended every week. Of the many playwrights of the period we may name along with Shakespeare (1564–1616) his early contemporary, Marlowe (1564–1593), and his later contemporary, Ben Jonson (1573–1637), poet laureate under James I. Shakespeare was a great poet and master of phrase, as well as a great dramatist and delineator of human character. *Hamlet* is probably the greatest tragedy ever written in any language. Shakespeare was also himself an actor and theatrical manager. The theaters were much like those of Spain; most of the audience stood in the uncovered "pit," and often talked, smoked, drank, played cards, got into fights, or had their pockets picked. The stage jutted out into the pit; only the back scene was curtained off. There were few scenic effects and stage properties, except in the case of masques at court for which Inigo Jones in 1604–1613 constructed elaborate settings, but costumes might be showy and varied. Boys played the female parts. Acting was therefore less emphasized than the plot or story of the play and the use of impressive language, in which the audience seems to have delighted, although they were also entertained by clowns and horse-play. They had few story-books and no magazines to read, and so went to the theater for their stories, as people are again going to moving pictures for the same purpose. Plots of the plays were sought from all sorts of sources: English history, Roman history, Italian literature, Greek literature, ancient legend, and medieval romance.

German culture of this period was first absorbed in the Protestant Reformation, then crippled in the Thirty Years War (1618–1648), of the horrors of which Grimmelshausen's novel, *Simplicius Simplicissimus* gives a vivid picture. We may also note, back in the sixteenth century, "Hans Sachs, the shoemaker-poet of Nürnberg, with his deep human sympathy and imperishable humor."

German Literature

BIBLIOGRAPHY

The *Lusiad,* Don Quixote, Cellini, and Tasso may be read in English translation; it is hardly necessary to list editions of the Elizabethan authors.

Bell, A. F. G. *Portuguese Literature,* 1902.

Blok, P. J. *History of the People of the Netherlands,* 1898–1912, 5 vols.

Bok, E. W. "Well! I didn't know that," in *Atlantic Monthly.* 130 (1922) 480–489; an entertaining summary of Dutch contributions to civilization.

Boulting, W. *Tasso and His Times,* 1907.

Bullen, A. H. *Elizabethans,* 1924.

Caffin, C. H. *Story of Spanish Painting,* 1911.

Calvert, A. F. *Murillo,* 1907; *Velasquez,* 1908.

Chambers, E. K. *The Elizabethan Stage,* 1923, 4 vols.; an elaborate work of scholarship paralleling his *The Medieval Stage.*

Chatfield-Taylor, H. C. *Goldoni,* 1913.

Dohme, R. *Barock- und Rokoko-Architektur,* 1884–1892, 3 vols.

Edmundson, George. *History of Holland,* 1922.

Félix, G. *Palestrina et la musique sacrée,* 1895.

Fitzmaurice-Kelley, J. *Chapters on Spanish Literature,* 1908; *History of Spanish Literature,* 1898; *Miguel de Cervantes Saavedra,* 1913.

Francke, Kuno. *Die Kulturwerte der Deutschen Literatur in ihrer Geschichtlichen Entwicklung,* II, "Von der Reformation bis zur Aufklärung," 1923. *History of German Literature,* English translation, 1903.

Froude, J. A. *English Seamen in the Sixteenth Century,* 1895.

Garden, R. W. *Life of Giorgio Vasari,* 1911.

Gardner, E. G. *Dukes and Poets at Ferrara,* 1904.

Garnett, R. *History of Italian Literature,* 1901.

Groot, C. Hofstede de. *A Catalogue Raisonné of the Works of the most Eminent Dutch Painters of the Seventeenth Century,* translated by E. G. Hawke, 1907–, 10 vols.

Hall, Hubert. *Society in the Elizabethan Age,* 1886.

Holroyd, C. *Michael Angelo Buonarroti,* 1903.

Hume, Martin. *Court of Philip IV,* 1907; *Spain, its greatness and decay, 1479–1788,* 1905.

Jamison, Ady, and Vernon. *Italy, Medieval and Modern,* 1917.

Kennard, J. S. *Goldoni and the Venice of His Time,* 1920.

Lee, Sidney. *Great Englishmen of the Sixteenth Century,* 1907.

Mallet, C. E. *A History of the University of Oxford,* 1924, vol. II, "the 16th and 17th centuries."

Molmenti, P. G. *Venice, its individual growth,* etc., translated by H. F. Brown, 1906–1908, 6 vols. Pt. II, "Golden Age," 2 vols.; Pt. III, "Decadence," 2 vols.

Oechsli, W. *History of Switzerland, 1499–1914,* English translation by E. and C. Paul, 1922.

Ogg, David. *Europe in the Seventeenth Century*, 1925.

Pfandl, Ludwig. *Spanische Kultur des 16 und 17 Jahrhunderts*, 1924; "One of the most useful books of the sort ever written." "Beautifully printed and lavishly illustrated."

Rennert, H. A. *The Life of Lope de Vega*, 1904; *The Spanish Stage in the Time of Lope de Vega*, 1909.

Robertson, J. M. *Elizabethan Literature*, 1914.

Rogers, Thorold. *History of the First Nine Years of the Bank of England*, 1887.

Saintsbury, G. E. B. *History of Elizabethan Literature*, 1887.

Shakespeare's England, 1916, 2 vols.

Smith, W. *The Commedia dell' Arte*, 1912.

Solon, M. L. *Old French Faience*, 1903.

Stephens, Morse. *History of Portugal*, 1891.

Stephenson, H. T. *The Elizabethan People*, 1910.

Symonds, J. A. *Life of Michael Angelo Buonarroti*, 1899, 2 vols.

Thorndike, A. H. *Shakespeare's Theater*, 1916.

Tréverret, A. de. *L'Italie au XVIe siècle: Machiavel, Castiglione, Sannazar*, 1877.

Vernon, H. M. *Italy from 1474 to 1790*, 1909.

Walsh, J. J. *What Civilization Owes to Italy*, 1923.

Wegg, Jervis. *The Decline of Antwerp under Philip of Spain*, 1924.

CHAPTER XXXVI

THE AGE OF LOUIS XIV

> If he was not the greatest king, he was the best actor of majesty at least, that ever filled a throne.—*Bolingbroke*

French
Culture
of the
Sixteenth
Century

FRANCE, whose feudal states and communes in the twelfth and thirteenth centuries had been leading centers of many activities of medieval civilization, in the sixteenth century largely turned aside from the remarkable past culture in which her various members had originated so much, to follow in the track of Italian humanism and to imitate the literature, architecture, and sculpture of classical antiquity. Ronsard (1524–1585) and the group of French poets known as The Pleiades (*La Pléiade*) attempted a union of music with poetry and an improvement of the French language as a literary medium, but were more favorable to antiquity and Italy than to new ideas. The French châteaux of the Loire region have a charm of their own, combining the picturesqueness of the feudal castle's towers and battlements with the refinement and regularity of the Renaissance palace, and are filled with attractive lesser works of art. One reason why cheap apartments still persist in having mock chimneyplaces with absurd mantels and mirrors above them is because the superb chimneyplaces and mantlepieces in the palaces of this period set a lasting fashion. The *Essays* of Montaigne (1533–1592), who was of a rich merchant family, reflected the culture attainable by the *bourgeoisie*. Unperturbed by the nine Wars of Religion which convulsed France from 1562 to 1598, they display knowledge of the world, moderate scepticism, common sense as well as broad erudition. They may be compared with Bacon's *Essays*. In the eighteenth century Bolingbroke speaks of "Montaigne whom I often quote, as I do Seneca, rather for the smartness of expression than the weight or newness of matter."

Richelieu
and Mazarin

The French wars of religion were not merely a struggle between Protestants and Catholics, but a last stand of feudal

446

states, local nobility, and towns against the central monarchy. By the Edict of Nantes in 1598 the Huguenots were granted religious toleration by Henry IV who had been their leader but who found it necessary to turn Catholic himself in order to remain king.   Cardinal Richelieu, chief minister for Louis XIII from 1624 to 1642, crushed the political power of the Huguenots and nobility, raised France to the leading position in the affairs of Europe by his foreign policy, and made the king the center of national activity and culture.   Richelieu protected the wealthy Protestant philanthropist, Renaudot, who founded benevolent pawnshops in imitation of those he had seen in Italy under the popes from which the poor might borrow at a low rate of interest, also an employment bureau to find work for the needy, and a clinic and hospital for poor patients.   He was furthermore the founder of the *Gazette de France*, while his *Bureau d'adresse*, containing the proceedings of literary and scientific conferences, was the forerunner of the *Journal des Savants*, the first literary periodical in modern Europe.   Richelieu's successor, another cardinal, the wily Italian, Mazarin, succeeded in maintaining what had been won during the difficult period of the minority of Louis XIV (1643–1661).   Mazarin also introduced Italian opera, founded an Academy of Painting and Sculpture, and had a fine library and librarian, Gabriel Naudé.

Building upon their foundation, Louis XIV, who reigned for over half a century (1661–1715) in his own name, made France replace decadent Spain as the leading nation of Europe, of which both politically and socially he became the dominant figure, so that the period is commonly spoken of as the Age of Louis XIV.   Politest of Frenchmen and gracious in manners to the humblest individual, Louis looked every inch a king.   He added to his inches by a tall wig and high-heeled shoes.   Of more importance was the fact that he believed in the kingship and in himself, holding a doctrine of divine right of kings which James I of England and others had already set forth.   Louis took his royal duties very seriously, working hard and conscientiously at "the trade of king."   Inasmuch as His Majesty condescended to employ such language, purists may pardon us for adding that he was always on the job, spending all his waking hours either at public business or in the public eye.   As he rose and dressed himself in the morning, first putting on his wig

Le Grand Monarque

and then his breeches with stockings attached, there were successively admitted the *Grand Entrée*, the First *Entrée*, the *Chambre*, the people of the *Antichambre*, and the general court. But everyone has read how one great noble was privileged to hand the king his shirt, another to offer him his cup of chocolate; after all, this was but a survival of the household officials and court attendance of feudalism.   When the *Lever* was over, the king announced his program for the coming day, so that everyone might know where to find him to a quarter of an hour. Usually he was busied with affairs of state in Council all the morning, dined at one o'clock, after which he went hunting or walking, then was further engaged with his Council.   Three evenings a week from seven to ten o'clock were given to the theater; the other three weekdays to court assemblies with cards and dancing.   At ten the king supped, he then retired for the night amid a *Coucher* ceremony analogous to the *Lever*.

His Court
and Its
Influence:
Versailles

Louis regarded this court life as of prime importance and "considered it the duty of every gentleman to come and pay court to him."   He seldom forgot a face; if someone was suggested as fitted for a position, or deserving of favor, who had not been at court, he would object, "But I do not know him; I have not seen him."   Office-holding carried with it great social prestige.   By such pressure and inducement the nobles of the provinces were brought to Paris and became courtiers, living expensively with large retinues of servants.   The king usually ate dinner alone at a small table while the courtiers looked on in silence.   If he spoke a few words to someone, or merely singled him out for recognition, that person's stock at once went up with a bound.   In 1682 Louis changed his residence from the Tuileries and Louvre in Paris to the new palace of Versailles outside the city, with accommodations for ten thousand persons, an elaborately decorated interior, and a surrounding park and gardens.   Exactly in the center of the vast structure was the royal bedchamber.   If such details seem somewhat trivial to us compared to the great currents of civilization, we must remember that they did not seem trivial to contemporaries.   Louis' magnificent court seemed to concentrate all the culture of France.   It captured the imagination of the time, and was imitated by all the other courts of Europe great and small until the French Revolution.   When the French court went under in that revolution, Edmund Burke felt that the age of gallantry and courtesy was dead, and that "the un-bought grace of life" was no more. Long after that revolution Taine could still compare the court life of the *ancien régime* to a rare perfume, distilled, it was true, at the cost of many flowers.

We must not idealize the court of Louis XIV too much and must remember that its grandeur and refinement were relative to its own age, that ordinary people today enjoy luxuries and comforts which were then denied to kings, and that even standards of politeness and etiquette have since much altered. Louis, for example, who was a large eater, used no fork and forbade his court to use forks. When Charles II of England and his wife supped with the French king and queen, both monarchs sat at the table with their hats on; but Charles, who had been educated in manners by a French mother, politely tipped his hat whenever Maria Theresa spoke to him. "By the end of the meal," said an eye-witness, "his hat was most terribly greasy." There was reason in Louis' keeping his hat on, since once when he laid it down for a moment at a court assembly, someone stole the diamonds off it. Charles II, for his part, was not above attending cock-fights; and he, his queen, and his mistresses played cards together daily.

Would not be so Admired Today

Not only was the court of Louis XIV more showy than any other in Europe, for the Grand Monarch knew how to advertise; his government was the most efficient. He was still, it is true, somewhat of a slave to the old superstition that it was a king's business to wage wars and extend his territories, although he actually accomplished more in that direction by skilful diplomacy than by military force. However, his foreign policy was aggressive; he aimed to annex the Spanish Netherlands, push the French frontier east to the Rhine, and establish Bourbon dynasties in Spain and Italy. In his early reign he had the best organized standing army in Europe, the ablest ministry of war, the best generals, the most skilful military engineers. Vauban invented the socket which made it possible for the soldier to shoot without removing the bayonet from his gun. Louvois' organization of the French standing army was so closely followed by other states that military terms in other European languages such as German, English, and Spanish are of French origin. Only as his ablest helpers died off, as Louis himself grew old, and as the other powers of Europe realized

Efficiency of Louis' Government

that they must all unite against him, were his aggressions checked. Even so, he acquired the County of Burgundy, Alsace-Lorraine, and for his grandson, the throne of Spain. His wars imposed a heavy financial burden on the country, and resulted in much misery for the people, while his devastation of the Palatinate of the Rhine and repeated battles in the Low Countries set back civilization° in those regions. "You are praised to the skies for having impoverished France," wrote Fénelon, "and you have built your throne on the ruin of all classes in the state."

Economic Policy of Colbert

More favorable to civilization than the military and diplomatic activity was the internal policy of Colbert, the energetic minister of finance during the first half of Louis' reign. He further superintended the royal household, public works, agriculture, commerce, and fine arts. After 1669 he took over the ministry of the marine. He introduced the budget system and other financial reforms which nearly trebled the public income. Some outlying regions of the realm, like Brittany, Gascony, and the Vivarais, revolted against the taxation but were suppressed by troops. Colbert further instituted the most extensive codification of law between Justinian and Napoleon. He tried to galvanize agricultural France into an industrial, commercial, and colonial nation by learning the industrial secrets of foreign lands, by regulating the local gilds by edicts, by persuading the church to reduce the number of religious holidays, by building harbors, canals, and roads; by organizing trading companies, by imposing a protective tariff against foreign imports and abolishing the internal customs between the twelve central provinces of France, and by purchasing, occupying, or capturing colonies. But these very efforts somewhat tended to embroil France with other commercial and colonial powers, such as England and the Netherlands, while on the industrial side Colbert's efforts were negatived by Louis' policy of religious persecution which drove Huguenot industries out of France to England and other Protestant countries. We suspect that some of the workers went because they did not find Colbert's paternal edicts any more palatable than the final revocation in 1685 of the Edict of Nantes.

Public Improvements

The Canal of Languedoc opened in 1681 between the Mediterranean and Bay of Biscay has been of use ever since. It was 162 miles in length with 75 locks to carry it over a watershed 830 feet high. As Versailles was a model for all other courts, so Paris set a bright and shining example for other cities. Some of the crowded medieval quarters were swept away. The streets were cleaned, widened, and paved. They were lighted from the first of November to the first of March by lanterns at either end and in the middle of the block. There were public conveyances, also public police and fire departments. The police not merely kept local order but served the absolute monarchy as spies. Indeed, the improvements at the capital were accompanied by a loss of autonomy in other municipalities. Control of their finances was transferred to the royal Intendants or representatives in the provinces; the offices of mayor and aldermen were made life-long or hereditary and sold to the profit of the central government to the highest bidder. But it is interesting to note that Dijon, the capital of Burgundy, after a vain attempt to purchase exemption from Louis' edict of 1697 extending the street lighting provisions for Paris to the provinces, became so satisfied with the installation of six hundred lanterns that it added others in the faubourgs. Glass shop fronts made their appearance in Paris about 1700, and sidewalks were introduced from England only in 1782.

Louis XIV wished to be a patron of arts and letters, and in 1662 ordered a list to be drawn up of authors and scientists in all countries, whom he intended to pension regardless of whether they were Frenchmen or not. This generous impulse was, however, never fully executed, but it was far from being Louis' only act of the sort. He gave Robert Talbor, who had been physician to the king of England, a large sum for the secret of the remedy (quinine) by which he had cured the Dauphin of fever, and then ordered its publication. Colbert, for his part, did more for the arts and sciences than any statesman since, and founded various academies. He cannot much be blamed for disagreeing with Bernini, master of the Baroque style, whose services the pope lent to Louis to complete the Louvre. Bernini, intent only on a grand external design, refused to give ear to Colbert's insistence on proper sanitary arrangements and plumbing, and in consequence was soon politely dismissed. But training, organization, and academic rules alone will not produce great artists. Furthermore, under Louis XIV art centered too much about the king and lost contact with nature and the life of the people. Louis Quatorze in a wig and

Louis as a Patron of the Arts

Roman toga on horseback as a conquering *imperator* was too artificial, not to say incongruous, a theme, but it was often encountered in the paintings at Versailles. Two of the leading French painters of the seventeenth century, Poussin and Claude Lorrain, preferred to spend most of their lives in Italy. Lebrun (1619–1690), as director of the Gobelins tapestry establishment, was in charge of the artistic enterprises at Louis' court. The similar dictator in music was Lully (1632–1687), a great violinist and leader of orchestras, into which he introduced brasses. He also developed a French opera distinct from the Italian and more in conformity with the French language. He further developed the overture and recitative, and greatly improved upon previous scenic effects.

French Literature of the Seventeenth Century

French literature of the seventeenth century is marked by good taste, clarity of style, and a definition of the language and grammar. The French Academy, founded in 1634, completed its Dictionary in 1694. Some words and idioms were lost because they did not suit the fastidious standards of good society. It was the age of salons presided over by cultivated ladies, and much of the literature, as well as conversation, of the age glorified the fair sex and was of an heroic or amorous character. We have already spoken of the first issue of the *Journal des Savants* in 1665. Of the three great French dramatists of this century, Corneille (1606–1684) and Racine (1639–1699) were primarily tragic poets. The former depicted sublimely heroic personages who are, if anything, a little too resolute and declamatory; the latter sometimes permitted the passion of love to override noble resolve. Molière (1622–1673), himself an actor, presented comedies which, while often extravagant or farcical, satirized contemporary morals and are true to human nature. All these were masters of felicitous expression. Other leading works of the reign were the *Maxims* of La Rochefoucauld, the *Letters* of Madame de Sevigné and of Fénelon, the *Art of Poetry* of Boileau, the critic, the *Fables* of La Fontaine, the *Characters* of La Bruyère, the religious and historical writings of Bossuet. This pure and well expressed literature also captivated the other courts and salons of Europe, and French became, to some extent, the language of diplomacy and of polite society abroad. In the eighteenth century French influence was strong in English, Italian, Spanish, and German literature. At the same time it should be remembered that the attitude of this French literature was narrowly classical. Racine could call the cathedral at Chartres "barbarous"; Molière said that Gothic art "waged mortal war with polite society," and described medieval sculptures as "those odious monsters of ignorant centuries."

Many of the states of Europe may be passed over as simply aping the French court and culture, but something should be said of contemporary developments in England and Russia. In England, after the Civil War, the execution of Charles I in 1649, the Commonwealth, and the Protectorate of Oliver Cromwell, the restoration of the monarchy in the person of the clever and pleasure-loving Charles II (1660–1685) left the relations between king and parliament still unsettled, restored the Established Episcopalian church, and marked a reaction from the austere morality of the Puritan period. The Revolution of 1688 drove James II from the throne, prevented the growth of an absolute monarchy like that of Louis XIV, and maintained the Established church. The two party system of government began with the Whigs and Tories. The country gentry or squires still formed the ruling class and were inclined to be Tories. A smaller number of London merchants and capitalists were threatening their supremacy and supported the Whigs. The cabinet system of government was developing, under which the ministers of the crown became an executive committee of parliament, whose majority opinion they must follow, or hold a new election in the hope of recovering their former majority, or resign. This is known as ministerial responsibility. The cabinet holds secret meetings of its own, but its members also regularly attend the public sessions of parliament to direct the course of legislation and to answer criticism.

London was the only large city, and the center of literary and social as well as political and financial life, of all which we may read in the contemporary diaries of Pepys and Evelyn. Prince Rupert, the dashing cavalry leader of the Royalists in the civil wars, will serve to illustrate some of the best sides of the court. As late as 1667 he was considered one of the best tennis players in England and "very sparkish in his dress." He was a member of the king's Privy Council and of the new council for trade and plantations. His expedition to Hudson's Bay to search for a northwest passage to the Indies resulted in the discovery of Rupert's Land and the foundation of the Hudson's Bay

Age of the Restoration in England

Company. The last coinage of silver pennies for general circulation was in 1661–1662; copper half-pence were introduced under Charles II, but copper pence not until 1797. Rupert had a scheme for coining farthings, performed scientific experiments, invented a gun, a certain kind of powder and shot, also Prince's Metal, an alloy, and Rupert's Drops, a sort of glass bulb.

Dryden and Wren

In literature Puritan and Non-Conformist writers turned their thoughts to the other world. Milton, who had become totally blind, wrote *Paradise Lost*. Bunyan, in jail until freed by the king's Declaration of Indulgence and licensed to preach by the Crown, wrote the first part of *Pilgrim's Progress* in prison. Presbyterianism was ridiculed in Butler's *Hudibras*, published 1663–1678.

> For his religion, it was fit
> To match his learning and his wit:
> 'Twas Presbyterian true blue,
> For he was of that stubborn crew
> Of errant saints, whom all men grant
> To be the true church militant;
> Such as do build their faith upon
> The holy text of pike and gun;
> Decide all controversies by
> Infallible artillery;
> And prove their doctrine orthodox
> By apostolic blows and knocks;
> Call fire, sword, and desolation
> A godly thorough reformation. . . .

Dryden, poet laureate from 1670 to 1688, changing his politics and religion to suit the times and king, was "the mouthpiece of the new period," and a great English exponent of classicism. He was a master both of prose style and of the heroic couplet, and also represents the decadent drama of the Restoration, when the theaters were reopened. Christopher Wren (1632–1723) was the leading name in art and left a vast amount of building as a result of his precocious genius and long career. Before he was sixteen he had "enriched astronomy, gnomics, statistics, and mechanics by brilliant inventions"; at twenty-two he was spoken of by Evelyn as "that prodigious young scholar"; at twenty-five he was professor of astronomy. His chief work is St. Paul's cathedral in London, which in some ways is better, in some worse, than St. Peter's at Rome. He also rebuilt over fifty London churches, after the great fire of 1666, with attractive steeples and with interiors adapted to the requirements of Protestant congregations. He constructed various college buildings and the Sheldonian theater at Oxford. A recent investigator of the great fire, however, believes that the new London which rose after it owed more to Charles II than to Wren. Wren had no feeling for Gothic architecture, and "ruthlessly pulled down charming old buildings," or spoiled them by unseemly restoration.

Peter the Great, czar of Russia from 1689 to 1725, raised that country to the position of a great European power and introduced western civilization. He was more particularly interested in those phases which would promote the material prosperity of Russia, such as shipbuilding, which he learned personally in western dockyards, canals, extraction of coal, iron, and naphtha from the earth, and the translation of technical and medical treatises from foreign languages into Russian. He visited Germany and Austria, England and the Netherlands, and remodelled the laws of Russia after the Swedish code. He was not directly influenced by France; and his rough ways, carelessness of his personal dignity, and frequent violence and cruelty bore little resemblance to the stately court of Versailles. However, Peter abolished beards, introduced western dress, gave women greater social freedom, forbade cruelty to serfs, simplified the alphabet, appointed sanitary inspectors in Moscow, founded St. Petersburg, now called Leningrad, and took the advice of Leibnitz in political science. Some think that these sudden changes, to a large extent put through by force and ill-understood by the people, did violence to the natural bent of Russian civilization and gave a regrettable turn to its subsequent development, which aped western ways without working out a satisfactory national culture.

Russia under Peter the Great

BIBLIOGRAPHY

Baird, H. M. *The Huguenots and the Revocation of the Edict of Nantes,* 1895.

Bastide, Ch. *Anglais et Français au XVIIe siècle,* 1912; deals in delightful style with cross-Channel travel then and with Frenchmen in England.

Battifol, Louis. *The Century of the Renaissance in France,* English translation by Elsie F. Buckley, 1916.

Bell, W. G. *The Great Fire of London,* 1920; brings out many new points concerning it. A work of pioneer research. *The Great Plague in London in 1665,* 1924; the first full and careful history of it.

Birch, Geo. *London Churches of the Seventeenth and Eighteenth Centuries,* 1896.

Blomfield, Reginald. *History of French Architecture from the reign of Charles VIII to the death of Mazarin,* 1911, 2 vols. 178 plates; *Renaissance Architecture in England, 1500–1800,* 1897, 2 vols.

Boulenger, J. R. *The Seventeenth Century,* 1920; an excellent survey of French life and literature.

Cook, T. A. *Old Touraine,* 1903, 2 vols.; a book for the traveler interested in history.

Dawson, J. C. *Toulouse in the Renaissance,* 1924.

Hind, A. M. *Wenceslaus Hollar and His Views of London in the Seventeenth Century,* 1922, 96 plates.

Macaulay, T. B. *History of England,* vol. I, chaps. 2, 3, 4; fascinating chapters on social conditions and culture from the most read of all histories of England.

Naudé, Gabriel. *Instructions concerning the erection of a library interpreted by John Evelyn,* 1661; reprinted 1903 by Houghton Mifflin Company. A quaint and interesting glimpse of libraries and books in the seventeenth century, written by the scholar who successively served Richelieu, Mazarin, and Christina of Sweden as librarian, and translated by the celebrated English diarist.

Nolhac, P. de. *Ronsard et l'humanisme,* 1921; by the leading French authority on humanism.

Normand, C. *La bourgeoisie française au XVIIᵉ siècle,* 1907.

Tilley, A. A. *Dawn of the French Renaissance,* 1918; *Literature of the French Renaissance,* 1904, 2 vols.; *Studies in the French Renaissance,* 1922; by the foremost writer in English on the Renaissance in France.

Trollope, H. M. *The Life of Molière,* 1905.

Viollet, Paul. *Histoire des institutions politiques et administratives de la France. Le roi et ses ministres pendant les trois derniers siècles de la monarchie,* 1912.

Voltaire, *Le Siècle de Louis Quatorze;* an eighteenth century contribution to the history of civilization by the famous wit, sceptic, and man of letters.

Ward, W. H. *The Architecture of the Renaissance in France,* 1911, 2 vols., 465 illus.

CHAPTER XXXVII

THE AGE OF REASON

> If it is true that this eighteenth century of ours may boast
> of some considerable advantages over all previous centuries,
> it is also true that we owe them exclusively to the freedom of
> thought and expression, to the propagation of a scientific and
> philosophic spirit, and to the popularization of those truths
> on which the welfare of society depends.—*L'Encyclopédie*.

THE eighteenth century has often been called the Age of Rea- The Spirit of the Eighteenth Century
son. The free-thinker, Thomas Paine, used the phrase as the
title of a book, published in 1794, which has been described as
"the first important English publication in which the Christian
scheme of salvation and the Bible are assailed in plain language
without any disguise or reserve," and as "written in such a way
as to reach the masses." Reason then was here put in opposition to revealed religion and the Christian church, and was of
a sort which the ordinary man could follow,—"Common Sense,"
as Paine entitled an earlier work of his in 1776 supporting the
independence of the American colonies. But the eighteenth
century was more than an age of free-thinking and common
sense. It also had confidence in reason as opposed to emotion.
The clarity, wit, and good taste of French literature of the previous century, combined with the empirical and practical philosophy of Locke and the mathematically simplified science of
Newton, had much influence on the spirit of the eighteenth century. This age of reason yet had its prejudices; in many
ways it seems an artificial, conventionalized period, especially in
dress and manners; it still cherished an excessive predilection
for classical antiquity and could see no good in the intervening
period. Voltaire said that Dante's reputation kept increasing
because he was never read; Oliver Goldsmith ascribed it to his
obscurity and the barbarous times in which he lived; Horace
Walpole, too, disliked Dante; and Goethe regarded the *Inferno*
as abominable, the *Purgatorio* as of dubious merit, and the
Paradiso as tiresome. Voltaire called Shakespeare "a drunken

savage without the least spark of good taste." To the glories of Gothic art he referred as "what unhappily remains of the architecture of those times." Even the sentimental Rousseau condemned the cathedrals as "a disgrace to those who had the patience to build them." Even the radical Shelley in the early nineteenth century could see no beauty in the mosaics of the mausoleum of Galla Placidia at Ravenna. In short, the age of reason was in many ways sadly deficient in æsthetic sense and artistic appreciation as well as in religious feeling and conviction. It has further been noted concerning the French writers of this century that their very vocabulary was limited and abstract, and that they seemed blind to "the diversities of life."

But there were at least two further merits of the age of reason. It sought information, and the progress of science went on apace during the eighteenth century. And it turned its attention to the subject of political and social reform with an earnestness that before the close of the century brought about the French Revolution. Narrow as its outlook was in some respects, the Age of Reason was concerned with humanity from the time that Pope, penning his *Essay on Man* at the suggestion of Bolingbroke, exhorted:

> Know then thyself; presume not God to scan;
> The proper study of mankind is Man!

to the "Declaration of the Rights of Man and of the Citizen" by the French National Assembly in 1789.

The French Philosophers: Voltaire

The French writers of the age of reason were known as the Philosophers, a term then employed about as Intellectuals is now. They were not pure philosophers or metaphysicians, and while some were specialists in natural science and others wrote treatises concerned with the social sciences, their number also included men like Voltaire, who was primarily a man of letters and satirist, and whose somewhat frothy publications appealed to a wide circle of readers. Parini called Voltaire "the master of those who make pretense to knowledge." Indeed, his influence was in part due to the mere volume of his literary work, for he wrote assiduously during a long lifetime (1694–1778), and in part due to its variety. He composed dramas, epics, and other poems. As historiographer of France he wrote a general history which is much less a history of civilization than its title might lead one to believe, *Essai sur les mœurs et l'esprit des nations,* and other histories of Charles XII of Sweden, Russia under Peter the Great, and the Age of Louis XIV. He also produced many works of criticism, popular science and philosophy, satire, as well as numerous pamphlets. The church, that "infamous thing," was the especial butt of his wit, and he found it advisable to reside on the outskirts of France where he might beat a quick retreat across the frontier. But he was tendered a great ovation when he visited Paris, his birth-place, once again in the last year of his life. We are told that the long hard journey from his retreat near Geneva proved too much for him, but he himself gave a different explanation. "I am dying," he said at the age of eighty-four during his last illness, "of two hundred and fifty thousand cups of coffee." The Café Procope, where he would stay, "talking and sipping coffee from morning until midnight," enjoyed an even longer life of over two centuries (1689–1891). Paris, however, was not yet the sole center of artistic appreciation and intellectual life in France; these were still alive in many of the provincial cities.

Both Voltaire and Montesquieu (1689–1755) resided in England for two or three years, and were much impressed by its political and intellectual freedom, its philosophy and science. In fact, they both presumed to criticize the customs of their own country, Montesquieu in *Persian Letters,* 1721, and Voltaire in *Letters upon the English,* 1733–1734, a book which the patriotic French judges ordered to be publicly burned. The French Academy, however, elected Montesquieu and Voltaire to its membership. Montesquieu's chief work, *L'Esprit des lois,* 1748, was a landmark in political science, discussing the natural grounds of constitutions, especially the influence of climate, urging the separation of the three powers, executive, legislative, and judicial, praising the government of England, and exposing the survival of feudal conditions in France. Of French writers on economics at this time the Marquis de Gournay promulgated the doctrine of *Laisser faire et laisser passer,* arguing against governmental regulation of economic activity and in favor of competition. His disciple, Turgot, a government official and finally chief minister under Louis XVI, in 1769–1770 published *Reflections on the Formation and Distribution of Wealth.* It was soon followed by the epoch- *Montesquieu and the Economists* making English work by Adam Smith, *The Wealth of Nations*, 1776, with which political economy may almost be said first to have become a distinct science, and which one historian of civilization, Buckle, has gone so far as to pronounce the most influential book ever written. Just as the great economic revolution of modern times was beginning, it exalted economic above political activity. The first professorship of political economy in Europe was established at Naples and held by Genovesi, who lived from 1712 to 1769.

Encyclopedias and Dictionaries

Diderot was almost as versatile a writer as Voltaire, but one work with which he was associated stands out above all others, namely, *L'Encyclopédie*, which, at first in cooperation with the astronomer, D'Alembert, he edited in seventeen great folio volumes from 1751 to 1765. The work especially emphasized natural science and industrial processes. Like Voltaire's more amateurish *Philosophical Dictionary*, it had great influence in increasing the interest in these fields and in dispelling old superstitions and errors. The ecclesiastical authorities twice had its publication suspended. While it was in process Johnson completed his famous English dictionary in 1755. The way for these two great successes had been prepared by earlier works of the same sort: Diderot's encyclopedia began as a revised translation of Chamber's *Cyclopedia* (1728), while Johnson's dictionary was based on that of Nathan Bailey (1721). It in turn was founded on the seventeenth century works of Blount, Coles, and others, while in France the *Dictionnaire historique et critique* (1696) of the sceptical philosopher Bayle had displayed something of the same spirit as Diderot's encyclopedia, which, however, laid a novel stress upon machinery. The numerous editions and revisions of these works demonstrate that the custom of looking things up in the encyclopedia or dictionary was now becoming well established among persons who did not read Latin, and that the Bible was losing its monopoly as a popular book of reference.

The Historical Attitude

It has been said that "the eighteenth century had more 'enlightenment' but hardly more 'historical sense' than the middle ages. It had certainly less learning and real criticism than the great seventeenth century scholars." We must not, however, forget the Italian, Vico (1668–1744), almost the first to reject Roman history before the Punic Wars as unreliable, to picture the Homeric age both critically and constructively, to study laws as the product and in the light of the state of society when they developed, and works of art or literature as the product of the artist's mind and surroundings. These attitudes were adopted later by Montesquieu and Wolf in the eighteenth, by Niebuhr and Taine in the nineteenth century. Winckelmann (1717–1768), who has been called the father of scientific archæology, showed in more detail how Greek art was a reflection of Greek life and environment. Herder (1744–1803), viewed history and literature as expressions of national life, recognizing with other German writers of the closing nineteenth century that ancient Greek literature was naïve, primitive, and close to nature, although continuing to idealize the Greek character excessively. In Italy, Muratori's *Scriptores* (1723–1751) and *Antiquitates* (1738–1742) were the first great attempt to collect all the medieval sources for one country. France soon followed suit in the *Histoire littéraire de la France* by the Congregation of St. Maur, begun in 1733, and Bouquet's collection of historians of Gaul and France, begun in 1738. The German *Monumenta* and British *Rolls Series* came only in the nineteenth century. But Bolingbroke wrote excellent *Letters on the Study and Use of History* in the first half of the eighteenth century, while in the second half Tom Paine even attacked the historical truth of the Gospel narrative.

Jean Jacques Rousseau (1712–1778) shows us that the century was not exclusively an age of reason. With passionate rhetoric he contended that the progress of science and literature had tended to corrupt morals, that men should revert to a simpler life and state of nature, that they were born free and equal but were now everywhere in chains. In a single year, 1762, he published two works which were to have a vast influence: *The Social Contract*, in which he advocated popular sovereignty and majority rule and which became the gospel of the leaders of the French Revolution; and *Emile*, in which he enlarged upon another of Locke's ideas, that of developing the nature of the child, and which has had much influence on modern pedagogy. As for Rousseau himself, far from putting this theory into practice with any of his own children, he turned all five over to the Foundling Asylum. But his intellectual offspring, sentimental democracy and sentimental education, are with us yet. Even his sentimental strain was not entirely a new departure, since already the writers of the closing years of

Rousseau

Louis XIV "by their tearful prose, their novel tenderness and pity . . . heralded the triumph of 'sensibility' and of Jean Jacques Rousseau." In the eighteenth century we have examples of the sentimental novel in various countries of Europe: Richardson's *Clarissa* (1748), Rousseau's *New Eloïse* (1761), Goethe's *The Sorrows of Young Werther* (1774), Karamsin's *Poor Lizzie*. The German poet, Klopstock (1724–1803), displayed the same tendency combined with dreamy religious idealism and pietism. The Italian Beccaria's *On Crimes and Punishments*, although "more sentimental than scientific," led to positive, practical penal reform.

German and Italian Literature

In literature Fielding, Diderot, and Lessing brought novel and drama down to the level of common, contemporary life. Lessing (1729–1781) founded an independent German drama, as a critic attacked French pseudo-classicism, urged further religious evolution through the spirit of free inquiry, and in his lost *Faust* expressed the eighteenth century ideal of enlightenment. Schiller (1759–1805) extolled the ideals of art, beauty, and self-sacrifice as essential to the progress of civilization. In Italy, Parini (1729–1799) was notable for sturdy independence of patronage, sympathy with the lowly and oppressed, and satire against the idle nobility and decadent society of his time. Alfieri (1749–1803) was the first Italian poet to write successful tragedies, directed against tyranny in terse style but with fiery ardor. Both these writers were disappointed by the French Revolution, but their works were to influence political revolution and social reform in the nineteenth century.

Discovery of New Elements

All through the middle ages the old Greek hypothesis of four elements, earth, air, fire, and water, had been repeatedly qualified and modified, yet it persisted to some extent among scientists until the eighteenth, and in popular speech and thought into the nineteenth century. From about the thirteenth century the alchemists began to speak rather in terms of sulphur, mercury, and salts. Paracelsus continued this practice. In the seventeenth century Becher and Stahl replaced the conception of an element, fire, by that of a principle of fire or combustible substance, called phlogiston, which was supposed to be expelled by heat. In the course of the eighteenth century new elements were discovered, and several "gases" were scientifically distinguished from air. In 1754 Joseph Black of Edinburgh, by treating limestone with acid, collected a gas heavier than air which would not support combustion or life.   This he called "fixed air"; it is now known as carbonic acid.   In 1766 Cavendish reported to the Royal Society his discovery of "inflammable air," or hydrogen, obtained by treating metals with sulphuric acid.   A Swede named Scheele in 1773, and Priestley, a versatile Unitarian clergyman of England, in 1774 discovered a gas which Priestley called "dephlogisticated air," but to which the French chemist Lavoisier in 1777 gave the name oxygen.   Later Cavendish showed that air was a compound of oxygen and nitrogen, and that water was composed of oxygen and hydrogen.   Scheele (1742–1786) further discovered the element chlorine, was the first to prepare glycerine, and laid the foundation for photography by first combining chemical and spectrum analysis.   Lavoisier carried further and systematized the experiments and results of Black, Priestley, and Cavendish.   Quantitative analysis may be said to date from this time.   Black made important experiments in physics as well as in chemistry, discovering both latent heat and specific heat.   The phlogiston theory, however, did not die out until the next century.   Priestley believed in it until his death in 1804.   The true nature of heat was not clearly comprehended until the middle of the nineteenth century.   Even Lavoisier regarded caloric as a simple substance, although many had already suggested that heat was only a property produced mechanically.   Count Rumford demonstrated this experimentally in 1798.

That disease was caused by germs or micro-organisms had been the view of Athanasius Kircher back in 1646 and 1658, and was a familiar contention in France early in the eighteenth century.   Spallanzani in 1767 reported successful experiments in hermetically sealing bottles so that living organisms did not afterwards develop in their contents, thus showing the way to modern canning processes for meat, fruit, vegetables, or "pasteurized" milk.   In 1786 the Dane, Müller, published a work on the classification of *infusoria*.   Linnæus systematized botany.   Haller, distinquished alike in botany and anatomy, medicine and surgery, made especial progress in physiology by vivisection of animals.   In 1761 Morgagni, at the age of nearly eighty, summed up the many dissections he had performed and *post-mortem* autopsies he had attended, in a work on morbid anatomy which entitles him to be called the Father of Pa-

Bacteriology, Physiology, Pathology, Histology

thology. It may be noted that he still wrote in Latin. Bichat (1771–1802), in his brief but tireless career, advanced anatomy and pathology to the study of the tissues composing the organs of the body, thus founding the science of histology.

Astronomical and Geographical Discovery

There was further progress in astronomical discovery; for instance, Bradley discovered the aberration of light and the nutation of the earth's axis; Herschel discovered the planet Uranus. Cook's voyages, which began in connection with an astronomical expedition to observe the transit of Venus in 1768, improved knowledge concerning Australia and New Zealand, various Pacific islands and the customs of their inhabitants—such as the Tahitians,—and of the regions about Behring Straits and the Antarctic Circle. Turgot induced the French government to grant immunity from all hostilities to Cook's ship on the ground that he was "a benefactor of every nation." The growth of the nebular hypothesis may be traced through the writings of Descartes, Leibnitz, and Kant (1755) to Laplace (1796). The nebular hypothesis was generally accepted by scientists during the nineteenth century, but now we are informed that "without radical reconstruction" it "can no longer serve as a reasonable theory of earth origin."

Foundation of Geology

Geology was a science unknown to the ancients. Despite some medieval discussion of the formation of mountains and the writings of Palissy in the sixteenth century, such an idea as that valleys are made by rivers rather than that rivers follow pre-existing valleys was hotly disputed even in the early nineteenth century. Darwin himself ascribed to the action of the sea valleys in Australia which have since been shown to have been produced by river action. Fossils, on the other hand, had long been noted and discussed, and were described and classified with some fulness in the early eighteenth century. In 1759 Arduino divided the rocks of northern Italy into Primitive, Secondary, Tertiary, and Volcanic. Werner, an able teacher of mineralogy at Freiberg, in 1786 classified rocks by their mineral composition. James Hutton's *Theory of the Earth, or an Investigation of the Laws observable in the Composition, Dissolution and Restoration of Land upon the Globe*, published in 1785 (more fully in 1795), held that past changes in the earth's crust could be explained by those which could still be seen in process, and that the changes of almost countless centuries were evidenced in present geological formation. The earth, in short, was not a comparatively recent creation, as was then commonly inferred by Christians from the Biblical account, but the outcome of a long and gradual evolution. Indeed, this view had already been set forth by a Frenchman, Benoît de Maillet, in a work printed in 1735, though not published until 1758. He had applied it not only to the geological structure of the earth but to species of living things, which he held had been produced by modification of preceding species. Thus was forecast Darwin's doctrine of the origin of species.

The early eighteenth century was a time of coldness and formality in religion—in England sermons were not much more than moral lectures such as Seneca or Epictetus might have delivered—and of scepticism on the part of the upper classes. Deism flourished in England and was taken up by the French philosophers. It rejected or at least criticized Christianity, but affirmed the existence of God and usually the immortality of the soul. The growth of the private pew system, an ecclesiastical equivalent of the private box at opera or theater, shows how class distinctions pervaded the Established church of England in this century. These enclosed spaces, often irregular in shape and scattered about here and there on the floor, "sometimes filled with sofas and tables, or even provided with fireplaces," provoked many allusions in contemporary literature to their cozy and soporific qualities, spoiled the architectural appearance of church interiors, and forced the poor parishioners back into cold, dark corners far from the choir and pulpit, or necessitated the building of galleries. It became evident that a new movement was needed, if to the poor the gospel was to be preached. This at first took the form of the Methodist or Wesleyan movement with outdoor preaching to great crowds by itinerant preachers, who reached workers in mines and others who were far removed by distance or neglect from any regular parish church. John Wesley (1703–1791) alone traveled in fifty years of itinerancy over 250,000 miles by land, mainly on horseback, and preached 40,000 sermons, rising at four o'clock every morning. Emphasis was laid on the importance of personal conversion and religious experience. Anyone who accepted Christ and gave evidence of living according to Christian principles was accepted. Under the name of the evangelical movement the new enthusiam spread

Deism and the Evangelical Movement

within the Established church and to other Non-Conformist bodies than the Wesleyan.

In England, in 1714, the Stuart dynasty had been replaced by George I, a king from the little German principality of Hanover. He could not speak English, so that it became more than ever the custom for the ministers to direct the government. The Tory party, which had hitherto supported the royal power, had split over the question of supporting the Stuart claimant to the throne, so that the Whigs now entered upon a long monopoly of office commonly described as the Whig Oligarchy, because a few great lords were the leaders, because owing to unequal distribution of seats and restricted suffrage only a small minority of the nation voted for members of parliament, and because only a minority of that minority were really Whig at heart. Nevertheless that party managed to control elections or the voting of members, by family influence, patronage, skilful party tactics, or outright corruption. Although Voltaire and Montesquieu had been favorably impressed by the British constitution and liberty, this government by an oligarchy was accompanied by social degradation in many quarters as well as by an easy-going prosperity in others. Gay's *Beggar's Opera* made lyrical even the sordid underworld of vice and crime, and Hogarth's caricatures show the picturesque side of corrupt electioneering, "Gin Lane," and the life of rake and prostitute. "No man," quoth Dr. Johnson, the heavy English counterpart of Voltaire, "will be a sailor who has contrivance enough to get himself into a jail; for being in a ship is being in jail with a chance of being drowned. . . . A man in jail has more room, better food, and commonly better company." Yet the conditions in prisons were horrible and evoked efforts at prison reform by Oglethorpe and Howard. The evangelical movement and the Quakers did something to reach the wretched and to awaken the public conscience, but excessive drinking of gin, whiskey, and port, brutal impressment in the navy and flogging in the army, employment of little children to climb chimneys and clean out the crooked, narrow flues, and general illiteracy of the masses continued well into the nineteenth century. The African slave-trade was not abolished until 1807. Yet the culture of the century was as noteworthy as its science. The composer, Handel, who came to England four years before his master, the Elector of Han-

over, became George I, found the country hardly ready for
opera, though he was very successful with the oratorio.   Wilson painted the first great English landscapes, and the portrait
painting of Reynolds, Romney, and Gainsborough made this
century "the golden age of English art."   Literature was still
dominated by classicism, yet such works as Gray's *Elegy Written in a Country Churchyard,* or Gibbon's *Decline and Fall of
the Roman Empire,* not only show a great mastery of language
but lead on to the romantic revival.   The foundation of the
British Museum in 1753 was an event in the annals of historical
research.   In this century Bishop Berkeley, building on the
philosophy of Locke, denied the existence of matter, holding
that the world is simply the expression of our human, and God's
infinite, mind.   On the other hand, Hume, noted also as a
historian, by his destructive criticism of Locke's empiricism
gave a great impetus to scepticism.

In the first year of the eighteenth century the Elector of   The Rise of
Brandenburg changed his title to King of Prussia, which thence-   Prussia
forth became an increasingly important state.   Friedrich Wil-
helm I (1713–1740) enforced that strict military discipline and
highly efficient administration which have been characteristic of
the country ever since.   Though only about twelfth in area
and population of the states of Europe at that time, Prussia
ranked fourth in the size of its army.   Its strength was not
exclusively military.   Agriculture and industry were pains-
takingly developed, the peasantry were to some extent freed
from servile restrictions and obligations, and compulsory education was established long before it was introduced in English-
speaking countries.   The land and people suffered greatly from
the wars of Frederick the Great (1740–1786), though a further gain was made thereby in military reputation and territory, but his administrative genius revived its prosperity
rapidly.   Frederick planned and supervised the execution of
everything himself, yet he allowed religious freedom, and freedom of speech and of the press.   It is perhaps worth noting
that in 1773 there were 25,000 French soldiers serving in the
Prussian army.   Prussian territory received further great increases by the partitions of Poland in 1772, 1793, and 1795
between herself, Austria, and Russia.

The leading representative of the intellectual life of eight-   Philosophy
eenth century Germany was the philosopher, Immanuel Kant   of Kant

(1724–1804). He agreed that this was the age of enlightenment; the German Illumination, it has often been called.
After lecturing in the university of his native town of Königs-
berg, from which he never stirred more than thirty miles, and
after writing on scientific subjects, he turned more exclusively
to metaphysics, completing in 1781 his most important work,
The Critique of Pure Reason, in which he discussed the powers,
possibilities, and limitations of theoretical intelligence. He reacted against the empiricism of Locke and the effort to account for knowledge simply on the basis of perceptions through
the senses, which Hume had carried to the sceptical conclusion
that human knowledge is only apparent and that the mind of
man is a mere kaleidoscope of shifting perceptions. Kant held
that space and time are intuitive forms of the reason without
which experience is impossible, and that similarly there are
certain concepts and principles of the pure understanding,
such as quantity and quality, cause and effect, without which
sensations cannot be put together and mean anything for us.
Such principles hold true for all human thought and give valid
judgments concerning phenomena as they appear to us, but to
know things as they really are is not given to the pure reason,
though it keeps striving to this end. Kant, however, wrote
another work, called *The Critique of Practical Reason,* in which
he held that conscience commands us unconditionally to will to
do right and to avoid wrong. "So act that in every case the
rule of your action shall be valid as a universal law." The
moral nature of man also requires belief in freedom of the will,
immortality of the soul, and the existence of God. It may not
be possible to prove these truths satisfactorily to others, Kant
grants, but they are necessary to the completeness of man's
ethical and spiritual nature, and hence may be accepted with
confidence. In other words, while knowledge is questioned as
subjective, the claims of personality are allowed; though the
reality of time is doubted, the existence of eternity is affirmed;
and though we can't know things as they are, there is a God.
If scientific materialism gives us truth without God, Kant gives
us God without truth. He also was too inclined to think of
virtue as doing what we don't want to do, and thus to elevate
a mere principle of contradiction into a universal moral law.

German and
Austrian
Music

Whether philosophy be, as Milton insisted, "musical as is
Apollo's lute" or not, the age of reason, although in litera-

ture a period of prose rather than poetry, was marked by some great masters of music. It was especially in the German-speaking world that music and philosophy flourished together and continued into the nineteenth century. Handel came from Prussia to England by way of Hanover. The Saxon, Bach (1685–1750, excelled as a composer of piano music and church music, the latter majestic and mystic, other-worldly and sublime. The prodigy, Mozart (1756–1791), son of a musician and participant in public performances from the age of five, was born and died in Austria. His brief life was all music, and he left over six hundred compositions. Beethoven (1770–1827) was also the son of a musician and began his musical education at four. He came to Vienna to complete it under Haydn the year after Mozart's death there. The first of Beethoven's nine great orchestral symphonies was composed in 1800, so that the greater part of his compositions were published in the nineteenth century. He had genius enough for two centuries, but other great creative musicians were to follow him.

"Since I mounted the throne, I have made philosophy the legislator," boasted Joseph II (1765–1790) of the Holy Roman Empire and Austria, who is regarded as the best example of the "benevolent despots" of the eighteenth century. He had reference to the reforms urged by the French "Philosophers" and economists, rather than to Kant's categorical imperative of the practical reason. Frederick the Great of Prussia had shared the same interest and had invited Voltaire for a time to his court. Various smaller German princes, kings of Naples, Spain, Portugal, and Denmark, and Catherine II (1762–1796) of Russia are put in the same category of benevolent despots. They commonly reformed the administration and judiciary. They restricted the past privileges of towns, clergy, and nobility, except that they usually permitted the nobles for the first time to engage in trade. They were hostile to the monks, Inquisition, and Jesuits. The last-named order was abolished by the pope from 1773 to 1814. Some of the enlightened despots freed the serfs, or swept away the last vestiges of feudalism; Portugal abolished slavery. While some rulers were truly humanitarian, others were simply shrewd enough to see the advantage to their own absolute power and to the economic prosperity of their country of such reforms, some of which,

The Benevolent Despots

however, were too sudden or too sweeping to be wise. The enlightened despots did nothing for popular participation in government; rather they did away with some of the old safeguards of local liberty. They tended, however, to reduce things to the same uniformity and dead level as democracy. They ceased to protect and endow the church as medieval rulers had done, they established protection for native industry, and they fostered business interests. Which will be the next to take its turn, perhaps in our own time, as the favored one and power behind the throne, Labor or Science?

Benjamin Franklin

Benjamin Franklin (1706–1790) well represents the developing civilization in the American colonies in the eighteenth century. He rose from poverty to distinction by his own efforts and merits, was largely self-educated, but also gave himself freely to public affairs. He displayed the qualities of thrift, shrewdness, ingenuity, urbanity, tact, and philosophical breadth of mind. He rapidly became the best known and most influential citizen of Philadelphia, participated in colonial conventions, acted as colonial agent for Pennsylvania in England for some fifteen years, and most worthily and adroitly represented the revolting colonies at the court of France during the revolutionary war. He was printer, journalist, autobiographer, postmaster, himself of an inventive turn of mind and always ready to encourage new ideas in others, one of the drafters of the Declaration of Independence and framers of the Constitution. Science remembers him as one of the first successful experimenters with electricity.

BIBLIOGRAPHY

Abbey and Overton. *The English Church in the Eighteenth Century,* 1878.

Benn, A. W. *History of English Rationalism,* 1906, 2 vols.

Besant, Sir Walter. *London in the Eighteenth Century,* 1903.

Botsford, J. B. *English Society in the Eighteenth Century as influenced from oversea,* 1924.

Bourne, H. E. *The Revolutionary Period in Europe,* 1914.

Cru, R. L. *Diderot as a Disciple of English Thought,* 1913.

Devas, C. S. *The Key to the World's Progress,* 1912.

Dilke, Lady. *French Painters of the Eighteenth Century,* 1899.

Gosse, Edmund. *A History of Eighteenth Century Literature,* 1911.

Graham, H. G. *Social Life in Scotland in the Eighteenth Century,* 1900.

Hettner, H. *Literaturgeschichte des Achtzehnten Jahrhunderts,* 1893–1894, 6 vols., 4th ed.

Higgs, Henry. *The Physiocrats*, 1897.

Lecky, W. E. H. *History of England in the Eighteenth Century*, 1907, 7 vols.

Legg, L. G. W. *Matthew Prior*, 1921.

Moore, E. C. *An Outline of the History of Christian Thought since Kant*, 1915.

Morley, Viscount John. *Diderot and the Encyclopedists*, 1878; *Rousseau*, 1873; *Voltaire*, 1903.

Redgrave, R. and S. *A Century of English Painters*, 1866.

Robertson, C. G. *England under the Hanoverians*, 1911.

Robertson, J. M. *A Short History of Free Thought*, 1915.

Roustan, M. *Les philosophes et la société française au XVIII* siècle*, 1906.

Sée, H. *La France économique et sociale au XVIII* siècle*, 1925.

Stephen, Leslie. *History of English Thought in the Eighteenth Century*, 3rd ed., 1902.

Stryienski, C. *The Eighteenth Century*, English translation by H. W. Dickinson, 1916.

Thorndike, Lynn. "L'Encyclopédie and the History of Science," in *Isis*, vol. VI (1924) pp. 361–86.

Thorpe, T. E. *Joseph Priestley*, 1906.

Ward, H. and Roberts, W. *Romney*, 1904.

Wesley Bicentennial, addresses by C. T. Winchester on "John Wesley the Man," and Woodrow Wilson on "John Wesley in History."

Winchester, C. T. *Life of John Wesley*, 1906.

Hazen, Charles. The Revolution, 1887.

Leadam, I. S. H., History of England in the Eighteenth Century, 1890.

Lecky, J. W., American Revolution, 1922.

..., The Revolution of the History of America Twenty-four Years, 1903.

Martin, Nicholas W. Law, The American Revolution, Number Sixty, Number ... Amherst College, 1888.

Paterson, Edward W., A History of England Fourteen, 1899.

Robertson, J. ..., Short History of Free Thought, 1912.

Humphrey, H. Action ...

..., Sons of Fortune Mythology XXXVII, Chapter ...

Palgrave, William, Twelfth XVIII Chapter, The Eighteenth Century, 1890.

BOOK VIII

THE GENESIS OF OUR PRESENT CIVILIZATION

CHAPTER XXXVIII

THE ECONOMIC REVOLUTION [1]

> If mere rapidity of change be the test of progress, then indeed the last generation—the age of the internal combustion engine, the turbine, the practical dynamo, and the filament lamp, of short-hand and the card index, the telephone and the typewriter, of the aeroplane and wireless telegraphy, of the girl clerk and the Labor Minister—easily eclipses the age of the steam engine. . . .—*Perris*

Chief Features of the Economic Revolution

INCREASED production and consumption by means of labor-saving devices, more scientific utilization of natural resources, and organization of effort on a larger scale commonly known as capitalistic, may be regarded as key-notes of the economic revolution, which began to manifest its Protean transformations in England in the eighteenth century and has continued to revolve rapidly to the present date.

Relative Lack of Change in the Long Previous Period

The life of the people in country and town and the means of communication and transport had not altered essentially from the thirteenth to the eighteenth or even nineteenth century. Streets and houses retained much of their quaint medieval aspect, labor was by hand, Roman ploughs had probably been superior to those used in the American colonies in the

[1] When in this and the following chapter a definite date is given for a new invention or a political change, it is for the sake of brief convenience rather than because the particular year is significant. An invention may have been conceived in one year, perfected in another, patented in a third, and not put into actual operation until still later. A law may have been enacted in one year to go into effect the year following, and have been reissued in improved form at some later date. But such dates help to orient the reader, and it is shorter to write and easier to take in at a glance a definite figure, such as 1805, than a phrase such as, "in the opening decade of the nineteenth century."

eighteenth century, "the Saxon farmer of the eighth century enjoyed most of the comforts known to the Saxon farmers of the eighteenth century." We have seen that the land system in France changed little from the thirteenth well into the nineteenth century, and that the medieval gilds lasted until the middle of that century upon the continent of Europe. Population also appears to have increased little between the thirteenth and eighteenth centuries. But now a great economic revolution, which began in England in the eighteenth century and spread to America and the continent of Europe in the nineteenth century, affected agriculture, industry, almost every side of daily life, and gave its distinctive character to present civilization. The new period has been called the age of machinery, of invention, and of applied science. It did not, however, begin without having been long prepared.

The free labor of the medieval gilds had been more inventive than the slave labor of antiquity, and the mechanical arts in better repute. Such machines as the printing-press, mechanical clock and watch, and stocking-knitting-frame with its 2500 parts, had been invented before 1600. The double-furrow or multiple plough was known in the seventeenth century but had not yet been made practicable. Simon Sturtevant patented the use of coal instead of charcoal in iron-smelting in 1611, and Dud Dudley made both cast and wrought iron in this way in 1619, but the hostility of the charcoal-burners stopped the new process for the time. As early as 1674 the airplane was faintly anticipated by a French locksmith who glided safely from high points with the aid of four collapsible frames which he worked with his hands and feet. By about 1700 there were fountain pens of a sort. There was now private capital available for investment in new undertakings, and, by the middle of the eighteenth century, a general interest in mechanical inventions which Diderot, himself the son of a cutler, both recognized and promoted by the special attention he gave to the subject of machines in the French *Encyclopedia.* Leupold's *Theatrum machinarum* had been published still earlier in 1725, while Jacques Besson had published a *Theater of Instruments and Machines* back in the sixteenth century in both French and Latin editions.

On the large estates of England in the eighteenth century, improved agricultural methods were applied, resulting in an

Yet Preparation for an Age of Mechanical Invention

The Agricultural Revolution

increased food supply for man and beast.　Jethro Tull's *Horse Hoeing Husbandry*, 1733, taught careful selection of seed, planting with drills at proper depths, and the advantage of keeping the soil loose and thoroughly pulverized.　Scientific rotation of crops was introduced from Flanders in place of allowing the land to lie fallow every second or third year. Townshend, abandoning politics for agriculture, increased his rents many times over by alternating clover and turnips with the cereals.　More attention was also given to fertilizers, irrigation, and drainage.　Robert Bakewell (1725–1795), by breeding stock for meat, doubled or trebled the weight of beeves and calves, sheep and lambs.　In the middle of the nineteenth century England was still regarded by French and German authorities as leading the world in scientific agriculture.　Another rather new source of increased food supply in Europe was the potato, which at first was thought fit only for the poor.　Frederick the Great promoted its introduction in Prussia, the Irish tenants with their tiny holdings came to depend upon it almost entirely for food, but in France the people would not touch potatoes until the nineteenth century.

The Enclosure Movement

In England the successful application of the new agricultural methods upon large estates completed the ruin of the open-field system, communal economy, and small landholder. A new enclosure movement began by private act of Parliament with the ultimate net result that the land came into a few hands.　The small holders, tenants, and persons with rights of common and pasture were dispossessed or bought out, and sank to the condition of agricultural laborers, poorly paid, ill housed, and ignorant, or else went off to work in the new factories.　In 1775 was repealed the Act of 1589 which had guaranteed each family a cottage and four acres of its own. An enclosure movement also occurred in Schleswig-Holstein, Denmark, and southern Sweden before the end of the eighteenth century.　In Denmark enlightened despotism regulated the change better than the English aristocracy had done and kept the consolidated lands in the hands of the peasants themselves. Prussia began to study the new methods as the nineteenth century opened, and from the close of the Napoleonic wars the junkers, east of the Elbe, "worked furiously at their estates."

In Germany, however, the peasants themselves have continued to hold between two-thirds and three-quarters of the land.

In France the holdings of the peasants are still scattered in Present Condition of the European Peasantry small strips in those regions where the open-field system existed of old; in 1908 there were over two million holdings of less than two and a half acres, while the forests still belong in large measure either to the local communes or the central government. In Russia serfdom was abolished only in 1861 —two years, however, before the emancipation of negro slaves in the United States,—and a feature of the recent Russian revolution has been the desire of the common people for more land. In 1861 too much of the best land was left in the possession of the landed nobility, while the peasants were burdened with an annual redemption tax to pay for their freedom. This tax was abolished only in 1905–1907. At about the same time the individual peasant was permitted to enclose and consolidate his different strips in the fields of the *mir* or village community. In the new states of Czecho-Slovakia and Jugoslavia, and in Rumania, laws have been passed dividing the great estates among small peasant landholders. With the overthrow of Stambulisky in 1923 the peasants lost control of the government of Bulgaria. Poland and Russia have both declared in favor of land ownership by the actual cultivators. In southern Italy and Sicily, too, since the war there was a movement to oust landlord and middleman, thus giving the peasant complete control of the soil he actually cultivates, but it has been checked by Fascism.

Returning to the eighteenth century, we note that with the Textile Inventions and the Factory System increased food supply went an increased production of clothing due to a series of inventions affecting textile industries in general and cotton goods in particular. Kay's Flying Shuttle, invented in 1733, the very year in which Tull's *Horse Hoeing Husbandry* was published, made it no longer necessary in weaving to pass the shuttle through from hand to hand. Thus it was possible to weave a greater breadth of cloth more rapidly. It therefore became difficult to find enough spinners to keep the weavers supplied with thread and yarn, although almost all women and children on the farm, as well as in town, spent their spare time at the old-fashioned spinning wheel, which produced only one thread at a time. As early as 1738 Paul and Wyatt devised a method of stretching and spinning the fibres between successive rollers but failed to make a practical success of it. In 1764 Hargreaves invented the

Spinning Jenny which revolved several spindles simultaneously and could be worked by a child. Arkwright first made a commercial success of such inventions, appropriating the ideas of others, employing first horse-power and then water-power, using alum-tawed leather on the rollers instead of sole leather as Paul had done, and further finding out the right way to put the leather on the rollers. Arkwright also built a spinning-mill where the workers toiled together at his machines instead of spinning in their homes. So he may be called the father of the factory system. His Water Frame first made possible the manufacture of true cotton cloth in England. An even finer and stronger thread was presently spun by Crompton's Mule, which combined the best features of the Spinning Jenny and the Water Frame. Machinery to card and comb the fibres was also soon invented. The year 1785 saw the slow process of printing calico by hand replaced by cylinder printing, the first employment of steam-power in a cotton mill, and the invention of a power-loom by Cartwright. The power-loom, however, came into use but slowly, so that the earnings of the hand-loom weavers were not seriously affected until after the Napoleonic wars. Cartwright was a clergyman, like a number of other modern inventors, the explanation perhaps being that they had more time to think and were more acustomed to think. Would-be inventors, however, often took counsel with experienced clock-makers. The new processes and factory system were first employed in the manufacture of cotton goods. It was therefore of great importance to increase the supply and reduce the price of raw cotton. This was made possible by the invention in 1792 by Whitney, a native of Massachusetts, of the cotton gin in which the teeth on a revolving disc pulled the lint off the seeds, while a brush removed the lint from the teeth. In recent years the world has produced and consumed about 20,000,000 bales of cotton annually.

Standard-ization of Machinery

Whitney, turning in 1798 to the manufacture of fire-arms, developed the idea of standard or interchangeable parts and relied for exact work upon his machines rather than his workmen. The early machines in England had been largely of wood; one of Watt's improvements in the steam engine was the use of iron for his gear and cog-wheels. Even so, if a screw broke, a new one usually could not be found that would

fit the nut.   In short, the best machines are machine-made,
and machinery, as Karl Marx has noted, seems to breed machinery.   In Great Britain standard patterns were introduced
by Maudsley and his followers, Clement, Murray, Whitworth,
and Nasmyth.   So the hardware business is very largely a
modern growth.   Such standardization naturally accompanied
the rise of the factory, where many similar machines are employed simultaneously and it is an obvious advantage to have
identical and interchangeable parts.   Standardization proceeded, however, more slowly than might be thought; in English
textile factories machinery entirely of metal came into general
use only from 1825 to 1840.

The earlier stages of the economic revolution in Great Britain
resulted in a great deal of human distress and demoralization.
The cotton factories ruined the hand spinners and eventually
the hand weavers, while the rural classes who had been partially
dependent upon these industries also often lost their income
from the land in the process of enclosure.   Such persons, it is
true, might and did seek employment in the factories and
towns.   But although the prices of yarn and cloth had fallen
greatly, and stock-breeding had increased the supply of meat,
prices as a whole advanced more rapidly than wages from 1750
to 1795.   During this period few poor families could afford
more than a pound of meat a week, made their own soap by
burning green fern, and seldom brewed even small-beer—drinking which had been a sign of extreme poverty back in the fourteenth century—except for rare occasions such as christenings.
The price of bread was kept up by duties on imported grain.
There was no governmental supervision of factories, no public
health regulation, or elementary education, and no adequate
local government, especially in the new industrial centers where
living conditions were disgusting.   The vicious practice of
giving poor relief to those who had large families or insufficient
wages was rapidly pauperizing the entire working class, encouraging manufacturers to keep down wages, and putting an in-
tolerable burden on the tax-payers.   The national wealth increased as a result of the economic growth, so that England was
able to finance the struggle against Napoleon and to lead the
world in trade, but the wealth was largely in the hands of the
landlords and manufacturers.   The hand worker had owned
his own tools, could work when he wished, and sell his product at

*Early Evil
Effects
of the
Economic
Revolution
in England*

market prices as opportunity offered; the machines were owned
by the factory, which employed labor only as it needed it, although it paid wages immediately. Population increased, but
declined in physical stamina as a result of the change from domestic to factory system and from country air to foul slum,
or as a result of employment underground for twelve or thirteen hours a day, in the narrow seams of coal mines, where
women and children on all fours dragged carts like beasts.

Effect in India

In distant India the native cotton industry collapsed completely before the competition of British factories and trade.
The Abbé Dubois, long a missionary in India, declared in a book
published in London in 1816, "This revolution threatens to
ruin India completely. Just before returning to Europe I
traveled through some of the manufacturing districts, and
nothing could equal the state of desolation prevailing in them.
All the work-rooms were closed, and hundreds of thousands of
the inhabitants, composing the weaver caste, were dying of hunger; for through the prejudices of the country they could not
adopt another profession without dishonoring themselves."
After showing how other classes had been indirectly affected,
the Abbé proceeds to state his opinion of "the much-vaunted
improvements in machinery which some nations glory in. Ah!
if only the inventors of these industrial developments could hear
the curses which this multitude of poor Hindus never tire of
heaping upon them! If only, like me, they had seen the fright-
ful misery which has overtaken whole provinces, owing entirely
to them and their inventive genius, they would no doubt, unless
they were entirely wanting in human pity, bitterly repent having carried their pernicious innovations so far, and having
thereby enriched a handful of men at the expense of millions
of poor people." At least we see the arrival of an age when
any great economic change in one part of the world reacts
swiftly on distant nations.

Spread of the New Inventions and Factory System Outside of England

A law against enticing English workmen abroad to set up
English industries in other countries had been passed as early
as 1718. Moreover, it was the general policy of the British
government well into the nineteenth century to forbid the exportation of British machinery or drawings and specifications
thereof. Workmen, nevertheless, emigrated to America and
reproduced some of the machines from memory aided by their
own ingenuity. As a result factories were in operation in the

New England states before the end of the century. In 1800, however, there were only six towns in Massachusetts besides Boston with a population of over 5000, and they were all east of it and depended for their prosperity mainly on shipping—Nantucket, Marblehead, Newburyport, Gloucester, Salem, and Bridgewater. Lowell with its looms was not incorporated until 1826. "In the Thirties we were still a nation of planters and farmers." The nations of the continent of Europe did not have much opportunity to learn and adopt the new processes until after the Napoleonic wars, by which time British trade and industry had a long start on them. Belgium was the only other country of Europe to keep up with England industrially in the first half of the nineteenth century. It took French industries some time to get back to where they were before 1789. Indeed, except for Alsace, where both the spinning machines and the power loom were rapidly adopted, the factory system was unusual in both France and Germany until about 1850. It hardly touched Russia until 1891, when Witte interested foreign capitalists in the industrial development of Russia.

But we must turn back to other phases of the industrial revolution in the eighteenth century. Next to food and clothing, dishes are the most frequent articles of household use. In this century the pottery became far superior in technique and mechanical perfection to anything previously produced, though inferior in artistic charm and individual interest to the older work. This was partly due to the employment of many mechanical appliances and to printing the patterns instead of painting them by hand, and partly to the great popular demand for the new "chinaware"—for earthenware was now for the first time manufactured that was white throughout,—while rich patrons of artists turned their attention largely to porcelain. True porcelain, hitherto obtainable only from China, was first manufactured in Europe by Böttger about 1710 at Meissen in Saxony. The leading name in connection with the aforesaid development of earthenware is that of Josiah Wedgwood (1730–1795). In the later nineteenth century pottery manufacture was extended to sanitary appliances and the chemical and electrical industries. Papier mâché, long known in the east, was introduced into Europe in the eighteenth century for trays, snuff-boxes, panels of coaches, furniture, and the like. Paper itself was first made by machinery in France in 1798.

Improved Pottery

Turning to arts concerned with fire and iron, as the ancient classification used to run, we have to note the increasing utilization of iron and coal. Owing chiefly, it would seem, to the growing scarcity of wood, the eighteenth century saw an enlarged demand for coal by industries. In France this led to state concessions to mining companies which were bitterly opposed by the proprietors of the soil. Smelting iron with coke and coal instead of charcoal now greatly increased the yield per furnace, especially with the better blast effected by use of the new steam engine after 1790. Rollers were used instead of hammers to press the impurities out of the metal and give the iron the desired shape. A rolling mill which produced sheet iron was established in 1728; in 1783 Cort by grooving the rollers turned out iron bars and rods. In 1784 came his puddling furnace for making wrought iron from pig iron, which was placed in a separate chamber from the fuel and heated by reverberation. It was now some three thousand years since the introduction of iron by the Hittites, when the first iron bridge of the iron age was constructed in 1779 over the Severn, and the first iron ship was launched in 1790. China, however, had an iron pagoda as early as the fourteenth century. Strictly speaking, railroads were in existence before locomotives were invented. Iron rails were being manufactured in 1767; in 1803 was opened the first public iron tramway on the outskirts of London, in 1811 there were 150 miles of iron tracks in connection with the mines, canals, and iron works of South Wales. Mining in general, and that of coal in particular, had been facilitated by the invention of steam pumps by Savery and Newcomen in 1698–1705. The danger from fire-damp was lessened in 1815 by Davy's invention of the safety lamp which gave him, he said, greater pleasure than any of his more purely scientific discoveries. Coal-mining has continued, however, to have its dangers; the deaths from accidents to miners numbered over one thousand *per annum* in the British Isles in the present century.

During the eighteenth century candles were the chief means of artificial lighting, while the common method of obtaining fire was by the tinder-box, flint and steel. Experiments with coal gas for illuminating purposes, however, had been made throughout the century. It first came into actual use in 1802 in the engine factory of Watt and his partner, Boulton, near Birming-

ham, and was first adopted for street lighting in Pall Mall,
1807, and in Paris in 1815.   Its use spread rapidly through
the chief towns of the British Isles for lighting streets, public
buildings, and shops, but more slowly into private dwellings.
The first practical friction matches were not produced until
1827, although attempts in that direction date back to the days
of Boyle.   Safety matches were not invented until about 1850,
in Sweden.   It was not until after 1859, when petroleum was
discovered in great quantities in Pennsylvania, that kerosene oil
began to be used in domestic lamps.

The use of power other than that of man and his domestic
animals has been a leading feature in our present civilization.
It may be said to have been initiated by Watt's invention or
improvement of the steam engine.   He introduced a separate
condenser, so that the cylinder need not be chilled in condens-
ing the steam.   In the steam pump the piston had worked up
and down, being raised by the force of steam admitted beneath
it and falling from atmospheric pressure as the steam was condensed by turning a jet of cold water into the cylinder.   Watt
kept the cylinder as hot as possible and admitted steam on
either side of the piston, thus driving it with greater rapidity
and making possible any position of the cylinder and circular
motion.   His first patent was obtained in 1769; many improvements were subsequently added.   In 1784 came the first trac-
tion engine; in 1785 the use of steam power in cotton factories;
in 1790 its application to the blast furnace; in 1814 *The London Times* was first printed by steam power; by 1818 there were
estimated to be over ten thousand steam engines with a total
of 225,000 horse power in Great Britain.   The steam hammer
was introduced by Nasmyth in 1838.   Compound engines, in
which high pressure steam expands successively in two or more
cylinders, which are thus kept at a more even temperature, were
devised from 1781 on, though they were not much used until
about 1850.   In the last decades of the nineteenth century was
developed the turbine, in which jets of steam revolve a shaft
fitted with series of blades and vanes.   Inventors were working
early at the problem of a gas or internal combustion engine, but
it became a commercial success only with Dr. Otto's patent in
1876.

Perhaps the most important use of the steam engine was to
improve communication, a need especially felt in Great Britain,

The Steam
Engine

Need of
Improved
Com-
munication

where the potteries, iron-works, mines, and factories needed to market their ever increasing output, and in America, where settlers were pushing far inland. This led to great activity in the building of roads and canals in both countries in the later eighteenth and early nineteenth centuries. There was nothing essentially novel in these means of communication, although some new processes such as macadamizing might be noted. However, the growing demand for more rapid and frequent transportation is seen in the marked improvement in mail coach service from 1784 on, and in the fact that "the coach and turnpike period" was at its height as late as 1837. For ocean trade rapid clipper ships were built which are said to have covered as much as 436 sea miles a day—under favoring conditions, of course. They continued to ply between Great Britain and its distant colonies in Australia and New Zealand, in the second half of the nineteenth century. Some of the best were American-built.

The
Steamboat

As early as 1787 John Fitch ran a steamboat propelled by six paddles on either side on the Delaware river. His claim to the invention was disputed by James Rumsey. Fitch failed to make money by carrying passengers and, becoming discouraged, committed suicide in 1798. Successful steamboat service began with Fulton's *Claremont* on the Hudson in 1807 and Bell's *Comet* on the Clyde in 1812. In 1819 the *Savannah* crossed the ocean from Savannah to Liverpool, in part under sail, taking thirty-two days. Successful transatlantic steamers began about twenty years later. The first iron steamship was built in 1821; in 1832 one was ascending the river Niger in Africa. In 1838 the iron screw propeller began slowly to replace the side-paddlewheel. The compound engine, introduced especially in the sixties, saved fuel and enabled the steamships to carry freight.

The Loco-
motive and
Railroad

Trevethick was experimenting with locomotives in the first decade of the nineteenth century; other locomotives were drawing loads on a small scale in the second decade, while steam omnibuses carried passengers on the highroads. The first regular steam railway was the Stockton and Darlington Railroad, opened in 1825 and intended to carry only freight. To meet the demand for passenger service a daily coach was added called "Experiment," which carried six persons inside, and from fifteen to twenty outside. In 1829 Stephenson's *Rocket* won the competition for a prize offered by the Liverpool and Manchester Railroad by making forty-four miles an hour, and the era of rapid communication and transportation opened. The ideal of speed began to dominate modern civilization as the ideal of permanence had dominated the old pyramid-builders. A veritable mania for railroad building seized the world in the middle of the nineteenth century. English capital, material, and navvies aided in the development of French railways; Belgium rather went ahead even of England in rapid execution of a network of state railways to catch the international traffic between England, France, Germany, and Holland; the German lines were the best continuous railway system in Europe. America at first largely employed British locomotives and depended on English capital, but rapidly outdistanced other lands in extent of tracks and in transcontinental lines, so that it now comprises half the mileage of the world. Indeed for a time the extension of railroads was pushed too rapidly. By about 1884 twice as many railroads had been built as the United States could then use with profit, and four times more securities had been issued than the country could pay interest or dividends on. "For forty years American railroad promoters, reckless optimists, gigantic thieves, huge confidence men—magnified a hundred times by the size of their transactions—had juggled and manipulated and exploited this great business for their own profit and the general loss of everyone else concerned." More acceptable was George Westinghouse's invention of the air-brake in 1868 and of automatic signals. About the same time Joseph Henry, secretary of the Smithsonian Institute at Washington from its foundation in 1846 until his death in 1878, was improving fog signals as a member of the lighthouse board, and making the first weather map.

The steam locomotive has been called "the iron horse," and if we possessed one-tenth the poetic ability of the author of *The Book of Job*, we would try to match his description quoted in our seventh chapter. Certainly the breath of a smoke-stack is more impressive than that of any horse's nostrils, the puffing and the shriek of the whistle more stirring. The iron horse not merely paws in the valley or swallows up the ground with fierceness and rage, but bounds over rivers, burrows through mountains, crosses the desert, and saith among the docks and factories, "Ha! Ha!" It increases the value of land without any effort on the part of the owner; it makes it

Results of the Railroad

"easier to feed five millions today than it was to feed fifty thousand three-quarters of a century ago." It never sleeps, for we can listen from our beds at night, across the silent, intervening spaces, to the distant sound of its bell, the clanking of loose chains and bars, the vibration of the heavy load upon the rails, and dream of distant lands and cities to which it might take us. But alas! it is making those distant lands and cities almost exactly like our own, and our own like them. Those six hundred thousand miles and more of steel rails form meshes that unite and bind closely together almost all parts of our tight little earth, which is only 25,000 miles in circumference. With its foul breath, unsightly roadbed, telegraph poles, and accompaniment of advertising signs, the monster spoils the scenery to which it might take us. Nevertheless a train in full course is a fine sight, especially at night when it seems some onrushing dragon belching forth fire, and even a slow-moving freight train by daylight is an interesting mosaic or moving picture in geography. Shortly before the recent world war the railroads were estimated to represent one-tenth of the wealth of the world and one-fourth of its invested capital. The longest railroad in the world is the Trans-Siberian, built by the Russian government in 1891–1900 with the aid of French loans. While the United States leads the world in railroad mileage, Great Britain still keeps ahead in merchant steam tonnage.

Agricultural Machinery

In the nineteenth century the agricultural revolution entered upon a second stage of advance with the introduction of the mechanical harvester. This advance took place not on English estates but on the much broader prairies of the American middle west with farms of great acreage where large machines can be employed to advantage. There had been British attempts to construct a machine to cut grain in the eighteenth century, several threshers had also been devised, and Bell's reaper of 1826 probably gave the idea of several American patents which followed. Cyrus McCormick, however, by moving his business out to Chicago in 1847 outdistanced his competitors. The scarcity of labor caused by enlistment in the Civil War brought agricultural machinery into further use. In 1872 the wire sheaf-binder was added to the harvester; in 1880 the machine bound the sheaves with twine. Today there are harrows twenty-five feet wide and harvesters which cut a swath fifty-two feet wide. Some other examples of nineteenth century agricultural machinery are the horse-rake, the machine for turning and spreading hay, the hay-loading machine, the hay-press, portable threshers, machines that not only harvest but husk, shuck, and shred corn, manure spreaders, the multiple plough, made practicable in 1873, the tractor, introduced only recently, and various dairy appliances, cream separators, and mechanical churns.

Planted and harvested by men who work their way north with the season from Oklahoma to Manitoba, stored in huge fireproof grain "elevators," transported to the eastern coasts by steamers on the Great Lakes and by the railroads, American wheat after 1870 so undersold the wheat grown in the British Isles that their acreage under wheat fell off one-half in thirty or forty years, and their population became increasingly dependent upon imported food-stuffs. Similarly wool shipped all the way from Australia, where sheep could be raised on a large scale, had reduced the price in England in 1893 to only a third of what it had been in 1840. From the sixties on tinned meat from Australia and canned meat from Chicago, sardines and salmon for which one fished with a can-opener, canned vegetables and fruits generally, cold storage meat and eggs, condensed milk, have been some of the numerous forms in which foods were shipped or stored.

Shipping and Storage of Commodities

Many attempts had been made to introduce a sewing-machine before the invention of Elias Howe of Massachusetts, which was patented in 1846, found general acceptance. Numerous later improvements were made upon it by others. A riveting machine for boots had already been invented in France. Machines that would sew leather were rapidly adopted in the shoemaking industry, which in the later nineteenth century in America became more and more specialized and was carried on in large factories rather than in the shops of individual shoemakers. Most shoes today are ready-made rather than made to order. Ready-made clothing began in America in the thirties and received a further impetus from the invention of the sewing-machine. Sewing-machines now have attachments which make buttonholes, hems, and ruffles, or darn and embroider. The hope, however, that the sewing-machine had forever rung the curtain on such sad exhibitions as that of the poor seamstress red-eyed over her stitches was somewhat disappointed by the employment of sewing-machines in sweatshops,—crowded work-

Sewing-Machine and Ready-made Clothing

rooms in the slums where conditions remained much worse than in the factories which had come to be well regulated.

Rise of the
Rubber
Industry

Not much attention was paid to caoutchouc, or rubber, for some time after the discovery of America. In the eighteenth century Frenchmen investigated the trees which were the source of the supply, and Priestley, discoverer of oxygen, sent bits of it to his English friends to use as erasers, on which account they were called India rubbers. The natives of Central and South America seem to have made some use of caoutchouc for shoes and clothing, but it became of use in modern manufacture only after Goodyear had discovered how to vulcanize it in 1839. Its use in tires, first for bicycles and then for automobiles, has created an ever-growing demand for it in recent years, so that the world's production of crude rubber increased from 56,890 long tons in 1900 to 70,500 in 1910 to 380,280 in 1922, of which last amount some 290,000 long tons were retained in the United States. The sources of supply, however, are at present largely controlled by British capitalists.

Rise of the
Oil Industry

Another raw material that came first to be used in large quantities in the second half of the nineteenth century was oil, or petroleum. Vegetable and animal oils had been much employed hitherto, and the ancients had some knowledge of asphalt, bitumen, and naphtha, but no such vast reservoir of mineral oil had previously been tapped as was found when Drake drilled for oil in Pennsylvania in 1859. It may be noted, however, that the method of drilling was borrowed or evolved from that of the artesian wells, so named from Artois where the method had been practiced since the middle ages. Indeed, springs of water seem to have been reached by deep boring in ancient times in Egypt, China, Persia, Asia Minor, and other regions. So great was the source of oil now unearthed that almost immediately pipe-lines were built to convey it. So many were the uses to which it could be put when properly refined and chemically treated—such as lubricants, vaseline, kerosene, gasoline or petrol,—that search was soon made for new oil fields, which have been discovered all over the world. Supplies of natural gas have also been found in the bowels of the earth and used as fuel from about 1872. Ocean liners and battleships have begun to burn oil instead of coal. It can be loaded more quickly and saves space, permitting the vessel to carry more freight or guns, or to make a longer cruise. Great

Britain's economic supremacy and naval power had hitherto been based largely upon her supply of coal, which her steamships would take out as ballast and sell abroad, returning with food-stuffs and other goods required at home. But she has realized the coming change and made haste to secure concessions to most of the oil fields the world over, including Central and South America, although by the San Remo agreement of 1920 France is allowed a share.

The iron industry became the steel industry after the English inventor, Bessemer, in trying to improve the metal employed in artillery, purified the iron by forcing a blast of air through it while it was in a molten state and at an extreme heat, thus securing a metal with less carbon than there had been in cast iron and less slag than there had been in wrought iron. Although it also differed somewhat in its properties from what had previously been known as steel, that name was henceforth given to it. Bessemer perfected his process in the years after 1856. He was less successful in his effort to avoid sea sickness by instituting a swinging saloon on steamboats crossing the Channel. The open-hearth process, introduced in 1864 by Siemens and Martin, is another method employed in the modern steel industry. Steel rails are now made by it rather than by the Bessemer process, and hydraulic presses are employed instead of hammers. The Thomas process of 1878 removed the sulphur and phosphorus from iron ore, making it possible to utilize hitherto neglected iron fields in France, Belgium, and Germany. Iron changes its form and properties readily at certain temperatures, or if cooled in certain ways, or if combined with other metals, so that different types of steel are manufactured. The new processes made possible better rails, superior cutting tools, steel construction of steamships and their screws, of railroad and subway carriages, of high city buildings, and many other improvements. This industry has forced or induced men to labor under extraordinarily trying and uncomfortable or perilous and exhausting conditions, standing amid the heat, noise, flames, and vapors of clanging foundries and scorching steel-mills which seem like the very pit of hell, or walking unconcernedly across single steel girders high aloft over ravine or river or crowded city pavement.

Steel construction and fire-proof buildings may be regarded as the chief achievement of modern architecture. The sky-

The Steel Industry

Steel Construction

scrapers and series of great bridges are certainly the most impressive feature of that most modern of cities, New York.   The towering office-buildings of the Wall Street district, concerted and yet menacing one another, like some highly magnified San Gimignano with its *torri dei grandi*, but many-windowed instead of thick-walled, express the financial feudalism of our trusts and corporations with their wider world outlook.   The hotels and elevator apartments further uptown, the cars of steel, containing not one rider and his charioteer but packed tighter with struggling humanity than ever was the Black Hole of Calcutta, which go crashing through subways and thundering over viaducts and bridges, reveal that close combination of palatial luxury and ease with acute discomfort, that glamour and clamor, which characterize our modern civilization.   The "I" beam, so important in steel and fireproof construction, dates in wrought iron form from 1855 on the eve of the Bessemer process.   Passenger lifts or elevators have come in since 1865.

Sky-
Scrapers

In a very high modern building the problem is similar to that which confronted the inventors of Gothic architecture, namely, to lessen the danger from fires, to admit more light to the interior of the building, and to remove the weight of the superstructure from the exterior walls, which must be filled with window glass.   This was done in the Gothic cathedral by the stone vault and the flying buttress which received and carried the stress of the vault to points outside the church.   In the modern building steel and cement are used to avoid fire. Instead of a single vault to be supported, there is a succession of steel and cement floors which are each laden with office furniture and human beings, or perhaps with stored wares and heavy machines.   Usually the outer walls bear only their own weight; often the masonry of upper stories is begun before that below them is finished, each floor supporting its own outer wall, and being tied by steel girders to an inner cage construction on which the weight is concentrated rather than, as in the case of the cathedral, on external buttresses.   This arrangement saves ground space, so costly in our great business centers, and the modern sky-scraper provides a great deal more floor space than any cathedral or previous building.   The steel columns which support the floors are composed of Z-shaped bars or angles, or lattice work, or plates and channels riveted together.   The foundations are of course sunk deep in the earth, but owing to

the height and slenderness of the total structure it is likely to
be swayed in the wind as cathedrals are not. The latest tendency, however, is to broaden the building at the base and narrow it by a series of terraces as it rises, making really a cluster
of buildings of different heights and producing an effect more
cathedral-like.

Modern bridges, if not made up of single arches of riveted   Bridges
steel springing from support to support, are either suspended
by great steel cables from high towers of steel or stone, or are
built on the cantilever principle, by which two huge, carefully
balanced intricacies of steel girders and trusses reach out little
by little across a great river or chasm until their ends meet
and are indissolubly riveted together, thus counteracting each
other's thrusts and stresses. Sometimes they receive and support between them a third steel trestle which is floated down the
river and fitted into its keystone position, spanning the gap
between the two great cantilevers,—an exceedingly delicate and
difficult operation which at Quebec resulted in repeated disaster.
The acute angles, zig-zags, and criss-crossing bars of steel
construction have thus far resulted in effects unpleasing to
the eye, and its rigidity is inferior to the solidity of stone or
masonry, its mechanical and artificial appearance lacking in
naturalness and grace. But in time steel construction should
achieve beauty as well as utility.

The railroads had not spread very far before they were ac-   Telegraph,
companied by lines of wires along which an electric current   Telephone,
transmitted the messages of human thought far more rapidly   and
than steam was transporting goods and human freight along the   Wireless
rails of steel. The electric telegraph, attempted by the Frenchman Lesage in 1774 and claimed by German writers as the simul-
taneous invention of Steinheil, Gauss, and Weber, was patented
by the American, Morse, in 1838 and installed both in England and the United States by 1844. It then rapidly followed
the railway lines, being of immense use in controlling their
traffic. This almost instantaneous method of communication
was then carried under water by laying cables, across the
English Channel in 1851, across the Atlantic in 1858–1865,
until its messages encircled the earth more rapidly than that
planet itself revolves, annihilating space and outstripping time.
This gave an enormous impetus to the daily newspaper, to
stock market transactions, to international trade and finance.

Edison's stock ticker gave added service in these last-named respects; his automatic telegraph and quadruplex telegraph facilitated the sending and receiving of messages and made it possible to send more messages on the wire together. Elisha Gray's telautograph transmits writing. The early telegraph, however, required a trained operator to translate its clicks into words and *vice versa*. The telephone, which carries the voice and words themselves over the wires and permits the conducting thus of ordinary conversation, was invented in 1861 by Reis and patented by Bell in 1876, but is not entirely satisfactory for long distance. Then appeared from Italy an electrician who needed no thread of wire to guide him through the labyrinth of wave-lengths of sound, and in 1899 Marconi was sending wireless messages across the English Channel. Today with a good radio set any home can hear speeches and concerts given out from broadcasting stations hundreds, or even thousands, of miles away. Soon we may be able to hear, better than we can see through the telescope, what is going on in distant planets—that "music of the spheres" after which yearned the ancient philosophers.

Further Introduction of Electricity

The telegraph was only one of the first of a host of inventions employing electricity. Of fundamental importance was the invention of the dynamo to transform mechanical into electrical energy in 1831 by Faraday, and the invention of the motor to transform the stored-up electrical energy into mechanical power. Cheap batteries and central power stations were other necessities before electricity could come into general use. Thus while Davy had discovered the voltaic arc, and De Moleyn had devised an incandescent electric light in 1841, and a Vermont blacksmith had driven an electric car in 1835, it was only after 1878 that electric lighting came in with the arc light of Charles F. Brush and the incandescent bulb of Thomas Edison. This last was the fruit of fourteen months' brain work and $40,000 expenditure in experimentation. The Welsbach mantle, patented in 1885, enabled illuminating gas to contest the field for a time longer. Then successive improvements, terminating in the Tungsten burner, led to the displacement of the other method of artificial illumination and to the spread of electric lighting into remote or backward regions which gas lighting had never penetrated. Electric railways began to develop in the eighties. After supplanting tramways drawn by horses and cable-cars in the cities, they spread to suburban and interurban lines which became serious competitors of the branch railroads. Now even the main railroad lines have begun to electrify their roads, replacing the smoky, sooty iron-horse by the quieter and cleaner electric locomotive. Meantime the rapid growth of the automobile industry, which employed the gas engine more than the electric motor, has driven the aforesaid interurban railways to the wall. But electric heaters and appliances of every sort are found more and more in the home, while electricity as power is taking an ever increasing part in industry. Already before 1900 the electric furnace made possible the commercial production of aluminum and gave us carborundum, magnesium, and calcium carbide. From the last comes acetylene, a most brilliant illuminating gas and also useful in severing or welding metals.

Chemicals and the application of chemical knowledge have been of great aid in modern agriculture and in the processes of preparing or refining rubber, petroleum, and steel. Industrial or commercial chemistry, in which Germany led the world before the war, has also busied itself with the utilization of waste- or by-products such as cotton seed, from which is now extracted oil, feed for cattle, and fertilizer, and such as the dyes and explosives derived from coal-tar. It has busied itself further with the making of chemical substitutes such as artificial flavors and perfumes, oleomargarin, peanut-butter and other fats, pyrotechnic fuel to imitate the flame of driftwood, leather substitutes, cellulose silks, or the production of new compounds such as celluloid. The Welsbach mantle was made with ninty-nine per cent of thorium oxide and one per cent of cerium oxide. Both thorium and cerium are rare metals —some sixty such have been discovered whose very names are unknown to most people—but the Germans found a sand on the shores of Brazil which contained both. They then made haste to corner the supply of this sand wherever it occurred the world over, until the war terminated their monopoly. Great Britain now gets a supply of her own from southern India and Ceylon. In making the Welsbach mantles the thrifty Germans used the cerium that was left over, and other rare elements such as didymium which occurred with it, to print the pink trade-mark on the mantle and to make cigarette- and gas-stove-lighters. Tungsten, which was once thrown away on the dumps of Corn-

Industrial and Commercial Chemistry

ish tin mines, is now not only employed in metal filament lamps, but is alloyed with steel for armor plate and for high speed tools which keep their temper when red-hot. Zirconium, another rare metal from Brazil, withstands the high temperature of the electric furnace, and is used in X-ray photography and automobile headlights. Iridium and osmium furnish points for the gold nibs of fountain pens. Tantalum, which is very hard, easily sterilized, and does not rust, is admirable for dental instruments. Of engines of destruction and poisonous gases devised for war the less said the better; one wonders who can have the heart to invent them, and one can only hope that they do not prove destructive of all civilization.

Man and Modern Machinery

No better illustration can be given of the speed and precision, the magnitude and complexity of modern machinery, and the numerous adjustments and improvements that are continually being made in it, than a comparison of the small printing-press of early days with the huge complexes of mechanism that take in great rolls of paper and turn out a complete copy of a daily newspaper with many pages of many-columned type. Instead of the typesetting by hand of a generation past there are linotype, monotype, and electrotype machines and methods. Typewriters have been in use since the years 1868–1871. In other industries the division of labor has been carried so far that one man or a girl at his or her machine constantly repeats some one simple operation, then passes on the article for the next step in the process, or the part for assemblage into the complete product. It has been remarked that machines not only do not make mistakes but often seem to display an uncanny automatic intelligence, while the human worker has grown mechanical in his constant repetition of the same motions like a ticking clock. Samuel Butler foresaw this fifty years ago in his satire *Erewhon* (1872), an imaginary land where men had revolted and smashed all the machines just in the nick of time before the machines were able to dispense with men entirely.

Increasingly Rapid Change since 1865

Yet the Reverend Oswald Cockayne, writing his *Anglo-Saxon Leechdoms* only eight years before *Erewhon*, could still thus compare the England of his day with ancient Greece and Rome:

Our great capitals are smaller than Rome, the fortunes of our men of millions are trifles to the wealth of a Crassus or a Lucullus, our houses are less carefully warmed in winter than the Roman villas, our poetry has no Homeros, our sculpture no Praxiteles, our architecture no Parthenon, our philosophy has never seen a century such as that between Pericles and Alexandros, those hundred years of Attic wit and wisdom have given us an education in dead languages, and in the lore and manners of two thousand years since, and are driving our native words from off our tongues and making them strange to our ears.

It is true that mid-Victorian England and America before the Civil War were very different from what those countries are today. Many of the inventions that we have mentioned were not made until the last quarter of the nineteenth century, or did not attain their full effect and spread until even the twentieth century. But from the time that Peel repealed the Corn Laws and introduced free trade in "the hungry forties," living conditions improved in England, and for about thirty years there was general prosperity. The United States recovered from the Civil War (1861–1865) with a rapidity that amazed Europe. Owing to its vast natural resources and greater opportunities for new developments, it has since outdistanced Europe both in the number of its millionaires, the more sumptuous living conditions of its people generally, and their far wider prospects of profitable employment. Germany, since the Franco-Prussian War in 1870 and the founding of the empire in 1871, was also making rapid, although somewhat forced, economic progress, until the harnessing of this horse with that of militarism in the race for power caused both to go down in the recent war, and perhaps will bring down all the other charioteers and their teams with it.

From this unpleasant possibility let us turn to the more pleasing prospect of how millionaires make their money and how the masses spend theirs. Such early eighteenth century experiences of the results of speculation and the workings of the credit system as Law's Mississippi Company in France and the bursting of the South Sea Bubble in England had made the general public somewhat wary about investing its hard-earned savings, or perhaps for a time afterwards it did not have any left to invest. At any rate for a season little was heard of joint stock companies. At the beginning of the nineteenth century the investment habit existed only in England and Holland, which since the sixteenth century had been the leading maritime and commercial powers of Europe. In America, too,

Growth of the Investment Habit

the richest men were merchants like John Hancock of Boston and Stephen Girard of Philadelphia. Even in England only venturesome persons would invest in anything except the government debt, Bank of England, East India Company, land, or a business known to them personally. After Law there was no bank in France that could be called national until, under Turgot's ministry in 1776, the *Caisse d'Escompte* was founded with power of note issue. In 1800 Napoleon founded the Bank of France, but cheques were still unknown in 1848. We should also mention the Jewish financiers of southern Germany, where the banking-house of Rothschild was founded in the second half of the eighteenth century. Nathan Rothschild, the third son of the founder, came to England about 1800 and financed the new cotton mills. The building of canals also attracted capital. In 1816 the income of those engaged in trade and industry in England was still not quite so large as the rents paid by occupiers of agricultural lands. In America the great firms of Wall Street almost all made their start in the dry goods or clothing business. Thus George Peabody, the founder of the firm of the Morgans, began at sixteen in 1811 as a dry goods clerk. Like Stephen Girard he justified his wealth by his philanthropy, an example which many later men of wealth have followed.

Growth of Speculation and Great Fortunes

Then came the period of reckless railroad speculation to which we before alluded, when Jay Gould and William H. Vanderbilt accumulated colossal fortunes, and of such large governmental credit transactions (for those times) as the national debt of the United States after the Civil War and the borrowing by France in 1871 to pay her indemnity to Germany. Andrew Carnegie (1835–1919) rose from a bobbin-boy in a cotton factory to be a multi-millionaire by shrewd speculation and the organization of great steel works. John D. Rockefeller made his fortune by controlling the oil of the country, in which the Standard Oil Company secured a practical monopoly until it was dissolved into a number of lesser companies by governmental action. Such corporations or "trusts," representing amalgamations of various firms and interests that would otherwise be competitive, have been a great problem of recent civilization. J. Pierpont Morgan (1837–1913) directed the investment of European capital in America and reorganized railroads. Other men grew rich by reaping the unearned increment upon lands which the growth of cities or discovery of unsuspected treasures of mineral wealth have produced.

Most great fortunes have been made, and most great busi- Stocks and Bonds nesses are carried on, not merely with the personal capital of the fortune-maker or members of the firm, but with the money of other investors which they have been allowed to use. This may be done by borrowing it of a bank which, however, is apt to grant only a short loan and to demand strong securities. Even in this case the bank passes on not its own money but that of its depositors and stock-holders for the use of the under-taking or business in question. Or the firm in question may issue stock which it puts on sale and which entitles those who buy it to a share in the profits or dividends of the concern, when and if there are any, in proportion to the amount of stock that they hold. Usually a corporation puts only a part of its stock on sale, retaining enough in its own hands to insure control of the business and board of directors, who determine how far earnings shall be paid out in dividends or put back into further development of the business. Or capital may be obtained by issuing bonds which are certificates of indebtedness to the person holding them and pay such interest rate as may be specified until the day when the bond falls due and the principal is to be repaid. When that day approaches, the company may very likely issue new bonds and pay off the old with the proceeds. Stocks and bonds may be bought and sold at any time a seller and purchaser can get together; their values fluctuate with the prosperity and standing of the business concerned, the needs of the sellers for ready cash, and in sym-pathy with the general condition of the stock-market. Com-monly they are bought and sold for customers by brokers who frequent the stock exchanges or bourses established for such purposes. There also are centers, like the cotton-clearing house established at Liverpool in 1876 and the wheat-pits of Chicago and Minneapolis, where one can buy and sell the crops themselves from a distance or deal in "futures" long before the harvest. The quantity of stocks and bonds issued by a business has long since ceased to be limited to the value of the property and stock-in-trade, or even to the present earning capacity of the undertaking, and is apt to be based upon its future possibilities and prospective earnings, as if these were already existent capital. Thus in the years from 1890 to

1915 the total capitalization of public service corporations in the United States in the shape of stocks and bonds increased one hundred times from one-fifth of a billion dollars to twenty billions.

Insurance and Trust Companies

Moreover, handier methods of getting the use of other people's money than the banks have come into existence, namely, the insurance companies and the trust companies. To the former comes a constant stream of money in the shape of premiums and installments which only at some later date do they repay in case of accident, fire, theft, and death. In the meantime they have the use of the money. Trust companies not only act as the trustees of estates, agents of investors, and ordinary bankers, but employ the money which they thus receive in underwriting and promoting various financial and industrial projects. In such activities they are subject to somewhat less strict regulations and safeguards than are commonly applied to the banks proper.

Credit and Panics

By all these devices actual money value or capital is turned over and over, and more is gotten out of it. As a farmer turns over the sods and admits air to the soil, so does credit permeate all the modern financial structure; and as soil is irrigated, so are stocks sometimes too well "watered." But when a great many investors suddenly and simultaneously want their money back, then comes the rub; and it takes high consultations in the office of J. Pierpont Morgan, or conferences between the Chancellor of the Exchequer and the Governor of the Bank of England, or the institution of a Federal Reserve Bank, to provide against the danger of sudden panics, which in the past have so frequently seized the world of finance. Following the terrible strain and drain of the great war, half the countries of Europe issued paper money in such quantities that it became either quite worthless or brought only a fraction of its face value. They furthermore have huge debts to other countries (usually Great Britain and the United States) on which they have as yet hardly begun to pay interest. In such arrangements for settling these debts as have thus far been made, the debtor nation has virtually been allowed to make only partial payment.

The Phonograph and Photography

We have alluded to cold storage warehouses, canned food, and chemical substitutes; we may go farther and speak of canned music and canned sound, and the substitution of mechanically or chemically made likenesses for painting or drawing by the human hand, in other words, of the phonograph and photography. Since 1807 successful efforts had been made to record sound vibration graphically upon moving surfaces, but Edison in his phonograph of 1877, which was much improved later, first succeeded in reproducing the sound vibrations so recorded. The scientific investigation of chemical and spectrum analysis by Scheele about 1782, and Ritter's discovery of ultra-violet rays in 1801, and of the action of light upon a chemically prepared plate or film, preceded Daguerre's pictures made by sunlight in 1839, as the daguerreotype preceded the popular camera or kodak of the eighties and the moving pictures of our own time.

Since the eighties travel by land and sea has been made increasingly comfortable. Mortimer Pullman devised the Pullman sleeping car and formed in 1867 the Pullman Palace Car Company; dining cars came in about 1881; the vestibuled railroad car was patented in 1887; ocean liners since the seventies have kept improving the accommodations for passengers. First the bicycle, then the motor cycle and automobile, have provided individual and family locomotion for an increasing number of persons. The pianola, phonograph, and automobile, together with the extension of telephone service, parcel post, and rural free delivery, have made life in agricultural communities in the United States, at least, more attractive and civilized, while the moving picture theater has added a new lure to the town. Steam heat and electric light warm and brighten shop and home.

Increasing Popular Comfort and Luxury

The average man in Europe and America today consumes a great deal more than he ever did before, despite the fact that in both continents the population has been steadily increasing. He also has more money to spend than before and, being generically so numerous, is consequently the incessant target of advertisements galore, which flood the pages of his daily morning newspaper and daily evening newspaper and cheap popular magazine, which confront him on bill boards wherever he goes and catch his eye in street-car or subway or on his theater program. It is essential for production on a large scale to have consumption also on a large scale, and business men figure that it is more profitable to sell at a low profit to a great many people than at a high price to a few, and that this end is best at-

Advertising and the Consumer

tained by extensive advertising. No doubt the business men understand their own interests best, but the consumers would probably be better off on the whole, if they bought less and paid more for it. Real necessities are seldom advertised as extensively as are the things one might do without. The average modern man perhaps eats no more than his predecessors, but he gets his food from more distant and varied sources. Through the nineteenth century international trade increased six times as rapidly as the growth of population, rapid as that was. The modern man's cheaper clothing wears out faster, but he buys new instead of patching the old. The sale of women's apparel is able to support a body of advertising that, at least in American daily papers, far exceeds any other interest visible in print except possibly the automobile advertising in the weeklies. Then the modern man consumes per capita a large quantity of iron and steel, of rubber and petroleum, while it may be questioned whether he saves or expends more time in rapid and continual transit to and fro.

Flying-Machines and Submarines

Let us close our chapter with one or two more inventions in this characteristically modern quest for speed and motion. Balloons lighter than air were introduced before 1800, but could not be guided except upward and downward. The first dirigible balloon driven by an engine was in 1852, but successful dirigibles date only from the Zeppelins of 1900, while the aeroplane heavier than air dates from the models of Langley in 1896 and the more successful flights of the Wright brothers in 1903. The internal combustion engine has been of great aid in aeronautics. Curtiss perfected the seaplane which rises from the water's surface. Records for speed, height, and sustained flight are so constantly being broken that we will record here only the first transatlantic flight in 1919. The submarine, in which Robert Fulton had tried to interest Napoleon by a test at Brest in 1801, was extensively employed during the recent war but seems better adapted to purposes of secret destruction than of useful communication.

BIBLIOGRAPHY

Some works on present economic civilization have already been listed at the close of the first chapter.

Ashton, T. S. *Iron and Steel in the Industrial Revolution,* 1924; an indispensable monograph for the student of that subject.

Bagehot, W. *Lombard Street: a description of the Money Market*, 1913.

Bishop, J. L. *History of American Manufactures*, 1868.

Bogart, E. L. *Economic History of the United States*, 1922.

Bogart, E. L., and Thompson, C. M. *Readings in the Economic History of the United States*, 1916.

Bowden, W. *The Rise of the Great Manufacturers of England*, 1919. *Industrial Society in England towards the End of the Eighteenth Century*, 1925.

Byrn, E. W. *Progress of Invention in the Nineteenth Century*, 1900.

Caldwell, O. T., and Slosson, E. E. *Science Remaking the World*, 1923.

Cheyney, E. P. *Industrial and Social History of England*, 1920.

Clapham, J. H. *Economic Development of France and Germany, 1815–1914*, 1921.

Clark, V. S. *History of Manufactures in the United States*, 1915.

Cleveland-Stevens, E. C. *English Railways, their development and relation to the state*, 1915.

Coman, K. *Industrial History of the United States*, 1911; *Economic Beginnings of the Far West*, 1912, 2 vols.

Conant, C. A. *History of Modern Banks of Issue*, 1909.

Cunningham, W. *Growth of English Industry and Commerce*, 1905–1907; *Progress of Capitalism in England*, 1916.

Dewey, D. R. *Financial History of the United States*, 1903.

Ely, R. T. *Evolution of Industrial Society*, 1906.

Faulkner, H. U. *American Economic History*, 1924.

Fay, C. R. *Life and Labor in the Nineteenth Century*, 1921; limited to England, but a fresh treatment with new material.

Galloway, R. L. *History of Coal Mining in Great Britain*, 1882; *The Steam Engine and Its Inventors*, 1881.

Gibbins, H. de B. *Economic and Industrial Progress of the Century*, 1901.

Hammond, J. C. and B. *The Village Laborer, 1760–1832*, 1911; *The Town Laborer, 1769–1832*, 1917; *The Skilled Laborer, 1770–1832*, 1919.

Hammond, M. B. *The Cotton Industry*, 1897.

Hendrick, B. J. *The Age of Big Business*, 1919; *The Story of Life Insurance*, 1907.

Howard, E. D. *The Cause and Extent of the Recent Economic Progress of Germany*, 1907.

Hulbert, A. B. *The Paths of Inland Commerce*, 1919.

Hyndman, H. M. *Commercial Crises of the Nineteenth Century*, 1892.

Kirkaldy, A. W., and Evans, A. D. *The History and Economics of Transport*, 1915.

Lardner, D. *Railway Economy; a treatise on the new art of transport*, 1850.

Levasseur, E. *Histoire des classes ouvriers de 1789 à 1870*, 1903, 2 vols.

Lippincott, I. *Economic Development of the United States*, 1921.

Lubbock, Basil. *The Colonial Clippers*, 2nd ed., 1921; *The China Clippers*, 1922.

Mackinnon, J. *Social and Industrial History of Scotland from the Union to the Present Time*, 1921.

Mantoux, P. *La révolution industrielle au XVIII° siècle*, 1906.

Mavor, James. *An Economic History of Russia*, 1914, 2 vols.; new ed. 1925.

Montague, G. H. *Rise and Progress of the Standard Oil Company*, 1903; *Trusts of Today*, 1904.

Moody, John. *The Masters of Capital*, 1919; *The Railroad Builders*, 1919.

Mowry, W. A. and A. M. *American Inventions and Inventors*, 1900.

Parsons, Wm. B. *Robert Fulton and the Submarine*, 1922.

Perris, G. H. *Industrial History of England*, 1914; material well selected and presented.

Powell, E. T. *The Evolution of the Money Market, 1385–1915*, 1916.

Pratt, E. A. *History of Inland Transport and Communication in England*, 1912.

Pratt, S. S. *The Work of Wall Street*, 1921; *The Rise of Rail-Power*, 1915.

Rees, J. F. *A Short Fiscal and Financial History of England, 1815–1918*, 1921.

Schmidt, L. B., and Ross, E. D. *Readings in the Economic History of American Agriculture*, 1925.

Slater, Gilbert. *The Making of Modern England*, 1915; a fresh treatment of the period since the industrial revolution.

Slosson, E. E. *Creative Chemistry*, 1920; maybe a trifle too pro-chemical.

Souvestre, P. *Histoire de l'automobile*, 1907.

Sumner, W. G. *History of American Currency*, 1878; *History of Banking in the United States*, 1896.

Tarbell, I. M. *History of the Standard Oil Company*, 1904.

Thompson, Holland. *The Age of Invention*, 1921.

Thurston, R. H. *A History of the Growth of the Steam Engine*, 1878.

Usher, A. P. *An Introduction to the Industrial History of England*, 1920.

Van Metre, *Economic History of the United States*, 1923.

Veblen, T. *Imperial Germany and the Industrial Revolution*, 1915.

Vierendeel, A. *Esquisse d'une histoire de la technique*, 1921, 2 vols.; concerned chiefly with modern machinery.

Warner, G. T. *Landmarks in English Industrial History*, 1912.

Webb, S. and B. *The Decay of Capitalist Civilization*, 1923.

Wood, H. T. *Industrial England in the Middle of the Eighteenth Century*, 1913.

CHAPTER XXXIX

POLITICAL REVOLUTION AND SOCIAL REFORM
(1776–1926)

Among enlightened business men, as well as among workingmen, statesmen, and writers on social subjects, there is a widespread tendency to look for some kind of reconstruction that
will carry industrial and social life forward to a more satisfactory state rather than to restore it to any earlier condition.

—Cheyney

DURING the last one hundred and fifty years have occurred a Intro-
number of political and social changes or movements that have Summary
affected, are affecting, or will affect civilization. First,
a change from the monarchical to the constitutional, or republican, type of government,—not accomplished without revolutions, reactions, and bloodshed. Second, the formation of
new, or revival of suppressed, nationalities either by separation
or unification. Third, the growth of liberalism, under which
term we may comprehend such ideals as individual liberty,
religious freedom, a free press, academic freedom, and free
speech,—perhaps also free trade and a tolerant attitude in
both religious and international questions. Fourth, a broadening of the citizenship in the direction of universal suffrage,
male and female, and what is commonly called democracy.
Fifth, popular education, lest popular rule be ignorant, blind,
misguided, and erring. Sixth, the development of trade unions
and organized labor with its political activities and class feeling. Seventh, socialist agitation, and social and industrial
legislation, based on the feeling that the individual liberty
advocated by the liberal is insufficient, and that society as
a whole must regulate itself. These changes and tendencies
came at different times in varying forms and ways in different
countries. With all such details we cannot begin to deal here,
but in the following pages we will try to suggest the general
current of development as far as may be in chronological outline.

501

An Age of
Revolutions

The relation of revolutions to the course of civilization was a favorite theme with the French Philosophers who edited the *Encyclopedia* about 1750, and they more than once darkly hinted that one was not far off. This prediction found a fulfilment in economic life and scientific thought of which we treat in other chapters, and it was speedily followed by a political revolution in a perhaps unexpected, but appropriate quarter, the new world.

The
American
Revolution

The American Revolution was in part a logical sequel of the separatist tendencies which had animated some of the colonists in their first settlements, and of the representative institutions of local government and the self-reliant attitude in trade and industry which had developed during the seventeenth and eighteenth centuries. It was partly the outcome of a gradually increasing, common feeling and action between the colonies. It was partly a sudden reaction against an ill-timed British reorganization of imperial control and a tactless effort on the part of George III and the Tory party to reassert the royal power and the Acts of Trade, and to force the colonists to pay a larger share of the expense of colonial defense. But it was also due to the liberal philosophy of the age of reason from Locke to Montesquieu. In 1776 the colonies drew up the *Declaration of Independence*, in which they arraigned the arbitrary government of George III and declared themselves a distinct people. They received aid from those European nations like France, Spain, and the Dutch who had suffered in their commerce and colonies in times past at the hands of Great Britain. Private individuals also came of their own accord from Europe to take part in the American Revolution, like the hero in Klinger's drama, *Sturm und Drang*, written in 1776, which has given its name to the Storm and Stress movement in German literature of that time, marked by a passionate agitation for individual freedom and even for free love. On the other hand, a considerable fraction of the colonists themselves remained loyal to the king, and when they lost their property in consequence, migrated to the British West Indies or Canada, which have remained loyal sections of the British Empire. Then again, the colonists had many supporters in England, especially within the Whig party. The affair of John Wilkes, who had opposed the use of general search warrants in London, as James Otis had opposed them in Boston, was a victory for freedom of the press, and seemed to establish the precedent that a candidate duly elected to parliament by a constituency could not be refused admission by that body.

After the revolutionary war (1775–1783) was over and the independence of the thirteen original colonies had been recognized, they for a time went on under loose articles of confederation, until in 1787–1789 they adopted a written constitution. It provided a stronger central government with such powers as to wage war and negotiate treaties, to coin money and levy taxes on foreign trade, but with separation of the three powers, executive, legislative, and judicial, somewhat as Montesquieu had advised. The constitution was, however, largely a compilation from the provisions and previous experience of the colonial governments themselves. At the head of the new central government was placed a strong executive, the president; elected indirectly by the people for a term of four years. He was limited in foreign policy and treaty-making power and in his administrative and judicial appointments by the requirement of confirmation by the senate. This upper house of the legislature, consisting of two members from each state, was at first somewhat in the nature of a conclave of plenipotentiaries from the thirteen original colonies to safeguard their rights as individual states and check, if necessary, the president and central government. But to pass a vote in the senate, a majority, or in some cases two-thirds, of the members present sufficed, so that one or two states could not block a measure. Not until 1913, however, was it made law that senators must be elected by popular vote of their states; previously they had been chosen by the state legislatures. In the lower house of representatives the states had members according to their population who were elected by all who could vote for members of the state legislature, but in some states a restricted suffrage persisted for a long time. To induce the southern states to sign the constitution, the Convention left the abolition of slavery to the individual states, assured the continuance of the African slave-trade until 1808, and permitted the slave-holding states to count three-fifths of their slaves as population, although none of the slaves could vote. On the other hand, slavery was forbidden in the new northwest territory between the Ohio and Mississippi rivers. The practice initiated by George Washington, the first presi-

The Constitution of the United States

dent, of an annual message to Congress enables the executive
to suggest the main points of the legislative program.   He
further has the power to veto acts of Congress, but these may
be passed over his veto by a two-thirds vote in each house.   On
the other hand, the constitution provides the power of impeach-
ment as a check by Congress upon the executive.

As for the judiciary there are both municipal courts, county
courts, state courts, and federal courts, the last named alone
being controlled by the central government.   The result has
been great diversity of law in different states.   Chief of the
federal courts is the Supreme Court, which has power to pass
upon the constitutionality of laws enacted by Congress and to
protect the individual citizen in his rights under the constitution.   To insure the liberty and privacy of the individual,
a number of amendments were almost immediately added to
the constitution.   Although not a perfect instrument, it has
worked remarkably long and well for a written document, and
has proved adaptable to rapidly changing conditions.   The
country so governed long served as a haven for the needy and
oppressed from other lands and as an example of free institutions and free opportunity.

The French
Revolution

Five days after Washington was ceremoniously inaugurated
in Federal Hall, New York, almost on the spot where the Stock
Exchange now stands, the Estates General of France met for
the first time since 1614, summoned to deal with the critical
financial condition of that country.   In other words, absolute
monarchy and benevolent despotism admitted its inability to
deal with the situation alone and revived the representative
institutions of the middle ages.   But these had rested in part
upon class distinctions and outworn institutions which the
philosophers had been attacking and which had lost their
original popularity.   Accordingly the six hundred representatives of the Third Estate, who alone were in any sense popularly
elected, refused to recognize the three hundred representatives
of the clergy and the three hundred representatives of the
nobility as separate estates, but invited them to join themselves
in a united body which should proceed to give France a new
constitution.   Since many representatives of the clergy were
parish priests who were in sympathy with the lower classes,
such a single house was sure to have a large popular majority.
It should be realized that while the American colonies had had

two centuries of constant experience with representative assemblies and also had gradually learned how to cooperate in
war and peace under conditions of storm and stress through
several decades before the adoption of the constitution, the
French since 1614 had never met in any general assembly, and,
with the exception of a few provinces and towns, had almost
no local legislative experience to guide them.   Also all educated persons had been trained to despise the middle ages,
feudalism, the church, and the gilds.

It was therefore quite to be expected that the assembly
should frame a theoretical constitution on the basis of ideal
general principles and reason, and that its members should
regard as fundamental a Declaration of the Rights of Man.
It is greatly to their credit that they concerned themselves with
the rights of human beings in general instead of merely with
those of Frenchmen in particular.   It must be added that they
failed to adopt a Declaration of the Rights of Women proposed by a few of that sex.   It was also not surprising that
all privileges of the nobility, all remnants of feudalism and
serfdom, and the gilds were abolished, that the lands of the
church were confiscated to save the state from bankruptcy, and
that the clergy were submitted to a Civil Constitution by which
they were to be chosen by the people and supported by the
state.   And it showed some insight that, in imposing a more
uniform local organization, the Assembly retained unchanged
the 44,000 (in 1921, 37,963) communes, rural and municipal,
which had been the vital cells of liberty and local government
back in the twelfth and thirteenth centuries.   The power of
the king and his ministers was greatly reduced.   At the same
time property, or rather tax-paying, qualifications were established both for voters and office-holders, but there was method
in this, since some of the patriots of France, then as now,
showed little inclination to pay the price of liberty in taxation.
What is most remarkable is that the work of the constitutional
assembly as outlined above has proved permanent with the
exception of the single house legislature and limited monarchy,
the property qualifications, and the popular election of the
clergy, which Napoleon, by the Concordat with the papacy
of 1801–1802, restored to the church and government.   The
chief criticism to be made of the Constitutional Assembly is
that it did not satisfactorily deal with the financial crisis

Work of the
Constitu-
tional
Assembly

which the Estates General had been summoned to settle, or with the riots in Paris and the revolts of the peasants, and thereby imperilled the entire revolutionary movement. This, however, was not so much its fault as that of the king and court who failed to maintain order, or to cooperate with the assembly, and of the localities and individual citizens who would not pay their taxes, or keep order. At the same time, it must be admitted that the revolutionary agitation in Paris and outbreaks of the peasants hastened the passing of reforms by the assembly.

Later Stages of the French Revolution

But then this violence got out of hand; fanatics and extremists struggled for control. Although the new constitution had renounced wars of conquest, France plunged into war with Austria, Prussia, and other states. There were conspiracies, executions, massacres, and great economic distress. France was declared a republic, but dictatorial power was exercised first by the Committee of Public Safety with from nine to twelve members and the Committee of the Commune of Paris with twenty members, then from 1795 to 1799 by the Directory, a board of five, then by Napoleon as First Consul (1799–1804) and Emperor (1804–1814). Theatrical gestures of equality and progress were made, such as the abolition of all other modes of address than "Citizen"—a title that was further conferred on foreigners like George Washington, Tom Paine, Jeremy Bentham, Priestley, and Wilberforce who were regarded as benefactors of humanity,—the changing of Notre Dame into a Temple of Reason, the abandoning of the Christian era for a new era of the French Republic beginning September 22, 1792, and substitution for Sunday of a holiday every tenth day. More sensible was the adoption of months of thirty days each with five intercalary days, which unfortunately proved only temporary, and the permanent adoption of the metric system of weights and measures—a great gain for science. Male attire has been simpler since the French Revolution, although the factory may have had something to do with this. Cottons and woolens replaced silks, satins, and velvets; pantaloons succeeded knee-breeches. The Revolutionists did much damage to churches and works of art.

Work of Napoleon

Napoleon made positive contributions to civilization, bringing the administrative system, local and central, into good working order, putting the finances on a sound basis, and giving France a national code of civil law.   The *Code Napoleon* was favorable to employers and unfavorable to organized labor. The Constitutional Assembly had declared for free elementary education, yet not much was accomplished in the way of public schools, probably from lack of funds, until Napoleon's time. In general he was ready to patronize almost any side of civilization, if it would only recognize his government, but he suppressed such inconvenient manifestations of liberty as the free press of Paris.   He carried still further the aggressive foreign policy of the republic, which had deluded itself into thinking that France was entitled to the frontiers of Roman Gaul and with the consoling thought that it was bestowing the blessings of liberty upon peoples whom it annexed.   Napoleon extended his administrative reforms to other parts of Europe, in which he continued the work of the benevolent despots rather than that of the French Revolution.   Nevertheless he freed the peasants of Poland from serfdom in 1807, and his government in Italy permitted that land to make rapid progress.

The first outbreak of the French Revolution aroused no little enthusiasm in England, where a Society for Constitutional Information, founded in 1780, was already agitating for parliamentary reform and universal suffrage by ballot, and the young Tory prime-minister, Pitt (1783–1801), had not yet grown reactionary.   But immediately the French revolutionists began to attack the hereditary nobility, vested privilege, and landed property, most respectable British public opinion adopted the same attitude to the French Revolution as most respectable public opinion in the United States adopted towards the Russian revolution after the Bolsheviks gained control of it.   When the French invaded the Austrian Netherlands, war with England became inevitable, just as when Germany invaded the same territory in 1914.   As the war went on, the ruling classes became as alarmed at the slightest manifestation of liberal sentiment or desire to improve the government, as the ruling classes in the United States were during the years 1917–1920, and a number of persons were heavily punished for such expressions, although in the main the laws of sedition and censorship which had been passed for this purpose were laxly enforced.   The result of this policy of repression upon ardent young geniuses like Byron and Shelley

Effect of the French Revolution on the Reform Movement in England

was to fan the higher the revolutionary spirit and detestation of existing institutions.   But except that 1802 saw a *Health and Morals Act to Regulate the Labor of Bound Children* (i. e. gangs of orphans and pauper apprentices) *in Cotton Factories,* and that Fox carried the abolition of the slave trade in 1806, there was little improvement in government or social reform until after the final defeat of Napoleon at Waterloo (1815).   Peace ended England's war time monopolies and markets, and brought bad harvests, high prices, and unemployment in its train.   There was great social misery and unrest on the part of the disillusioned people, while the government for several years continued its repressive attitude towards all public agitation for reform.   Equally reactionary were the governments just after 1815 in most other countries of Europe.   Finland and Russian Poland, however, had constitutions of their own under the Czar.

National
Revolutions
of the Early
Nineteenth
Century
The example of the United States and the reaction against Napoleon's rule in the European states conquered by him, or, following these wars of liberation, against the rule of their returning monarchs, which was often more inefficient, burdensome, and unenlightened than the Napoleonic regime, produced a series of national revolutions in the early nineteenth century. During the struggle against Napoleon the Spaniards had proclaimed the Constitution of 1812 which gave legal equality, popular sovereignty, and religious freedom.   But the restored Bourbon monarch suppressed it.   Indeed, both he and the restored Bourbon king in Naples ruled so tyrannically that their subjects forced them by revolts to grant constitutions.   But other monarchs of Europe intervened and repressed these movements and a third in Piedmont.   The Bourbon kings of Spain and the Two Sicilies then took a vengeance on the liberals that made the reign of terror of the French Revolution seem mild by comparison.   The colonies of Spain and Portugal in Central and South America had, however, in the meantime established independent republics or empires.   When the monarchs of continental Europe proposed to reduce them, too, to obedience, James Monroe, president of the United States, warned them off the western hemisphere in the famous Monroe Doctrine of 1823, and Great Britain, which generally favors small nationalities outside her own empire, recognized the South American republics.   Portugal from 1820 to 1834 was

in the throes of a struggle for constitutional government.   The war of the Greeks for independence from Turkey (1821–1829) aroused widespread feeling in their favor and finally the intervention of Russia, France, and England on their behalf, while the Serbs were granted local autonomy in 1830.

In America something almost revolutionary occurred when the people finally succeeded in electing as president Andrew Jackson (1829–1837), who was not one of the office-holding class but a product of the frontier.   Until 1820 the presidential electors had been chosen in most cases by the state legislatures, but in 1824 in eighteen out of twenty-four states they were elected directly by the people.   Of the four candidates Jackson then received the most votes though not the necessary majority.   The House of Representatives, however, decided in favor of another candidate.   Jackson's supporters complained that the voice of the people had been disregarded, and in 1828, when in all except two states the people voted directly for the presidential electors, Jackson was triumphantly returned, and again in 1832 by an even larger majority.   When the constitution was adopted, all thirteen original states had property qualifications for the suffrage; by 1837 universal manhood suffrage prevailed in most of the northern and western states.   Jackson's success in 1828 was also due to a well-organized presidential campaign carried on for three years previously, and to the fact that he introduced into the federal government the spoils system, already not unknown in the states, rewarding his supporters with public offices.   Ever since that time political parties have tended to run for office a candidate who would make a popular appeal, and all sorts of public demonstrations, mass-meetings, fervid oratory, profuse promises, and "spell-binding" have been employed to charm the ear and secure the vote of the ordinary citizen who has no very clear idea what it is all about.   In more recent times the newspapers mould to a large extent the mind of the average citizen, and in their turn are moulded by it.

Popular Sovereignty and Manhood Suffrage in America

In France the restored Bourbon monarch had granted representative government patterned more nearly after the English parliament than after the American Congress or French revolutionary assemblies.   There was, however, no ministerial responsibility.   In general, reforming European governments in the nineteenth century inclined to follow the British model,

The July Revolution of 1830

probably as more consonant with European conditions, especially with monarchy and aristocracy. In France at this particular time a high tax-paying suffrage resulted in the election of parliaments less liberal than the king himself. His reactionary successor, Charles X, was overthrown by the July Revolution of 1830, when Louis Philippe was installed in his stead as a strictly constitutional monarch, but the voters were increased to only about 200,000. France was still able to touch the spark in Europe. Her Revolution of 1830 led Belgium in the same year to declare its national independence of the Netherlands, with which since the overthrow of Napoleon it had been united in one monarchy. There were also revolutionary movements in Germany, Poland, Switzerland, and Italy, but all failed, and Russian Poland lost its constitution of 1815.

The English Reform Act of 1832

In England during the previous decade there had been reform of prisons and the penal code, and other humanitarian measures, improvement of the police, finances, and tariff, and further steps towards religious liberty, of which the chief was the admission in 1829 of Roman Catholics to parliament. By this time the demand for parliamentary reform had become irresistible. As a result of the economic revolution the density of population had shifted from the southeast to the center of England. By 1820 Manchester and Liverpool had over 130,000 inhabitants; in the next ten years these and Sheffield, Birmingham, Leeds, and Bradford increased forty per cent more. Yet these great manufacturing and trading centers had no representatives in parliament, while ancient boroughs which now were quite deserted still had two members each, who were almost always nominees of some great landowner. But the governing classes stubbornly resisted any redistribution of seats. On the other hand, there was a great demand from the radicals and lower classes for a broadening of the suffrage as well as for a redistribution of seats. After two years of agitation and struggle, during which the country sometimes seemed on the point of rebellion, the third attempt in the way of a reform bill finally went through as the Reform Act of 1832. This, on the whole, satisfied the new centers of population by its redistribution of seats in parliament, but it did not greatly broaden the suffrage (about 700,000 voters) and so left the lower classes discontented. The new parliament, however, pro-

ceeded to institute a more democratic type of government in
the municipalities, to reform the poor law—more in the interest
of the tax-payer than of the poor,—to make the first grant
for public education, to emancipate the slaves in British dominions, and to pass the first really effective factory legislation, regulating child labor.

Meanwhile new schools of social and political thought had
been developing. In 1789 Jeremy Bentham (1748–1832) had
published his *Introduction to the Principles of Morals and
Legislation,* which he based upon utilitarianism, or the greatest happiness of the greatest number. "Every man is to count
for one, and no man for more than one," or as Goethe (1749–
1832), whose lifetime was almost coincident with Bentham's,
more poetically put it, "Nur alle Menschen zusammen machen
die Menschheit aus." Of course, some kindly oriental sages
had long before carried this line of thought much further, and,
holding that every living creature had a right to count for
one and no more than one, had cheerfully allowed themselves
to be bitten by myriads of mosquitoes for the sake of the greatest happiness of the greatest number, or, like Buddha, had
offered their bare flesh to the eagle pursuing the dove. But
Bentham, limiting his consideration to the happiness of human beings, held that the best way to secure the public good
was to allow each man to pursue his own self-interest and then
let the majority rule or overrule the minority. Furthermore
he was always asking concerning any institution or practice,
"What is the use of it?" He attacked the devotion of so
much time to the study of Latin and Greek, heartily disliked
every kind of religion, and held that any popular form of
amusement such as skittles—or jazz, to bring Bentham's philosophy more up-to-date,—if it furnishes more general pleasure
than such cultured pursuits as the arts and sciences, music and
poetry, is more valuable than they. He also had little or no
respect for the historic past, contending that the English
common law and constitution were unsystematic and unscientific, and that he could legislate offhand for any people with
much better results than their existing government. He emphasized the need of technical training and business methods
in government, and was full of specific practical schemes and
devices for the public good. It is evident that his philosophy
was a popular and easy one, suited to ordinary human nature,

Utilitari-
anism

to the rapidly increasing population, to the new conditions resulting from the economic revolution, to the democratic and humanitarian and social service ideals of the past century, but unsympathetic with what had hitherto been considered the highest aims of civilization and attributes of human nature.

Comte

The French philosopher and sociologist, Comte (1798–1857), on the other hand, while emphasizing the importance of sociability, held that intellectual development is the most important and the determining power in the history of human progress. In other words, he introduced a qualitative instead of merely a quantitative standard.

The Problem of Capital and Labor

The problem of labor and capital in the modern sense and the grievances of workingmen against the existing economic system had hardly existed until the economic revolution had gotten well under way. The framers of the American constitution and the French revolutionists had considered such problems as negro slavery, the peasantry, and the gilds, but were unacquainted with the masses of labor employed together in large industrial undertakings and with the business corporations of today. In the course of the nineteenth century, however, the condition and attitude of the laboring class began to attract or force itself upon public attention. It is a question whether in any previous stage of civilization the workers had been any better off than they have been since the economic revolution, and whether their present discontent is not largely due to the fact that they see so many more persons than formerly who are vastly better off than themselves.

Period of So-called *Laisser-faire* in England

The modern labor problem began in England where the economic revolution and factory system began. The doctrine of *laisser-faire* in favor with economists in the late eighteenth and early nineteenth centuries, that the state should not interfere with business or try to control economic forces, would seem to be the very antithesis of socialism, and is often blamed for all the trouble that resulted. As a matter of fact, *laisser-faire* was never given a fair trial. Had the English government scrupulously abstained from any legislation whatever of an economic character during the beginnings of the economic revolution, labor might have worked out its own salvation then and there, and the evils of the present capitalistic system have been avoided. Instead, the government put through all sorts of legislation in favor of English landlords and manu-

facturers and merchants, while it erased from the statute book
the old laws that were designed for the protection of the laborers. The artisans struggled hard for the retention of the
Statute of Apprentices which empowered the justices of the
peace to maintain just wages, but the justices allowed the
employers to pay inadequate wages and then supplemented
these by pauper doles at the expense of the tax-payer. In
1813 the wage clause of the Statute of Apprentices was
formally repealed, "practically," we are told, "at the dictation
of Ricardo and other economists." But why did they not
dictate the repeal of the Combination Acts of 1799–1800, which
forbade any agreement of workingmen to advance their wages,
shorten their hours, or determine who their fellow laborers
should be, and which have been called "an undisguised exercise
of power of the employing class to use their membership in
parliament to legislate in their own interest"? Nor were the
Acts of Enclosure, the protective duties on industries, the
Corn Laws, the laws against the exportation of English machinery and specifications, or even against artisans leaving the
country, in any way in accordance with the spirit or letter of
laisser-faire.

No sooner were the aforesaid Combination Acts repealed in
1824, than labor showed its teeth by numerous strikes, whereupon parliament made haste to pass a new act greatly limiting the activities of trade unions and strikers. The new parliament after the Reform Act of 1832 was no more favorable
to trade unions. Six men were sentenced to seven years penal
transportation for founding a Friendly Society of Agricultural Laborers who were to be urged not to work for less than
ten shillings a week. The nation-wide unions founded in this
period did not have much permanence, often collapsing as
rapidly as they were formed. Sometimes their treasurers ab-
sconded with the societies' funds; indeed, one of the great
difficulties has been to obtain legal protection of trade union
funds from conservative judges. Parliament in the forties
passed some further factory legislation on behalf of child
and female labor, while an exposure of the horrible conditions
in the mines led in 1842 to an act forbidding all work underground by women and children. Meanwhile the British workingmen were interesting themselves mainly in the People's
Charter, a demand for universal male suffrage, in cooperative

The Labor
Movement
and
Socialism
in England

stores and societies, and in the socialism of Robert Owen (1771–1858) who, after conducting model mills as an employer, was less successful in the ideal communities that he founded. Socialism may be briefly defined as public control of all means of production and public distribution of the wealth so produced.

Revolutions of 1848

Another year of revolutions in Europe came in 1848. In France artisans of Paris, who were not yet workers in factories but who wished the establishment of national workshops to insure them employment, were largely instrumental in the uprising of 1848 which led to the Second Republic with universal male suffrage. But the Assembly, representing France as a whole, used troops to suppress them with much bloodshed, and the resulting government under Louis Napoleon, first as president, then as emperor, was very much in the interest of the *bourgeoisie* and of business enterprise. In the British Isles Chartism, i. e. the movement for the People's Charter, ended tamely in 1848. An attempted revolution in Ireland was even more of a fiasco. The revolutionary movement spread, however, from France to the various states of Germany, Central Europe, and the Italian peninsula. But in the end the concessions which had resulted were withdrawn, or amounted to little, except in the kingdoms of Sardinia, Denmark, Holland, and the smaller states of Germany. Many German liberals of 1848 came to the United States for the freedom that was lacking in Prussia and Austria. There was also a great stream of immigration from Ireland, where a terrible potato famine in 1846 had been followed by wholesale eviction of small tenants.

The Crimean War and Russian Progress

A series of wars now occurred which rather gave the impression that national ends could be served, even best served, by deceitful and unscrupulous diplomacy. In the Crimean War (1854–1856), England, France, and Sardinia came to the aid of Turkey against Russia, postponing the independence of the Balkan states, although Moldavia and Wallachia were now granted local autonomy and were later united as Rumania. After the war the policy of Nicholas I (1825–1855), of keeping Russia free from western ideas, education, and liberalism, was for a time abandoned by Alexander II (1855–1881), who emancipated the peasants, instituted administrative and judicial reforms, and gave some powers of local government to the Zemstvos or elective district assemblies. Meanwhile

MODERN STEEL STRUCTURES

Left, a 24-story building in the course of construction; right, the Woolworth Tower, New York City.

MODERN TRANSPORTATION

Above, the S. S. *Leviathan*, the largest trans-Atlantic liner; below, a modern steam locomotive.

many of the educated classes became Nihilists (that is, nothing in Russia satisfied them) and attempted to spread their views to the peasants.   The government then reverted to a repressive policy, while the Nihilists resorted to assassinations and secret terrorism, culminating in the assassination of Alexander II himself.

Sardinia, which had entered the Crimean War to gain European standing and prestige, was now helped by Louis Napoleon in the Austro-Sardinian War of 1859 to annex Lombardy.   This success led the other states of Italy to overthrow their existing governments and unite under the king of Sardinia, who became king of Italy in 1861, with a parliament. By three successive wars with Denmark (1864), Austria (1866), and France (1870), Bismarck united the petty German states into one empire with the king of Prussia as emperor.   A Bundesrath of sixty-one members representing the monarchs of the component states, initiated legislation, and had more power than the popularly elected Reichstag, which served chiefly as a place for the expression of public opinion.

Unification of Italy and Germany

In the American Civil War (1861–1865) the southern slave-holding states failed to make good their claim to independent sovereignty and the right of secession from the Union.   Human slavery was abolished, but the negro problem still remains.   For a decade following the war Congress tried to force the southern states to admit all negroes to full citizenship.   Corrupt "carpet-bag" politicians from the north organized and controlled the negro vote to the great detriment of property holders and public decency.   In the end the native white population everywhere regained control, and the North has since left the South to solve its own problems.   In other ways the period of reconstruction following the war was a trying one for the South.   But since in race, language, and institutions it was really homogeneous with the North, the breach was soon healed, and the United States became a stronger and more united nation.   On the contrary, when the Polish rebellion of 1863 against Russia failed, it was followed by a policy of Russification which only served to alienate the Poles the more.

Civil War and Reconstruction in the United States

Again in the Russo-Turkish War of 1877–1878, Russia came to the relief of the oppressed Balkans and would have almost wholly freed the peninsula from Turkish control, establishing

The Near East Problem

the complete independence of Rumania, Serbia, Montenegro, and a "Greater Bulgaria," had not the powers of central and western Europe again interfered in this Near Eastern question. We cannot pursue further the vexed history of these Balkan nationalities whose very names as well as boundaries have kept fluctuating ever since and very likely will continue to do so, who have been the source of repeated wars, who have committed as revolting atrocities at one another's expense as they ever suffered from the Turks, and who have as yet contributed little to civilization. But this is only the natural outcome of the fall of Byzantine civilization centuries ago before nomadic and Slavic stagnation. Perhaps had Germany been allowed to carry out her Berlin to Bagdad policy of pacific exploitation of the Near East, she would have galvanized these regions and Turkey itself into new life; perhaps they will now proceed to work out their own salvation.

The Labor Movement from 1848 to 1867

In 1848 had been issued at Brussels the Communist Manifesto urging the workingmen or proletariat of all countries to unite against the bourgeoisie or capitalistic regime. No international organization, however, resulted until 1864. In 1859 the British parliament allowed the trade unions to take action involving other workmen than their members and to persuade others to join them in striking. But a London firm in the building trades promptly discharged one of its employees for daring to present a petition of the carpenters, masons, and bricklayers for a nine-hour day, and although the unions struck, they ultimately had to return to work on the old conditions. In 1860, however, the first conciliation board, composed of employers and employees, was formed in the Nottingham hosiery trade, connected with the oldest of textile machines, the stocking-knitting-frame. In 1864 and 1868 France for the first time permitted strikes and labor organizations, but only to a limited extent. Almost the first piece of labor legislation in the United States was when Massachusetts in 1867 limited the work of children under fourteen to ten hours a day. Labor organization, too, began chiefly after the Civil War when prices had risen much more rapidly than wages.

Karl Marx

One of the authors of the Communist Manifesto of 1848 was Karl Marx. Instead of allowing him to effervesce daily as a newspaper editor against the government at Cologne and be soon forgotten, the authorities first drove him to Paris, where

he absorbed the notions of the Utopians, and then into the
British Museum where he could read and think and bottle up
his ideas for years, with the consequence that in his book,
Das Kapital (1867), which has been translated into almost
every civilized tongue, they acquired such a "kick" that they
seem to intoxicate every member of the proletariat who reads
it with the spirit of "Arise, ye Goths, and glut your ire."

For some time after 1867, however, conditions were not **The Labor**
favorable for any such proletariat uprising.   In England the **Movement**
Second Reform Act of 1867 extended the suffrage so as to **after 1867**
include most skilled laborers and members of unions, and was
followed by considerable legislation regulating industries in
the interests of the employees.   By such means the two political parties of Conservatives and Liberals angled for the
labor vote.   Although two labor members appeared in parliament as early as 1874, there was no important labor party
until the present century.   In France, the unpatriotic outbreak of the Commune at Paris in the nation's hour of distress
following the Franco-Prussian War, brought socialism into
general disfavor for many years.   In 1884, nevertheless, the
restrictions were removed as regards strikes and trade unions,
which thereupon increased within a decade from 68 to 2178.
Bismarck's policy of suppression was unsuccessful against the
German socialists.   His national insurance laws of 1883, 1884,
and 1889 against sickness, accident and old age, and in-
capacity respectively, were really themselves socialistic.   They
did much to content the laboring classes, and have been since
imitated by other European countries.   On the other hand,
through the organization of the Socialist party, the workers of
Germany were securing the necessary political experience to
enable them some day to take the helm of government.

The success of military Prussia in unifying Germany caused **Militarism**
the adoption of universal military service as a fundamental institution of the German Empire, in which the army and its
general staff were largely uncontrolled by the civil government
and popular representatives.   Thus German liberty yielded to
those Roman ideals of militarism, imperialism, and a disciplined
and dutiful people, against which its barbarian warriors had
successfully struggled many centuries before.   The other nations of the continent followed the same path of conscription
and great standing armies.   England, which in 1628 had de-

clared against martial law and since 1689 had sanctioned military discipline in a small standing army for only a year at a time, relied rather on its navy.   In the United States the armies of the Civil War were at once disbanded and resumed peaceful pursuits, for which the rapidly developing country afforded plenty of opportunities.

State Education

The other states of Europe were also behind Prussia in provision for public education.   After Horace Mann became secretary of the state board of education in Massachusetts, where in 1839 he established the first normal school in the United States, he visited schools abroad and found those of Prussia the best.   He was much impressed by such points as that the teacher never held the book open before him, never remained seated while conducting the class, and held the attention and interest of the children without resort to punishment. England first adopted universal public elementary education in 1870, made it compulsory in 1876, and free in 1891.   Italy adopted a program of free, compulsory, secular education in 1877, but began really to enforce it only in 1904.   By 1914 illiteracy was reduced to about one-fourth of the population. In France laws of 1881–1882 made education free, compulsory, and secular.   In the United States the process of registration for conscription in the recent war revealed an alarming percentage of illiteracy.   In Spain in 1910 nearly two-thirds of the population could not read or write, so that universal male suffrage, introduced in 1890, would seem to provide a very unenlightened basis for government.   Most European cabinets include a minister of education, but in America state universities at the top as well as elementary schools at the bottom of the public educational system are the creation of the individual states.   Nearly all of the states now have compulsory education laws.

Church and State

In England, France, and Portugal the setting up of a public school system was hampered by the existence of schools supported by religious bodies which had hitherto been favored by the state, and by the question what, if any, religious instruction should be given in the public schools.   In England, with its Established church and general respect for Christianity, these questions were compromised; the schools maintained by religious bodies continued to receive some financial aid from the state, and in the new secular elementary schools the Bible might be read and explained to those children whose parents did not object to this, but there was to be no denominational religious instruction.   Somewhat the same arrangement as to religious exercises in the public schools prevails in some of the United States.   In the anti-clerical French and Portuguese republics the school question was bound up with the relations of the state to the Roman Catholic church.   In 1901–1905, France first suppressed the religious orders or congregations, closing or secularizing their schools and confiscating their property; then completely separated church and state, depriving all religious bodies of any state support and also freeing them from political interference.   Portugal followed the same course in 1910, and then established free, compulsory, secular education in 1911.

Defeat in the Franco-Prussian War had sealed the fate of Louis Napoleon and the Second Empire, and led to the gradual and somewhat reluctant establishment of the Third French Republic, for monarchical sentiment was still strong in France whose people had grown conservative.   The governments of the French Republic and the new Kingdom of Italy were in many ways similar.   Both had parliaments of two houses, a senate, in one case indirectly elected for nine years, in the other appointed for life, and a popularly elected Chamber of Deputies which exercised the main legislative authority.   Both had the English cabinet system and ministerial responsibility to the lower house, but lacked the two party system which had hitherto prevailed in England and the United States, and so made frequent ministerial changes to satisfy the different conflicting interests represented in the Chamber without resorting to dissolution of the Chamber and a new popular election.   In both states local government was strongly centralized in the hands of prefects appointed by the central government over artificially created areas which purposely disregarded local history and sentiment, if not convenience.   This in itself is almost proof enough that both these "nations," for all their pretense of popular government, are arbitrary machines, well adapted to the purposes of certain "interests" and politicians, but mortally afraid of any spontaneous and natural expression of actual self-government or local autonomy by the people themselves.   It is idle to prate of natural national boundaries when the very nations concerned disregard immemorial local

Recent Republics and Parliamentary Governments

areas, associations, and traditions within their own recent boundaries. Both the French and Italian governments were also too often marked by venality, corruption, and political scandals in contrast to the honest and efficient government of the German Empire. Spain adopted parliamentary government in 1876; Japan did so in 1889, but without ministerial responsibility to parliament. In the same year Brazil became a republic; Portugal, in 1910; China, in 1912. England in 1911 reduced the legislative power of the House of Lords to a suspensive veto over acts passed by the House of Commons, and became virtually a democracy. The long, unwilling union of Roman Catholic and Gaelic Ireland with the United Kingdom of England, Wales, and Scotland was at last, after much grievance, bitterness, strife, and suffering, dissolved in 1922 by the creation of the Irish Free State. It includes all Ireland except a few northern counties which are Protestant and remain loyal, owing to their having been occupied by English and Scotch settlers in the sixteenth and seventeenth centuries. The Irish Free State remains a member of the British Empire, and represents a compromise between various previous proposals of Home Rule for Ireland and the Irish Republic attempted in 1919.

Growth of Self-Government in the British Empire

Those British colonies which were largely settled by English-speaking people, such as Canada, Cape Colony, Australia, and New Zealand, acquired self-government with representative parliaments and ministerial responsibility about the middle of the nineteenth century. In matters of foreign policy, however, they remained under the British foreign office, and they had governor-generals representing the crown. The Boers, or original Dutch settlers at the Cape of Good Hope, did not accept with a good grace their home government's surrender of them in 1815 to Great Britain. In 1836, having become further disgusted with various features of British rule, they made the Great Trek into the interior, where they founded the Orange Free State and the South African Republic, or Transvaal. These two tiny republics of fighting farmers carried on a long and plucky struggle against the repeated efforts of the British Empire to absorb them and against the influx of foreign population, attracted by the discovery of gold and diamond mines, which threatened to swamp them. Finally in the Boer War of 1899–1902 they were forced to enter the British Empire, but were soon granted self-government, and are now members of the South African Union. With the French population of Canada the British government dealt more wisely from the start, perhaps because in Quebec there were neither other races nor gold and diamond mines to complicate the situation.

Since the world war there has been an increasing demand and agitation from non-English and non-European peoples under British rule for the control of their own affairs. The 1919 Reforms Bill for India granted the natives an increased share in the government. They have continued to agitate, however, for more complete self-government. Macaulay wrote in 1833 that "the proudest day in English history" would be when the people of India became so "instructed in European knowledge" and advanced in "the capacity for better government" as to "demand European institutions"; but there seems to be some disagreement whether that day has now arrived. Egypt, where England, although nominally present only in an advisory capacity, controlled the government from 1882 to 1914, when she took advantage of the war to change her dubious status into a protectorate, in 1922 as a result of Nationalist agitation was recognized as an independent sovereign state. Just what this will mean remains to be seen, as various matters have been reserved for future discussion. Since this sentence was written, the assassination by Egyptians of General Sir Lee Stack, Sirdar of the Egyptian Army and Governor-General of the Sudan, has resulted in a British ultimatum and practical resumption of control, while an appeal of the Egyptian parliament to the League of Nations has passed unheard, the British Government insisting that this is "a domestic matter."

Agitation for Self-Government in India and Egypt

Manhood suffrage, which had been adopted in France in 1848 and in most of the United States even earlier, was realized in England only with the Franchise Act of 1884 and then with some exceptions. In the next year single member constituencies for parliament were adopted, as has been the practice in the Third French Republic except from 1885 to 1889. Italy in 1882 increased the number of voters from 628,000 to over two millions by reducing the age limit from twenty-five to twenty-one and by cutting the property qualification in half. In 1912 the property qualification was totally abolished, and

Progress Towards Universal Suffrage

even illiterate males were allowed to vote, if over thirty.   This raised the voting body to 8,635,000.   Australia and New Zealand adopted women's suffrage before America or any of the European states.   Recently there has been a widespread tendency, both in national and municipal government, towards proportional representation.

Feminism

Modern agitation for women's rights dates, as we have seen, from the French Revolution, when in 1792 Mary Wollstonecraft published her *Vindication of the Rights of Women.*   The movement for women's suffrage dates in England from about 1847, and that for the equal education of women from the foundation of Mount Holyoke Seminary in Massachusetts in 1837, of Oberlin Collegiate Institution in Ohio as co-educational in 1833, and of Queen's College, London, in 1848. The cause found a prominent male advocate in John Stuart Mill who in 1866 founded the National Society for Women's Suffrage in England and in 1869 published his work, *Subjection of Women.*   The economic and legal position of women, as well as their political and educational status, have been the objects of criticism and reform.   The women's movement, which has been strongest in Scandinavia, England, and America, made itself sufficiently felt in France by the nineties to receive the name *feminism* there.

Increasing Social Sympathy and Science

The closing decades of the nineteenth century were marked by a growing public interest in social welfare work, charity organization, and "the submerged tenth" of the population. The sympathy towards the poor was partly caused by the hard times in the nineties, but an increasing tenderness was shown even towards the criminal.   The Salvation Army and the social settlement were founded.   Social science and statistics strove to solve the problems in a sound, scientific manner.   In Great Britain at least trade unions made up of skilled laborers had become respectable and were accepted without much question as a social and industrial institution.   Moreover, public sympathy was aroused by strikes in such humble and precarious occupations as those of the match girls and dock workers. Legislation was enacted to regulate dangerous and unhealthful occupations, sweatshops, and laundries.

Municipal Ownership and Nationalization

Municipal ownership of public utilities had also been making rapid strides in various countries.   Parks, libraries, galleries and museums, golf-links and playgrounds, baths and markets, waterworks, gasworks, electricity and telephone, docks and ferries, tramways and subways, have been to a greater or less degree controlled by the city government for the use of the populace.   While no one thinks of objecting to national postal service as socialistic, there is more difference of opinion as to the advisability of state railways, which have worked well in Australia, New Zealand, Germany, Switzerland, Norway, and Sweden, but not in France and Italy.   New Zealand, with a purer English population than England itself, early showed the way in compulsory arbitration (1895)—which, however, has sometimes failed to avert strikes—and old age pensions (1898). In Great Britain Lloyd George's budget of 1909 taxed wealth, especially unearned wealth and land, so heavily in order to pay for old age pensions and a war on poverty as well as an increased navy against Germany that it was attacked as socialistic and confiscatory at the time, though it was mild compared to the taxation of large estates and incomes during and since the war.   Public opinion in the United States is growing more and more concerned at the way in which its rich natural resources have been let slip into private hands to be recklessly exploited for immediate profit instead of having been carefully conserved and controlled by the state for the benefit of the nation's future.

With the twentieth century European organized labor and socialists became increasingly aggressive; the cost of living mounted more rapidly than wages; and the consuming public became irritated and alarmed at the frequency and magnitude of strikes and industrial disturbances, from which it suffered more than did capital or labor.   Rightly or wrongly, the general public has got the impression that the attitude of organized labor toward it is the same as that often attributed to the capitalistic corporation, namely, "The public be damned."   The sour, disagreeable, gruff attitude of many street-car conductors, plumbers, carpet-layers, furniture-movers, electricians, and the like to the ordinary householder, occupant of an apartment, or citizen and passenger, has probably lost labor more friends than all its "dangerous doctrines" put together.   Labor legislation, however, has grown apace, England generally leading in this respect.   When in 1901 the House of Lords, acting in its capacity as a court of appeal, held that a trade union could be sued for damages for the acts of its members, parliament, against

The Labor Movement in the Twentieth Century

whose decision there is no court of appeal in the British constitution, passed the Trades Disputes Act of 1906 which made it impossible to bring civil suit against a trade union. Over against this may be set the decision of the United States Supreme Court in the Coronado Coal Case of 1922, that a labor union, although unincorporated, may be sued for its acts as an organization, and prosecuted under the Sherman Anti-Trust Law for restraint of interstate commerce. Until 1911 the members of the British House of Commons received no salaries, and the Labor party was accustomed to pay its campaign expenses and support its representatives in parliament from the funds of the trade unions. The Osbourne Judgment of the House of Lords in 1909 forbade this use of trade union funds for political purposes. Whereupon parliament declared it legal except for those members of the unions who objected to such use of their contributions, and further decreed regular salaries for all members of parliament. In 1908 the Coal Mines Act gave an eight-hour day; in 1909 the state instituted boards to set a minimum wage in certain trades where wages were too low; in 1912 a coal strike resulted in the passage of a Minimum Wage Bill for coal mines. In the United States Massachusetts, in 1912, was the first state to enact a minimum wage law. England set up labor exchanges to relieve unemployment in 1909, and public employment offices now exist in about half of the United States. About two-thirds of the states have provisions for conciliation and arbitration boards; a still greater fraction have workingmen's compensation laws.

Syndicalism and I.W.W.

Just before the world war the socialist and labor parties had made marked gains in the parliaments of Europe, and there had been a great series of strikes involving basic industries such as coal and transportation, and culminating in the Italian general strike of 1914 when all industrial activity was suspended for forty-eight hours. Behind such strikes lay not only specific grievances as to hours and wages, but a demand for nationalization of mines, railroads, and the like. In France, where there has been least labor legislation and the workingmen form a smaller fraction of the population than in more industrial countries, the trade unions have tended to syndicalism, or united "direct action" against their employers by general strikes which cripple both industry and society, and even by steady *sabotage*, that is, doing as slovenly and imperfect work and damaging the machinery and property of the industry as much as possible in order to hasten the downfall of the entire present system.   This tendency was represented in America by the formation in 1905 of the Industrial Workers of the World, but the more conservative and law-abiding American Federation of Labor has, on the whole, kept the guiding hand.   When the world war broke out in Europe, the socialist parties and labor unions in the various lands involved, instead of proclaiming themselves international pacifists and uniting together against the capitalistic state, patriotically supported their respective countries.

In Russia, however, revolution came before the end of the war.   Indeed, it had really begun in 1905, when nationalist uprisings and a general strike had forced Nicholas II to grant Finland a constitution with women's suffrage, and to grant Russia a Duma or legislature of two houses with freedom of speech and of religion.   But these concessions had been largely whittled away, the peasants had been satisfied for the time being with abolition of the redemption tax, foreign capital and the middle classes had been alarmed by the demands and depradations of the artisans, and the army was loyal to the Czar, when the war began.   Misconduct of the war by officialdom and war-weariness of troops and people led to the overthrow of the Czar and ultimately to the establishment of a Republic of Soviets, or local associations of workingmen and soldiers.   At last the proletariat had its chance to make actual experiment of the socialistic state.   The reason why this movement occurred first in Russia and thus far has not spread permanently anywhere else, is not very hard to see.   In Russia the industrial revolution was very recent and had been largely put through by foreign capital.   There was no strongly entrenched, native class of manufacturers and business men with its roots going down into Russian society.   Therefore there was no very strong economic opposition to the Soviets in Russia itself; the great outcry of indignation against them has come from those foreign countries which had *their* capital invested in Russian means of production, which the Soviets now proceeded to confiscate.   The Russian nobility and governmental officials naturally were opposed to the Soviets and lost everything, often even their lives, by the revolution.   As they

The Russian Revolution

were comparatively few, it was not difficult for a few determined men to seize the control from them, especially after all discipline in the army had disappeared, and the soldiers had killed their former officers or elected new ones.   The peasants seem satisfied with the abolition of private property in land, which has been made the common property of the people, since large estates are thus done away with, and collectively at least the actual cultivators have more than before.

The Soviet Experiment   But in the supreme political body, the All-Russian Congress of Soviets, the peasants are allowed only one delegate for every 125,000 as against one for every 25,000 townsmen or artisans.   However, for several centuries the peasants have been unaccustomed to participate in the government of Russia.   Furthermore in the past the government of Russia has never done much for the popular benefit; the Soviets therefore do not have to live up to any very high standard, and they seem to be doing more for popular education than the Czar ever did.   Persons who do not engage in productive labor, for instance priests and monks, and those who employ others for profit, are excluded from the franchise.   The Soviets at first not only nationalized the land, but took over all the instruments of production, such as factories, mines, and railways. They did not succeed in playing these instruments as easily as they had expected, however, and have now leased out the majority of them to private individuals, although a large number are leased to cooperative associations.   They have also largely ceased the compulsory requisitioning of grain from the peasants to supply the towns and soldiers, and have authorized free trading in food and other necessities.   Thus they seem to have failed of full realization of the ideal socialist state, or to have showed that that ideal was somewhat impracticable.   They have had to accept foreign charity to keep the population from starving; after hopelessly depreciating the paper currency and vainly experimenting with index numbers to correlate prices, they have returned to a currency on a gold basis; and their failure to balance their budget and effort to obtain loans from foreign capitalists make a close approach to an admission of failure.   However, their interesting experiment is not yet completed.   While it is of course a dangerous experiment, performed on the living body politic and society by persons perhaps in no sense qualified, and while it resulted like the French Revolution in a reign of terror and damage to civilization, still there was not a vast and widespread amount of civilization in Russia to be destroyed, and the civilized world may congratulate itself that the experiment was not tried elsewhere.

What has made the world generally so afraid of the Soviet experiment, its novelty, is what rather commends it to the historian and the student of civilization. But that old, old, sickeningly monotonous, and heart-rendingly antiquated, oft-repeated experiment of militarism and war, that was tried again in 1914–1918, how the historian of civilization hates to record it, although most historians are still hovering over the field of carnage like so many recording vultures. Brief will be our picture: Germany, Austria, Bulgaria, and Turkey arrayed against France, Russia, Serbia, Belgium, England, Japan, Italy, Rumania, and at last America; brown men from India, black men from Africa, and peasants from Siberia all hurled into the maelstrom of Europe; blonde giants from the Baltic, lanky mountaineers from Tennesse, tall white men from the Antipodes, all of the same Nordic ancestry, meeting now for the first time in wholesale massacre; months in stinking trenches, years in prison camps, lungs poisoned by gases, limbs shattered and features effaced by explosives, minds distraught. We would not derogate from the high motives, heroism and patient endurance of the actual combatants or the devotion of the civilian populations that seconded and supported them, or deny the stupendous character of the conflict which has captivated the popular imagination, but we are writing a history of civilization, not of human sacrifice. And after having slighted the strategy of a Hannibal, Cæsar, Frederick the Great, and Napoleon, we may omit the military operations of the late war, which were colossal in size, but mediocre in mentality except in the use of new inventions. We fear, however, that the great conflict has inculcated, rather than cured the world of, militarism, and has let loose a third dog of war, the air force, in addition to armies and navies.

Before the war various arbitration treaties between nations had been signed, and several international peace conferences had been held. The treaty of peace, thanks to President Wilson, contained a scheme for a league of nations, to which unfortunately the selfish nationalism manifested in other articles

The World War of 1914–1918

The League of Nations

gave the lie.   Moreover, instead of sweeping reforms to remove the economic causes of war there was merely a poorly
planned effort to make exhausted Germany pay the whole cost
of the war, with very unsatisfactory results to all concerned
until the adoption of the Dawes plan in 1924.   Disillusioned
and alarmed by the immediate reversion of our European allies
to their selfish, grasping, pre-war attitude, unselfish American
public opinion was inadequate to force the League of Nations
upon selfish American nationalism, which had been offered
nothing but burdens by the treaty and refused to sink more
billions in helping ungrateful Europe.   Many other states,
however, including neutrals in the recent war and the Central
and South American republics, joined the League of Nations,
which has engaged in various activities and settled some minor
international disputes.   In 1920 it adopted the plan for a
Permanent International Court of Justice, which the Senate
of the United States accepted with reservations in January,
1926.

New Nations and Universal Suffrage
More satisfactory than most other provisions of the treaty
and sequels of the war was the revival of suppressed nationalities such as Poland and Bohemia (the core of Czecho-Slovakia),
Finland, Esthonia, Lithuania, and Latvia; the rectification
of certain national boundaries; the replacing of monarchical
by democratic governments in Germany, Austria, and Turkey
as well as in the new states; and a rather widespread introduction of universal suffrage of both men and women, which
was partly in recognition of war work by women.   In Europe France, Spain, and the Balkan states are now the chief
exceptions to the rule of women's suffrage; in Great Britain
women cannot vote until thirty.   The United States adopted
women's suffrage in 1920 by the Nineteenth Amendment to
the constitution.   Universal suffrage increased the electorate
in Italy to 11,821,168, while in recent elections in Germany
28,196,202 persons actually voted as against 26,661,606 voting in the United States.   It remains, of course, to be seen
how long these new nations, governments, and boundaries will
endure, and whether from the present confusion and turmoil
civilization will emerge triumphant.

Labor on Trial
Socialists derived some crumbs of comfort from war-time
economic activity by noting the efficiency of joint effort with
the means of production placed under state control and directed

by common enthusiasm instead of towards individual profit. Others noted the profiteers, high wages, and uninterrupted employment. The international labor bureau of the league of nations has been called its most flourishing department; its aim is to make the conditions of labor more uniform the world over by raising the standard where it is too low. But there have been many strikes and much radical agitation since the war, together with much persecution of the radicals. In Italy, with nominal universal suffrage, economic activities and society were becoming demoralized when the Fascisti seized the power everywhere and, with Mussolini as dictator, instituted a regime of forced labor, sobriety, and order, seasoned with much sententious bombast, imperialistic "flapdoodle," and occasional bloodshed. The Fascisti, like the Bolsheviks in Russia, are a well-organized minority, only they represent property rather than labor. Great Britain, with longer training in parliamentary and party politics, has followed her usual moderate, unbroken course, and, without revolution or bloodshed, in 1923 placed in power for the first time a ministry representing a plurality in parliament of the labor party, supported for the moment by the Liberals. This British labor party includes intellectuals as well as manual workers, it knows more than its own grievances, and may prove to be the first step in a far more gradual and successful experiment in political and social reform than the too headlong and disruptive Soviet movement. In the election of 1924, however, the Conservatives were returned to power by a large majority but with the threatening problem of unemployment to face. In Germany, since it became a republic, the socialists have been much of the time in power, and they now seem likely to hold the controlling vote in France. Political parties are, however, badly split up in both countries, and coalitions are apt to be of short duration.

BIBLIOGRAPHY

We cannot here sift the immense literature on the war and kindred topics, or do more than mention the works of Gooch, Hayes, Hazen, Robinson and Beard, Schapiro, and E. R. Turner on modern European history, and, in the field of United States history, the two excellent series of volumes by different authors known as *The American Nation Series* (ed. A. B. Hart), and *Chronicles of America* (ed. Allen Johnson), or the briefer *Riverside History of the United States* in 4 vols. and the works of Basset, D. S. Muzzey, and of Hockett and Schlesinger. Some of the books listed at the close of the last chapter apply also to the reforms in England treated of in this chapter. For current events may be recommended *Current History* and the "Record of Political Events" issued annually by the *Political Science Quarterly*. With some exceptions the following books are concerned with the history of the labor movement and socialism:

Ashley, W. J. *Progress of the German Working Classes during the last quarter of a century*, 1904.

Beard, C. A. *Contemporary American History*, 1918; *Cross Currents in Europe Today*, 1923.

Beer, M. *A History of English Socialism*, 1919–1920, 2 vols.

Carlton, F. T. *History and Problems of Organized Labor*, 1920.

Dutcher, Geo. M. *The Political Awakening of the East: studies of political progress in Egypt, India, China, Japan, and the Philippines*, 1925.

Ellis, Havelock. *The Nineteenth Century, An Utopian Retrospect*, 1901; a brief and witty satire.

Ely, R. T. *The Labor Movement in America*, 1902.

Graham, M. W. and Binkley, R. C. *New Governments of Central Europe*, 1924.

Hall, H. D. *The British Commonwealth of Nations*, 1920.

Hayes, C. J. H. *British Social Politics*, 1913.

Hilquit, M. *History of Socialism in the United States*, 1910.

Hutchins, B. L. and Harrison, L. *A History of Factory Legislation*, 1903.

James, H. G. *Brazil after a Century of Independence*, 1925.

Leroy-Beaulieu, P. *The United States in the Twentieth Century*, 1907.

Lingley, C. R. *Since the Civil War*, 1920.

Macdonald, J. Ramsay. *The Socialist Movement*, 1911; by the leader of the British Labor Party and recent prime-minister.

McBain, H. L. and Rogers, L. *The New Constitutions of Europe*, 1922; translated with notes.

Mitchell, John. *Organized Labor*, 1903.

Noyes, J. *History of American Socialisms*, 1870.

Ogg, F. A. *Social Progress in Contemporary Europe*, 1912; *Governments of Europe*, 1913.

Oman, C. W. C. *England in the Nineteenth Century*, 1901; mainly political and imperial.

Orth, S. P. *Socialism and Democracy in Europe*, 1913.

Platonov, S. *A History of Russia*, 1925.

Porter, K. H. *A History of Suffrage in the United States*, 1919.

Rose, J. H. *The Rise of Democracy*, 1904; i.e. in nineteenth century England; well written.

Schlesinger, A. M. *New Viewpoints in American History*, 1922.

Snowden, Ethel. *The Feminist Movement*, 1913.

These Eventful Years; the twentieth century in the making, etc., Encyclopedia Britannica, Inc. 1924, 2 vols.

Webb, S. and B. *History of Trade Unionism*, 1920.

CHAPTER XL

IMPERIALISM AND EXPANSION:
THE GREAT CITY

How is Montaudon, where you have more people?
—*God to a troubadour, just arriving in heaven.*

THE greatly increased production, the great acceleration and multiplication of means of communication, resulting from the economic revolution, have led to a world-wide search for new sources of raw materials and for new markets in which to sell the manufactured products, to a large increase in population, and to the rapid acquisition of new and distant territories or the exploitation of their natural resources by those nations with the most highly developed economic civilization. Other causes have somewhat contributed to these same ends. The desire to continue the old agricultural life undisturbed, or the temporary distress caused by the introduction of new industrial processes or by periods of depression and unemployment have led settlers to move on to new lands or colonies. The advance of medical science has increased population by lessening infant mortality and the ravages of infectious diesases, although this increase has been somewhat counteracted by the greater spread of disease with modern multiplied communication and by the unwholesome conditions of city life. *Causes of Expansion and Increasing Population*

As Great Britain was first in the economic revolution and had already wrested the primacy in sea power from the Dutch and in colonial possessions from the French, she naturally took the lead in world trade and empire. Her loss of colonies in the American Revolution was partially compensated by the strengthening of her hold in Canada and the West Indies through Tory refugees from the United States. In 1788 she began the white settlement of the great southern continent of Australia with convicts. Later the abolition of the slave-trade and then of slavery itself in the West Indies, and the *Growth of the British Empire* introduction of beet-sugar in Europe, ruined the economic prosperity of the British West Indies which had depended on growing sugar-cane. During the French Revolution and Napoleonic wars England acquired almost complete control in India. Through the remainder of the nineteenth century she annexed Burma and pushed forward the northwestern frontier far beyond the Indus into Afghanistan. In 1815 she had been confirmed in various conquests and annexations in both hemispheres, of which the chief was Cape Colony, an entering wedge for her present great possessions in South Africa. Free settlers soon came to Australia, especially with the successive discovery of coal, introduction of sheep-raising, and discovery of gold. Convict settlement and labor were gradually abolished. New Zealand was annexed in 1840. Both it and Australia, located in the neighborhood of overpopulated oriental nations with cheap labor, have thus far maintained the standard of admitting only white immigrants. In 1921 the white population of Australia was 5,436,794; that of New Zealand, 1,218,913. Canada, which did not increase very rapidly in population from 1870 to 1900, has grown faster since 1900, reaching in 1921 the figure of 8,788,483 inhabitants who are almost entirely of white race. On the other hand, in the Union of South Africa in 1921 the white population was 1,519,488 and the colored was 5,409,092, which of course did not include the many millions of British East Africa, Uganda, Rhodesia, Nigeria, and the Gold Coast. When we add India with 247,000,000 natives in British territory and 72,000,000 in native states, we see that the British Empire has been less an expansion of British colonists, although that has been very noticeable, than a search for trade with vast native populations and for territories rich in natural resources which may be developed by British capital and native labor.

Merits and Defects of British Rule

The British take pride in the administration of their empire, which many observers agree has been on the whole more honest, efficient, and enlightened than that of the native rulers who preceded it or who would follow it, should British rule be withdrawn. The further justification is given of British rule that, without unduly interfering with native customs, prejudices, or ideals, it has held an even balance of justice between different classes, colors, races, and interests. The Earl of Cromer's reform of the Egyptian finances and army, and construction of the great dam at Assouan, contributed greatly to the popular welfare and general prosperity of that country. But any officialdom is apt to lose touch and sympathy with popular needs and feeling, to get tied up with red tape, disregard public opinion and grievances, and persist in egregious blunders. This is especially true of a handful of officials—however well-meaning—in the midst of a great mass of native population, with which they have no means of communication or coming to any real understanding, and to which they regard themselves as superior in race, education, political training and knowledge, and general civilization. The natives are naturally less inclined to admit their inferiority, and too often western civilization has been almost forced on them at the mouth of cannon rather than accepted by them. Thus in the case of the Malay States, of which the last were annexed in 1909, it is admitted by British writers that the Malays "seem to have preferred consistently the benighted rule of their own princes to the blessings of government by European methods." Gandhi, who recently aroused a great wave of passive resistance to British rule, European manufactures, and western civilization, is more of a leader after India's heart than any British viceroy. And how can the Chinese feel otherwise about Hong-Kong, which was taken from them in 1842 primarily because they tried by a sort of Boston Tea Party to prevent the importation of opium into China, than most Americans would feel if some foreign power should occupy New York or San Francisco in order to violate the Volstead Act? This is how the Chinese emperor in his Manifesto of 1847 expressed himself concerning the lucrative traffic that has shipped twelve tons of opium into China every day until 1911: "I cannot prevent the introduction of the flaming poison; keen-seeking and corrupt men will, for profit and sensuality, defeat my wishes; but nothing will induce me to derive a revenue from the vice and misery of my people."

In occupying Hong-Kong, however, Great Britain sought trade with China in many other things than opium, so that by 1900 she had in her hands sixty per cent of all China's foreign trade. In general, at that time British trade was even more extensive than the British Empire. The rapid growth of German industry and trade then alarmed Great Britain, but the recent economic chaos of Germany was found to hurt instead

Europe's Far Eastern Trade

of help England, while Japan and the United States have come
to rival her in the far eastern trade.   Japan was forced by a
naval expedition to make a commercial treaty with the United
States in 1854, and soon after admitted other European nations to trade with her.   Other powers of Europe also followed England's example in forcing China to open "treaty
ports" and grant trade concessions.   France gradually took
Indo-China unto herself.

**Different
Reception
of Western
Civilization
in Japan
and in
China**

Japan soon realized the military and economic superiority
of western civilization, and even to a certain extent of western
social and political institutions, which she proceeded to study
and adopt with great gusto.   Feudalism and serfdom were
abolished, the industrial revolution took place almost over
night, a national army was organized like Germany's, a navy
like Great Britain's, a parliamentary government somewhat
less so, legal codes like those of the continent of Europe, compulsory elementary education in public schools like those of
the United States.   Japan did not much mind throwing over-
board her old civilization because it was largely of foreign,
not native, origin, having been in the main borrowed from
China.   In China the old civilization was more ingrained and
deep-seated, the vast area and population more unwieldly, local and voluntary associations stronger, and the bitterness
against foreigners more extreme as a consequence of many
wars of aggression by European powers in the nineteenth century.   Lack of government, or misgovernment under the Manchu dynasty and repeated rebellions also operated as a blight
upon the land.   Therefore western civilization made little head-
way in China.   In 1899–1900 a secret society known as The
League of United Patriots headed an attack upon the foreign
legations and native Christians.   This of course was suppressed, resulting simply in loss to Chinese property and civilization, and in increased foreign influence.   With the overthrow of the Manchu dynasty in 1912 there have come to the
front leaders educated in Europe and America who will perhaps succeed in effecting somewhat the same development in
China as has already occurred in Japan.   But at present
China is still in a chaotic condition.   The greatest change has
been in education and literature; the time-honored examination
system was abolished in 1905, and schools were introduced to
teach "western learning."   In 1918–1919 there were 4,500,-

000 pupils in 134,000 schools. A phonetic script has been adopted, and the simpler spoken language is replacing the literary characters in printed books and periodicals. The following criticism by an Englishman, if just, suggests that there is danger that the Chinese leaders who have been educated abroad may go too far in their imitation of western ways. "I met in Canton some of the chief officials of the revolutionary government . . . I was astounded. They were exactly like American undergraduates. Their whole mentality, so far as I could see, was American. They had not only the manners, the dress, the speech; they had the confidence, the light-heartedness, the easy and disconcerting superficiality." But our English author somewhat dulls the edge of his criticism of modern China and America by complacently continuing, "On the other hand, those educated in England were comparatively critical, sober, and cautious."

The only expansion comparable to that of the British Empire during the past century has been the westward movement of European immigrants to the western hemisphere and of the eastern settlers in the United States and Canada to new lands in the interior and far west. As soon as the revolutionary war was over, settlers from the thirteen original states began to cross the Appalachian Mountains, either transporting their household effects in a covered wagon—known in later days when settlement had passed on to the region west of the Mississippi as a "prairie schooner"—or floating down the Ohio and other rivers on flatboats. Then they would build rude log cabins for shelter and begin the work of making a clearing for crops in the forest. At first the pioneers followed Indian trails and turnpikes, then they profited by the period of road and canal building, marked by the Cumberland or National Turnpike carried as far as Wheeling by 1818 and to Vandalia, Illinois by 1838, and by the Erie Canal, opened from Albany to Buffalo in 1825. Then the railroads and agricultural machinery made possible the development of the wide western prairie. By 1821 eleven new states had been admitted to the Union, two of them, Louisiana and Missouri, in territory which Napoleon had taken from Spain and sold to President Jefferson for $15,000,000 in 1803. Most of the territorial gains of the United States have been at the expense of Spain or Mexico, from whom Florida, Texas, California, and the intervening

The Westward Movement in America

states were purchased or conquered in the mid-nineteenth century. By 1861 there were thirty-five states; now there are forty-eight.

European Immigration

Immigration from Europe ceased during the wars there from 1793 to 1815, after which it resumed a steady flow, becoming especially marked after the Irish Potato Famine of 1846 and the unsuccessful revolutionary movements of 1848. In overpopulated Europe employment has been much more uncertain, and wages and living standards lower than in America, so that the average workingman has poverty, if not starvation, staring him in the face. As a result, in 1861–1900, over 14,000,000 immigrants poured into the United States, and in 1901–1920 as many more. In all from 1820–1921, 34,435,332 immigrants came to the United States. Brazil received 3,648,374 during practically the same period (1820–1922), and the Argentine Republic welcomed 5,121,958 in the years 1857–1920. Before 1880 immigrants to the United States were largely British, German, and Scandinavian. Since that date immigrants from Mediterranean lands and central and eastern Europe have predominated, who represent a greater racial and linguistic divergence from the earlier settlers. These newer comers have also been more prone to remain aliens; at the time of the recent war about one-tenth of the total population of the United States was unnaturalized. The negroes make up another tenth. Canada's immigration, on the other hand, has remained largely English-speaking, with a considerable influx from the United States across the northwest border. But the total population of Canada is less than the negro or alien population in the United States. Although the United States had forced Japan and China to open their ports to its products and capital, it soon refused to admit Asiatic labor to its shores. Since the Civil War the majority of European immigrants have been absorbed by the large industrial cities of the eastern United States, while the original colonial stock of that region has to a large extent moved west.

Russian Expansion in Asia

Russia's overland expansion and the settlement of Siberia have been another noteworthy modern development. The arctic coasts and vast interior of Siberia had been explored by a series of scientific expeditions in 1733–1742, but Siberia was used for a time chiefly by fur hunters and as a penal colony for convicts and political exiles. The peasants were not at liberty to migrate there so long as they were bound to the soil of their villages in Russia. Many of them ran away to Siberia, nevertheless. After their emancipation in 1861, the number of free immigrants swelled greatly. Perhaps two millions went between 1870 and 1895, despite the severity of the Siberian climate and the fact that great stretches of the country are unfit for agriculture. In 1900 the penal system was discontinued, and the Trans-Siberian Railway aided settlement, so that the population grew from 5,784,832 in 1897, to 11,069,550 in 1922. The later immigrants, coming in larger numbers, have ceased to intermarry with the natives as some of the first settlers did, and the population has become largely pure Russian. Before this development took place Russia had sold Alaska in 1867 to the United States; but she now was not satisfied with Siberia and began to extend her influence into Manchuria and Korea in order to have a good outlet on the Pacific. This led in 1904–1905 to war with Japan, who preferred to exploit those regions herself, and Russia was defeated and had to withdraw from Korea and southern Manchuria. Her advance in Turkestan in the direction of India had for some time given Great Britain grave concern, but they now agreed to leave Afghanistan as a buffer state between them and to divide Persia amicably for exploitation by their capitalists. Soviet Russia has since renounced the Russian interests and claims in Persia, leaving the British government the chief creditor of Persia and in control of such things as the main telegraph lines. Persia, however, has discontinued an army that was commanded by British officers. Before the world war Germany had been endeavoring to extend her influence to the Near East by building railroads between Constantinople and Bagdad and by cultivating the friendship of Turkey.

Turning back again in time, we may note that the Ottoman Empire under the suzerainty of the Turkish Sultan in 1800 still stretched far and wide, extending into Europe to the Adriatic and lower Danube, and nominally controlling the Mediterranean coast of Africa as far as Morocco, which had its own sultan. France, which in the course of the eighteenth century lost most of her colonial possessions to England, has in the years 1815–1914 expanded especially in Africa, although also in Indo-China. She began with Algeria, which lies within

European Annexation and Exploitation of Africa

easy reach directly south across the Mediterranean and which was conquered in 1830–1834. From it and from Senegal on the west coast France has gradually extended her control over most of the Sahara and Sudan. Egypt had become practically independent of Turkey under Mehemet Ali, who died in 1849. The Suez Canal, engineered by the Frenchman, de Lesseps, was opened in 1869, greatly shortening the water route from Europe to the Indian Ocean and assisting the process which we are tracing in this chapter of bringing the whole world into close association. The Egyptian ruler at this time had been spending money very freely on this and other ambitious projects, encouraged by the loans which European capitalists offered him. Now they demanded payment. He sold his shares in the canal to Great Britain, but even with this sum he could not meet his obligations. England and France then jointly assumed charge of the Egyptian finances; there was an Egyptian nationalist revolt against both their chosen ruler and his financial advisers; France, who was busy occupying Tunis, withdrew; but England sent an army and remained in control both of the Suez Canal and Egypt. Meanwhile Du Chaillu, in the fifties and sixties, Livingstone until his death in 1873, and Stanley thereafter, had begun the exploration of equatorial Africa. The appetites of the European powers were whetted by the publications of such explorers, and in 1876 Leopold II of Belgium formed an International Association for the Exploration and Civilization of Africa, which was to have national committees in the several powers. The so-called Congo Free State which resulted gave the natives nothing but cruel treatment and forced labor in collecting rubber. The great scramble among the powers of Europe for the remaining regions of Africa came in the closing years of the nineteenth and opening years of the twentieth centuries. Great Britain aimed to connect her possessions and protectorates in South Africa with Egypt and its hinterland in the Sudan and to construct a railroad from Cairo to the Cape. France had continuous possessions in the northwest third of the continent from Mediterranean to equator, not to mention the large island of Madagascar in the Indian Ocean, added in 1895. The other powers of Europe, or more particularly Germany and Italy, who had only recently become nations and thereby privileged to plunder, had to be content with annexing widely separated districts. These, together with the scattered remnants of the Portuguese empire, made the map of Africa look like a crazy patchwork quilt. The slave trade in Africa itself was condemned, however, by a conference of European powers in 1890.

Japan, having adopted western civilization with a vim, saw that it was more blessed to civilize than to be civilized, and, defeating China and Russia in successive wars, possessed herself of Formosa and Korea. In 1915 she was about to imitate the British example in Egypt, Persia, and the native states of India, by becoming China's capitalist and "adviser" in political, financial, military, and commercial matters, when the United States heeded China's protest that this infringed upon her sovereignty and induced Japan to withdraw most of her demands, and to maintain the "open door" policy to all foreign nations. Meanwhile the United States had itself expanded into both the Atlantic and Pacific Oceans, taking Porto Rico and the Philippines from Spain, annexing Hawaii with an assenting vote of the natives, and purchasing—thanks to a Central American revolution—the control of the Panama Canal zone which unites the two oceans. The Danish West Indies were bought later in 1917. The free public schools established by the United States in the Philippine Islands were attended in 1921 by one-tenth of the entire population. This may be compared with India, of whose population of 315,156,-396 in 1911 only 18,539,431 could read and write. The Philippine schools are co-educational; of the literate Hindus only 1,600,763 were females.

Japanese and American Imperialism

In the recent war Germany lost its colonies in Africa and the Pacific to Great Britain, Belgium, France, and Japan; and Turkey was shorn of Mesopotamia, Palestine, and Syria by Great Britain and France. These territories are administered under mandated authority from the League of Nations, and some advance in civilization should result in the regions taken from the Turks. In these very regions, however, the mandatory powers have met with no little opposition and have too often had to employ force.

Parcelling Out of German Colonies and Turkish Possessions

The imperialistic and economic exploitation of Asia and Africa by western powers has been accompanied by foreign missionary activity based, for the most part, on higher and more disinterested motives. The natives, however, are apt

Christian Missions

to resent this attempt to introduce what seems to them simply a foreign religion as much as they resent the introduction of foreign government, foreign manufactures, and economic competition. But just as many of them none the less buy the superior western wares, so many accept the industrial and other schools and the medical assistance which the missionaries freely offer them. In general the Christian faith has made few converts in Mohammedan countries or in the older civilizations of the east such as India, where less than two per cent of the population are Christian, or China, where less than one per cent are Christian. On the other hand, in Korea, in some of the islands of Oceania, and in parts of Africa which are not Mohammedan, a large percentage of the native population, or entire tribes, like the Baganda, have been converted. What the lasting effect of this will be upon their morale and mode of life it is not yet possible to say.

Disastrous Effect of Contact with Western Civilization upon Primitive Peoples

In general western civilization does not seem to agree well with "inferior peoples." A few years ago the ancient town of Jenné, situated near the Niger in the French Sudan, was a commercial capital and a place of much architectural interest. Since then modern transportation has made it a dead city; "one French governor has accomplished more destruction than twelve centuries of war, and the splendid walls have been levelled to make way for an imitation Parisian boulevard." But there has been opened the first French school in the Niger valley where little blackamoors are being taught the fables of La Fontaine. What progress! As a result of the spread of European settlers or rulers and business interests over the face of the globe, various native peoples and cultures who once sparsely populated large areas, like the North American Indians, the Maoris of New Zealand, and the Australian aborigines, have tended to disappear rather than to prosper under the new conditions. If vigorous and intelligent, like the Maoris, they resist the European invasion and weaken themselves by wars. If low in the scale of civilization and mentality, they are apt to be demoralized rather than improved by contact with the white man and his ways. The Tasmanians, about two thousand in number at the time of British occupation, were reduced to two hundred by 1831, and the last survivor of the race died in 1877. The Veddahs of the forests of Ceylon, nomads without even pottery, fell off in population in fifty years from about eight thousand to only fifty or sixty. Howitt says of the tribes of southeastern Australia: "All those who have had to do with the native race in its primitive state will agree with me that there are men in the tribes who have tried to live up to the standard of tribal morality, and who were faithful friends and true to their word; in fact men for whom, although savages, one must feel a kindly respect. Such men are not to be found in the later generation, which has grown up under our civilization, and is rapidly being exterminated by it." Even when they are not exploited or cheated or ill-treated or worked to death, as the natives in Africa too often have been, the savages find their environment altered and restricted, and are unable to adapt themselves to the change. Inasmuch as many of them inhabit tropical climates where white men cannot live and labor, it seems questionable if the extermination of the natives or the attempt to make them like us will help civilization.

But on the whole, the world over, there has been a great increase in population during the past century or more. This has been true of lands dependent mainly upon agriculture for subsistence, such as Russia, India, and Egypt, as well as of those marked by the industrial revolution. Thus India, with an area only about one-third that of the United States, has a population three times as great, yet over two-thirds of them are engaged in tillage, or pastoral pursuits, and there are only three cities with a population above 500,000. The eighteen provinces of China proper have about the same population as India, but reliable figures are lacking, and it is also difficult to say whether the population has increased during the last century or had already reached about its maximum under prevailing conditions. At any rate China, too, is primarily agricultural, though without the internal peace and modern improvements introduced by the British in India.

General Increase in World Population

In most lands, however, the growing population has tended to congregate in the large city and the densely populated industrial area. Modern rapid transportation has made it possible not only to feed these great metropolitan centers, but for many who live outside the city limits to come in to their work every morning and return to their suburban or even country home in the evening. Indeed, the city itself covers so much ground that most workers have to make similar trips

The Great Modern City

from their place of residence to the business center or factory. Many persons reside not in a house or even a suite of rooms but in what is little more than a single room apartment, into which the bed is let down at night from a recess in the wall, and off which open tiny closets in which restricted cooking and ablutions may be performed. It is, however, not so much preciousness of space as high cost of building and reluctance to do housework that leads to the populating of these little cells in apartment-house hives, and they offer slightly more privacy and independence than the boarding-house or lodgings. The city dweller goes to his work by riding in a crowded subway or surface electric tram-car or bus, or perhaps threads his way through the dense traffic in his own automobile. If a clerk or stenographer in a business office, he or she then ascends in an elevator to the fifth or sixth, or nineteenth or twentieth floor of a steel building, there to work at a desk in a space little larger than the close quarters where the night was spent. Or, as the husband goes to work in the factory or steel mill, his wife may be riding in the elevator of some great department store on the different floors of which are acres of space offering for sale almost every conceivable sort of commodity— groceries, meat and fish, clothing, hardware, dishes, bedding, furniture, rugs and carpets, books, drugs, perfumes, sporting goods, confectionary, stationery, toys and games, electrical appliances, and so on—like no bazaar or market in all the world's previous history. While these articles are to be found here displayed in greater profusion and variety, for most of the immediate requirements of her family she would not need to go farther than the smaller shops located in the same city block in which she lives and which can be reached without crossing the street or hardly venturing out-of-doors. For lunch the city dweller usually has not the time to return home, except in Mediterranean countries where the noontime siesta is customary, but eats in a crowded restaurant, which the shopper can find in the department store itself, while the manual worker perhaps eats from a dinner pail which he has brought with him.

Recreation and Amusements

In the evening the more ambitious may frequent night schools of law, or business and the extension courses of universities and the Young Men's Christian Association, or more elementary schools where foreigners may learn English, or labor and socialist meetings, or lodges, or institutional churches which offer entertainments and improvement.   Others go to basket-ball games or boxing exhibitions, to skating rinks or dance halls, to clubs and pool-rooms and crowded moving-picture theaters.   There the films present more interesting and excit-ing scenes, situations, and stories than the ordinary run of their daily experience, although they derive similar sensational and emotional matter from the daily newspapers read on the way to and from work.   Others may stay at home and read a book from the public library, or listen to music produced by the graphophone or heard over the radio with little effort and no skill on their own part.   But the temptation is to go out.   All day they have been confined, first in a crowded bus, subway coach, or surface car, then in a packed elevator, then behind a counter, or in an office or workshop full of people, files, machines, and goods, then elbowed in a steaming lunch-room, then back to elevator, shop, office, counter, and crowds homeward bound.   Now at night they miss the tumult and the throng, they fail to enjoy their own thoughts and society, they want something to take them outside themselves.   They go out where the streets are bright with electric illuminations and the pavement is encumbered with passers-by.   They over-whelm their jaded nerves with jazz.   Or they carry on long conversations over the telephone.   The city dweller commonly has no garden of his own, but in warm weather he may go to the public parks, or sit in the open air at a baseball or foot-ball match on a spare afternoon, or on a Sunday ride out into the country.   The great popularity of the automobile and the radio are partly due to the relief they give the city dweller, enabling him to get away from his immediate environment and giving him a feeling of greater freedom and reach.

At the same time, the smooth organization of the multifari-ous activities of millions or hundreds of thousands of human beings, all carried on without conflict or confusion within so restricted an urban area, stirs our admiration as one of the greatest triumphs of modern civilization.   From systematic regulation of traffic in the crowded streets to detailed codes of laws concerning the erection of new buildings, from succes-sive editions of newspapers to almost hourly collection and

Municipal Organiza-tion

delivery of mail, from provision of pure daily food for the vast
population to the removal of garbage and ashes, many instances might be noted of the complexity and efficiency of
present muncipal administration and business enterprise.   With
living so compressed, yet on such a gigantic scale, it is not
surprising if there has been a strong tendency for competing
firms and business undertakings in any single field, such as
street railways or bakeries, to amalgamate into one all-
embracing organization which shall insure more harmonious
and effective operation.   It is also not surprising if there is
a marked demand for increasing municipal ownership or direction and control.

BIBLIOGRAPHY

Adams, R. G. *A History of the Foreign Policy of the United States,*
1924.

Dewey, John. *Letters from China and Japan,* 1921.

Gonnard, R. *Histoire des doctrines de la population,* 1923.

Grice, J. W. *The Resources of the Empire,* 1917.

Harris, N. D. *Europe and the East,* 1926.

Hawke, E. G. *The British Empire and its History,* 1911.

Johnston, Sir Harry. *A History of the Colonization of Africa by Alien
Races,* 1899.

King-Hall, Stephen. *Western Civilization and the Far East,* 1924; a
stimulating and informing review of recent conditions.

Lucas, C. K. *The Partition and Colonization of Africa,* 1922.

Macdonald, A. J. *Trade, Politics, and Christianity in Africa and the
East,* 1916.

Martin, P. F. *The Sudan in Evolution,* 1921.

Marvin, F. S. *Western Races and the World,* 1922.

Maxwell, Sir H. *A Century of Empire, 1801–1900,* 1909–1912.

Millard. F. F. *The New Far East,* 1906.

Moon, P. T. *Imperialism and World Politics,* 1925.

Norton, H. K. *The Far Eastern Republic of Siberia,* 1923.

Pasvolsky, Leo. *Russia in the Far East,* 1921.

Pollard, A. F. *The British Empire,* 1909.

Price, M. G. *Siberia,* 1912.

Price, M. T. *Christain Missions and Oriental Civilization: a study in
culture contact,* 1924; sociological and psychological.

Robinson, Howard. *The Development of the British Empire,* 1922.

Roosevelt, T. *The Winning of the West,* 1905, 6 vols.

Ross, E. A. *The Old World in the New,* 1914.

Russell, Bertrand. *The Problem of China,* 1922.

Satomi, K. *Japanese Civilization: its significance and realization,* 1923.
Sparks. E. E. *Expansion of the American People,* 1899.
Tenney, A. A. *Social Democracy and Population,* 1907.
Turner, F. J. *The Rise of the New West,* 1906.
Weale, B. L. P. *The Truth about China and Japan,* 1921.
Williamson, J. A. *A Short History of British Expansion,* 1922.

CHAPTER XLI

THE PROBLEM OF MODERN CULTURE

Criticism and the continuity of human thought are just as important to man as mastery of the outer world.—Tatlock

Effect of Increased Population and Rapid Communication on Culture

THREE considerations exert a vast influence upon our present civilization and culture: the great increase in population, in the number of voters and active citizens, in the number of persons who can read and write; their increased facilities for moving about and coming into varied relations with one another instead of remaining in little local groups; the ease of communicating almost simultaneously with great numbers of them. These things have led to big business and the rapid consumption of natural resources, upon which present humanity descends not like a cloud of locusts or horde of nomads, for these scour and denude only the surface of the ground, but more like an army of leeches sucking the life blood out of poor old mother earth in the form of oil and coal and steel. These three considerations have produced the omnipresent propagandist and advertiser, a very Mephistopheles of insinuating suggestion or compelling demand, who constantly dogs the footsteps or rather poisons the stream of precepts of the individual, preventing him from ever having an honest, independent thought of his own, keeping him from contact with nature, telling him what he is to think or do, always tempting him to consume, consume, consume, and waste, waste, waste. With this goes the popular press, the morning and evening newspaper, the cheap magazine, sold at low prices which lead everyone to buy, paid for immediately by its advertisers or rich proprietors but ultimately, perhaps dearly, paid for by the consumer, whose vote, purchases, and whole view of the world it influences.

The Modern Newspaper

Yet the newspaper, at least, brings him precious information. From it he can learn the present price of stocks, bonds, and other possible financial investments the world over, or read

546

an account of social functions to which he was not invited, thrilling deeds of heroism in which he did not participate, dramatic performances, outdoor sports, and political meetings which he was unable to attend, for he could only be present at one of them at a time.   In a sense, the doings of the whole world the day before are set before his eyes in type, and the daily perusal of this should have a most beneficial, broadening effect upon his mind.   Unfortunately this ideal is very imperfectly realized in the average newspaper.   The individual is not thought capable of taking a broad social view of world society.   He is fed with stories of human heart interest agreeable to his limited personal outlook and experience, with all the crimes of abnormal individuals, with anything that borders on the sensational, marvelous, superstitious, or humorous. Thus the newspaper is affected by the capacity of its audience, to whose interests it must conform if it would have readers. If it truly reflects contemporary civilization, it should prove invaluable to future historians as an index to the state of our society.   On the other hand, although history daily repeats itself in the newspapers, few follow its course continuously, and it rolls off the ordinary reader like water from a duck's back.   Yet there can be little doubt that he takes to the many columns of his favorite journal as a duck does to water, and the next morning or evening he is always back again for another refreshing shower bath in the daily deluge of the world's happenings and utterances.   There is even something ceremonial and sacramental in this daily communion of the individual with the great world about him through the printed page recording the sayings and doings of yesterday.   Undoubtedly there are great possibilities in it of inculcating true public spirit, disseminating culture, and humanizing knowledge. And undoubtedly an effort is made to realize these possibilities by the best edited papers.   It is to be regretted that newspaper men are usually too intent on the news of the day to digest or compare or verify or amend what has gone before. Working under constant pressure, they can hardly be expected to produce enduring literature despite their advantages of contact with real life and daily practice in writing.   Or if they do turn off some gems of literature now and then, who will ever collect and preserve these jewels from the vast mass of columns?

Difficulty in
Estimating
the Vast
Output of
Modern
Writers

This difficulty, indeed, applies to current writing in general. There are so many readers, so many periodicals, so many publishers, that there is no longer any general literary tribunal to say who are our best authors. Some read one; others, another; no single story or book is any longer read universally. Considering the number of persons now supposed to be educated, we ought to have an increasing number of first-rate writers and literary geniuses .in proportion, and the number of their writings should increase with the speed of typewriters and other modern facilities for composition. If we do not have them, it must be because we do not take time to think in our reading and writing. At any rate, as we approach our own times, it becomes increasingly difficult to select individuals from the various countries and languages as the leaders, or even as representative, of their epoch, society, and civilization. If in 1800, when the population of Great Britain was less than a fourth what it is now, there were Crabbe, Blake, Wordsworth, Coleridge, Southey, Scott, Godwin, Edgeworth, we ought to be able to enumerate thirty-two present British authors of like rank, or, if that be too many for our space and notice, we should omit and forget six of the eight named and find eight today to compare with the two remaining names. If we admit that poets and novelists have fallen off, ought we not to find a compensating increase in some other field, such as music or the short story? Or are we to admit that individuals do not stand out now as they did once, except as millionaires or captains of industry, and that culture has become socialized in advance of the state and the economic means of production? Certainly in our crowded, communicative, standardized society the individual finds it increasingly difficult to live his own life or develop his own thought.

Can the
Human
Mind
Assimilate
the Great
Advances of
Knowledge?

Furthermore, not only with the mass of contemporary writing is it difficult to keep track of the past masters in many lands, or *vice versa*, but science and learning have so ramified, so specialized, so progressed, that knowledge and theory have perhaps grown even faster than population or popular education. No one man, however learned and characterized by breadth of interest, can even fully appreciate, to say nothing of mastering, the achievements in all the different fields, while the ordinary man has no conception of the present state of knowledge. If the system of public education were more truly disciplinary, if the newspapers largely replaced crime, sensation, and sentimental matter by straightforward statement of political, social, and economic happenings, and the progress of knowledge, if the magazines minimized love stories, adventure, and personality in favor of matters of more moment to civilization, if advertisements gave sound advice as to good manners in public thoroughfares and conveyances, or sensible medical, legal, and financial counsel, if the moving pictures were employed more for purposes of instruction,—perhaps the average man could keep up better with the onward march of civilization. Can science shepherd the herd? That is the question. Has scientific specialization proved fatal to the humanism which enabled many leaders of thought in previous generations to publish their views in an acceptable, graceful, and forceful form? Can we have only a caste of intellectuals, as in China and India? Will the popular demand, vulgar taste, and utilitarian attitude lower everything to its own level and swamp civilization? Or is civilization now unfolding in more varied flower than ever before with more individuals of high rank in each field and with an ever increasing public following which is able to appreciate their work?

At the beginning of the nineteenth century a broad mind like Goethe's could still take an intelligent interest in almost everything; literature was still able to give some fairly satisfactory reflection of knowledge. This was because scholarship was still largely restricted to the classics, while experimental science had not yet become so technical and specialized. With the vast increase of knowledge in the last century, literature has become more and more divorced from learning, and, like religion, has tended to limit itself to the emotional or mystical side of life, or to realism, and to make its appeal largely to the untutored mind.

Goethe the Last Great Mind in Literature

In the Romantic Movement of the early nineteenth century literature began somewhat tardily to awake to the meaning of the labors of Muratori, Bouquet, and other scholars in medieval records in the eighteenth century, although, with the flightiness and the distaste for sound learning and hard sense that has too often marked the literary mind and artistic temperament of late, it was more carried away by alleged works of the ancient Gaelic poet Ossian and the forgeries fabricated by young Chatterton from medieval charters. But

The Romantic Movement

the narrow outlook of classicism was broadened, and the romantic imagination began to play with a wider past and the world of nature, or to drift away into the realms of faëry land. The movement appeared in most of the countries of Europe, albeit at somewhat different times. It was often combined with the restless revolutionary spirit stirred up by the French Revolution. And the somewhat prosaic character of much eighteenth-century literature was now replaced by a more lyrical note. Particularly in England women writers became more common than before, and today women perhaps constitute the majority of readers, especially in English-speaking lands. The Oxford or Tractarian movement in the church, the pre-Raphaelites in painting, the Gothic revival in architecture, were other manifestations and accompaniments of the Romantic movement.

Victor Hugo

In the brief space at our command we can perhaps best give some idea of modern literature by a few single representatives of its tendencies in different languages and countries. Victor Hugo (1802–1885) was the giant of the romantic movement and the greatest French author of the century. With indefatigable exuberance of language, imagination, and vivid descriptive power he galloped for more than sixty years over the whole field of literature: poetry, romantic dramas, historical novels that vie with those of Scott and Dumas if not quite equal to Thackeray's, satire, literary criticism, political and historical essays. *Les Misérables*, a work in ten volumes which appeared simultaneously, in 1862, in ten European languages, is probably despite its faults the greatest novel of modern times, a broad canvas depicting the misery and abuses in modern social conditions. Hugo was perhaps greatest as a lyric poet, possessing a wonderful feeling for melody, while he also had many epic qualities. *La légende des siècles* (The Story of the Ages) is his most noted poem. His work as a whole suggests a Gothic cathedral in words, like that which he makes live for us in *Notre-Dame de Paris*, vast and rich, full of color and shadows, with grandly aspiring towers and a wealth of faithfully executed detail. But he is not equal to the cathedral in perfection of structure, in proportion, or in sense of humor, for Hugo is sometimes grotesque when he does not mean to be.

Charles Dickens (1812–1870), on the contrary, founded his

success on humor, which in *Pickwick Papers* (1837) took the world by storm.   In it, too, began that dramatic presentation of a wealth of personalities from the common people and ordinary walks of contemporary life, hitherto almost unportrayed in literature except by Balzac (1799–1850), but put forth by Dickens in his succeeding novels with a profusion that harmonized well with the increasing population and broadening suffrage of our age.   Similarly Balzac's *Comédie humaine* contains about five thousand characters.   In Dickens' glass the people could see themselves, and even if the mirror distorted them a little too comically or sentimentally, still they preferred to have a good laugh or cry over themselves once in a while rather than stare forever at oil paintings, however artistic and exquisite, of ancestors of the nobility, at romantic maidens and heroes of the past, or at self-centred Byronic replicas and Heine's one variety.   Dickens possessed neither Hugo's mastery of words and lyrical style nor Balzac's power of character analysis, but he was a great story-teller and master of plots.   He rivalled Hugo in imaginative power which, combined with his prismatic humor, enabled his readers to see ordinary contemporary life with rainbow tints.   He nevertheless exposed and denounced many social abuses that cried for reform.   But he kept his faith in good cheer, and if it be combined with justice, there is hardly a sounder or more tolerant working creed.

Dickens' New Departure

The more recent realistic school have chased away the rainbow and dwelt on the commonplace, the sordid, and the degraded in current civilization.   No longer content to mirror, they take an X-ray photograph of the diseased and reveal the skeleton of human psychology, but their presentation lacks light.   They have taken their cue from the scientific historian and the natural scientist, devoting themselves to minute observation of "the little facts" and to "human documents."   But they have gone on beyond the middle and lower classes to study the dregs of society, and it is questionable if they are right in thinking that human nature can best be studied in its pathological manifestations.

Realism or Naturalism

Madame de Staël could say at the beginning of the nineteenth century, "In Russia a few noblemen are occupied with literature."   Russia has since come to have more of a national literature, and the Russian novel may perhaps be regarded

The Russian Novel: Tolstoi

as leading the realistic reaction from romanticism. Gogol, founder of the Russian naturalistic school, "first made men ashamed of life." His *Dead Souls* (1842) "does not contain a single honest character." Turgeniev (1818–1883), Dostoievsky (1821–1881), and Tolstoi (1828–1910) continued the movement with increasing fidelity of delineation, psychological analysis, and morbidity. Tolstoi ended by condemning civilization and modern progress, preaching and practicing individual self-improvement, Christian simplicity, and the life of the common peasant, which is indeed perhaps the safest refuge from the Russian tendency to morbidity or mysticism. But enough of novels! They are not to be taken too seriously as an index of civilization.

The Modern Drama

The leader in dramatic literature of the past century has been the Norwegian, Ibsen (1828–1906), whose satirical social plays, uncovering the shams of modern conventional middle class life, and whose allegorical poetic dramas interpreting life's problems symbolically, have been continued by Shaw, Sudermann, and Hauptmann in the generation following.

Carducci

Carducci (1836–1907), the greatest poet of modern Italy, reacted from romanticism not to realism but to classicism. Himself a critic and university professor, Carducci refused to write down to his readers and strove to elevate them to his purity of language and form, his deeply cultured thought and wide range of learning. He revived the spirit of paganism, attacking the church and Christianity; he revelled both in Italian scenery and history.

Wagner and the Problem of Art Today

Richard Wagner (1813–1883) brought originality, intellectual vigor, and dramatic power into the realm of music. In his operas we see the genius of poet, stage-manager, dramatist, and musician fused in one grand harmony. As an exile after the Revolution of 1848 he urged that art, which had become divorced from productive work through the degradation of manual labor and individual skill and the triumph of machinery, factory, and mass-production, and divorced from religion by the failure of Christianity any longer to command universal intellectual respect or to inspire artistic creation, should be reanimated by the social ideal and by pantheism, and become, not dilettantism in the pay of the rich, but expressive of the highest aspirations of the entire people and inspired by the conviction that all life is divine.   This ambitious goal seems still to be farther from realization in literature and other fine arts than in music.   There can be little doubt, however, that Wagner thus early correctly analyzed the causes of decline in art in modern times and of the restless, often crude and naïve, experimentation in art and literature which we today behold.   Victorian poets like Tennyson and Browning strove to blend the theory of evolution with Christian faith, and the probing of human moral psychology with optimism as to the divine government of the universe.   But most continental authors would reject their attitude as one of shallow compromise and vague hope, which shrivels before the cool wit of an Anatole France or the hot passion of a D'Annunzio.

Another weakness of modern art seems to be in the matter of structure and form.   Here again the reproach applies less to modern music, for just as we have a great dramatist in Wagner, so we may almost be said to have a great architect in Brahms (1833–1897), who always raises his superstructure of melody upon firm and solid foundations, with every chord clear-cut, exactly fitted to its place, and essential to the whole. The progress of modern music has not, however, been confined to German composers.   Poland had its Chopin (1810–1849); Russia, its Tschaikowsky (1840–1893); France, its Debussy (1862–1918). *Other Composers of Music*

Painting, since 1800, has displayed many of the same tendencies as literature, being swayed now by romanticism and now by realism and naturalism, becoming increasingly democratic in its choice of subjects, in its study of the lower classes, tragedies of everyday life, and out-of-the-way places, and its desire to neglect nothing that may afford material somewhat resembling the contents of the naturalistic, if not the pathological, novel.   Landscape painting has maintained a prominent place since the great works of Constable (1776–1837) and Turner (1775–1851) early in the century.   Historical painters were for a time notable, but not of recent years.   France on the whole was the greatest center of painting in the nineteenth century.   Corot (1796–1875) excelled in intimate pictures of nature; Millet (1814–1875), in representations of peasant life; Courbet (1819–1877), in somewhat emphatic and showy naturalism.   France also saw a great *Modern Painting* revival of mural painting in such public buildings at Paris as the Opéra, Pantheon, Sorbonne, Palais de Justice, and Hôtel de Ville, whose walls and ceilings show scenes far more interesting and attractive to the modern eye than those at Versailles of pre-revolutionary days. Among the artists Cabanel and Chavannes may be mentioned. Water-color painting began towards the close of the eighteenth century. The lively etchings of Whistler (1834–1903) should at least be mentioned, if not his oil paintings, pastels, and lithographs. The painting of still life and of the nude female form received more attention in the past century than before, and there was also a new style of depicting things in full daylight (*plein air*) rather than in subdued tones, and of depicting space more adequately. There was conflict as to the relative importance of color or of line and form, and an increasing growth of impressionism, the catching of momentary effects and of general impressions. There has been individuality in giving expression to each artist's personality, but as most recent painters have tended each to specialize in some one field, such as trees, or flowers, or town streets and squares, or marine subjects, there has perhaps been some narrowness and loss of universality. And as yet, despite the increasing number of municipal art galleries and local exhibitions open to the public, painting cannot be called a popular, or universal art, but remains largely limited to wealthy purchasers and the cultured few.

Popular Education in America

In the United States of America of recent years there has been a feverish activity in education, more perhaps of the sociological than the scholarly variety. At any rate, great sums of money have been expended on school and university buildings and equipment, including numerous costly athletic stadiums. There also has been a great rush of youth to secondary schools and colleges, overwhelming many institutions with classes of almost unmanageable size. It would seem that the future outcome of this great movement or increase cannot but be favorable to the growth of higher sides of civilization. Temporarily it proves difficult to assimilate the numbers, standards tend to fall off, and England, with only about 30,000 persons attending her universities, still compares favorably in culture and learning with the United States where there are now about twenty times that number in attendance on higher institutions of learning.

BIBLIOGRAPHY

Baldensperger, F. *L'Avant-guerre dans la littérature française (1900–1914)*, 1919.

Bell, Clive. *Since Cezanne*, 1922.

Brandes, *Main Currents in Nineteenth Century Literature.*

Cheney, S. W. *Primer of Modern Art*, 1923.

Collison-Morley, L. *Modern Italian Literature*, 1911.

Francke, Kuno. *German Ideals of Today*, 1907.

Gordon, Jan. *Modern French Art.*

Halévy, E. *A History of the English People in 1815*, (English translation) 1924.

Marvin, F. S. *The Century of Hope*, 1919.

Morris, W. *Hopes and Fears for Art*, 4th edition, 1896.

Muther, Richard. *History of Modern Painting*, English translation, 1907.

Nitze and Dardan, *History of French Literature, from the earliest times to the great war*, 1922.

Pellissier, G. *Le mouvement littéraire au XIXe siècle*, 1908.

Phelps, W. L. *Essays on Russian Novelists*, 1911; *The Pure Gold of Nineteenth Century Literature*, 1907.

Shotwell, J. T. "Mechanism and Culture," in *The Historical Outlook*, Jan. 1925.

Thomson, D. C. *The Barbizon School of Painters*, 1891.

Thorndike, A. H. *Literature in a Changing Age*, 1920.

Tittoni, Tommaso. *Modern Italy, its Intellectual, Cultural, and Financial Aspects*, 1922.

Trevelyan, G. M. *The Nineteenth Century*, 1922.

Wells, B. W. *Modern French Literature*, 1896.

Wolkonsky, *Lectures on Russian History and Literature.*

CHAPTER XLII

THE ADVANCE OF SCIENCE

When all treasure is tried, Truth is the best.
—The Vision of Piers the Ploughman

Unveiling
the Past:
the Comparative
Method;
Archæology

MAN'S knowledge of himself and his fellow men has been tremendously extended in time, space, and intensity since the eighteenth century. The study of Sanskrit in the last quarter of that century not only introduced western scholars to the riches of Hindu literature, but, from the connections that were noted with other Indo-European languages, led to the development of the sciences of comparative philology, comparative literature, and comparative mythology, and to the use of the comparative method generally in scientific inquiry. In the domain of natural science, for example, Cuvier about 1815 established comparative anatomy as a distinct branch. But to return to the disclosure of the remote past. By aid of the Rosetta stone, which Napoleon had found in Egypt, Champollion deciphered the hieroglyphic writing which for so long had veiled the wonderful civilization of ancient Egypt. The deciphering of cuneiform by Rawlinson followed in 1847 and 1850. Ever since that date excavation in Egypt, Mesopotamia, and other lands of the ancient orient has vastly increased the number both of inscriptions and works of art. Towards the end of the nineteenth century, excavation in the Ægean area opened up a long period of high civilization before the Homeric poems; investigation in Palestine revealed remains antedating the Hebraic occupation of that region; in Asia Minor the home of the Hittites was found, and now their language is being read. Systematic search for, and scientific study of papyri since 1890 have also greatly increased our knowledge of the historic Greek and Roman period and its literature. Scientific archæology has broadened our knowledge and appreciation of medieval and renaissance as well as ancient art. Meanwhile with the assistance of geology human

556

implements, bones, and places of habitation were being dated farther and farther back into remote periods.

Anthropology, ethnology, and sociology now first arose and measured the many primitive and savage races of the world, classifying their languages, recording their customs and institutions. The study of folklore dates back to the Grimm brothers, of whom Jacob (1785–1863) was also a great comparative philologist. Modern psychology has added its contribution by scientific scrutiny of human mental processes, behaviour, and personality. Its ever ramifying branches of animal psychology, educational psychology, experimental psychology, pathological psychology, and the like, are more than matched by the varied departments and specialization of present medical investigation. When to all these new points of view, methods of inquiry, and collections of data, we add the light cast upon human development by the scientific investigation of a greatly increased number of other forms of life, and by the theory of evolution,—we see how different our view of man's past, nature, and destiny must be from that of the most enlightened eighteenth century Philosophers. They still accepted, for want of a better, the Old Testament account of natural creation and short chronology of human history, they limited their survey of civilized rational development by the Homeric poems and classical literature, they thought of primitive man as a fully developed species living in a state of nature, innocence, and equality. But now civilization and human history and society are seen to be a far more intricate game than they imagined,—chess rather than tit-tat-to.

Rise of Anthropology, Folklore, and Psychology

These social problems have led to an increasingly specialized study of economics, political science, and sociology, a name invented by the philosopher Comte (1798–1857) for the science of society, which he aimed to make as positive as mathematics and the natural sciences. While it is as yet far from this goal, these social sciences have none the less been very influential in directing that movement of political revolution and social reform which we have traced in a previous chapter.

The Social Sciences

Scholarship during the past century has been growing more and more precise, painstaking, conscientious, open, reliable, convincing, and scientific in method. It keeps criticizing the older authorities and so-called standard works and revising their

Growth of Critical Scholarship: the Monograph

estimates, sifting the hasty assumptions and over-ready beliefs of the past with greater care, as well as discovering additional sources of information or rendering existing sources more
available.   Just as modern science and medicine have rejected
much ancient and medieval superstition and magic, so history
has discarded many legends of the past.   The scholar has little
use for any book from which he cannot derive definite, exact
information with clear indication of the sources whence it was
drawn.   For statements that are simply repeated from other
books he has no liking, he would rather read the other books
for these, he wishes first-hand information.   William Grimm
well expressed at least one side of the scholarly method when
he said, "Exact and careful monographs . . . may be small
in volume, but their influence is incalculable and their value
is imperishable."   On the other hand, with the ever onward
march of scholarship, general works rapidly grow obsolete so
that the scholar looks first for the most recent work published
on a subject.   The mass of known, accepted fact alters so
continually, old points being rejected and new ones added, that
the philosophizing and interpretation of the facts in which
writers used to indulge, and even general narratives or treatments, have of late years perhaps grown too rare, at least from
the hands of the true scholars alone competent to attempt
them.   This is a real loss to the reading public.   Cooperative works by a number of scholars have been put forth on
the ground that with the existing specialization of knowledge
no one man can cover even a single department or considerable
period, but such works commonly have less literary quality
and unity of presentation than if one individual had been responsible and felt responsible for the whole.

Scientific
Measure-
ment

Perhaps the greatest achievement of modern science is its
ever increasing capacity to measure.   Matters that were
formerly entirely outside man's ken are now measured with
superhuman mechanical accuracy.   Data are accumulated of
a minuteness or a stupendousness, and in such multitudinous
quantity, that the average human mind is as little able
to take them in as the defective human senses are to
make the precise instrumental and experimental observations
upon which they have been based by a vast army of devoted
scientific workers.   Thus Aristotle enumerated about 500
species of animals; Linnæus in 1758 named 4236; Ludwig in

1886 gave 273,000; Pratt in 1911 listed 522,400 living species. This is a fair illustration of the enormously increased amount of knowledge in practically every department of science and learning. Indeed, the defects of the senses were but vaguely realized until such precise measurement began; for instance, Dalton in 1794 is said to have first called attention to color-blindness. A hard black rock can now be cut into slices only one-thousandth of an inch in thickness, so thin that print can be read through it, while the minutest structures present in it are revealed to the geologist by the petrographic micro-scope. As a result, almost all the known rocks have been "ex-haustively studied and minutely described." The calorimeter, which measures the heat generated or emitted by a body, is useful not only in physics but in recording chemical action, and in such subjects as nutrition and psychology, since the effects of foods or emotional excitement upon the temperature of the individual who is secluded in the respiration calorimeter can be determined. Various other apparatus has been de-vised to record vital activities such as blood pressure, and the time rate of the response of nerves and muscles to stimula-tion.

Measurement of the vast scale of the starry heavens made a great advance in 1839, with the determination of the stellar parallax of *61 Cygni* by Bessel and of *a Centauri* by Hender-son. The invention of the spectroscope in 1859–1860, by Kirchhoff and Bunsen permitted minute examination and measurement of the spectra of celestial bodies against a scale, and consequently, by comparison with the spectra of known terrestrial substances, the determination of their chemical composition, and, from the shifting of lines in the spectrum, their velocity. In making such a scale for solar work about the year 1891, twenty thousand parallel gratings to the inch were marked on glass. The application of photography by Huggins in 1876 brought out the ultra-violet rays invisible to human sight. In many other ways stellar photography has multiplied astronomical knowledge. About 1850 began the measurement of the velocity of light by passing it through the teeth of a revolving wheel, whose speed can be measured, to a mirror and back again. In 1920 by Michelson's interferometer method the angular diameter of the star Betelgeuse was meas-ured.

Measuring the Stars and Light

Investigating the Atom

Dalton had formulated his atomic theory in 1804, but atomic weights were not established on a basis of experimental measurement until the sixties, when the graphic and structural formulæ of chemistry were also defined.   Now science has reached the point of measuring the concourse of electrons within the atom, which is itself so tiny that it has always been regarded as indivisible as well as invisible, and has been described as "so small that 500,000 could repose in a row on the period at the end of this sentence." Yet scientists find that electrons speed around the nucleus of the atom in elliptical orbits like those of the planets about the sun and at a speed almost that of light.   They find furthermore that the number of satellite electrons varies in atoms of the different chemical elements from only one in hydrogen, the lightest element, up to ninety-two electrons in uranium, the heaviest of the ninety-two elements now known.   Thus the old views of the Greek philosophers concerning macrocosm and microcosm, and of a universe of tiniest particles all in incessant motion and of like substance, find something of a modern scientific justification. And no occult virtues ascribed to animals, plants, and minerals by past magicians are more marvelous than the calculation of Mme. Curie that "the energy of one gram of radium would suffice to lift a weight of five hundred tons to the height of one mile."

Modern Mathematics

We may only very briefly suggest a few of the directions in which progress has been made in the various sciences. Mathematics continues to be of the greatest service to investigators in other fields as well as to pursue new marches of its own, such as the theory of functions and imaginary numbers.   Medical research requires its aid; the theory of statistics is of obvious importance for the social sciences and modern government; the investigation of electric and magnetic fields has called for further application of mathematical analysis to physics.   As a sequel to Kant's questioning the conception of space has come the non-Euclidean geometry with its further questioning of Euclid's axioms, and today we have the non-Newtonian mechanics of Einstein and others.   While applied mathematics continues to guide science, pure mathematics has become so complex and imaginative in its methods that it has outstripped metaphysics both in logic and fearless idealism.

In astronomy we may add to spectrum analysis and the other advances mentioned above, the discovery of the planet Neptune in 1846, and the initiation in 1904 of a new stage in the investigation of sidereal systems with Kapteyn's discovery of two star-streams. In physics the principle of the conservation of energy was promulgated by Helmholtz in 1847, and thermodynamics became a distinct subject about the same time. The discovery of X-rays by Röntgen in 1895 was epoch-making in the investigation of light, has led to further advance in spectrum analysis, has been of great practical service in medicine, surgery, and dentistry, and has shown that changes in mass do occur. The great progress in knowledge of electricity in modern times has been somewhat indicated in speaking of its practical applications in a previous chapter, where we also noted the discovery of new metals and elements.

Astronomy and Physics

In these fields and that of radioactivity the sciences of physics and chemistry meet and cooperate. Faraday (1791–1867) by electrolysis decomposed chemical compounds and solutions. The kinetic theory of gases, that the molecules dart about in straight lines at approximately the speed of a rifle shot, was developed in the nineteenth century. In 1898 Professor and Madame Curie discovered the element radium, which has been employed since to bombard other elements, disintegrating their atomic structure and showing that all their atoms have a similar structure of hydrogen nuclei and revolving electrons, as above suggested, and so fundamentally affecting our conceptions of matter and chemical change. Organic chemistry scarcely existed apart from pharmacy and medicine in 1800, although Scheele had added eight more organic acids to the four then known. The development of this field during the following century was mainly the work of German chemists. Recent investigation in nutrition by many scientists has revealed the existence in foodstuffs of the vitamins, hitherto unsuspected substances which are present only in very small amounts and "defy chemical separation or identification except by their physiological effects," which are to promote bodily growth and to prevent certain diseases. They again remind us of the occult virtues in nature which were posited by medieval science.

Physical and Organic Chemistry

Organic chemistry thus leads us on to biology and medicine, the sciences of life and how to preserve it. In the thirties

Protoplasm,
the Cell
Theory, and
Evolution

came the discovery of protoplasm, the "living jelly endowed with all the properties of life," and the enunciation of the cell theory that all animals and plants are composed of similar cells, and that the cell is the unit in all organisms. Evolutionary theories of the universe date back at least as early as the ancient Greek philosophers. During the eighteenth century there was a growing tendency to think of religious evolution and to account for laws and societies as outgrowths of their environment. Lamarck in 1801 had already advanced the doctrine of evolution for the world of nature, but it was the publication of Darwin's *Origin of Species* in 1859 which brought about general acceptance, at least on the part of scientists, of the view that existing species have evolved out of earlier species by natural selection. All the half million and more species of animals, for example, from protozoa to vertebrates, are seen to be related structurally, physiologically, and psychologically, and to have a common ancestry if we trace them back far enough. Of course the relationship between the five main groups of vertebrates—fish, amphibia, reptiles, birds, and mammals—is closer than that between vertebrates and molluscs or flatworms, while man is most closely related to the other mammals and in particular to the anthropoid apes. Geology and the study of fossils of extinct species of plants and animals in the strata, tell the same story of gradual evolution. Indeed, before Darwin chalk, marl, and some limestones had been found to consist of the skeletons of tiny organisms. But we have already presented the evolutionary view of the universe and organic life in our first chapter. Since Darwin the evidence in its favor has been constantly added to, and no cogent evidence has been deduced against it.

The discovery of a single fossil creature in a geological stratum of a wrong period, the detection of a single anatomical or physiological fact irreconcilable with origin by descent with modification, would have been destructive of the theory and would have made the reputation of the observer. But in the prodigious number of supporting discoveries that have been made no single negative factor has appeared, and the evolution from their predecessors of the forms of life existing now or at any other period must be taken as proved. (*Encyclopedia Britannica*)

The protoplasm, cell, and evolution theories all harmonized with, and confirmed, each other. Schultze in 1860 defined the cell as "a mass of protoplasm containing a nucleus." About 1865, all eggs and sperms were seen to be cells, and it was recognized that all organisms, even the most complex, begin their existence as a single cell, which by dividing keeps forming additional cells.

A natural next step was the experimental study of heredity. The Austrian botanist and abbot, Mendel, in publications of 1865 and 1869, which did not become generally known until the twentieth century, led the way. Roughly speaking, he proved that interbreeding of two opposite stocks will in the first generation produce a half-way, intermediate, hybrid stock, but that when these hybrids interbreed, about half of their offspring will revert to the original two opposite stocks. Further experimentation along this line has confirmed the view that heredity depends upon the cell, and more particularly upon chromosomes within the nucleus of the germ cells, derived in equal quantities from the male and female parent and so always found in pairs. These chromosomes carry the various hereditary characters or factors, which number 7500 in the case of the fruit fly, and which probably lie in longitudinal order in the microscopic chromosomes. In the individuals of the species these hereditary characters, which are variable, appear to be combined and distributed by chance like the shuffling of so many cards. How far these hereditary characteristics may be affected by nutrition and like influences, and whether they may be affected at all by characteristics which the parents have acquired and which therefore were not present in the chromosomes of *their* original germ-cells, are still disputed problems. Obviously this experimental study of heredity is of great importance for the future of mankind and civilization.

Experimental Study of Heredity

The physiology of the nervous system was greatly advanced by the work of Sir Charles Bell and others in the earlier nineteenth century. Claude Bernard (1823–1878), discovered the formation of glycogen or sugar in the liver, the importance of the pancreatic juice in digestion, and the nervous regulation of the blood-vessels. Now the investigation of glands is absorbing attention. Bacteriology developed apace in the nineteenth century with the researches of Pasteur (1822–1895)

Physiology and Bacteriology

Cohn, and Koch. Pasteur showed that various fermentations were the work of living organisms, not merely chemical change, and that diseases of wine, beer, and silk-worms were similarly caused.

Progress of Modern Medicine and Surgery

Thus we are brought to the investigation of the germs responsible for various human diseases, and the cure or prevention of such diseases by some treatment that will kill the germs, such as the use of mercury for syphilis, or that will accustom the system to the disease by a very light inoculation, as in Pasteur's treatment of hydrophobia. Before Pasteur almost the only use of an antitoxin had been in 1798, when Jenner proved by experiment the truth of the popular belief in Gloucestershire that persons who had contracted cow-pox were immune from small-pox, and thus introduced vaccination. Since Pasteur's time a chief concern of medical research has been on the one hand, to discover the particular micro-organism that produces a given disease, and on the other hand to find an antitoxin against it. The discoveries that the parasites which produce malaria and yellow fever are transmitted to human beings only by the bite of certain mosquitoes have made it possible to prevent most cases of those diseases. Looking back again into the nineteenth century, we may note between 1798 and 1847 the introduction of new anæsthetics, nitrous oxide or "laughing gas," ether, and chloroform; the foundation of cellular pathology by Virchow (1821–1902) and of modern antiseptic surgery by Lister (1827–1912). Surgery and dentistry have made great strides in recent years, aided by modern appliances and by inventions such as X-ray photography. The terrible reckoning of physical injury and dismemberment and mental derangement exacted in the recent war gave surgeons and psychoanalysts a great field of observation and activity, which led to further advance in bone-grafting, blood-transfusion, brain and heart surgery, and pathological psychology. Marvelous as such mending is, human life has been preserved and the population increased more by public sanitary and preventive measures to guard against the germs of disease and against infant mortality, although epidemics of such diseases as influenza still show that the old demon can assume new forms when baffled in one quarter, and that modern communication spreads diseases as never before. Possibly our age reposes a little too much confidence in medicine and surgical operations.   Christian Science, however, which has many adherents, contends that disease is a mental error.

Besides the exploration of equatorial Africa alluded to in another chapter, central Asia and other remote parts of the globe have recently been scientifically explored.   The twentieth century has also seen the discovery of both poles, the North Pole by Peary in 1909, the South Pole by Amundsen in 1912. Meteorology and climatology are recently developed sciences. The aeroplane makes possible exploration and observation both of the upper regions of the atmosphere and of certain parts of the earth's surface as never before. *Geographic Exploration*

The progress of science and human invention have exerted a much more positive influence in the spheres of religion and ethics than is sometimes recognized.   Thus as early as 1794 and 1802 Paley's *Evidences of Christianity* and *Natural Theology* show the conception of God altered by the recent progress in science and applied science.   In the words of Leslie Stephen, "God has been civilized like man; he has become scientific and ingenious; he is superior to Watt or Priestley in devising mechanical and chemical contrivances, and is therefore made in the image of that generation of which Watt and Priestley were conspicuous lights."   But after all, why should not God reveal Himself through science?   Philosophy since Comte, however, has tended to abandon theology and metaphysics, as earlier stages in the evolution of human thought, for science, on the ground that knowledge is limited to phenomena.   Comte nevertheless believed in social progress by development of the higher human activities, as against the lower animal activities, under the impulse of social altruism and intellectual vivacity, as against natural inertia and selfishness.   It has recently been affirmed that, despite the general uncertainty as to theological creeds and loosening of ecclesiastical ties, if not decline in religious sentiment, the great growth of modern science has brought with it a marked improvement in both public and private morality. *Effect of Scientific Progress on Religion and Ethics*

The scientist has all the serene courage, inner peace, and trained mind of the ancient philosopher, and in addition a vastly broader view over past and present, a much deeper and more solid foundation of measured and classified observation. The student of historical and social sciences is consequently more open-minded and better balanced than his fellows.   If *Science and Society*

society can be imbued with this attitude, its restless waves of passions, superstitions, harmful habits, idle thoughts, incompetent, unscientific leadership, and woeful ambitions may soon be stilled. Science has already made great contributions to modern industry, communication and comfort, and public health. It has lengthened our days and the years of our lives, enriched our sensations and filled our minds. Science does not exclude art and beauty from our lives, since art is close to nature where the beautiful especially resides, while nothing else reveals nature to us as science has done. Moreover, as a modern theologian has said, "A greater gain to the world . . . than all the growth of scientific knowledge is the growth of the scientific spirit." And as a modern historian of science has said, "The only human activity which is truly cumulative and progressive is scientific activity." It has opened the past to our gaze; it orients us in the present; no better guide can be found for the future destiny of civilization.

BIBLIOGRAPHY

Bury, J. B. *The Idea of Progress,* 1921; *A History of Freedom of Thought,* 1914.

Cox, J. *Beyond the Atom,* 1913.

Curtis, W. C. *Science and Human Affairs,* 1921; Parts II and III, a very clear exposition of the cell theory, and stimulating discussion of the relation of science to human life.

Darwin Anniversary Number of *The Popular Science Monthly* (now *The Scientific Monthly*), April, 1909.

Fifty Years of Darwinism; centennial addresses before the American Association for the Advancement of Science, 1909.

Gooch, G. P. *History and Historians in the Nineteenth Century,* 1913.

Harris, F. S. and Butt, N. I. *Scientific Research and Human Welfare,* 1924.

Leighton, J. A. *Religion and the Mind of Today,* 1924.

Marvin, F. S. *Recent Development in European Thought,* 1921.

Matthews, A. P. "Science and Morality," in *The Scientific Monthly,* March, 1909.

Merz, J. T. *A History of European Thought in the Nineteenth Century,* 1896–1903, 2 vols.

Mills, John. *Within the Atom,* 1921; *Radio-Communication,* 1917; *Realities of Modern Science,* 1919.

Seward, A. C. *Darwin and Modern Science, Commemoration Essays,* 1909.

Slosson, E. E. *Keeping up with Science: notes on recent progress in the various sciences for unscientific readers,* 1924.

Thompson, S. P. *Michael Faraday*, 1898.

Tilden, Sir W. A. *Progress of Scientific Chemistry in Our Own Time*, 1913; *Chemical Discovery and Invention in the Twentieth Century*, 1916; *Famous Chemists, the Men and Their Work*, 1921.

Veblen, T. *The Place of Science in Modern Civilization*, 1920.

Wallace, A. R. *The Wonderful Century*, 1899; *Social Environment and Moral Progress*, 1914.

Whitehead, A. N. *Science and the Modern World*, 1925; metaphysical.

Whittaker, E. F. *History of the Theories of Æther and Electricity*, 1910.

Williams, H. S. and E. H. *A History of Science*, 1904, 5 vols., of which vols. 3–5 deal with the nineteenth century.

Windle, B. C. A. *A Century of Scientific Thought and Other Essays*, 1915.

APPENDIX

GENERAL BIBLIOGRAPHY

(Works on more particular periods and topics are listed in the bibliographies at the close of each chapter.)

I. GENERAL HISTORIES OF CIVILIZATION

The work of Guizot, translated into English in 1846, is now somewhat out-of-date. H. G. Wells' *Outline of History,* except for its compelling sketch of evolution and early man, is a summary of history in the old sense rather than a history of civilization. Alfred A. Knopf Inc. announces a History of Civilization series to comprise more than two hundred volumes, of which a few have begun to appear. They are in part translations of the French series, *L'Evolution de l'humanité,* of which 15 vols. appeared 1920–1925. *The Records of Civilization,* issued by the Department of History, Columbia University, ed. A. P. Evans, are a series of volumes presenting the original sources in English translation with scholarly notes and introductions. F. S. Marvin has edited various collections of essays and co-operative works bearing upon the history of civilization such as *Science and Civilization,* 1923, and *The Making of the Western Mind* with F. M. Stawell. For works in German on Kulturgeschichte see L. J. Paetow, *Guide to the Study of Medieval History,* p. 74, and *Ibid.* pp. 36–37 for a list of universal or world histories. W. G. DeBurgh's *The Legacy of the Ancient World,* 1924, opens a series on the contributions of the past to our civilization. The best current bibliographies for the history of civilization will be found annually in *Isis* (Official Organ of the History of Science Society) ed. Geo. Sarton. Lists of Books on History and of Historical Articles in Current Periodicals appear more frequently in *The Historical Outlook,* McKinley Publishing Co., Phila. A periodical devoted exclusively to the history of civilization is the *Archiv für Kulturgeschichte,* ed. W. Goetz and G. Steinhausen, Teubner, 1903–.

II. WORKS COVERING LONG PERIODS

Breasted, J. H., *Ancient Times,* 1916.
Baikie, J., *The Life of the Ancient East,* 1923.
Hall, H. R., *Ancient History of the Near East,* 5th ed., 1920; fuller than
   Breasted for the ancient orient, handier and more unified than the
   following.
Cambridge Ancient History, vols. 1–3, 1923–1925.
Cambridge History of India.
Cambridge Medieval History.
Cambridge Modern History; unfortunately gives slight attention to civilization.

Cambridge History of English Literature. All these Cambridge Histories are elaborate works with different chapters written by specialists and varying much in heaviness or readability; only the last two have as yet been completed.

Botsford, G. W., *Hellenic History,* 1922.

Botsford and Sihler, *Hellenic Civilization,* 1915; a translation of selections from the ancient authors and records.

Stobart, J. C., *The Glory that was Greece,* 1915. *The Grandeur that was Rome,* 1920.

Thorndike, Lynn, *The History of Medieval Europe,* 1917.

Hearnshaw, F. J. C., *Medieval Contributions to Modern Civilization,* 1921; lectures by specialists in various fields.

Munro, D. C. and Sellery, G., *Medieval Civilization,* 1907; extracts translated from notable French and German works.

Bateson, Mary, *Medieval England,* 1904.

Tilley, A., *Medieval France,* 1922; by various contributors.

Guerard, A. L., *French Civilization from the Origins to the Close of the Middle Ages,* 1920.

Lacroix, A., Various richly illustrated works in French or English translation on art, science and literature, institutions, usages, and costume in the middle ages, the renaissance, and the seventeenth and eighteenth centuries.

Traill, H. D., *Social England,* illustrated and revised edition, 1901–1904, 6 vols.; treatment by topics under periods.

Lavisse, E. and Rambaud, A., *Histoire générale du IV* e *siècle à nos jours,* 1893–1901, 12 vols.

Lavisse, E., *Histoire de France depuis les origines,* 1900–1912, 8 vols.

Hanotaux, G., *Histoire de la nation française,* vol. 11 deals with the history of the arts; vol. 14, with that of the sciences; and so on.

Lindsay, T. M., *History of the Reformation,* 1906–1907, 2 vols.

Smith, Preserved, *Age of the Reformation,* 1921; the best work on the period.

Hayes, C. J. H., *Political and Social History of Modern Europe,* 1916 and 1924, 2 vols.

Schevill, Ferdinand, *A History of Europe from the Reformation to the Present Day,* 1925.

III. HISTORIES OF SPECIAL TOPICS AND DEPARTMENTS OF CIVILIZATION

André-Pontier, L., *Histoire de la pharmacie,* 1900; deals with France from the thirteenth century.

Apthorp, Wm. F., *The Opera, Past and Present,* 1901.

Arnold, J. P., *Origin and History of Beer and Brewing,* 1911.

Ashley, W. J., *Economic Organization of England,* 1914; excellent.

Ashton, J., *History of Bread,* 1904.

Austin, S., *History of Engraving,* 1910.

Bapst, G., *Études sur l'étain dans l'antiquité et au moyen âge,* 1884.

Bassermann-Jordan, F., *Geschichte des Weinbaus unter besonder. Berücks- icht der bayer. Rheinpfalz,* 1907.

Bennett, R. and Elton, J., *History of Corn Milling,* 1898–1904, 4 vols.

Berendes, Z., *Die Pharmacie bei den alten Culturvölkern,* 1892. *Das Apothekenwesen . . . bis zum 20 Jahrh.,* 1907.

Blümner, H., *Technologie und Terminologie der Gewerbe und Künste bei Greichen und Römern,* 1875–1887.

Brett, G. S., *A History of Psychology,* 1912–1921, 3 vols.

Brieuves, Mme. M. de, *Historique de la broderie à travers les âges et les pays,* 1907.

Briggs, C. A., *History of the Study of Theology,* 1916, 2 vols.

Brown, G. B., *The Fine Arts,* 4th ed., 1916.

Bury, J. B., *History of the Freedom of Thought,* 1913. *The Idea of Progress,* 1920.

Cajori, Florian, *History of Mathematics,* 2nd ed., 1919.

Cantor, Moritz, *Vorlesungen über Geschichte der Mathematik,* 1880–1892, 3 vols. (and subsequent re-editions); the fullest scholarly treatment.

Clement, Mrs. C. E., *Women in the Fine Arts from the seventh century* B. C. *to the twentieth century* A. D., 1904.

Cunningham, W., *Western Civilization in its Economic Aspects,* 1900; standard, but all too brief.

d'Allemagne, H. R., *Récréations et passétemps,* 1905; and other works on amusements of the past.

Dannemann, Friedrich, *Die Naturwissenschaften in ihrer Entwicklung und in ihrem Zusammenhange,* 1910–1913, 4 vols.; this first edition is out of print; vols. 1–2 of a 2nd ed. appeared 1920–1921.

Dargan, E. C., *History of Preaching, A. D. 70–1572,* 1905.

Darmstädter, L., *4000 Jahre Pionier-Arbeit in den Exakten Wissenschaften,* 1904. *Handbuch zur Geschichte der Naturwiss. und Technik,* 2nd ed., 1908.

Day, Clive, *A History of Commerce,* 1907; rather elementary.

Dock, L. and Stewart, I. M., *A Short History of Nursing,* 1920.

Dock, L. and Nutting, M. A., *A History of Nursing,* 1907, 2 vols.

Dreyer, J. L. E., *History of Planetary Systems,* 1906.

Dunning, Wm. A., *A History of Political Theories, Ancient and Medieval,* 1902. *A History of Political Theories from Luther to Montesquieu,* 1905.

Falke, J., *Costümgeschichte der Culturvölker;* 378 illustrations.

Feldhaus, F. M., *Lexicon der Erfindungen und Entdeckungen auf den Gebieten der naturwissenschaften und Technik,* 1904; the best work available for the history of inventions.

Fergusson, J., *A History of Architecture in All Countries,* 3rd ed., 1891–1893, 5 vols.

Fiske, B. A., *Invention, the Master-Key to Progress,* 1921; an interpretation of history in terms of inventions, especially military ones. Unfortunately a crude piece of work, full of historical errors.

Flueckiger, F. A. and Hanbury, D., *Pharmacographia: a history of the principal drugs of vegetable origin met with in Great Britain and British India,* 2nd ed., 1879.

Fowler, H. N., *A History of Sculpture*, 1916; illustrated.

Garrison, F. H., *Introduction to the History of Medicine*, 3rd ed., 1921; the fullest history of medicine in English.

Gerland, E., *Geschichte der Physik von den ältesten Zeiten bis zum Ausgange des achtzehnten Jahrhunderts*, 1913.

Gerland, E. and Traumüller, F., *Geschichte der Physikalischen Experimentierkunst*, 1899; valuable for its pictures of early apparatus, machinery, and inventions.

Gettell, R. G., *History of Political Thought*, 1924.

Gothein, M. L., *Geschichte der Gartenkunst*, 1914, 2 vols.

Gras, N. S. B., *A History of Agriculture in Europe and America*, 1925.

Grousset, René, *Histoire de l'Asie*, 1922, 3 vols.

Guerini, V., *History of Dentistry from the most ancient times until the end of the eighteenth century*, 1909.

Gurlt, E., *Geschichte der Chirurgie*, 1898, 3 vols.; copious analyses of, and extracts from, past surgical writings.

Hamlin, A. D. F., *History of Architecture*, 1898.

Hefner-Alteneck, J. H. v., *Trachten, Kunstwerke und Geräthschaften vom frühen Mittelalter bis Ende des achtzehnten Jahrh.*, 1879–1889, 10 vols.

Helbing, Franz, *Die Tortur: Geschichte der Folter im Kriminal-Verfahren aller Völker und Zeiten*, 1913.

Heller, A., *Geschichte der Physik von Aristoteles bis auf die neueste Zeit*, 1882–1884, 2 vols.

Henderson, W. J., *Early History of Singing*, 1921.

Henslow, Geo., *Origin and History of Our Garden Vegetables*, 1912, 71 pp.

Herrick, C. A., *History of Commerce and Industry*, 1917.

Heuzey, L., *L'histoire du costume antique*, 1922; brief and attractive.

Hind, A. M., *A History of Engraving and Etching, from the fifteenth century to 1914*, 3rd ed., 1923.

Histoire générale des arts appliquées à l'industrie.

Histoire universelle du travail, general editor, Geo. Renard.

Holmes, G. V., *Ancient and Modern Ships*, 1906.

Hunter, G. L., *Tapestries, their origin, history and renaissance*, 1912.

Jenks, E., *A Short History of English Law*, 1912.

Jenkins, J. T., *History of Whale Fisheries*, 1921.

Johnston, H. H., *History of Colonization*, 1899.

Karpinski, L. C., *History of Arithmetic*, 1924.

Kisa, Anton, *Das Glas im Altertums*, 1908, 3 vols.

Kocourek, A. and Wigmore, J. H., *Evolution of Law: select readings*, 1915.

Lange, C. L., *Histoire de l'internationalisme*: I. (to the peace of Westphalia), 1919.

Lange, F. A., *Geschichte des Materialismus und Kritik seiner Bedeutung in der Gegenwart*, 1908, 2 vols.

Lating, G., *A Record of European Armour and Arms through Seven Centuries*, 1920, 2 vols.

Lecky, W. E. H., *History of European Morals from Augustus to Charlemagne*, 1872, 2 vols. *History of the Rise and Influence of the Spirit of Rationalism in Europe*, 1870.

Lectures on Literature, "delivered by members of the Faculty of Columbia

University giving a comprehensive view of the great literatures of the world."

Lethaby, W. R., *Medieval Art . . . 312-1350*, 1912; a handy volume.

Libby, W., *An Introduction to the History of Science*, 1917. *The History of Medicine*, 1922; two brief, well-written surveys of salient features.

Lichtenfelt, *Die Geschichte der Ernährung*, 1913.

Lindsay, W. S., *History of Merchant Shipping and Ancient Commerce,* 1874, 4 vols.

Lippman, E. O. v., *Entstehung und Ausbreitung der Alchemie*, 1919.

Loisel, G., *Histoire des ménageries*, 1912, 3 vols.

Maddox, H. A., *Paper: its History, Sources, and Manufacture*, 1916.

Mason, W. A., *History of the Art of Writing*, 1920.

Mathews, W. S. B., *A Popular History of the Art of Music*, 1907.

Michel, A., *Histoire de l'art*, 10 vols.

Monroe, Paul, *A Text Book in the History of Education*, 1905.

Navarre, A., *Histoire générale de la sténographie et de l'écriture à travers les âges*, 1909.

Oxford History of Music, ed. W. H. Hadow, 1901 etc., 6 vols.

Parmentier, A., *Album historique*, 3rd and 4th eds., 1907–1910, 4 vols.

Philip, Alexander, *The Calendar: its History, Structure, and Improvement*, 1921.

Porter, A. K., *Beyond Architecture*, 1918; concise, penetrating, entertaining.

Pound, Roscoe, *Interpretation of Legal History*, 1923.

Puschmann, Th., *A History of Medical Education*, 1891.

Racinet, A., *Le costume historique*, 1876–1888, 6 vols.

Radcliffe, Wm., *Fishing from the Earliest Times*, 1921.

Reinach, S., *Apollo: an illustrated manual of the history of art*, 1907.

Richard, E., *History of German Civilization*, 1911.

Riemann, E., *Handbuch der Musikgeschichte*, 1904, etc.

Riverside, P. L., *Romantic and Historic Background of Agriculture and Plant Study*, 1921.

Ruckstull, F. W., *Great Works of Art and What Makes them Great*, 1925.

Sandys, J. E., *A History of Classical Scholarship*, 1903–1906, 3 vols. and subsequent editions.

Sarton, Geo., *Introduction to the History of Science*. Vol. I, *From Homer to the end of the XIth century*. Forthcoming.

Sedgwick, W. T. and Tyler, H. W., *A Short History of Science*, 1917.

Simpson, F. M., *A History of Architectural Development*, 1905–1911, 3 vols.

Singer, Chas., *Studies in the History and Method of Science*, 1917, 1921, etc.; handsomely illustrated.

Smith, D. E., *History of Mathematics*, 1923–1925, 2 vols.

Stillman, J. M., *Story of Early Chemistry*, 1924.

Sturgis, R., *A Short History of Architecture*, 1908.

Taylor, H. O., *The Classical Heritage*, 1901. *The Medieval Mind*, 1911, 2 vols. *Thought and Expression of the Sixteenth Century*, 1920, 2 vols.

Thorndike, Lynn, *A History of Magic and Experimental Science*, 1923, 2 vols.

Walsh, Wm. F., *Outlines of the History of English and American Law,* 1923.

Wauthoz, H. A., *Les ambulances et les ambulanciers à travers les siècles,* c. 1907.

Windelband, W., *A History of Philosophy,* 2nd ed., 1901.

Withington, E. T., *Medical History from the Earliest Times,* 1894.

Woltmann, A. and Woermann, *History of Painting,* 4 vols.

Women Painters of the World from Caterina Vigri (1413–1463) to Rosa Bonheur, 1905.

Wootton, A. C., *Chronicles of Pharmacy,* 1910, 2 vols.

Zimmerman, A., *Geschichte der Stenographie,* 1912.

Histories of literature have for the most part been omitted from the foregoing list as better known and more accessible than works in most of the fields above-mentioned, or as so numerous as to make selection difficult, or as cited earlier in the bibliographies of particular chapters.

ALPHABETICAL LIST OF TOPICS AND DEPARTMENTS OF CIVILIZATION WITH THE NAMES OF THE AUTHORS TREATING THEM IN THE FOREGOING BIBLIOGRAPHY

Agriculture: Gras, Riverside.

Album, historical: Parmentier.

Alchemy: Lippmann.

Ambulances: Wauthoz.

Amusements: d'Allemange.

Architecture: Fergusson, Hamlin, Simpson, Sturgis.

Arithmetic: Karpinski.

Arms and Armor: Lating.

Art: Brown, Clement, Lethaby, Michel, Porter, Reinach, Ruckstull.

Asia: Grousset.

Astronomy: Dreyer.

Beer: Arnold.

Bread: Ashton.

Calendar: Philip.

Chemistry: Stillman.

Classical scholarship: Sandys.

Colonization: Johnston.

Commerce: Day, Herrick, Lindsay.

Corn milling: Bennett.

Costume: Falke, Heuzey, Racinet.

Dentistry: Guerini.

Economic history: Ashley, Cunningham.

Education: Monroe, Puschmann.

Embroidery: Brieuves.

Engraving and Etching: Austin, Hind.

Fishing: Jenkins, Radcliffe.

Free Thought: see Rationalism.

Gardening: Gothein, Henslow.

Germany: Richard.

Glass: Kisa.

Industry and Industrial Arts: Blümner, Hefner-Alteneck, Herrick, *Histoire, etc.*

Internationalism: Lange.

Inventions: Feldhaus, Fiske, Garland and Traumüller.

Labor: *Histoire universelle du travail.*

Law: Jenks, Kocourek, Pound, Walsh.

Literature: *Lectures on*

Magic: Thorndike.

Materialism: Lange.

Mathematics: Cajori, Cantor, Smith.

Medicine: Garrison, Libby, Puschmann, Withington.

Menageries: Loisel.

Morals: Lecky.

Music: Mathews, *Oxford History of,* Riemann.

Nursing: Dock.

Nutrition: Lichtenfelt.

Opera: Apthorp.

Painting: Woltmann.

Paper: Maddox.

Pharmacy: André-Pontier, Berendes, Flueckiger, Wootton.

Philosophy: Windelband, and see Thought.

Physics: Gerland, Heller.

Political Thought: Dunning, Gettell.

Preaching: Dargan.

Progress: Bury.

Psychology: Brett.

Rationalism: Bury, Lecky.

Science: Dannemann, Darmstädter, Libby, Sarton, Sedgwick, Singer, Thorndike.

Sculpture: Fowler.

Shipping: Lindsay, Holmes.

Singing: Henderson.

Stenography: Navarre, Zimmerman.

Surgery: Gurlt.

Tapestries: Hunter.

Theology: Briggs.

Thought: Taylor, and see Rationalism, Philosophy.

Tin: Bapst.

Torture: Helbing.

Vine-culture: Bassermann-Jordan.

Women: Clement.

Writing: Mason, Navarre.

STEPS IN THE DEVELOPMENT OF CIVILIZATION

(It is impossible to date with any accuracy the advances made during the stone age and prehistoric period. Many of the other dates are only approximate.)

OLD STONE AGE

Eoliths.
Fist-hatchet.
Mousterian point: practice of ceremonial burial.
Paintings of cave men mark the birth of the fine arts.
Height of flint-flaking reached in Solutrean period.
Bone implements and sculpture: the harpoon, throwing-stick, lamp, etc.

NEW STONE AGE

New stone age of polished implements with a ground edge and handles.
Development of pottery (perhaps 15,000–13,000 B. C.).
Domestication of animals and cultivation of plants.
Boats and lake-villages on piles.
Spinning and mining.
Invention of the plough and the wheel.
Monoliths, tombs and great circles of stone.
Pre-dynastic graves in Egypt: linen, glazed beads, amulets, face-paint, beginnings of picture-writing.
Use of gold, silver, and copper; followed by the Bronze Age.

B. C.

4241 Possible origin of Egyptian calendar.
4200 Apparent date of first dynasty (Sumerian) at Nippur in the Tigris-Euphrates Valley.
3400 First Dynasty of the Old Kingdom in Egypt.
2900–2750 Fourth Dynasty, builders of the largest pyramids.
2650–2500 "Oldest chapter of human thought extant"; hieroglyphic texts from Sakkara; family life and common occupations also portrayed; the temple, column, and capital.
Remains of Sumerian cities and cuneiform tablets in the Tigris-Euphrates Valley.
2500 Second city of Troy.
2200–1500 Culture of the palace at Cnossus in Crete.
2100 Code of Hammurabi at Babylon.
2000–1788 Middle Kingdom in Egypt; Twelfth Dynasty; literary remains in ink on papyrus; feudalism.

1926 Hittites raid Babylonia: Indo-Europeans soon begin to enter the Greek and Italian peninsulas.

1746 Horse introduced in Babylonia by the Kassites, and about the same date by the Hyksos into Egypt.

1580–1090 The Empire in Egypt; temple of Karnak; Book of the Dead; magical and medical papyri.

1400–1200 Mycenaean civilization at its height.

1400 Hebrews and Aramaeans begin to invade Syria.

1272 Treaty of Rameses II and the king of the Hittites; iron mines of the Hittites.

1200 Hymns of the Rigveda, the oldest Indo-European literature. Alphabet spread by Phoenicians and Aramaeans.

1000–800 Homeric poems.

c900 Carthage founded by the Phoenicians. Spread of the leaf-shaped Hallstatt sword.

850 Bronze reliefs on the gate of Shalmaneser II of Assyria.

846–777 Hesiod.

776 First Olympiad of Greek chronology begins: solar eclipse recorded in China.

732–606 Assyrian Empire at its height: cotton growing introduced from India.

722–479 Feudal age in China: Etruscan civilization and Greek colonies in Italy.

675–670 Colony at Shantung founded by traders from the Indian Ocean. Coinage invented in Lydia; the trireme, in Phoenicia.

640–548 Thales of Miletus, roughly contemporary with Zoroaster of Persia and the Upanishads of India.

604–561 Babylon under Nebuchadnezzar.

594 Reforms of Solon at Athens.

568–488 Buddha (Siddhattha Gotama), roughly contemporary with Mahavira, the founder of Jainism.

551–478 Confucius, roughly contemporary with The Old Sage, founder of Taoism.

550–330 Persian Empire from the Indus to the Aegean.

c500 Greek transition from lyric to dramatic poetry, black- to red-figure vase-painting, archaic to developed sculpture: in India Yaska marks the beginning of scientific philology.

484–425 Herodotus, father of history.

460–377 Hippocrates, father of medicine.

451–449 Twelve Tables of Roman Law.

447–438 Parthenon built; sculptures of Phidias; age of Pericles.

431–404 Peloponnesian War.

399 Martyrdom of Socrates: Plato leaves Athens.

390 Sack of Rome by the Gauls.

384–322 Aristotle.

372–289 Mencius.

c341 Births of Epicurus and Menander: Hermes of Praxiteles.

338 Chaeronea ends Greek freedom.

336–323 Reign of Alexander the Great.

311 Zeno founds the Stoic school at Athens.

Ptolemy I founds the Museum at Alexandria.

287–212 Archimedes.

264–146 Punic Wars: Roman expansion in eastern Mediterranean.

263–226 Reign of Asoka in India; rock edicts, pillars.

206 B. C.–221 A. D. Han Dynasty in China; Great Wall built.

184 Admission of Ennius, father of Latin literature, to Roman citizenship.

176 *Lex Aebutia;* change from Twelve Tables to the Praetorian Edict Hindu epics, *Mahabharata* and *Ramayana.*

145–87 Ssu-ma Ch'ien, father of Chinese history.

c120 Greek Grammar of Dionysius Thrax.

106–43 Cicero.

104 China adopts Meton's cycle.

98 Earliest letters of Chinese soldiers in Central Asia.

78 Rock-cut temple of Karli in India.

58–50 Caesar conquers Gaul.

31 B. C.–14 A. D. Reign of Augustus Caesar and foundation of Roman Empire.

20 B. C.–20 A. D. Glass blown by Neikon and Artas at Sidon.

A. D.

1–700 Maya Empire in Central America.

65 Introduction of Buddhism into China.

70 Destruction of Jerusalem.

77 Pliny's *Natural History.*

69–96 Roman sculpture at its height under the Flavian Dynasty.

98 *Germania* of Tacitus.

106–270 Roman occupation of Dacia.

117–138 Reign of Hadrian; Pantheon completed.

127–151 Astronomical observations of Ptolemy.

129–200 Galen.

226–651 Sassanid Dynasty in Persia.

228 Murder of the jurist Ulpian by the praetorian guards.

319 Beginning in India of Gupta Empire and Golden Age of Sanskrit literature.

Oldest extant Chinese painting by Ku K'ai-chih.

325 Council of Nicaea.

330 Constantinople replaces Rome as capital.

372 Huns cross the Volga, initiating the barbarian invasions.

413–426 Augustine composes *The City of God.*

Coptic art in Egypt.

476 Transition to the Byzantine Empire.

529 Rule of St. Benedict.

527–565 Reign of Justinian; *Code* and *Digest;* Church of St. Sophia.

588 Buddhism enters Japan via Korea.

590–604 Pope Gregory the Great.

618–907 T'ang Dynasty in China; flowering of art and poetry.

622 Hegira of Mohammed.

Celtic art in Irish monasteries.

Persian Magi, Manichean, and Nestorian refugees in China.

Culture of the Toltecs in Mexico.

732 Westward wave of Moslem conquest checked at Tours.

750–1258 Abbasid Dynasty at Bagdad.

755–1036 Emirate and Caliphate of Cordova.

800 Imperial coronation of Charlemagne: close of the best period of Sanskrit literature.

871–900 Reign of Alfred the Great in England.

910 Foundation of the Abbey of Cluny.

911 Origin of Normandy.

955 Battle of the Lechfeld ends barbarian invasions of western Europe.

960–1280 Sung Dynasty in China.

987–1328 Capetian Dynasty.

999–1003 Pope Sylvester II, previously as Gerbert acquainted with the Hindu-Arabic numerals.

1015 Genoa and Pisa expel the Saracens from Sardinia.

1031 Alberuni's *Inquiry into India.*

1037 Death of Avicenna.

1055 Death of Guido d'Arezzo, inventor of staff-notation in music.

1063 Romanesque cathedral of Pisa begun.

1066 Norman conquest of England.

1071 Battle of Manzikert seals the fate of civilization in Asia Minor.

1079–1142 Abelard: origin of universities and scholasticism.

1086–1127 William X of Aquitaine, first known troubadour.

1087 Death of Constantinus Africanus.

1095–1099 The First Crusade.

1105 First mention of wind-mills in a Norman charter.

Study of Roman Law revived at Bologna by Irnerius.

Questions about Nature of Adelard of Bath.

1126–1198 Averroës.

c1134–1532 Dynasty of the Incas in Peru.

Decretum of Gratian; *Sentences* of Peter Lombard; Geography of Edrisi.

1157–1217 Alexander Neckam mentions the mariner's compass and glass mirrors.

1163 Gothic cathedral of Notre-Dame at Paris begun.

1171 Venice institutes a public debt.

1176–1183 Lombard communes establish their complete independence.

1193–1280 Albertus Magnus.

1198–1216 Pope Innocent III: Latin Empire of Constantinople; Albigensian Crusade; Dominican and Franciscan Orders founded; Fourth Lateran Council.

1202 *Liber Abaci* of Leonard of Pisa.

1215 Magna Carta: Capture of Peking by Jenghiz Khan.

1225–1274 Thomas Aquinas.

1238–1241 Mongol invasion of Europe.

1265–1321 Dante.

1266 *Opus Maius* of Roger Bacon; gunpowder already in use.

c1266–1337 Giotto.

1271–1295 Marco Polo in the Far East.

1291 Turks take Acre, the last stronghold of the crusaders in Syria.

1295 Model Parliament of Edward I.

1302 First meeting of the French Estates General.

Most of the present coal-fields of England were already being worked. Invention of clock-work.

1306–1320 Antiseptic surgery of Henry of Mondeville.

1324 *Defensor pacis* of Marsiglio of Padua.

c1325 Aztecs found the city of Mexico.

1341 Petrarch crowned poet laureate at Rome by King Robert of Naples.

1348 The Black Death.

1351 Laurentian Portolano.

1353 Ottoman Turks enter Europe.

1368–1370 Mongols expelled from China.

1370–1405 Ravages of Tamerlane from northern India to Asia Minor.

1378–1382 Failure of popular risings in western Europe.

1386–1466 Donatello.

1405–1457 Lorenzo Valla.

c1446 First mentions of movable metal types in Europe.

1452–1519 Leonardo da Vinci.

1453 Turks take Constantinople: end of Hundred Years War.

1483–1520 Raphael.

1486 Diaz rounds the Cape of Good Hope.

1492 Columbus discovers America.

1493–1541 Paracelsus.

1497–1499 Voyage of Vasco da Gama to India.

1509 *The Praise of Folly* by Erasmus.

1513 *The Prince* of Machiavelli.

1517 Luther posts his Ninety-Five Theses.

1518–1580 Palladio.

1519–1522 Circumnavigation of the globe by Magellan.

1525–1529 Erection of the late-Gothic Town Hall of Oudenaarde.

1526 Baber makes Delhi the Great Mogul's capital.

1526–1594 Palestrina.

1527 Sack of Rome by imperial troops.

1536 Calvin's *Institute of Christianity*.

1540 Society of Jesus confirmed by Pope Paul III.

1543 Publication of Copernican theory and anatomy of Vesalius.

1545–1563 Council of Trent.

1556–1605 Reign of Akbar in India.

1562–1598 French Wars of Religion.

1564 Death of Michelangelo: births of Galileo and Shakespeare.

1572 *Lusiad* of Camoens.

Mexico now a Europeanized city of 165,000.

1574–1688 Golden Age of the Dutch Netherlands.

1586–1628 Reign of Abbas I of Persia at Isfahan.

1596–1650 Descartes.

1599–1660 Velasquez.

1600 First performance of opera at Florence: East India Co. chartered.

1604–1605 *Don Quixote* of Cervantes.

1607 Settlement of Virginia.

1609 Bank of Amsterdam founded: telescope in use.

1615 End of feudal anarchy in Japan.

1618–1648 Thirty Years War.

1625 Grotius' *De iure belli et pacis.*

1628 Harvey's *De motu.*

1634 Foundation of the French Academy.

1640–1660 Period of the Puritan Revolution in England.

1642–1727 Sir Isaac Newton.

1644 Ming Dynasty in China replaced by foreign Manchu invaders.

1660 Royal Society of London.

1661–1715 Age of Louis XIV.

1665 *Journal des Savants* founded.

1675 Leeuwenhoek discovers protozoa through the microscope.

1685–1750 Johann Sebastian Bach.

1688–1689 Revolution of, in England.

1689–1725 Reign of Peter the Great in Russia.

1690 Locke's *Essay Concerning Human Understanding.*

1694–1778 Voltaire.

1696 Bayle's *Dictionnaire historique et critique.*

1703–1791 John Wesley.

1706–1790 Benjamin Franklin.

1723–1751 Muratori's *Scriptores.*

1728 First iron rolling mill.

1730–1795 Josiah Wedgwood.

1733 Tull's *Horse-Hoeing Husbandry:* Kay's flying shuttle.

1740–1786 Reign of Frederick the Great in Prussia.

1748 Montesquieu's *L'esprit des lois:* Richardson's *Clarissa.*

1749–1832 Goethe.

1751–1765 First edition of *L'encyclopédie.*

1756–1791 Mozart.

1762 Rousseau's *Social Contract* and *Emile.*

1764 Hargreaves' spinning jenny.

1765–1790 Reign of Joseph II in Austria.

1769 Watt's first patent on the steam engine.

1773–1776 Discovery of oxygen.

1774–1785 Warren Hastings governor-general of India.

1776 Declaration of Independence of the American Colonies: Adam Smith's *Wealth of Nations:* Gibbon's *Decline and Fall of the Roman Empire.*

1779 First iron bridge.

1781 Kant's *Critique of Pure Reason.*

1787–1789 United States Constitution adopted.

1788 British colonization of Australia begun.

1789 Declaration of the Rights of Man by the French Constitutional Assembly; Bentham's *Introduction to the Principles of Morals and Legislation.*

1790 First iron ship.

1792 Whitney's cotton gin.

1794 Tom Paine's *Age of Reason.*

1798–1857 Comte.

1799–1814 Napoleon in power.

1800 Beethoven's first symphony.

1801 Ritter discovers ultra-violet rays: Lamarck's doctrine of evolution.

1804 Dalton's atomic theory.

1807 Fulton's Claremont the first commercially successful steamboat.

1813–1883 Richard Wagner.

1815 Waterloo.

1820–1921 34,435,332 immigrants enter the United States.

1822 Champollion deciphers hieroglyphics.

1822–1859 Pasteur.

1823 Monroe Doctrine enunciated.

1825 Opening of the Stockton and Darlington Railroad.

1827 Invention of friction matches.

1828 Andrew Jackson elected president of the United States.

1830 July Revolution in France.

1831 Farraday invents the dynamo.

1832 First Reform Act, England.

1833 Co-education begun at Oberlin.

1837 Dickens' *Pickwick Papers.*

1838 Morse patents the telegraph.

1839 Goodyear process of vulcanizing rubber: determination of stellar parallaxes by Bessel and Henderson: Horace Mann establishes the first normal school in America.

1846 Howe's sewing-machine: discovery of planet Neptune.

1847 McCormick's reaper becomes a commercial success: Rawlinson deciphers cuneiform.

1848 European Revolutions: the Communist Manifesto.

1856 Bessemer steel process.

1858 First Transatlantic cable.

1859 Darwin's *Origin of Species:* discovery of oil-fields in Pennsylvania.

1859–1860 Spectroscope invented by Kirchhoff and Bunsen.

1861 Unification of Italy; emancipation of the Russian peasants.

1861–1865 Civil War in the United States: emancipation of the negroes.

1862 Victor Hugo's *Les misérables.*

1867 Massachusetts limits child labor to 10 hours a day: *Das Kapital* of Karl Marx: Second Reform Act in England.

1868–1871 Invention of typewriters.

1869 Suez Canal opened.

1870 England adopts universal public elementary education.

1871 Unification of Germany: abolition of feudalism in Japan.

1876 Otto's internal combustion engine: Koch proves the germ theory of disease: International Association for the Exploration and Civilization of Africa.

1877 Edison s phonograph: extinction of the Tasmanians.

1882 England enters Egypt.

1889 Japan adopts parliamentary government without ministerial responsibility.

1891–1900 Trans-Siberian Railroad constructed.

1895 Röntgen discovers x-rays: Linde makes liquid air.

1895–1899 Malarial infection traced to the anopheles genus of mosquitoes.

1898 Discovery of radium by the Curies.

1899 Marconi transmits wireless messages across the English Channel.

1900–1901 Yellow fever traced to bite of female Stegomyia mosquito.

1901–1905 France suppresses religious orders and secularizes their schools.

1903 First successful aeroplane flight by the Wright brothers.

1905 Czar forced to grant Russia a Duma: China introduces "western learning."

1906 Death of Ibsen.

1909 North Pole discovered by Peary: Lloyd George's budget.

1910 Death of Tolstoi.

1911 522,400 different living species known to science.

1912 South Pole discovered by Amundsen: Chinese Republic: Flexner's antitoxin for cerebro-spinal meningitis.

1914–1918 World War.

1917 Russian Revolution.

1919 First Transatlantic flight.

1920 Michelson's interferometer: women's suffrage in the United States.

1923 Labor Party in power for the first time in England: Republic of Turkey.

1924 Dawes' Plan: abolition of the caliphate.

1925 Treaty of Locarno.

INDEX

Arabic numerals refer to pages; Roman, to chapters.